OSBORNE & HAMILTON'S

ORIGINAL RECORD COLLECTORS PRICE GUIDE

1st Edition

Presleyana

Pres • ley • an • a (pres lē an′ə) *N.* Of or having to do with the personal, public, singing or acting career of Elvis Presley. Usually used in connection with those who untiringly seek to collect said memorabilia, past and present.

Published by

O'SULLIVAN WOODSIDE & COMPANY

This book is dedicated to both DAVE KENT and the LOUISIANA HAYRIDE.

*To Dave. . . for the extreme confidence he placed in us,
and to the Hayride. . . for giving the Memphis newcomer a start. Had
they not. . . this book may have never been.*

—Jerry & Bruce

Published in the United States of America

First Edition.
First Printing.
Second Printing.

Manufactured in the United States of America.

ISBN: 0-89019-073-9

FOLLETT: T 1508

Distributed to Booksellers by:
Follett Publishing Company
1010 West Washington Blvd.
Chicago, Illinois, 60607

(Presleyana is a listing of records and their current market values and is not a catalog of records for sale.)

PRESLEYANA SEQUENCE OF CONTENTS

Acknowledgements

Of the one dozen nationally distributed major music publications from us at Jellyroll, this is the book in which we share the greatest pride.

Its accuracy and comprehensiveness is, honestly, second to none.

Attaining that goal, though, would not have been possible without the valued assistance and contributions of the following Elvis fans and collectors.

In addition, we'd like to thank both Phil Gelormine, and his fine publication *Elvis World*, for many of this book's photos of the King.

Special appreciation is also extended to Randy Jones, co-author of *The Complete Elvis*, for valuable assistance on this project.

As always, there are those whose writing was illegible and therefore whose names could not be included. Please accept our thanks. . . you know who you are!

KEN ALPER
LOUIS ANTONICELLO
JAMES ARNOLD
JOHN ASHE
DAVE BAKER
RAY BENJAMIN
BILL BRAM
BUFFALO RECORDS & TAPES
ALAN W. BUNCH
FRANK CARAVELLO
BOB CATTANEO
JOHN CLARK
RUSS COCHRAN
WILLIAM CONLEY
BILL CONROY
SHARON CORNELISON
LEE COTTON
TOM COTTON
IAN CRAIG
ROBERT CRANSWICK
MIKE CZAPKAY
JOAN DEARY
BILL DEPEW JR.
DAWN MICHELLE DOTSON
PAUL DOWLING
LEN EISENSTEIN
ELVIS WORLD
SCOTT EMBERSON
DEAN FAULKISON
JERRY FENSKE
FRANK FODOR
JIM FRIES
ROBERT A. FURRER
PHIL GELORMINE
JERRY GIBSON
ERIC D. GOETTSCH
BOBBY GOFF
SUSAN GREENSPAN

BILL GRIGGS
RICHARD HAGGETT
GEORGE T. HAMILTON
DENNIS HENDLEY
JACK HELINSKI
LARRY HILBURN
BUDDY HOLLY MEMORIAL SOCIETY
DAN HOWE
RONALD E. HOYER
JEFF HUBBARD
BILL JACKSON
FELTON JARVIS
GLEN JOHNSON
WILLIAM B. JOHNSON
LARRY JONES
NITAYA KANCHANAWAN
BILL KELLY
DAVE KENT
TOM KOEHLER
MICHAEL KOLONEL
ANNA LABBATE
ALLAN G. LATAWIEC
RIP LAY
W. LISMORE
DANTE LORENZI
ERIC MACHE
BUTCH MACKIMMIE
MICKIE MALBROUGH
GARY L. MALONE
PATRICIA MARSOLAIS
JON MCAULIFFE
JIM MCKEE
JIM MCMANES
LARRY MCNABB
ALAN MCQUISTIN
LON MELTON
FRANK MERRILL
E. J. MEULENBELT

ANNA MIESZCZAK
KATHY MILLER
RICHARD MINOR
WALT MITCHELL
DEREK MYERS
WILLIAM R. NICHOLSON
HOWARD NORRELL.
JOEL O'BRIEN
ALLAN OERLE
GERI-ANNE OSBORNE
COL. TOM PARKER
GEORGE PARKHILL
BRUNO PAUSE
GARETH PAWLOWSKI
ROGER PEARL
VICTOR PEARLIN
TERRY POGUE
JANICE RAMSAY
KAL RAUDOJA
RECORD RESEARCH PUBLICATIONS
BOB REEVES
GEORGE RITTENHOUSE
RED ROBINSON
GER RYFF
JIM SAITTA
DICK SCHMITT
JOSEPH A. SEDLAK
BARRY SHABANSKY
DEAN SILVERSTONE
ROBERT SNYDER
AL SZABO
GENE TOMLINSON
MICHAEL VACANTI
DAN WELLS
WENZEL'S MUSIC TOWN
JOEL WHITBURN
FRED WHOBREY
MIKE WILLIAMS

Individual acknowledgements for each of the international correspondents are included in the section containing their contributions to this edition.

DO YOU KNOW IF YOUR RECORD COLLECTION IS ADEQUATELY PROTECTED AGAINST LOSS?

LIST YOUR RECORD COLLECTION UNDER A GENERAL HOMEOWNERS POLICY

If you do not have your record collection listed separately in your general homeowners policy, in the event of a loss, you would be paid only a fraction of your collection's actual value.

For example, if your Elvis Presley, Milkcow Blues Boogie, (Sun 215) worth $300.00 in mint condition, is destroyed in a fire, the insurance company would only be able to give you 10% of the ORIGINAL COST of the record. Since this record was released in 1955 and sold for 89¢, you would receive 9¢ for your record!

OBTAIN COMPLETE COVERAGE FOR YOUR COLLECTION

Getting FULL coverage for your record valuables is SIMPLE. It can be accomplished in two easy steps:

1. Make a list of your records. Using the Osborne/Hamilton Price Guide for Collectible Records, write down:

*
1. Name of artist
2. Title of record
3. Label and number
4. Price value

2. Call your insurance agent and tell him you have an itemized list of records that you want protected with your household goods on your homeowners or renters policy or highlight your record collection in the Osborne/Hamilton Guide and turn the guide in to your agent.

* If you do not have all the information listed above, simply inform your insurance agent that you have records which need to be listed with your general household goods. Many insurance companies are currently using the Record Collector's Price Guides to appraise collections.

WELCOME TO THE WORLD OF PRESLEYANA

To the eyes of the whole world our cover is unmistakably Elvis, and what a tribute to the man that it is not even necessary to see his face to know that! We'd like to extend our thanks many times over to the photographer, Phil Gelormine, a true Elvis fan of the first rank (and publisher of *Elvis World*), for the use of this magnificent on-stage shot!

We're very happy with the photographic content of *Presleyana,* not just for the quality of the photos of the King that came to us from such divergent sources as Dave Kent of the Louisiana Hayride and Collector's Bookstore of Hollywood (many of which we've run full page), but for the fact that we are able to show fans many dozens of the rarest Elvis records, some never before published and many so rare as to be thought not to exist or only rumored so until now!

WHAT CAME BEFORE

This book sets the Elvis standard for all time. The only publication to even compare with it was the widely distributed *Complete Elvis* magazine. *T.C.E.* was not a price guide, however, and its principle photographic content was a thorough representation of the covers of all commercial Elvis Presley picture sleeves for singles and jackets for EPs and albums.

Even though *T.C.E.* was also a Jellyroll product, we had no quality control over its production and some of the typical problems that result from having a staff of uninformed layout people found their way into print. We still hope to issue an updated and far more "complete" *Complete Elvis* because of the mass market audience that can be reached, but to the readers of *Presleyana,* what you'll find in the pages of *this* book is without precedent!

COMING OF AGE

This is a book that will come to mean more and more to you, as you familiarize yourself with it. This is a book that will settle arguments, end confusion, correct misconceptions and add to the knowledge of anyone who owns a copy. If it could ever be said before, *now* collecting Elvis Presley records has come of age!

A few collectors may be surprised by the quadruple price structure. The spread—that is, what collectors will pay for a record in "good" average used condition compared to what they will put out for a record in "mint" unplayed condition—is constantly expanding. The "spread" is spreading.

Five or six years ago it was obvious the difference meant less, as the standard of double (a range, for example, of $10 to $20, versus a range today of $10 to $40) prevailed. As prices have arisen, however, and big money has often come into the picture, it was inevitable that collectors who weren't so particular before would increasingly demand perfection as protection to their investment. This is as logical as it was inevitable.

NOT PEAKED OUT

We can look for the prices asked and realized (not always the same thing) to increase on Elvis records, as the demand shows no signs of having peaked out. And we probably can assume records will follow the path of coins and some other collectibles that will zero in, eventually, on price spreads of ten times difference between "good" and "mint". That is why, to the uninitiated—and that includes the swap meet dealer and the thrift shop owner—we advise you *not* to look only at the right-hand column of our prices and tell yourself that's what your records are worth. In almost all cases you'll be wrong. Prices do not start at "mint" and work down, according to defects. They start at the average condition usually found, which is "good," and work up, if their condition warrants. Stated in another way, collectors do not pay *less* for a record in lesser condition—they think of themselves as being willing to pay *more* (perhaps than they think it's really worth) if it's in top, "near mint" condition.

As an aside to new collectors or investors, this growing spread has good aspects to it from whatever your viewpoint. If you're just interested in the music, in many cases as the "spread" widens and the value of "mint" goes up, the price of "good" does *not* go up. So, as you fill holes in your collection, taking inflation into consideration, you might be able to pick up some records "cheaper" in the future (in "good," remember) than you can today.

On the other hand, if investment is a factor in your determination and you buy only "fine" to "mint", that's where your future profit will be, even though you have to lay out more money now.

If, on the third hand, you want both "mint" condition and bargain "good" prices . . . well, good luck.

ESTABLISH THE CONDITION

To arrive at the value of any record, the condition must be established first. If a record has, say, a $10 to $40 "spread" and you have a copy that's about halfway between "good" and "fine" ("fine" is considered to be exactly halfway between "good" and "mint"), you have a "very good" record and will figure its value at halfway between "good" and "fine," which is halfway between $10 and $25, or $17.50. With a little practice, you can compute these pinpointed estimations very quickly. "Fair" condition depreciates value rapidly, in this example to about $5, or *half* "good." If you were to sell a "very good" copy of such a record to a dealer, don't expect him to pay you over 50% of what he eventually will expect to sell it for ($17.50).

MORE FOR MORE, LESS FOR LESS

A dealer tends to pay higher percentages for records the more valuable they are. Whereas he might offer you half the value for a record in the $10 to $20 range, he might pay $300 for a record he thinks he can sell right away for $400. Conversely, he may not offer you *anything* for your boxful of $2 to $3 records, or he may bid for the lot at 10¢ apiece and just shrug if you refuse to sell. If he already has a lot of the type you're selling he knows he's going to sit on most of them for a long time.

As you add records to your collection you might want to utilize the multi-purpose checklist boxes that accompany all variations in this book. A classic "for instance" would be the second Elvis long play album with its eleven-known cover variations. A checklist box has been provided for each, so no matter what variation, or pressing, or re-issue you may add to your collection of this or any record, if you pencil in the condition in the appropriate box, that's all the bookkeeping you'll need to do to have a complete record of your Elvis discs.

ALSO NOTE: please refer to the page on insuring your records in the last section of this book. The combined efforts of Elvis fandom in the United States would be enough to change the insurance company practices concerning coverage of records at collector values!

Be sure to note that singles and picture sleeves are priced separately and to arrive at a total for both, add the prices for each. It is necessary that we keep the prices apart, since singles are commonly sold without sleeves (and vice versa), while albums and EPs are almost never sold without jackets.

HERE A DOG, THERE A DOG

Some other miscellaneous thoughts about the contents of this book:
. . . all original pressings are priced.
. . . all later pressings are identified.
. . . generally, each later pressing of a record goes down in value by half the pressing before (exceptions are noted).
. . . the r.p.m. speeds of singles are shown in parentheses, and to look for that is often the fastest way to find what you want.
. . . Gold Standard singles are in their own section, as are special and promotional singles.
. . . the recently renumbered RCA catalog, printed here for the first time, is going to end a lot of frustration and grief for completists.
. . . the International Elvis Directory, unlike the Collector's Directory in our Popular & Rock singles and albums books, doesn't need to specifically go into the wants of the names listed since they all want the same things!

CHEATING ONESELF

Jellyroll has noticed that collectors and dealers advertising Elvis records have consistently been cheating themselves and confusing their customers by not knowing how to identify various pressings of Elvis records that have significantly different values.

The most classic example we can recall is the 1964 Roustabout stereo album, LSP 2999. The first pressing is the "silvertop" label, with RCA's logo printed in silver lettering. The *second* pressing, which is much more common, is with the logo printed in white lettering. Since the first is worth many times as much as the second, this is vital information to know, as buyer or seller!

ODDITIES UNENDING

This book doesn't price or attempt to document the countless oddities that have been created over the years by manufacturing or production errors, such as partial labels, something missing from a label, the same label on both sides of the record, the labels reversed, or even the labels for a different artist being stuck on a Presley disc (or vice versa). While such oddities may increase value in stamps, there has been no discernable interest among Elvis collectors beyond, perhaps, a vague curiosity.

Though dealers have been known to give away these "rarities" in contempt for their value, it does not mean that interest might not change someday. Our best guess at this time, however, is that it is unlikely.

Other errors that resulted in a press run "recall" to correct an error from continuing to be repeated, are sometimes another story. Very recently "There's A Honky Tonk Angel" appeared with vocal backing and orchestral credits on this Elvis record, when the whole point of the release was that it had none! When RCA caught the error, the presses were stopped and the error corrected, but now the "credits label" record (as it's called) has become a collector's item.

There have been others. One side of the "He Touched Me" single came out on some copies pressed at a speed of about 35 r.p.m. instead of at 45 (a *very* strange production error). Another example: the copies that got out of "It's Now Or Never" with the entire piano track missing! These oddities have established their own values and the demand for them is high.

WHAT IS AND ISN'T LEGAL

We want to be sure readers understand the difference between "unauthorized" and "bootleg." If a record contains Elvis' speaking voice, but no singing, it is probably not illegal, even if "unauthorized" by RCA. These records are identified as such.

A "bootleg", of course, contains illegally released material that deprives the artists and writers of their royalties and the true licensee his recording rights. A "counterfeit" is an attempted reproduction of an existing record or tape, also illegal, and often done in large operations to sell currently advertised and salable material at "bargain" prices. Not only do the record companies suffer, but naturally on these, too, no royalties are paid.

The "fake" is almost always designed to fool collectors, such as in the examples given in our introduction to the International Listings section.

Neither boots nor counterfeits are priced in this guide. Some bootlegs have been documented to account for "alternate takes and alternate mixes".

WHAT IS UNDISCOVERED?

Finally, as complete as this book is—or as nearly complete—we believe collectible Elvis records still exist that no modern-day fan has yet to discover. If so, we are particularly interested in turning up these remaining mavericks. If you think you've found something completely new—and not just a printing or label oddity—please drop us a line at the Jellyroll address below.

Without mentioning several other books, magazines and records, *Presleyana* is our eighth price guide! It, and our recently completed guide pricing *Blues/Rhythm & Blues/Soul,* we feel are the two books that most firmly establish Jellyroll's credentials in this most difficult business.

We're especially proud of these two works because we feel they are fine books, well-researched and accurately cross-referenced. And, most important, we feel they sincerely represent true, unbiased pricing based on the current market.

AXES TO GRIND

Imitation, they say, is the highest form of flattery, but the injustices resulting from some of the new axe-to-grind price guides that have hit the market recently are grossly unfair to the unsuspecting who buy them. An entire series of guides has apparently been started by a large house that "manufactures" price guides. They've stolen so much material from our guides, that they've picked up our old errors as well as our out-of-date prices. Everything they do is two years behind.

Another recent guide attempts to cover all of record collecting in one book, a task *we* know to be nice only in theory but highly impractical. The promise it makes is grandiose, but the fulfillment is weak. Beware to the buyer who tries to look up much! What makes books like these dangerous is that they try to force the market down on the most sought-after items. Why they appear to have this axe-to-grind philosophy, we don't know.

OUR BEST TO YOU

In any case, our pledge to you remains constant: the Osborne-Hamilton Original Price Guide series is DEDICATED to reporting the record market *as it really is,* and we know we're getting better at it with every book!

Incidentally, there are a *very limited number* of deluxe, permanent hardbound copies of each of our books that may be ordered directly from Jellyroll, while the supply lasts (autographed, if you wish) @ $25.00 for *Presleyana* and $18.95 for *Blues/Rhythm & Blues/Soul,* plus $1.00 for shipping.

Thank you for reading this far, and let us hear from you!   —Jerry and Bruce
April, 1980

Jellyroll Productions
Box 3017
Scottsdale, Arizona 85257

Author Jerry Osborne has been a serious student of Elvis Presley's career for 20 years. His countless newspaper and magazine articles on the subject have been read worldwide by millions. Added to this, his numerous meetings with Elvis, his massive collection of "The King's" records and his involvement in the business of putting out record collecting guides and publications make it easy to see why it's been said, "there simply wasn't anyone else who could have done this book."

Osborne had two primary objectives in mind for *Presleyana*. First, to share with Elvis fans and collectors the information and photographs contained within these pages and building upon that foundation toward his ultimate goal to document every Elvis record on earth. And second, to add fresh impetus to what is already the fastest growing phase of record collecting. New Collectors, just coming into the hobby, need dependable and comprehensive reference material. *Presleyana* fills that need.

Osborne feels that *Presleyana* will serve as a handbook, a checklist and a workbook, as well as providing some fascinating insights into the recording career of the greatest entertainer of them all.

We think that you'll agree with him. We know that we do.

Bruce Hamilton's involvement in music began with a seventeen year stint as a disc jockey and program director for radio stations during the golden age of "pop and rock" in the 50s and 60s. This personal, critical involvement included a first hand study of the records released, the public's shifting reactions to them, and of the artists themselves, many of whom (including Presley) he had the privilege of meeting. Even before getting out of broadcasting, Hamilton's interest in collecting records and other items of nostalgia began.

Since the late 60s he's been professionally involved in one aspect or another of collecting, including dealing and acting as an advisor to the preparation of price guides. This background lead to a perspective and an understanding that gave additional depth to the formation of the Osborne-Hamilton team that was formed in 1975 to tackle the "impossible" task of documenting record values.

CONDITION: YOU NEED TO KNOW
WHAT SHAPE YOUR RECORDS ARE IN

Just because a record is old does not necessarily make it valuable. There *has* to be a demand for it. For the value to continue to rise, the demand must always be greater than the supply. Another factor is condition. The most accurate grading system and the easiest one to explain and understand is as follows:

M - MINT

Mint means the record must be in perfect condition. There can be no compromise. If you have two mint records, but can tell a slight difference between the two, one is not mint. It is for this reason that the term "near mint" appears as the highest grade listed in our books. Label defects—such as stickers, writing, rubbing, fading, or warping and wrinkling—will detract from its value. If a record is, indeed, perfect in every way, it will bring somewhat more than the near mint listing.

VG - VERY GOOD

The halfway mark between good and near mint. The disc should have only a minimum amount of foreign, or surface noise and it should not detract at all from the recorded sound. A VG record may show some label wear, but as with audio, it would be minimal.

G - GOOD

The most misunderstood of all grades. Good should not mean bad! A record in good condition will show signs of wear, with an audible amount of foreign noises. There may be scratches and it may be obvious it was never properly cared for (such as being stacked with other records not in sleeves). Nevertheless, it still plays "good" enough to enjoy.

F - FAIR

Fair is the beginning of bad. A fair record will play all the way through without skips, but will contain a distracting amount of noises.

P-POOR

Stepped on by an elephant and it sells for peanuts.

TWO COLUMNS OF PRICING - WHAT IT REALLY MEANS:

The values of Elvis' recordings on the current collector's market are shown in two columns. The figure on the right is always four times that of the figure on the left. An explanation of the quadruple price structure appears on page viii of the introduction.

The first price reflects the collector's market value for copies in "good" condition. The higher price is for copies that are in "near-mint" condition. Obviously, a copy in "very good" condition would have a value of about halfway between the two figures. Strict grading standards must also apply to the jackets and picture sleeves, as well as any other materials that accompany the record.

ELVIS' SINGLES

A

A BIG HUNK O' LOVE/MY WISH CAME TRUE

- ☐ *RCA Victor 47-7600* (45) 1.50   6.00
- ☐ *RCA Victor 47-7600* (Picture sleeve). . . 4.00   16.00

A FOOL SUCH AS I/I NEED YOUR LOVE TONIGHT

- ☐ *RCA Victor 47-7506* (45) 1.50   6.00
- ☐☐ *RCA Victor 47-7506* (Picture sleeve). . . 4.00   16.00

NOTE: Two variations are known to exist for this picture sleeve. One has an ad for the EP "Elvis Sails" on the back, the other carries a listing of available Elvis records on the back. No difference in value has yet been established.

One of the back cover versions of the 47-7506 sleeve.

A LITTLE LESS CONVERSATION/ALMOST IN LOVE

- ☐ *RCA Victor 47-9610* (45) . . . . −   3.00
- ☐ *RCA Victor 47-9610* (Promo 45) 2.00   8.00
- ☐ *RCA Victor 47-9610* (Picture sleeve) . . 2.00   8.00

AIN'T THAT LOVING YOU BABY/ASK ME

- ☐ *RCA Victor 47-8440* (45) 1.00   4.00
- ☐ *RCA Victor 47-8440* (Promo 45) 4.00   16.00
- ☐☐ *RCA Victor 47-8440* (Picture sleeve) . . . 3.00   12.00

NOTE: Two variations are known to exist for this picture sleeve. First issue reads "Coming Soon!" whereas second issue reads "Ask For!" with regard to "Roustabout" LP promotional announcement at bottom of sleeve. No difference in value has yet been established.

ALL SHOOK UP/THAT'S WHEN YOUR HEARTACHES BEGIN

- ☐ *RCA Victor 20-6870* (78) 8.00   32.00
- ☐ *RCA Victor 47-6870* (45) 1.50   6.00
- ☐ *RCA Victor 47-6870* (Picture sleeve) . . . 7.00   28.00

AN AMERICAN TRILOGY/THE FIRST TIME EVER I SAW YOUR FACE

- ☐ *RCA 74-0672* (45) 1.00   4.00
- ☐ *RCA 74-0672* (Promo 45). 2.50   10.00
- ☐ *RCA 74-0672* (Picture sleeve) 2.50   10.00

NOTE: Do not be confused by the promotional announcement at the bottom of this sleeve refering to Elvis' "Standing Room Only" LP. There was never an Elvis album issued by RCA using this title. The idea was simply scrapped, but after the sleeves for this single were already printed.

ARE YOU LONESOME TO-NIGHT?/I GOTTA KNOW

- ☐ *RCA Victor 47-7810* (45) 1.00   4.00
- ☐ *RCA Victor 47-7810* (Picture sleeve) . . . 3.00   12.00
- ☐ *RCA Victor 61-7810* (Living Stereo 45) . 60.00   240.00

ARE YOU SINCERE/SOLITAIRE

- ☐ *RCA PB-11533* (45) . . . . −   2.00
- ☐ *RCA PB-11533* (Promo 45) 1.50   6.00
- ☐ *RCA PB-11533* (Picture sleeve) 1.00   4.00

B

BABY LET'S PLAY HOUSE/I'M LEFT, YOU'RE RIGHT, SHE'S GONE

- ☐ *Sun 217* (78) 25.00   100.00
- ☐ *Sun 217* (45) 60.00   240.00
- ☐ *RCA Victor 20-6383* (78) 9.00   36.00
- ☐ *RCA Victor 47-6383* (45) 4.00   16.00

NOTE: No RCA original picture sleeve exists for this release. Any 47-6383 sleeve you may find is a bootleg.

BIG BOSS MAN/YOU DON'T KNOW ME

☐ *RCA Victor 47-9341* (45) 1.00   4.00
☐ *RCA Victor 47-9341* (Promo 45). 4.00   16.00
☐ *RCA Victor 47-9341* (Picture sleeve) . . . 2.50   10.00

BLUE MOON/JUST BECAUSE

☐ *RCA Victor 20-6640* (78) 9.00   36.00
☐ *RCA Victor 47-6640* (45) 3.00   12.00
NOTE: No RCA original picture sleeve exists for this release. Any 47-6640 sleeve you may find is a bootleg.

BLUE SUEDE SHOES/TUTTI FRUTTI

☐ *RCA Victor 20-6636* (78) 10.00   40.00
☐ *RCA Victor 47-6636* (45) 5.00   20.00
NOTE: No RCA original picture sleeve exists for this release. Any 47-6636 sleeve you may find is a bootleg.

BOSSA NOVA BABY/WITCHCRAFT

☐ *RCA Victor 47-8243* (45) 1.00   4.00
☐☐ *RCA Victor 47-8343* (Picture sleeve) . . . 3.00   12.00
NOTE: Two variations are known to exist for this picture sleeve. First issue reads "Coming Soon!" with regard to Elvis' new LP. Second version makes no mention of the new LP. No difference in value has yet been established.

BURNING LOVE/IT'S A MATTER OF TIME

☐ *RCA 74-0679* (45: Orange label) . . . . —   3.00
☐ *RCA 74-0679* (45: Gray label) 12.50   50.00
☐ *RCA 74-0679* (Promo 45) 1.50   6.00
☐ *RCA 74-0679* (Picture sleeve) 1.50   6.00

C

CAN'T HELP FALLING IN LOVE/ROCK-A-HULA BABY

☐ *RCA Victor 47-7968* (45) 1.00   4.00
☐ *RCA Victor 47-7968* (Picture sleeve) . . . 3.00   12.00
☐ *RCA Victor 37-7968* (Compact 33 single) 125.00   500.00
☐ *RCA Victor 37-7968* (Picture sleeve for Compact 33 single) 75.00   300.00

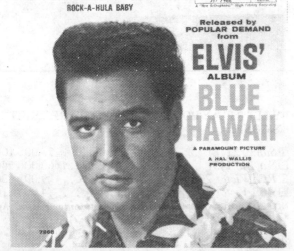

CLEAN UP YOUR OWN BACK YARD/THE FAIR IS MOVING ON

☐ *RCA 47-9747* (45) . . . . —   3.00
☐ *RCA 47-9747* (Promo 45) 1.50   6.00
☐ *RCA 47-9747* (Picture sleeve) 1.50   6.00

D

(YOU'RE THE) DEVIL IN DISGUISE/PLEASE DON'T DRAG THAT STRING AROUND

☐ *RCA Victor 47-8188* (45) . . . . —   3.00
☐ *RCA Victor 47-8188* (Picture sleeve) . . . 3.00   12.00

DO THE CLAM/YOU'LL BE GONE

☐ *RCA Victor 47-8500* (45) 1.00   4.00
☐ *RCA Victor 47-8500* (Promo 45) 4.00   16.00
☐ *RCA Victor 47-8500* (Picture sleeve) . . . 3.00   12.00

DON'T/I BEG OF YOU

☐ *RCA Victor 20-7150* (78) 9.00   36.00
☐ *RCA Victor 47-7150* (45) 1.00   4.00
☐ *RCA Victor 47-7150* (Picture sleeve) . . . 4.00   16.00

DON'T/WEAR MY RING AROUND YOUR NECK: *See our section on SPECIAL/PROMOTIONAL SINGLES*

DON'T BE CRUEL/HOUND DOG

- ☐ *RCA Victor 20-6604* (78) 7.00   28.00
- ☐ *RCA Victor 47-6604* (45) 1.50   6.00
- ☐ *RCA Victor 47-6604* (Picture sleeve: has "Don't Be Cruel" in larger letters than "Hound Dog") 10.00   40.00
- ☐ *RCA Victor 47-6604* (Picture sleeve: has "Hound Dog" in larger letters than "Don't Be Cruel") 7.00   28.00

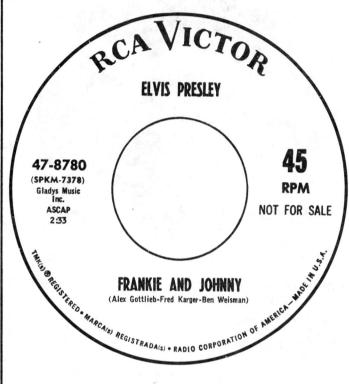

DON'T CRY DADDY/RUBBERNECKIN'

- ☐ *RCA 47-9768* (45) . . . .   —   3.00
- ☐ *RCA 47-9768* (Promo 45) 1.50   6.00
- ☐ *RCA 47-9768* (Picture sleeve) 1.50   6.00

E

(SUCH AN) EASY QUESTION/IT FEELS SO RIGHT

- ☐ *RCA Victor 47-8585* (45) 1.00   4.00
- ☐ *RCA Victor 47-8585* (Promo 45) 4.00   16.00
- ☐ *RCA Victor 47-8585* (Picture sleeve) . . 2.50   10.00

ELVIS: A SIX HOUR SPECIAL: *See our section on SOUNDSHEETS*

ELVIS SPEAKS (THE TRUTH ABOUT ME): *See our section on SOUNDSHEETS*

ELVIS PRESLEY STORY, THE: *See our section on SOUNDSHEETS*

F

15 GOLDEN RECORDS - 30 GOLDEN HITS: *See our section on SPECIAL/PROMOTIONAL singles*

FRANKIE AND JOHNNY/PLEASE DON'T STOP LOVING ME

- ☐ *RCA Victor 47-8780* (45) 1.00   4.00
- ☐ *RCA Victor 47-8780* (Promo 45) 4.00   16.00
- ☐ *RCA Victor 47-8780* (Picture sleeve) . . . 2.50   10.00

G

GOOD LUCK CHARM/ANYTHING THAT'S PART OF YOU

- ☐ *RCA Victor 47-7992* (45) 1.00   4.00
- ☐☐ *RCA Victor 47-7992* (Picture sleeve) . . . 3.00   12.00
- ☐ *RCA Victor 37-7992* (Compact 33 single) 150.00   600.00
- ☐ *RCA Victor 37-7992* (Picture sleeve for Compact 33 single) 100.00   400.00

NOTE: Two variations are known to exist for this picture sleeve, as issued with the 45 single. Although slight, the difference is certainly worth noting. One version has the song titles in blue and pink colors whereas the alternate sleeve has them printed in rust and lavender colors. No price difference has yet been established.

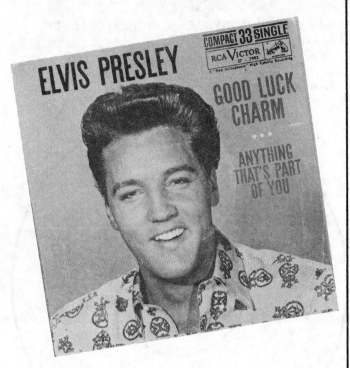

GOOD ROCKIN' TONIGHT/I DON'T CARE IF THE SUN DON'T SHINE

☐ *Sun 210* (78)	25.00	100.00
☐ *Sun 210* (45)	60.00	240.00
☐ *RCA Victor 20-6381* (78)	9.00	36.00
☐ *RCA Victor 47-6381* (45)	4.00	16.00

NOTE: No RCA original picture sleeve exists for this release. Any 47-6381 sleeve you may find is a bootleg.

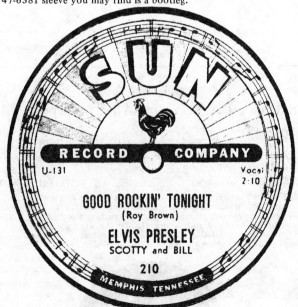

GUITAR MAN/HIGH HEEL SNEAKERS

☐ *RCA Victor 47-9425* (45)	—	3.00
☐ *RCA Victor 47-9425* (Promo 45)	2.00	8.00
☐☐ *RCA Victor 47-9425* (Picture sleeve) ...	2.00	8.00

NOTE: Two variations are known to exist for this picture sleeve. The first issue says "Coming Soon" "Elvis Gold Records Volume 4," whereas the second issue says "Ask For" the LP. No difference in value has yet been established.

HARD HEADED WOMAN/DON'T ASK ME WHY

☐ *RCA Victor 20-7280* (78)	12.00	48.00
☐ *RCA Victor 47-7280* (45)	1.00	4.00
☐ *RCA Victor 47-7280* (Picture sleeve) ...	4.00	16.00

HE TOUCHED ME/BOSOM OF ABRAHAM

☐ *RCA 74-0651* (45)	1.50	6.00
☐ *RCA 74-0651* (Promo 45)	12.50	50.00
☐ *RCA 74-0651* (Picture sleeve)	8.00	32.00

NOTE: An error in production resulted in some copies of the commercial release of this record to be pressed at 35rpm (approximately) on the "He Touched Me" side. The flip of these copies runs at the proper 45rpm. Since this book does not price oddities created simply by errors, values are entirely negotiable between buyers and sellers.

HEARTBREAK HOTEL/I WAS THE ONE

☐ *RCA Victor 20-6420* (78)	7.00	28.00
☐ *RCA Victor 47-6420* (45)	1.50	6.00

NOTE: No RCA original picture sleeve exists for this release. Any 47-6420 sleeve you may find is a bootleg.

HIS LATEST FLAME/LITTLE SISTER

☐ *RCA Victor 47-7908* (45)	1.00	4.00
☐ *RCA Victor 47-7908* (Picture sleeve) ...	3.00	12.00
☐ *RCA Victor 37-7908* (Compact 33 single)	125.00	500.00
☐ *RCA Victor 37-7908* (Picture sleeve for Compact 33 single)	75.00	300.00

(See photos on the following page)

HOME IS WHERE THE HEART IS/KING OF THE WHOLE WIDE WORLD: *See KING OF THE WHOLE WIDE WORLD in our section on SPECIAL/PROMOTIONAL SINGLES*

HOW GREAT THOU ART/HIS HAND IN MINE

☐ *RCA 74-0130* (45)	4.00	16.00
☐ *RCA 74-0130* (Promo 45)	5.00	20.00
☐ *RCA 74-0130* (Picture sleeve)	15.00	60.00

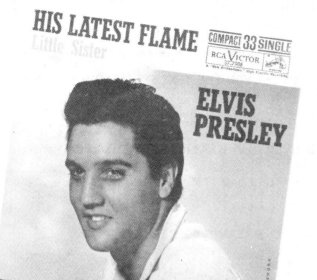

HOW GREAT THOU ART/SO HIGH: *See our section on* *SPECIAL/PROMOTIONAL SINGLES*

HURT/FOR THE HEART

☐ *RCA PB-10601* (45) . . . .   –   2.00
☐ *RCA PB-10601* (Promo 45) 1.00   4.00
☐ *RCA PB-10601* (Picture sleeve) 1.00   4.00

I FEEL SO BAD/WILD IN THE COUNTRY

☐ *RCA Victor 47-7880* (45) 1.00   4.00
☐ *RCA Victor 47-7880* (Picture sleeve) . .   4.00   12.00
☐ *RCA Victor 37-7880* (Compact 33 single) 60.00 240.00
☐ *RCA Victor 37-7880* (Picture sleeve for
  Compact 33 single) 60.00 240.00

I GOT A WOMAN/I'M COUNTING ON YOU

☐ *RCA Victor 20-6637* (78) 9.00   36.00
☐ *RCA Victor 47-6637* (45) 3.00   12.00
NOTE: No RCA original picture sleeve exists for this release. Any
47-6637 sleeve you may find is a bootleg.

I REALLY DON'T WANT TO KNOW/THERE GOES MY EVERYTHING

- ☐ *RCA 47-9960* (45) .... — 3.00
- ☐ *RCA 47-9960* (Promo 45) 1.50 6.00
- ☐☐ *RCA 47-9960* (Picture sleeve) 1.50 6.00

NOTE: Two variations are known to exist for this picture sleeve. The first issue says "Coming Soon" new album "Elvis Country," whereas the second issue says "Now Available." No difference in value has yet been established.

I WANT YOU, I NEED YOU, I LOVE YOU/MY BABY LEFT ME

- ☐ *RCA Victor 20-6540* (78) 7.00 28.00
- ☐ *RCA Victor 47-6540* (45) 1.50 6.00
- ☐ *RCA Victor 47-6540* (Promotional picture sleeve) 75.00 300.00

NOTE: This special picture sleeve was issued as a part of a lengthy series of "cartoon sleeves" used by RCA. Each sleeve depicted "the life story" of the artist. This Elvis sleeve, which does not have the catalog number on it, was issued prior to "Don't Be Cruel"/"Hound Dog" (47-6604) and thus becomes the very first Elvis picture sleeve used on 45rpm by RCA.

I'LL NEVER LET YOU GO/I'M GONNA SIT RIGHT DOWN AND CRY

- ☐ *RCA Victor 20-6638* (78) 9.00 36.00
- ☐ *RCA Victor 47-6638* (45) 4.00 16.00

NOTE: No RCA original picture sleeve exists for this release. Any 47-6638 sleeve you may find is a bootleg.

I'M LEAVIN'/HEART OF ROME

- ☐ *RCA 47-9998* (45) .... — 3.00
- ☐ *RCA 47-9998* (Promo 45) 1.50 6.00
- ☐ *RCA 47-9998* (Picture sleeve) 1.50 6.00

I'M YOURS/ (IT'S A) LONG LONELY HIGHWAY

- ☐ *RCA Victor 47-8657* (45) 1.00 4.00
- ☐ *RCA Victor 47-8657* (Promo 45) 4.00 16.00
- ☐ *RCA Victor 47-8657* (Picture sleeve) ... 3.00 12.00

I'VE GOT A THING ABOUT YOU BABY/TAKE GOOD CARE OF HER

- ☐ *RCA APBO-0916* (45) .... — 3.00
- ☐ *RCA APBO-0916* (Promo 45) 1.50 6.00
- ☐ *RCA APBO-0916* (Picture sleeve) 1.50 6.00

I'VE LOST YOU/THE NEXT STEP IS LOVE

- ☐ *RCA 47-9873* (45) .... — 3.00
- ☐ *RCA 47-9873* (Promo 45) 1.50 6.00
- ☐ *RCA 47-9873* (Picture sleeve)........ 1.50 6.00

IF EVERYDAY WAS LIKE CHRISTMAS/HOW WOULD YOU LIKE TO BE

- ☐ *RCA Victor 47-8950* (45) 1.25 5.00
- ☐ *RCA Victor 47-8950* (Promo 45) 4.00 16.00
- ☐ *RCA Victor 47-8950* (Picture sleeve) .. 4.00 16.00

IF I CAN DREAM/EDGE OF REALITY

- ☐ *RCA 47-9670* (45) .... — 3.00
- ☐ *RCA 47-9670* (Promo 45) 1.50 6.00
- ☐ *RCA 47-9670* (Picture sleeve: First issue with "As Featured On His NBC-TV Special" printed under song title) 2.50 10.00
- ☐ *RCA 47-9670* (Picture sleeve: Second issue, no mention of NBC-TV Special on this sleeve) 1.50 6.00

IF YOU TALK IN YOUR SLEEP/HELP ME

- ☐ *RCA APBO-0280* (45) .... — 2.00
- ☐ *RCA APBO-0280* (Promo 45) 1.50 6.00
- ☐ *RCA APBO-0280* (Picture sleeve) 1.00 4.00

IN THE GHETTO/ANY DAY NOW

- ☐ *RCA 47-9741* (45) .... — 3.00
- ☐ *RCA 47-9741* (Promo 45) 1.50 6.00
- ☐☐ *RCA 47-9741* (Picture sleeve) 1.50 6.00

NOTE: Two variations are known to exist for this picture sleeve. First issue reads "Coming Soon" with regard to Elvis' new album, "From Elvis in Memphis." Second issue says "Ask For" the new LP. No difference in value has yet been established.

INDESCRIBABLY BLUE/FOOLS FALL IN LOVE

- ☐ *RCA Victor 47-9056* (45) 1.00 4.00
- ☐ *RCA Victor 47-9056* (Promo 45) 4.00 16.00
- ☐ *RCA Victor 47-9056* (Picture sleeve) .. 2.50 10.00

IT'S NOW OR NEVER/A MESS OF BLUES

- ☐ *RCA Victor 47-7777* (45) 1.00 4.00
- ☐ *RCA Victor 47-7777* (Picture sleeve) .. 3.00 12.00
- ☐ *RCA Victor 61-7777* (Living Stereo 45) 60.00 240.00

NOTE: An error in production resulted in a small number of copies of this record to be pressed without the piano track. Since this book does not price oddities created simply by errors, values are entirely negotiable between buyers and sellers.

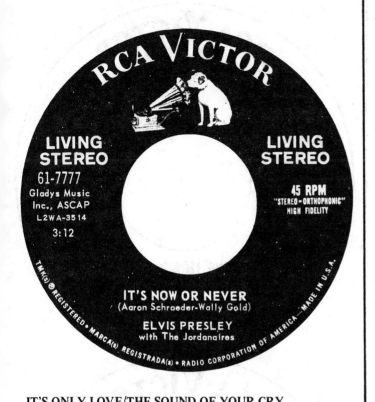

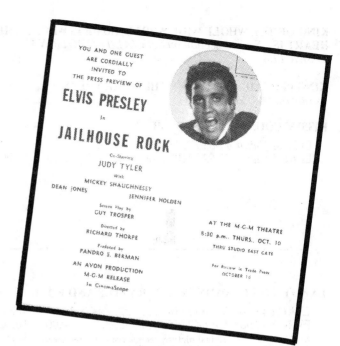

ELVIS PRESLEY
In
JAILHOUSE ROCK
Co-Starring
JUDY TYLER
With
MICKEY SHAUGHNESSY
DEAN JONES   JENNIFER HOLDEN

IT'S ONLY LOVE/THE SOUND OF YOUR CRY

☐ *RCA 48-1017* (45)	–	3.00
☐ *RCA 48-1017* (Promo 45)...........	1.50	6.00
☐ *RCA 48-1017* (Picture sleeve)........	1.50	6.00

J

JAILHOUSE ROCK/TREAT ME NICE

☐ *RCA Victor 20-7035* (78)	7.00	28.00
☐ *RCA Victor 47-7035* (45)	1.50	6.00
☐ *RCA Victor 47-7035* (Picture sleeve)..	7.00	28.00
☐ *Special MGM "Jailhouse Rock" jacket*	50.00	200.00

NOTE: As a novel way of inviting the trade press to the special press review of Elvis' film, "Jailhouse Rock," MGM prepared a large theatre ticket that actually wrapped around the commercial RCA single picture sleeve, die-cut to allow the Elvis facial photo to show through. The entire package, record, picture sleeve and invitational ticket, was then sent to the selected media.

TEAR HERE
- - - - - - - - - - - - - - - - - - - -

ADMIT BEARER AND GUEST
TO THE SPECIAL PRESS SCREENING OF
"JAILHOUSE ROCK"
THURSDAY EVENING, OCTOBER 10
AT 8:30 P.M.

JUDY/THERE'S ALWAYS ME

☐ *RCA Victor 47-9287* (45)	1.00	4.00
☐ *RCA Victor 47-9287* (Promo 45).....	4.00	16.00
☐ *RCA Victor 47-9287* (Picture sleeve)..	2.50	10.00

K

KENTUCKY RAIN/MY LITTLE FRIEND

☐ *RCA 47-9791* (45)	–	3.00
☐ *RCA 47-9791* (Promo 45).........	1.50	6.00
☐ *RCA 47-9791* (Picture sleeve).......	1.50	6.00

KING OF THE WHOLE WIDE WORLD/HOME IS WHERE THE HEART IS: *See our section on SPECIAL/PROMOTIONAL SINGLES*

KING IS DEAD - LONG LIVE THE KING, THE: *See our section on SOUNDSHEETS*

KISSIN' COUSINS/IT HURTS ME

☐ *RCA Victor 47-8307 (45)* 1.00   4.00
☐ *RCA Victor 47-8307 (Picture sleeve)* . .   3.00   12.00

L

LAWDY MISS CLAWDY/SHAKE, RATTLE AND ROLL

☐ *RCA Victor 20-6642 (78)* 10.00   40.00
☐ *RCA Victor 47-6642 (45)* 4.00   16.00

NOTE: No RCA original picture sleeve exists for this release. Any 47-6642 sleeve you may find is a bootleg.

LET ME BE THERE: *See our section on SPECIAL PROMOTIONAL SINGLES*

LIFE/ONLY BELIEVE

☐ *RCA 47-9985 (45)* . . . .   –   3.00
☐ *RCA 47-9985 (Promo 45)* 1.50   6.00
☐ *RCA 47-9985 (Picture sleeve)* 1.50   6.00

LONG LEGGED GIRL (WITH THE SHORT DRESS ON)/ THAT'S SOMEONE YOU NEVER FORGET

☐ *RCA Victor 47-9115 (45)* 1.00   4.00
☐ *RCA Victor 47-9115 (Promo 45)* 4.00   16.00
☐☐ *RCA Victor 47-9115 (Picture sleeve)* . .   2.50   10.00

NOTE: Two variations are known to exist for this picture sleeve. First issue reads "Coming Soon" with regard to Elvis' "Double Trouble" album. Second issue says "Ask For" the LP. No difference in value has yet been established.

NOTE: The two promotional copies of 47-9115 pictured on this page serve to point out the type of label variations that can be found on nearly every RCA release issued prior to the time (1968) the company switched to the orange label.

Singles, extended plays and albums from the first 13-plus years of RCA's Elvis releases, including both black and yellow labels as well as promotional issues, can usually be found to exist in more than one label design.

In most cases, like the example shown, the differences in type style or size, or overall layout, is obvious at a glance. A Few, however, require a closer inspection to detect the variations.

Although no difference in value has yet and perhaps never will be attached to these seemingly endless label variations, from a serious collector's viewpoint they are worth both noting and collecting.

In a future edition of this guide, we will provide a complete listing of Elvis' label variations.

LOVE LETTERS/COME WHAT MAY

☐ *RCA Victor 47-8870 (45)* 1.00   4.00
☐ *RCA Victor 47-8870 (Promo 45)* 4.00   16.00
☐☐ *RCA Victor 47-8870 (Picture sleeve)* . .   2.50   10.00

NOTE: Two variations are known to exist for this picture sleeve. First issue reads "Coming Soon," with regard to Elvis' new album, "Paradise Hawaiian Style." Second issue says "Ask For" the new LP.

LOVE ME TENDER/ANY WAY YOU WANT ME (THAT'S HOW I'LL BE)

- ☐ *RCA Victor 20-6643* (78) 6.00 24.00
- ☐ *RCA Victor 47-6643* (45) 1.50 6.00
- ☐ *RCA Victor 47-6643* (Picture sleeve: Black and White colors) 25.00 100.00
- ☐ *RCA Victor 47-6643* (Picture sleeve: Black and Green colors) 12.00 48.00
- ☐☐ *RCA Victor 47-6643* (Picture sleeve: Black and Pink colors) 4.00 16.00

NOTE: Two variations are known to exist for the PINK 47-6643 sleeve. One is light pink, the other a darker pink. It may be necessary to have them both in hand to know which is which. No significant difference in value has yet been established between the two pink sleeves.

NOTE: Copies of this 78rpm single have been found on very thick plastic as well as on a much thinner stock. In addition to the varying thickness, different labels (some with catalog number on left; others on right side) have also been found. While many other Elvis 78s have the label variation, fewer seem to have been issued on the noticably different stock.

M

MEMORIES/CHARRO

- ☐ *RCA 47-9731* (45) . . . . – 3.00
- ☐ *RCA 47-9731* (Promo 45) 1.50 6.00
- ☐ *RCA 47-9731* (Picture sleeve) 1.50 6.00

MERRY CHRISTMAS BABY/O COME ALL YE FAITHFUL

- ☐ *RCA 74-0572* (45) 1.00 4.00
- ☐ *RCA 74-0572* (Promo 45) 2.50 10.00
- ☐ *RCA 74-0572* (Picture sleeve) 2.50 10.00

MONEY HONEY/ONE SIDED LOVE AFFAIR

- ☐ *RCA Victor 20-6641* (78) 9.00 36.00
- ☐ *RCA Victor 47-6641* (45) 3.00 12.00

NOTE: No RCA original picture sleeve exists for this release. Any 47-6641 sleeve you may find is a bootleg.

MOODY BLUE/SHE THINKS I STILL CARE

- ☐ *RCA PB-10857* (45) . . . . – 2.00
- ☐ *RCA PB-10857* (Promo 45) 1.50 6.00
- ☐ *RCA PB-10857* (Picture sleeve) 1.00 4.00

MY BOY/THINKING ABOUT YOU

- ☐ *RCA PB-10191* (45) . . . . – 2.00
- ☐ *RCA PB-10191* (Promo 45) 2.00 8.00
- ☐ *RCA PB-10191* (Picture sleeve) 1.00 6.00

NOTE: Promotional copies of this single were issued with "My Boy" on both sides. The intent was to concentrate all promotion on that song. One side of the promo 45 had the song in monaural, the reverse offered the stereo version. This was the only time, despite its widespread use in the industry, that RCA issued an Elvis promotional single that didn't feature the same two sides as the commercial issue. It should be noted that "Let Me Be There" was also produced on a mono/stereo 45, but it was neither released by RCA, nor was it a commercial single release.

MY WAY/AMERICA

- ☐ *RCA PB-11165* (45) . . . . — 2.00
- ☐ *RCA PB-11165* (Promo 45) 1.50 6.00
- ☐ *RCA PB-11165* (Picture sleeve) 1.00 4.00

  NOTE: Also see MY WAY/AMERICA THE BEAUTIFUL

MY WAY/AMERICA THE BEAUTIFUL

- ☐ *RCA PB-11165* (45) 6.00 24.00
- ☐ *RCA PB-11165* (Picture sleeve) 6.00 24.00

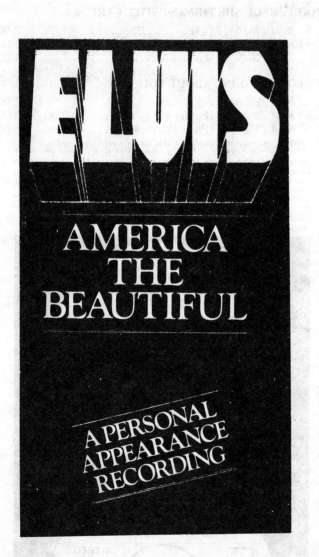

MYSTERY TRAIN/I FORGOT TO REMEMBER TO FORGET

- ☐ *Sun 223* (78) 20.00 80.00
- ☐ *Sun 223* (45) 40.00 160.00
- ☐ *RCA Victor 20-6357* (78) 9.00 36.00
- ☐ *RCA Victor 47-6357* (45) 4.00 16.00
- ☐ *RCA Victor 47-6357* (Promo 45) 15.00 60.00

O

OLD SHEP: *See our section on SPECIAL/PROMOTIONAL SINGLES*

ONE BROKEN HEART FOR SALE/THEY REMIND ME TOO MUCH OF YOU
- ☐ *RCA Victor 47-8134* (45) 1.00 4.00
- ☐ *RCA Victor 47-8134* (Picture sleeve) . . 3.00 12.00

ONE NIGHT/I GOT STUNG
- ☐ *RCA Victor 20-7410* (78) 50.00 200.00
- ☐ *RCA Victor 47-7410* (45) 1.50 6.00
- ☐ *RCA Victor 47-7410* (Picture sleeve) . . 4.00 16.00

P

PIECES OF MY LIFE/BRINGING IT BACK
- ☐ *RCA PB-10401* (45) . . . . — 3.00
- ☐ *RCA PB-10401* (Promo 45) 1.50 6.00
- ☐ *RCA PB-10401* (Picture sleeve) 1.50 6.00

PROMISED LAND/IT'S MIDNIGHT
- ☐ *RCA PB-10074* (45) . . . . — 2.00
- ☐ *RCA PB-10074* (Promo 45) 1.50 6.00
- ☐ *RCA PB-10074* (Picture sleeve) 1.50 6.00

R

RAGS TO RICHES/WHERE DID THEY GO LORD
- ☐ *RCA 47-9980* (45) . . . . — 3.00
- ☐ *RCA 47-9980* (Promo 45) 1.50 6.00
- ☐ *RCA 47-9980* (Picture sleeve) 1.50 6.00

RAISED ON ROCK/FOR OLD TIMES SAKE
- ☐ *RCA APBO-0088* (45) . . . . — 3.00
- ☐ *RCA APBO-0088* (Promo 45) 2.50 10.00
- ☐ *RCA APBO-0088* (Picture sleeve) 1.50 6.00

RETURN TO SENDER/WHERE DO YOU COME FROM
- ☐ *RCA Victor 47-8100* (45) 1.00 4.00
- ☐ *RCA Victor 47-8100* (Picture sleeve) . 3.00 12.00

ROUSTABOUT/ONE TRACK HEART: *See our section on SPECIAL/PROMOTIONAL SINGLES*

ROUSTABOUT (THEATRE LOBBY SPOT): *See our section on SPECIAL/PROMOTIONAL SINGLES*

S

SEPARATE WAYS/ALWAYS ON MY MIND
- ☐ *RCA 74-0815* (45) . . . . — 3.00
- ☐ *RCA 74-0815* (Promo 45) 1.50 6.00
- ☐ *RCA 74-0815* (Picture sleeve) 1.50 6.00

SHE'S NOT YOU/JUST TELL HER JIM SAID HELLO
- ☐ *RCA Victor 47-8041* (45) 1.00 4.00
- ☐ *RCA Victor 47-8041* (Picture sleeve) . 3.00 12.00

SO HIGH/HOW GREAT THOU ART: *See our section on SPECIAL/PROMOTIONAL SINGLES*

SOFTLY, AS I LEAVE YOU/UNCHAINED MELODY
- ☐ *RCA PB-11212* (45) . . . . — 2.00
- ☐ *RCA PB-11212* (Promo 45) 1.50 6.00
- ☐ *RCA PB-11212* (Picture sleeve) 1.00 4.00

SPINOUT/ALL THAT I AM
- ☐ *RCA Victor 47-8941* (45) 1.00 4.00
- ☐ *RCA Victor 47-8941* (Promo 45) . . . 4.00 16.00
- ☐☐ *RCA Victor 47-8941* (Picture sleeve) 2.50 10.00

NOTE: Two variations are known to exist to this picture sleeve. First issue reads "Watch For," with regard to Elvis' new album, "Spinout." Second issue says "Ask For" the LP.

WATCH FOR ELVIS' "SPINOUT" LP ALBUM

ASK FOR ELVIS' "SPINOUT" LP ALBUM

STEAMROLLER BLUES/FOOL

- ☐ *RCA 74-0910* (45) . . . .   —   3.00
- ☐ *RCA 74-0910* (Promo 45) 1.50   6.00
- ☐ *RCA 74-0910* (Picture sleeve) 1.50   6.00

STUCK ON YOU/FAME AND FORTUNE

- ☐ *RCA Victor 47-7740* (45) 1.00   4.00
- ☐ *RCA Victor 47-7740* (Picture sleeve) . .   1.25   5.00
- ☐ *RCA Victor 61-7740* (Living Stereo 45)   40.00   160.00

NOTE: Totally unlike any other Elvis picture sleeves, the one for this release had a die-cut, label-size, hole in its center. The actual record label was then on display while still inside the sleeve.

SUCH A NIGHT/NEVER ENDING

- ☐ *RCA Victor 47-8400* (45) 1.00   4.00
- ☐ *RCA Victor 47-8400* (Promo 45) 60.00   240.00
- ☐ *RCA Victor 47-8400* (Picture sleeve) . .   3.00   12.00

When it comes to Elvis promotional releases of standard RCA catalog issues, "Such A Night"/"Never Ending" ranks as the world's rarest!

12

SURRENDER/LONELY MAN

☐ *RCA Victor 47-7850* (45)	1.00	4.00
☐ *RCA Victor 47-7850* (Picture sleeve) . .	3.00	12.00
☐ *RCA Victor 37-7850* (Compact 33 single)	40.00	160.00
☐ *RCA Victor 37-7850* (Picture sleeve for Compact 33 single)	40.00	160.00
☐ *RCA Victor 61-7850* (Living Stereo 45)	60.00	240.00
☐ *RCA Victor 68-7850* (Living Stereo Compact 33 single)	200.00	800.00

NOTE: The Living Stereo Compact 33 single of "Surrender"/ "Lonely Man" was the only commercial stereo 33 compact ever made using Elvis' voice. As a one time experiment, there was never a special picture sleeve made for the stereo compact. The few copies known to exist were said to have been packaged in the 37-7850, monaural Compact 33 single, sleeve.

If nothing else, RCA's release of "Surrender"/ "Lonely Man" single in every conceivable format helped establish where the public's interest was; still in the good ol' 45rpm.

A grand total of four Living Stereo singles were made during 1960-61. Five 33-Compacts —all with special picture sleeves— appeared from 1961-62. And never again did RCA do an Elvis Stereo 33-Compact.

SUSPICIOUS MINDS/YOU'LL THINK OF ME

- ☐ *RCA 47-9764* (45) .... — 3.00
- ☐ *RCA 47-9764* (Promo 45) 1.50 6.00
- ☐ *RCA 47-9764* (Picture sleeve) 1.50 6.00

T

(LET ME BE YOUR) TEDDY BEAR/LOVING YOU

- ☐ *RCA Victor 20-7000* (78) 7.00 28.00
- ☐ *RCA Victor 47-7000* (45) 1.50 6.00
- ☐ *RCA Victor 47-7000* (Picture sleeve) .. 7.00 28.00

(LET ME BE YOUR) TEDDY BEAR/PUPPET ON A STRING

- ☐ *RCA PB-11320* (45) .... — 2.00
- ☐ *RCA PB-11320* (Promo 45) 1.50 6.00
- ☐ *RCA PB-11320* (Picture sleeve) 1.00 4.00

TELL ME WHY/BLUE RIVER

- ☐ *RCA Victor 47-8740* (45) 1.00 4.00
- ☐ *RCA Victor 47-8740* (Promo 45) 4.00 16.00
- ☐ *RCA Vietor 47-8740* (Picture sleeve) .. 3.00 12.00

THAT'S ALL RIGHT/BLUE MOON OF KENTUCKY

- ☐ *Sun 209* (78) 30.00 120.00
- ☐ *Sun 209* (45) 70.00 280.00
- ☐ *RCA Victor 20-6380* (78) 9.00 36.00
- ☐ *RCA Victor 47-6380* (45) 4.00 16.00

NOTE: No RCA original picture sleeve exists for this release. Any 47-6380 sleeve you may find is a bootleg.

THERE'S A HONKY TONK ANGEL (WHO'LL TAKE ME BACK IN/I GOT A FEELIN' IN MY BODY

- ☐ *RCA PB-11679* (45) .... — 2.00
- ☐ *RCA PB-11679* (45: Credits label) ... 2.00 8.00
- ☐ *RCA PB-11679* (Promo 45) 1.50 6.00
- ☐ *RCA PB-11679* (Picture sleeve) 1.50 6.00

NOTE: First commercial pressings of this single had printed credits on the label for vocal accompaniment and for strings arrangement. Since this single was lifted from the "Our Memories of Elvis Vol. 2" LP, which featured the "pure Elvis" (sans vocal and string accompaniment) sound, it did not have the backing shown by the credits. RCA, quickly discovering the error, stopped the presses, eliminated the credits, then continued production using the proper information on the label. All promo 45 singles have the credits, as they were done prior to the first commercial pressings.

TOO MUCH/PLAYING FOR KEEPS

- ☐ *RCA Victor 20-6800* (78) 8.00 32.00
- ☐ *RCA Victor 47-6800* (45) 1.50 6.00
- ☐ *RCA Victor 47-6800* (Picture sleeve) .. 7.00 28.00

NOTE: It would appear that 47-6800 was the only Elvis single on RCA's dogless label.

You'll find a number of extended plays that were available on dogless labels, as well as more information on this interesting RCA pressing variation, further on in this book.

A photo of the dogless "Too Much" appears on the following page.

UNTIL IT'S TIME FOR YOU TO GO/WE CAN MAKE THE MORNING

- ☐ *RCA 74-0619* (45) .... − 3.00
- ☐ *RCA 74-0619* (Promo 45)........... 1.50 6.00
- ☐ *RCA 74-0619* (Picture sleeve)........ 1.50 6.00

V

VIVA LAS VEGAS/WHAT'D I SAY

- ☐ *RCA Victor 47-8360* (45) 1.00 4.00
- ☐ *RCA Victor 47-8360* (Promo 45)..... 4.00 16.00
- ☐ *RCA Victor 47-8360* (Picture sleeve).. 3.00 12.00

T-R-O-U-B-L-E/MR. SONGMAN

- ☐ *RCA PB-10278* (45) .... − 3.00
- ☐ *RCA PB-10278* (Promo 45) 1.50 6.00
- ☐ *RCA PB-10278* (Picture sleeve) 1.00 4.00

TRUTH ABOUT ME, THE: *See our section on SOUNDSHEETS*

TRYIN' TO GET TO YOU/I LOVE YOU BECAUSE

- ☐ *RCA Victor 20-6639* (78) 9.00 36.00
- ☐ *RCA Victor 47-6639* (45) 4.00 16.00

NOTE: No RCA original picture sleeve exists for this release. Any 47-6639 sleeve you may find is a bootleg.

20 GOLDEN HITS IN FULL COLOR SLEEVES: *See our section on SPECIAL/PROMOTIONAL SINGLES*

U

U.S. MALE/STAY AWAY

- ☐ *RCA Victor 47-9465* (45) 1.00 4.00
- ☐ *RCA Victor 47-9465* (Promo 45)..... 2.00 8.00
- ☐ *RCA Victor 47-9465* (Picture sleeve).. 2.00 8.00

ELVIS PRESLEY

WAY DOWN/PLEDGING MY LOVE

- ☐ *RCA PB-10998* (45) . . . .   —   2.00
- ☐ *RCA PB-10998* (Promo 45). 1.50   6.00
- ☐ *RCA PB-10998* (White label promo 45) 20.00 80.00
- ☐ *RCA PB-10998* (Picture sleeve). 1.00   4.00

NOTE: Prior to the release of the standard yellow (or cream color) label promotional copies of PB-10998, RCA rush released a white label promotional version.

NOTE: "Way Down"/"Pledging My Love" was the first of a few of RCA's Elvis releases that had a kind of reddish-brown tint to the vinyl (polystyrene) when held up to a bright light. Although not an intentional variation by RCA, some collectors have placed somewhat of a premium of these pressings. The Price Guide's position is to not attach specific values to discs that are the result of errors or quirks in production, leaving that to negotiation between buyer and seller. We do, however, include such information in the Guide for the sake of providing a more useful and comprehensive publication.

WEAR MY RING AROUND YOUR NECK/DONCHA' THINK IT'S TIME

- ☐ *RCA Victor 20-7240* (78) 11.00 44.00
- ☐ *RCA Victor 47-7240* (45) 1.50   6.00
- ☐ *RCA Victor 47-7240* (Picture sleeve) . . 4.00 16.00

WEAR MY RING AROUND YOUR NECK/DON'T: *See our section on SPECIAL/PROMOTIONAL SINGLES*

WONDER OF YOU, THE/MAMA LIKED THE ROSES

- ☐ *RCA 47-9835* (45) . . . .   —   3.00
- ☐ *RCA 47-9835* (Promo 45). 1.50   6.00
- ☐ *RCA 47-9835* (Picture sleeve). 1.50   6.00

YOU DON'T HAVE TO SAY YOU LOVE ME/PATCH IT UP

- ☐ *RCA 47-9916* (45) . . . .   —   3.00
- ☐ *RCA 47-9916* (Promo 45). 1.50   6.00
- ☐ *RCA 47-9916* (Picture sleeve). 1.50   6.00

YOU'LL NEVER WALK ALONE/WE CALL ON HIM

- ☐ *RCA Victor 47-9600* (45) 1.25   5.00
- ☐ *RCA Victor 47-9600* (Promo 45). 4.00 16.00
- ☐ *RCA Victor 47-9600* (Picture sleeve) . . 9.00 36.00

YOUR TIME HASN'T COME YET BABY/LET YOURSELF GO

- ☐ *RCA Victor 47-9547* (45) 1.00   4.00
- ☐ *RCA Victor 47-9547* (Promo 45). 2.00   8.00
- ☐☐ *RCA Victor 47-9547* (Picture sleeve) . . 2.00   8.00

NOTE: Two variations are known to exist for this picture sleeve. First issue reads "Coming Soon," with regard to Elvis' new album, "Speedway." Second issue says "Ask For" the new LP.

YOU'RE A HEARTBREAKER/MILKCOW BLUES BOOGIE

Sun 215 (78)	30.00	120.00
Sun 215 (45)	75.00	300.00
RCA Victor 20-6382 (78)	9.00	36.00
RCA Victor 47-6382 (45)	4.00	16.00

NOTE: No RCA original picture sleeve exists for this release. Any 47-6382 sleeve you may find is a bootleg.

SPECIAL U.S. AIR FORCE SINGLES

The following two singles were issued as part of the U.S. Air Force's "Music In The Air" series, sent to radio stations for public service broadcast. One side of each disc features Elvis.

IT'S NOW OR NEVER/I WALK THE LINE (by Jaye P. Morgan)

☐ *U.S.A.F. Program No. 125* 50.00 200.00

NOTE: The ending of the song has been edited so as to cut down on the overall playing time.

SURRENDER/OUT OF A CLEAR BLUE SKY (by Lawrence Welk)

☐ *U.S.A.F. Program No. 159* 50.00 200.00

SINGLES ISSUED WITH HORIZONTAL SILVER LINE:

The following singles were pressed using a silver horizontal line across the label, in addition to the slightly more common issues that do not have the line. Copies of these singles with the line seem to bring more —from 25% to double— than those copies that were pressed without the line.

☐ *47-6357 MYSTERY TRAIN/I FORGOT TO REMEMBER TO FORGET*
☐ *47-6380 THAT'S ALL RIGHT/BLUE MOON OF KEN-TUCKY*
☐ *47-6381 GOOD ROCKIN' TONIGHT/I DON'T CARE IF THE SUN DON'T SHINE*
☐ *47-6382 YOU'RE A HEARTBREAKER/MILKCOW BLUES BOOGIE*
☐ *47-6383 BABY LET'S PLAY HOUSE/I'M LEFT, YOU'RE RIGHT, SHE'S GONE*
☐ *47-6420 HEARTBREAK HOTEL/I WAS THE ONE*
☐ *47-6540 I WANT YOU, I NEED YOU, I LOVE YOU/ MY BABY LEFT ME*
☐ *47-6604 DON'T BE CRUEL/HOUND DOG*
☐ *47-6636 BLUE SUEDE SHOES/TUTTI FRUTTI*
☐ *47-6637 I GOT A WOMAN/I'M COUNTING ON YOU*
☐ *47-6638 I'LL NEVER LET YOU GO/I'M GONNA SIT RIGHT DOWN AND CRY*
☐ *47-6639 TRYIN' TO GET TO YOU/I LOVE YOU BECAUSE*
☐ *47-6640 BLUE MOON/JUST BECAUSE*
☐ *47-6641 MONEY HONEY/ONE SIDED LOVE AFFAIR*
☐ *47-6642 LAWDY MISS CLAWDY/SHAKE, RATTLE AND ROLL*
☐ *47-6643 LOVE ME TENDER/ANY WAY YOU WANT ME*
☐ *47-6800 TOO MUCH/PLAYING FOR KEEPS*
☐ *47-6870 ALL SHOOK UP/THAT'S WHEN YOUR HEART-ACHES BEGIN*
☐ *47-7000 TEDDY BEAR/LOVING YOU*
☐ *47-7035 JAILHOUSE ROCK/TREAT ME NICE*

(Copies of 47-6870, with and without the silver line, are shown below)

ALPHABETICAL LISTING OF FLIP SIDES

When you can only think of one side of an Elvis disc, and when that one tune happens to be listed as a flip side in our pricing section, use this handy listing to discover the "A" side. Then, simply look up that title.

TO LOCATE: LOOK FOR:

A MESS OF BLUES/**IT'S NOW OR NEVER**
ALL THAT I AM/**SPINOUT**
ALMOST IN LOVE/**A LITTLE LESS CONVERSATION**
ALWAYS ON MY MIND/**SEPARATE WAYS**
AMERICA/**MY WAY**
AMERICA THE BEAUTIFUL/**MY WAY**
ANY DAY NOW/**IN THE GHETTO**
ANY WAY YOU WANT ME/**LOVE ME TENDER**
ANYTHING THAT'S PART OF YOU/**GOOD LUCK CHARM**
ASK ME/**AIN'T THAT LOVING YOU BABY**
BLUE MOON OF KENTUCKY/**THAT'S ALL RIGHT**
BLUE RIVER/**TELL ME WHY**
BOSOM OF ABRAHAM/**HE TOUCHED ME**
BRINGING IT BACK/**PIECES OF MY LIFE**
CHARRO/**MEMORIES**
COME WHAT MAY/**LOVE LETTERS**
DONCHA' THINK IT'S TIME/**WEAR MY RING AROUND YOUR NECK**
DON'T ASK ME WHY/**HARD HEADED WOMAN**
EDGE OF REALITY/**IF I CAN DREAM**
FAIR IS MOVING ON, THE/**CLEAN UP YOUR OWN BACK-YARD**
FAME AND FORTUNE/**STUCK ON YOU**
FIRST TIME EVER I SAW YOUR FACE, THE/**AN AMERICAN TRILOGY**
FOOL/**STEAMROLLER BLUES**
FOOLS FALL IN LOVE/**INDESCRIBABLY BLUE**
FOR OLD TIMES SAKE/**RAISED ON ROCK**
FOR THE HEART/**HURT**
HEART OF ROME/**I'M LEAVIN'**
HELP ME/**IF YOU TALK IN YOUR SLEEP**
HIGH HEEL SNEAKERS/**GUITAR MAN**
HIS HAND IN MINE/**HOW GREAT THOU ART**
HOUND DOG/**DON'T BE CRUEL**
HOW WOULD YOU LIKE TO BE/**IF EVERYDAY WAS LIKE CHRISTMAS**
I BEG OF YOU/**DON'T**
I DON'T CARE IF THE SUN DON'T SHINE/**GOOD ROCKIN' TONIGHT**
I FORGOT TO REMEMBER TO FORGET/**MYSTERY TRAIN**
I GOT A FEELIN' IN MY BODY/**THERE'S A HONKY TONK ANGEL (WHO'LL TAKE ME BACK IN)**
I GOT STUNG/**ONE NIGHT**
I GOTTA KNOW/**ARE YOU LONESOME TONIGHT**
I LOVE YOU BECAUSE/**TRYIN' TO GET TO YOU**
I NEED YOUR LOVE TONIGHT/**A FOOL SUCH AS I**
I WAS THE ONE/**HEARTBREAK HOTEL**
I'M COUNTING ON YOU/**I GOT A WOMAN**
I'M GONNA SIT RIGHT DOWN AND CRY/**I'LL NEVER LET YOU GO**
I'M LEFT, YOU'RE RIGHT, SHE'S GONE/**BABY LET'S PLAY HOUSE**
IT FEELS SO RIGHT/**EASY QUESTION**

IT HURTS ME/**KISSIN' COUSINS**
IT'S A MATTER OF TIME/**BURNING LOVE**
IT'S MIDNIGHT/**PROMISED LAND**
JUST BECAUSE/**BLUE MOON**
JUST TELL HER JIM SAID HELLO/**SHE'S NOT YOU**
LET YOURSELF GO/**YOUR TIME HASN'T COME YET BABY**
LITTLE SISTER/**HIS LATEST FLAME**
LONELY MAN/**SURRENDER**
LONG LONELY HIGHWAY/**I'M YOURS**
LOVING YOU/**TEDDY BEAR**
MAMA LIKED THE ROSES/**WONDER OF YOU, THE**
MILKCOW BLUES BOOGIE/**YOU'RE A HEARTBREAKER**
MR. SONGMAN/**T-R-O-U-B-L-E**
MY BABY LEFT ME/**I WANT YOU, I NEED YOU, I LOVE YOU**
MY LITTLE FRIEND/**KENTUCKY RAIN**
MY WISH CAME TRUE/**A BIG HUNK O' LOVE**
NEVER ENDING/**SUCH A NIGHT**
NEXT STEP IS LOVE, THE/**I'VE LOST YOU**
O COME, ALL YE FAITHFUL/**MERRY CHRISTMAS BABY**
ONE SIDED LOVE AFFAIR/**MONEY HONEY**
ONLY BELIEVE/**LIFE**
PATCH IT UP/**YOU DON'T HAVE TO SAY YOU LOVE ME**
PLAYING FOR KEEPS/**TOO MUCH**
PLEASE DON'T DRAG THAT STRING AROUND/**DEVIL IN DESGUISE**
PLEASE DON'T STOP LOVING ME/**FRANKIE AND JOHNNY**
PLEDGING MY LOVE/**WAY DOWN**
PUPPET ON A STRING/**TEDDY BEAR**
ROCK-A-HULA BABY/**CAN'T HELP FALLING IN LOVE**
RUBBERNECKIN'/**DON'T CRY DADDY**
SHAKE, RATTLE AND ROLL/**LAWDY MISS CLAWDY**
SHE THINKS I STILL CARE/**MOODY BLUE**
SOLITAIRE/**ARE YOU SINCERE**
SOUND OF YOUR CRY, THE/**IT'S ONLY LOVE**
STAY AWAY/**U.S. MALE**
TAKE GOOD CARE OF HER/**I'VE GOT A THING ABOUT YOU BABY**
THAT'S SOMEONE YOU NEVER FORGET/**LONG LEGGED GIRL (WITH THE SHORT DRESS ON)**
THAT'S WHEN YOUR HEARTACHES BEGIN/**ALL SHOOK UP**
THERE GOES MY EVERYTHING/**I REALLY DON'T WANT TO KNOW**
THERE'S ALWAYS ME/**JUDY**
THEY REMIND ME TOO MUCH OF YOU/**ONE BROKEN HEART FOR SALE**
THINKING ABOUT YOU/**MY BOY**
TREAT ME NICE/**JAILHOUSE ROCK**
TUTTI FRUTTI/**BLUE SUEDE SHOES**
UNCHAINED MELODY/**SOFTLY, AS I LEAVE YOU**
WE CALL ON HIM/**YOU'LL NEVER WALK ALONE**
WE CAN MAKE THE MORNING/**UNTIL IT'S TIME FOR YOU TO GO**
WHAT'D I SAY/**VIVA LAS VEGAS**
WHERE DID THEY GO LORD/**RAGS TO RICHES**
WHERE DO YOU COME FROM/**RETURN TO SENDER**
WILD IN THE COUNTRY/**I FEEL SO BAD**
WITCHCRAFT/**BOSSA NOVA BABY**
YOU DON'T KNOW ME/**BIG BOSS MAN**
YOU'LL BE GONE/**DO THE CLAM**
YOU'LL THINK OF ME/**SUSPICIOUS MINDS**

RCA began the Gold Standard series of reissues in 1959 as a means of making their biggest hits of years gone by available again.

This practice became widespread in the industry, and by the late sixties every major label had a similar series whereby their "oldies" were available for purchase.

With Elvis, the first 18 Gold Standard singles were issued in early '59. All were songs that had appeared on 45 between 1955 and 1957.

RCA did not add to the number of Elvis' Gold Standard releases until 1964, when they added quite a few new titles to the series. In addition, they also repressed most of the original 1959 numbers. In keeping with the times, RCA selected five of their original 18 singles and packaged them in brand new picture sleeves. White label promotional copies were also issued on these five discs.

The five singles that were reissued with picture sleeves and simultaneous promotional copies were:

447-0601   *THAT'S ALL RIGHT/BLUE MOON OF KENTUCKY*

447-0602   *GOOD ROCKIN' TONIGHT/I DON'T CARE IF THE SUN DON'T SHINE*

447-0605   *HEARTBREAK HOTEL/I WAS THE ONE*

447-0608   *DON'T BE CRUEL/HOUND DOG*

447-0618   *ALL SHOOK UP/THAT'S WHEN YOUR HEARTACHES BEGIN*

Trying to determine whether you have a copy of one of the 1959 issues, or if its a 1964 pressing, can be very difficult, but you can be certain that you have a sixties pressing if the black RCA label is a shiny, or glossy type stock.

One must also keep in mind the fact that RCA did continue pressing the 1959 issues in the same manner right up until the change in 1964. You could easily have a 1962 or '63 issue that would be identical to the very first 1959 copies.

About all that collectors require is to have the record in its original label design and original label color. For a quick determination on original Gold Standard pressings, use the following chart.

FROM 447-0600	TO 447-0646	BLACK LABEL WITH DOG ON TOP
FROM 447-0647	TO 447-0658	BLACK LABEL WITH DOG ON SIDE
FROM 447-0659	TO 447-0685	RED LABEL
FROM GB-10156	TO GB-10489	RED LABEL
FROM GB-11326	TO ???	BLACK LABEL WITH RCA LOGO INSTEAD OF RCA "VICTOR."

Please note the following exceptions:

The 1977 black label reissue of 447-0647, "Blue Christmas"/"Santa Claus Is Back In Town," differs from the original in that it uses only the RCA log, not the older RCA VICTOR logo.

The 1964 issue of 447-0720, "Blue Christmas"/"Wooden Heart" carries an unusual catalog number, with the use of a "7" instead of a "6." Do not be confused by this. This was originally issued with the black label, dog on top, like all of the other earlier issues. It was, however, deleted a few months after its release and each of its two sides turned up on later numbers in the Gold Standard series.

As of this writing, RCA has not changed from the newer black label, thus the placement of the question marks in this chart.

In this book we have chosen to list, by description, and to price only the original pressing of each Gold Standard single. Also, it is the original pressings that most collectors seek.

Most of the popular songs that appeared originally on a black label, with dog on top, were later pressed on the RCA orange label, then pressed again on the red label, and may now be available again on the newer black label.

The following guidelines apply to second and third pressings, with regard to pricing.

If the original is BLACK LABEL with DOG ON TOP:
- *Estimate the value of a DOG ON SIDE pressing at about half.*
- *Estimate the value of an ORANGE pressing at about two-thirds to full value of original. Orange label Gold Standards are quite scarce.*
- *Estimate the value of a RED pressing at about one-quarter of original.*

If the original is BLACK LABEL with DOG ON SIDE:
- *Estimate the value of a RED pressing at about half.*

Two other points to remember about the orange label Gold Standards:

Only singles that originally appeared on black label with dog on top were issued on the orange label.

Likewise, there was never a Gold Standard single that appeared for the first time on an orange label.

As of press time, only 13 of the Gold Standard singles have appeared in picture sleeves. 12 of these same issues were pressed on special promotional copies. Only the 1977 reissue of 447-0647 was not pressed on promo 45.

The first five, 447-0601, 447-0602, 447-0605, 447-0608, and 447-0618, were listed earlier. The next seven issues were songs that had never appeared on 45rpm singles prior to 1964. *Continued on next page.*

447-0639 *KISS ME QUICK/SUSPICION*
447-0720 *BLUE CHRISTMAS/WOODEN HEART*
447-0643 *CRYING IN THE CHAPEL/I BELIEVE IN THE MAN IN THE SKY*
447-0647 *BLUE CHRISTMAS/SANTA CLAUS IS BACK IN TOWN*
447-0650 *PUPPET ON A STRING/WOODEN HEART*
447-0651 *JOSHUA FIT THE BATTLE/KNOWN ONLY TO HIM*
447-0652 *MILKY WHITE WAY/SWING DOWN SWEET CHARIOT*

Four Gold Standard singles have been issued with flip sides that were different than was featured on the original hit single.

447-0685 *AN AMERICAN TRILOGY/UNTIL IT'S TIME FOR YOU TO GO*
GB-10156 *BURNING LOVE/STEAMROLLER BLUES*
GB-10157 *IF YOU TALK IN YOUR SLEEP/RAISED ON ROCK*
GB-11326 *MOODY BLUE/FOR THE HEART*

Of all of Elvis' hit singles, only 20 of his songs that originally appeared on 45rpm have *NOT* yet appeared on Gold Standard singles.

AMERICA
ARE YOU SINCERE
BOSOM OF ABRAHAM
BRINGING IT BACK
FIRST TIME EVER I SAW YOUR FACE, THE
FOOL
HE TOUCHED ME
HELP ME
HURT
I GOT A FEELIN' IN MY BODY
IT'S A MATTER OF TIME
MERRY CHRISTMAS BABY
O COME, ALL YE FAITHFUL
PIECES OF MY LIFE
PLEDGING MY LOVE
SOFTLY, AS I LEAVE YOU
SOLITAIRE
THERE'S A HONKY TONK ANGEL
UNCHAINED MELODY
WE CAN MAKE THE MORNING

A BIG HUNK O' LOVE/MY WISH CAME TRUE

☐ *RCA Victor 447-0626* (45: black label - dog on top) 2.00 8.00

A FOOL SUCH AS I/I NEED YOUR LOVE TONIGHT

☐ *RCA Victor 447-0625* (45: black label - dog on top) 2.00 8.00

A LITTLE LESS CONVERSATION/ALMOST IN LOVE

☐ *RCA Victor 447-0667* (45: red label) .. — 3.00

AIN'T THAT LOVING YOU BABY/ASK ME

☐ *RCA Victor 447-0649* (45: black label - dog on side) 1.25 5.00

ALL SHOOK UP/THAT'S WHEN YOUR HEARTACHES BEGIN

☐ *RCA Victor 447-0618* (45: black label - dog on top) 3.00 12.00
☐ *RCA Victor 447-0618* (Promo 45) 6.00 24.00
☐ *RCA Victor 447-0618* (Picture sleeve) . 10.00 40.00

AN AMERICAN TRILOGY/UNTIL IT'S TIME FOR YOU TO GO

☐ *RCA Victor 447-0685* (45: red label) .. 1.00 4.00

ARE YOU LONESOME TONIGHT/I GOTTA KNOW

☐ *RCA Victor 447-0629* (45: black label - dog on top) 1.50 6.00

BABY LET'S PLAY HOUSE/I'M LEFT, YOU'RE RIGHT, SHE'S GONE

☐ *RCA Victor 447-0604* (45: black
label - dog on top) 2.00   8.00

BIG BOSS MAN/YOU DON'T KNOW ME

☐ *RCA Victor 447-0662* (45: red label) . .   1.50   6.00

BLUE CHRISTMAS/SANTA CLAUS IN BACK IN TOWN

☐ *RCA Victor 447-0647* (45: black
label - dog on side) 1.50   6.00
☐ *RCA Victor 447-0647* (Promo 45) 3.00   12.00
☐ *RCA Victor 447-0647* (Picture sleeve) .   5.00   20.00
☐ *RCA 447-0647* (45: black label 1977
issue) . . . .   —   2.00
☐ *RCA 447-0647* (Picture sleeve: 1977
issue) 1.00   4.00

NOTE RCA repackaged 447-0647 in a completely
new picture sleeve and issued it in 1977. Notice
that the original Gold Standard release was on the
RCA VICTOR label, whereas the 1977 issue was
on RCA. Both disc and sleeve can be easily identified
using this information.

NOTE: In our chapter on standard commercial singles, we
discussed the fact that just about every RCA Elvis release,
prior to late 1968, can be found in more than one label
style. Gold Standards are no exception.

Pictured here are two label styles for 447-0647. Besides
the obvious difference in style and size of type, note that
the label in the next column has the recording date included,
whereas the photo above does not. Reportedly, Gold
Standards that were made available both with and without
recording dates can be placed into the following sequence:
First pressing; no date given. Later pressings; date given.

BLUE CHRISTMAS/WOODEN HEART

☐ *RCA Victor 447-0720* (45: black
label - dog on top) 2.00   8.00
☐ *RCA Victor 447-0720* (Promo 45) 4.00   16.00
☐ *RCA Victor 447-0720* (Picture sleeve) .   7.00   28.00

NOTE: Despite a higher Gold Standard catalog number,
this single was actually released one year before 447-0647,
"Blue Christmas"/"Santa Claus Is Back In Town." Shortly
after its release, this record was deleted from the series. One
side, "Blue Christmas," became one half of the 1965 issue,
447-0647, whereas "Wooden Heart" was put on the reverse
side of "Puppet On a String," also released in 1965.

BLUE MOON/JUST BECAUSE

☐ *RCA Victor 447-0613* (45: black
label - dog on top) 2.00   8.00

BLUE SUEDE SHOES/TUTTI FRUTTI

☐ *RCA Victor 447-0609* (45: black
label - dog on top) 2.00   8.00

BOSSA NOVA BABY/WITCHCRAFT

☐ *RCA Victor 447-0642* (45: black
label - dog on top) 3.00   12.00

BURNING LOVE/STEAMROLLER BLUES

☐ *RCA Victor GB-10156* (45: red label) . 1.00   4.00

C

CAN'T HELP FALLING IN LOVE/ROCK-A-HULA BABY

☐ *RCA Victor 447-0635* (45: black
label - dog on top) 3.00   12.00

CLEAN UP YOUR OWN BACK YARD/THE FAIR IS MOVING ON

☐ *RCA Victor 447-0672* (45: red label) .. —   3.00

CRYING IN THE CHAPEL/I BELIEVE IN THE MAN IN THE SKY

☐ *RCA Victor 447-0643* (45: black
label - dog on side) 1.00   4.00
☐ *RCA Victor 447-0643* (Promo 45) 2.50   10.00
☐ *RCA Victor 447-0643* (Picture sleeve) . 4.00   16.00

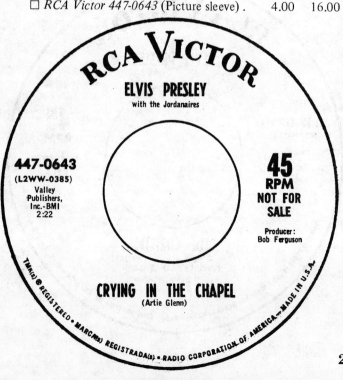

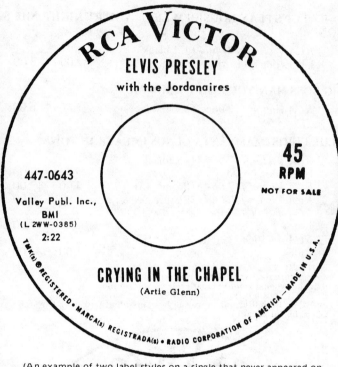

(An example of two label styles on a single that never appeared on 45rpm until its release as part of the Gold Standard Series.)

D

(YOU'RE THE) DEVIL IN DISGUISE/PLEASE DON'T DRAG THAT STRING AROUND

☐ *RCA Victor 447-0641* (45: black
label - dog on top) 3.00   12.00

DO THE CLAM/YOU'LL BE GONE

☐ *RCA Victor 447-0648* (45: black
label - dog on side) 1.25   5.00

DON'T/I BEG OF YOU

☐ *RCA Victor 447-0621* (45: black
label - dog on top) 1.50   6.00

DON'T BE CRUEL/HOUND DOG

☐ *RCA Victor 447-0608* (45: black
label - dog on top) 3.00   12.00
☐ *RCA Victor 447-0608* (Promo 45) 6.00   24.00
☐ *RCA Victor 447-0608* (Picture sleeve) . 10.00   40.00

DON'T CRY DADDY/RUBBERNECKIN'

☐ *RCA Victor 447-0674* (45: red label) .. —   3.00

(SUCH AN) EASY QUESTION/IT FEELS SO RIGHT

☐ *RCA Victor 447-0653* (45: black
label - dog on side) 1.25   5.00

F

FRANKIE AND JOHNNY/PLEASE DON'T STOP LOVING ME

☐ *RCA Victor 447-0656* (45: black
label - dog on side) 1.25   5.00

G

GOOD LUCK CHARM/ANYTHING THAT'S PART OF YOU

☐ *RCA Victor 447-0636* (45: black
label - dog on top) 1.50   6.00

GOOD ROCKIN' TONIGHT/I DON'T CARE IF THE SUN DON'T SHINE

☐ *RCA Victor 447-0602* (45: black
label - dog on top) 3.00   12.00
☐ *RCA Victor 447-0602* (Promo 45) 6.00   24.00
☐ *RCA Victor 447-0602* (Picture sleeve) . 10.00   40.00

GUITAR MAN/HIGH HEEL SNEAKERS

☐ *RCA Victor 447-0663* (45: red label) . .   —   3.00

H

HARD HEADED WOMAN/DON'T ASK ME WHY

☐ *RCA Victor 447-0623* (45: black
label - dog on top) 1.50   6.00

HEARTBREAK HOTEL/I WAS THE ONE

☐ *RCA Victor 447-0605* (45: black
label - dog on top) 3.00   12.00
☐ *RCA Victor 447-0605* (Promo 45) 6.00   24.00
☐ *RCA Victor 447-0605* (Picture sleeve) . 10.00   40.00

HIS LATEST FLAME/LITTLE SISTER

☐ *RCA Victor 447-0634* (45: black
label - dog on top) 1.50   6.00

HOW GREAT THOU ART/HIS HAND IN MINE

☐ *RCA Victor 447-0670* (45: red label) . .   —   3.00

I

I FEEL SO BAD/WILD IN THE COUNTRY

☐ *RCA Victor 447-0631* (45: black
label - dog on top) 1.50   6.00

I GOT A WOMAN/I'M COUNTING ON YOU

☐ *RCA Victor 447-0610* (45: black
label - dog on top) 2.00   8.00

I REALLY DON'T WANT TO KNOW/THERE GOES MY EVERYTHING

☐ *RCA Victor 447-0679* (45: red label) . .   —   3.00

I WANT YOU, I NEED YOU, I LOVE YOU/MY BABY LEFT ME

☐ *RCA Victor 447-0607* (45: black
label - dog on top) 2.00   8.00

I'LL NEVER LET YOU GO/I'M GONNA SIT RIGHT DOWN AND CRY

☐ *RCA Victor 447-0611* (45: black
label - dog on top) 2.00   8.00

I'M LEAVIN'/HEART OF ROME

☐ *RCA Victor 447-0683* (45: red label) . .   —   3.00

I'M YOURS/(IT'S A) LONG LONELY HIGHWAY
☐ *RCA Victor 447-0654* (45: black
label - dog on side) 1.25 5.00

I'VE GOT A THING ABOUT YOU BABY/TAKE GOOD CARE OF HER
☐ *RCA Victor GB-10485* (45: red label)..   — 3.00

I'VE LOST YOU/THE NEXT STEP IS LOVE
☐ *RCA Victor 447-0677* (45: red label) ..   — 3.00

IF EVERYDAY WAS LIKE CHRISTMAS/HOW WOULD YOU LIKE TO BE
☐ *RCA Victor 447-0681* (45: red label) ..   — 3.00

IF I CAN DREAM/EDGE OF REALITY
☐ *RCA Victor 447-0668* (45: red label) ..   — 3.00

IF YOU TALK IN YOUR SLEEP/RAISED ON ROCK
☐ *RCA Victor GB-10157* (45: red label).. 1.00 4.00

IN THE GHETTO/ANY DAY NOW
☐ *RCA Victor 447-0671* (45: red label) ..   — 3.00

INDESCRIBABLY BLUE/FOOLS FALL IN LOVE
☐ *RCA Victor 447-0659* (45: red label) .. 2.50 10.00

IT'S NOW OR NEVER/A MESS OF BLUES
☐ *RCA Victor 447-0628* (45: black
label - dog on top) 1.50 6.00

IT'S ONLY LOVE/THE SOUND OF YOUR CRY
☐ *RCA Victor 447-0684* (45: red label) ..   — 3.00

J

JAILHOUSE ROCK/TREAT ME NICE
☐ *RCA Victor 447-0619* (45: black
label - dog on top) 1.50 6.00

JOSHUA FIT THE BATTLE/KNOWN ONLY TO HIM
☐ *RCA Victor 4470651* (45: black
label - dog on side) 2.50 10.00
☐ *RCA Victor 447-0651* (Promo 45) 5.00 20.00
☐ *RCA Victor 447-0651* (Picture sleeve) . 9.00 36.00

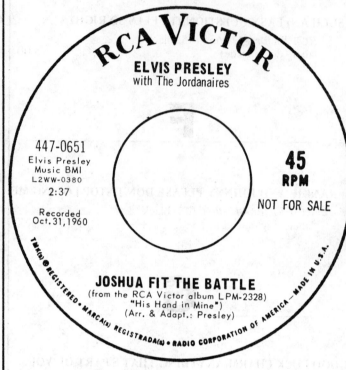

JUDY/THERE'S ALWAYS ME
☐ *RCA Victor 447-0661* (45: red label) .. 2.50 10.00

K

KENTUCKY RAIN/MY LITTLE FRIEND
☐ *RCA Victor 447-0657* (45: red label) ..   — 3.00

KISS ME QUICK/SUSPICION
☐ *RCA Victor 447-0639* (45: black
label - dog on top) 1.50 6.00
☐ *RCA Victor 447-0639* (Promo 45) 3.00 12.00
☐ *RCA Victor 447-0639* (Picture sleeve) . 5.00 20.00
(See photo on next page)

KISSIN' COUSINS/IT HURTS ME
☐ *RCA Victor 447-0644* (45 black
label - dog on top) 1.50 6.00

GOLD STANDARD SERIES
Elvis

447-0639
M2WW-0857
Recorded June 25, 1961

45 RPM
NOT FOR SALE

KISS ME QUICK
(Doc Pomus Mort Shuman)
ELVIS PRESLEY
with The Jordanaires

L

MEMORIES/CHARRO
- ☐ *RCA Victor 447-0669* (45: red label) . .   —   3.00

MILKY WHITE WAY/SWING DOWN SWEET CHARIOT
- ☐ *RCA Victor 447-0652* (45: black label - dog on side) 2.50   10.00
- ☐ *RCA Victor 447-0652* (Promo 45) 5.00   20.00
- ☐ *RCA Victor 447-0652* (Picture sleeve) .   9.00   36.00

447-0652
Elvis Presley Music BMI
L2WW-0373
2:10
Recorded Oct. 30, 1960

ELVIS PRESLEY
with The Jordanaires

45 RPM
NOT FOR SALE

MILKY WHITE WAY
(from the RCA Victor album LPM-2328
"His Hand in Mine")
(Arr. & Adapt.: Presley)

LAWDY MISS CLAWDY/SHAKE, RATTLE AND ROLL
- ☐ *RCA Victor 447-0615* (45: black label - dog on top) 2.00   8.00

LIFE/ONLY BELIEVE
- ☐ *RCA Victor 447-0682* (45: red label) . .   —   3.00

LONG LEGGED GIRL (WITH THE SHORT DRESS ON)/ THAT'S SOMEONE YOU NEVER FORGET
- ☐ *RCA Victor 447-0660* (45: red label) . .   4.00   16.00

LOVE LETTERS/COME WHAT MAY
- ☐ *RCA Victor 447-0657* (45: black label - dog on side) 1.25   5.00

LOVE ME TENDER/ANY WAY YOU WANT ME (THAT'S HOW I'LL BE)
- ☐ *RCA Victor 447-0616* (45: black label - dog on top) 2.00   8.00

MONEY HONEY/ONE SIDED LOVE AFFAIR
- ☐ *RCA Victor 447-0614* (45: black label - dog on top) 2.00   8.00

MOODY BLUE/FOR THE HEART
- ☐ *RCA GB-11326* (45: black label) . . . .   —   2.00

MY BOY/THINKING ABOUT YOU
- ☐ *RCA Victor GB-10489* (45: red label) . .   —   3.00

MYSTERY TRAIN/I FORGOT TO REMEMBER TO FORGET
- ☐ *RCA Victor 447-0600* (45: black label - dog on top) 2.00   8.00

O

ONE BROKEN HEART FOR SALE/THEY REMIND ME TOO MUCH OF YOU
- ☐ *RCA Victor 447-0640* (45: black label - dog on top) 3.00 12.00

ONE NIGHT/I GOT STUNG
- ☐ *RCA Victor 447-0624* (45: black label - dog on top) 1.50 6.00

P

PROMISED LAND/IT'S MIDNIGHT
- ☐ *RCA Victor GB-10488* (45: red label). . — 3.00

PUPPET ON A STRING/WOODEN HEART
- ☐ *RCA Victor 447-0650* (45: black label - dog on side) 1.50 6.00
- ☐ *RCA Victor 447-0650* (Promo 45) 3.00 12.00
- ☐ *RCA Victor 447-0650* (Picture sleeve) . 5.00 20.00

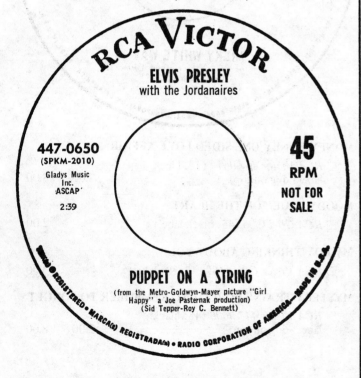

R

RAGS TO RICHES/WHERE DID THEY GO LORD
- ☐ *RCA Victor 447-0680* (45: red label) . . — 3.00

RAISED ON ROCK: *See IF YOU TALK IN YOUR SLEEP*

RETURN TO SENDER/WHERE DO YOU COME FROM
- ☐ *RCA Victor 447-0638* (45: black label - dog on top) 1.50 6.00

S

SEPARATE WAYS/ALWAYS ON MY MIND
- ☐ *RCA Victor GB-10486* (45: red label) . — 3.00

SHE'S NOT YOU/JUST TELL HER JIM SAID HELLO
- ☐ *RCA Victor 447-0637* (45: black label - dog on top) 1.50 6.00

SPINOUT/ALL THAT I AM
- ☐ *RCA Victor 447-0658* (45: black label - dog on side) 1.25 5.00

STEAMROLLER BLUES: *See BURNING LOVE*

STUCK ON YOU/FAME AND FORTUNE
- ☐ *RCA Victor 447-0627* (45: black label - dog on top) 1.50 6.00

SUCH A NIGHT/NEVER ENDING
- ☐ *RCA Victor 447-0645* (45: black label - dog on top) 1.50 6.00

SURRENDER/LONELY MAN
- ☐ *RCA Victor 447-0630* (45: black label - dog on top) 3.00 12.00

SUSPICIOUS MINDS/YOU'LL THINK OF ME
- ☐ *RCA Victor 447-0673* (45: red label) . . — 3.00

T-R-O-U-B-L-E/MR. SONGMAN
☐ *RCA Victor GB-10487* (45: red label) .   —   3.00

(LET ME BE YOUR) TEDDY BEAR/LOVING YOU
☐ *RCA Victor 447-0620* (45: black
label - dog on top) 1.50   6.00

TELL ME WHY/BLUE RIVER
☐ *RCA Victor 447-0655* (45: black
label - dog on side) 1.25   5.00

THAT'S ALL RIGHT/BLUE MOON OF KENTUCKY
☐ *RCA Victor 447-0601* (45: black
label - dog on top) 3.00   12.00
☐ *RCA Victor 447-0601* (Promo 45) 6.00   24.00
☐ *RCA Victor 447-0601* (Picture sleeve) .   10.00   40.00

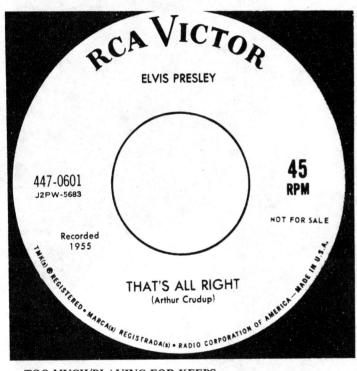

TOO MUCH/PLAYING FOR KEEPS
☐ *RCA Victor 447-0617* (45: black
label - dog on top) 2.00   8.00

TRYIN' TO GET TO YOU/I LOVE YOU BECAUSE
☐ *RCA Victor 447-0612* (45: black
label - dog on top) 2.00   8.00

U

U.S. MALE/STAY AWAY
☐ *RCA Victor 447-0664* (45: red label) . .   —   3.00

UNTIL IT'S TIME FOR YOU TO GO: *See AN AMERICAN TRILOGY*

V

VIVA LAS VEGAS/WHAT'D I SAY
☐ *RCA Victor 447-0646* (45: black
label - dog on top) 1.50   6.00

W

WAY DOWN/MY WAY
☐ *RCA GB-11504* (black label) . . . .   —   2.00

WEAR MY RING AROUND YOUR NECK/DONCHA' THINK IT'S TIME
☐ *RCA Victor 447-0622* (45: black
label - dog on top) 1.50   6.00

WONDER OF YOU, THE/MAMA LIKED THE ROSES
☐ *RCA Victor 447-0676* (45: red label) . .   —   3.00

Y

YOU DON'T HAVE TO SAY YOU LOVE ME/PATCH IT UP
☐ *RCA Victor 447-0678* (45: red label) . .   —   3.00

YOU'LL NEVER WALK ALONE/WE CALL ON HIM
☐ *RCA Victor 447-0665* (45: red label) . .   —   3.00

YOUR TIME HASN'T COME YET BABY/LET YOURSELF GO
☐ *RCA Victor 447-0666* (45: red label) . .   —   3.00

YOU'RE A HEARTBREAKER/MILKCOW BLUES BOOGIE
☐ *RCA Victor 447-0603* (45: black
label - dog on top) 2.00   8.00

COLLECTOR'S CHECKLISTS:

Using these handy checklists, collectors can tell at a glance which picture sleeves, promotional copies and 78rpm singles they already have, as well as which ones they still need.

When applicable, additional space is provided so that you can write in those releases that appear on the scene after this book has gone to press.

ELVIS

I'VE LOST YOU

FOOL

ONE BROKEN HEART FOR SALE

BLUE RIVER

(SUCH AN) EASY QUESTION

YOU DON'T KNOW ME

THERE'S A HONKY TONK ANGEL (Who Will Take Me Back In)

I GOT A FEELIN' IN MY BODY

TELL ME WHY

WOODEN HEART

BIG BOSS MAN

(Let Me Be Your) TEDDY BEAR PUPPET ON A STRING

THEY REMIND ME TOO MUCH OF YOU

CRYING IN THE CHAPEL

☐ 47-6540   *I WANT YOU, I NEED YOU, I LOVE YOU/MY BABY LEFT ME ("This Is His Life" cartoon sleeve)*

☐ 47-6604   *DON'T BE CRUEL/HOUND DOG (With "Don't Be Cruel" on top)*

☐ 47-6604   *HOUND DOG/DON'T BE CRUEL (With "Hound Dog" on top)*

☐ 47-6643   *LOVE ME TENDER/ANY WAY YOU WANT ME (Black and white)*

☐ 47-6643   *LOVE ME TENDER/ANY WAY YOU WANT ME (Green)*

☐ 47-6643   *LOVE ME TENDER/ANY WAY YOU WANT ME (Dark Pink)*

☐ 47-6643   *LOVE ME TENDER/ANY WAY YOU WANT ME (Light Pink)*

☐ 47-6800   *TOO MUCH/PLAYING FOR KEEPS*

☐ 47-6870   *ALL SHOOK UP/THAT'S WHEN YOUR HEART-ACHES BEGIN*

☐ 47-7000   *TEDDY BEAR/LOVING YOU*

☐ 47-7035   *JAILHOUSE ROCK/TREAT ME NICE*

☐ 47-7035   *JAILHOUSE ROCK/TREAT ME NICE (Special MGM theatre ticket sleeve)*

☐ 47-7150   *DON'T/I BEG OF YOU*

☐ 47-7240   *WEAR MY RING AROUND YOUR NECK/ DONCHA' THINK IT'S TIME*

☐ 47-7280   *HARD HEADED WOMAN/DON'T ASK ME WHY*

☐ 47-7410   *ONE NIGHT/I GOT STUNG*

☐ 47-7506   *A FOOL SUCH AS I/I NEED YOUR LOVE TO-NIGHT (With "Elvis Sails" ad on back)*

☐ 47-7506   *A FOOL SUCH AS I/I NEED YOUR LOVE TO-NIGHT (With Gold Standard singles listed on back)*

☐ 47-7600   *A BIG HUNK O' LOVE/MY WISH CAME TRUE*

☐ 47-7740   *STUCK ON YOU/FAME AND FORTUNE*

☐ 47-7777   *IT'S NOW OR NEVER/A MESS OF BLUES*

☐ 47-7810   *ARE YOU LONESOME TONIGHT/I GOTTA KNOW*

☐ 47-7850   *SURRENDER/LONELY MAN (45)*

☐ 37-7850   *SURRENDER/LONELY MAN (Compact 33 single)*

☐ 47-7880   *I FEEL SO BAD/WILD IN THE COUNTRY (45)*

☐ 37-7880   *I FEEL SO BAD/WILD IN THE COUNTRY (Compact 33 single)*

☐ 47-7908   *HIS LATEST FLAME/LITTLE SISTER (45)*

☐ 37-7908   *HIS LATEST FLAME/LITTLE SISTER (Compact 33 single)*

☐ 47-7968   *CAN'T HELP FALLING IN LOVE/ROCK-A-HULA BABY (45)*

☐ 37-7968   *CAN'T HELP FALLING IN LOVE/ROCK-A-HULA BABY (Compact 33 single)*

☐ 47-7992   *GOOD LUCK CHARM/ANYTHING THAT'S PART OF YOU (45: Blue and pink titles)*

☐ 47-7992   *GOOD LUCK CHARM/ANYTHING THAT'S PART OF YOU (45: Rust and lavender titles)*

☐ 37-7992   *GOOD LUCK CHARM/ANYTHING THAT'S PART OF YOU (Compact 33 single)*

☐ 47-8041   *SHE'S NOT YOU/JUST TELL HER JIM SAID HELLO*

☐ 47-8100   *RETURN TO SENDER/WHERE DO YOU COME FROM*

☐ 47-8134   *ONE BROKEN HEART FOR SALE/THEY RE-MIND ME TOO MUCH OF YOU*

☐ 47-8188   *DEVIL IN DISGUISE/PLEASE DON'T DRAG THAT STRING AROUND*

☐ 47-8243   *BOSSA NOVA BABY/WITCHCRAFT*

☐ 47-8307   *KISSIN' COUSINS/IT HURTS ME*

☐ 47-8360   *VIVA LAS VEGAS/WHAT'D I SAY*

☐ 47-8400   *SUCH A NIGHT/NEVER ENDING*

☐ 47-8440   *AIN'T THAT LOVING YOU BABY/ASK ME ("Coming Soon")*

☐ 47-8440   *AIN'T THAT LOVING YOU BABY/ASK ME ("Ask For")*

☐ 47-8500   *DO THE CLAM/YOU'LL BE GONE*

☐ 47-8585   *EASY QUESTION/IT FEELS SO RIGHT*

☐ 47-8657   *I'M YOURS/LONG LONELY HIGHWAY*

☐ 47-8740   *TELL ME WHY/BLUE RIVER*

☐ 47-8740   *FRANKIE AND JOHNNY/PLEASE DON'T STOP LOVING ME*

☐ 47-8870   *LOVE LETTERS/COME WHAT MAY ("Coming Soon")*

☐ 47-8870   *LOVE LETTERS/COME WHAT MAY ("Ask For")*

☐ 47-8941   *SPINOUT/ALL THAT I AM ("Watch For")*

☐ 47-8941   *SPINOUT/ALL THAT I AM ("Ask For")*

☐ 47-8950   *IF EVERYDAY WAS LIKE CHRISTMAS/HOW WOULD YOU LIKE TO BE*

☐ 47-9056   *INDESCRIBABLY BLUE/FOOLS FALL IN LOVE*

☐ 47-9115   *LONG LEGGED GIRL/THAT'S SOMEONE YOU NEVER FORGET ("Coming Soon")*

☐ 47-9115   *LONG LEGGED GIRL/THAT'S SOMEONE YOU NEVER FORGET ("Ask For")*

☐ 47-9287   *JUDY/THERE'S ALWAYS ME*

☐ 47-9341   *BIG BOSS MAN/YOU DON'T KNOW ME*

☐ 47-9425   *GUITAR MAN/HIGH HEEL SNEAKERS ("Coming Soon")*

☐ 47-9425   *GUITAR MAN/HIGH HEEL SNEAKERS ("Ask For")*

☐ 47-9465   *U.S. MALE/STAY AWAY*

☐ 47-9547 *YOUR TIME HASN'T COME YET BABY/LET YOURSELF GO ("Coming Soon")*

☐ 47-9547 *YOUR TIME HASN'T COME YET BABY/LET YOURSELF GO ("Ask For")*

☐ 47-9600 *YOU'LL NEVER WALK ALONE/WE CALL ON HIM*

☐ 47-9610 *A LITTLE LESS CONVERSATION/ALMOST IN LOVE*

☐ 47-9670 *IF I CAN DREAM/EDGE OF REALITY (With "NBC-TV Special" mention)*

☐ 47-9670 *IF I CAN DREAM/EDGE OF REALITY (No mention of TV Special)*

☐ 47-9731 *MEMORIES/CHARRO*

☐ 47-9741 *IN THE GHETTO/ANY DAY NOW ("Coming Soon")*

☐ 47-9741 *IN THE GHETTO/ANY DAY NOW ("Ask For")*

☐ 47-9747 *CLEAN UP YOUR OWN BACK YARD/THE FAIR IS MOVING ON*

☐ 47-9764 *SUSPICIOUS MINDS/YOU'LL THINK OF ME*

☐ 47-9768 *DON'T CRY DADDY/RUBBERNECKIN'*

☐ 47-9791 *KENTUCKY RAIN/MY LITTLE FRIEND*

☐ 47-9835 *THE WONDER OF YOU/MAMA LIKED THE ROSES*

☐ 47-9873 *I'VE LOST YOU/THE NEXT STEP IS LOVE*

☐ 47-9916 *YOU DON'T HAVE TO SAY YOU LOVE ME/ PATCH IT UP*

☐ 47-9960 *I REALLY DON'T WANT TO KNOW/THERE GOES MY EVERYTHING ("Coming Soon")*

☐ 47-9960 *I REALLY DON'T WANT TO KNOW/THERE GOES MY EVERYTHING ("Now Available")*

☐ 47-9980 *RAGS TO RICHES/WHERE DID THEY GO LORD*

☐ 47-9985 *LIFE/ONLY BELIEVE*

☐ 47-9998 *I'M LEAVIN'/HEART OF ROME*

☐ 48-1017 *IT'S ONLY LOVE/THE SOUND OF YOUR CRY*

☐ 74-0130 *HOW GREAT THOU ART/HIS HAND IN MINE*

☐ 74-0572 *MERRY CHRISTMAS BABY/O COME, ALL YE FAITHFUL*

☐ 74-0619 *UNTIL IT'S TIME FOR YOU TO GO/WE CAN MAKE THE MORNING*

☐ 74-0651 *HE TOUCHED ME/BOSOM OF ABRAHAM*

☐ 74-0672 *AN AMERICAN TRILOGY/THE FIRST TIME EVER I SAW YOUR FACE*

☐ 74-0769 *BURNING LOVE/IT'S A MATTER OF TIME*

☐ 74-0815 *SEPARATE WAYS/ALWAYS ON MY MIND*

☐ 74-0910 *STEAMROLLER BLUES/FOOL*

☐ APBO-0088 *RAISED ON ROCK/FOR OLD TIMES SAKE*

☐ APBO-0280 *IF YOU TALK IN YOUR SLEEP/HELP ME*

☐ APBO-0916 *I'VE GOT A THING ABOUT YOU BABY/ TAKE GOOD CARE OF HER*

☐ PB-10074 *PROMISED LAND/IT'S MIDNIGHT*

☐ PB-10191 *MY BOY/THINKING ABOUT YOU*

☐ PB-10278 *T-R-O-U-B-L-E/MR. SONGMAN*

☐ PB-10401 *PIECES OF MY LIFE/BRINGING IT BACK*

☐ PB-10601 *HURT/FOR THE HEART*

☐ PB-10857 *MOODY BLUE/SHE THINKS I STILL CARE*

☐ PB-10998 *WAY DOWN/PLEDGING MY LOVE*

☐ PB-11165 *MY WAY/AMERICA*

☐ PB-11165 *MY WAY/AMERICA THE BEAUTIFUL*

☐ PB-11212 *SOFTLY, AS I LEAVE YOU/UNCHAINED MELODY*

☐ PB-11320 *TEDDY BEAR/PUPPET ON A STRING*

☐ PB-11533 *ARE YOU SINCERE/SOLITAIRE*

☐ PB-11679 *THERE'S A HONKY TONK ANGEL/I GOT A FEELIN' IN MY BODY*

GOLD STANDARD PICTURE SLEEVES:

☐ 447-0601 *THAT'S ALL RIGHT/BLUE MOON OF KEN-TUCKY*

☐ 447-0602 *GOOD ROCKIN' TONIGHT/I DON'T CARE IF THE SUN DON'T SHINE*

☐ 447-0605 *HEARTBREAK HOTEL/I WAS THE ONE*

☐ 447-0608 *DON'T BE CRUEL/HOUND DOG*

☐ 447-0618 *ALL SHOOK UP/THAT'S WHEN YOUR HEART-ACHES BEGIN*

☐ 447-0639 *KISS ME QUICK/SUSPICION*

☐ 447-0643 *CRYING IN THE CHAPEL/I BELIEVE IN THE MAN IN THE SKY*

☐ 447-0647 *BLUE CHRISTMAS/SANTA CLAUS IS BACK IN TOWN (1964 issue - RCA VICTOR logo)*

☐ 447-0647 *BLUE CHRISTMAS/SANTA CLAUS IS BACK IN TOWN (1977 issue - RCA logo, red sleeve)*

☐ 447-0650 *PUPPET ON A STRING/WOODEN HEART*

☐ 447-0651 *JOSHUA FIT THE BATTLE/KNOWN ONLY TO HIM*

☐ 447-0652 *MILKY WHITE WAY/SWING DOWN SWEET CHARIOT*

☐ 447-0720 *BLUE CHRISTMAS/WOODEN HEART*

PICTURE SLEEVES FOR SPECIAL SINGLE ISSUES

☐ SP 45-76 *WEAR MY RING AROUND YOUR NECK/DON'T*

☐ SP 45-118 *KING OF THE WHOLE WIDE WORLD/HOME IS WHERE THE HEART IS*

☐ SP 45-162 *HOW GREAT THOU ART/SO HIGH*

☐ PB-11099 *DON'T BE CRUEL/HOUND DOG*

☐ PB-11100 *IN THE GHETTO/ANY DAY NOW*

☐ PB-11101 *JAILHOUSE ROCK/TREAT ME NICE*

☐ PB-11102 *CAN'T HELP FALLING IN LOVE/ROCK-A-HULA BABY*

☐ PB-11103 *SUSPICIOUS MINDS/YOU'LL THINK OF ME*

☐ *PB-11104* *ARE YOU LONESOME TONIGHT/I GOTTA KNOW*

☐ *PB-11105* *HEARTBREAK HOTEL/I WAS THE ONE*

☐ *PB-11106* *ALL SHOOK UP/THAT'S WHEN YOUR HEART-ACHES BEGIN*

☐ *PB-11107* *BLUE SUEDE SHOES/TUTTI FRUTTI*

☐ *PB-11108* *LOVE ME TENDER/ANY WAY YOU WANT ME*

☐ *PB-11109* *TEDDY BEAR/LOVING YOU*

☐ *PB-11110* *IT'S NOW OR NEVER/A MESS OF BLUES*

☐ *PB-11111* *RETURN TO SENDER/WHERE DO YOU COME FROM*

☐ *PB-11112* *ONE NIGHT/I GOT STUNG*

☐ *PB-11113* *CRYING IN THE CHAPEL/I BELIEVE IN THE MAN IN THE SKY*

PICTURE SLEEVE ADDITIONS:

_____

_____

_____

_____

_____

THE FOLLOWING WERE ISSUED ON RCA'S WHITE LABEL

- ☐ 47-6357   *MYSTERY TRAIN/I FORGOT TO REMEMBER TO FORGET*
- ☐ 47-8360   *VIVA LAS VEGAS/WHAT'D I SAY*
- ☐ 47-8400   *SUCH A NIGHT/NEVER ENDING*
- ☐ 47-8440   *AIN'T THAT LOVING YOU BABY/ASK ME*
- ☐ 47-8500   *DO THE CLAM/YOU'LL BE GONE*
- ☐ 47-8585   *EASY QUESTION/IT FEELS SO RIGHT*
- ☐ 47-8657   *I'M YOURS/LONG LONELY HIGHWAY*
- ☐ 47-8740   *TELL ME WHY/BLUE RIVER*
- ☐ 47-8780   *FRANKIE AND JOHNNY/PLEASE DON'T STOP LOVING ME*
- ☐ 47-8870   *LOVE LETTERS/COME WHAT MAY*
- ☐ 47-8941   *SPINOUT/ALL THAT I AM*
- ☐ 47-8950   *IF EVERYDAY WAS LIKE CHRISTMAS/HOW WOULD YOU LIKE TO BE*
- ☐ 47-9056   *INDESCRIBABLY BLUE/FOOLS FALL IN LOVE*
- ☐ 47-9115   *LONG LEGGED GIRL/THAT'S SOMEONE YOU NEVER FORGET*
- ☐ 47-9287   *JUDY/THERE'S ALWAYS ME*
- ☐ 47-9341   *BIG BOSS MAN/YOU DON'T KNOW ME*

THE FOLLOWING WERE ISSUED ON RCA'S YELLOW LABEL

- ☐ 47-9425   *GUITAR MAN/HIGH HEEL SNEAKERS*
- ☐ 47-9465   *U.S. MALE/STAY AWAY*
- ☐ 47-9547   *YOUR TIME HASN'T COME YET BABY/LET YOURSELF GO*
- ☐ 47-9600   *YOU'LL NEVER WALK ALONE/WE CALL ON HIM*
- ☐ 47-9610   *A LITTLE LESS CONVERSATION/ALMOST IN LOVE*
- ☐ 47-9670   *IF I CAN DREAM/EDGE OF REALITY*
- ☐ 47-9731   *MEMORIES/CHARRO*
- ☐ 47-9741   *IN THE GHETTO/ANY DAY NOW*
- ☐ 47-9747   *CLEAN UP YOUR OWN BACK YARD/THE FAIR IS MOVING ON*
- ☐ 47-9764   *SUSPICIOUS MINDS/YOU'LL THINK OF ME*
- ☐ 47-9768   *DON'T CRY DADDY/RUBBERNECKIN'*
- ☐ 47-9791   *KENTUCKY RAIN/MY LITTLE FRIEND*
- ☐ 47-9835   *THE WONDER OF YOU/MAMA LIKED THE ROSES*
- ☐ 47-9873   *I'VE LOST YOU/THE NEXT STEP IS LOVE*
- ☐ 47-9916   *YOU DON'T HAVE TO SAY YOU LOVE ME/PATCH IT UP*
- ☐ 47-9960   *I REALLY DON'T WANT TO KNOW/THERE GOES MY EVERYTHING*
- ☐ 47-9980   *RAGS TO RICHES/WHERE DID THEY GO LORD*
- ☐ 47-9985   *LIFE/ONLY BELIEVE*
- ☐ 47-9998   *I'M LEAVIN'/HEART OF ROME*

- ☐ 48-1017   *IT'S ONLY LOVE/THE SOUND OF YOUR CRY*
- ☐ 74-0130   *HOW GREAT THOU ART/HIS HAND IN MINE*
- ☐ 74-0572   *MERRY CHRISTMAS BABY/O COME, ALL YE FAITHFUL*
- ☐ 74-0619   *UNTIL IT'S TIME FOR YOU TO GO/WE CAN MAKE THE MORNING*
- ☐ 74-0651   *HE TOUCHED ME/BOSOM OF ABRAHAM*
- ☐ 74-0672   *AN AMERICAN TRILOGY/THE FIRST TIME EVER I SAW YOUR FACE*
- ☐ 74-0769   *BURNING LOVE/IT'S A MATTER OF TIME*
- ☐ 74-0815   *SEPARATE WAYS/ALWAYS ON MY MIND*

THE FOLLOWING WERE ISSUED ON RCA'S CREAM COLOR (LIGHT YELLOW) LABEL

- ☐ 74-0910   *STEAMROLLER BLUES/FOOL*
- ☐ APBO-0088   *RAISED ON ROCK*
- ☐ APBO-0280   *I'VE GOT A THING ABOUT YOU BABY/ TAKE GOOD CARE OF HER*
- ☐ APBO-0916   *I'VE GOT A THING ABOUT YOU BABY/ TAKE GOOD CARE OF HER*
- ☐ PB-10074   *PROMISED LAND/IT'S MIDNIGHT*
- ☐ PB-10191   *MY BOY (Monaural)/MY BOY (Stereo)*
- ☐ PB-10278   *T-R-O-U-B-L-E/MR. SONGMAN*
- ☐ PB-10401   *PIECES OF MY LIFE/BRINGING IT BACK*
- ☐ PB-10601   *HURT/FOR THE HEART*
- ☐ PB-10857   *MOODY BLUE/SHE THINKS I STILL CARE*
- ☐ PB-10998   *WAY DOWN/PLEDGING MY LOVE (Special WHITE label advance copy)*
- ☐ PB-10998   *WAY DOWN/PLEDGING MY LOVE*
- ☐ PB-11165   *MY WAY/AMERICA*
- ☐ PB-11212   *SOFTLY, AS I LEAVE YOU/UNCHAINED MELODY*
- ☐ PB-11320   *TEDDY BEAR/PUPPET ON A STRING*
- ☐ PB-11533   *ARE YOU SINCERE/SOLITAIRE*
- ☐ PB-11679   *THERE'S A HONKY TONK ANGEL/I GOT A FEELIN' IN MY BODY*

NOTE: Promo singles from the mid-seventies, especially 1976, may turn up in colors that vary from that which is indicated above. We have seen "Hurt" on a tan color promo label, for example. RCA was also sporadic during those years with their commercial label colors.

SPECIAL SINGLE ISSUES ON PROMO LABELS:

- ☐ CR-15   *OLD SHEP/(Blank Groove)* [white]
- ☐ JH-10951   *LET ME BE THERE (Monaural)/LET ME BE THERE (Stereo)* [cream]
- ☐ SP 45-76   *WEAR MY RING AROUND YOUR NECK/DON'T* [black - Not For Sale]
- ☐ SP 45-118   *KING OF THE WHOLE WIDE WORLD/HOME IS WHERE THE HEART IS* [black - Not For Sale]
- ☐ SP 45-139   *ROUSTABOUT/ONE TRACK HEART* [white]
- ☐ SP 45-162   *HOW GREAT THOU ART/SO HIGH* [white]
- ☐ HO-0808   *BLUE CHRISTMAS/BLUE CHRISTMAS* [white]

PROMOTIONAL COPY ADDITIONS:

_____
_____
_____
_____
_____

78 RPM SINGLES:

THE FOLLOWING ARE ON SUN RECORDS

☐ 209   *THAT'S ALL RIGHT/BLUE MOON OF KEN-TUCKY*

☐ 210   *GOOD ROCKIN' TONIGHT/I DON'T CARE IF THE SUN DON'T SHINE*

☐ 215   *YOU'RE A HEARTBREAKER/MILKCOW BLUES BOOGIE*

☐ 217   *BABY, LET'S PLAY HOUSE/I'M LEFT, YOU'RE RIGHT, SHE'S GONE*

☐ 223   *MYSTERY TRAIN/I FORGOT TO REMEMBER TO FORGET*

THE FOLLOWING ARE ON RCA VICTOR RECORDS

☐ 20-6357   *MYSTERY TRAIN/I FORGOT TO REMEMBER TO FORGET*

☐ 20-6380   *THAT'S ALL RIGHT/BLUE MOON OF KEN-TUCKY*

☐ 20-6381   *GOOD ROCKIN' TONIGHT/I DON'T CARE IF THE SUN DON'T SHINE*

☐ 20-6382   *YOU'RE A HEARTBREAKER/MILKCOW BLUES BOOGIE*

☐ 20-6383   *BABY, LET'S PLAY HOUSE/I'M LEFT, YOU'RE RIGHT, SHE'S GONE*

☐ 20-6420   *HEARTBREAK HOTEL/I WAS THE ONE*

☐ 20-6540   *I WANT YOU, I NEED YOU, I LOVE YOU/MY BABY LEFT ME*

☐ 20-6604   *DON'T BE CRUEL/HOUND DOG*

☐ 20-6636   *BLUE SUEDE SHOES/TUTTI FRUTTI*

☐ 20-6637   *I GOT A WOMAN/I'M COUNTING ON YOU*

☐ 20-6638   *I'LL NEVER LET YOU GO/I'M GONNA SIT RIGHT DOWN AND CRY*

☐ 20-6639   *TRYIN' TO GET TO YOU/I LOVE YOU BECAUSE*

☐ 20-6640   *BLUE MOON/JUST BECAUSE*

☐ 20-6641   *MONEY HONEY/ONE SIDED LOVE AFFAIR*

☐ 20-6642   *LAWDY MISS CLAWDY/SHAKE, RATTLE AND ROLL*

☐ 20-6643   *LOVE ME TENDER/ANY WAY YOU WANT ME*

☐ 20-6800   *TOO MUCH/PLAYING FOR KEEPS*

☐ 20-6870   *ALL SHOOK UP/THAT'S WHEN YOUR HEART-ACHES BEGIN*

☐ 20-7000   *TEDDY BEAR/LOVING YOU*

☐ 20-7035   *JAILHOUSE ROCK/TREAT ME NICE*

☐ 20-7150   *DON'T/I BEG OF YOU*

☐ 20-7240   *WEAR MY RING AROUND YOUR NECK/DONCHA' THINK IT'S TIME*

☐ 20-7280   *HARD HEADED WOMAN/DON'T ASK ME WHY*

☐ 20-7410   *ONE NIGHT/I GOT STUNG*

SPECIAL SINGLES— UNIQUE PROMO SINGLES—

AMAZING WORLD OF SHORT WAVE LISTENING: *See WORLD OF SHORT WAVE LISTENING.*

BLUE CHRISTMAS/BLUE CHRISTMAS

☐ *RCA Victor HO-0808* 200.00 800.00
NOTE: A special single issued for radio stations, to encourage play of this selection from "Elvis' Christmas Album."

ELVIS REMEMBERED: *See our section on SPECIAL/PROMOTIONAL ALBUMS.*

15 GOLDEN RECORDS - 30 GOLDEN HITS

☐ *RCA PB-11301* (Collector's Series
Limited Edition) 8.00   32.00

15 record box set, containing the following singles:

PB-11099 - *DON'T BE CRUEL/HOUND DOG*
PB-11100 - *IN THE GHETTO/ANY DAY NOW*
PB-11101 - *JAILHOUSE ROCK/TREAT ME NICE*
PB-11102 - *CAN'T HELP FALLING IN LOVE/ROCK-A-HULA BABY*
PB-11103 - *SUSPICIOUS MINDS/YOU'LL THINK OF ME*
PB-11104 - *ARE YOU LONESOME TONIGHT/I GOTTA KNOW*
PB-11105 - *HEARTBREAK HOTEL/I WAS THE ONE*
PB-11106 - *ALL SHOOK UP/THAT'S WHEN YOUR HEARTACHES BEGIN*
PB-11107 - *BLUE SUEDE SHOES/TUTTI FRUTTI*
PB-11108 - *LOVE ME TENDER/ANY WAY YOU WANT ME (THAT'S HOW I'LL BE)*
PB-11109 - *(LET ME BE YOUR) TEDDY BEAR/LOVING YOU*
PB-11110 - *IT'S NOW OR NEVER/A MESS OF BLUES*
PB-11111 - *RETURN TO SENDER/WHERE DO YOU COME FROM*
PB-11112 - *ONE NIGHT/I GOT STUNG*
PB-11113 - *CRYING IN THE CHAPEL/I BELIEVE IN THE MAN IN THE SKY*

☐ Special browser box, especially made for this release, containing six complete box sets. To qualify for the near-mint price, outer box must not have yet been cut into browser bin configuration. 90.00   360.00

COLLECTORS' SERIES LIMITED EDITION — COLLECTORS' SERIES LIMITED EDITION
ELVIS PRESLEY
15 GOLDEN RECORDS — 30 GOLDEN HITS
INDIVIDUALLY PACKED IN FULL COLOR PHOTO SLEEVES
IT'S NOW OR NEVER/A MESS OF BLUES · JAILHOUSE ROCK/TREAT ME NICE
ANY WAY YOU WANT ME/LOVE ME TENDER · IN THE GHETTO/ANY DAY NOW
HOUND DOG/DON'T BE CRUEL · RETURN TO SENDER/WHERE DO YOU COME FROM
LOVING YOU/TEDDY BEAR · CAN'T HELP FALLING IN LOVE/ROCK-A-HULA BABY
BLUE SUEDE SHOES/TUTTI FRUTTI · ARE YOU LONESOME TONIGHT/I GOTTA KNOW
HEARTBREAK HOTEL/I WAS THE ONE · SUSPICIOUS MINDS/YOU'LL THINK OF ME
I GOT STUNG/ONE NIGHT · ALL SHOOK UP/THAT'S WHEN YOUR HEARTACHES BEGIN
CRYING IN THE CHAPEL/I BELIEVE IN THE MAN IN THE SKY
PP-11301

HOW GREAT THOU ART/SO HIGH (Air Play Special)

☐ *RCA Victor SP-45-162* (45) 25.00   100.00
☐ *RCA Victor SP-45-162* (Picture sleeve) . 15.00   60.00
NOTE: Two years before the release of Elvis' popular sacred song, "How Great Thou Art," on commercial 45 (RCA 74-0130), the tune was distributed to radio stations on this special single. Backed with "So High," also from the "How Great Thou Art" album, this release coincided with both the new sacred LP and the special Elvis Palm Sunday program in 1967.

FOR RADIO STATIONS ONLY
ELVIS
SIDE 1—"HOW GREAT THOU ART"
(MANNA MUSIC INC.) (BMI) (2:58)
SIDE 2—"SO HIGH"
(ELVIS PRESLEY MUSIC INC.) (BMI) (1:55)
BOTH SELECTIONS FROM ELVIS'
NEW SACRED ALBUM
"HOW GREAT THOU ART" LPM/LSP-3578
FOR PROGRAMMING ONLY — NOT FOR SALE

KING OF THE WHOLE WIDE WORLD/HOME IS WHERE THE HEART IS (Promotional Special)

RCA Victor SP-45-118 (45) 50.00 200.00
RCA Victor SP-45-118 (Sleeve) 40.00 160.00

NOTE: This promotional single spotlighted two songs from Elvis' new EP, "Kid Galahad" (EPA-4371). The special sleeve had no picture of Elvis, just a description of the record contained within.

LET ME BE THERE (Stereo)/**LET ME BE THERE** (Mono)

RCA JH-10951 (45) 12.50 50.00

NOTE: This single was reportedly issued by the song's publisher, Al Gallico Music Corp., and not by RCA. Regardless, it does appear on an single using RCA's logo and numbering system and for that reason is included in this book.

NOTE: The price range given above reflects the average transaction involving this record at press time. Although only pressed in a quantity of about 2000 copies, the song's publisher reportedly has most of those copies stored. If they were to suddenly dump a large quantity on the market the price range would surely drop, perhaps only temporarily, before settling at a new price range.

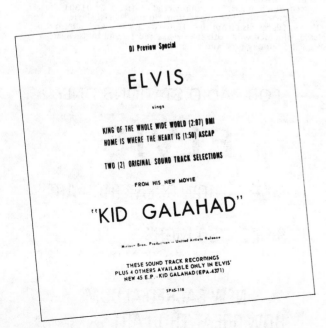

OLD SHEP/(Blank Groove)

☐ *RCA Victor CR-15* (45) 125.00 500.00

NOTE: RCA issued this single, pressed only on one side, in 1956 as a vehicle to promote sales of Elvis' second album, "Elvis." The tune was considered one of the lead songs in the LP, and producing a 45 single of it made it easier for dee jays to play it.

ROUSTABOUT/ONE TRACK HEART (Promotional Special)

☐ *RCA Victor SP-45-139* (45) 25.00 100.00

NOTE: This disc coupled two songs from the "Roustabout" LP, and was serviced to radio stations. Unlike some of the other "SPs" there was no special sleeve made for this issue.

ROUSTABOUT (Coming Soon)/**ROUSTABOUT** (Now Playing)

☐ *Paramount Pictures SP-2414* (45) 200.00 800.00

NOTE: This 45 was distributed to select theatres by Paramount Pictures. It contains an announcer pitching the film, but more importantly, it contains an alternate take of the song "Roustabout." This is a complete, studio, version and is heard on both sides of the record. The only difference between sides one and two is the announcer's closing comment that the movie is either "coming soon" or is "now playing." The disc was meant to be played in the theatre's lobby, over and over.

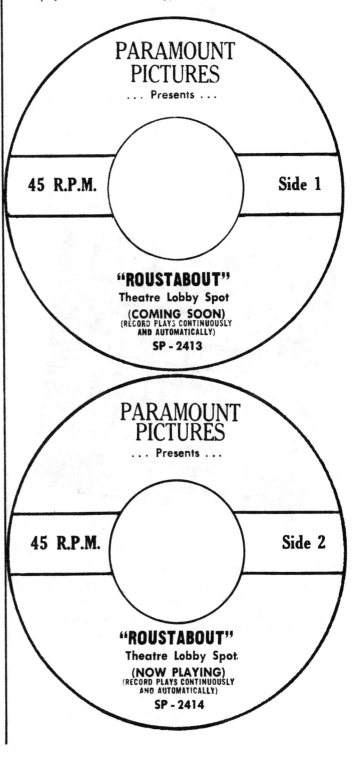

20 GOLDEN HITS IN FULL COLOR SLEEVES

☐ *RCA PB-11301* (Collector's Series
Limited Edition) 10.00 40.00

10 record box set, containing the following singles:

PB-11099 - *DON'T BE CRUEL/HOUND DOG*
PB-11100 - *IN THE GHETTO/ANY DAY NOW*
PB-11102 - *CAN'T HELP FALLING IN LOVE/ROCK-A-
          HULA BABY*
PB-11104 - *ARE YOU LONESOME TONIGHT/I GOTTA
          KNOW*
PB-11105 - *HEARTBREAK HOTEL/I WAS THE ONE*
PB-11106 - *ALL SHOOK UP/THAT'S WHEN YOUR
          HEARTACHES BEGIN*
PB-11107 - *BLUE SUEDE SHOES/TUTTI FRUTTI*
PB-11108 - *LOVE ME TENDER/ANY WAY YOU WANT
          ME (THAT'S HOW I'LL BE)*
PB-11109 - *(LET ME BE YOUR) TEDDY BEAR/LOVING
          YOU*
PB-11111 - *RETURN TO SENDER/WHERE DO YOU
          COME FROM*

NOTE: All 10 of these singles, plus five others also in color
sleeves, appeared in the 15-record box set, "15 Golden Records
30 Golden Hits," which was released prior to this 10-record set.

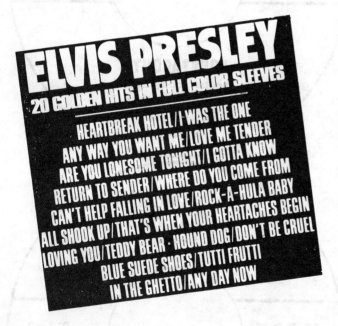

WEAR MY RING AROUND YOUR NECK/DON'T

☐ *RCA Victor SP-45-76* (45) 90.00 360.00
☐ *RCA Victor SP-45-76* (Picture sleeve). . 100.00 400.00

NOTE: RCA chose these two songs from "Elvis Gold Records
Vol 2" and issued them back-to-back for promotional purposes.
The intention, of course, was that air play of these songs would
promote sales of the album.

WORLD OF SHORT WAVE LISTENING

☐ *Hallicrafters (N9MW-4435)* 10.00 40.00
A sampler of radio broadcasts picked up
by short wave, including an excerpt of a
French station playing "Loving You."
A 1957 promotional item from Hallicrafters, a manufacturer of short wave
radios.

ELVIS' EXTENDED PLAY RELEASES

A TOUCH OF GOLD

☐ *RCA Victor EPA-5088* (black
   label - dog on top)   12.50   50.00
☐ *RCA Victor EPA-5088* (maroon
   label) 50.00   200.00

A TOUCH OF GOLD VOLUME II

☐ *RCA Victor EPA-5101* (black
   label - dog on top)   12.50   50.00
☐ *RCA Victor EPA-5101* (maroon
   label) 50.00   200.00

A TOUCH OF GOLD VOLUME 3

☐ *RCA Victor EPA-5141* (black
   label - dog on top) 12.50   50.00
☐ *RCA Victor EPA-5141* (maroon
   label) 50.00   200.00

NOTE: Some copies of the maroon label "Touch Of Gold" EP
releases were sold with a "Thank you for buying this and other
RCA records" paper insert. Add 10% to 20% to the values shown
above for the insert.

ALOHA FROM HAWAII VIA SATELLITE: *See our section on
SPECIAL/PROMOTIONAL EXTENDED PLAYS.*

ANYWAY YOU WANT ME

☐ *RCA Victor EPA-965* (black
   label - dog on top) 10.00   40.00

CHRISTMAS WITH ELVIS

☐ *RCA Victor EPA-4340* (black
   label - dog on top) 10.00   40.00

EASY COME, EASY GO

☐ *RCA Victor EPA-4387* (black
   label - dog on side) 7.00   28.00
☐☐ *RCA Victor EPA-4387* (Promo
   copy - white label) 9.00   36.00

NOTE: This was the only commercial EP release that was
also pressed on special promotional copies in addition to
the standard catalog issues. There are two variations of
the promo copy known to exist. One has "RCA Victor
Presents Elvis in the original soundtrack recording from the
Paramount Picture Easy Come, Easy Go a Hal Wallis
Production" at the top of the label. The other version
simply has "Easy Come, Easy Go - Elvis Presley" at the
top of the label.

ELVIS (VOLUME 1)

☐ *RCA Victor EPA-992* (black
   label - dog on top) 8.00   32.00

ELVIS (VOLUME 2)

☐ *RCA Victor EPA-993* (black
   label - dog on top) 9.00   36.00

ELVIS (VOLUME 3): *See STRICTLY ELVIS*

ELVIS BY REQUEST (FLAMING STAR)

☐ *RCA Victor EPC-128* (Compact 33
   double) 9.00   36.00

ELVIS PRESLEY

☐☐ *RCA Victor EPA-747* (black
☐☐ label - dog on top) 10.00   40.00
   ☐ *RCA Victor EPA-747* (special sleeve
   used to merchandise the EP until
   the regular jackets were available). 125.00 500.00

NOTE: There are four variations known to exist
for this EP. All variations are with regard to the
back of the jacket. One version has Elvis' photo
along with a brief story. Three versions are known
that promote assorted RCA releases, with each of
the three spotlighting different releases.

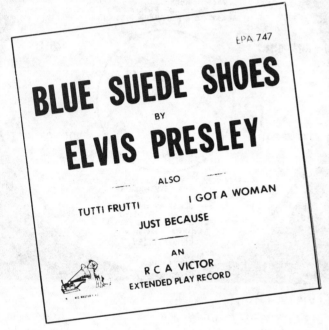

ELVIS PRESLEY

☐ *RCA Victor EPA-830* (black
   label - dog on top) 10.00   40.00

A copy of EPA-830, as is commonly found, is shown above.
Below is the rarer "dogless" version of the same EP. Recent
trends have shown that collectors will pay double or triple the
guide prices for the dogless extended plays.

NOTE: Pictured above is a copy of the actual letter that
RCA sent to its distributors, on March 7, 1956, advising
them of the delay in shipping EPA-747 in its planned
jacket.

Also shown is the temporary envelope-sleeve that the
EP was shipped in, and sold in. . . for a few days anyway.

ELVIS PRESLEY

☐ *RCA Victor EPB-1254* (Two disc,
☐☐ double pocket set) 50.00 200.00

NOTE: There are three known variations of
this EP. Two versions have photos of various
RCA releases (each of the two showing different RCA product), and the other variation has
a photo of Elvis on the back cover.

ELVIS SAILS

☐ *RCA Victor EPA-4325* (black
label - dog on top) 12.50 50.00

NOTE: Original pressings of this jacket
have a 1959 calander on the back cover, as
well as a hole (for hanging calander) punched
in the top center of the jacket. Prices shown
here are for original pressings.

ELVIS SINGS CHRISTMAS SONGS

☐ *RCA Victor EPA-4108* (black
label - dog on top) 6.00 24.00

FLAMING STAR: *See ELVIS BY REQUEST*

FOLLOW THAT DREAM

☐ *RCA Victor EPA-4368* (black
label - dog on top) 6.00 24.00
☐ *RCA Victor EPA-4368* (sleeve
used for special mailing of "Coin
Operator/DJ prevue" copies) 30.00 120.00

HEARTBREAK HOTEL

☐ *RCA Victor EPA-821* (black
label - dog on top) 10.00 40.00

JAILHOUSE ROCK

☐ *RCA Victor EPA-4114* (black
label - dog on top) 8.00 32.00

JUST FOR YOU

☐ *RCA Victor EPA-4041* (black
label - dog on top) 10.00 40.00

KID GALAHAD

☐ *RCA Victor EPA-4371* (black
label - dog on top) 6.00 24.00

KING CREOLE

☐ *RCA Victor EPA-4319* (black
label - dog on top) 8.00 32.00
☐ *RCA Victor EPA-5122* (maroon
label) 60.00 240.00

KING CREOLE VOL. 2

☐ *RCA Victor EPA-4321* (black
label - dog on top) 10.00 40.00

LOVE ME TENDER

☐ *RCA Victor EPA-4006* (black
label - dog on top) 8.00 32.00

LOVING YOU VOL I

☐ *RCA Victor EPA-1-1515* (black
label - dog on top) 8.00 32.00

LOVING YOU VOL II

☐ *RCA Victor EPA-2-1515* (black
label - dog on top) 9.00 36.00

PEACE IN THE VALLEY

☐ *RCA Victor EPA-4054* (black
label - dog on top) 9.00 36.00
☐ *RCA Victor EPA-5121* (maroon
label) 60.00 240.00

REAL ELVIS, THE

☐ *RCA Victor EPA-940* (black
label - dog on top) 10.00 40.00
☐ *RCA Victor EPA-5120* (maroon
label) 60.00 240.00

STRICTLY ELVIS

☐ *RCA Victor EPA-994* (black
label - dog on top) 10.00 40.00

NOTE: This was actually Vol. 3 of the three EP
series began with EPA-992 and EPA-993.

TICKLE ME

☐ *RCA Victor EPA-4383* (black
label - dog on side) 6.00 24.00

NOTE: Two variations are known to exist for
this cover. One says "Coming Soon" Special LP,
the second issue reads "Ask For" the album.

VIVA LAS VEGAS

☐ *RCA Victor EPA-4382* (black
label - dog on top) 6.00 24.00

COIN OPERATOR / DJ PREVUE
EPA 4368

ELVIS

SINGS

FOUR GREAT SONGS

Side 1 Follow That Dream (1:38 ASCAP)
        Angel (2:40 ASCAP)
Side 2 What A Wonderful Life (2:28 ASCAP)
        I'm Not The Marrying Kind (2:00 ASCAP)

FROM HIS NEW MOVIE

"FOLLOW THAT DREAM"

AVAILABLE NOW ONLY ON 45 EP

SPECIAL EXTENDED PLAY RELEASES

BECAUSE MANY ARE UNTITLED, WE ARE LISTING THESE IN ALPHA–NUMERICAL ORDER

ALOHA FROM HAWAII VIA SATELLITE

☐ *RCA DTFO-2006* (Issued to juke box operators, designed for coin machine play) 10.00   40.00

NOTE: Since it was manufactured for juke box use, this EP was issued in stereo; the only Elvis EP to have appeared in stereo. It was also packaged with factory prepared juke box title strips. If the title strips are missing, deduct about 10% from prices shown.

DJ-7 (47-6643) PROMOTIONAL EP

☐ White label - Not for sale 15.00   60.00
Contains the following Elvis selections:
LOVE ME TENDER
ANYWAY YOU WANT ME

DJ-56 (47-6800) PROMOTIONAL EP

☐ White label - Not for sale 15.00   60.00
Contains the following Elvis selections:
TOO MUCH
PLAYING FOR KEEPS

RCA VICTOR

EPB-1254
SIDE 4
547-0793
(G2WH-1853)

45 EP
"NEW ORTHOPHONIC"
HIGH FIDELITY

1—I'LL NEVER LET YOU GO (Little Darlin')
(Jimmy Wakely)
2—BLUE MOON (Rodgers–Hart)
3—MONEY HONEY (Jesse Stone)
Elvis Presley

TRADE MARKS® REGISTERED • MARCAS REGISTRADAS • RADIO CORPORATION OF AMERICA—CAMDEN, N. J.—MADE IN U.S.A.

*EPB-1254, Special Edition:
Listing appears on
following page.*

RCA VICTOR

EPB-1254
SIDE 3
547-0794
(G2WH-1852)

45 EP
"NEW ORTHOPHONIC"
HIGH FIDELITY

1—TUTTI FRUTTI
(Dorothy LaBostrie–Richard Penniman)
2—TRYIN' TO GET TO YOU (Singleton–McCoy)
3—I'M GONNA SIT RIGHT DOWN AND CRY
(Over You) (Thomas–Biggs)
Elvis Presley

TRADE MARKS® REGISTERED • MARCAS REGISTRADAS • RADIO CORPORATION OF AMERICA—CAMDEN, N. J.—MADE IN U.S.A.

EPB-1254 THE MOST TALKED-ABOUT NEW PERSONALITY IN THE LAST TEN YEARS OF RECORDED MUSIC. 12 GREAT NEW SIDES FROM HIS NEW ALBUMS; LPM-1254; EPB-1254; EPA-747

☐ Black label - Two disc, double
   pocket set (discs only) 100.00 400.00
☐ Picture sleeve 125.00 500.00
   Contains the following Elvis selections:
   BLUE SUEDE SHOES
   I'M COUNTING ON YOU
   I GOT A WOMAN
   ONE SIDED LOVE AFFAIR
   I LOVE YOU BECAUSE
   JUST BECAUSE
   TUTTI FRUTTI
   TRYIN' TO GET TO YOU
   I'M GONNA SIT RIGHT DOWN AND CRY
   I'LL NEVER LET YOU GO (LITTLE DARLIN')
   BLUE MOON
   MONEY HONEY

NOTE: The two discs in this set each contain six songs. Together they present all 12 songs contained on Elvis' first LP, "Elvis Presley" (LPM-1254), in the same sequence as featured on the album. This special EP should not be confused with the more common EPB-1254, which has only eight songs on its two discs.

PR-121 RCA FAMILY RECORD CENTER

☐ White label - Promotional record
   Not for sale (Compact 33 single) 200.00 800.00
   Contains the following Elvis selection:
   GOOD LUCK CHARM

NOTE: This very unusual EP was specifically prepared for repeated play in record shops. The disc has an announcer pitching new RCA releases, while playing portions of selected songs.

PRO-12 PROMOTION DISC

☐ White label - Not for sale 200.00 800.00
   Contains the following Elvis selection:
   OLD SHEP

SDS 7-2 DEALER'S PREVUE PROMOTIONAL DISC

☐ White label - Not for sale
  (disc only) 175.00 700.00
☐ Special sleeve 125.00 500.00
  Contains the following Elvis selections:
    TEDDY BEAR
    LOVING YOU

SDS 57-39 DEALER'S PREVUE PROMOTIONAL DISC

☐ White label - Not for sale
  (disc only) 150.00 600.00
☐ Special sleeve 125.00 500.00
  Contains the following Elvis selections:
    JAILHOUSE ROCK
    TREAT ME NICE

SPA 7-27 SAVE-ON-RECORDS (BULLETIN FOR JUNE, 1956)

☐ Black label (disc only) 50.00 200.00
Picture sleeve : 100.00 400.00

Contains the following Elvis selection:
  GONNA SIT RIGHT DOWN AND CRY

NOTE: This EP was intended to give record buyers, who
bought certain records at a discount prices through use of
a coupon book, a sampling of the different artists whose
records RCA was promoting at the time.

SPA 7-37 PERFECT FOR PARTIES HIGHLIGHT ALBUM

☐☐ Black label - Not for sale
  (disc only) 20.00 80.00
☐ Picture sleeve 20.00 80.00

Contains the following Elvis selection:
  LOVE ME

NOTE: Two variations are known to exist for this
record label. Although there are other differences,
the most obvious is the fact that "Not For Sale" appears
on the left side of the label on one version, and on the
right side of the label on the other.

SPA 7-61 EXTENDED PLAY SAMPLER

☐ Black label - Not for sale 250.00 1000.00
Contains the following Elvis selection:
JAILHOUSE ROCK

NOTE: This EP was sent to select radio stations for
the purpose of promoting RCA's latest extended play
releases. The Elvis EP highlighted was, of course,
"Jailhouse Rock."

SPD·15

SPD 15 PACKAGE OF 10 EXTENDED PLAYS

- ☐ Gray label (Elvis disc only;
  Sides 7 and 14) 150.00 600.00
- ☐ Complete box set (10 EPs, box, special
  paper inserts and sleeves) 600.00 2400.00
  Contains the following Elvis selections:
  *THAT'S ALL RIGHT
  BABY LET'S PLAY HOUSE
  I FORGOT TO REMEMBER TO FORGET
  MYSTERY TRAIN*

SPD·19

THE SOUND OF LEADERSHIP

In 1928, when nearly every American was eating three times a day and millionaires were becoming multimillionaires, the nation's taste in music tended toward the nostalgic, romantic ballad. Everyone who had a musical bone in his body was humming, whistling or singing *Ramona*, ...

recorded *Vesti la giubba* and *O sole mio*, both of which in later years soared past the million mark in sales.

Then, as now, the Sound of Leadership was artistically grooved into every Victor record, an achievement recognized and appreciated by music lovers throughout the world. As the leader in the industry, RCA Victor and its predecessor company, the Victor Talking Machine Co., ...

Side 1	1907	Vesti la giubba *Enrico Caruso*	Side 9	1946	Prisoner of Love *Perry Como*
	1916	O sole mio *Enrico Caruso*		1947	Ballerina *Vaughn Monroe*
Side 2	1928	Ramona *Gene Austin*	Side 10	1947	Whiffenpoof Song *Robert Merrill*
	1937	Marie *Tommy Dorsey*		1948	Bouquet of Roses *Eddy Arnold*
Side 3	1938	Boogie Woogie *Tommy Dorsey*	Side 11	1950	Be My Love *Mario Lanza*
	1938	Jalousie *Boston Pops Orchestra*		1951	Anytime *Eddie Fisher*
Side 4	1938	Beer Barrel Polka *Will Glahé*	Side 12	1951	The Loveliest Night of the Year *Mario Lanza*
	1938	Begin the Beguine *Artie Shaw*		1951	Slow Poke *Pee Wee King*
Side 5	1939	In the Mood *Glenn Miller*	Side 13	1952	Don't Let the Stars Get in Your Eyes *Perry Como*
	1939	Sunrise Serenade *Glenn Miller*		1953	You You You *The Ames Brothers*
Side 6	1939	Blue Danube Waltz *Leopold Stokowski*	Side 14	1954	I Need You Now *Eddie Fisher*
	1940	Tuxedo Junction *Glenn Miller*		1954	Cherry Pink and Apple Blossom White *Perez Prado*
Side 7	1940	Star Dust *Artie Shaw*	Side 15	1954	Naughty Lady from Shady Lane *Ames Brothers*
	1941	Tchaikovsky Piano Concerto *Freddy Martin*		1955	Rock and Roll Waltz *Kay Starr*
Side 8	1941	Chattanooga Choo Choo *Glenn Miller*	Side 16	1956	Hot Diggity *Perry Como*
	1941	Racing with the Moon *Vaughn Monroe*		1956	Heartbreak Hotel *Elvis Presley*

SPD-19-4

TMKS ® © Radio Corporation of America
Marcas Registradas

Printed in U.S.A.

© by Radio Corporation of America, 1956

SPD 19 THE SOUND OF LEADERSHIP (PACKAGE OF 8 EXTENDED PLAYS - SOUVENIR OF THE MIAMI MEETING JUNE, 1956)

☐ Gray label (Elvis disc only:
Side 16 - Track 2) 200.00 800.00
☐ Complete box set (8 EPs, box, paper
insert/contents list) 600.00 2400.00
Contains the following Elvis selection:
HEARTBREAK HOTEL

NOTE: In June, 1956 RCA held its company distributor meeting in Miami, Florida. The SPD-19 box set was prepared, a compilation of 32 of the label's million sellers from 1907 to 1956, and given as a souvenir of that meeting. This set was never sold commercially or offered to the general public in any way.

SPD-22

SPD 22 ELVIS PRESLEY (MERCHANDISE PREMIUM)

☐ Black label - Two disc, double
   pocket set) 125.00   500.00
   Contains the following Elvis selections:
   BLUE SUEDE SHOES
   I'M COUNTING ON YOU
   I GOT A WOMAN
   ONE SIDED LOVE AFFAIR
   TUTTI FRUTTI
   TRYIN' TO GET TO YOU
   I'M GONNA SIT RIGHT DOWN AND CRY
   I'LL NEVER LET YOU GO

Newspaper ads like this one appeared nationwide offering SPD-22 as a bonus, for a limited time, to buyers of RCA's $32.95 Victrola.

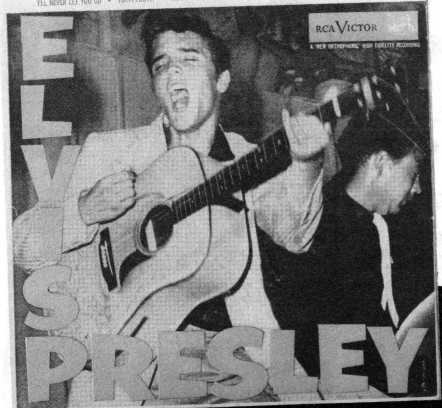

BLUE SUEDE SHOES • I'M COUNTING ON YOU
I GOT A WOMAN • ONE SIDED LOVE AFFAIR
I'M GONNA SIT RIGHT DOWN AND CRY
I'LL NEVER LET YOU GO • TUTTI FRUTTI • TRYIN' TO GET TO YOU

SPD-22

RCA VICTOR
A "NEW ORTHOPHONIC" HIGH FIDELITY RECORDING

ELVIS PRESLEY

RCA VICTOR

SPD-22
599-9121
(G2WH-1852)

45 EP
Side 4
"NEW ORTHOPHONIC"
HIGH FIDELITY

1—TUTTI FRUTTI
(Dorothy LaBostrie-Richard Penniman)
2—TRYIN' TO GET TO YOU
(Singleton-McCoy)
Elvis Presley

TRADE MARKS ® REGISTERED • MARCAS REGISTRADAS • RADIO CORPORATION OF AMERICA—CAMDEN, N.J.—MADE IN U.S.A.

SPD·23

Free! 12-SONG RECORD ALBUM BY ELVIS PRESLEY **PLUS 12 POP RECORDS** BY OTHER LEADING RCA ARTISTS ($10 VALUE)

With Your Purchase of this Elvis Presley Autographed

RCA VICTOR

Automatic '45' Portable "Victrola" ®

HEAR THESE FAMOUS ELVIS PRESLEY HITS

- Blue Suede Shoes
- I'm Counting On You
- I Got a Woman
- One Sided Love Affair
- I'm Gonna Sit Right Down and Cry
- I'll Never Let You Go
- Tutti Frutti
- Don't Be Cruel
- I Want You—I Need You—I Love You
- Hound Dog
- My Baby Left Me

ALL FOR ONLY

$47⁹⁵

$1 DOWN and per WEEK

® RCA Trade Mark for Record Players

- Plays up to 14 Records Automatically

- Separate tone and volume control. In smart luggage-type carry case.

Elvis Presley Autograph in Gold on "Victrola"

NO INTEREST OR CARRYING CHARGE

SPD 23 ELVIS PRESLEY (MERCHANDISE PREMIUM)

☐ Black label - Three disc, triple
pocket set) 500.00 2000.00
Contains the following Elvis selections:
BLUE SUEDE SHOES
I'M COUNTING ON YOU
I GOT A WOMAN
ONE SIDED LOVE AFFAIR
I'M GONNA SIT RIGHT DOWN AND CRY
I'LL NEVER LET YOU GO
TUTTI FRUTTI
DON'T BE CRUEL
I WANT YOU, I NEED YOU, I LOVE YOU
HOUND DOG
MY BABY LEFT ME
TRYIN' TO GET TO YOU

NOTE: This EP was offered, for a limited time, as a
bonus to buyers of the $47.95 Victrola.

ELVIS PRESLEY
SPD-23

It was a cold, rainy night on Broadway. The time, January 1956. The place, a TV theater-studio between 53rd and 54th Streets. The occasion, the first network telecast of a country singer unknown to the pop world, a youngster of unusual talents with some uncertainty about displaying them before a national audience.

Although Elvis Presley's debut was gained through spectacular local fame and following, its publicity had not attracted the world at large. An artist wh... numerous Southern centers on their... facing a majority of viewers as... as the citizens of Siberia.

In New York very few... theater was sparsely f... and Saturday night... from the weather... past the marque... before show ti... box office wit... them away o...

What ha... following,... pivoted to...

transformed into a deluge of acclaim all over the country. In the South, people understood and were delighted by the success of their 21-year-old prodigy. Elsewhere this enthusiasm was carried first by amazement, later by a sizzling controversy.

At its source was the "Why?" of Elvis Presley's wildfire popularity. The answer to this "Why?" lies somewhere in the welter of feelings and trends which... ...d through Presley's powerful style. ...ls (country, gospel, rhythm ...he is unique in music ...e influences behind ...t, or better yet ...gins)—leave ...sic.

...surpassed ...an even ...e chill ...rable ...into ...alize

1956

SPD-23

RCA VICTOR

SPD-23
599-9124
(G2WH-6136)

45 EP
Side 5
"NEW ORTHOPHONIC"
HIGH FIDELITY

1—DON'T BE CRUEL
(Otis Blackwell)
2—I WANT YOU, I NEED YOU, I LOVE YOU
(Maurice Mysels-Ira Kosloff)
Elvis Presley

RCA VICTOR

SPD-23
599-9125
(G2WH-1852)

45 EP
Side 4
"NEW ORTHOPHONIC"
HIGH FIDELITY

1—TUTTI FRUTTI
(Dorothy LaBostrie-Richard Penniman)
2—TRYIN' TO GET TO YOU
(Singleton-McCoy)
Elvis Presley

RCA VICTOR

SPD-23
599-9123
G2WH-1850

45 EP
Side 1
NEW ORTHOPHONIC
HIGH FIDELITY

1—BLUE SUEDE SHOES
(Carl Perkins)
2—I'M COUNTING ON YOU
(Don Robertson)
Elvis Presley

SPD-26

SPD-26
SIDE **15**
599-9141
(H2WH-1997)

RCA VICTOR

45 EP
"NEW ORTHOPHONIC"
HIGH FIDELITY

1—MYSTERY TRAIN (Parker-Phillips)
2—MILKCOW BOOGIE BLUES (Arnold)

Elvis Presley
1. with Scotty and Bill

Here are the hits and the great artists
who made them famous!
RCA VICTOR
All-Time Pop Best Sellers

SOFT AND SWEET		MUSIC FOR RELAXATION		PERFECT FOR DANCING
The Three Suns	EPB-1041	The Melachrino Strings	EPB-1001	WALTZES	EPB
I LOVE YOU		"MARK TWAIN" AND OTHER		PERFECT FOR DANCING
Eddie Fisher	EPB-1097	FOLK FAVORITES		TEMPOS	EPB
		Harry Belafonte	EPB-1022	
MAMBO MANIA				GREAT LOVE THEMES
Perez Prado	EPB-1075	MUSIC FOR TWO PEOPLE		Max Steiner and his Orchestra
		ALONE		EP
THE ONE — THE ONLY		The Melachrino Orchestra	EPB-1027	EP
Kay Starr	EPA-677			
	EPB-1149	SO SMOOTH		SAX IN SILK
		Perry Como	EPB-1085	Bobby Dukoff
PICKIN' THE HITS				
Chet Atkins	EPA-594	FLIRTATION WALK		ELVIS PRESLEY
		The Voices of Walter Schumann		Elvis Presley	EP
GLENN MILLER	EPA-148		EPA-711	
			EPB-1202	J. P. MORGAN
BELAFONTE		PERFECT FOR DANCING —		Jaye P. Morgan	EP
Harry Belafonte	EPA-693	JITTERBUG or LINDY		
	EPA-694		EPB-1071	ESCAPADE IN SOUND
	EPA-695			Al Nevins and his Orchestra
		PERFECT FOR DANCING —		EP
MUSIC FOR DINING		FOX-		EP
The Melachrino Strings	EPB-1000	TROTS	EPB-1070	

45 EP-POP Insert-1

IMRS & © Radio Corporation of America
Marcas Registradas   Printed

Paper inserts, like the one shown above, were used in this
to separate the discs.

SPD-26
SIDE **6**
599-9141
(H2WH-1996)

RCA VICTOR

45 EP
"NEW ORTHOPHONIC"
HIGH FIDELITY

1—BLUE MOON OF KENTUCKY (Bill Monroe)
2—LOVE ME TENDER (from the 20th Century-F.
CinemaScope production "Love Me Tender")
(Elvis Presley-Vera Matson)

Elvis Presley

SPD 26 GREAT COUNTRY/WESTERN HITS (10 EP SET)

☐ Black label (Elvis disc only;
Sides 6 and 15) 50.00   200.00
☐ Complete box set (10 EPs, box, special
paper inserts and outer sleeve) 200.00   800.00
Contains the following Elvis selections:
BLUE MOON OF KENTUCKY
LOVE ME TENDER
MYSTERY TRAIN
MILKCOW BOOGIE BLUES

NOTE: The title of the second song on side 15
should have read "Milkcow Blues Boogie," but
somehow the words were transposed on this label.

Eddy Arnold · Chet Atkins
Jim Edward, Maxine and Bonnie Brown
Homer and Jethro · Johnnie and Jack · Pee Wee King
Elvis Presley · Jim Reeves · Hank Snow
Sons of the Pioneers · Porter Wagoner · Del Wood
GREAT COUNTRY/WESTERN HITS

TV GUIDE PRESENTS ELVIS PRESLEY (Promotional Special)

☐ *RCA Victor GB-MW-8705* (45) 300.00 1200.00

☐ *RCA Victor GB-MW-8705* (Green insert with four paragraphs telling the story of TV Guide's interview with Elvis) 200.00   800.00

☐ *RCA Victor GB-MW-8705* (Pink insert with "Suggested Continuity" for conducting the open-end interview using Elvis' voice as provided on the disc) . .   150.00   600.00

 **ELVIS EXCLUSIVELY**

One hot, sticky night a few weeks ago in Lakeland, Florida, a TV GUIDE reporter switched on a tape recorder. He extended the microphone to the young man from Mississippi who has taken the country by storm with his energetic style of singing.

The result was one of the most unusual interviews in show-business as Elvis Presley talked freely about his nickname, "The Pelvis"; his impact on teenagers, and the singing style that has sold millions of records in an incredibly short time.

From a half-hour of tape intended originally only as background material for TV GUIDE's three-part series on Elvis, we have lifted four brief, independent excerpts of Presleyana . . . Elvis' off-the-cuff responses to questions of interest to every person who is at all curious about the Presley phenomenon.

We are informed by RCA Victor that this represents the very first occasion on which the famous Presley voice has been preserved on a record . . . sans music. If this constitutes a collector's item—make the most of it!"

*Especially from now until Sept. 30!

AMERICA'S TELEVISION MAGAZINE

ELVIS EXCLUSIVELY

SUGGESTED CONTINUITY

CUT #1

LIVE ANNOUNCER:

Sometimes a nickname helps a performer. Remember when everyone called Frank Sinatra "The Voice"? It certainly didn't hurt Sinatra. Bing Crosby, Georgia Gibbs, Satchmo . . . *their* nicknames all helped make them famous. Nowadays . . . everyone's talking about "Elvis The Pelvis." But even though it's a nickname everyone will remember, it's not exactly a pretty tag to hang onto Elvis Presley. In fact, Elvis isn't happy with it at all. Elvis told a TV GUIDE reporter all about it in an exclusive interview for the magazine's series on Presley. Listen as Elvis discusses his now-famous nickname . . .

TV GUIDE—PRESLEY RECORDING—CUT #1:

("I DON'T LIKE TO BE CALLED ELVIS THE PELVIS, BUT ER . . . I MEAN IT'S ONE OF THE MOST CHILDISH EXPRESSIONS I EVER HEARD COMING FROM AN ADULT, ELVIS THE PELVIS . . . BUT ER . . IF THEY WANT TO CALL ME THAT THERE'S NOTHING I CAN DO ABOUT IT SO I JUST HAVE TO ACCEPT IT. YOU GOT TO ACCEPT THE GOOD WITH THE BAD . . . THE BAD WITH THE GOOD.")

LIVE ANNOUNCER:

Well, what do *you* think? Can Elvis' nickname hurt his career? We think he's taking it like a pretty good sport! . . . That of course, was Elvis, himself, talking to a TV GUIDE reporter for the magazine's current series on the nation's Number 1 recording star. And here's more of Elvis . . . this time, his current record for RCA Victor . . . (TITLE OF RECORD).

Most of the standard catalog commercial extended plays were reissued by RCA at one time or another. There were 26 EPs that originally appeared on RCA's dog on top label that were reissued with dog on side. Two EPs were issued originally with the dog on the side. All 28 of these EPs were later reissued on RCA's orange label. As with the Gold Standard singles, there was never an EP that appeared originally on the orange label.

Prices given in this book are for original pressings, unless noted otherwise, and such is the case in the EP section. A description of the label, dog on top, dog on side, black label, white label, etc., is given to assist you in the important identification of first pressings. To estimate the value of unlisted reissues, use the following guidelines:

If the original is BLACK LABEL with DOG ON TOP:

- *Estimate the value of a DOG ON SIDE pressing at about half.*
- *Estimate the value of an ORANGE pressing at about half to two-thirds the value of the original. As with Gold Standard singles, orange label EPs are both scarce and popular with collectors.*

If the original is BLACK LABEL with DOG ON SIDE:

- *Estimate the value of an ORANGE pressing at about two-thirds.*

Three EPs appeared for the first time on RCA's Gold Standard series. Upon their release, RCA selected three previously issued EPs and all six were pressed on the RCA maroon label. All of the highly sought-after maroon pressings were packaged in the standard Gold Standard series jackets.

Some of the black label EPs appeared on labels using more than one style of printing and layout. With both variations being considered originals, no value difference has yet been established between these variations.

The following checklist will detail the most noteworthy variations, as well as pointing out which EPs were also pressed on RCA's dogless black label and which EPs were pressed both with and without the silver horizontal line.

EPA 747 ELVIS PRESLEY
- ☐ *Black label - dog on top*
- ☐ *Black label - dog on side*
- ☐ *Black label - dogless*
- ☐ *Black label - with line*
- ☐ *Black label - without line*
- ☐ *Orange label*

EPA 821 HEARTBREAK HOTEL
- ☐ *Black label - dog on top*
- ☐ *Black label - dog on side*
- ☐ *Black label - dogless*
- ☐ *Black label - with line*
- ☐ *Black label - without line*
- ☐ *Orange label*

EPA 830 ELVIS PRESLEY
- ☐ *Black label - dog on top*
- ☐ *Black label - dog on side*
- ☐ *Black label - dogless*
- ☐ *Black label - with line*
- ☐ *Black label - without line*
- ☐ *Orange label*

EPA 940 THE REAL ELVIS
- ☐ *Black label - dog on top*
- ☐ *Black label - dogless*
- ☐ *Black label with line*
- ☐ *Black label without line*
  - ALSO SEE: EPA-5120

EPA 965 ANY WAY YOU WANT ME
- ☐ *Black label - dog on top*
- ☐ *Black label - dog on side*
- ☐ *Black label - dogless*
- ☐ *Black label - with line*
- ☐ *Black label - without line*
- ☐ *Orange label*

EPA 992 ELVIS (VOL. 1)
- ☐ *Black label - dog on top*
- ☐ *Black label - dog on side*
- ☐ *Black label - dogless*
- ☐ *Black label - with line*
- ☐ *Black label - without line*
- ☐ *Orange label*

EPA 993 ELVIS (VOL. 2)
- ☐ *Black label - dog on top*
- ☐ *Black label - dog on side*
- ☐ *Black label - dogless*
- ☐ *Black label - with line*
- ☐ *Black label - without line*
- ☐ *Orange label*

EPA 994 STRICTLY ELVIS (VOL. 3)
- [ ] *Black label - dog on top*
- [ ] *Black label - dog on side*
- [ ] *Black label - dogless*
- [ ] *Black label - with line*
- [ ] *Black label - without line*
- [ ] *Orange label*

EPA 1-1515 LOVING YOU (VOL. I)
- [ ] *Black label - dog on top*
- [ ] *Black label - dog on side*
- [ ] *Black label - with line*
- [ ] *Black label - without line*
- [ ] *Orange label*

EPA 2-1515 LOVING YOU (VOL. II)
- [ ] *Black label - dog on top*
- [ ] *Black label - dog on side*
- [ ] *Black label - with line*
- [ ] *Black label - without line*
- [ ] *Orange label*

EPA 4006 LOVE ME TENDER
- [ ] *Black label - dog on top*
- [ ] *Black label - dog on side*
- [ ] *Black label - dogless*
- [ ] *Orange label*

EPA 4041 JUST FOR YOU
- [ ] *Black label - dog on top*
- [ ] *Black label - dog on side*
- [ ] *Black label - with line*
- [ ] *Black label - without line*
- [ ] *Orange label*

EPA 4054 PEACE IN THE VALLEY
- [ ] *Black label - dog on top*
  - ALSO SEE: EPA-5121

EPA 4108 ELVIS SINGS CHRISTMAS SONGS
- [ ] *Black label - dog on top*
- [ ] *Black label - dog on side*
- [ ] *Orange label*

EPA 4114 JAILHOUSE ROCK
- [ ] *Black label - dog on top*
- [ ] *Black label - dog on side*
- [ ] *Orange label*

EPA 4319 KING CREOLE
- [ ] *Black label - dog on top*
  - ALSO SEE: EPA-5122

EPA 4321 KING CREOLE VOL. 2
- [ ] *Black label - dog on top*
- [ ] *Black label - dog on side*
- [ ] *Orange label*

EPA 4325 ELVIS SAILS
- [ ] *Black label - dog on top*
  - ALSO SEE: EPA-5123

EPA 4340 CHRISTMAS WITH ELVIS
- [ ] *Black label - dog on top*
- [ ] *Black label - dog on side*
- [ ] *Orange label*

EPA 4368 FOLLOW THAT DREAM
- [ ] *Black label - dog on top*
- [ ] *Black label - dog on side*
- [ ] *Orange label*

EPA 4371 KID GALAHAD
- [ ] *Black label - dog on top*
- [ ] *Black label - dog on side*
- [ ] *Orange label*

EPA 4382 VIVA LAS VEGAS
- [ ] *Black label - dog on top*
- [ ] *Black label - dog on side*
- [ ] *Orange label*

EPA 4383 TICKLE ME
- [ ] *Black label - dog on side*
- [ ] *Orange label*

EPA 4387 EASY COME EASY GO
- [ ] *Black label - dog on side*
- [ ] *Orange label*
- [ ] *White label - promo; studio credit at top*
- [ ] *White label - promo; studio credit at bottom*

EPB 1254 ELVIS PRESLEY
- [ ] *Black label - dog on top*
- [ ] *Black label - with lines*
- [ ] *Black label - without lines*

EPC 128 ELVIS BY REQUEST (FLAMING STAR)
- [ ] *Black label - dog on top*
  - THIS COMPACT 33 WAS NEVER REISSUED, THERE ARE NO LABEL VARIATIONS.

GOLD STANDARD EXTENDED PLAYS:

EPA 5088 A TOUCH OF GOLD
- [ ] *Black label - dog on top*
- [ ] *Black label - dog on side*
- [ ] *Maroon label*
- [ ] *Orange label*

EPA 5101 A TOUCH OF GOLD VOLUME II
- [ ] *Black label - dog on top*
- [ ] *Black label - dog on side*
- [ ] *Maroon label*
- [ ] *Orange label*

EPA 5120 THE REAL ELVIS
- [ ] *Black label - dog on top*
- [ ] *Black label - dog on side*
- [ ] *Maroon label*
- [ ] *Orange label*
  - ORIGINALLY ISSUED AS EPA-940

EPA 5121 PEACE IN THE VALLEY
☐ *Black label - dog on top*
☐ *Black label - dog on side*
☐ *Maroon label*
☐ *Orange label*
    ORIGINALLY ISSUED AS EPA-4054

EPA 5122 KING CREOLE
☐ *Black label - dog on top*
☐ *Black label - dog on side*
☐ *Maroon label*
☐ *Orange label*
    ORIGINALLY ISSUED AS EPA-4319

EPA ELVIS SAILS
☐ *Black label - dog on top*
☐ *Black label - dog on side*
☐ *Orange label*
    ORIGINALLY ISSUED AS EPA-4325

EPA 5141 A TOUCH OF GOLD VOLUME 3
☐ *Black label - dog on top*
☐ *Black label - dog on side*
☐ *Maroon label*
☐ *Orange label*

As shown in this checklist, there were six Elvis extended play releases manufactured on the special maroon label. At the time of purchase, the buyer didn't know until breaking the seal [bag] if the enclosed EP was black label or maroon. Both sold for the same $1.29 suggested retail price.

Since they were not reissued, special and promotional extended plays are not included in the checklist.

Those EPs that were pressed on the dogless RCA label are highly sought after by Elvis collectors. And, naturally, they will command higher prices. How much higher? It would be safe to expect to pay double, maybe even triple, for a dogless EP.

Although the dogless EPs do boost the value a bit, those EPs that were pressed both with and without the horizontal line don't seem to vary in price. Should any trend in collecting develop to the contrary, it will be so noted in future editions.

REPRODUCTION OF RCA'S ACTUAL MAGAZINE AD COPY OFFERING THE "PERFECT FOR PARTIES" EP. . . FOR JUST 25-CENTS!

ELVIS' LONG PLAY RELEASES

Album prices are given for original pressings, or variations of original pressings, unless a particular reissue or promotional recording requires individual pricing.

Descriptive information necessary in the important identification of original pressings will be provided with each listing. In some cases, an original pressing may have first, temporarily perhaps, been issued with a titles sticker on the cover. In such instances, copies of the original pressing without the sticker are no less original than those with the sticker. This simply constitutes a variation of the original. All known variations of this type will be separately priced in the Guide.

Albums intended for promotional use were so-marked by RCA in a number of different ways. Some were pressed on white label promotional labels, others were even specially pressed on banded discs for air play, most, however, were indicated as promotional copies by the use of a stamp or sticker on the jacket, making no changes on the disc or label.

Because many LPs were designated as promotional copies by stamping —or letter-punching— the covers, most collectors place only a slight increase, if any at all, in their value. On the other hand, those promo LPs that were special pressings are worth much more than their more common commercial issues.

In this edition, we will list, price and describe only those promotional albums that are different enough from the commercial releases to be sought-after by most Elvis collectors.

The following albums were commercially released (including promotional variations of commercially issued product). Following this section, you'll find a listing of special promotional LPs, not commercially released, and their prices.

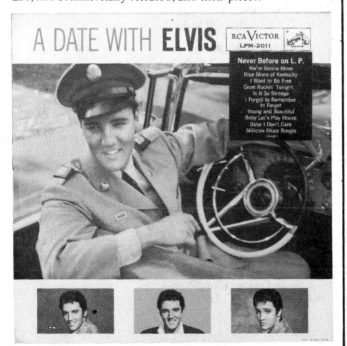

A DATE WITH ELVIS

- [ ] *RCA Victor LPM-2011* (Mono) ... 30.00 120.00
- ✓ Label: Black - reads "Long 33 1/3 Play" at bottom
- ✓ Cover: Single pocket - opens up like a book cover. Song titles are listed on a red sticker applied to front of jacket. Back cover is a 1960 calendar.
- [ ] *RCA Victor LPM-2011* (Mono) ... 10.00 40.00
- ✓ Label: Black - reads "Long 33 1/3 Play" at bottom
- ✓ Cover: Single pocket - catalog number under RCA logo in upper right *RCA Victor LSP-2011(e)* (Reprocessed Stereo) 9.00 36.00
- ✓ Label: The circular RCA VICTOR logo at the top of label is in white.
- ✓ Cover: Has ads for the first three volumes of "Elvis' Gold" on back

A JOURNEY INTO YESTERDAY

- [ ] *Economic Consultants Inc.* (A series
- [ ] of various artists albums, each LP featuring the hits of a different year. Both the 1956 and 1969 LPs contain Elvis songs. Price is for either 8.00 32.00

A LEGENDARY PERFORMER: *See ELVIS: A LEGENDARY PERFORMER*

AGE OF ROCK: *See our section on SPECIAL/PROMOTIONAL ALBUMS*

ALL-TIME CHRISTMAS FAVORITES: *See our section on SPECIAL/PROMOTIONAL ALBUMS*

ALL-STAR ROCK (VOL. 11): *See ROCK, ROCK, ROCK (ALL-STAR ROCK VOL. 11) in this section*

ALMOST IN LOVE

- [ ] *RCA Camden CAS-2440* 2.00 8.00
- ✓ Label: Blue - contains the title "Stay Away Joe."
- ✓ Cover: Also lists "Stay Away Joe" (on back).

NOTE: Any copy of this LP that contains the song "Stay Away Joe" is a first issue. Subsequent Camden (and Pickwick) pressings replaced "Stay Away Joe" with "Stay Away," a completely different Elvis song. Both songs were from the film "Stay Away Joe." The later pressings marked the first appearance of "Stay Away" on an LP.

ALOHA FROM HAWAII VIA SATELLITE (Double Album)

☐ *RCA VPSX-6089* 8.00   32.00
✓ Label: Reddish-Orange
✓ Cover: First issue covers did not list
the song titles. The titles were shown
on an adhesive-backed sticker that was
affixed to the front of the jacket.

☐ *RCA VPSX-6089* (Title sticker) . . .   4.00   16.00

☐ *RCA VPSX-6089* (Chicken Of
The Sea in-house promotional
package; consists of standard
copy of the LP plus "sneak preview" and "ad schedule" printed
materials) 125.00   500.00

NOTE: After our 1978 investigation into this
Chicken Of The Sea variation, it was proven
conclusively that RCA neither authorized this
packaging nor was involved in its production.
In fact, until we brought it to their attention,
they were not aware of its existance. Our conversation with the Chicken Of The Sea (Van
Camps) executives revealed that only a few
dozen, perhaps 50, copies were made of this
package, all of which were distributed within
the organization.

☐ *RCA VPSX-6089* (Promotional
copy - titles and times on white
sticker pasted on front cover) 20.00   80.00

☐ *RCA R-213736* (RCA Record
Club issue) 5.00   20.00
✓ Label: Orange
✓ Cover: Solid front, not die-cut with
circle hole

NOTE: Unlike the first commercial pressings,
the RCA Record Club version was in STEREO.
The commercial release of this LP was the first
appearance of an Elvis recording in Quadraphonic,
the ill-fated four channel system.

This LP's first "Stereo" appearance in the U.S. was available
through the RCA Record Club. The first pressings, like the
one pictured above, were on the orange label.

APRIL POP SAMPLERS: *See our section on SPECIAL/PRO-
MOTIONAL ALBUMS.*

AUGUST 1959 SAMPLER: *See our section on SPECIAL/
PROMOTIONAL ALBUMS.*

BACK IN MEMPHIS

☐ *RCA LSP-4429* 2.50   10.00
✓ Label: Orange
✓ Cover: RCA logo/catalog number is in
upper left

BLUE HAWAII

☐ *RCA Victor LPM-2426* (Mono) . . .   9.00   36.00
✓ Label: Black - reads "Long 33 1/3
Play" at bottom
✓ Cover: Catalog number is in lower
left

☐ *RCA Victor LSP-2426* (Stereo) . . .   12.50   50.00
✓ Label: Black - reads "Living
Stereo" at bottom
✓ Cover: Reads "Living Stereo" in
upper right

BRIGHTEST STARS OF CHRISTMAS, THE

☐ *RCA DLP1-0086* 5.00 20.00
✓ Label: Blue - reads "Special
Products"
✓ Cover: RCA/Special Products logo
in lower right
NOTE: Elvis' "Here Comes Santa Claus" is
one of 11 songs on this LP. The other tracks
are by various RCA artists. No other Presley
selections are featured. This LP was made for
the J.C. Penny's chain of stores and was sold
only in their stores.

BURNING LOVE (AND HITS FROM HIS MOVIES VOL. 2)

☐ *RCA Camden CAS-2595* 2.00 8.00
✓ Label: Blue
✓ Cover: Reads "Limited offer
special bonus photo inside" in
lower left
☐ *Bonus Photo:* 7 X 9 color — 3.00

CHRISTMAS PROGRAMMING FROM RCA VICTOR: *See
our section on SPECIAL/PROMOTIONAL ALBUMS*

CLAMBAKE

☐ *RCA Victor LPM-3893* (Mono) . . . 25.00 100.00
✓ Label: Black - reads "Monaural"
✓ Cover: Catalog number is in
lower left - bonus photo mention
☐ *RCA Victor LSP-3893* (Stereo) . . . 7.00 28.00
✓ Label: Black - reads "Stereo"
✓ Cover: Catalog number is in
upper left - bonus photo mention
☐ *Bonus Photo:* 12 X 12 color 3.00 12.00

C'MON EVERYBODY

☐ *RCA Camden CAL-2518* 2.00 8.00
✓ Label: Blue
✓ Cover: RCA logo is in upper left

COUNTRY MEMORIES (Double Album)

☐ *RCA R-244069* (RCA Record
Club issue) 3.00 12.00
✓ Label: Black
✓ Cover: RCA logo in lower right

COUNTRY MUSIC IN THE MODERN ERA: *See our section
on SPECIAL/PROMOTIONAL ALBUMS*

COUNTRY SUPER SOUNDS

☐ *Omega Sales Inc.* (A 16 volume
☐ set, one for each year 1956-1971.
☐ Three ('56, '57 & '58) contain
Elvis tracks. Price is for any of the
three featuring Elvis) 8.00 32.00

COUNTRY & WESTERN CLASSICS

☐ *Economic Consultants Inc.* (A series
☐ of volumes, one for each year. Four
☐ ('55, '56, '57 & '58) contain Elvis
☐ tracks. Price is for any of the four that
feature Elvis) 8.00 32.00

CURRENT AUDIO MAGAZINE – ELVIS: HIS FIRST AND ONLY PRESS CONFERENCE

☐ *Current Audio Magazine CM-Vol.1
No. 1 (Dist. by Buddah Records)* . . 5.00 20.00
✓ Label: Red
✓ Cover: Single pocket - opens up
like a book cover

DECEMBER '63 POP SAMPLER: *See our section on
SPECIAL/PROMOTIONAL ALBUMS*

DOUBLE DYNAMITE (Double Album)

☐ *RCA Camden/Pickwick DL 2-5001* 2.00 8.00
✓ Label: Black - Pickwick name at
top, Camden at bottom
✓ Cover: Camden name in upper
left, Pickwick logo in lower right

DOUBLE TROUBLE

☐ *RCA Victor LPM-3787* (Mono) . . . 8.00 32.00
✓ Label: Black - reads "Monaural"
✓ Cover: Catalog number in lower
left. Lower (of the two) film
strip frame plugs the "Special
Bonus" photo.
☐ *Bonus Photo:* 7 X 9 color 1.00 4.00

☐ *RCA Victor LSP-3787* (Stereo) . . . 7.00 28.00
✓ Label: Black - reads "Stereo"
✓ Cover: Catalog number in upper
left. Lower (of the two) film
strip frame plugs the "Special
Bonus" photo. Later pressings
replaced this with the words
"Trouble Double."
☐ *Bonus Photo:* 7 X 9 color 1.00 4.00

EARTH NEWS: *See our section on SPECIAL/PROMOTIONAL
ALBUMS*

ELVIS

☐ *RCA Victor LPM-1382* (Mono) . . . 40.00 160.00
✓ Label: Black - reads "Long 33 1/3
Play" at bottom. This variation
lists the song tracks as "Band 1,"
"Band 2," etc., whereas the more
common versions list only the
numbers 1 through 6.
✓ Cover: Catalog number under the
RCA logo in upper right
☐ ☐ *RCA Victor LPM-1382* (Mono) . . . 10.00 40.00
☐ ✓ Label: Black - reads "Long 33 1/3
☐ Play" at bottom
☐ ✓ Cover: Catalog number under the
☐ RCA logo in upper right
☐ ☐ *RCA Victor LSP-1382*(e) (Reprocessed
☐ ☐ Stereo) 12.50 50.00
✓ Label: The circular RCA VICTOR
logo at the top of the label is in
silver. Later pressings had those
letters in white.
✓ Cover: Catalog number in upper
left
NOTE: There are eleven known variations of the back cover to
this LP, each picturing other RCA album releases. We have pro-
vided a checklist box for each variation.

RCA VICTOR

LPM-1382

A "NEW ORTHOPHONIC" HIGH FIDELITY RECORDING

RCA VICTOR

"HIS MASTER'S VOICE"

"NEW ORTHOPHONIC" HIGH FIDELITY

LPM
1382
(G2WP-7207)

SIDE
1

ELVIS

Band 1—RIP IT UP (Robert Blackwell-John Marascalco)
Band 2—LOVE ME (Jerry Leiber-Mike Stoller)
Band 3—WHEN MY BLUE MOON TURNS TO GOLD AGAIN
(Wiley Walker-Gene Sullivan)
Band 4—LONG TALL SALLY (Enotris Johnson)
Band 5—FIRST IN LINE (Aaron Schroeder-Ben Weisman)
Band 6—PARALYZED (Otis Blackwell)

ELVIS PRESLEY

TRADE MARKS ® REGISTERED • MARCAS REGISTRADAS • RADIO CORPORATION OF AMERICA—CAMDEN, N.J.—MADE IN U.S.A.

LONG 33⅓ PLAY

RCA VICTOR

"HIS MASTER'S VOICE"

"NEW ORTHOPHONIC" HIGH FIDELITY

LPM
1382
(G2WP-7208)

SIDE
2

ELVIS

Band 1—SO GLAD YOU'RE MINE (Arthur Crudup)
Band 2—OLD SHEP (Red Foley)
Band 3—READY TEDDY (Blackwell-Marascalco)
Band 4—ANYPLACE IS PARADISE (Joe Thomas)
Band 5—HOW'S THE WORLD TREATING YOU
(Chet Atkins- Boudleaux Bryant)
Band 6—HOW DO YOU THINK I FEEL
(Walker-Pierce)

ELVIS PRESLEY

TRADE MARKS ® REGISTERED • MARCAS REGISTRADAS • RADIO CORPORATION OF AMERICA—CAMDEN, N.J.—MADE IN U.S.A.

LONG 33⅓ PLAY

ELVIS (Including FOOL)

☐ *RCA APL1-0283* 4.00   16.00
✓ Label: Orange
✓ Cover: RCA logo in lower left

ELVIS (Double Album)

☐ *RCA Victor DPL2-0056(e)*. 8.00   32.00
(Marketed through Brookville Records)
✓ Label: Tan
✓ Cover: Has "Brookville Records" in
upper right

NOTE: All of the selections on this release were
later issued, in the same sequence, on the "Elvis
Commerative Album." Both label and cover were
changed for the latter issue.

ELVIS (FROM HIS NBC-TV SPECIAL)

☐ *RCA LPM-4088* 2.50   10.00
✓ Label: Orange
✓ Cover: RCA in upper left, VICTOR
in upper right

ELVIS (SPEAKS TO YOU) (Double Album)

☐ *Green Valley GV-2001/2003* 3.00   12.00
✓ Label: GV-2001 is green, GV-2003
is red.
✓ Cover: Double pocket - yellow banner
across upper right corner.

NOTE: One of the two discs in this set, GV-2001,
was previously issued as "Elvis Exclusive Live
Press Conference." See that listing for more
information.

ELVIS: A CANADIAN TRIBUTE

☐ *RCA KKL1-7065* 6.00   24.00
✓ Label: Custom; Elvis' photo on label
✓ Cover: Has "Gold Collectors Edition
Serial No." gold sticker on front. Copies
without the sticker are later pressings
and are still available as of press time.

NOTE: This LP was originally manufactured in Canada. RCA in
the States began distribution and production after its impressive
sales in Canada.

ELVIS — A COLLECTORS EDITION (Five LP Import Set)

☐ *RCA TB-1* 10.00   40.00
✓ Label: Brown
✓ Cover: Box; Tee Vee logo at top

NOTE: This set was manufactured in Canada,
but is included here because it was offered to U.S.
buyers through TV ads. Included in the box were
the following albums:

☐ *RCA KSL 1-7053* - *"Elvis In Hollywood"*
☐ *RCA KSL 2-7031* - *"Elvis Forever"*
☐ *RCA DPL2-0056(e)* - *"Elvis"*
☐ *Bonus Photo Booklet:* 20 Pages in color

ELVIS (VOLUME 1): A LEGENDARY PERFORMER

☐ *RCA CPL1-0341* 2.50   10.00
✓ Label: Black with gold letters
✓ Cover: Large die-cut hole in center
☐ *RCA CPL1-0341 - Bonus booklet, "The
Early Years."* (Included in value
given for LP package above)

ELVIS (VOLUME 2): A LEGENDARY PERFORMER

☐ *RCA CPL1-1349* 2.50   10.00
✓ Label: Black with gold letters
✓ Cover: Large die-cut hole in center
☐ *RCA CPL1-1349 - Bonus booklet, "The
Early Years. . .Continued."* (Included in
value given for LP package above)

ELVIS (VOLUME 3): A LEGENDARY PERFORMER

☐ *RCA CPL1-1378* (Picture disc) . . .   4.00   16.00
✓ Label: Photo of Elvis covers entire
disc, different one on each side.
✓ Cover: Large die-cut hole in center
☐ *RCA CPL1-1378 - Bonus booklet,
"Yesterdays."* (Included in value
given for LP package above)
☐ *RCA CPL1-1382* 2.50   10.00
✓ Label: Black with gold letters
✓ Cover: Large die-cut hole in center
☐ *RCA CPL1-1382 - Bonus booklet,
"Yesterdays."* (Included in value
given for LP package above)

ELVIS: ALOHA FROM HAWAII VIA SATELLITE:
See: ALOHA FROM HAWAII VIA SATELLITE

ELVIS AS RECORDED AT MADISON SQUARE GARDEN

☐ *RCA LSP-4776* 2.50   10.00
✓ Label: Orange
✓ Cover: RCA logo in upper left
☐ *RCA LSP-4776* (Promotional copy)   10.00   40.00
✓ Label: Orange
✓ Cover: White "Promotional Album -
Not For Sale" sticker on front
☐ *RCA SPS 33-571-1 (LSP 4776)*
(Special double album promotional
pressing). 60.00   240.00
✓ Label: White
✓ Cover: Double pocket, plain white
with programming information on
white stickers.

NOTE: In order to enable dee jays to select
a particular track from this album, this special
banded (space between each track) pressing
was shipped to select radio stations. The commercial version had no bands on the disc.

ELVIS BACK IN MEMPHIS: *See BACK IN MEMPHIS*

ELVIS' CHRISTMAS ALBUM

☐ *RCA Victor LOC-1035* 100.00 400.00
    Label: Black
    Cover: Single pocket - opens up
    like a book cover. Contains bound-in
    10 page Elvis photo section. First
    copies issued came with gold cover
    sticker listing titles. Sticker could
    also be used when giving the album
    as a Christmas gift. LP must have
    this sticker to fall within the above
    price range.

☐ *RCA Victor LOC-1035* (Without
    special gold cover sticker. Listed
    separately since most copies found
    are missing the sticker) 60.00 240.00
☐ *RCA Victor LPM-1951* (Mono) ...   10.00 40.00
✓ Label: Black - reads "Long 33 1/3
    Play" at bottom
✓ Cover: Catalog number under the
    RCA logo in upper right
☐ *RCA Victor LSP-1951(e)* (Reprocessed
    Stereo) 9.00 36.00
✓ Label: Black - RCA VICTOR is in
    white circular latters at top
✓ Cover: Catalog number in upper left
☐ *RCA Camden CAL-2428* 2.00 8.00

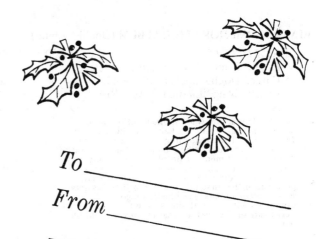

To _____

From _____

ELVIS SINGS

Santa Claus Is Back in Town • White
Christmas • Here Comes Santa Claus •
I'll Be Home for Christmas • Blue
Christmas • Santa Bring My Baby Back
(to Me) • Oh Little Town of Bethlehem •
Silent Night • Peace in the Valley •
I Believe • Take My Hand,
Precious Lord • It Is No Secret

ELVIS COMMEMORATIVE ALBUM (Double Album)

☐ *RCA DPL2-0056(e)* 12.50   50.00
✓ Label: Black RCA "Special Products"
✓ Cover: Double pocket - with gold sticker giving "Limited Edition Reg. No."

NOTE: This album was a limited edition, numbered, repackage of the earlier Brookville Records LP, "Elvis." The catalog number is the same as the Brookville set, but nowhere on the "Commemorative Album" does it mention Brookville. The copy of the earlier set that is pictured on this LP's cover is even missing the Brookville Records logo, as were later pressings of the first LP. This LP, which was only sold through TV ads, was pressed on gold vinyl. Contained within the album is a printed "Registered Certificate of Ownership" that the buyer could fill out.

ELVIS COUNTRY ("I'M 10,000 YEARS OLD")

☐ *RCA LSP-4460* 2.50   10.00
✓ Label: Orange
✓ Cover: RCA logo is upper left
☐ *Bonus Photo:* 7 X 9 color

ELVIS EXCLUSIVE LIVE PRESS CONFERENCE (MEMPHIS, TENNESSEE – FEBRUARY 1961)

☐ *Green Valley GV-2001* 6.00   24.00
✓ Label: Green
✓ Cover: Only by examining the cover closely can you determine a first pressing, of which there were only 5000 made. The cover is the softer, European style, stock. The black 1½-inch bar on the back should not touch or wrap around the spine. Later pressings would be valued at about one-half prices given for original issues.

ELVIS FOR EVERYONE

☐ *RCA Victor LPM-3450* (Mono) . . . 8.00   32.00
✓ Label: Black - reads "Monaural"
✓ Cover: Catalog number in lower left
☐ *RCA Victor LSP-3450* (Stereo) . . . 7.00   28.00
✓ Label: Black - reads "Stereo"
✓ Cover: Catalog number in upper left

ELVIS FOREVER (Double Album)

☐ *RCA KSL2-7031* 6.00   24.00
✓ Label: Tan
✓ Cover: Single pocket - RCA "Special Products" logo in lower right.

NOTE: This album was manufactured in Canada, but distributed to U.S. buyers through TV ads. Since it was widely available in the States, we are including it in this book.

NOTE: The four volumes of "Elvis' Gold," are listed in the order of their release, in the next column. To do this, it was necessary to take them out of proper alphabetical order.

ELVIS' GOLDEN RECORDS

☐ *RCA Victor LPM-1707* (Mono) . . . 20.00   80.00
✓ Label: Black - reads "Long 33 1/3 Play" at bottom
✓ Cover: LP title, "Elvis Golden Records" printed in light blue. No song titles shown on front cover. Catalog number under RCA logo in upper right.
☐ *RCA Victor LSP-1707(e)* (Reprocessed Stereo) 12.50   50.00
✓ Label: The circular RCA VICTOR logo at the top of the label is silver. Later pressings had those letters in white.
✓ Cover: Catalog number in upper left

ELVIS' GOLD RECORDS – VOLUME 2 (50,000,000 ELVIS FANS CAN'T BE WRONG)

☐ *RCA Victor LPM-2075* (Mono) . . . 10.00   40.00
✓ Label: Black - reads "Long 33 1/3 Play" at bottom
✓ Cover: Catalog number is under the RCA logo in upper right
☐ *RCA Victor LSP-2075(e)* (Reprocessed Stereo) 12.50   50.00
✓ Label: The circular RCA VICTOR logo at the top of the label is silver. Later pressings had those letters in white.
✓ Cover: Catalog number in upper left

NOTE: Some second pressings show the title on the label as "Elvis' Gold Records, Vol. 2," dropping the reference to "50,000,000 Elvis Fans."

ELVIS' GOLDEN RECORDS – VOLUME 3

☐ *RCA Victor LPM-2765* (Mono) 8.00   32.00
✓ Label: Black - reads "MONO"
✓ Cover: Catalog number in lower left.
☐ *RCA Victor LSP-2765* (Stereo) 7.00   28.00
✓ Label: Black - RCA Victor logo at top in silver print.
✓ Cover: Catalog number in upper left.

ELVIS' GOLD RECORDS – VOLUME 4

☐ *RCA Victor LPM-3921* (Mono) 125.00   500.00
✓ Label: Black - reads "Monaural"
✓ Cover: Catalog number in lower left.
☐ *Bonus Photo:* 7 X 9 color.

☐ *RCA Victor LSP-3921* (Stereo) 7.00   28.00
✓ Label: Black - reads "Stereo"
✓ Cover: Catalog number in upper left.
☐ *Bonus Photo:* 7 X 9 color.

ELVIS: HIS FIRST AND ONLY PRESS CONFERENCE: *See CURRENT AUDIO MAGAZINE – ELVIS HIS FIRST AND ONLY PRESS CONFERENCE*

ELVIS IN CONCERT (Double Album)

☐ *RCA APL2-2587* 2.50   10.00
✓ Label: Blue - custom
✓ Cover: Double pocket - blue banner
across lower right describing source
of the material on the LP.

NOTE: Packaged inside this album was a
color flyer, listing other Elvis albums available. No noteworthy value has yet been
attached to the flyer.

ELVIS IN HOLLYWOOD (Double Album)

☐ *RCA DPL2-0168* 6.00   24.00
(Marketed through Brookville Records)
✓ Label: Blue - RCA Special Products
✓ Cover: Single pocket - Brookville
Records logo in upper right
☐ *Bonus Photo Booklet:* 20 pages in
color 2.50   10.00

ELVIS IN PERSON AT THE INTERNATIONAL HOTEL, LAS VEGAS, NEVADA

☐ *RCA LSP-4428* 2.50   10.00
✓ Label: Orange
✓ Cover: RCA logo in upper left

NOTE: This album originally appeared as one of
the two LPs contained in the double album "From
Memphis to Vegas/From Vegas to Memphis."

ELVIS IS BACK

☐ *RCA Victor LPM-2231* (Mono) . . .   15.00   60.00
✓ Label: Black - reads "Long 33 1/3
Play" at bottom
✓ Cover: Catalog number is under the
RCA logo in upper right. Jacket has
no song titles printed on it. Titles
are not printed on cover. They may
be on yellow sticker applied to cover.
☐ *RCA Victor LSP-2231* (Stereo) . . .   15.00   60.00
✓ Label: Black - reads "Living Stereo"
at bottom
✓ Cover: Reads "Living Stereo" at top.
Song titles are on yellow sticker and
do not appear on the jacket itself.
Cover for both mono and stereo
opens up like a book cover.

NOTE: Copies of this LP exist with an additional cover
variation. One side of the double pocket jacket has a photo
of Elvis in civilian clothes (front), the other in Army garb.
In some cases the record is held in the front pocket, in other
pressings the disc is contained in the back pocket.

ELVIS NOW

☐ *RCA LSP-4671* 2.50   10.00
✓ Label: Orange
✓ Cover: RCA logo in upper right
☐ *RCA LSP-4671* (Promotional Copy)   10.00   40.00
✓ Label: Commercial orange
✓ Cover: Song titles and programming
information on white sticker, applied
to front cover.

ELVIS MEMORIES: *See our section on SPECIAL/PRO-MOTIONAL ALBUMS*

ELVIS PRESLEY

☐ *RCA Victor LPM-1254* (Mono) . . .   10.00   40.00
✓ Label: Black - reads "Long 33 1/3
Play" at bottom
✓ Cover: Catalog number is under RCA
logo in upper right
☐ *RCA Victor LSP-1254(e)* (Reprocessed
Stereo) 12.50   50.00
✓ Label: The circular RCA VICTOR
logo at the top of the label is in
silver. Later pressings had those
letters in white
✓ Cover: Catalog number is in upper
left

NOTE: The word "Elvis" on the left side of
the LP cover was first printed using a light pink
color. In later pressings, a dark pink was used on
these letters.

ELVIS PRESLEY STORY, THE (By Watermark Inc.): *See our section on SPECIAL/PROMOTIONAL ALBUMS*

ELVIS PRESLEY STORY, THE (By Candlelite Music Inc.)

☐ *RCA DML5-0263* (Five LP box set)   5.00   20.00
✓ Label: Black - RCA Special Products
✓ Cover: Candlelite logo at top, RCA
logo in lower right.
☐ *RCA DML1-0264* (Bonus LP, titled
"Elvis: His Songs of Inspiration,"
originally sent with above box set)   2.50   10.00
✓ Label: Black - RCA Special Products
✓ Cover: Candlelite logo at top, RCA
logo in lower right.

NOTE: Although at press time this LP package
was still being offered by Candlelite Music, for
a few dollars less than the combined figures shown
above, these values reflect sales on the collector's
market.

ELVIS RECORDED LIVE ON STAGE IN MEMPHIS

☐ *RCA CPL1-0606* 2.50   10.00
✓ Label: Orange
✓ Cover: RCA logo in upper left
☐ *RCA DJL1-0606* (Promotional Copy)   50.00   200.00
✓ Label: Orange - disc is special "banded"
pressing (space between each track) for
radio station use.
✓ Cover: Has white sticker on front cover
giving programming information.
☐ *RCA APD1-0606* (Quadradisc) . . .   25.00   100.00
✓ Label: Orange. Not repressed on black.
✓ Cover: Black border around front
cover. Quadradisc logo at top-center.

ELVIS SINGS FLAMING STAR

☐ *RCA Camden CAS-2304* 2.00   8.00
✓ Label: Blue
✓ Cover: RCA logo in upper left

NOTE: This LP was a reissue, slightly altered
in design, of "Singer Presents Elvis Singing
Flaming Star and Others" (RCA PRS-279.
See that listing for more information.

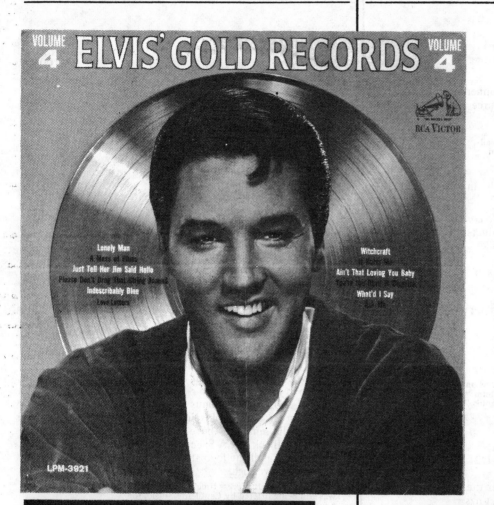

ELVIS SINGS FOR CHILDREN AND GROWNUPS TOO!
- ☐ *RCA Victor CPL1-2901.........* 2.00 8.00
- ✓ Label: Black
- ✓ Cover. Catalog number in upper right
- ☐ *Bonus Elvis Greeting Card* (Removable greeting card was attached to back of LP) .... − 2.00

ELVIS SINGS HITS FROM HIS MOVIES VOLUME 1
- ☐ *RCA Camden CAS-2304* 2.00 8.00
- ✓ Label: Blue
- ✓ Cover: RCA logo in upper right

ELVIS SINGS THE WONDERFUL WORLD OF CHRISTMAS
- ☐ *RCA LSP-4579* 2.50 10.00
- ✓ Label: Orange
- ✓ Cover: RCA logo in upper left

ELVIS TAPES, THE
- ☐ *The Great Northwest Music Company GNW-4005* 2.00 8.00
- ✓ Label: Green
- ✓ Cover: GNW logo in lower right

ELVIS: THE OTHER SIDES: *See WORLDWIDE GOLD AWARD HITS VOL. 2 – THE OTHER SIDES*

ELVIS TODAY
- ☐ *RCA APL1-1039* 2.50 10.00
- ✓ Label: Orange
- ✓ Cover: Catalog number in lower right
- ☐ *RCA APD1-1039 (Quadradisc)* ... 25.00 100.00
- ✓ Label: Orange
- ✓ Cover: Quadradisc logo in upper left

NOTE: This quad LP, like all of the other quad releases except for APD1-0606, was repressed on RCA's newer black label.

E-Z PROGRAMMING (POP & COUNTRY): *See our section on SPECIAL/PROMOTIONAL ALBUMS*

50,000,000 ELVIS FANS CAN'T BE WRONG: *See ELVIS GOLD RECORDS – VOLUME 2*

FIRST YEARS, THE
- ☐ *HALW-00001* 7.00 28.00
- ✓ Label: Pink - side one is labeled "The First Years" but side two is titled "Elvis Presley Live."
- ✓ Cover: Says "Special Limited Edition 10,000 Albums." Should have an issue number imprinted in upper right corner.

FOR LP FANS ONLY
- ☐ *RCA Victor LPM-1990* (Mono) ... 10.00 40.00
- ✓ Label: Black - reads "Long 33 1/3 Play" at bottom.
- ✓ Cover: Catalog number is under RCA logo in upper right
- ☐ *RCA LSP-1990(e)* (Reprocessed Stereo) 9.00 36.00
- ✓ Label: The circular RCA VICTOR logo at the top is in white letters
- ✓ Cover: Catalog number in upper left

FRANKIE AND JOHNNY
- ☐ *RCA Victor LPM-3553* (Mono) ... 9.00 36.00
- ✓ Label: Black - reads "Monaural"
- ✓ Cover: Catalog number in lower left
- ☐ *Bonus Photo:* 12 X 12 color 3.00 12.00
- ☐ *RCA Victor LSP-3553* (Stereo) ... 7.00 28.00
- ✓ Label: Black - reads "Stereo"
- ✓ Cover: Catalog number in upper left
- ☐ *Bonus Photo:* 12 X 12 color 3.00 12.00

FROM ELVIS IN MEMPHIS
- ☐ *RCA LSP-4155* 2.50 10.00
- ✓ Label: Orange
- ✓ Cover: RCA logo in upper left, VICTOR logo in upper right
- ☐ *Bonus Photo:* 8 X 10 color 1.25 5.00

FROM ELVIS PRESLEY BOULEVARD, MEMPHIS, TENNESSEE
- ☐ *RCA APL1-1506* 2.50 10.00
- ✓ Label: Tan
- ✓ Cover: RCA logo in lower left

FROM ELVIS WITH LOVE (Double Album)
- ☐ *RCA Victor R-234340* (RCA Record Club issue) 3.00 12.00
- ✓ Label: Black
- ✓ Cover: Single pocket - RCA logo in upper right

FROM MEMPHIS TO VEGAS/FROM VEGAS TO MEMPHIS (Double Album)
- ☐ *RCA LSP-6020* 4.00 16.00
- ✓ Label: Orange
- ✓ Cover: Double pocket - RCA logo in upper left, VICTOR logo in upper right.
- ☐☐ *Bonus Photos:* Two 8 X 10 black and white. Price range is for both 1.50 6.00

NOTE: Shortly after this LP was released, RCA took the two records that make up this set and issued them individually. Each of the two, "Elvis In Person At The International Hotel, Las Vegas, Nevada" and "Elvis Back In Memphis" was given a new catalog number. See those titles for more information.

FUN IN ACAPULCO
- ☐ *RCA Victor LPM-2756* (Mono) ... 8.00 32.00
- ✓ Label: Black - reads "MONO"
- ✓ Cover: Catalog number in lower left
- ☐ *RCA Victor LSP-2756* (Stereo) ... 7.00 28.00
- ✓ Label: Black - RCA VICTOR, at top, is in silver letters. Later pressings have those letters in white.
- ✓ Cover: Catalog number in upper left

G.I. BLUES
- ☐ *RCA Victor LPM-2256* (Mono) ... 9.00 36.00
- ✓ Label: Black - reads "Long 33 1/3 Play" at bottom
- ✓ Cover: Catalog number in lower left
- ☐ *RCA Victor LSP-2256* (Stereo) ... 12.50 50.00
- ✓ Label: Black - reads "Living Stereo"
- ✓ Cover: Catalog number in upper left

GIRL HAPPY

- ☐ *RCA Victor LPM-3338* (Mono) ...   8.00   32.00
- ✓ Label: Black - reads "Monaural"
- ✓ Cover: Catalog number in lower left
- ☐ *RCA Victor LSP-3338* (Stereo) ...   7.00   28.00
- ✓ Label: Black - reads "Stereo"
- ✓ Cover: Catalog number in upper left

GIRLS! GIRLS! GIRLS!

- ☐ *RCA Victor LPM-2621* (Mono) ...   9.00   36.00
- ✓ Label: Black - reads "Long 33 1/3 Play" at bottom
- ✓ Cover: Catalog number in lower left
- ☐ *RCA Victor LSP-2621* (Stereo) ... 12.50   50.00
- ✓ Label: Black - reads "Living Stereo"
- ✓ Cover: Catalog number in upper left

GOOD TIMES

- ☐ *RCA CPL1-0475* 2.50   10.00
- ✓ Label: Orange
- ✓ Cover: RCA logo in upper left

GREATEST SHOW ON EARTH, THE: *See MEMORIES OF ELVIS*

HARUM SCARUM

- ☐ *RCA Victor LPM-3468* (Mono) ...   8.00   32.00
- ✓ Label: Black - reads "Monaural"
- ✓ Cover: Catalog number in lower left
- ☐ *Bonus Photo:* 12 X 12 color 3.00   12.00
- ☐ *RCA Victor LSP-3468* (Stereo) ...   7.00   28.00
- ✓ Label: Black - reads "Stereo"
- ✓ Cover: Catalog number in upper left
- ☐ *Bonus Photo:* 12 X 12 color 3.00   12.00

HAVING FUN WITH ELVIS ON STAGE

- ☐ *Boxcar (No number given)* 7.00   28.00
- ✓ Label: White - has "Elvis 1" and "Elvis 2" stamped in the vinyl
- ✓ Cover: Boxcar logo in upper left
- NOTE: This album was later reissued by RCA on their own label. As of press time this reissue was easily available.

HE TOUCHED ME

- ☐ *RCA LSP-4690* 2.50   10.00
- ✓ Label: Orange
- ✓ Cover: RCA logo in upper right
- ☐ *RCA LSP-4690* (Promotional copy) 10.00   40.00
- ✓ Label: Commercial orange
- ✓ Cover: Song titles and programming information on white sticker, applied to front cover.

HE WALKS BESIDE ME

- ☐ *RCA Victor AFL1-2772* 2.00   8.00
- ✓ Label: Black
- ✓ Cover: Catalog number in upper left
- ☐ *Bonus Photo Booklet:* 20 pages; color   —   2.00

HIS HAND IN MINE

- ☐ *RCA Victor LPM-2328* (Mono) ...   9.00   36.00
- ✓ Label: Black - reads "Long 33 1/3 Play" at bottom
- ✓ Cover: Catalog number in lower left
- ☐ *RCA Victor LSP-2328* (Stereo) ... 12.50   50.00
- ✓ Label: Black - reads "Living Stereo"
- ✓ Cover: Catalog number in upper left

HIS SONGS OF INSPIRATION: *See ELVIS PRESLEY STORY, THE*

HOW GREAT THOU ART

- ☐ *RCA Victor LPM-3758* (Mono) ...   8.00   32.00
- ✓ Label: Black - reads "Monaural"
- ✓ Cover: Catalog number in lower left
- ☐ *RCA Victor LSP-3758* (Stereo) ...   7.00   28.00
- ✓ Label: Black - reads "Stereo"
- ✓ Cover: Catalog number in upper left

I GOT LUCKY

- ☐ *RCA Camden CAL-2533* 2.00   8.00
- ✓ Label: Blue
- ✓ Cover: RCA logo in upper left

INTERNATIONAL HOTEL, LAS VEGAS, NEVADA PRESENTS ELVIS - (BOX SETS): *See our section on SPECIAL/PROMOTIONAL ALBUMS*

IT HAPPENED AT THE WORLD'S FAIR

- ☐ *RCA Victor LPM-2697* (Mono) ...   9.00   32.00
- ✓ Label: Black - reads "Long 33 1/3 Play" at bottom
- ✓ Cover: Catalog number in lower left
- ☐ *RCA Victor LSP-2697* (Stereo) ... 12.50   50.00
- ✓ Label: Black - reads "Living Stereo"
- ✓ Cover: Catalog number in upper left

KING CREOLE

- ☐ *RCA Victor LPM-1884* (Mono) ... 10.00   40.00
- ✓ Label: Black - reads "Long 33 1/3 Play" at bottom
- ✓ Cover: Catalog number is under RCA logo in upper right
- ☐ *RCA Victor LSP-1884(e)* (Reprocessed Stereo) 12.50   50.00
- ✓ Label: The circular RCA VICTOR logo at the top of the label is in silver letters. Later pressings have those letters in white.
- ✓ Cover: Catalog number in upper left

KISSIN' COUSINS

- ☐ *RCA Victor LPM-2894* (Mono) ...   8.00   32.00
- ✓ Label: Black - reads "MONO"
- ✓ Cover: Catalog number in lower left
- ☐ *RCA Victor LSP-2894* (Stereo) ...   7.00   28.00
- ✓ Label: Black - RCA VICTOR, at top, is in silver letters. White letters are on later pressings.
- ✓ Cover: Catalog number in upper left

LE DISQUE D'OR (French Import)

☐ *RCA 6886 807* 3.00   12.00
✓ Label: Red with silver printing
✓ Cover: RCA logo in lower right
NOTE: Included since this LP was widely distributed and sold in U.S. stores.

LEGENDARY CONCERT PERFORMANCES (Double Album)

☐ *RCA Victor R-244047* (RCA Record Club issue). 3.00   12.00
✓ Label: Black
✓ Cover: Single pocket - RCA logo in lower left

LET'S BE FRIENDS

☐ *RCA Camden CAS-2408* 2.00   8.00
✓ Label: Blue
✓ Cover: RCA logo in upper left

LOVE LETTERS FROM ELVIS

☐ *RCA LSP-4530* 2.50   10.00
✓ Label: Orange
✓ Cover: First issue has the small letters RE in the lower left corner. Even advance promotional copies had the RE.

LOVING YOU

☐ *RCA Victor LPM-1515* (Mono) . . .   10.00   40.00
✓ Label: Black - reads "Long 33 1/3 Play" at bottom
✓ Cover: Catalog number is under the RCA logo in upper right
☐ *RCA Victor LSP-1515(e)* (Reprocessed Stereo) 12.50   50.00
✓ Label: The circular RCA VICTOR logo at the top is in silver letters. Later pressings had those letters in white.
✓ Cover: Catalog number in upper left

MAHALO FROM ELVIS

☐ *RCA Camden/Pickwick ACL-7064* . . .   2.00   8.00
✓ Label: Black
✓ Cover: Pickwick logo in upper left, Camden logo in upper right.

MARCH OF DIMES GALAXY OF STARS: *See our section on SPECIAL/PROMOTIONAL ALBUMS*

MEMORIES OF ELVIS (Multi-album Set)

☐ *RCA DML5-0347* (Five LP box set)   5.00   20.00
✓ Label: Black - RCA Special Products
✓ Cover: Candlelite logo at top, RCA dog in lower right.
☐ *RCA DML1-0348* (Bonus LP, titled "Elvis, The Greatest Show On Earth," originally sent with above box set . .   2.50   10.00
✓ Label: Black - RCA Special Products
✓ Cover: Candlelite logo in upper left, RCA dog in lower right.
☐ *Bonus Booklet:* 16-pages; titled "Musical History's Finest Hour.". . .   —   2.00

ALSO SEE: "ELVIS PRESLEY STORY, THE"

MICHELOB PRESENTS HIGHLIGHTS OF ELVIS MEMORIES: *See our section on SPECIAL/PROMOTIONAL ALBUMS*

MOODY BLUE

☐ *RCA Victor AFL1-2428* 2.00   8.00
✓ Label: Black - First pressings, including promotional copies, were on blue vinyl.
✓ Cover: Catalog number in upper right
☐ *RCA Victor AFL1-2428* 20.00   80.00
✓ Label: Black - The first copies of the second pressing of this LP were made using black vinyl. It was at this time that the nation learned of Elvis' death. In a commemorative action, RCA quickly switched back to blue vinyl. As of press time, this LP is still being pressed on blue vinyl.
✓ Cover: Catalog number in upper right

OCTOBER CHRISTMAS SAMPLER: *See our section on SPECIAL/PROMOTIONAL ALBUMS*

OLD & HEAVY GOLD

☐ *Economic Consultants Inc.* (A
☐ series of various artists albums,
☐ each one spotlighting a different
☐ year. The LPs for '56, '57, '58,
☐ '60 & '61 contain Elvis songs.
Price is for any of the albums . . .   8.00   32.00

ON STAGE – FEBRUARY, 1970

☐ *RCA LSP-4362* 2.50   10.00
✓ Label: Orange
✓ Cover: RCA logo in upper left, Victor in upper right. Other than on the spine, Elvis' name does not appear on the jacket anywhere.

ON THE RECORD - EVENTS OF 1977: *See our section on SPECIAL/PROMOTIONAL ALBUMS*

OUR MEMORIES OF ELVIS

☐ *RCA Victor AQL1-3279* 2.00   8.00
✓ Label: Black
✓ Cover: Other than on spine, catalog number and logo do not appear on jacket anywhere

OUR MEMORIES OF ELVIS VOLUME 2

☐ *RCA Victor AQL1-3448* 2.00   8.00
✓ Label: Black
✓ Cover: Catalog number in lower left

NOTE: Also see "Pure Elvis," listed in our section on SPECIAL/PROMOTIONAL ALBUMS.

PARADISE HAWAIIAN STYLE

☐ *RCA Victor LPM-3643* (Mono) . . .   8.00   32.00
✓ Label: Black - reads "Monaural"
✓ Cover: Catalog number in lower left
☐ *RCA Victor LSP-3643* (Stereo) . . .   7.00   28.00
✓ Label: Black - reads "Stereo"
✓ Cover: Catalog number in upper left

POT LUCK

□ *RCA Victor LPM-2523* (Mono) ...   9.00 36.00
✓ Label: Black - reads "Long 33 1/3 Play" at bottom
✓ Cover: Catalog number in lower left
□ *RCA Victor LSP-2523* (Stereo) ...   12.50 50.00
✓ Label: Black - reads "Living Stereo" at bottom
✓ Cover: Catalog number in upper left

PROMISED LAND

□ *RCA APL1-0873* 2.50 10.00
✓ Label: Orange
✓ Cover: RCA logo at bottom
□ *RCA APD1-0873* (Quadradisc) ...   20.00 80.00
✓ Label: Orange
✓ Cover: Quadradisc logo in upper left

PURE ELVIS: *See our section on SPECIAL/ PROMOTIONAL ALBUMS*

PURE GOLD

□ *RCA ANL1-0971(e)* 2.00 8.00
✓ Label: Orange
✓ Cover: RCA logo in lower left

RAISED ON ROCK/FOR OL' TIMES SAKE

□ *RCA APL1-0388* 2.50 10.00
✓ Label: Orange
✓ Cover: Catalog number is right/center

ROCK ROCK ROCK (ALL STAR ROCK - VOLUME 11)

□ *Original Sound Recordings OSR-11*   6.00 24.00
✓ Label: Orange
✓ Cover: Catalog number in upper right

NOTE: Elvis' "Until It's Time For You To Go" is one of 14 songs on this LP. No other Presley selections are featured on this album. This LP was issued with two completely different covers. One says "All-Star Rock, Vol. 11... As Advertised On TV," whereas the other uses the title shown above for this listing.

ROUSTABOUT

□ *RCA Victor LPM-2999* (Mono) ...   8.00 32.00
✓ Label: Black - reads "MONO"
✓ Cover: Catalog number in lower left
□ *RCA Victor LSP-2999* (Stereo) ...   15.00 60.00
✓ Label: Black - RCA VICTOR, at top, is in silver letters. Later pressings have those letters in white.
✓ Cover: Catalog number in upper left

SEPARATE WAYS

□ *RCA Camden CAS-2611* 2.00 8.00
✓ Label: Blue
✓ Cover: RCA/Camden logo at bottom-center

SINGER PRESENTS ELVIS SINGING FLAMING STAR & OTHERS

□ *RCA PRS-279* 12.50 50.00
✓ Label: Tan
✓ Cover: RCA logo in upper left

NOTE: Singer (sewing machines) sponsored the 1968 Elvis NBC-TV special, and this special LP was sold only in Singer Sewing Centers. The contents was later reissued by RCA as "Elvis Sings Flaming Star." See that listing for more information.

SOMETHING FOR EVERYBODY

□ *RCA Victor LPM-2370* (Mono) ...   9.00 36.00
✓ Label: Black - reads "Long 33 1/3 Play" at bottom
✓ Cover: Catalog number in lower left. Back cover has ads for two Compact 33 releases and a scene pictured from the film "Wild In The Country."
□ *RCA Victor LSP-2370* (Stereo) ...   12.50 50.00
✓ Label: Black - reads "Living Stereo"
✓ Cover: Catalog number in upper left. Back cover, same as described above for mono issue.

SPECIAL PALM SUNDAY PROGRAMMING: *See our section on SPECIAL/PROMOTIONAL ALBUMS*

SPEEDWAY

□ *RCA Victor LPM-3989* (Mono) ...   300.00 1200.00
✓ Label: Black - reads "Monaural"
✓ Cover: Catalog number in lower left
□ *RCA Victor LSP-3989* (Stereo) ...   7.00 28.00
✓ Label: Black - reads "Stereo"
✓ Cover: Catalog number in upper left
□ *Bonus Photo:* 8 X 10 color 1.25 5.00

NOTE: With declining consumer and industry interest in monaural recordings, in the late sixties, RCA was pressing fewer mono copies of each new Elvis album. By the time "Speedway" was issued, the pressing of both a mono and a stereo version of each LP was a dying practice. "Speedway" was not the last LP issued in mono, but it was the last LP issued in both mono and stereo. As its value indicates, it is very, very rare in mono. The same applies, to lesser degrees, to the two LPs before "Speedway," "Elvis Gold Records Volume 4" and "Clambake." See those listings for more information.

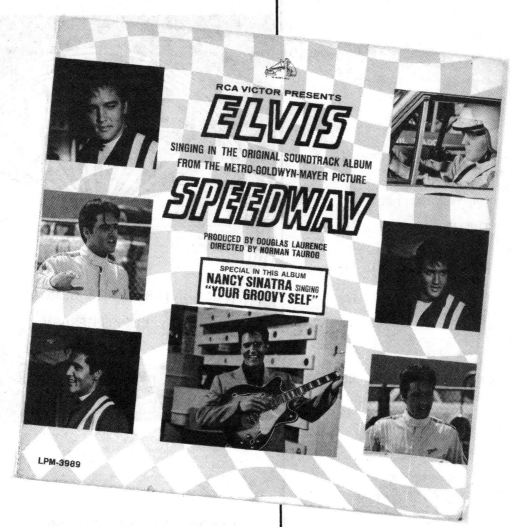

RCA VICTOR PRESENTS
ELVIS
SINGING IN THE ORIGINAL SOUNDTRACK ALBUM
FROM THE METRO-GOLDWYN-MAYER PICTURE
SPEEDWAY
PRODUCED BY DOUGLAS LAURENCE
DIRECTED BY NORMAN TAUROG

SPECIAL IN THIS ALBUM
NANCY SINATRA SINGING
"YOUR GROOVY SELF"

LPM-3989

SPINOUT

□ *RCA Victor LPM-3702* (Mono) ... 8.00 32.00
√ Label: Black - reads "Monaural"
√ Cover: Catalog number in lower left
□ *Bonus Photo:* 12 X 12 color.

□ *RCA Victor LSP-3702* (Stereo) ... 7.00 28.00
√ Label: Black - reads "Stereo"
√ Cover: Catalog number in upper left
□ *Bonus Photo:* 12 X 12 color 3.00 12.00

SUN COLLECTION, THE

□ *RCA HY-1001* (English import) ... 4.00 16.00
√ Label: Green (Two versions known
to exist, one says "Starcall" whereas
the other does not.
√ Cover: Two versions known to exist,
one has ads for other Starcall series
LPs on the back, the other has the
discography and Sun Records story,
the same as "The Sun Sessions."

NOTE: This album was manufactured in
England but was imported and widely distributed in the U.S., by Peters International
of New York. U.S. collectors have yet to
place differing values on the two versions
of this LP. RCA, the following year, issued
the same package in the States, changing
the title to "The Sun Sessions." See that
listing for more information.

SUN SESSIONS, THE

□ *RCA AMP1-1675* 2.00 8.00
√ Label: Tan
√ Cover: RCA logo in lower right

SUN YEARS, THE (INTERVIEWS AND MEMORIES)

□ *Sun-1001* 10.00 40.00
√ Label: Yellow - Has the outer circle
of musical notes and staff around the
entire label, with exception of the bar
wherein "Memphis, Tennessee" appears.
√ Cover: Light yellow; cream color.
Printing is done in light brown.

□ *Sun-1001* (Variation) 2.50 10.00
√ Label: Yellow - Outer circle of notes
and staff rims only top half of label.
Says "Nashville, U.S.A." at bottom,
does not say "Memphis."
√ Cover: Dark yellow - Printing is done
in dark brown.

□ *Sun-1001* (Cover variation) 6.00 24.00
√ Label: Yellow, same as shown above
for *Sun-1001* (Variation)
√ Cover: White with brown printing

NOTE: As a result of successful legal action by
RCA, Sun Records manufacture and distribution
of this LP was halted shortly after its release.
Since there were never any second pressings,
and since all of the variations appeared at about
the same time, we have listed them all.

THAT'S THE WAY IT IS
- ☐ *RCA LSP-4445* 2.50 10.00
- ✓ Label: Orange
- ✓ Cover: RCA logo in upper left, Victor logo in upper right.

TODAY: *See ELVIS TODAY*

WELCOME TO MY WORLD
- ☐ *RCA Victor APL1-2274* 2.00 8.00
- ✓ Label: Black
- ✓ Cover: Catalog number in upper right

WORLD IN SOUND, THE (1977): *See our section on SPECIAL/PROMOTIONAL ALBUMS*

WORLDWIDE 50 GOLD AWARD HITS, VOL. 1 (Four LP Box Set)
- ☐ *RCA LPM-6401* 5.00 20.00
- ✓ Label: Orange
- ✓ Cover: Box; carries a mention for the bonus booklet on front cover.
- ☐ *Bonus Photo Booklet:* 20 pages, color 4.00 16.00

WORLDWIDE GOLD AWARD HITS VOL. 2 – ELVIS - THE OTHER SIDES (Four LP Box Set)
- ☐ *RCA LPM-6402* 5.00 20.00
- ✓ Label: Orange
- ✓ Cover: Box; Plugs "Special Bonus Number one" in upper left and "Special Bonus Number Two" in upper right
- ☐ *Bonus One:* Specially made envelope containing, supposedly, a piece of Elvis' wardrobe 1.00 4.00
- ☐ *Bonus Two:* Large folded color portrait print of Elvis 2.00 8.00

WORLDWIDE GOLD AWARD HITS, PARTS 1 & 2 (Double Album)
- ☐ *RCA Victor R-213690* (RCA Record Club issue) 9.00 36.00
- ✓ Label: Orange (Rarely did an orange label carry the word "Victor")
- ✓ Cover: Single pocket

NOTE: The two records in this set represented half of the four LP set, LPM-6401

WORLDWIDE GOLD AWARD HITS, PARTS 3 & 4 (Double Album)
- ☐ *RCA Victor R-214657* (RCA Record Club issue) 3.00 12.00
- ✓ Label: Black
- ✓ Cover: Single pocket

NOTE: The two records in this set represented half of the four LP set, LPM-6401

YOU'LL NEVER WALK ALONE
- ☐ *RCA Camden CALX-2472* 2.00 8.00
- ✓ Label: Blue
- ✓ Cover: Except for the word "Elvis," front cover has no writing.

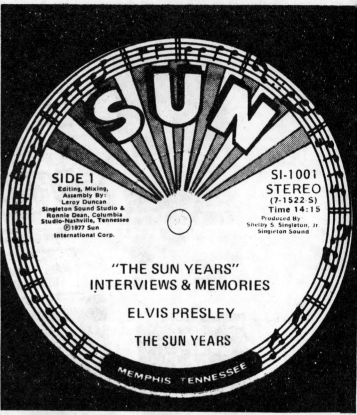

A limited edition of "The Sun Years" LP was pressed using the old "Memphis" style Sun label.

AGE OF ROCK, THE

☐ *EMR Enterprises EMR RH-8* 12.50   50.00
Issued to promote the book, "The
Age of Rock," now out of print.
No special cover exists for this disc.
Contains the following Elvis selection:
TUTTI FRUTTI
LOVE ME TENDER
BLUE SUEDE SHOES

THE AGE OF ROCK

Produced for Random House and Vintage
Books by EMR Enterprises, Ltd.

PART I

Side 1   EMR RH 8
33⅓ RPM   ◯   Time: 23:49

Based on the Random House book
THE AGE OF ROCK: Sounds of the American
Cultural Revolution
Also available as a Vintage Paperback
Written By: Williams James
Produced By: John Snell
Executive Producer: Robert L. Walter
Copyright 1969
EMR Enterprises Ltd.
YB-320

An interesting sidenote on this release is the fact that Random House,
at the time of this issue, was owned by RCA.

ALL-TIME CHRISTMAS FAVORITES (Five LP Box Set)

☐ *Collector's Edition CE-505* 40.00   160.00
One entire side of one of the five LPs
features Elvis songs. This set is iden-
tical in construction to the two box
sets issued through Candlelite Music.
Contains the following Elvis selections:
O COME, ALL YE FAITHFUL (shown on the
label as COME ALL YE FAITHFUL)
THE FIRST NOEL (shown on the label as NOEL)
IF I GET HOME ON CHRISTMAS DAY (shown on
the label as I'LL BE HOME FOR CHRISTMAS)
SILVER BELLS
WINTER WONDERLAND (shown on the label
as WALKING IN A WINTER WONDERLAND)

NOTE: It's interesting that out of five Elvis song titles, this
company was only able to list one properly. Along those lines,
a number of signs point to the possibility that this set was
unauthorized. Nonetheless, because of its quality packaging
and Elvis content it will still bring the prices shown here.
We have chosen to list this LP in this section, unauthorized
though it may be, for the same reason as we list "The Sun
Years" in the section of standard LPs. It is another example
of an unauthorized LP that most collectors will agree doesn't
belong in the bootleg, counterfeit and underground section.

BILLBOARD'S 1979 YEARBOOK: *See 1979 YEARBOOK*

COUNTRY MUSIC IN THE MODERN ERA 1940s - 1970s

☐ *New World Records NW-207* 25.00   100.00
This superb LP contains 18 country-western
tracks, one of which is by Elvis. In addition,
the book-like cover has a bound-in six page
booklet detailing singer and song history,
as well as lyrics to all of the songs. This LP
was never made available commercially.
Contains the following Elvis selection:
MYSTERY TRAIN

81

EARTH NEWS (FOR THE WEEK AUGUST 29, 1977)

☐ *Earth News EN 8-22-77*. 50.00   200.00
There is no number given on the label,
the number above is etched in the vinyl.
Disc contains the material needed for
member stations to broadcast two
5-minute segments daily, for one week.
12 of the segments feature Elvis songs
and interviews, much of which has
never been commercially released.
Contains the following Elvis selections:
BLUE SUEDE SHOES (Live, 1956)
DON'T BE CRUEL (Live, 1956)
HEARTBREAK HOTEL (Live, 1956)
HOUND DOG

NOTE: Only excerpts of the above songs are featured.
In addition, excerpts from "Elvis Sails" and "The
Truth About Me," and other interviews are heard.
Finally, excerpts of songs about Elvis are included
in this six day tribute to Elvis, aired the week
following his death. No special cover exists for
this disc.

ELVIS MEMORIES

☐ *ABC Radio ASP-1003* (Three LP box set; including 16-page "Program Operation Instructions" booklet and four pages of "Commercial/Final Program Instructions") 125.00 500.00

☐ *ABC Radio Special Reel-to-reel Tape* (Contains spot inserts and advance promotional announcement for the actual three hour "Elvis Memories" show) 12.50 50.00

NOTE: The special reel tape came in a box clearly identified as a part of the "Elvis Memories" package. Also see "Michelob Presents Highlights of Elvis Memories" for another important disc, appurtenant to this show.

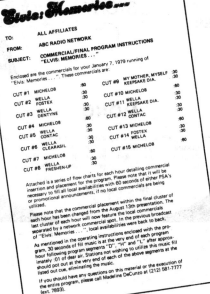

This program is cleared for one time only broadcast on affiliates of the ABC Radio Network. "Elvis: Memories…" is for the sole broadcast use of the ABC Radio Network, and may not be copied or offered for resale.

℗1978 American Broadcasting Companies, Inc.

ELVIS PRESLEY STORY, THE (By Watermark Inc.)

☐ *EPS 1A - 13B* (13 LP set) 150.00 600.00
A complete 13-hour program, containing interviews, commentary and dozens of Elvis' songs. No special box or jacket exists for this set. Made available only to radio stations, with options for exclusivity in each market. Stations purchased the program from Watermark Inc. The above set was issued in 1975 and had a copyright 1975 at the bottom of the label.

☐ *PROGRAMMER'S BOOKLET (included in price given)*

☐ *EPS 1A - 13B* (13 LP set, 1977 edition) 125.00 500.00
Because of Elvis' death, it was necessary to revise the beginning and ending of "The Elvis Presley Story." Only discs 1 and 13 were updated, with the remainder of the show being unchanged. The 1975 version had the title on the label in pink letters, this 1977 version had those letters in blue. Of course, the copyright date was changed to 1977.

☐ *PROGRAMMER'S BOOKLET (included in price given)*

NOTE: Even though this program was first aired in 1970, only the 1975 and 1977 versions were on disc. The 1970 program was on reel tapes which were sent to stations, along with a script and programming information packet. Also, the 1970 program was only a 12-hour show.

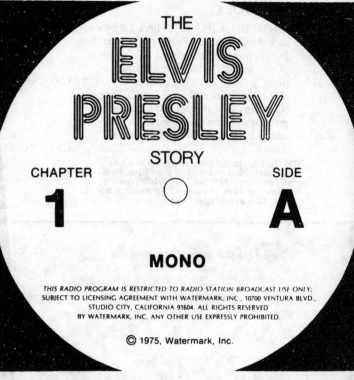

ABOVE: The 1975 edition of "The Elvis Presley Story.
BELOW: The 1977 edition of "The Elvis Presley Story.

THE ELVIS PRESLEY STORY
Manual of Operations
Index

	Page
	1
	2
Index	3
Delivery	4
The Package	5
Quality Check	7
Technical Specs	8
Programming	10
Sample Hour Clock	11
Cueing Instructions	12
The Cue Sheet	
Promotion	GREEN SECTION
Cue Sheets	TAN SECTION
Music List	PINK SECTION
Timing Sheets	
Press Kit (Special unbound insert, inside back cover)	

(Note: Cue Sheets and Timing Sheets may be removed for convenience in Production)

WATERMARK, INC.
10700 Ventura Boulevard
North Hollywood, California 91604

1

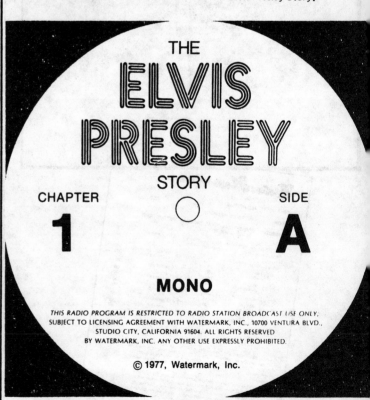

ELVIS REMEMBERED (By Creative Radio Shows)

☐ *CRS 1A-3B* (3-LP set) 60.00   240.00
   Another Elvis "life story," told in a
   series of interviews and a wide selection
   of Presley songs. Contains previously
   unreleased live versions of "I Can't Stop
   Loving You," "I Got A Woman/Amen,"
   "Hurt" and "See See Rider."

☐ *Sales Demo for "Elvis Remembered"*
   (7-inch single) 10.00   40.00
   This 33 1/3 single advertised the three
   hour show through the use of excerpts
   from the actual program. The flip side
   promoted the "Frank Sinatra" and
   "Nat King Cole" programs, two other
   prepared shows available for syndication
   from Creative Radio Shows.

☐ *Programming Packet for "Elvis
   Remembered"* 6.00   24.00
   Includes a program "cue sheet" (script
   information for broadcaster) and a
   cover letter advising stations that the
   discs **must** be returned after the stations
   had aired the program. Another insert
   promoted the company's catalog of
   syndicated shows available.

NOTE: The three discs had no special label,
whereas the small single did have a custom label.
Since our copies were among the first pressed,
the possibility does exist that labels were made
for the LP discs later. First issues, "hot off the
press" had handwritten labels. No special box
or jacket exists for this set.

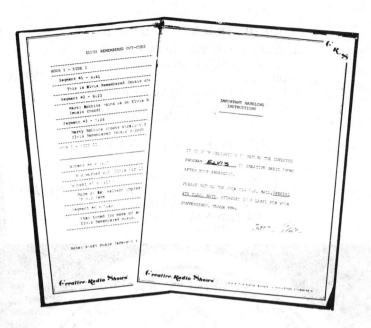

EPIC OF THE 70'S

☐ *Century 21 Productions Inc. (1A-6B)*   30.00   120.00
   A three hour program, highlighting the
   decade of the seventies. No special
   cover or jacket exists.
   Contains the following Elvis selection:
   BURNING LOVE
   *Plus an excerpt from an Elvis interview
   that we have never heard before.*

E-Z COUNTRY PROGRAMMING NO. 2

☐ *RCA Victor G7OL-0108/9* (10-inch sampler of RCA's country-western product) 50.00 200.00
Contains the following Elvis selections:
    MYSTERY TRAIN
    I FORGOT TO REMEMBER TO FORGET

E-Z COUNTRY PROGRAMMING NO. 3

☐ *RCA Victor G8OL-0199/200* (10-inch sampler of RCA's country-western product) 50.00 200.00
Contains the following Elvis selections:
    HEARTBREAK HOTEL
    I WAS THE ONE

E-Z POP PROGRAMMING NO. 1: *Copies of this disc have been found that were manufactured in Canada. The possibility that it was issued in the U.S. does, therefore, exist. We are simply listing it here in hopes that someone may know of a U.S. issue of E-Z Pop Programming No. 1.*
Contains the following Elvis selections:
    TUTTI FRUTTI
    HEARTBREAK HOTEL

86

E-Z POP PROGRAMMING NO. 5

☐ *RCA Victor F7OP-9681/2* 50.00   200.00
(12-inch sampler of RCA's pop product)
Contains the following Elvis selections:
   MYSTERY TRAIN
   I FORGOT TO REMEMBER TO FORGET

E-Z POP PROGRAMMING NO. 6

☐ *RCA Victor G7OL-0197/8* (10-inch
sampler of RCA's pop product) 50.00   200.00
Contains the following Elvis selection:
   I WAS THE ONE

NOTE: There were no special covers or jackets
made for any of the E-Z Pop or E-Z Country discs.

INTERNATIONAL HOTEL, LAS VEGAS, NEVADA PRESENTS ELVIS – AUGUST 1969 (Box Set)

☐ *RCA* (A specially prepared box, con-
taining the following items:
☐ *Copy of "Elvis NBC-TV Special" LP*
☐ *Copy of "From Elvis in Memphis" LP*
☐ *Nine page letter from RCA and The Col.*
☐ *Elvis record and tape catalog*
☐ *1969 Elvis pocket calendar*
☐ *Two 8 X 10 black & white Elvis pictures*
☐ *One 8 X 10 color Elvis picture*
   Total package 250.00 1000.00

NOTE: Price range is given for complete box set
only. Based on that information, incomplete sets
can easily be negotiated.

INTERNATIONAL HOTEL, LAS VEGAS, NEVADA PRESENTS ELVIS – 1970 (Box Set)

☐ *RCA* (A specially prepared box, dif-
ferent than the one issued in 1969,
containing the following items:
☐ *Copy of "From Memphis to Vegas/From Vegas to Memphis"*
☐ *One 8 X 10 black & white photo of Elvis*
☐ *1970 Elvis pocket calendar*
☐ *Elvis record and tape catalog*
☐ *Souvenir photo album*
☐ *Single of "Kentucky Rain" with picture sleeve*
☐ *International Hotel menu*
☐ *Introductory note from Elvis and The Col.*
   Total package 250.00 1000.00

NOTE: Obviously, the greatest portion of the value
shown is the box itself. Beyond that, the only items
of noteworthy value, in either this or the 1969 set,
are those that were not commonly available. For
example, the nine page letter would be much more
valuable than any of the records, all of which were
identical to store stock copies.

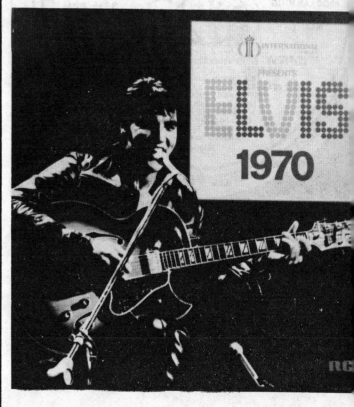

LOUISIANA HAYRIDE, THE

☐ *Louisiana Hayride NR-8454* (12-inch disc that contains Elvis' version of "Tweedle Dee." 200.00 800.00

MARCH OF DIMES GALAXY OF STARS, 1957

☐ *GM-8M-0653/4* (16-inch disc, contains spoken statements from Elvis and other entertainment personalities.......... 300.00 1200.00

☐ *GM-8M-0657/8* (16-inch disc, contains both spoken statements and songs by Elvis and others. The Elvis song played is "Love Me Tender." The remainder of the Elvis segment is an open-end interview...................... 300.00 1200.00

☐ *Cover Letter and Interview Script* (Here is the necessary script needed to conduct the open-end interview 25.00 100.00

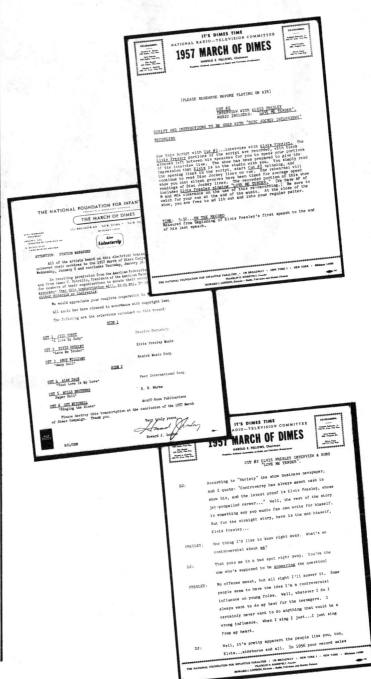

MICHELOB PRESENTS HIGHLIGHTS OF ELVIS MEMORIES

☐ *ABC 0CC810* 40.00 160.00
(ABC prepared this special LP, with its
custom jacket, for executives of the
Michelob Beer Co. As a sponsor for
the three hour ABC radio special,
"Elvis Memories," the network showed
its appreciation by sending them this
preview of the show.

NOTE: Also see "Elvis Memories," in this section.

(BILLBOARD'S) 1979 YEARBOOK

☐ *Billboard Publications (Sides 1-10)* 40.00 160.00
A five hour program, reviewing the
hits and events of 1979. The Elvis
song is played in conjunction with
the mention of "Elvis: The Movie."
Contains the following Elvis selection:
HOUND DOG
This program came packaged in a box
set, including script copy for air play.

Also see "Sound Of '77," in this section.

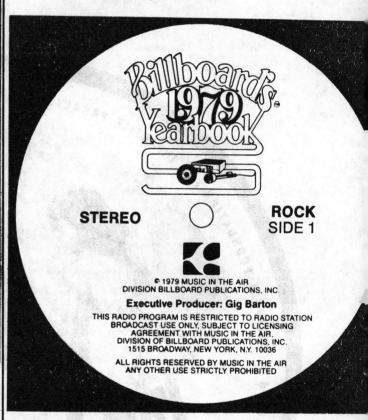

ON THE RECORD – EVENTS OF 1977

☐ *Caedmon TC-1572* 12.50 50.00
(United Press International put together
this LP, highlighting the news events of
1977. A recap of Elvis' death plus excerpts
of the following two songs are included:
ALL SHOOK UP (Live)
HOUND DOG
NOTE: Each of the two major wire services, UPI
and AP, issued news highlights of 1977 albums.
Both had a picture of Elvis on their covers.
See "World In Sound, The" in this section
for more information.

PURE ELVIS (OUR MEMORIES OF ELVIS, VOL. 2)

☐ *RCA (DJL1-3455)* 60.00 240.00

This most unusual promotional LP contained four songs just as they were originally issued, on one side. On the reverse, those same four songs exactly as recorded by Elvis, before the vocal and instrumental overdubbing was added. A custom black and white jacket was made for this release, which, reports RCA, was limited to a press run of only 400 copies. Contains the following Elvis selections:

> *I GOT A FEELIN' IN MY BODY*
> *FOR THE HEART*
> *SHE WEARS MY RING*
> *FIND OUT WHAT'S HAPPENING*

RCA 12-INCH SAMPLERS

The first 12-inch RCA programming sampler was issued in 1956. It was one of the "E-Z Pop Programming" series and the only one of that series to be issued on a 12-inch disc (in the U.S.) According to RCA's files, the next time an Elvis track appeared on a 12-inch sampler was in 1958. By this time the "E-Z" series had been replaced with the "SP" and, shortly thereafter, the "SPS" discs. The "SP," or Special Products, records were made in very limited quantity and distributed to select radio stations. Even today, the most likely place to turn up one of these treasures is in some radio station's dusty library. Only one of these RCA samplers was issued with a special cover, SP 33-66. The possibility that there are other samplers —or perhaps covers— does certainly exist. Any additions to this section are strongly encouraged.

☐ *RCA Victor SP 33-10P* (1958) 200.00 800.00
Contains the following Elvis selection:
KING CREOLE

☐ *RCA Victor SP 33-27* (Titled "August 1959 Sampler") 150.00 600.00
Contains the following Elvis selection:
BLUE MOON OF KENTUCKY

NOTE: This sampler was the first issued in "Living Stereo," that contained an Elvis song. Of course, "Blue Moon of Kentucky" was not one of the stereo tracks on the LP.

☐ *RCA Victor SPS 33-54* (Titled "October Christmas Sampler")(1959)
Contains the following Elvis selection: 150.00 600.00
BLUE CHRISTMAS

NOTE: This sampler was in "Living Stereo." The Elvis song was not in stereo.

□ *RCA Victor SP 33-66* (Titled "Christmas Programming from RCA Victor") (1960) 100.00 400.00

□ *RCA Victor SP 33-66* (Special jacket-sleeve; has Elvis' Christmas Album, LPM-1951, pictured —and therefore Elvis' photo— on back in addition to other RCA Christmas product) 100.00 400.00
Contains the following Elvis selection:
I'LL BE HOME FOR CHRISTMAS

☐ *RCA Victor SPS 33-141* (Titled "October '61 Pop Sampler) 100.00 400.00
Contains the following Elvis selection:
BLUE HAWAII

☐ *RCA Victor SPS 33-191* (1962) 100.00 400.00
Contains the following Elvis selections:
I DON'T WANT TO BE TIED
WHERE DO YOU COME FROM

☐ *RCA Victor SPS 33-219* (1963) 100.00 400.00
Contains the following Elvis selection:
ARE YOU LONESOME TONIGHT

☐ *RCA Victor SP 33-247* (Titled "December '63 Pop Sampler") 100.00 400.00
Contains the following Elvis selection:
FUN IN ACAPULCO

☐ *RCA Victor SPS 33-273* (1964) 100.00 400.00
Contains the following Elvis selection:
KISSIN' COUSINS (NO. 2)

☐ *RCA Victor SPS 33-331* (Titled "April '65 Pop Sampler") 100.00 400.00
Contains the following Elvis selection:
THE MEANEST GIRL IN TOWN

NOTE: Unlike any of Elvis' standard catalog LPs, this sampler was issued on RCA's "Dynagroove Stereo" label. The Elvis song was in stereo.

☐ *RCA Victor SPS 33-347* (1966) 100.00 400.00
Contains the following Elvis selection:
THIS IS MY HEAVEN

☐ *RCA Victor SPS 33-403* (1967) 100.00 400.00
Contains the following Elvis selection:
CRYING IN THE CHAPEL

ROCK AND ROLL ROOTS

Another of the syndicated radio shows that was shipped to subscribing stations on disc. Any of those discs that feature Elvis could be expected to bring about $10.00.

ROCK, ROLL & REMEMBER

☐ *Dick Clark Productions (DPE-402)*   40.00 160.00
  A three hour program covering the
  subject of rock & roll.
  Contains the following Elvis selections:
    I WANT YOU, I NEED YOU, I LOVE YOU
    WEAR MY RING AROUND YOUR NECK
    Plus the 1959 Elvis/Dick Clark-American
    Bandstand telephone conversation.

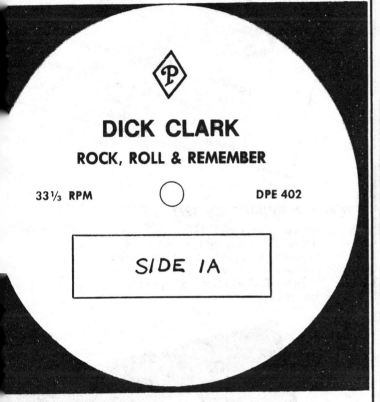

(DICK CLARK'S) SOLID GOLD

This is a syndicated radio program, provided to subscribing
stations on discs. There are too many weekly discs in the
series to list, but, generally speaking, any of the discs that
contain an Elvis song could be expected to bring around
$10.00. In addition to the 12-inch programming discs, a
7-inch demo record was made for this show.

SOUND OF '77

☐ *Billboard Publications (Sides 1-10)* . . .   50.00 200.00
  A five hour program, reviewing the hits
  and events of 1977. One complete
  segment of the show is devoted to Elvis.
  Issued in a special box and includes a
  programmer's script.
  Also see "1979 Yearbook," in this section.

SPECIAL PALM SUNDAY PROGRAMMING

☐ *RCA Victor SP 33-461* 150.00   600.00
(A complete 30-minute program, issued
to approximately 300 select radio stations.
No special jacket or cover exists for this
disc.) Contains the following Elvis songs:
HOW GREAT THOU ART
IN THE GARDEN
SOMEBODY BIGGER THAN YOU AND I
STAND BY ME
WITHOUT HIM
WHERE COULD I GO BUT TO THE LORD
WHERE NO ONE STANDS ALONE
CRYING IN THE CHAPEL
HOW GREAT THOU ART (Excerpt)
☐ *Script and Programming Information*. . .   25.00   100.00

TO ELVIS: LOVE STILL BURNING: *See our section of ELVIS TRIBUTE ALBUMS*

UNITED STATES ARMED FORCES PROGRAMS

Hundreds of programming discs have been made by the
various branches of the armed forces. Usually they contain
a produced show, aimed at a particular music format, that
radio stations can use to log public service time with. Many
of the discs contain an Elvis song or songs. Individually,
these discs usually fall into the $10-$20 range, depending
on how much Elvis is heard.

There were a number of box sets, containing several discs,
that included Elvis tracks. Complete box sets are often
traded in the $30-$75 range. Again, it depends on how
much Elvis is included in the set.

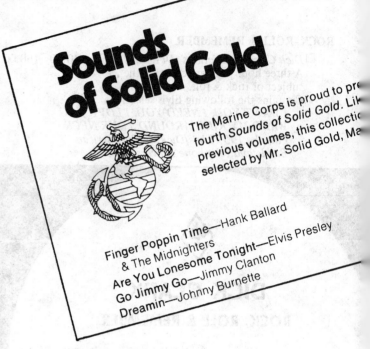

Sounds of Solid Gold

The Marine Corps is proud to pr[e]
fourth *Sounds of Solid Gold*. Lik
previous volumes, this collectio
selected by Mr. Solid Gold, Ma

Finger Poppin Time—Hank Ballard
& The Midnighters
Are You Lonesome Tonight—Elvis Presley
Go Jimmy Go—Jimmy Clanton
Dreamin—Johnny Burnette

WORLD IN SOUND, THE — 1977

☐ *Associated Press AP-1977* 25.00   100.00
(Included in this album's review of 1977
news stories is a portion on Elvis' death.)
Contains the following Elvis selection:
HOUND DOG (Live - excerpt only)
NOTE: Also see "On the Record - Events of 1977,"
in this section.

SOUNDSHEETS

Soundsheets, or plastic flexi-discs as they are sometimes called, containing Elvis' voice, first appeared in 1956. Most of these plastic recordings, however, appeared after Elvis' death in 1977. Although RCA Victor has never issued a soundsheet themselves, they have authorized a few. Most Elvis record collectors are as avid in their quest for a complete collection of soundsheets as any other of his recordings.

All plastic and vinyl soundsheets have one thing in common. They are always given away, either as an added bonus or as an insert in a magazine.

Each soundsheet listed in this section features the voice of Elvis Presley, either singing or speaking.

ELVIS LIVE (1961 PRESS CONFERENCE MEMPHIS, TENN.

☐ *Eva-Tone 1037710A&BX* (Bound-in
   the magazine "Collector's Issue! Elvis,"
   published by Green Valley Record
   Store Inc.) 10.00   40.00
☐ *Eva-Tone 1037710A&BX* (Disc only)   5.00   20.00
NOTE: The material contained on this disc was issued twice before by Green Valley Record Store. See the LPs "Elvis Exclusive Live Press Conference (Memphis, Tennessee — February 1961" and "Elvis (Elvis Speaks to You."

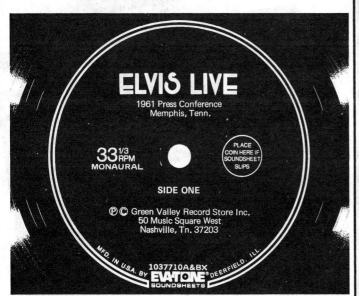

ELVIS PRESLEY STORY, THE (SAMPLER)

☐ *Eva-Tone 726771XS* (Made for Candle-
   lite Music) 2.50   10.00
NOTE: Most Eva-Tone numbers represent the date the job was run. In this case, July 26, 1977 was the manufacturing date. This particular disc was produced for distribution to RCA record club members, promoting the Candlelite Music box set of the same name. The idea was scrapped and the unused soundsheets were sold to dealers in the collector's market.

ELVIS PRESLEY "SPEAKS — IN PERSON"

☐ *Rainbo Records 78rpm* (Dark blue label disc, attached to front cover of "Elvis Answers Back!" magazine) 70.00   280.00

☐ *Rainbow Records 78rpm* (Disc only) . .   20.00   80.00

NOTE: The spoken material on this disc, by Elvis, was also issued as "The Truth About Me" and later as "Elvis Speaks." See those listings in this section for more information.

ELVIS PRESLEY "THE TRUTH ABOUT ME"

☐ *Rainbow Records 78rpm* (Light blue label disc, attached to front cover of "Elvis Answers Back" magazine) 70.00   280.00

☐ *Rainbow Records 78rpm* (Disc only) . .   20.00   80.00

NOTE: There is a noteworthy variation in the actual magazines used in conjunction with these two Rainbow Records soundsheets. The version of the disc described as dark blue was affixed to copies of the magazine using red ink on much of the cover. The light blue disc, with a slightly different label, appeared on a version of the book that used green ink instead of red.

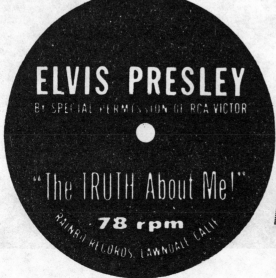

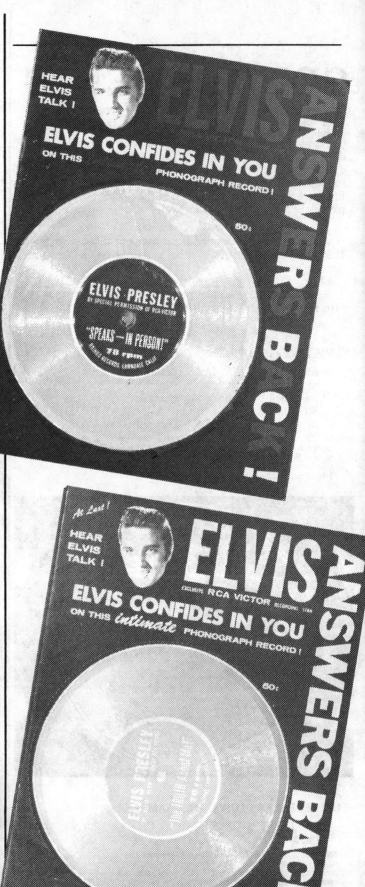

ELVIS: SIX HOUR SPECIAL (SAMPLER)

☐ *Eva-Tone 10287733BX* (Made for the
Chicago Radio Syndicate) 5.00   20.00

NOTE: This soundsheet was included in an
issue of Billboard magazine, and sampled the
Elvis special they were offering for syndication,
as well another special, "Jamboree USA," which
did not contain Elvis.

ELVIS SPEAKS! "THE TRUTH ABOUT ME"

☐ *Eva-Tone EL-38713T* (45rpm version
of this previously issued material, done
for Teen Parade magazine) 8.00   32.00

ELVIS SPEAKS!! "THE TRUTH ABOUT ME"

☐ *Lynchburg Audio 1404-1L 45rpm*
(Made for Teen Parade magazine. First
time on 45 for this recording) 25.00   100.00

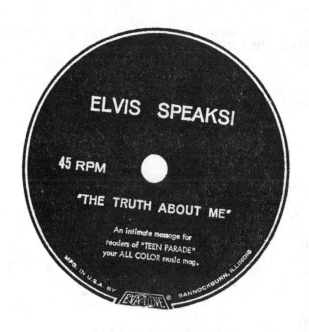

GRACELAND TOUR, THE (Elvis Break-in)

☐ *Record Digest 25794* 1.25   5.00
Buyers of the Record Digest feature
book "Our Best To You" received this
soundsheet as a bonus. Only 500 copies
of the book, and 600 of the disc, were
made. Break-in by Jerry Osborne.

NOTE: This soundsheet was pressed on red vinyl.

KING IS DEAD LONG LIVE THE KING, THE (ELVIS PRESLEY IS STILL THE KING! (SAMPLER)

☐ *Eva-Tone 52578X* (Made for Universal
Sounds Unlimited) 20.00   80.00

NOTE: This soundsheet was pressed on yellow vinyl.

THE
KING IS DEAD
LONG LIVE THE KING

33 1/3 RPM
MONAURAL   PLACE
                           COIN HERE IF
                           SOUNDSHEET
                           SLIPS

Elvis Presley is still the KING!

DEMO

℗ COPYRIGHT 1977
UNIVERSAL SOUNDS UNLIMITED

525787X

EVATONE®
SOUNDSHEETS

102

ELVIS' EXTENDED PLAY CONTENTS

A TOUCH OF GOLD *RCA Victor (EPA-5088)* 1959
SIDE 1: HARD HEADED WOMAN; GOOD ROCKIN' TONIGHT
SIDE 2: DON'T; I BEG OF YOU

A TOUCH OF GOLD VOLUME II *RCA Victor (EPA-5101)* 1959
SIDE 1: WEAR MY RING AROUND YOUR NECK; TREAT
ME NICE
SIDE 2: ONE NIGHT; THAT'S ALL RIGHT

A TOUCH OF GOLD VOLUME 3 *RCA Victor (EPA-5141)* 1959
SIDE 1: ALL SHOOK UP; DON'T ASK ME WHY
SIDE 2: TOO MUCH; BLUE MOON OF KENTUCKY

ALOHA FROM HAWAII VIA SATELLITE *RCA (DTFO-2006)*
1973
SIDE 1: SOMETHING; YOU GAVE ME A MOUNTAIN; I CAN'T
STOP LOVING YOU
SIDE 2: MY WAY; WHAT NOW MY LOVE; I'M SO LONESOME
I COULD CRY

ANYWAY YOU WANT ME *RCA Victor (EPA-965)* 1956
SIDE 1: ANYWAY YOU WANT ME; I'M LEFT, YOU'RE RIGHT,
SHE'S GONE
SIDE 2: I DON'T CARE IF THE SUN DON'T SHINE; MYSTERY
TRAIN

CHRISTMAS WITH ELVIS *RCA Victor (EPA-4340)* 1958
SIDE 1: WHITE CHRISTMAS; HERE COMES SANTA CLAUS,
SIDE 2: OH LITTLE TOWN OF BETHLEHEM; SILENT NIGHT

DEALER'S PREVUE *RCA Victor (SDS 7-2)* 1957
SIDE 1: LOVING YOU (Elvis Presley); TEDDY BEAR (Elvis Presley);
NOW STOP (Martha Carson); JUST WHISTLE OR CALL
(Martha Carson)
SIDE 2: THE WIFE (Lou Monte); MUSICA BELLA (Lou Monte);
MAILMAN, BRING ME NO MORE BLUES (Herb Jeffries);
SO SHY (Herb Jeffries)

DEALER'S PREVUE *RCA Victor (SDS 57-39)* 1957
SIDE 1: THE OLD RUGGED CROSS (Stuart Hamblen); OLD TIME
RELIGION (Stuart Hamblen); JAILHOUSE ROCK (Elvis
Presley); TREAT ME NICE (Elvis Presley); TILL THE LAST
LEAF SHALL FALL (Statesmen Quartet); EVERY HOUR
AND EVERY DAY (Statesmen Quartet)
SIDE 2: A SLIP OF THE LIP (Kathy Barr); WELCOME MAT (Kathy
Barr); JUST BORN (Perry Como); IVY ROSE (Perry Como);
SAYONARA (Eddie Fisher); THAT'S THE WAY IT GOES
(Eddie Fisher)

EASY COME, EASY GO *RCA Victor (EPA-4387)* 1967
SIDE 1: EASY COME, EASY GO; THE LOVE MACHINE; YOGA IS
AS YOGA DOES
SIDE 2: YOU GOTTA STOP; SING YOU CHILDREN; I'LL TAKE
LOVE

ELVIS, VOLUME I *RCA Victor (EPA-992)* 1956
SIDE 1: RIP IT UP; LOVE ME
SIDE 2: WHEN MY BLUE MOON TURNS TO GOLD AGAIN;
PARALYZED

ELVIS, VOLUME II *RCA Victor (EPA-993)* 1956
SIDE 1: SO GLAD YOU'RE MINE; OLD SHEP
SIDE 2: REDDY TEDDY; ANYPLACE IS PARADISE

ELVIS BY REQUEST *RCA Victor (LPC-128)* 1961
SIDE 1: FLAMING STAR; SUMMER KISSES, WINTER TEARS
SIDE 2: ARE YOU LONESOME TONIGHT; IT'S NOW OR NEVER

ELVIS PRESLEY *RCA Victor (EPA-747)* 1956
SIDE 1: BLUE SUEDE SHOES; TUTTI FRUTTI
SIDE 2: I GOT A WOMAN; JUST BECAUSE

ELVIS PRESLEY *RCA Victor (EPB-1254)* 1956
SIDE 1: BLUE SUEDE SHOES; I'M COUNTING ON YOU
SIDE 2: I GOT A WOMAN; ONE-SIDED LOVE AFFAIR
SIDE 3: TUTTI FRUTTI; TRYIN' TO GET TO YOU
SIDE 4: I'M GONNA SIT RIGHT DOWN AND CRY; I'LL NEVER
LET YOU GO

ELVIS PRESLEY *RCA Victor (SPD-22)* 1956
SIDE 1: BLUE SUEDE SHOES; I'M COUNTING ON YOU
SIDE 2: I GOT A WOMAN; ONE-SIDED LOVE AFFAIR
SIDE 3: TUTTI FRUTTI; TRYIN' TO GET TO YOU
SIDE 4: I'M GONNA SIT RIGHT DOWN AND CRY; I'LL NEVER
LET YOU GO

ELVIS PRESLEY *RCA Victor (SPD-23)* 1956
SIDE 1: BLUE SUEDE SHOES; I'M COUNTING ON YOU
SIDE 2: I GOT A WOMAN; ONE SIDED LOVE AFFAIR
SIDE 3: I'M GONNA SIT RIGHT DOWN AND CRY; I'LL NEVER
LET YOU GO
SIDE 4: TUTTI FRUTTI; TRYIN' TO GET TO YOU
SIDE 5: DON'T BE CRUEL; I WANT YOU, I NEED YOU, I LOVE
YOU
SIDE 6: HOUND DOG; MY BABY LEFT ME

ELVIS PRESLEY *RCA Victor (EPA-830)* 1956
SIDE 1: SHAKE, RATTLE AND ROLL; I LOVE YOU BECAUSE
SIDE 2: BLUE MOON; LAWDY, MISS CLAWDY

ELVIS SAILS *RCA Victor (EPA-4325)* 1958
SIDE 1: PRESS INTERVIEWS WITH ELVIS PRESLEY
SIDE 2: ELVIS PRESLEY'S NEWSREEL INTERVIEW; PAT
HERNON INTERVIEWS ELVIS IN THE LIBRARY OF
THE U.S.S. RANDALL AT SAILING

ELVIS SINGS CHRISTMAS SONGS *RCA Victor (EPA-4108)*
1957
SIDE 1: SANTA BRING MY BABY BACK; BLUE CHRISTMAS
SIDE 2: SANTA CLAUS IS BACK IN TOWN; I'LL BE HOME FOR
CHRISTMAS

FOLLOW THAT DREAM *RCA Victor (EPA-4368)* 1962
SIDE 1: FOLLOW THAT DREAM; ANGEL
SIDE 2: WHAT A WONDERFUL LIFE; I'M NOT THE
MARRYING KIND

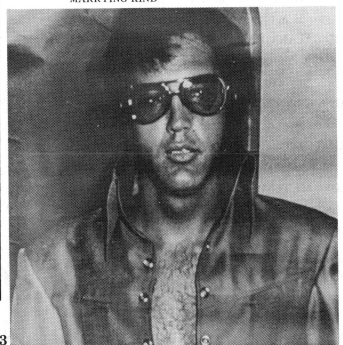

GREAT COUNTRY/WESTERN HITS *RCA Victor (SPD-26)*
1956

SIDE 1: BOUQUET OF ROSES; MOLLY DARLING (Eddy Arnold)
SIDE 2: ALABAMA JUBILEE; UNCHAINED MELODY (Chet Atkins)
SIDE 3: THE BANANA BOAT SONG; SLOW POISON (Johnnie and Jack)
SIDE 4: I'M MY OWN GRANDPAW; CIGAREETES, WHUSKY AND WILD, WILD WOMEN (Homer & Jethro)
SIDE 5: LOOKING BACK TO SEE; DRAGGIN' MAIN STREET (Jim Edward and Maxine Brown)
SIDE 6: BLUE MOON OF KENTUCKY; LOVE ME TENDER (Elvis Presley)
SIDE 7: ACCORDING TO MY HEART; AM I LOSING YOU (Jim Reeves)
SIDE 8: I DON'T HURT ANYMORE; I'M MOVING ON (Hank Snow)
SIDE 9: COOL WATER; THE EVERLASTING HILLS OF OKLA-HOMA (Sons of the Pioneers)
SIDE 10: COMPANY'S COMING; A SATISFIED MIND (Porter Wagoner)
SIDE 11: SEEING HER ONLY REMINDED ME OF YOU; EAT, DRINK, AND BE MERRY (Porter Wagoner)
SIDE 12: I WONDER WHEN WE'LL EVER KNOW; RED RIVER VALLEY (Sons of the Pioneers)
SIDE 13: OLD DOC BROWN; GRANDFATHER'S CLOCK (Hank Snow)
SIDE 14: YONDER COMES A SUCKER; WAITIN' FOR A TRAIN (Jim Reeves)
SIDE 15: MYSTERY TRAIN; MILKCOW BOOGIE BLUES (Elvis Presley)
SIDE 16: DOWN YONDER; ALOHA OE (Del Wood)
SIDE 17: SLOW POKE; OVER THE WAVES (Homer & Jethro)
SIDE 18: LOVE, LOVE, LOVE; WE LIVE IN TWO DIFFERENT WORLDS (Johnnie and Jack)
SIDE 19: SAN ANTONIO ROSE; ARKANSAS TRAVELER (Chet Atkins)
SIDE 20: THE CATTLE CALL; I WOULDN'T KNOW WHERE TO BEGIN (Eddy Arnold)

NOTE: The Elvis song "Milkcow Blues Boogie," that appears on side 15 is incorrectly labeled "Milkcow Boogie Blues."

HEARTBREAK HOTEL *RCA Victor (EPA-821)* *1956*
SIDE 1: HEARTBREAK HOTEL; I WAS THE ONE
SIDE 2: MONEY HONEY; I FORGOT TO REMEMBER TO FORGET

JAILHOUSE ROCK *RCA Victor (EPA-4114)* *1957*
SIDE 1: JAILHOUSE ROCK; YOUNG AND BEAUTIFUL
SIDE 2: I WANT TO BE FREE; DON'T LEAVE ME NOW; BABY I DON'T CARE

JUST FOR YOU *RCA Victor (EPA-4041)* *1957*
SIDE 1: I NEED YOU SO; HAVE I TOLD YOU LATELY THAT I LOVE YOU
SIDE 2: BLUEBERRY HILL; IS IT SO STRANGE

KID GALAHAD *RCA Victor (EPA-4371)* *1962*
SIDE 1: KING OF THE WHOLE WIDE WORLD; THIS IS LIVING; RIDING THE RAINBOW
SIDE 2: HOME IS WHERE THE HEART IS; I GOT LUCKY; A WHISTLING TUNE

KING CREOLE *RCA Victor (EPA-4319)* *1958*
SIDE 1: KING CREOLE; NEW ORLEANS
SIDE 2: AS LONG AS I HAVE YOU; LOVER DOLL

KING CREOLE VOL. II *RCA Victor (EPA-4321)* *1958*
SIDE 1: TROUBLE; YOUNG DREAMS
SIDE 2: CRAWFISH; DIXIELAND ROCK

LOVE ME TENDER *RCA Victor (EPA-4006)* *1956*
SIDE 1: LOVE ME TENDER; LET ME
SIDE 2: POOR BOY; WE'RE GONNA MOVE

LOVING YOU VOL. I *RCA Victor (EPA1-1515)* *1957*
SIDE 1: LOVING YOU; PARTY
SIDE 2: TEDDY BEAR; TRUE LOVE

LOVING YOU VOL. II *RCA Victor (EPA2-1515)* *1957*
SIDE 1: LONESOME COWBOY; HOT DOG
SIDE 2: MEAN WOMAN BLUES; GOT A LOT O' LIVIN' TO DO

MOST TALKED-ABOUT NEW PERSONALITY IN THE LAST TEN YEARS OF RECORDED MUSIC *RCA Victor (EPB-1254)*
1956

SIDE 1: BLUE SUEDE SHOES; I'M COUNTING ON YOU; I GOT A WOMAN
SIDE 2: ONE-SIDED LOVE AFFAIR; I LOVE YOU BECAUSE; JUST BECAUSE
SIDE 3: TUTTI FRUTTI; TRYIN' TO GET TO YOU; I'M GONNA SIT RIGHT DOWN AND CRY
SIDE 4: I'LL NEVER LET YOU GO; BLUE MOON; MONEY HONEY

PERFECT FOR PARTIES HIGHLIGHTER
SIDE 1: LOVE ME (Elvis Presley); ANCHORS AWEIGH (Tony Cabot); THAT'S A PUENTE (Tito Puente)
SIDE 2: ROCK ME BUT DON'T ROLL ME (Tony Scott); HAPPY FACE BABY (The Three Suns); PROM TO PROM (Dave Pell)

PEACE IN THE VALLEY *RCA Victor (EPA-4054)* *1957*
SIDE 1: PEACE IN THE VALLEY; IT IS NO SECRET
SIDE 2: I BELIEVE; TAKE MY HAND, PRECIOUS LORD

RCA FAMILY RECORD CENTER *RCA Victor (PR-121)* *1962*
SIDE 1: GOOD LUCK CHARM (Elvis Presley); THE WAY YOU LOOK TONIGHT (Peter Nero); YOUNGER THAN SPRING-TIME (Paul Anka); FRENESI (Living Strings)
SIDE 2: TWISTIN' THE NIGHT AWAY (Sam Cooke); EASY STREET (Al Hirt); MAKE SOMEONE HAPPY (Perry Como); MOON RIVER (Henry Mancini)

REAL ELVIS, THE *RCA Victor (EPA-940)* *1956*
SIDE 1: DON'T BE CRUEL; I WANT YOU, I NEED YOU, I LOVE YOU
SIDE 2: HOUND DOG; MY BABY LEFT ME

SAVE-ON-RECORDS *RCA Victor (SPA 7-27)* *1956*
SIDE 1: INTERMEZZO (Frankie Carle); MOONLIGHT COCKTAIL (Al Nevins); GONNA SIT RIGHT DOWN AND CRY (Elvis Presley); ADVENTURE IN TIME (Sauter-Finegan Orch.); GREAT GETTIN' UP MORNING (Harry Belafonte)
SIDE 2: LIEBESTRAUM (Rubinstein); VOI CHE SAPETE (Rise Stevens); BEETHOVEN: SYMPHONY NO. 9 (Arturo Toscanini); JALOUSIE (Arthur Fiedler & Boston Pops); SYMPHONIE FANTASTIQUE (Boston Symphony Orch.)

SOUND OF LEADERSHIP, THE (SOUVENIR OF THE MIAMI MEETING JUNE, 1956) *RCA Victor (SPD-19)* *1956*
SIDE 1: VESTI LA GIUBBA [1907] (Enrico Caruso); O SOLE MIO [1916] (Enrico Caruso)
SIDE 2: RAMONA [1928] (Gene Austin); MARIE [1937] (Tommy Dorsey)
SIDE 3: BOOGIE WOOGIE [1938] (Tommy Dorsey); JALOUSIE [1938] (Boston Pops Orch.)
SIDE 4: BEER BARREL POLKA [1938] (Will Glahe); BEGIN THE BEGUINE [1938] (Artie Shaw)
SIDE 5: IN THE MOOD [1939] (Glenn Miller); SUNRISE SEREN-ADE [1939] (Glenn Miller)
SIDE 6: BLUE DANUBE WALTZ [1939] (Leopold Stokowski); TUXEDO JUNCTION [1940] (Glenn Miller)
SIDE 7: STAR DUST [1940] (Artie Shaw); TCHAIKOVSKY PIANO CONCERTO [1941] (Freddy Martin)
SIDE 8: CHATTANOOGA CHOO CHOO [1941] (Glenn Miller); RACING WITH THE MOON [1941] (Vaughn Monroe)
SIDE 9: PRISONER OF LOVE [1946] (Perry Como); BALLERINA [1947] (Vaughn Monroe)
SIDE 10: WHIFFENPOOF SONG [1947] (Robert Merrill); BOUQUET OF ROSES [1948] (Eddy Arnold)
SIDE 11: BE MY LOVE [1950] (Mario Lanza); ANYTIME [1951] (Eddie Fisher)
SIDE 12: THE LOVELIEST NIGHT OF THE YEAR [1951] (Mario Lanza); SLOW POKE [1951] (Pee Wee King)
SIDE 13: DON'T LET THE STARS GET IN YOUR EYES [1952] (Perry Como); YOU, YOU, YOU [1953] (Ames Bros.)
SIDE 14: I NEED YOU NOW [1954] (Eddie Fisher); CHERRY PINK AND APPLE BLOSSOM WHITE [1954] (Perez Prado)
SIDE 15: NAUGHTY LADY OF SHADY LANE [1954] (Ames Bros.); ROCK AND ROLL WALTZ [1955] (Kay Starr)
SIDE 16: HOT DIGGITY [1956] (Perry Como); HEARTBREAK HOTEL [1956] (Elvis Presley)

STRICTLY ELVIS *RCA Victor (EPA-994)*   *1956*
    SIDE 1: LONG TALL SALLY; FIRST IN LINE
    SIDE 2: HOW DO YOU THINK I FEEL; HOW'S THE WORLD
              TREATING YOU

TICKLE ME *RCA Victor (EPA-4383)*   *1965*
    SIDE 1: I FEEL THAT I'VE KNOWN YOU FOREVER; SLOWLY
              BUT SURELY
    SIDE 2: NIGHT RIDER; PUT THE BLAME ON ME; DIRTY, DIRTY
              FEELING

VIVA LAS VEGAS *RCA Victor (EPA-4382)*   *1964*
    SIDE 1: IF YOU THINK I DON'T NEED YOU; I NEED SOMEBODY
              TO LEAN ON
    SIDE 2: C'MON EVERYBODY; TODAY, TOMORROW AND FOR-
              EVER

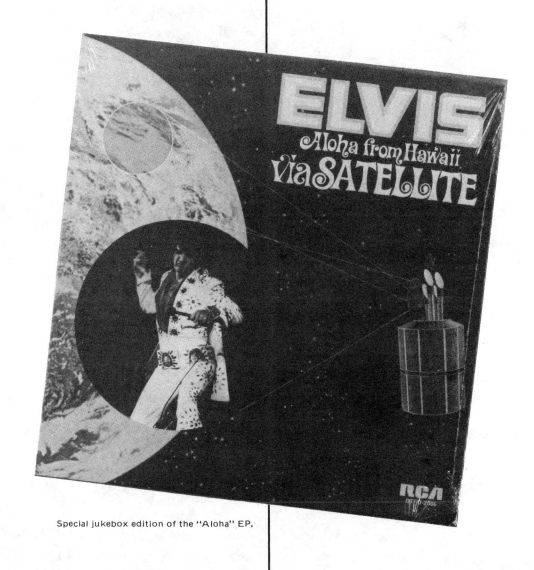

Special jukebox edition of the "Aloha" EP.

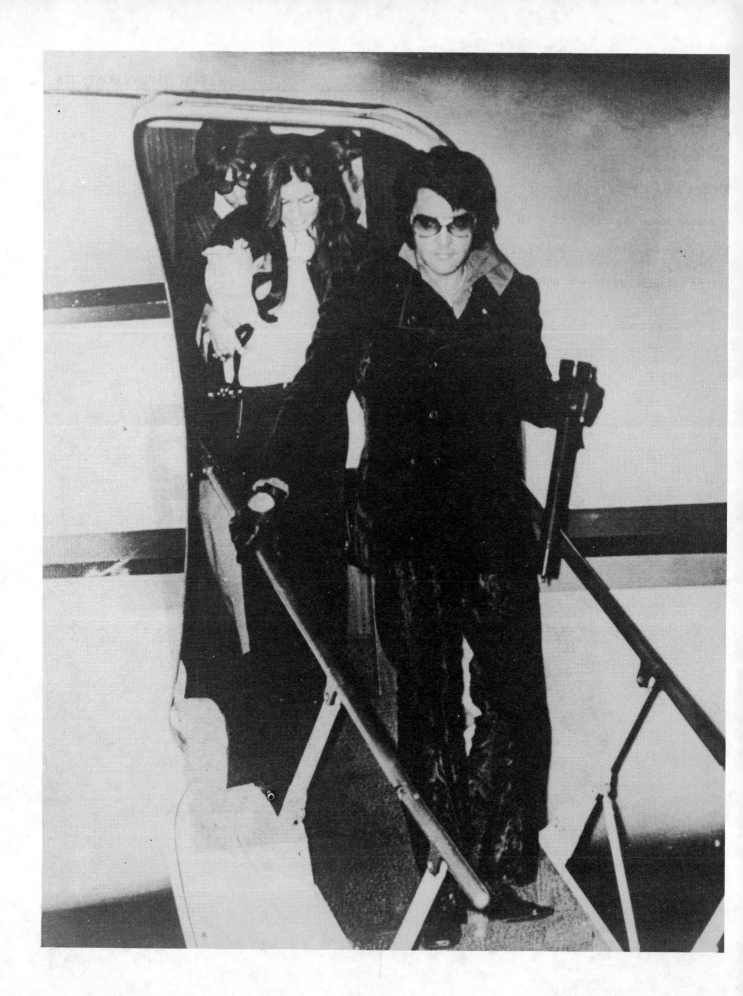

ELVIS'
LONG PLAY CONTENTS

A DATE WITH ELVIS *RCA Victor (LPM-2011)*   *1959*
SIDE 1: BLUE MOON OF KENTUCKY; YOUNG AND BEAUTIFUL; (YOU'RE SO SQUARE) BABY I DON'T CARE; MILKCOW BLUES BOOGIE; BABY LET'S PLAY HOUSE
SIDE 2: GOOD ROCKIN' TONIGHT; IS IT SO STRANGE; WE'RE GONNA MOVE; I WANT TO BE FREE; I FORGOT TO REMEMBER TO FORGET

ALL-TIME CHRISTMAS FAVORITES *Collector's Edition*
(CE-505)   *1976*
SIDE 1a: LYNN ANDERSON – DING-A-LING THE CHRISTMAS BELL; FROSTY THE SNOWMAN; A WISTLE A WISKER AWAY; RUDOLPH THE RED NOSED RAINDEER; SOON IT WILL BE CHRISTMAS
SIDE 1b: CHARLIE PRIDE – CHRISTMAS IN MY HOME TOWN; LITTLE DRUMMER BOY; DECK THE HALLS; O HOLY NIGHT; SILENT NIGHT
SIDE 2a: BARBARA STREISAND – JINGLE BELLS; GOUNOD'S AVE MARIA; THE BEST GIFT; THE CHRISTMAS SONG; SLEEP IN HEAVENLY PEACE
SIDE 2b: FRANK SINATRA – THE CHRISTMAS SONG; MISTLETOE AND HOLLY; I'LL BE HOME FOR CHRISTMAS; THE FIRST NOEL; SILENT NIGHT
SIDE 3a: ANDY WILLIAMS – SLEIGH RIDE; CHRISTMAS HOLIDAY; WINTER WONDERLAND; MARY'S LITTLE BOY CHILD; SILVER BELLS
SIDE 3b: GLEN CAMPBELL – IT MUST BE GETTING CLOSE TO CHRISTMAS; HAVE YOURSELF A MERRY CHRISTMAS; BLUE CHRISTMAS; THE CHRISTMAS; PRETTY PAPER
SIDE 4a: DEAN MARTIN – I'M DREAMING OF A WHITE CHRISTMAS; IT'S A MARSHMELLOW WORLD IN THE WINTER; SILVER BELLS; WALKING IN A WINTER WONDERLAND; SILENT NIGHT
SIDE 4b: ELVIS PRESLEY – COME ALL YE FAITHFUL; NOEL; I'LL BE HOME FOR CHRISTMAS; SILVER BELLS; WALKING IN A WINTER WONDERLAND
SIDE 5a: TAMMY WYNETTE – AWAY IN THE MANGER; SILENT NIGHT; O LITTLE TOWN OF BETHLEHEM; JOY TO THE WORLD; IT CAME UPON A MIDNIGHT CLEAR
SIDE 5b: JOHNNY MATHIS – WALKIN' IN A WINTER WONDERLAND; SLEIGH RIDE; I'M DREAMING OF A WHITE XMAS; SILVER BELLS; BLUE CHRISTMAS

NOTE: All information given on this album has been copied from the actual record labels. We have, therefore, reprinted their numerous errors.

ALMOST IN LOVE *RCA Camden (CAS-2440)*   *1970*
SIDE 1: ALMOST IN LOVE; LONG LEGGED GIRL; EDGE OF REALITY; MY LITTLE FRIEND; A LITTLE LESS CONVERSATION
SIDE 2: RUBBERNECKIN'; CLEAN UP YOUR OWN BACKYARD; U.S. MALE; CHARRO; STAY AWAY, JOE

ALMOST IN LOVE *RCA Camden (CAS-2440)*   *1973*
SIDE 1: ALMOST IN LOVE; LONG LEGGED GIRL; EDGE OF REALITY; MY LITTLE FRIEND; A LITTLE LESS CONVERSATION
SIDE 2: RUBBERNECKIN'; CLEAN UP YOUR OWN BACKYARD; U.S. MALE; CHARRO; STAY AWAY

ALOHA FROM HAWAII VIA SATELLITE *RCA (VPSX-6089)*
1973
SIDE 1: INTRODUCTION: ALSO SPRACH ZARATHUSTRA; SEE SEE RIDER; BURNING LOVE; SOMETHING; YOU GAVE ME A MOUNTAIN; STEAMROLLER
SIDE 2: MY WAY; LOVE ME; JOHNNY B. GOODE; IT'S OVER; BLUE SUEDE SHOES; I'M SO LONESOME I COULD CRY; I CAN'T STOP LOVING YOU; HOUND DOG
SIDE 3: WHAT NOW MY LOVE; FEVER; WELCOME TO MY WORLD; SUSPICIOUS MINDS; INTRODUCTIONS BY ELVIS
SIDE 4: I'LL REMEMBER YOU; MEDLEY: LONG TALL SALLY/ WHOLE LOT-TA SHAKIN' GOIN ON; AN AMERICAN TRILOGY; A BIG HUNK O' LOVE; CAN'T HELP FALLING IN LOVE

BLUE HAWAII *RCA Victor (LPM/LSP-2426)*   *1961*
SIDE 1: BLUE HAWAII; ALMOST ALWAYS TRUE; ALOHA OE; NO MORE; CAN'T HELP FALLING IN LOVE; ROCK-A-HULA BABY; MOONLIGHT SWIM
SIDE 2: KU-U-I-PO; ITO EATS; SLICIN' SAND; HAWAIIAN SUNSET; BEACH BOY BLUES; ISLAND OF LOVE; HAWAIIAN WEDDING SONG

BRIGHTEST STARS OF CHRISTMAS, THE *RCA (DLP1-0086)*
1974
SIDE 1: WE WISH YOU A MERRY CHRISTMAS (Eugene Ormandy & the Philadelphia Orch.); HERE COMES SANTA CLAUS (Elvis Presley); WINTER WONDERLAND (Danny Davis & the Nashville Brass); HOME FOR THE HOLIDAYS (Perry Como); MEDLEY: IT CAME UPON A MIDNIGHT CLEAR/ THE FIRST NOEL/AWAY IN A MANGER
SIDE 2: JINGLE BELLS (Julie Andrews); JOY TO THE WORLD (Ed Ames); SLEIGH RIDE (Arthur Fiedler & the Boston Pops); CHRISTMAS IN MY HOME TOWN (Charley Pride); HARK! THE HERALD ANGLES SING (Robert Shaw Chorale); SILENT NIGHT (Sergio Franchi)

BURNING LOVE (AND HITS FROM HIS MOVIES VOL. 2)
RCA/Camden (CAS-2595) *1972*
SIDE 1: BURNING LOVE; TENDER FEELING; AM I READY; TONIGHT IS SO RIGHT FOR LOVE; GUADALAJARA
SIDE 2: IT'S A MATTER OF TIME; NO MORE; SANTA LUCIA; WE'LL BE TOGETHER; I LOVE ONLY ONE GIRL

CLAMBAKE *RCA Victor (LPM/LSP-3893)*   *1967*
SIDE 1: GUITAR MAN; CLAMBAKE; WHO NEEDS MONEY; A HOUSE THAT HAS EVERYTHING; CONFIDENCE; HEY, HEY, HEY
SIDE 2: YOU DON'T KNOW ME; THE GIRL I NEVER LOVED; HOW CAN YOU LOSE WHAT YOU NEVER HAD; BIG BOSS MAN; SINGING TREE; JUST CALL ME LONESOME

C'MON EVERYONE *RCA/Camden (CAL-2518)*   *1971*
SIDE 1: C'MON EVERYBODY; ANGEL; EASY COME, EASY GO; A WHISTLING TUNE; FOLLOW THAT DREAM
SIDE 2: KING OF THE WHOLE WIDE WORLD; I'LL TAKE LOVE; TODAY, TOMORROW AND FOREVER; I'M NOT THE MARRYING KIND; THIS IS LIVING

COUNTRY MEMORIES *RCA Record Club (R-244069)*   *1978*
SIDE 1:: I'LL HOLD YOU IN MY HEART; WELCOME TO MY WORLD; IT KEEPS RIGHT ON A-HURTIN'; RELEASE ME; MAKE THE WORLD GO AWAY
SIDE 2: SNOWBIRD; EARLY MORNING RAIN; I'M SO LONESOME I COULD CRY; FUNNY HOW TIME SLIPS AWAY; I'M MOVING ON
SIDE 3: HELP ME MAKE IT THROUGH THE NIGHT; YOU DON'T KNOW ME; HOW GREAT THOU ART; I WASHED MY HANDS IN MUDDY WATER; I FORGOT TO REMEMBER TO FORGET
SIDE 4: YOUR CHEATIN' HEART; BABY LET'S PLAY HOUSE; WHOLE LOT-TA SHAKIN' GOIN' ON; GENTLE ON MY MIND; FOR THE GOOD TIMES

COUNTRY MUSIC IN THE MODERN ERA 1940s - 1970s
New World Records (NW-207)   *1976*
SIDE 1: BOUQUET OF ROSES (Eddy Arnold); NEVER NO MORE BLUES (Lefty Frizzell); MUCH TOO YOUNG TO DIE (Ray Price); SQUID JIGGIN' GROUND (Hank Snow); THERE'S POISON IN YOUR HEART (Kitty Wells); TRY ME ONE MORE TIME (Ernest Tubb); LOVE LETTERS IN THE SAND (Patsy Cline); JEAN'S SONG (Chet Atkins); MYSTERY TRAIN (Elvis Presley)
SIDE 2: LITTLE OLE YOU (Jim Reeves); JIMMY MARTINEZ (Marty Robbins); I'M A HONKY-TONK GIRL (Loretta Lynn); LORENA (Johnny Cash); DON'T LET HER KNOW (Buck Owens); ALL I LOVE IS YOU (Roger Miller) SING A SAD SONG (Merle Haggard); COAT OF MANY COLORS (Dolly Parton) HELP ME MAKE IT THROUGH THE NIGHT (Kris Kristofferson)

CURRENT AUDIO MAGAZINE – ELVIS: HIS FIRST AND ONLY PRESS CONFERENCE *Current Audio Magazine (CM) Vol. 1 No. 1 August/September 1972*   *1972*
SIDE 1: MICK JAGGER SPEAKS; MANSON WILL ESCAPE; ROBERT KLEIN; TEDDY KENNEDY; ANGELA DAVIS; MONTY PYTHON'S FLYING CIRCUS "SPAM"
SIDE 2: ELVIS PRESLEY; THE KILLER WAS A NARC; BELLA ABZUG LOSES; SCOOP'S COLUMN; NADER GROUP HITS VEGA; CRIME WATCH; SENSUOUS YOU

DOUBLE DYNAMITE *RCA/Camden-Pickwick (DL 2-5001)*   *1975*
SIDE 1: BURNING LOVE; I'LL BE THERE; FOOLS FALL IN LOVE; FOLLOW THAT DREAM; YOU'LL NEVER WALK ALONE
SIDE 2: FLAMING STAR; YELLOW ROSE OF TEXAS/THE EYES OF TEXAS; OLD SHEP; MAMA
SIDE 3: RUBBERNECKIN'; U.S. MALE; FRANKIE & JOHNNY; IF YOU THINK I DON'T NEED YOU; EASY COME, EASY GO
SIDE 4: SEPARATE WAYS; PEACE IN THE VALLEY; BIG BOSS MAN; IT'S A MATTER OF TIME

DOUBLE TROUBLE *RCA Victor (LPM/LSP-3787)*   *1967*
SIDE 1: DOUBLE TROUBLE; BABY IF YOU'LL GIVE ME ALL YOUR LOVE; COULD I FALL IN LOVE; LONG LEGGED GIRL; CITY BY NIGHT; OLD MACDONALD
SIDE 2: I LOVE ONLY ONE GIRL; THERE IS SO MUCH WORLD TOO SEE; IT WON'T BE LONG; NEVER ENDING; WHAT NOW, WHAT NEXT, WHERE TO

EARTH NEWS *Earth News (Aug. 22 - 29)*   *1977*
SIDE 1: 1956 ELVIS INTERVIEW; BLUE SUEDE SHOES (from the Dorsey Bros. Stage Show); 1956 ELVIS INTERVIEW; DON'T BE CRUEL (from Ed Sullivan show); HEARTBREAK HOTEL (from Dorsey Show); 1956 ELVIS INTERVIEW; JAY THOMPSON'S ELVIS INTERVIEW; ELVIS SAILS INTERVIEW; DICK CLARK/ELVIS PHONE CALL; THE TRUTH ABOUT ME
SIDE 2: 1956 ELVIS INTERVIEW; 1961 ELVIS INTERVIEW; RED WEST INTERVIEW; THE TRUTH ABOUT ME; HOUND DOG; WILLIE MAE THORNTON INTERVIEW; THE TRUTH ABOUT ME; IN THE GHETTO; STEVE BENDER INTERVIEW; MEDLEY: HEY MR. PRESLEY/I DREAMED I WAS ELVIS/MY BABY'S CRAZY ABOUT ELVIS/ELVIS PRESLEY FOR PRESIDENT

ELVIS *RCA Victor (LPM-1382)*   *1956*
SIDE 1: RIP IT UP; LOVE ME; WHEN MY BLUE MOON TURNS TO GOLD AGAIN; LONG TALL SALLY; FIRST IN LINE; PARALYZED
SIDE 2: SO GLAD YOU'RE MINE; OLD SHEP; REDDY TEDDY; ANYPLACE IS PARADISE; HOW'S THE WORLD TREATING YOU; HOW DO YOU THINK I FEEL

ELVIS (Brookville Records) *RCA Victor (DPL2-0056e)*   *1973*
SIDE 1: HOUND DOG; I WANT YOU, I NEED YOU, I LOVE YOU; ALL SHOOK UP; DON'T; I BEG OF YOU
SIDE 2: A BIG HUNK O' LOVE; LOVE ME; STUCK ON YOU; GOOD LUCK CHARM; RETURN TO SENDER
SIDE 3: DON'T BE CRUEL; LOVING YOU; JAILHOUSE ROCK; CAN'T HELP FALLING IN LOVE; I GOT STUNG
SIDE 4: TEDDY BEAR; LOVE ME TENDER; HARD HEADED WOMAN; IT'S NOW OR NEVER; SURRENDER

ELVIS (FROM HIS NBC-TV SPECIAL) *RCA (LPM-4088) 1968*
SIDE 1: TROUBLE/GUITAR MAN; LAWDY MISS CLAWDY/BABY WHAT DO YOU WANT ME TO DO; MEDLEY: HEARTBREAK HOTEL/HOUND DOG/ALL SHOOK UP/CAN'T HELP FALLING IN LOVE/JAILHOUSE ROCK; LOVE ME TENDER
SIDE 2: WHERE COULD I GO BUT TO THE LORD/UP ABOVE MY HEAD/SAVED; BLUE CHRISTMAS; ONE NIGHT; MEMORIES; MEDLEY: NOTHINGVILLE/BIG BOSS MAN/GUITAR MAN/LITTLE EGYPT/TROUBLE/GUITAR MAN; IF I CAN DREAM

ELVIS (Including FOOL) *RCA (APL1-0283)*   *1973*
SIDE 1: FOOL; WHERE DO I GO FROM HERE; LOVE ME, LOVE THE LIFE I LEAD; IT'S STILL HERE; IT'S IMPOSSIBLE
SIDE 2: FOR LOVIN' ME; PADRE; I'LL TAKE YOU HOME AGAIN KATHLEEN; I WILL BE TRUE; DON'T THINK TWICE, IT'S ALL RIGHT

ELVIS – A COLLECTORS EDITION

This five album box set contained the following LPs, all of which can be looked up elsewhere in this chapter for contents.
ELVIS (RCA DPL2-0056e) Double LP
ELVIS FOREVER (RCA KSL 2-7031) Double LP
ELVIS IN HOLLYWOOD (RCA KSL 1-7053)

ELVIS – A CANADIAN TRIBUTE *RCA (KKL1-7065)*   *1978*
SIDE 1: INTRO. . .JAILHOUSE ROCK; INTRO. . .TEDDY BEAR; LOVING YOU; UNTIL IT'S TIME FOR YOU TO GO; EARLY MORNING RAIN; VANCOUVER PRESS CONFERENCE (1957)
SIDE 2: I'M MOVIN' ON; SNOWBIRD; FOR LOVIN' ME; PUT YOUR HAND IN THE HAND; LITTLE DARLIN'; MY WAY

ELVIS (VOLUME 1): A LEGENDARY PERFORMER *RCA (CPL1-0341)*   *1974*
SIDE 1: THAT'S ALL RIGHT; I LOVE YOU BECAUSE (Unreleased version); HEARTBREAK HOTEL; DON'T BE CRUEL; LOVE ME (Unreleased version); TRYING TO GET TO YOU; (Unreleased live version).
SIDE 2: LOVE ME TENDER; PEACE IN THE VALLEY; A FOOL SUCH AS I; TONIGHT'S ALL RIGHT FOR LOVE (Unreleased in English speaking countries); ARE YOU LONESOME TONIGHT (Unreleased live version); CAN'T HELP FALLING IN LOVE

ELVIS (VOLUME 2): A LEGENDARY PERFORMER *RCA (CPL1-1349)*   *1976*
SIDE 1: HARBOR LIGHTS; JAY THOMPSON INTERVIEWS ELVIS (1956); I WANT YOU, I NEED YOU, I LOVE YOU (Unreleased alternate take); BLUE SUEDE SHOES (Unreleased live version); BLUE CHRISTMAS; JAILHOUSE ROCK; IT'S NOW OR NEVER
SIDE 2: A CANE AND A HIGH STARCHED COLLAR; PRESENTATION OF AWARDS TO ELVIS; BLUE HAWAII (Unreleased version); SUCH A NIGHT (with false starts); BABY WHAT DO YOU WANT ME TO DO (Unreleased live version); HOW GREAT THOU ART; IF I CAN DREAM

ELVIS (VOLUME 3): A LEGENDARY PERFORMER *RCA (CPL1-1378)*   *1978*
SIDE 1: HOUND DOG; 1956 (TV GUIDE) INTERVIEW; DANNY; FAME AND FORTUNE (Unreleased alternate take); FRANKFORT SPECIAL (Unreleased alternate version); BRITCHES; CRYING IN THE CHAPEL
SIDE 2: SURRENDER; GUADALAJARA (Unreleased alternate version); IT HURTS ME (Unreleased version); LET YOURSELF GO (Unreleased version); IN THE GHETTO; LET IT BE ME (Unreleased live version)

ELVIS AS RECORDED AT MADISON SQUARE GARDEN *RCA (LSP-4776)* 1972
SIDE 1: INTRODUCTION: ALSO SPRACH ZARATHUSTRA; THAT'S ALL RIGHT; PROUD MARY; NEVER BEEN TO SPAIN; YOU DON'T HAVE TO SAY YOU LOVE ME; YOU'VE LOST THAT LOVIN' FEELIN'; POLK SALAD ANNIE; LOVE ME; ALL SHOOK UP; HEARTBREAK HOTEL; MEDLEY: TEDDY BEAR/DON'T BE CRUEL; LOVE ME TENDER
SIDE 2: THE IMPOSSIBLE DREAM; INTRODUCTIONS BY ELVIS; HOUND DOG; SUSPICIOUS MINDS; FOR THE GOOD TIMES; AMERICAN TRILOGY; FUNNY HOW TIME SLIPS AWAY; I CAN'T STOP LOVING YOU; CAN'T HELP FALLING IN LOVE; EXIT MUSIC

ELVIS BACK IN MEMPHIS *RCA (LSP-4429)* 1970
SIDE 1: INHERIT THE WIND; THIS IS MY STORY; STRANGER IN MY OWN HOME TOWN; A LITTLE BIT OG GREEN; AND THE GRASS WON'T PAY NO MIND
SIDE 2: DO YOU KNOW WHO I AM; FROM A JACK TO A KING; THE FAIR IS MOVING ON; YOU'LL THINK OF ME; WITHOUT LOVE

ELVIS' CHRISTMAS ALBUM *RCA Victor (LOC-1035)* 1957
SIDE 1: SANTA CLAUS IS BACK IN TOWN; WHITE CHRISTMAS; HERE COMES SANTA CLAUS; I'LL BE HOME FOR CHRISTMAS; BLUE CHRISTMAS; SANTA BRING MY BABY BACK
SIDE 2: OH LITTLE TOWN OF BETHLEHEM; SILENT NIGHT; PEACE IN THE VALLEY; I BELIEVE; TAKE MY HAND, PRECIOUS LORD, IT IS NO SECRET
NOTE: Copies of "Elvis' Christmas Album," LPM-1951 (and LSP-1951 reprocessed stereo) contain the same tracks as shown above. In 1970, RCA issued another "Elvis' Christmas Album," this time on their Camden label. Contents of that album are shown in the following listing.

ELVIS' CHRISTMAS ALBUM *RCA Camden (CAL-2428)* 1970
SIDE 1: BLUE CHRISTMAS; SILENT NIGHT; WHITE CHRISTMAS; SANTA CLAUS IS BACK IN TOWN; I'LL BE HOME FOR CHRISTMAS
SIDE 2: IF EVERY DAY WAS LIKE CHRISTMAS; HERE COMES SANTA CLAUS; OH LITTLE TOWN OF BETHLEHEM; SANTA BRING MY BABY BACK; MAMA LIKED THE ROSES
NOTE: Like all of the RCA Camden albums by Elvis, this LP was reissued in 1975 by Pickwick. The contents remained unchanged.

ELVIS COMMEMORATIVE ALBUM *RCA (DPL2-0056e)* 1978
NOTE: This double album set is a repackage of "Elvis (Brookville Records)." See that listing for complete contents.

ELVIS COUNTRY ("I'M 10,000 YEARS OLD") *RCA (LSP-4460)* 1971
SIDE 1: SNOWBIRD; TOMORROW NEVER COMES; LITTLE CABIN ON THE HILL; WHOLE LOT-TA SHAKIN' GOIN' ON; FUNNY HOW TIME SLIPS AWAY; I REALLY DON'T WANT TO KNOW
SIDE 2: THERE GOES MY EVERYTHING; IT'S YOUR BABY, YOU ROCK IT; THE FOOL; FADED LOVE; I WASHED MY HANDS IN MUDDY WATER; MAKE THE WORLD GO AWAY
NOTE: Excerpts of the song "I Was Born About 10,000 Years Ago" are heard following each track on this LP. The song can be heard in its entirety on the LP "Elvis Now."

ELVIS FOREVER *RCA (KSL2-7031)* 1974
SIDE 1: TREAT ME NICE; I NEED YOUR LOVE TONIGHT; THAT'S WHEN YOUR HEARTACHES BEGIN; G.I. BLUES; BLUE HAWAII; EASY COME, EASY GO
SIDE 2: SUSPICION; PUPPET ON A STRING; HEARTBREAK HOTEL; ONE NIGHT; MEMORIES; BLUE SUEDE SHOES
SIDE 3: ARE YOU LONESOME TONIGHT; HI HEEL SNEAKERS; OLD SHEP; RIP IT UP; SUCH A NIGHT; A FOOL SUCH AS I
SIDE 4: TUTTI FRUTTI; IN THE GHETTO; WEAR MY RING AROUND YOUR NECK; WOODEN HEART; CRYING IN THE CHAPEL; DON'T CRY DADDY

ELVIS FOR EVERYONE *RCA Victor (LPM/LSP-3450)* 1965
SIDE 1: YOUR CHEATIN' HEART; SUMMER KISSES, WINTER TEARS; FINDERS KEEPERS, LOSERS WEEPERS; IN MY WAY; TOMORROW NIGHT; MEMPHIS, TENNESSEE
SIDE 2: FOR THE MILLIONTH AND THE LAST TIME; FORGET ME NEVER; SOUND ADVICE; SANTA LUCIA; I MET HER TODAY; WHEN IT RAINS IT REALLY POURS

ELVIS' GOLDEN RECORDS *RCA Victor (LPM-1707)* 1958
SIDE 1: HOUND DOG; LOVING YOU; ALL SHOOK UP; HEARTBREAK HOTEL; JAILHOUSE ROCK; LOVE ME; TOO MUCH
SIDE 2: DON'T BE CRUEL; THAT'S WHEN YOUR HEARTACHES BEGIN; TEDDY BEAR; LOVE ME TENDER; TREAT ME NICE; ANYWAY YOU WANT ME; I WANT YOU, I NEED YOU, I LOVE YOU

ELVIS' GOLD RECORDS – VOLUME 2 (50,000,000 ELVIS FANS CAN'T BE WRONG) *RCA Victor (LPM-2075)* 1959
SIDE 1: I NEED YOUR LOVE TONIGHT; DON'T; WEAR MY RING AROUND YOUR NECK; MY WISH CAME TRUE; I GOT STUNG
SIDE 2: ONE NIGHT; A BIG HUNK O' LOVE; I BEG OF YOU; A FOOL SUCH AS I; DONCHA' THINK IT'S TIME

ELVIS' GOLDEN RECORDS VOLUME 3 *RCA Victor (LPM/LSP-2765)* 1963
SIDE 1: IT'S NOW OR NEVER; STUCK ON YOU; FAME AND FORTUNE; I GOTTA KNOW; SURRENDER; I FEEL SO BAD
SIDE 2: ARE YOU LONESOME TONIGHT; HIS LATEST FLAME; LITTLE SISTER; GOOD LUCK CHARM; ANYTHING THAT'S PART OF YOU; SHE'S NOT YOU

ELVIS' GOLD RECORDS VOLUME 4 *RCA Victor (LPM/LSP-3921)* 1968
SIDE 1: LOVE LETTERS; WITCHCRAFT; IT HURTS ME; WHAT'D I SAY; PLEASE DON'T DRAG THAT STRING AROUND; INDESCRIBABLY BLUE
SIDE 2: DEVIL IN DISGUISE; LONELY MAN; A MESS OF BLUES; ASK ME; AIN'T THAT LOVING YOU BABY; JUST TELL HER JIM SAID HELLO

ELVIS IN CONCERT *RCA (APL2-2587)* 1977
SIDE 1: ELVIS' FANS COMMENTS/OPENING RIFF; ALSO SPRACH ZARATHUSTRA (THEME FROM 2001: A SPACE ODYSSEY)/OPENING RIFF (REPRISE); SEE SEE RIDER; THAT'S ALL RIGHT; ARE YOU LONESOME TONIGHT; MEDLEY: TEDDY BEAR/DON'T BE CRUEL; ELVIS' FANS COMMENTS; YOU GAVE ME A MOUNTAIN; JAILHOUSE ROCK
SIDE 2: ELVIS' FANS COMMENTS; HOW GREAT THOU ARE; ELVIS' FANS COMMENTS; I REALLY DON'T WANT TO KNOW; ELVIS INTRODUCES HIS FATHER; CLOSING RIFF; SPECIAL MESSAGE FROM ELVIS' FATHER, VERNON PRESLEY
SIDE 3: MEDLEY: I GOT A WOMAN/AMEN; ELVIS TALKS; LOVE ME; IF YOU LOVE ME (LET ME KNOW); MEDLEY: O SOLO MIO – SHERRILL NIELSEN SOLO/IT'S NOW OR NEVER; TRYING TO GET TO YOU
SIDE 4: HAWAIIAN WEDDING SONG; FAIRYTALE; LITTLE SISTER; EARLY MORNING RAIN; WHAT'D I SAY; JOHNNY B. GOODE; AND I LOVE YOU SO

ELVIS IN HOLLYWOOD *RCA (DPL2-0168)* 1976
SIDE 1: JAILHOUSE ROCK; ROCK-A-HULA BABY; G.I. BLUES; KISSIN' COUSINS; WILD IN THE COUNTRY
SIDE 2: KING CREOLE; BLUE HAWAII; FUN IN ACAPULCO; FOLLOW THAT DREAM; GIRLS! GIRLS! GIRLS!
SIDE 3: VIVA LAS VEGAS; BOSSA NOVA BABY; FLAMING STAR; GIRL HAPPY; FRANKIE AND JOHNNY
SIDE 4: ROUSTABOUT; SPINOUT; DOUBLE TROUBLE; CHARRO; THEY REMIND ME TOO MUCH OF YOU

ELVIS IN PERSON AT THE INTERNATIONAL HOTEL, LAS VEGAS, NEVADA *RCA (LSP-4428)* 1970
SIDE 1: BLUE SUEDE SHOES; JOHNNY B. GOODE; ALL SHOOK UP; ARE YOU LONESOME TONIGHT; HOUND DOG; I CAN'T STOP LOVING YOU; MY BABE
SIDE 2: MEDLEY: MYSTERY TRAIN/TIGER MAN; WORDS; IN THE GHETTO; SUSPICIOUS MINDS; CAN'T HELP FALLING IN LOVE

ELVIS IS BACK *RCA Victor (LPM/LSP-2231)* 1960
SIDE 1: MAKE ME KNOW IT; FEVER; THE GIRL OF MY BEST FRIEND; I WILL BE HOME AGAIN; DIRTY, DIRTY FEELING; THRILL OF YOUR LOVE
SIDE 2: SOLDIER BOY; SUCH A NIGHT; IT FEELS SO RIGHT; THE GIRL NEXT DOOR; LIKE A BABY; RECONSIDER, BABY

ELVIS MEMORIES *ABC Radio (ASP-1003)* 1978
SIDE 1: MEMORIES; ELVIS MEMORIES (Jingle/Logo); THAT'S ALL RIGHT; GOOD ROCKIN' TONIGHT; MYSTERY TRAIN; I WANT YOU, I NEED YOU, I LOVE YOU; HEARTBREAK HOTEL
SIDE 2: BURNING LOVE; RIP IT UP; FOLLOW THAT DREAM; LOVING YOU; LOVE ME TENDER; HOUND DOG; DON'T BE CRUEL; WAY DOWN; MOODY BLUE; DEVIL IN DISGUISE; SUSPICION
SIDE 3: ELVIS MEMORIES (Jingle/Logo); HIS LATEST FLAME; ALL SHOOK UP; TEDDY BEAR; JAILHOUSE ROCK; IT'S NOW OR NEVER; ELVIS MEMORIES (Jingle/Logo); I GOT STUNG; ONE NIGHT; WEAR MY RING AROUND YOUR NECK; STUCK ON YOU
SIDE 4: ELVIS MEMORIES (Jingle/Logo); MY WISH CAME TRUE; GOOD LUCK CHARM; THE GRASS WON'T PAY NO MIND; FAME AND FORTUNE; KENTUCKY RAIN; IN THE GHETTO
SIDE 5: VIVA LAS VEGAS; DON'T CRY DADDY; SEPARATE WAYS; YOU DON'T HAVE TO SAY YOU LOVE ME; ELVIS MEMORIES (Jingle/Logo); BLUE CHRISTMAS; ARE YOU LONESOME TONIGHT; CAN'T HELP FALLING IN LOVE
SIDE 6: ELVIS MEMORIES (Jingle/Logo); MY WAY; HOW GREAT THOU ART; CRYING IN THE CHAPEL; IF I CAN DREAM; THE WONDER OF YOU; MEMORIES
NOTE: ABC Radio clearly states that "Elvis Memories" is a copyrighted feature and may not be offered for resale or copied.

ELVIS NOW *RCA (LSP-4671)* 1972
SIDE 1: HELP ME MAKE IT THROUGH THE NIGHT; MIRACLE OF THE ROSARY; HEY JUDE; PUT YOUR HAND IN THE HAND; UNTIL IT'S TIME FOR YOU TO GO
SIDE 2: WE CAN MAKE THE MORNING; EARLY MORNING RAIN; SYLVIA; FOOLS RUSH IN; I WAS BORN ABOUT TEN THOUSAND YEARS AGO

ELVIS PRESLEY *RCA Victor (LPM-1254)* 1956
SIDE 1: BLUE SUEDE SHOES; I'M COUNTING ON YOU; I GOT A WOMAN; ONE-SIDED LOVE AFFAIR; I LOVE YOU BECAUSE; JUST BECAUSE
SIDE 2: TUTTI FRUTTI; TRYIN' TO GET TO YOU; I'M GONNA SIT RIGHT DOWN AND CRY; I'LL NEVER LET YOU GO; BLUE MOON; MONEY HONEY

ELVIS PRESLEY STORY, THE *RCA (DML5-0263)* 1977
—By Candlelite Music Inc.
SIDE 1: IT'S NOW OR NEVER; TREAT ME NICE; FOR THE GOOD TIMES; I GOT STUNG; ASK ME; RETURN TO SENDER
SIDE 2: THE WONDER OF YOU; HOUND DOG; MAKE THE WORLD GO AWAY; HIS LATEST FLAME; LOVING YOU
SIDE 3: ONE NIGHT; YOU DON'T KNOW ME; BLUE CHRISTMAS; GOOD LUCK CHARM; BLUE SUEDE SHOES; SURRENDER
SIDE 4: IN THE GHETTO; TOO MUCH; HELP ME MAKE IT THROUGH THE NIGHT; I WAS THE ONE; LOVE ME; LITTLE SISTER
SIDE 5: CAN'T HELP FALLING IN LOVE; TROUBLE; MEMORIES; WEAR MY RING AROUND YOUR NECK; BLUE HAWAII; BURNING LOVE
SIDE 6: LOVE ME TENDER; STUCK ON YOU; FUNNY HOW TIME SLIPS AWAY; ALL SHOOK UP; PUPPET ON A STRING; JAILHOUSE ROCK
SIDE 7: HEARTBREAK HOTEL; I JUST CAN'T HELP BELIEVIN'; I BEG OF YOU; DON'T CRY DADDY; HARD HEADED WOMAN; ARE YOU LONESOME TONIGHT
SIDE 8: TEDDY BEAR; HAWAIIAN WEDDING SONG; A BIG HUNK O' LOVE; I'M YOURS; A FOOL SUCH AS I; DON'T
SIDE 9: I WANT YOU, I NEED YOU, I LOVE YOU; KISSIN' COUSINS; I CAN'T STOP LOVING YOU; DEVIL IN DISGUISE; SUSPICION; DON'T BE CRUEL
SIDE 10: SHE'S NOT YOU; FROM A JACK TO A KING; I NEED YOUR LOVE TONIGHT; WOODEN HEART; HAVE I TOLD YOU LATELY THAT I LOVE YOU; YOU DON'T HAVE TO SAY YOU LOVE ME

ELVIS PRESLEY STORY, THE *Watermark (EPS 1A - 13B)*
—By Watermark Inc. 1975
SIDE 1: INTRODUCTION: MEDLEY OF ELVIS HITS; OLD SHEP; JESUS KNOWS WHAT I NEED (Comparison of versions by the Statesmen Quartet and by Elvis)
SIDE 2: THAT'S ALL RIGHT (Arthur Crudup); HOUND DOG (Willie Mae Thornton); EARLY FIFTIES MEDLEY: HARBOR LIGHTS (Sammy Kaye)/RAG MOP (Ames Bros.)/ TENNESSEE WALTZ (Patti Page)/CRY OF THE WILD GOOSE (Frankie Laine)/YOU BELONG TO ME (Jo Stafford)/MY HEART CRIES FOR YOU (Guy Mitchell)/COME-ON-A MY HOUSE (Rosemary Clooney)/CRY (Johnny Ray); WORKING ON THE BUILDING (Comparison of versions by the Blackwood Bros. and by Elvis)
SIDE 3: THAT'S ALL RIGHT; BLUE MOON OF KENTUCKY; GOOD ROCKIN' TONIGHT; YOU'RE A HEARTBREAKER; JUST BECAUSE
SIDE 4: MILKCOW BLUES BOOGIE; THE TRUTH ABOUT ME; BABY LET'S PLAY HOUSE; I'M LEFT, YOU'RE RIGHT, SHE'S GONE; BLUE MOON; I FORGOT TO REMEMBER TO FORGET; MYSTERY TRAIN
SIDE 5: HEARTBREAK HOTEL; I WAS THE ONE; HEARTBREAK HOTEL (Stan Freberg); MEDLEY: REDDY BLUE-BERRY HILL/MONEY HONEY/RIP IT UP/I GOT A WOMAN/LAWDY MISS CLAWDY/LONG TALL SALLY/ SHAKE, RATTLE AND ROLL/TUTTI FRUTTI; BLUE SUEDE SHOES; I WANT YOU, I NEED YOU, I LOVE YOU
SIDE 6: HOUND DOG; DON'T BE CRUEL; LOVE ME; LOVE ME TENDER; ONE-SIDED LOVE AFFAIR; TOO MUCH
SIDE 7: ALL SHOOK UP; LOVING YOU; TEDDY BEAR; GOT A LOT OF LIVING TO DO; PEACE IN THE VALLEY
SIDE 8: MEDLEY OF SONGS ABOUT ELVIS; PARTY; JAILHOUSE ROCK; BABY I DON'T CARE; OH LITTLE TOWN OF BETHLEHEM; BLUE CHRISTMAS; DON'T
SIDE 9: KING CREOLE; DEAR 53310761 (Thirteens); WON'T YOU WEAR MY RING AROUND YOUR NECK; HARD HEADED WOMAN; IF WE NEVER MEET AGAIN; ELVIS SAILS INTERVIEW
SIDE 10: TROUBLE; I GOT STUNG; A FOOL SUCH AS I; MY WISH CAME TRUE; A BIG HUNK O' LOVE; I WILL BE HOME AGAIN
SIDE 11: I'M HANGING' UP MY RIFLE (Bill [Bobby Bare] Parsons); DIRTY, DIRTY FEELING; STUCK ON YOU; IT'S NOW OR NEVER; FEVER; G. I. BLUES
SIDE 12: WOODEN HEART; FLAMING STAR; ARE YOU LONESOME TONIGHT; I SLIPPED, I STUMBLED, I FELL; HIS HAND IN MINE; SURRENDER; I'M COMING HOME
SIDE 13: MEDLEY OF ELVIS' FILM SONGS; BLUE HAWAII; I FEEL SO BAD; CAN'T HELP FALLING IN LOVE; GOOD LUCK CHARM; RETURN TO SENDER
SIDE 14: ONE BROKEN HEART FOR SALE; MEDLEY: ELVIS' FILM SONGS; BOSSA NOVA BABY; HAPPY ENDING; MEMPHIS, TENNESSEE; FUN IN ACAPULCO
SIDE 15: DEVIL IN DISGUISE; SANTA LUCIA; WHAT'S I SAY; CRYING IN THE CHAPEL; AIN'T THAT LOVING YOU BABY; YOUR CHEATIN' HEART
SIDE 16: LITTLE EGYPT; MEDLEY OF SILLY ELVIS FILM SONGS; DOWN BY THE RIVERSIDE/WHEN THE SAINTS GO MARCHING IN; PUPPET ON A STRING; DO THE CLAM; WHEN IT RAINS IT REALLY POURS
SIDE 17: OLD MACDONALD; LONG LONELY HIGHWAY; DOWN IN THE ALLEY; TOMORROW IS A LONG TIME; PARADISE HAWAIIAN STYLE
SIDE 18: IF EVERYDAY WAS LIKE CHRISTMAS; THERE AIN'T NOTHING LIKE A SONG; HE'S YOUR UNCLE, NOT YOUR DAD; BIG BOSS MAN; HOW GREAT THOU ART
SIDE 19: GUITAR MAN; U.S. MALE; A LITTLE LESS CONVERSATION; MEMORIES; YELLOW ROSE OF TEXAS/THE EYES OF TEXAS; IF I CAN DREAM
SIDE 20: SONGS FROM NBC-TV SPECIAL; ONLY THE STRONG SURVIVE; GENTLE ON MY MIND; IN THE GHETTO
SIDE 21: SONGS FROM "ELVIS LIVE AT THE INTERNATIONAL HOTEL, LAS VEGAS, NEVADA" LP; DON'T CRY DADDY; KENTUCKY RAIN
SIDE 22: SONGS FROM "ON STAGE" LP: YOU'VE LOST THAT LOVIN' FEELING; THE WONDER OF YOU; THE NEXT STEP IS LOVE
SIDE 23: PATCH IT UP; BRIDGE OVER TROUBLED WATER; RAGS TO RICHES; THERE GOES MY EVERYTHING; WHOLE LOT-TA SHAKIN' GOIN' ON; I'M LEAVIN'

(Continued on following page)

ELVIS PRESLEY STORY (Continued from previous page)

SIDE 24: HELP ME MAKE IT THROUGH THE NIGHT; AMERICAN TRILOGY; DON'T THINK TWICE; ALSO SPRACH ZARATHUSTRA/SEE SEE RIDER; HOUND DOG; BURNING LOVE; IT'S A MATTER OF TIME

SIDE 25: SEPARATE WAYS; MY WAY; I'M SO LONESOME I COULD CRY; RAISED ON ROCK; TALK ABOUT THE GOOD TIMES; STEAMROLLER BLUES

SIDE 26: MEDLEY OF ELVIS HITS; I'VE GOT A THING ABOUT YOU BABY; HELP ME; PROMISED LAND

ELVIS PRESLEY STORY, THE *Watermark (EPS 1A - 13B)* —By Watermark Inc. *1977*

SIDE 1: INTRODUCTION: MEDLEY OF ELVIS HITS; OLD SHEP; JESUS KNOWS WHAT I NEED (Comparison of versions by the Statesmen Quartet and by Elvis)

SIDE 2: THAT'S ALL RIGHT (Arthur Crudup); HOUND DOG (Willie Mae Thornton); EARLY FIFTIES MEDLEY: HARBOR LIGHTS (Sammy Kaye)/RAG MOP (Ames Bros.)/ TENNESSEE WALTZ (Patti Page)/CRY OF THE WILD GOOSE (Frankie Laine)/YOU BELONG TO ME (Jo Stafford)/MY HEART CRIES FOR YOU (Guy Mitchell)/COME-ON-A MY HOUSE (Rosemary Clooney)/CRY (Johnny Ray); WORKING ON THE BUILDING (Comparison of versions by the Blackwood Bros. and by Elvis)

SIDE 3: THAT'S ALL RIGHT; BLUE MOON OF KENTUCKY; GOOD ROCKIN' TONIGHT; YOU'RE A HEARTBREAKER; JUST BECAUSE

SIDE 4: MILKCOW BLUES BOOGIE; THE TRUTH ABOUT ME; BABY LET'S PLAY HOUSE; I'M LEFT, YOU'RE RIGHT, SHE'S GONE; BLUE MOON; I FORGOT TO REMEMBER TO FORGET; MYSTERY TRAIN

SIDE 5: HEARTBREAK HOTEL; I WAS THE ONE; HEARTBREAK HOTEL (Stan Freberg); MEDLEY: REDDY TEDDY/BLUEBERRY HILL/MONEY HONEY/RIP IT UP/I GOT A WOMAN/LAWDY MISS CLAWDY/LONG TALL SALLY/SHAKE, RATTLE AND ROLL/TUTTI FRUTTI; BLUE SUEDE SHOES; I WANT YOU, I NEED YOU, I LOVE YOU

SIDE 6: HOUND DOG; DON'T BE CRUEL; LOVE ME; LOVE ME TENDER; ONE-SIDED LOVE AFFAIR; TOO MUCH

SIDE 7: ALL SHOOK UP; LOVING YOU; TEDDY BEAR; GOT A LOT OF LIVING TO DO; PEACE IN THE VALLEY

SIDE 8: MEDLEY OF SONGS ABOUT ELVIS; PARTY; JAILHOUSE ROCK; BABY I DON'T CARE; OH LITTLE TOWN OF BETHLEHEM; BLUE CHRISTMAS; DON'T

SIDE 9: KING CREOLE; DEAR 53310761 (Thirteens); WON'T YOU WEAR MY RING AROUND YOUR NECK; HARD HEADED WOMAN; IF WE NEVER MEET AGAIN; ELVIS SAILS INTERVIEW

SIDE 10: TROUBLE; I GOT STUNG; A FOOL SUCH AS I; MY WISH CAME TRUE; A BIG HUNK O' LOVE; I WILL BE HOME AGAIN

SIDE 11: I'M HANGING' UP MY RIFLE (Bill [Bobby Bare] Parsons); DIRTY, DIRTY FEELING; STUCK ON YOU; IT'S NOW OR NEVER; FEVER; G. I. BLUES

SIDE 12: WOODEN HEART; FLAMING STAR; ARE YOU LONESOME TONIGHT; I SLIPPED, I STUMBLED, I FELL; HIS HAND IN MINE; SURRENDER; I'M COMING HOME

SIDE 13: MEDLEY OF ELVIS' FILM SONGS; BLUE HAWAII; I FEEL SO BAD; CAN'T HELP FALLING IN LOVE; GOOD LUCK CHARM; RETURN TO SENDER

SIDE 14: ONE BROKEN HEART FOR SALE; MEDLEY: ELVIS' FILM SONGS; BOSSA NOVA BABY; HAPPY ENDING; MEMPHIS, TENNESSEE; FUN IN ACAPULCO

SIDE 15: DEVIL IN DISGUISE; SANTA LUCIA; WHAT'S I SAY; CRYING IN THE CHAPEL; AIN'T THAT LOVING YOU BABY; YOUR CHEATIN' HEART

SIDE 16: LITTLE EGYPT; MEDLEY OF SILLY ELVIS FILM SONGS; DOWN BY THE RIVERSIDE/WHEN THE SAINTS GO MARCHING IN; PUPPET ON A STRING; DO THE CLAM; WHEN IT RAINS IT REALLY POURS

SIDE 17: OLD MACDONALD; LONG LONELY HIGHWAY; DOWN IN THE ALLEY; TOMORROW IS A LONG TIME; PARADISE HAWAIIAN STYLE

SIDE 18: IF EVERYDAY WAS LIKE CHRISTMAS; THERE AIN'T NOTHING LIKE A SONG; HE'S YOUR UNCLE, NOT YOUR DAD; BIG BOSS MAN; HOW GREAT THOU ART

SIDE 19: GUITAR MAN; U.S. MALE; A LITTLE LESS CONVERSATION; MEMORIES; YELLOW ROSE OF TEXAS/THE EYES OF TEXAS; IF I CAN DREAM

SIDE 20: SONGS FROM NBC-TV SPECIAL; ONLY THE STRONG SURVIVE; GENTLE ON MY MIND; IN THE GHETTO

SIDE 21: SONGS FROM "ELVIS LIVE AT THE INTERNATIONAL HOTEL, LAS VEGAS, NEVADA" LP; DON'T CRY DADDY; KENTUCKY RAIN

SIDE 22: SONGS FROM "ON STAGE" LP: YOU'VE LOST THAT LOVIN' FEELING; THE WONDER OF YOU; THE NEXT STEP IS LOVE

SIDE 23: PATCH IT UP; BRIDGE OVER TROUBLED WATER; RAGS TO RICHES; THERE GOES MY EVERYTHING; WHOLE LOT-TA SHAKIN' GOIN' ON; I'M LEAVIN'

SIDE 24: HELP ME MAKE IT THROUGH THE NIGHT; AMERICAN TRILOGY; DON'T THINK TWICE; ALSO SPRACH ZARATHUSTRA/SEE SEE RIDER; HOUND DOG; BURNING LOVE; IT'S A MATTER OF TIME

SIDE 25: SEPARATE WAYS; MY WAY; I'M SO LONESOME I COULD CRY; RAISED ON ROCK; TALK ABOUT THE GOOD TIMES; STEAMROLLER BLUES

SIDE 26: MEDLEY OF ELVIS' HITS; I'VE GOT A THING ABOUT YOU BABY; MEDLEY OF ELVIS' HITS THROUGH 1977

NOTE: Only the beginning and ending of this show was changed to reflect Elvis' death. The remainder of the program was unchanged in this 1977 reissue.

ELVIS RECORDED LIVE ON STAGE IN MEMPHIS *RCA (CPL1-0606) 1974*

SIDE 1: SEE SEE RIDER; I GOT A WOMAN; LOVE ME; TRYIN' TO GET TO YOU; MEDLEY: LONG TALL SALLY/WHOLE LOT-TA SHAKIN' GOIN' ON/YOUR MAMA DON'T DANCE/FLIP, FLOP AND FLY; JAILHOUSE ROCK/HOUND DOG; WHY ME; HOW GREAT THOU ART

SIDE 2: MEDLEY: BLUEBERRY HILL/I CAN'T STOP LOVING YOU; HELP ME; AMERICAN TRILOGY; LET ME BE THERE; MY BABY LEFT ME; LAWDY MISS CLAWDY; CAN'T HELP FALLING IN LOVE; CLOSING VAMP

ELVIS REMEMBERED *Creative Radio (CRS 1A - 3B) 1979*

SIDE 1: HEARTBREAK HOTEL; MEDLEY: YOUR CHEATIN' HEART/WHEN THE SAINTS GO MARCHING IN/WON'T YOU WEAR MY RING AROUND YOUR NECK; MEDLEY: HOUND DOG/KING CREOLE/DON'T BE CRUEL/TEDDY BEAR/BLUE SUEDE SHOES/RECONSIDER, BABY/HARD HEADED WOMAN/LOVING YOU; ALL SHOOK UP; THAT'S ALL RIGHT; I REALLY DON'T WANT TO KNOW; HOUND DOG; MAKE THE WORLD GO AWAY

SIDE 2: JAILHOUSE ROCK; I FORGOT TO REMEMBER TO FORGET; MONEY HONEY; ARE YOU SINCERE; YOU GAVE ME A MOUNTAIN; SUCH A NIGHT; FAME AND FORTUNE

SIDE 3: MEDLEY: I GOT STUNG/A BIG HUNK O' LOVE/ONE BROKEN HEART FOR SALE/RETURN TO SENDER/SURRENDER/DOWN BY THE RIVERSIDE; HOW GREAT THOU ART; TREAT ME NICE; I CAN'T STOP LOVING YOU/I GOT A WOMAN/AMEN (Unreleased version); I WANT YOU, I NEED YOU, I LOVE YOU

SIDE 4: IN THE GHETTO; IT'S NOW OR NEVER; I BEG OF YOU; SHE WEARS MY RING; WEAR MY RING AROUND YOUR NECK; WHERE DID THEY GO LORD

SIDE 5: LOVE ME TENDER; I CAN HELP; A FOOL SUCH AS I; CRYING IN THE CHAPEL; IF I CAN DREAM; SUSPICIOUS MINDS

SIDE 6: SEE SEE RIDER (Unreleased version); HURT (Unreleased version); THERE GOES MY EVERYTHING; GREEN, GREEN GRASS OF HOME; THERE'S A HONKY-TONK ANGEL (WHO'LL TAKE ME BACK IN); MEMORIES; MY WAY

NOTE: All previously unreleased versions in this show were recorded live, in concert.

ELVIS SINGS FLAMING STAR *RCA Camden (CAS-2304)*
1969

SIDE 1: FLAMING STAR; WONDERFUL WORLD; NIGHT LIFE; ALL I NEEDED WAS THE RAIN; TOO MUCH MONKEY BUSINESS

SIDE 2: YELLOW ROSE OF TEXAS/THE EYES OF TEXAS; SHE'S A MACHINE; DO THE VEGA; TIGER MAN

ELVIS SINGS FOR CHILDREN AND GROWNUPS TOO!
RCA Victor (CPL1-2901) *1978*

SIDE 1: TEDDY BEAR; WOODEN HEART; FIVE SLEEPYHEADS; PUPPET ON A STRING; ANGEL; OLD MACDONALD

SIDE 2: HOW WOULD YOU LIKE TO BE; COTTON CANDY LAND; OLD SHEP; BIG BOOTS; HAVE A HAPPY

ELVIS SINGS HITS FROM HIS MOVIES VOLUME 1 *RCA*
RCA Camden (CAS-2304) *1972*

SIDE 1: DOWN BY THE RIVERSIDE/WHEN THE SAINTS GO MARCHING IN; THEY REMIND ME TOO MUCH OF YOU; CONFIDENCE; FRANKIE AND JOHNNY; GUITAR MAN

SIDE 2: LONG LEGGED GIRL; YOU DON'T KNOW ME; HOW WOULD YOU LIKE TO BE; BIG BOSS MAN; OLD MACDONALD

ELVIS SINGS THE WONDERFUL WORLD OF CHRISTMAS
RCA (LSP-4579) *1971*

SIDE 1: O COME, ALL YE FAITHFUL; THE FIRST NOEL; ON A ANOWY CHRISTMAS NIGHT; WINTER WONDERLAND; THE WONDERFUL WORLD OF CHRISTMAS; IT WON'T SEEM LIKE CHRISTMAS (WITHOUT YOU)

SIDE 2: I'LL BE HOME ON CHRISTMAS DAY; IF I GET HOME ON CHRISTMAS DAY; HOLLY LEAVES AND CHRISTMAS TREES; MERRY CHRISTMAS BABY; SILVER BELLS

ELVIS TODAY *RCA (APL1-1039)* *1975*

SIDE 1: T-R-O-U-B-L-E; AND I LOVE YOU SO; SUSAN WHEN SHE TRIED; WOMAN WITHOUT LOVE; SHAKE A HAND

SIDE 2: PIECES OF MY LIFE; FAIRYTALE; I CAN HELP; BRINGING IT BACK; GREEN GRASS OF HOME

E-Z COUNTRY PROGRAMMING NO. 2 *RCA Victor* *1956*

SIDE 1: (G7OL-0108) WHEN YOU SAID GOODBYE (Eddy Arnold); HI DE ANK TUM (Nick, Rita & Ruby); MYSTERY TRAIN (Elvis Presley); HONEY (Chet Atkins); THESE HANDS (Hank Snow); THE LAST FRONTIER (Sons of the Pioneers)

SIDE 2: (G7OL-0109) I FORGOT TO REMEMBER TO FORGET; I WORE DARK GLASSES (Anita Carter); ROCK-A-BYE (Skeeter Bonn); LOVE AND MARRIAGE (Homer & Jethro); LOVE OR SPITE (Hank Locklin); HANDFUL OF SUNSHINE (STUART HAMBLEN

E-Z COUNTRY PROGRAMMING NO. 3 *RCA Victor* *1956*

SIDE 1: (G8OL-0199) HEARTBREAK HOTEL (Elvis Presley); I'M MOVING IN (Hank Snow); IF IT AIN'T ON THE MENU (Hawkshaw Hawkins); THE POOR PEOPLE OF PARIS (Chet Atkins); I WANT TO BE LOVED (Johnny & Jack & Ruby Wells); THAT'S A SAD AFFAIR (Jim Reeves)

SIDE 2: (G8OL-0200) DO YOU KNOW WHERE GOD LIVES (Eddy Arnold); IF YOU WERE MINE (Jim Reeves); THE LITTLE WHITE DUCK (Dorthy Olsen); BORROWING (Hawkshaw Hawkins); WHAT WOULD YOU DO (Porter Wagoner); I WAS THE ONE (Elvis Presley)

E-Z POP PROGRAMMING NO. 5 *RCA Victor* *1956*

SIDE 1: (F7OP-9681) DUNGAREE DOLL (Eddie Fisher); STOLEN LOVE (Dinah Shore); TAKE MY HAND (SHOW ME THE WAY) Rhythmettes; NOT ONE GOODBYE (Jaye P. Morgan); DON'T GO TO STRANGERS (Vaughn Monroe); THE ROCK AND ROLL WALTZ (Kay Starr); I FORGOT TO REMEMBER TO FORGET (Elvis Presley); THE LITTLE LAPLANDER (Henri Rene)

SIDE 2: (F7OP-9682) THE LARGE, LARGE HOUSE (Mike Pedicin); ALL AT ONCE YOU LOVE HER (Perry Como); WHEN YOU SAID GOODBYE (Eddy Arnold); MY BEWILDERED HEART (Jaye P. Morgan); MYSTERY TRAIN (Elvis Presley); THAT'S ALL THERE IS TO THAT (Dinah Shore); JEAN'S SONG (Chet Atkins); EVERYBODY'S GOT A HOME BUT ME (Eddie Fisher)

E-Z POP PROGRAMMING NO. 6 *RCA Victor* *1956*

SIDE 1: (G7OL-0197) LIPSTICK AND CANDY AND RUBBERSOLE SHOES (Julius La Rosa); MR. WONDERFUL (Teddi King); THE BITTER WITH THE SWEET (Bill Eckstine); FOREVER DARLING (Ames Bros.) SWEET LIPS (Jaye P. Morgan); DO YOU KNOW WHERE GOD LIVES (Eddy Arnold)

SIDE 2: (G7OL-0198) GRAPEVINE (Billy Eckstine); THE POOR PEOPLE OF PARIS (Chet Atkins); JUKE BOX BABY (Perry Como); LITTLE WHITE DUCK (Dorthy Olsen); I WAS THE ONE (Elvis Presley); HOT DOG ROCK AND ROLL (The Singing Dogs)

FIRST YEARS, THE *HALW (00001)* *1978*

SIDE 1: SCOTTY MOORE TALKS ABOUT ELVIS

SIDE 2: GOOD ROCKIN' TONIGHT; BABY LET'S PLAY HOUSE; BLUE MOON OF KENTUCKY; I GOT A WOMAN; THAT'S ALL RIGHT

NOTE: The proper song titles are shown above. On this LP the only titles that were shown correctly were BABY LET'S PLAY HOUSE and BLUE MOON OF KENTUCKY. The others were shown as THERE'S GOOD ROCKIN' TONIGHT, I'VE GOT A WOMAN and THAT'S ALRIGHT LITTLE MAMA.

FOR LP FANS ONLY *RCA Victor (LPM-1990)* *1979*

SIDE 1: THAT'S ALL RIGHT; LAWDY MISS CLAWDY; MYSTERY TRAIN; PLAYING FOR KEEPS; POOR BOY

SIDE 2: MY BABY LEFT ME; I WAS THE ONE; SHAKE, RATTLE AND ROLL; I'M LEFT, YOU'RE RIGHT, SHE'S GONE; YOU'RE A HEARTBREAKER

FRANKIE AND JOHNNY *RCA Victor (LPM/LSP-3553)* *1966*

SIDE 1: FRANKIE AND JOHNNY; COME ALONG; PETUNIA, THE GARDNER'S DAUGHTER; CHESAY; WHAT EVERY WOMAN LIVES FOR; LOOK OUT, BROADWAY

SIDE 2: BEGINNER'S LUCK; DOWN BY THE RIVERSIDE/WHEN THE SAINTS GO MARCHING IN; SHOUT IT OUT; HARD LUCK; PLEASE DON'T STOP LOVING ME; EVERYBODY COME ABOARD

FRANKIE & JOHNNY *RCA Camden-Pickwick (ACL-7007)*
1976

SIDE 1: FRANKIE AND JOHNNY; COME ALONG; WHAT EVERY WOMAN LIVES FOR; HARD LUCK; PLEASE DON'T STOP LOVING ME

SIDE 2: DOWN BY THE RIVERSIDE AND WHEN THE SAINTS GO MARCHING IN; PETUNIA, THE GARDNER'S DAUGHTER; BEGINNER'S LUCK; SHOUT IT OUT

NOTE: Since RCA had deleated the original FRANKIE AND JOHNNY LP, Pickwick was given permission to reissue it in 1976. In doing so, the cover, both front and back, was completely changed. The AND in "Frankie AND Johnny" was replaced with an ampersand, and three of the original 12 tunes were dropped. They are "Chesay," "Everybody Come Aboard " and "Look Out Broadway."

FROM ELVIS IN MEMPHIS *RCA (LSP-4155)* *1969*

SIDE 1: WEARIN' THAT LOVED ON LOOK; ONLY THE STRONG SURVIVE; I'LL HOLD YOU IN MY ARMS (TILL I CAN HOLD YOU IN MY HEART); LONG BLACK LIMOUSINE; IT KEEPS RIGHT ON A-HURTIN'; I'M MOVING ON

SIDE 2: POWER OF MY LOVE; GENTLE ON MY MIND; AFTER LOVING YOU; TRUE LOVE TRAVELS ON A GRAVEL ROAD; ANY DAY NOW; IN THE GHETTO

FROM ELVIS PRESLEY BOULEVARD, MEMPHIS, TENNESSEE
RCA (APL1-1506) *1976*

SIDE 1: HURT; NEVER AGAIN; BLUE EYES CRYING IN THE RAIN; DANNY BOY; THE LAST FAREWELL

SIDE 2: FOR THE HEART; BITTER THEY ARE, HARDER THEY FALL; SOLITAIRE; LOVE COMING DOWN; I'LL NEVER FALL IN LOVE AGAIN

Elvis Presley

FROM ELVIS WITH LOVE *RCA Record Club (R234340) 1978*
—Songs With LOVE in the title—
SIDE 1: LOVE ME TENDER; CAN'T HELP FALLING IN LOVE; THE NEXT STEP IS LOVE; I NEED YOUR LOVE TONIGHT; I CAN'T STOP LOVING YOU
SIDE 2: I WANT YOU, I NEED YOU, I LOVE YOU; I LOVE YOU BECAUSE; LOVE LETTERS; A THING CALLED LOVE; A BIG HUNK O' LOVE
SIDE 3: LOVE ME; WITHOUT LOVE; FADED LOVE (Alternate version); LOVING YOU; YOU'VE LOST THAT LOVIN' FEELING
SIDE 4: HAVE I TOLD YOU LATELY THAT I LOVE YOU; YOU DON'T HAVE TO SAY YOU LOVE ME; TRUE LOVE; AIN'T THAT LOVING YOU BABY; PLEASE DON'T STOP LOVING ME

FROM MEMPHIS TO VEGAS/FROM VEGAS TO MEMPHIS
RCA (LSP-6020) 1969
SIDE 1: BLUE SUEDE SHOES; JOHNNY B. GOODE; ALL SHOOK UP; ARE YOU LONESOME TONIGHT; HOUND DOG; I CAN'T STOP LOVING YOU; MY BABE
SIDE 2: MEDLEY: MYSTERY TRAIN/TIGER MAN; WORDS; IN THE GHETTO; SUSPICIOUS MINDS; CAN'T HELP FALLING IN LOVE
SIDE 3: INHERIT THE WIND; THIS IS MY STORY; STRANGER IN MY OWN HOME TOWN; A LITTLE BIT OF GREEN; AND THE GRASS WON'T PAY NO MIND
SIDE 4: DO YOU KNOW WHO I AM; FROM A JACK TO A KING; THE FAIR IS MOVING ON; YOU'LL THINK OF ME; WITHOUT LOVE (THERE IS NOTHING)

FUN IN ACAPULCO *RCA Victor (LPM/LSP-2756)* 1963
SIDE 1: FUN IN ACAPULCO; VINO, DINERO Y AMOR; MEXICO; EL TORO; MARGUERITA; THE LADY WAS A BULLFIGHTER; NO ROOM TO RHUMBA IN A SPORTS CAR
SIDE 2: I THINK I'M GONNA LIKE IT HERE; BOSSA NOVA BABY; YOU CAN'T SAY NO IN ACAPULCO; GUADALAJARA; LOVE ME TONIGHT; SLOWLY BUT SURELY

G.I. BLUES *RCA Victor (LPM/LSP-2256)* 1960
SIDE 1: TONIGHT IS SO RIGHT FOR LOVE; WHAT'S SHE REALLY LIKE; FRANKFORT SPECIAL; WOODEN HEART; G.I. BLUES
SIDE 2: POCKET FULL OF RAINBOWS; SHOPPIN' AROUND; BIG BOOTS; DIDJA' EVER; BLUE SUEDE SHOES; DOIN' THE BEST I CAN

GIRL HAPPY *RCA Victor (LPM/LSP-3338)* 1965
SIDE 1: GIRL HAPPY; SPRING FEVER; FORT LAUDERDALE CHAMBER OF COMMERCE; STARTIN' TONIGHT; WOLF CALL; DO NOT DISTURB
SIDE 2: CROSS MY HEART AND HOPE TO DIE; THE MEANEST GIRL IN TOWN; DO THE CLAM; PUPPET ON A STRING; I'VE GOT TO FIND MY BABY; YOU'LL BE GONE

GIRLS! GIRLS! GIRLS! *RCA Victor (LPM/LSP-2621)* 1962
SIDE 1: GIRLS! GIRLS! GIRLS!; I DON'T WANT TO BE TIED; WHERE DO YOU COME FROM; I DON'T WANT TO; WE'LL BE TOGETHER; A BOY LIKE ME, A GIRL LIKE YOU; EARTH BOY
SIDE 2: RETURN TO SENDER; BECAUSE OF LOVE; THANKS TO THE ROLLING SEA; SONG OF THE SHRIMP; THE WALLS HAVE EARS; WE'RE COMING IN LOADED

GOOD TIMES *RCA (CPL1-0475)* 1974
SIDE 1: TAKE GOOD CARE OF HER; LOVING ARMS; I GOT A FEELIN' IN MY BODY; IF THAT ISN'T LOVE; SHE WEARS MY RING
SIDE 2: I'VE GOT A THING ABOUT YOU BABY; MY BOY; SPANISH EYES; TALK ABOUT THE GOOD TIMES; GOOD TIME CHARLIE'S GOT THE BLUES

GREATEST SHOW ON EARTH, THE *RCA Special Products (DML1-0348)* 1978
—By Candlelite Music Inc.
SIDE 1: I'LL REMEMBER YOU; WITHOUT LOVE; GENTLE ON MY MIND; IT'S IMPOSSIBLE; WHAT NOW MY LOVE
SIDE 2: UNTIL IT'S TIME FOR YOU TO GO; EARLY MORNING RAIN; SOMETHING; THE FIRST TIME EVER I SAW YOUR FACE; THE IMPOSSIBLE DREAM

HARUM SCARUM *RCA Victor (LPM/LSP-3468)* 1965
SIDE 1: HAREM HOLIDAY; MY DESERT SERENADE; GO EAST, YOUNG MAN; MIRAGE; KISMET; SHAKE THAT TAMBOURINE
SIDE 2: HEY LITTLE GIRL; GOLDEN COINS; SO CLOSE, YET SO FAR; ANIMAL INSTINCT; WISDOM OF THE AGES

HE TOUCHED ME *RCA (LSP-4690)* 1972
SIDE 1: HE TOUCHED ME; I'VE GOT CONFIDENCE; AMAZING GRACE; SEEING IS BELIEVING; HE IS MY EVERYTHING; BOSOM OF ABRAHAM
SIDE 2: AN EVENING PRAYER; LEAD ME, GUIDE ME; THERE IS NO GOD BUT GOD; A THING CALLED LOVE; I, JOHN; REACH OUT TO JESUS

HE WALKS BESIDE ME *RCA Victor (AFL1-2772)* 1978
SIDE 1: HE IS MY EVERYTHING; MIRACLE OF THE ROSARY; WHERE DID THEY GO LORD; SOMEBODY BIGGER THAN YOU AND I; AN EVENING PRAYER; THE IMPOSSIBLE DREAM
SIDE 2: IF I CAN DREAM; PADRE; KNOWN ONLY TO HIM; WHO AM I; HOW GREAT THOU ART
NOTE: IF I CAN DREAM and THE IMPOSSIBLE DREAM, as contained in this LP, were previously unreleased takes.

HIS HAND IN MINE *RCA Victor (LPM/LSP-2328)* 1960
SIDE 1: HIS HAND IN MINE; I'M GONNA WALK DEM GOLDEN STAIRS; IN MY FATHER'S HOUSE; MILKY WHITE WAY; KNOWN ONLY TO HIM; I BELIEVE IN THE MAN IN THE SKY
SIDE 2: JOSHUA FIT THE BATTLE; JESUS KNOWS WHAT I NEED; SWING DOWN SWEET CHARIOT; MANSION OVER THE HILLTOP; IF WE NEVER MEET AGAIN; WORKING ON THE BUILDING

HIS SONGS OF INSPIRATION *RCA Special Products (DML1-0264)* 1977
—By Candlelite Music Inc.
SIDE 1: CRYING IN THE CHAPEL; PUT YOUR HAND IN THE HAND; I BELIEVE; HOW GREAT THOU ART; IF I CAN DREAM
SIDE 2: PEACE IN THE VALLEY; AMAZING GRACE; AN AMERICAN TRILOGY; FOLLOW THAT DREAM; YOU'LL NEVER WALK ALONE

HOW GREAT THOU ART *RCA Victor (LPM/LSP-3758)* 1967
SIDE 1: HOW GREAT THOU ART; IN THE GARDEN; SOMEBODY BIGGER THAN YOU AND I; FARTHER ALONG; STAND BY ME; WITHOUT HIM
SIDE 2: SO HIGH; WHERE COULD I GO BUT TO THE LORD; BY AND BY; IF THE LORD WASN'T WALKING BY MY SIDE; RUN ON; WHERE NO ONE STANDS ALONE; CRYING IN THE CHAPEL

I GOT LUCKY *RCA Camden (CAL-2533)* 1971
SIDE 1: I GOT LUCKY; WHAT A WONDERFUL LIFE; I NEED SOMEBODY TO LEAN ON; YOGA IS AS YOGA DOES; RIDIN' THE RAINBOW
SIDE 2: FOOLS FALL IN LOVE; THE LOVE MACHINE; HOME IS WHERE THE HEART IS; YOU GOTTA STOP; IF YOU THINK I DON'T NEED YOU

IT HAPPENED AT THE WORLD'S FAIR *RCA Victor (LPM/LSP-2697)* 1963
SIDE 1: BEYOND THE BEND; RELAX; TAKE ME TO THE FAIR; THEY REMIND ME TOO MUCH OF YOU; ONE BROKEN HEART FOR SALE
SIDE 2: I'M FALLING IN LOVE TONIGHT; COTTON CANDY LAND; A WORLD OF OUR OWN; HOW WOULD YOU LIKE TO BE

KING CREOLE *RCA Victor (LPM-1884)* 1958
SIDE 1: KING CREOLE; AS LONG AS I HAVE YOU; HARD HEADED WOMAN; TROUBLE; DIXIELAND ROCK
SIDE 2: DON'T ASK ME WHY; LOVER DOLL; CRAWFISH; YOUNG DREAMS; STEADFAST, LOYAL AND TRUE; NEW ORLEANS

KISSIN' COUSINS *RCA Victor (LPM/LSP-2894)* *1964*
SIDE 1: KISSIN' COUSINS (NO. 2); SMOKEY MOUNTAIN BOY;
THERE'S GOLD IN THE MOUNTAINS; ONE BOY, TWO
LITTLE GIRLS; CATCHIN' ON FAST; TENDER FEELING;
SIDE 2: ANYONE (COULD FALL IN LOVE WITH YOU); BARE-
FOOT BALLAD; KISSIN' COUSINS; ECHOES OF LOVE;
(IT'S A) LONG LONELY HIGHWAY

LE DISQUE D'OR *RCA French Import (6886 807)* *1978*
SIDE 1: C'MON EVERYBODY; A WHISTLING TUNE; I'LL BE
THERE (IF YOU WANT ME); I LOVE ONLY ONE GIRL;
EASY COME, EASY GO; SANTA LUCIA
SIDE 2: TONIGHT IS SO RIGHT FOR LOVE; GUADALAJARA;
ANGEL; A LITTLE LESS CONVERSATION; FOLLOW
THAT DREAM; LONG LEGGED GIRL

LEGENDARY CONCERT PERFORMANCES *RCA Victor Record*
Club (R-244047) *1978*
SIDE 1: BLUE SUEDE SHOES; SWEET CAROLINE; BURNING
LOVE; RUNAWAY; MY BABE
SIDE 2: JOHNNY B. GOODE; YESTERDAY; MEDLEY: MYSTERY
TRAIN/TIGER MAN; YOU GAVE ME A MOUNTAIN;
NEVER BEEN TO SPAIN
SIDE 3: SEE SEE RIDER; WORDS; PROUD MARY; WALK A MILE
IN MY SHOES; STEAMROLLER BLUES
SIDE 4: POLK SALAD ANNIE; SOMETHING; LET IT BE ME (JE
T'APPARTIENS); THE IMPOSSIBLE DREAM; MY WAY

LET'S BE FRIENDS *RCA Camden (CAS-2408)* *1970*
SIDE 1: STAY AWAY JOE; IF I'M A FOOL (FOR LOVING YOU);
LET'S BE FRIENDS; LET'S FORGET ABOUT THE STARS;
MAMA
SIDE 2: I'LL BE THERE (IF EVER YOU WANT ME); ALMOST;
CHANGE OF HABIT; HAVE A HAPPY

LOVE LETTERS FROM ELVIS *RCA (LSP-4530)* *1971*
SIDE 1: LOVE LETTERS; WHEN I'M OVER YOU; IF I WERE YOU;
GOT MY MOJO WORKING; HEART OF ROME
SIDE 2: ONLY BELIEVE; THIS IS OUR DANCE; CINDY CINDY;
I'LL NEVER KNOW; IT AIN'T NO BIG THING; LIFE

LOVING YOU *RCA Victor (LPM-1515)* *1957*
SIDE 1: MEAN WOMAN BLUES; TEDDY BEAR; LOVING YOU;
GOT A LOT O' LIVIN' TO DO; LONESOME COWBOY;
HOT DOG; PARTY
SIDE 2: BLUEBERRY HILL; TRUE LOVE; DON'T LEAVE ME
NOW; HAVE I TOLD YOU LATELY THAT I LOVE YOU;
I NEED YOU SO

MAHALO FROM ELVIS *RCA Camden/Pickwick (ACL-7064)*
1978
SIDE 1: BLUE HAWAII; EARLY MORNING RAIN; HAWAIIAN
WEDDING SONG; KU-U-I-PO (The preceeding four songs
were newly recorded in 1973 for the "Aloha From Hawaii
Via Satellite" TV special, and were included in that show
but not on the RCA soundtrack LP of the show.); NO
MORE (Recorded at the same time as the other four songs
on this side, but NOT included in the TV special.)
SIDE 2: RELAX; BABY, IF YOU'LL GIVE ME ALL YOUR LOVE;
ONE BROKEN HEART FOR SALE; SO CLOSE, YET SO
FAR (FROM PARADISE); HAPPY ENDING

NOTE: The appearance of this version of NO MORE on this LP marked
the first time this particular recording had been heard by the general
public.

MARCH OF DIMES GALAXY OF STARS, 1957
SIDE 1: (GM-8M-0653) DISCS FOR DIMES: HOWARD MILLER
(Instructions - not for broadcast); EDDIE FISHER; JULIE
LONDON; DENISE LOR; JIM LOWE; MILLS BROS.; GUY
MITCHELL; VAUGHN MONROE; ELVIS PRESLEY;
GALE ROBBINS
SIDE 2: (GM-8M-0654) DISCS FOR DIMES: PAT BOONE;
SAMMY DAVIS JR.; GOGI GRANT; BILL HAYES;
EARTHA KITT; RAY PRICE; JOHNNIE RAY; HENRI
RENE; DINAH SHORE; MARGARET WHITING; ANDY
WILLIAMS

NOTE: Each of the above entertainers gives a statement for the March
of Dimes 1957 campaign.

MARCH OF DIMES GALAXY OF STARS, 1957
SIDE 1: (GM-8M-0657) I LOVE MY BABY (Jill Corey); LOVE ME
TENDER (Elvis Presley); BABY DOLL (Andy Williams)
SIDE 2: (GM-8M-0658) YOUR LOVE IS MY LOVE (Alan Dale);
PAPER DOLL (Mills Bros.); SINGING THE BLUES (Guy
Mitchell)

NOTE: In addition to the songs, each of the six entertainers provides
an open-end interview. A guideline script was provided with the disc.

MEMORIES OF ELVIS *RCA (DML5-0347)* *1978*
—By Candlelite Music Inc.
SIDE 1: ONE BROKEN HEART FOR SALE; YOUNG AND BEAUTI-
FUL; A MESS OF BLUES; THE NEXT STEP IS LOVE; I
GOTTA KNOW; LOVE LETTERS
SIDE 2: WHEN MY BLUE MOON TURNS TO GOLD AGAIN; IF
EVERYDAY WAS LIKE CHRISTMAS; STEAMROLLER
BLUES; ANYWAY YOU WANT ME; (SUCH AN) EASY
QUESTION; THAT'S WHEN YOUR HEARTACHES BEGIN
SIDE 3: KENTUCKY RAIN; MONEY HONEY; MY WAY; GIRLS!
GIRLS! GIRLS!; LONELY MAN; U.S. MALE
SIDE 4: MY WISH CAME TRUE; KISS ME QUICK; AS LONG AS I
HAVE YOU; BOSSA NOVA BABY; I FORGOT TO
REMEMBER TO FORGET; SUCH A NIGHT
SIDE 5: I REALLY DON'T WANT TO KNOW; DONCHA' THINK
IT'S TIME; HIS HAND IN MINE; THAT'S ALL RIGHT;
NOTHINGVILLE MEDLEY; BABY, I DON'T CARE;
SIDE 6: PLAYING FOR KEEPS; KING OF THE WHOLE WIDE
WORLD; DON'T ASK ME WHY; FLAMING STAR; I'M
LEFT, YOU'RE RIGHT, SHE'S GONE; WHAT'D I SAY
SIDE 7: THERE GOES MY EVERYTHING; PATCH IT UP; RECON-
SIDER BABY; GOOD ROCKIN' TONIGHT; YOU GAVE
ME A MOUNTAIN; ROCK-A-HULA BABY
SIDE 8: MEAN WOMAN BLUES; IT HURTS ME; FEVER; I WANT
TO BE FREE; VIVA LAS VEGAS; OLD SHEP
SIDE 9: ANYTHING THAT'S PART OF YOU; MY BABY LEFT
ME; WILD IN THE COUNTRY; MEMPHIS, TENNESSEE;
DON'T LEAVE ME NOW; I FEEL SO BAD
SIDE 10: SEPARATE WAYS; POLK SALAD ANNIE; FAME AND
FORTUNE; TRYING TO GET TO YOU; I'VE LOST YOU;
KING CREOLE

MICHELOB PRESENTS HIGHLIGHTS OF ELVIS MEMORIES
ABC (0CC810) —By ABC Radio *1978*
SIDE 1: MEMORIES; HEARTBREAK HOTEL; LOVE ME TENDER;
HOUND DOG; DON'T BE CRUEL; JAILHOUSE ROCK;
IT'S NOW OR NEVER
SIDE 2: VIVA LAS VEGAS; SEPARATE WAYS; YOU DON'T HAVE
TO SAY YOU LOVE ME; ARE YOU LONESOME
TONIGHT; CAN'T HELP FALLING IN LOVE: IF I
CAN DREAM

MOODY BLUE *RCA Victor (AFL1-2428)* *1977*
SIDE 1: UNCHAINED MELODY; IF YOU LOVE ME (LET ME
KNOW); LITTLE DARLIN'; HE'LL HAVE TO GO; LET
ME BE THERE
SIDE 2: WAY DOWN; PLEDGING MY LOVE; MOODY BLUE; SHE
THINKS I STILL CARE; IT'S EASY FOR YOU

ON STAGE — FEBRUARY, 1970 *(LSP-4362)* *1970*
SIDE 1: SEE SEE RIDER; RELEASE ME; SWEET CAROLINE;
RUNAWAY; THE WONDER OF YOU
SIDE 2: POLK SALAD ANNIE; YESTERDAY; PROUD MARY;
WALK A MILE IN MY SHOES; LET IT BE ME (JE
T'APPARTIENS)

OUR MEMORIES OF ELVIS *RCA Victor (AQL1-3279)* *1979*
SIDE 1: ARE YOU SINCERE (Unreleased version); IT'S MID-
NIGHT; MY BOY; GIRL OF MINE; TAKE GOOD CARE
OF HER; I'LL NEVER FALL IN LOVE AGAIN
SIDE 2: YOUR LOVE'S BEEN A LONG TIME COMING; SPANISH
EYES; NEVER AGAIN; SHE THINKS I STILL CARE;
SOLITAIRE

115

OUR MEMORIES OF ELVIS VOLUME 2 *RCA Victor*
(AQL1-3448)   1979
SIDE 1: I GOT A FEELIN' IN MY BODY; GREEN GREEN GRASS OF HOME; FOR THE HEART; SHE WEARS MY RING; I CAN HELP
SIDE 2: WAY DOWN; THERE'S A HONKY TONK ANGEL (WHO'LL TAKE ME BACK IN); FIND OUT WHAT'S HAPPENING; THINKING ABOUT YOU; DON'T THINK TWICE, IT'S ALL RIGHT (Unreleased complete studio jam session)

PARADISE HAWAIIAN STYLE *RCA Victor (LPM/LSP-3643)*
1966
SIDE 1: PARADISE HAWAIIAN STYLE; QUEENIE WAHINE'S PAPAYA; SCRATCH MY BACK (I'LL SCRATCH YOURS); DRUMS OF THE ISLANDS; DATIN'
SIDE 2: A DOG'S LIFE; A HOUSE OF SAND; STOP WHERE YOU ARE; THIS IS MY HEAVEN; SAND CASTLES

POT LUCK *RCA Victor (LPM/LSP-2523)*   1962
SIDE 1: KISS ME QUICK; JUST FOR OLD TIMES SAKE; GONNA GET BACK HOME SOMEHOW; (SUCH AN) EASY QUESTION; STEPPIN' OUT OF LINE; I'M YOURS
SIDE 2: SOMETHING BLUE; SUSPICION; I FEEL THAT I'VE KNOWN YOU FOREVER; NIGHT RIDER; FOUNTAIN OF LOVE; THAT'S SOMEONE YOU NEVER FORGET

PROMISED LAND *RCA (APL1- 0873)*   1975
SIDE 1: PROMISED LAND; THERE'S A HONKY TONK ANGEL (WHO'LL TAKE ME BACK IN); HELP ME; MR. SONGMAN; LOVE SONG OF THE YEAR
SIDE 2: IT'S MIDNIGHT; YOUR LOVE'S BEEN A LONG TIME COMING; IF YOU TALK IN YOUR SLEEP; THINKING ABOUT YOU; YOU ASKED ME TO

PURE ELVIS *RCA (DJL1-3455)*   1979
SIDE 1: I GOT A FEELIN' IN MY BODY; FOR THE HEART; SHE WEARS MY RING; FIND OUT WHAT'S HAPPENING
SIDE 2: I GOT A FEELIN' IN MY BODY; FOR THE HEART; SHE WEARS MY RING; FIND OUT WHAT'S HAPPENING

PURE GOLD *RCA (ANL1-0097e)*   1975
SIDE 1: KENTUCKY RAIN; FEVER; IT'S IMPOSSIBLE; JAILHOUSE ROCK; DON'T BE CRUEL
SIDE 2: I GOT A WOMAN; ALL SHOOK UP; LOVING YOU; IN THE GHETTO; LOVE ME TENDER

RAISED ON ROCK/FOR OL' TIMES SAKE *RCA (APL1-0388)*
1973
SIDE 1: RAISED ON ROCK; ARE YOU SINCERE; FIND OUT WHAT'S AHPPENING; I MISS YOU; GIRL OF MINE
SIDE 2: FOR OL' TIMES SAKE; IF YOU DON'T COME BACK; JUST A LITTLE BIT; SWEET ANGELINE; THREE CORN PATCHES

ROCK ROCK ROCK (ALL STAR ROCK - VOLUME 11)
Original Sound (OSR-11)   1972
SIDE 1: AMERICAN PIE (Don McLean); BRAND NEW KEY (Melanie); LET'S STAY TOGETHER (Al Green); DAY AFTER DAY (Badfinger); NEVER BEEN TO SPAIN (Three Dog Night); UNTIL IT'S TIME FOR YOU TO GO (Elvis Presley); COUNTRY WINE (The Raiders)
SIDE 2: THE WAY OF LOVE (Cher); HURTING EACH OTHER (The Carpenters); JOY (Apollo 100); MY WORLD (Bee Gees); EVERYTHING I OWN (Bread); FEELIN' ALRIGHT (Joe Cocker); DOWN BY THE LAZY RIVER (Osmonds)

ROUSTABOUT   *RCA Victor (LPM/LSP-2999)*   1964
SIDE 1: ROUSTABOUT; LITTLE EGYPT; POISON IVY LEAGUE; HARD KNOCKS; IT'S A WONDERFUL WORLD; BIG LOVE, BIG HEARTACHE
SIDE 2: ONE TRACK HEART; IT'S CARNIVAL TIME; CARNY TOWN; THERE'S A BRAND NEW DAY ON THE HORIZON; WHEELS ON MY HEELS

SEPARATE WAYS *RCA Camden (CAS-2611)*   1973
SIDE 1: SEPARATE WAYS; SENTIMENTAL ME; IN MY WAY; I MET HER TODAY; WHAT NOW, WHAT NEXT, WHERE TO
SIDE 2: ALWAYS ON MY MIND; I SLIPPED, I STUMBLED, I FELL; IS IT SO STRANGE; FORGET ME NEVER; OLD SHEP

SINGER PRESENTS ELVIS SINGING FLAMING STAR AND OTHERS: *See ELVIS SINGS FLAMING STAR, as contents are identical for both albums.*

SOMETHING FOR EVERYBODY *RCA Victor (LPM/LSP-2370)*
1961
SIDE 1: THERE'S ALWAYS ME; GIVE ME THE RIGHT; IT'S A SIN; SENTIMENTAL ME; STARTING TODAY; GENTLY
SIDE 2: I'M COMIN' HOME; IN YOUR ARMS; PUT THE BLAME ON ME; JUDY; I WANT YOU WITH ME; I SLIPPED, I STUMBLED, I FELL

SPECIAL PALM SUNDAY PROGRAMMING *RCA Victor*
(SP 33-461)   1967
SIDE 1: HOW GREAT THOU ART; IN THE GARDEN; SOMEBODY BIGGER THAN YOU AND I; STAND BY ME
SIDE 2: WITHOUT HIM; WHERE COULD I GO BUT TO THE LORD; WHERE NO ONE STANDS ALONE; CRYING IN THE CHAPEL; HOW GREAT THOU ART (excerpt)

SPEEDWAY *RCA Victor (LPM/LSP-3989)*   1968
SIDE 1: SPEEDWAY; THERE AIN'T NOTHING LIKE A SONG (Duet with Nancy Sinatra); YOUR TIME HASN'T COME YET, BABY; WHO ARE YOU (WHO AM I); HE'S YOUR UNCLE, NOT YOUR DAD; LET YOURSELF GO
SIDE 2: YOUR GROOVY SELF (Nancy Sinatra solo); FIVE SLEEPY HEADS; WESTERN UNION; MINE; GOIN' HOME; SUPPOSE

SPINOUT *RCA Victor (LPM/LSP-3702)*   1966
SIDE 1: STOP, LOOK AND LISTEN; ADAM AND EVIL; ALL THAT I AM; NEVER SAY YES; AM I READY; BEACH SHACK
SIDE 2: SPINOUT; SMORGASBORD; I'LL BE BACK; TOMORROW IS A LONG TIME; DOWN IN THE ALLEY; I'LL REMEMBER YOU

SUN COLLECTION, THE *RCA English Import (HY-1001) and*
SUN SESSIONS, THE *RCA (AMP1-1675)*   1976
SIDE 1: THAT'S ALL RIGHT; BLUE MOON OF KENTUCKY; I DON'T CARE IF THE SUN DON'T SHINE; GOOD ROCKIN' TONIGHT; MILKCOW BLUES BOOGIE; YOU'RE A HEARTBREAKER; I'M LEFT, YOU'RE RIGHT, SHE'S GONE; BABY LET'S PLAY HOUSE
SIDE 2: MYSTERY TRAIN; I FORGOT TO REMEMBER TO FORGET; I'LL NEVER LET YOU GO; TRYIN' TO GET TO YOU; I LOVE YOU BECAUSE (standard version); BLUE MOON; JUST BECAUSE; I LOVE YOU BECAUSE (Newly discovered track)

NOTE: Although the English LP "The Sun Collection" was actually issued in 1975 in the U.K., it was not widely distributed in the U.S. until 1976.

THAT'S THE WAY IT IS *RCA (LSP-4445)*   1970
SIDE 1: I JUST CAN'T HELP BELIEVIN'; TWENTY DAYS AND TWENTY NIGHTS; HOW THE WEB WAS WOVEN; PATCH IT UP; MARY IN THE MORNING; YOU DON'T HAVE TO SAY YOU LOVE ME
SIDE 2: YOU'VE LOST THAT LOVIN' FEELIN'; I'VE LOST YOU; JUST PRETEND; STRANGER IN THE CROWD; THE NEXT STEP IS LOVE; BRIDGE OVER TROUBLED WATER

WELCOME TO MY WORLD *RCA Victor (APL1-2274)*   1977
SIDE 1: WELCOME TO MY WORLD; HELP ME MAKE IT THROUGH THE NIGHT; RELEASE ME (AND LET ME LOVE AGAIN); I REALLY DON'T WANT TO KNOW; FOR THE GOOD TIMES
SIDE 2: MAKE THE WORLD GO AWAY; GENTLE ON MY MIND; I'M SO LONESOME I COULD CRY; YOUR CHEATIN' HEART; I CAN'T STOP LOVING YOU (Unreleased live version)

WORLDWIDE 50 GOLD AWARD HITS, VOL. 1 *RCA*
(LPM-6401) *1970*
SIDE 1: HEARTBREAK HOTEL; I WAS THE ONE; I WANT YOU,
I NEED YOU, I LOVE YOU; DON'T BE CRUEL; HOUND
DOG; LOVE ME TENDER
SIDE 2: ANYWAY YOU WANT ME; TOO MUCH; PLAYING FOR
KEEPS; ALL SHOOK UP; THAT'S WHEN YOUR HEART-
ACHES BEGIN; LOVING YOU
SIDE 3: TEDDY BEAR; JAILHOUSE ROCK; TREAT ME NICE;
I BEG OF YOU; DON'T; WEAR MY RING AROUND YOUR
NECK: HARD HEADED WOMAN
SIDE 4: I GOT STUNG; A FOOL SUCH AS I; A BIG HUNK O' LOVE;
STUCK ON YOU; A MESS OF BLUES; IT'S NOW OR
NEVER
SIDE 5: I GOTTA KNOW; ARE YOU LONESOME TONIGHT; SUR-
RENDER; I FEEL SO BAD; LITTLE SISTER; CAN'T HELP
FALLING IN LOVE
SIDE 6: ROCK-A-HULA BABY; ANYTHING THAT'S PART OF YOU;
GOOD LUCK CHARM; SHE'S NOT YOU; RETURN TO
SENDER; WHERE DO YOU COME FROM; ONE BROKEN
HEART FOR SALE
SIDE 7: DEVIL IN DISGUISE; BOSSA NOVA BABY; KISSIN' COU-
SINS; VIVA LAS VEGAS; AIN'T THAT LOVING YOU
BABY; WOODEN HEART
SIDE 8: CRYING IN THE CHAPEL; IF I CAN DREAM; IN THE
GHETTO; SUSPICIOUS MINDS; DON'T CRY DADDY;
KENTUCKY RAIN; EXCERPTS FROM "ELVIS SAILS"

**WORLDWIDE GOLD AWARD HITS VOL. 2 – ELVIS : THE
OTHER SIDES** *RCA (LPM-6402)* *1971*
SIDE 1: PUPPET ON A STRING; WITCHCRAFT; TROUBLE; POOR
BOY; I WANT TO BE FREE; DONCHA' THINK IT'S TIME;
YOUNG DREAMS
SIDE 2: THE NEXT STEP IS LOVE; YOU DON'T HAVE TO SAY
YOU LOVE ME; PARALYZED; MY WISH CAME TRUE;
WHEN MY BLUE MOON TURNS TO GOLD AGAIN; LONE-
SOME COWBOY
SIDE 3: MY BABY LEFT ME; IT HURTS ME; I NEED YOUR LOVE
TONIGHT; TELL ME WHY; PLEASE DON'T DRAG THAT
STRING AROUND; YOUNG AND BEAUTIFUL
SIDE 4: HOT DOG; NEW ORLEANS; WE'RE GONNA MOVE; CRAW-
FISH; KING CREOLE; I BELIEVE IN THE MAN IN THE
SKY; DIXIELAND ROCK
SIDE 5: THE WONDER OF YOU; THEY REMIND ME TOO MUCH
OF YOU; MEAN WOMAN BLUES; LONELY MAN; ANY
DAY NOW; DON'T ASK ME WHY
SIDE 6: HIS LATEST FLAME; I REALLY DON'T WANT TO
KNOW; BABY I DON'T CARE; I'VE LOST YOU; LET ME;
LOVE ME
SIDE 7: GOT A LOT O' LIVIN' TO DO; FAME AND FORTUNE;
RIP IT UP; THERE GOES MY EVERYTHING; LOVER
DOLL; ONE NIGHT
SIDE 8: JUST TELL HER JIM SAID HELLO; ASK ME; PATCH IT
UP; AS LONG AS I HAVE YOU; YOU'LL THINK OF ME;
WILD IN THE COUNTRY

WORLDWIDE GOLD AWARD HITS, PARTS 1 & 2 *RCA
Record Club (R213690): Same as contents of WORLDWIDE
50 GOLD AWARD HITS, VOL. 1, sides 1, 2, 3 and 4.*

WORLDWIDE GOLD AWARD HITS, PARTS 3 & 4 *RCA
Record Club (R214657): Same as contents of WORLDWIDE
50 GOLD AWARD HITS, VOL. 1, sides 5, 6, 7 and 8.*

YOU'LL NEVER WALK ALONE *RCA Camden (CALX-2472)*
1971
SIDE 1: YOU'LL NEVER WALK ALONE; WHO AM I; LET US
PRAY; PEACE IN THE VALLEY; WE CALL ON HIM
SIDE 2: I BELIEVE; IT IS NO SECRET; SING YOU CHILDREN;
TAKE MY HAND PRECIOUS LORD

IDENTIFICATION OF FIRST, SECOND AND THIRD PRESSINGS OF LONG PLAY LABELS

CATALOG NUMBER-LP TITLE	FIRST PRESSING	SECOND	THIRD
LPM-1254 ELVIS PRESLEY	LONG PLAY	MONO	MONAURAL
LSP-1254 ELVIS PRESLEY	SILVER LOGO	WHITE LOGO	ORANGE
LPM-1382 ELVIS	LONG PLAY	MONO	MONAURAL
LSP-1382 ELVIS	SILVER LOGO	WHITE LOGO	ORANGE
LPM-1515 LOVING YOU	LONG PLAY	MONO	MONAURAL
LSP-1515 LOVING YOU	SILVER LOGO	WHITE LOGO	ORANGE
LOC-1035 ELVIS' CHRISTMAS ALBUM	LONG PLAY	—	—
LPM-1707 ELVIS' GOLDEN RECORDS	LONG PLAY	MONO	MONAURAL
LSP-1707 ELVIS' GOLDEN RECORDS	SILVER LOGO	WHITE LOGO	ORANGE
LPM-1884 KING CREOLE	LONG PLAY	MONO	MONAURAL
LSP-1884 KING CREOLE	SILVER LOGO	WHITE LOGO	ORANGE
LPM-1951 ELVIS' CHRISTMAS ALBUM	LONG PLAY	MONO	MONAURAL
LSP-1951 ELVIS' CHRISTMAS ALBUM	WHITE LOGO	—	—
LPM-1990 FOR LP FANS ONLY	LONG PLAY	MONO	MONAURAL
LSP-1990 FOR LP FANS ONLY	WHITE LOGO	ORANGE	NEW BLACK
LPM-2011 A DATE WITH ELVIS	LONG PLAY	MONO	MONAURAL
LSP-2011 A DATE WITH ELVIS	WHITE LOGO	ORANGE	NEW BLACK
LPM-2075 ELVIS GOLD RECORDS VOL. 2	LONG PLAY	MONO	MONAURAL
LSP-2075 ELVIS GOLD RECORDS VOL. 2	SILVER LOGO	WHITE LOGO	ORANGE
LPM-2231 ELVIS IS BACK	LONG PLAY	MONO	MONAURAL
LSP-2231 ELVIS IS BACK	LIVING STEREO	STEREO	ORANGE
LPM-2256 G.I. BLUES	LONG PLAY	MONO	MONAURAL
LSP-2256 G.I. BLUES	LIVING STEREO	STEREO	ORANGE
LPM-2328 HIS HAND IN MINE	LONG PLAY	MONO	MONAURAL
LSP-2328 HIS HAND IN MINE	LIVING STEREO	STEREO	ORANGE
LPM-2370 SOMETHING FOR EVERYBODY	LONG PLAY	MONO	MONAURAL
LSP-2370 SOMETHING FOR EVERYBODY	LIVING STEREO	STEREO	ORANGE
LPM-2426 BLUE HAWAII	LONG PLAY	MONO	MONAURAL
LSP-2426 BLUE HAWAII	LIVING STEREO	STEREO	ORANGE
LPM-2523 POT LUCK	LONG PLAY	MONO	MONAURAL
LSP-2523 POT LUCK	LIVING STEREO	STEREO	ORANGE
LPM-2621 GIRLS! GIRLS! GIRLS!	LONG PLAY	MONO	MONAURAL
LSP-2621 GIRLS! GIRLS! GIRLS!	LIVING STEREO	STEREO	ORANGE
LPM-2697 AT THE WORLD'S FAIR	LONG PLAY	MONO	MONAURAL
LSP-2697 AT THE WORLD'S FAIR	LIVING STEREO	STEREO	NEW BLACK
LPM-2756 FUN IN ACAPULCO	MONO	MONAURAL	ORANGE
LSP-2756 FUN IN ACAPULCO	SILVER TOP STEREO	WHITE TOP STEREO	ORANGE
LPM-2765 ELVIS' GOLD VOL. 3	MONO	MONAURAL	ORANGE
LSP-2765 ELVIS' GOLD VOL. 3	SILVER TOP STEREO	WHITE TOP STEREO	ORANGE
LPM-2894 KISSIN' COUSINS	MONO	MONAURAL	ORANGE
LSP-2894 KISSIN' COUSINS	SILVER TOP STEREO	WHITE TOP STEREO	ORANGE
LPM-2999 ROUSTABOUT	MONO	MONAURAL	ORANGE
LSP-2999 ROUSTABOUT	SILVER TOP STEREO	WHITE TOP STEREO	ORANGE
LPM-3338 GIRL HAPPY	MONAURAL	ORANGE	NEW BLACK
LSP-3338 GIRL HAPPY	STEREO	ORANGE	NEW BLACK
LPM-3450 ELVIS FOR EVERYONE	MONAURAL	ORANGE	NEW BLACK
LSP-3450 ELVIS FOR EVERYONE	STEREO	ORANGE	NEW BLACK
LPM-3468 HARUM SCARUM	MONAURAL	—	—
LSP-3468 HARUM SCARUM	STEREO	NEW BLACK	—
LPM-3553 FRANKIE AND JOHNNY	MONAURAL	—	—
LSP-3553 FRANKIE AND JOHNNY	STEREO	NEW BLACK	—

CATALOG NUMBER-LP TITLE	FIRST PRESSING	SECOND	THIRD
LPM-3643 PARADISE HAWAIIAN STYLE	MONAURAL	–	–
LSP-3643 PARADISE HAWAIIAN STYLE	STEREO	ORANGE	NEW BLACK
LPM-3702 SPINOUT	MONAURAL	–	–
LSP-3702 SPINOUT	STEREO	NEW BLACK	–
LPM-3758 HOW GREAT THOU ART	MONAURAL	–	–
LSP-3758 HOW GREAT THOU ART	STEREO	ORANGE	NEW BLACK
LPM-3787 DOUBLE TROUBLE	MONAURAL	–	–
LSP-3787 DOUBLE TROUBLE	STEREO	NEW BLACK	–
LPM-3893 CLAMBAKE	MONAURAL	–	–
LSP-3893 CLAMBAKE	STEREO	NEW BLACK	–
LPM-3921 ELVIS' GOLD VOL. 4	MONAURAL	–	–
LSP-3921 ELVIS' GOLD VOL. 4	STEREO	ORANGE	NEW BLACK
LPM-3989 SPEEDWAY	MONAURAL	–	–
LSP-3989 SPEEDWAY	STEREO	ORANGE	NEW BLACK
LPM-4088 ELVIS (TV SPECIAL)	ORANGE	NEW BLACK	–
LSP-4155 FROM ELVIS IN MEMPHIS	ORANGE	NEW BLACK	–
LSP-6020 MEMPHIS TO VEGAS	ORANGE	NEW BLACK	–
LSP-4362 ON STAGE - FEBRUARY, 1970	ORANGE	NEW BLACK	–
LPM-6401 WORLDWIDE 50 GOLD	ORANGE	NEW BLACK	–
LSP-4428 AT INTERNATIONAL HOTEL	ORANGE	NEW BLACK	–
LSP-4429 BACK IN MEMPHIS	ORANGE	NEW BLACK	–
LSP-4445 THAT'S THE WAY IT IS	ORANGE	NEW BLACK	–
LSP-4460 ELVIS COUNTRY	ORANGE	NEW BLACK	–
LSP-4530 LOVE LETTERS	ORANGE	NEW BLACK	–
LPM-6402 THE OTHER SIDES	ORANGE	NEW BLACK	–
LSP-4579 WONDERFUL WORLD OF XMAS	ORANGE	NEW BLACK	–
LSP-4671 ELVIS NOW	ORANGE	NEW BLACK	–
LSP-4690 HE TOUCHED ME	ORANGE	NEW BLACK	–
LSP-4776 AT MADISON SQUARE GARDEN	ORANGE	NEW BLACK	–
VPSX-6089 ALOHA FROM HAWAII	RED	NEW BLACK	
APL1-0283 ELVIS	ORANGE	–	–
APL1-0388 RAISED ON ROCK	ORANGE	NEW BLACK	–
CPL1-0341 LEGENDARY VOL. 1	CUSTOM BLACK	–	–
CPL1-0475 GOOD TIMES	ORANGE	NEW BLACK	–
APD1-0606 LIVE IN MEMPHIS	ORANGE	NEW BLACK	–
CPM1-0818 HAVING FUN WITH ELVIS	ORANGE	NEW BLACK	–
APL1-0873 PROMISED LAND	ORANGE	NEW BLACK	–
ANL1-0971 PURE GOLD	ORANGE	NEW BLACK	–
APL1-1039 TODAY	ORANGE	NEW BLACK	–
CPL1-1349 LEGENDARY VOL. 2	CUSTOM BLACK	–	–
ANL1-1319 HIS HAND IN MINE	ORANGE	NEW BLACK	–
AMP1-1675 THE SUN SESSIONS	TAN	NEW BLACK	–
APL1-1506 ELVIS PRESLEY BLVD.	TAN	NEW BLACK	–
APL1-2274 WELCOME TO MY WORLD	NEW BLACK	–	–
AFL1-2428 MOODY BLUE	NEW BLACK	–	–
APL2-2587 ELVIS IN CONCERT	CUSTOM BLUE	–	–
AFL1-2772 HE WALKS BESIDE ME	NEW BLACK	–	–
CPL1-2901 ELVIS SINGS FOR CHILDREN	NEW BLACK	–	–
CPL1-3078 LEGENDARY VOL. 3	PICTURE DISC	–	–
CPL1-3082 LEGENDARY VOL. 3	CUSTOM BLACK	–	–
AQL1-3279 OUR MEMORIES OF ELVIS	NEW BLACK	–	–
AQL1-3448 OUR MEMORIES VOL. 2	NEW BLACK	–	–

Key to label descriptions used on this chart:

LONG PLAY: Original black RCA label with the term "Long 33 1/3 Play" at the bottom of the label.

MONO: The term "Mono" appears at the bottom of the label.

MONAURAL: The word "Monaural" appears at the bottom of the label.

SILVER LOGO: The circular words "RCA Victor" are in silver print around the top of the label.

WHITE LOGO: The circular words "RCA Victor" are in white print around the top of the label.

LIVING STEREO: The words "Living Stereo" appear at the bottom of the label.

STEREO: The word "Stereo" appears at the bottom of the label.

ORANGE: RCA's orange label.

NEW BLACK: The current style black label being used by RCA.

Note: Some albums may have been pressed on the tan label in 1976, prior to the switchover to the new black label. There is no satisfactory documentation as to which ones were repressed on tan labels.

ELVIS' TV APPEARANCES

Here is a complete listing of guest television appearances made by Elvis, along with the air dates and songs he sang.

JANUARY 28, 1956: *THE JACKIE GLEASON STAGE SHOW STARRING TOMMY & JIMMY DORSEY*

Elvis sang "Blue Suede Shoes" and "Heartbreak Hotel." The Dorsey Brothers orchestra provided a most unusual backing for "Heartbreak Hotel" on this show.

FEBRUARY 4, 1956: *THE JACKIE GLEASON STAGE SHOW STARRING TOMMY & JIMMY DORSEY*

Elvis sang "Tutti Frutti" and "I Was The One."

FEBRUARY 11, 1956: *THE JACKIE GLEASON STAGE SHOW STARRING TOMMY & JIMMY DORSEY*

Elvis sang "Shake, Rattle And Roll" with a portion of "Flip, Flop And Fly" thrown in at the ending. A medley is thus made of the two Joe Turner hits. He then sang "I Got A Woman."

FEBRUARY 18, 1956: *THE JACKIE GLEASON STAGE SHOW STARRING TOMMY & JIMMY DORSEY*

Elvis sang "Baby Let's Play House," the only time in the fifties he performed one of his original Sun recordings. He then sang "Tutti Frutti."

MARCH 17, 1956: *THE JACKIE GLEASON STAGE SHOW STARRING TOMMY & JIMMY DORSEY*

Elvis sang "Blue Suede Shoes" and "Heartbreak Hotel," the same two songs he performed on his first TV appearance.

MARCH 24, 1956: *THE JACKIE GLEASON STAGE SHOW STARRING TOMMY & JIMMY DORSEY*

Elvis sang "Money Honey" and "Heartbreak Hotel."

APRIL 3, 1956: *THE MILTON BERLE SHOW*

Elvis sang "Heartbreak Hotel," "Money Honey" and "Blue Suede Shoes."

JUNE 5, 1956: *THE MILTON BERLE SHOW*

Elvis sang "Hound Dog" and used the bump and grind blues style ending. This was not the first time he had ended the song in that style, however, as we have heard recordings made while on the Louisiana Hayride that have Elvis doing his famous ending to this song. As you know, his live concert albums from the seventies prove that he still got a kick out of this rendition of "Hound Dog." The second and last song done on this show was "I Want You, I Need You, I Love You."

JULY 1, 1956: *THE STEVE ALLEN SHOW*

Elvis sang "I Want You, I Need You, I Love You" and "Hound Dog." It was on this show that Elvis was dressed in the tuxedo and tails, and was persueded to sing the song to a live hound dog. Elvis then joined the cast in a cowboy comedy routine, as "Tumbleweed Presley," wherein he sings a verse of a song that we can only title "Yippie Yi Yo."

SEPTEMBER 9, 1956: *ED SULLIVAN'S TOAST OF THE TOWN SHOW*

Elvis sang "Don't Be Cruel," "Love Me Tender," Reddy Teddy" and "Hound Dog."

OCTOBER 28, 1956: *ED SULLIVAN'S TOAST OF THE TOWN SHOW*

Elvis sang "Don't Be Cruel," "Love Me Tender," "Love Me" and "Hound Dog."

JANUARY 6, 1957: *ED SULLIVAN'S TOAST OF THE TOWN SHOW*

Elvis sang "Hound Dog," "Love Me Tender," "Heartbreak Hotel," "Don't Be Cruel," "Too Much," "When My Blue Moon Turns To Gold Again" and "Peace In The Valley." It was on this broadcast of the Sullivan show that Elvis was filmed only from the waist up.

MARCH 26, 1960: *THE FRANK SINATRA (TIMEX) SPECIAL*

Elvis sang the opening line "It's very nice to go traveling, but it's oh so nice to come home," afterwhich the rest of the cast completed the tune. He then sang "Fame and Fortune" and "Stuck On You," followed by a few lines of "Witchcraft" in a duet with Frank Sinatra (who sang "Love Me Tender).

ELVIS' TAPES

PRE-RECORDED REEL TO REEL TAPES AT 7½ INCHES PER SECOND SPEED:

- ☐ ELVIS IS BACK (FTP-1024)
- ☐ G.I. BLUES (FTP-1045)
- ☐ SOMETHING FOR EVERYBODY (FTP-1084)
- ☐ BLUE HAWAII (FTP-1132)
- ☐ POT LUCK (FTP-1137)
- ☐ GIRLS! GIRLS! GIRLS! (FTP-1173)
- ☐ IT HAPPENED AT THE WORLD'S FAIR (FTP-1199)
- ☐ FUN IN ACAPULCO (FTP-1226)
- ☐ ELVIS' GOLDEN RECORDS VOLUME 3 (FTP-1228)
- ☐ KISSIN' COUSINS (FTP-1269)
- ☐ ROUSTABOUT (FTP-1291)
- ☐ GIRL HAPPY (FTP-1297)
- ☐ HIS HAND IN MINE (FTP-1320)
- ☐ HARUM SCARUM (FTP-1321)
- ☐ FRANKIE AND JOHNNY (FTP-1326)

The following five reel tapes were not manufactured by RCA, but *were* authorized by them. Production was done by Magtec, of Hollywood, California, probably on a one-year contract with RCA.

- ☐ ELVIS AS RECORDED AT MADISON SQUARE GARDEN (EPPA-4776C)
- ☐ ALOHA FROM HAWAII VIA SATELLITE (EPPB-6089-P-DP) [stereo]
- ☐ ALOHA FROM HAWAII VIA SATELLITE (EPQB-6089-QM-DP) [quad]
- ☐ ELVIS (EPPI-0283C)
- ☐ RAISED ON ROCK (EPPI-0388C)

PRE-RECORDED REEL TO REEL TAPES AT 3¾ INCHES PER SECOND SPEED:

- ☐ ELVIS (TV SPECIAL) (TP3-1008)
- ☐ FROM ELVIS IN MEMPHIS (TP3-1013)
- ☐ ON STAGE - FEBRUARY, 1970 (TP3-1043)
- ☐ G.I. BLUES (TP3-1052)
- ☐ ELVIS' GOLDEN RECORDS VOLUME 3 (TP3-1054)
- ☐ ELVIS COUNTRY (TP3-1066)
- ☐ LOVE LETTERS FROM ELVIS (TP3-1072)
- ☐ THAT'S THE WAY IT IS (TP3-1062)
- ☐ ELVIS FOR EVERYONE/PARADISE HAWAIIAN STYLE (TP3-5019)
- ☐ SPINOUT/DOUBLE TROUBLE (TP3-5034)
- ☐ FROM MEMPHIS TO VEGAS/FROM VEGAS TO MEMPHIS (TP3-5077)

As the popularity of reel to reel tapes began to give way to the smaller, more convenient, cassettes and 8-track cartridges, RCA geared up to meet the demand by issuing all of Elvis' post-army albums on both 8-track and cassette tapes.

Even though "stereo" was the byword, one of Elvis' pre-army LPs was even included in the new tape line ("Elvis' Golden Records"). The other earlier albums, which were not recorded in true stereo, were never made available on tapes.

Just as reel-to-reel tapes are nearly a thing of the past, as far as commercial sales of pre-recorded albums are concerned, it seems that 8-track tapes will soon begin to fade. The bulky cartridge and annoying change of tracks, sometimes in the midst of a song, cannot compete with the far superior cassette. It would seem, perhaps, that one with an interest in collecting the 8-tracks should get them while they're still easily available.

There hasn't been enough collector interest and trading of Elvis' reel tapes to either justify pricing them, or, in fact, to provide necessary information on which pricing could be estimated.

The only tape releases that are heavily sought after by Elvis record collectors are listed next, complete with pricing.

ELVIS PRESLEY SPECIAL CHRISTMAS PROGRAM *(RCA* ☐ *EPC-1)* Full Track @ 7½ inches per second   80.00   240.00

Here is the complete Elvis Christmas special that was aired nationally December 3, 1967. This reel tape was packaged in its own special box and includes a custom, full color, insert containing the entire script for the program.

WORLDWIDE 50 GOLD AWARD HITS, VOL. 1 (BOX SET)

RCA *(P8S-6401) for 8-track tapes* 40.00 160.00
RCA *(PK-6401) for cassettes* 50.00 200.00

In an unusual move, RCA packaged the two tapes in a box set, pretty much like the four-LP box only larger. The tape box sets included the same bonus photo booklet as buyers of the LP sets received.

As of press time, we have learned of a set of the 24 reel tapes used for the original 1971 broadcast of "The Elvis Presley Story" being offered for sale.

Since the emphisis among collectors has always been on the disc version of this program, and since we know of no previous sales of the tapes, we cannot accurately offer pricing on the tape set at this time.

Perhaps, if the tapes sell or are traded, we will have a basis for pricing that can be included in the second edition of this guide.

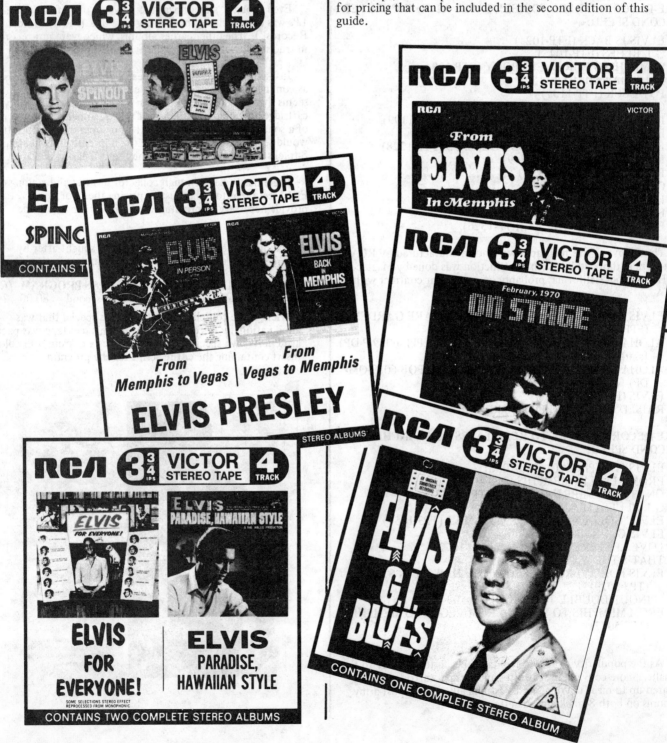

COMPLETE LISTING OF ELVIS' SONGS

Unlike anything we've ever seen in print before, this section gives you an analysis of every song that Elvis has had on record. The format is kept simple, making for easy reference. All song titles are alphabetical, exactly as they read on the actual record. Titles that begin with the article THE are listed in that proper sequence, under the letter "T."

Using a sample of our layout, here is what you'll find in this chapter:

COMPLETE SONG TITLE (Composer, full names when known)

RECORDED: Month and year Elvis first recorded the song for records. In nearly every case, this date will be correct. There are, however, a few recording dates that cannot yet be pinpointed. In those instances, our date should not be more than one month off. As more information surfaces on Elvis' recordings, those dates should become known, and, of course, reported in the second edition of this book.

RELEASED: Month and year that Elvis' first recording of the song appeared commercially in the United States. Advance promotional releases and special pressings are disregraded in this section.

FIRST APPEARANCE: A description of the first release of the song, be it single, EP or LP. We have chosen to identify monaural and stereo differences, but have not gone so far as to identify 33-compacts, Living Stereo 45s and quad LP releases. These items are thouroughly covered in other chapters of this book.

HIT PRIOR TO ELVIS: A listing of previous, nationally charted, versions of the song. Our guidelines limit information contained here pretty much to the forties, fifties, sixties and seventies. When possible, we relate data from the earlier years.

HIT AFTER ELVIS: A listing of nationally charted versions of the song after Elvis had recorded his version, even if his version had not yet been released.

OTHER SIGNIFICANT RECORDINGS: Here we will list any other versions of the song, usually not of "hit" status, that we feel would be of interest. In cases where there are other songs using the same title, but different in content, we will relate that to you.

A BIG HUNK O' LOVE (Sid Wyche - Aaron Schroeder)

RECORDED: June, 1958
RELEASED: July, 1959
FIRST APPEARANCE: RCA Victor (45rpm single) 47-7600
HIT PRIOR TO ELVIS: None
HIT AFTER ELVIS: None
OTHER SIGNIFICANT RECORDINGS: None

A BOY LIKE ME, A GIRL LIKE YOU (Sid Tepper - Roy C. Bennett)

RECORDED: March, 1962
RELEASED: November, 1962
FIRST APPEARANCE: RCA Victor (LP) LPM-2621 (mono) and LSP-2621 (stereo) GIRLS! GIRLS! GIRLS!
HIT PRIOR TO ELVIS: None
HIT AFTER ELVIS: None
OTHER SIGNIFICANT RECORDINGS: None

A DOG'S LIFE (Sid Wayne - Ben Weisman)

RECORDED: August, 1965
RELEASED: June, 1966
FIRST APPEARANCE: RCA Victor (LP) LPM-3643 (mono) and LSP-3643 (stereo) PARADISE HAWAIIAN STYLE
HIT PRIOR TO ELVIS: None
HIT AFTER ELVIS: None
OTHER SIGNIFICANT RECORDINGS: None

(NOW AND THEN THERE'S) A FOOL SUCH AS I (Bill Trader)

RECORDED: June, 1958
RELEASED: March, 1959
FIRST APPEARANCE: RCA Victor (45rpm single) 47-7506)
HIT PRIOR TO ELVIS: December, 1952 by Hank Snow (RCA Victor 47-5034); February, 1953 by Jo Stafford (Columbia 39930)
HIT AFTER ELVIS: December, 1973 by Bob Dylan (Columbia 45982); December, 1978 by Bill Green (NSD-11)
OTHER SIGNIFICANT RECORDINGS: February, 1953 by The Robins (RCA Victor 47-5175).

A HOUSE THAT HAS EVERYTHING (Sid Tepper - Roy C. Bennett)

RECORDED: February, 1967
RELEASED: November, 1967
FIRST APPEARANCE: RCA Victor (LP) LPM-3893 (mono) and LSP-3893 (stereo) CLAMBAKE
HIT PRIOR TO ELVIS: None
HIT AFTER ELVIS: None
OTHER SIGNIFICANT RECORDINGS: None

A LITTLE BIT OF GREEN (Arnold - Morrow - Martin)

RECORDED: January, 1969
RELEASED: November, 1969
FIRST APPEARANCE: RCA (LP) LSP-6020 (stereo) FROM MEMPHIS TO VEGAS/FROM VEGAS TO MEMPHIS
HIT PRIOR TO ELVIS: None
HIT AFTER ELVIS: None
OTHER SIGNIFICANT RECORDINGS: None

A LITTLE LESS CONVERSATION (Scott "Mac" Davis - Strange)

RECORDED: March, 1968
RELEASED: September, 1968
FIRST APPEARANCE: RCA Victor (45rpm single) 47-9610
HIT PRIOR TO ELVIS: None
HIT AFTER ELVIS: None
OTHER SIGNIFICANT RECORDINGS: None

A MESS OF BLUES (Doc Pomus - Mort Shuman)

RECORDED: March, 1960
RELEASED: July, 1960
FIRST APPEARANCE: RCA Victor (45rpm single) 47-7777
HIT PRIOR TO ELVIS: None
HIT AFTER ELVIS: None
OTHER SIGNIFICANT RECORDINGS: None

A THING CALLED LOVE (Jerry "Reed" Hubbard)

RECORDED: May, 1971
RELEASED: April, 1972
FIRST APPEARANCE: RCA (LP) LSP-4690 (stereo)
  HE TOUCHED ME
HIT PRIOR TO ELVIS: March, 1968 by Jimmy Dean
  (RCA Victor 47-9454); January, 1972 by Johnny Cash
  (Columbia 45534)
HIT AFTER ELVIS: None, although Johnny Cash did
  actually record his version *after* Elvis recorded the song.
  The Cash single was, however, issued prior to the Elvis
  album.
OTHER SIGNIFICANT RECORDINGS: August, 1969 by
  Jerry Reed (RCA 74-0242)

A WHISTLING TUNE (Hal David - Sherman Edwards)

RECORDED: November, 1961
RELEASED: August, 1962
FIRST APPEARANCE: RCA Victor (EP) EPA-4371 (mono)
  KID GALAHAD
HIT PRIOR TO ELVIS: None
HIT AFTER ELVIS: None
OTHER SIGNIFICANT RECORDINGS: None

A WORLD OF OUR OWN (Bill Giant - Bernie Baum - Florence
  Kaye)
RECORDED: October, 1962
RELEASED: March, 1963
FIRST APPEARANCE: RCA Victor (LP) LPM-2697 (mono)
  and LSP-2697 (stereo) IT HAPPENED AT THE WORLD'S
  FAIR
HIT PRIOR TO ELVIS: None
HIT AFTER ELVIS: None, however in 1965 The Seekers did
  have a hit with a completely different song that had the
  same title as this Elvis tune (Capitol 5430).
OTHER SIGNIFICANT RECORDINGS: None

ADAM AND EVIL (Fred Wise - Randy Starr)

RECORDED: February, 1966
RELEASED: October, 1966
FIRST APPEARANCE: RCA Victor (LP) LPM-3702 (mono)
  and LSP-3702 (stereo) SPINOUT
HIT PRIOR TO ELVIS: None
HIT AFTER ELVIS: None
OTHER SIGNIFICANT RECORDINGS: None

AFTER LOVING YOU (E. Miller - J. Lantz)

RECORDED: February, 1969
RELEASED: May, 1969
FIRST APPEARANCE: RCA (LP) LSP-4155 (stereo)
  FROM ELVIS IN MEMPHIS
HIT PRIOR TO ELVIS: None
HIT AFTER ELVIS: None
OTHER SIGNIFICANT RECORDINGS: September, 1962,
  this song appeared on the flip side of BIG LOVE, by Joe
  Henderson (Todd 1077), a minor hit.

AIN'T THAT LOVING YOU BABY (Clyde Otis - Ivory Joe
  Hunter)
RECORDED: June, 1958
RELEASED: September, 1964
FIRST APPEARANCE: RCA Victor (45rpm single) 47-8840
HIT PRIOR TO ELVIS: None
HIT AFTER ELVIS: None
OTHER SIGNIFICANT RECORDINGS: None, however it is
  important to not confuse this song with the January 1956
  hit by Jimmy Reed titled AIN'T THAT *LOVIN'* YOU
  BABY, a completely different song (Vee Jay 168).

ALL I NEEDED WAS THE RAIN (Fred Wise - Ben Weisman)

RECORDED: October, 1967
RELEASED: November, 1968
FIRST APPEARANCE: RCA (LP) PRS-279 (stereo)
  SINGER PRESENTS ELVIS SINGING FLAMING STAR
  AND OTHERS
HIT PRIOR TO ELVIS: None
HIT AFTER ELVIS: None
OTHER SIGNIFICANT RECORDINGS: None

ALL SHOOK UP (Otis Blackwell - Elvis Presley)

RECORDED: January, 1957
RELEASED: March, 1957
FIRST APPEARANCE: RCA Victor (45rpm single) 47-6870
  and (78rpm single) 20-6870
HIT PRIOR TO ELVIS: None
HIT AFTER ELVIS: September, 1974 by Suzi Quatro
  (Bell 45, 477)
OTHER SIGNIFICANT RECORDINGS: November, 1977
  by the song's co-writer, Otis Blackwell, on his LP
  THESE ARE MY SONGS (Inner City 1032).

ALL THAT I AM (Sid Tepper - Roy C. Bennett)

RECORDED: February, 1966
RELEASED: October, 1966
FIRST APPEARANCE: RCA Victor (45rpm single) 47-8941
HIT PRIOR TO ELVIS: None
HIT AFTER ELVIS: None
OTHER SIGNIFICANT RECORDINGS: None

ALMOST (Florence Kaye - Ben Weisman)

RECORDED: October, 1968
RELEASED: April, 1970
FIRST APPEARANCE: RCA Camden (LP) CAS-2408
  LET'S BE FRIENDS
HIT PRIOR TO ELVIS: None
HIT AFTER ELVIS: None
OTHER SIGNIFICANT RECORDINGS: None

ALMOST ALWAYS TRUE (Fred Wise - Ben Weisman)

RECORDED: March, 1961
RELEASED: October, 1961
FIRST APPEARANCE: RCA Victor (LP) LPM-2426 (mono)
  and LSP-2426 (stereo) BLUE HAWAII
HIT PRIOR TO ELVIS: None
HIT AFTER ELVIS: None
OTHER SIGNIFICANT RECORDINGS: None

ALOHA OE (Hawaiian Traditional - Adapted and Arranged by
  Elvis Presley)
RECORDED: March, 1961
RELEASED: October, 1961
FIRST APPEARANCE: RCA Victor (LP) LPM-2426 (mono)
  and LSP-2426 (stereo) BLUE HAWAII
HIT PRIOR TO ELVIS: None
OTHER SIGNIFICANT RECORDINGS: December, 1957 by
  Marty Robbins on his LP SONG OF THE ISLANDS (Colum-
  bia CL-1087). Also included, no doubt, on dozens of
  Hawaiian music albums.

**ALSO SPRACH ZARATHUSTRA (THEME FROM "2001: A
  SPACE ODYSSEY")** (Richard Strauss)
Although Elvis never sang to this music, it is included in this
section because it was used for his in-concert introduction
and, as such, appeared on several of his recordings.

FIRST APPEARANCE: June, 1972 - RCA (LP) LSP-4776
  ELVIS AS RECORDED AT MADISON SQUARE GARDEN
  (stereo)
HIT PRIOR TO ELVIS: June, 1968 on the original sound-
  track 2001: A SPACE ODYSSEY (MGM-13)
HIT AFTER ELVIS: January, 1973 by Deodato (CTI-12)
OTHER SIGNIFICANT RECORDINGS: None

ALWAYS ON MY MIND (Wayne Carson - Mark James - Johnny
  Christopher)
RECORDED: March, 1972
RELEASED: November, 1972
FIRST APPEARANCE: RCA (45rpm single) 74-0815
HIT PRIOR TO ELVIS: June, 1972 by Brenda Lee
  (Decca 32975)
HIT AFTER ELVIS: None, although Brenda Lee actually
  recorded her version *after* Elvis' recording. Her single was
  issued five months earlier than his, however.

AM I READY (Sid Tepper - Roy C. Bennett)

RECORDED: February, 1966
RELEASED: October, 1966
FIRST APPEARANCE: RCA Victor (LP) LPM-3702 (mono)
  and LSP-3702 (stereo)
HIT PRIOR TO ELVIS: None
HIT AFTER ELVIS: None
OTHER SIGNIFICANT RECORDINGS: None

AM I TO BE THE ONE - This song is listed here since there have
  been some collectors who thought Elvis sang along with Jerry
  Lee Lewis on this Sun recording. The singer on the track with
  Jerry Lee is Charlie Rich! Elvis is *not* heard on this song!

AMAZING GRACE (Traditional - Arranged and Adapted by
  Elvis Presley)
RECORDED: March, 1971
RELEASED: April, 1972
FIRST APPEARANCE: RCA (LP) LSP-4690 (stereo)
HIT PRIOR TO ELVIS: November, 1970 by Judy Collins
  (Elektra 45709)
HIT AFTER ELVIS: May, 1972 by The Pipes and Drums and
  the Military Band of the Royal Scots Dragoon Guards
  (RCA 74-0709)
OTHER SIGNIFICANT RECORDINGS: Contained in count-
  less sacred and religious albums.
NOTE: This song should never be confused with "Amazing Grace"
(Used To Be Her Favorite Song) by the Amazing Rhythm Aces. They
are two completely different songs.

AMEN (John W. Pate Sr. - Curtis Mayfield)
Elvis never sang this song in its entirety; rather in a sort of
medley at the end of "I Got A Woman" during his concert
appearances. For that reason it is included in this section.

FIRST APPEARANCE: June, 1974 - RCA (LP) CPL1-0606
(stereo) ELVIS RECORDED LIVE ON STAGE IN MEMPHIS.
HIT PRIOR TO ELVIS: November, 1964 by The Impressions
  (ABC Paramount 10602); June, 1968 by Otis Redding
  (Atco 6592)
HIT AFTER ELVIS: None
OTHER SIGNIFICANT RECORDINGS: None
NOTE: The song was originally written by The Impressions and record-
ed by them as a Christmas song. Even though Elvis sang the song many
different ways, he never —to our knowledge— included the lyrics that
pertain to Christmas.

AMERICA (THE BEAUTIFUL) (Traditional - Arranged and
  Adapted by Elvis Presley)
RECORDED: In concert - 1976 or 1977 performance
RELEASED: November, 1977
FIRST APPEARANCE: RCA (45rpm single) PB-11165
HIT PRIOR TO ELVIS: None
HIT AFTER ELVIS: None
OTHER SIGNIFICANT RECORDINGS: None, although
  hasn't everyone sung this at one time or another? Elvis
  began using it in concert in conjunction with the U.S.
  bi-centenial.

AN AMERICAN TRILOGY (Traditional - Arranged by Mickey
  Newbury)
RECORDED: February, 1972 in concert at the Hilton Hotel,
  Las Vegas, Nevada.
RELEASED: May, 1972
FIRST APPEARANCE: RCA (45rpm single) 74-0672
HIT PRIOR TO ELVIS: October, 1971 by Mickey Newbury
  (Elektra 45750)
HIT AFTER ELVIS: None
OTHER SIGNIFICANT RECORDINGS: None

AN EVENING PRAYER (C. M. Battersby - Charles H. Gabriel)

RECORDED: May, 1971
RELEASED: April, 1972
FIRST APPEARANCE: RCA (LP) LSP-4690) HE TOUCHED
  ME (stereo)
HIT PRIOR TO ELVIS: None
HIT AFTER ELVIS: None
OTHER SIGNIFICANT RECORDINGS: None

AND I LOVE YOU SO (Don McLean)

RECORDED: March, 1975
RELEASED: May, 1975
FIRST APPEARANCE: RCA (LP) APL1-1039 TODAY (stereo)
HIT PRIOR TO ELVIS: April, 1971 by Bobby Goldsboro (United Artists 50776); April, 1973 by Perry Como (RCA 74-0906)
HIT AFTER ELVIS: None
OTHER SIGNIFICANT RECORDINGS: None

AND THE GRASS WON'T PAY NO MIND (Neil Diamond)

RECORDED: February, 1969
RELEASED: November, 1969
FIRST APPEARANCE: RCA (LP) LSP-6020 (stereo) FROM MEMPHIS TO VEGAS/FROM VEGAS TO MEMPHIS
HIT PRIOR TO ELVIS: August, 1970 by Mark Lindsay (Columbia 45229)
HIT AFTER ELVIS: None
OTHER SIGNIFICANT RECORDINGS: April, 1970 by Neil Diamond, the song's composer, on the flip side of "Soolaimon" (UNI 55224)

ANGEL (Sid Tepper - Roy C. Bennett)

RECORDED: July, 1961
RELEASED: April, 1962
FIRST APPEARANCE: RCA Victor (EP) EPA-4368 FOLLOW THAT DREAM (mono)
HIT PRIOR TO ELVIS: None
HIT AFTER ELVIS: None
OTHER SIGNIFICANT RECORDINGS: None, although there have been several other, completely different, songs using the same title.

ANIMAL INSTINCT (Bill Giant - Bernie Baum - Florence Kaye)

RECORDED: February, 1965
RELEASED: October, 1965
FIRST APPEARANCE: RCA Victor (LP) LPM-3468 (mono) and LSP-3468 (stereo)
HIT PRIOR TO ELVIS: None
HIT AFTER ELVIS: None
OTHER SIGNIFICANT RECORDINGS: None

ANY DAY NOW (Bob Hillard - Burt Bacharach)

RECORDED: February, 1969
RELEASED: April, 1969
FIRST APPEARANCE: RCA (45rpm single) 47-9741
HIT PRIOR TO ELVIS: April, 1962 by Chuck Jackson (Wand 122); March, 1969 by Percy Sledge (Atlantic 2616)
HIT AFTER ELVIS: None
OTHER SIGNIFICANT RECORDINGS: None

ANY WAY YOU WANT ME (THAT'S HOW I'LL BE) (Aaron Schroeder - Cliff Owens)

RECORDED: July, 1956
RELEASED: October, 1956
FIRST APPEARANCE: RCA Victor (45rpm single) 47-6643 and (78rpm single) 20-6643.
HIT PRIOR TO ELVIS: None
HIT AFTER ELVIS: None
OTHER SIGNIFICANT RECORDINGS: None, however a completely different song titled "Any Way You Want Me," recorded by The Sylvers (Capitol 4493) was issued in 1977.

ANYONE (COULD FALL IN LOVE WITH YOU) (Bennie Benjamin - Sol Marcus - A. Dejesus)

RECORDED: October, 1963
RELEASED: March, 1964
FIRST APPEARANCE: RCA Victor (LP) LPM-2894 (mono) and LSP-2894 (stereo) KISSIN' COUSINS
HIT PRIOR TO ELVIS: None
HIT AFTER ELVIS: None
OTHER SIGNIFICANT RECORDINGS: None

ANYPLACE IS PARADISE (Joe Thomas)

RECORDED: September, 1956
RELEASED: November, 1956
FIRST APPEARANCE: RCA Victor (LP) LPM-1382 (mono)
HIT PRIOR TO ELVIS: None
HIT AFTER ELVIS: None
OTHER SIGNIFICANT RECORDINGS: None

ANYTHING THAT'S PART OF YOU (Don Robertson)

RECORDED: October, 1961
RELEASED: March, 1962
FIRST APPEARANCE: RCA Victor (45rpm single) 47-7992
HIT PRIOR TO ELVIS: None
HIT AFTER ELVIS: None
OTHER SIGNIFICANT RECORDINGS: None

ARE YOU LONESOME TO-NIGHT (Roy Turk - Lou Handman)

RECORDED: April, 1960
RELEASED: November, 1960
FIRST APPEARANCE: RCA Victor (45rpm single) 47-7810
HIT PRIOR TO ELVIS: This song, written in 1926, was a popular number by Al Jolson prior to the period generally covered by us in this section (1940 - 1979). The song was again a hit in April, 1950, by The Blue Barron (MGM-10628). In January, 1959 Jaye P. Morgan brought it back to the charts (MGM-12752).
HIT AFTER ELVIS: November, 1973 by Donnie Osmond (MGM-14677
OTHER SIGNIFICANT RECORDINGS: January, 1961 by Lenny Stone, "Are You Wonesome Tonight," a novelty parody (Triodex 105); January, 1961 by Homer & Jethro, a comedy version (RCA Victor 47-7852); January, 1961 by Dodie Stevens, an answer song titled "Yes, I'm Lonesome Tonight" (Dot 16167).

ARE YOU SINCERE (Wayne Walker)

RECORDED: September, 1973
RELEASED: November, 1973
FIRST APPEARANCE: RCA (LP) APL1-0388 (stereo)
    RAISED ON ROCK
HIT PRIOR TO ELVIS: January, 1958 by Andy Williams
    (Cadence 1340); June, 1965 by Trini Lopez (Reprise 0376).
HIT AFTER ELVIS: None
OTHER SIGNIFICANT RECORDINGS: In 1979, RCA re-
    leased an alternate take of this song on the LP "Our Memo-
    ries Of Elvis," and later on 45rpm single.

AS LONG AS I HAVE YOU (Fred Wise - Ben Weisman)

RECORDED: January, 1958
RELEASED: August, 1958
FIRST APPEARANCE: RCA Victor (LP) LPM-1884 (mono)
HIT PRIOR TO ELVIS: None
HIT AFTER ELVIS: None
OTHER SIGNIFICANT RECORDINGS: None

ASK ME (Domenico Modungo - Bill Giant - Bernie Baum -
    Florence Kaye)

RECORDED: January, 1964
RELEASED: October, 1964
FIRST APPEARANCE: RCA Victor (45rpm single) 47-8440
HIT PRIOR TO ELVIS: None
HIT AFTER ELVIS: None
OTHER SIGNIFICANT RECORDINGS: None, however there
    have been four other hit songs titled "Ask Me." None are
    the same song as performed by Elvis.

(YOU'RE SO SQUARE) BABY, I DON'T CARE (Jerry Leiber -
    Mike Stoller)
RECORDED: May, 1957
RELEASED: October, 1957
FIRST APPEARANCE: RCA Victor (EP) EPA-4114 (mono)
    JAILHOUSE ROCK
HIT PRIOR TO ELVIS: None
HIT AFTER ELVIS: None
OTHER SIGNIFICANT RECORDINGS: A great version of
    this song can be heard by Buddy Holly on his LP "Buddy
    Holly" (Coral 57210), shown as "You're So Square."

BABY, IF YOU'LL GIVE ME ALL OF YOUR LOVE (Joy Byers)
RECORDED: June, 1966
RELEASED: June, 1967
FIRST APPEARANCE: RCA Victor (LP) LPM-3787 (mono)
    and LSP-3787 (stereo)
HIT PRIOR TO ELVIS: None
HIT AFTER ELVIS: None
OTHER SIGNIFICANT RECORDINGS: None

BABY LET'S PLAY HOUSE (Arthur Gunter)

RECORDED: February, 1955
RELEASED: April, 1955
FIRST APPEARANCE: Sun 217 (45 and 78rpm)
HIT PRIOR TO ELVIS: Late 1954 by Arthur Gunter)
    (Excello 2047)
HIT AFTER ELVIS: None
OTHER SIGNIFICANT RECORDINGS: By Buddy Holly on
    his LP "Holly In The Hills" (Coral 57463) shown as "I
    Wanna Play House With You." An interesting Elvis sound-
    a like version is done by Vince Everett (ABC Paramount
    10472), issued in August, 1963.

BABY, WHAT YOU WANT ME TO DO (Jimmy Reed)

RECORDED: June, 1968
RELEASED: Segments of this recording first appeared in
    December, 1968.
FIRST APPEARANCE: RCA (LP) LPM-4088 (mono prefix,
    but LP does contain some stereo tracks) ELVIS (NBC-TV
    SPECIAL). Although only a portion of the song was on
    the TV Special LP, a complete song can be heard on the
    LP "Elvis: A Legendary Performer Vol. 2" (CPL1-1349).
HIT PRIOR TO ELVIS: February, 1960 by Jimmy Reed
    (Vee Jay 333); January, 1964 by Etta James (Argo 5459)
HIT AFTER ELVIS: None
OTHER SIGNIFICANT RECORDINGS: None, however this
    song should not be confused with "Baby, What Do You
    Want Me To Do," as recorded by Barbara Lewis, a com-
    pletely different song.

BAREFOOT BALLAD (Dolores Fuller - Lee Morris)

RECORDED: October, 1963
RELEASED: March, 1964
FIRST APPEARANCE: RCA Victor (LP) LPM-2894 (mono)
    and LSP-2894 (stereo) KISSIN' COUSINS
HIT PRIOR TO ELVIS: None
HIT AFTER ELVIS: None
OTHER SIGNIFICANT RECORDINGS: None

BEACH BOY BLUES (Sid Tepper - Roy C. Bennett)

RECORDED: March, 1961
RELEASED: October, 1961
FIRST APPEARANCE: RCA Victor (LP) LPM-2426 (mono)
    and LSP-2426 (stereo) BLUE HAWAII
HIT PRIOR TO ELVIS: None
HIT AFTER ELVIS: None
OTHER SIGNIFICANT RECORDINGS: None

BEACH SHACK (Bill Giant - Bernie Baum - Florence Kaye)
RECORDED: February, 1966
RELEASED: October, 1966
FIRST APPEARANCE: RCA Victor (LP) LPM-3702 (mono)
    and LSP-3702 (stereo) SPINOUT
HIT PRIOR TO ELVIS: None
HIT AFTER ELVIS: None
OTHER SIGNIFICANT RECORDINGS: None

BECAUSE OF LOVE (Ruth Batchelor - Bob Roberts)

RECORDED: March, 1962
RELEASED: November, 1962
FIRST APPEARANCE: RCA Victor (LP) LPM-2621 (mono)
    and LSP-2621 (stereo) GIRLS! GIRLS! GIRLS!
HIT PRIOR TO ELVIS: None
HIT AFTER ELVIS: None
OTHER SIGNIFICANT RECORDINGS: None

BEGINNER'S LUCK (Sid Tepper - Roy C. Bennett)

RECORDED: May, 1965
RELEASED: April, 1966
FIRST APPEARANCE: RCA Victor (LP) LPM-3553 (mono)
    and LSP-3553 (stereo) FRANKIE AND JOHNNY
HIT PRIOR TO ELVIS: None
HIT AFTER ELVIS: None
OTHER SIGNIFICANT RECORDINGS: None

BEYOND THE BEND (Fred Wise - Ben Weisman - Dolores Fuller)

RECORDED: October, 1962
RELEASED: March, 1963
FIRST APPEARANCE: RCA Victor (LP) LPM-2697 (mono)
    and LSP-2697 (stereo) IT HAPPENED AT THE WORLD'S
    FAIR
HIT PRIOR TO ELVIS: None
HIT AFTER ELVIS: None
OTHER SIGNIFICANT RECORDINGS: None

BIG BOOTS (Sid Wayne - Sherman Edwards)

RECORDED: April, 1960
RELEASED: October, 1960
FIRST APPEARANCE: RCA Victor (LP) LPM-2256 (mono)
    and LSP-2256 (stereo) G.I. BLUES
HIT PRIOR TO ELVIS: None
HIT AFTER ELVIS: None
OTHER SIGNIFICANT RECORDINGS: None

BIG BOSS MAN (Luther Dixon - Jimmy Reed - Jerry Smith)

RECORDED: September, 1967
RELEASED: October, 1967
FIRST APPEARANCE: RCA Victor (45rpm single) 47-9341
HIT PRIOR TO ELVIS: May, 1961 by Jimmy Reed (Vee Jay
    380); March, 1964 by Gene Chandler (Constellation 114)
    with the title "Soul Hootenanny."
HIT AFTER ELVIS: None
OTHER SIGNIFICANT RECORDINGS: None, however there
    seems to be continuing confusion over the writer(s) of this
    song. Jimmy Reed's single credits SMITH - DIXON; Gene
    Chandler's single credits DIXON - REED; Elvis' single just
    credits REED; Elvis' LP version of the song credits SMITH -
    DIXON. So as not to leave anyone out, we've credited them
    all (something none of the records have done).

BIG LOVE, BIG HEARTACHE (Dolores Fuller - Lee Morris -
    James Hendrix)

RECORDED: February, 1964
RELEASED: October, 1964
FIRST APPEARANCE: RCA Victor (LP) LPM-2999 (mono)
    and LSP-2999 (stereo) ROUSTABOUT
HIT PRIOR TO ELVIS: None
HIT AFTER ELVIS: None
OTHER SIGNIFICANT RECORDINGS: None

BITTER THEY ARE, HARDER THEY FALL (THE)
    (Larry Gatlin)

RECORDED: February, 1976
RELEASED: May, 1976
FIRST APPEARANCE: RCA (LP) APL1-1506 (stereo)
    FROM ELVIS PRESLEY BOULEVARD, MEMPHIS,
    TENNESSEE
HIT PRIOR TO ELVIS: March, 1974 by Larry Gatlin
    (Monument 8602)
HIT AFTER ELVIS: None
OTHER SIGNIFICANT RECORDINGS: None
(The article "The" in the title appeared on the Larry Gatlin
recording, but not on Elvis' version.)

BLUE CHRISTMAS (Billy Hayes - Jay Johnson)

RECORDED: September, 1957
RELEASED: November, 1957
FIRST APPEARANCE: RCA Victor (LP) LOC-1035
    ELVIS' CHRISTMAS ALBUM
HIT PRIOR TO ELVIS: December, 1949 by Russ Morgan
    (Decca 24766); December, 1949 by Hugo Winterhalter
    (Columbia 38635); December, 1949 by Ernest Tubb
    (Decca 46186)
HIT AFTER ELVIS: November, 1960 by The Browns
    (RCA Victor 47-7820)
OTHER SIGNIFICANT RECORDINGS: This song can
    be found on countless Christmas music albums.

BLUE EYES CRYING IN THE RAIN (Leon Rose)

RECORDED: February, 1976
RELEASED: May, 1976
FIRST APPEARANCE: RCA (LP) APL1-1506 (stereo)
    FROM ELVIS PRESLEY BOULEVARD, MEMPHIS,
    TENNESSEE
HIT PRIOR TO ELVIS: July, 1975 by Willie Nelson
    (Columbia 10176)
HIT AFTER ELVIS: February, 1977 by Ace Cannon
    (Hi 2313)
OTHER SIGNIFICANT RECORDINGS: None

BLUE HAWAII (Leo Robin - Ralph Rainger)

RECORDED: March, 1961
RELEASED: October, 1961
FIRST APPEARANCE: RCA Victor (LP) LPM-2426 (mono)
    and LSP-2426 (stereo) BLUE HAWAII
HIT PRIOR TO ELVIS: January, 1959 by Billy Vaughn
    (Dot 15879)
HIT AFTER ELVIS: None
OTHER SIGNIFICANT RECORDINGS: None, however it
    is interesting that since this song was written, in 1937,
    only Billy Vaughn has had a hit single with it. Of course,
    the tune appears on numerous albums, with Elvis' being
    the most famous (and the most successful).

BLUE MOON (Lorenz Hart - Richard Rogers)

RECORDED: July, 1954
RELEASED: March, 1956
FIRST APPEARANCE: RCA Victor (LP) LPM-1254 (mono)
HIT PRIOR TO ELVIS: March, 1949 by Mel Torme
   (Capitol 15428)
HIT AFTER ELVIS: February, 1961 by Herb Lance & The
   Classics (Promo 1010); March, 1961 by The Marcels
   (Colpix 186); October, 1961 by The Ventures (Dolton 47)
OTHER SIGNIFICANT RECORDINGS: Mid-1956 by The
   Emanons (Josie 801), regarded as the first rock and roll
   version of "Blue Moon," such as later performed by The
   Marcels. Perhaps the first attempt to make the tune a
   rhythm and blues hit was the 1951 instrumental version
   by Lynn Hope (Aladdin 3095). This song was originally
   written in 1934.

BLUE MOON OF KENTUCKY (Bill Monroe)

RECORDED: July, 1954
RELEASED: July, 1954
FIRST APPEARANCE: Sun 209 (45 and 78rpm singles)
HIT PRIOR TO ELVIS: No versions of this song could be
   classified as hits prior to Elvis, however the original
   recording, by Bill Monroe's Blue Grass Boys (Columbia
   20370), should be noted.
HIT AFTER ELVIS: None
OTHER SIGNIFICANT RECORDINGS: None

BLUE RIVER (Paul Evans - Fred Tobias)

RECORDED: May, 1963
RELEASED: December, 1965
FIRST APPEARANCE: RCA Victor (45rpm single) 47-8740
HIT PRIOR TO ELVIS: None
HIT AFTER ELVIS: None
OTHER SIGNIFICANT RECORDINGS: None

BLUE SUEDE SHOES (Carl Perkins)

RECORDED: January, 1956
RELEASED: March, 1956
FIRST APPEARANCE: RCA Victor (EP) EPA-747
   ELVIS PRESLEY
HIT PRIOR TO ELVIS: January, 1956 by Carl Perkins
   (Sun 234)
HIT AFTER ELVIS: April, 1956 by Boyd Bennett & His
   Rockets (King 4903); March, 1973 by Johnny Rivers
   (United Artists 198)
OTHER SIGNIFICANT RECORDINGS: None

BLUEBERRY HILL (Al Lewis - Larry Stock - Vincent Rose)

RECORDED: January, 1957
RELEASED: July, 1957
FIRST APPEARANCE: RCA Victor (LP) LPM-1515 (mono)
   LOVING YOU
HIT PRIOR TO ELVIS: July, 1940 by Glenn Miller
   (Bluebird 10768); September, 1956 by Fats Domino
   (Imperial 5407); October, 1956 by Louis Armstrong
   (Decca 30091).
HIT AFTER ELVIS: None
OTHER SIGNIFICANT RECORDINGS: None

BOSOM OF ABRAHAM (William Johnson - George McFadden -
   Ted Brooks)

RECORDED: June, 1971
RELEASED: March, 1972
FIRST APPEARANCE: RCA (45rpm single) 74-0651
HIT PRIOR TO ELVIS: None
HIT AFTER ELVIS: None
OTHER SIGNIFICANT RECORDINGS: None
NOTE: The picture sleeve for the single release of this song gives the
title as "THE Bosom of Abraham," whereas the label, LP label and LP
jacket do not use the article "The."

BOSSA NOVA BABY (Jerry Leiber - Mike Stoller)

RECORDED: January, 1963
RELEASED: October, 1963
FIRST APPEARANCE: RCA Victor (45rpm single) 47-8243
HIT PRIOR TO ELVIS: None
HIT AFTER ELVIS: None
OTHER SIGNIFICANT RECORDINGS: The original version
   of this song was released in 1962 by Tippie & The Clovers
   (Tiger 201)

BRIDGE OVER TROUBLED WATER (Paul Simon)

RECORDED: June, 1970
RELEASED: December, 1970
FIRST APPEARANCE: RCA (LP) LSP-4445 (stereo)
   THAT'S THE WAY IT IS
HIT PRIOR TO ELVIS: January, 1970 by Simon and
   Garfunkle (Columbia 45079)
HIT AFTER ELVIS: January, 1971 by Buck Owens (Capitol
   3023); April, 1971 by Aretha Franklin (Atlantic 2796);
   March, 1979, disco version by Linda Clifford (RSO 921).
OTHER SIGNIFICANT RECORDINGS: None

BRINGING IT BACK (G. Gordon)

RECORDED: March, 1975
RELEASED: May, 1975
FIRST APPEARANCE: RCA (LP) APL1-1039 (stereo)
   TODAY
HIT PRIOR TO ELVIS: None
HIT AFTER ELVIS: July, 1975 by Brenda Lee (MCA 40442)
OTHER SIGNIFICANT RECORDINGS: None

BRITCHES (Sid Wayne - Sherman Edwards)

RECORDED: August, 1960
RELEASED: December, 1978
FIRST APPEARANCE: RCA Victor (LP) CPL1-3078 (stereo)
   ELVIS: A LEGENDARY PERFORMER VOL. 3
HIT PRIOR TO ELVIS: None
HIT AFTER ELVIS: None
OTHER SIGNIFICANT RECORDINGS: None

BURNING LOVE (Dennis Linde)

RECORDED: March, 1972
RELEASED: August, 1972
FIRST APPEARANCE: RCA (45rpm single) 74-0769
HIT PRIOR TO ELVIS: None
HIT AFTER ELVIS: None
OTHER SIGNIFICANT RECORDINGS: None

BY AND BY (Traditional - Arranged and Adapted by Elvis Presley)
RECORDED: May, 1966
RELEASED: March, 1967
FIRST APPEARANCE: RCA Victor (LP) LPM-3758 (mono) and LSP-3758 (stereo)
HIT PRIOR TO ELVIS: None
HIT AFTER ELVIS: None
OTHER SIGNIFICANT RECORDINGS: None

CANE AND A HIGH STARCHED COLLAR (Sid Tepper - Roy C. Bennett)
RECORDED: If you'll check the liner notes on the back of the LP "Elvis: A Legendary Performer Vol. 2" you'll note that RCA gives February 1961 as the recording date for this song. Our position is that this is an error. All evidence points to this song being recorded at the same time as the other songs for "Flaming Star," August of 1960. Furthermore, we find no record of Elvis even being in the studio in February 1961. It is possible that RCA confused the actual recording date with the hand-over date (date that the film studio hands their recordings over to RCA), which in this case should have been February 1961.
RELEASED: January, 1976
FIRST APPEARANCE: RCA (LP) CPL1-1349 (stereo) ELVIS: A LEGENDARY PERFORMER VOL. 2
HIT PRIOR TO ELVIS: None
HIT AFTER ELVIS: None
OTHER SIGNIFICANT RECORDINGS: None

CAN'T HELP FALLING IN LOVE (Hugo Peretti - Luigi Creatore - George Weiss)
RECORDED: March, 1961
RELEASED: October, 1961
FIRST APPEARANCE: RCA Victor (LP) LPM-2426 (mono) and LSP-2426 (stereo) BLUE HAWAII
HIT PRIOR TO ELVIS: None
HIT AFTER ELVIS: February, 1970 by Al Martino (Capitol 2746); February, 1970 by Andy Williams (Columbia 45094)
OTHER SIGNIFICANT RECORDINGS: None

CARNY TOWN (Fred Wise - Randy Starr)
RECORDED: February, 1964)
RELEASED: October, 1964
FIRST APPEARANCE: RCA Victor (LP) LPM-2999 (mono) and LSP-2999 (Stereo) ROUSTABOUT
HIT PRIOR TO ELVIS: None
HIT AFTER ELVIS: None
OTHER SIGNIFICANT RECORDINGS: None

CATCHIN' ON FAST (Bill Giant - Bernie Baum - Florence Kaye)
RECORDED: October, 1963
RELEASED: March, 1964
FIRST APPEARANCE: RCA Victor (LP) LPM-2894 (mono) and LSP-2894 (stereo) KISSIN' COUSINS
HIT PRIOR TO ELVIS: None
HIT AFTER ELVIS: None
OTHER SIGNIFICANT RECORDINGS: None

CHANGE OF HABIT (Florence Kaye - Ben Weisman)
RECORDED: March, 1969
RELEASED: April, 1970
FIRST APPEARANCE: RCA Camden (LP) CAS-2408 (stereo)
HIT PRIOR TO ELVIS: None
HIT AFTER ELVIS: None
OTHER SIGNIFICANT RECORDINGS: None

CHARRO (Scott Davis - Strange)
RECORDED: July, 1968
RELEASED: March, 1969
FIRST APPEARANCE: RCA (45rpm single) 47-9731
HIT PRIOR TO ELVIS: None
HIT AFTER ELVIS: None
OTHER SIGNIFICANT RECORDINGS: None

CHESAY (Fred Karger - Ben Weisman - Sid Wayne)
RECORDED: May, 1965
RELEASED: April, 1966
FIRST APPEARANCE: RCA Victor (LP) LPM-3553 (mono) and LSP-3553 (stereo) FRANKIE AND JOHNNY
HIT PRIOR TO ELVIS: None
HIT AFTER ELVIS: None
OTHER SIGNIFICANT RECORDINGS: None

CINDY, CINDY (Florence Kaye - Ben Weisman - Dolores Fuller)
RECORDED: June, 1970
RELEASED: May, 1971
FIRST APPEARANCE: RCA (LP) lsp-4530 (stereo) LOVE LETTERS FROM ELVIS
HIT PRIOR TO ELVIS: None
HIT AFTER ELVIS: None
OTHER SIGNIFICANT RECORDINGS: Each time this song was performed it seemed that the lyrics were slightly altered. As a matter of fact, so was the title. In 1959, the song was called "Get Along Home Cindy, Cindy" and was sung in the film "Rio Bravo" by Ricky Nelson, assisted by Dean Martin and Walter Brennan. In February, 1960, it was titled "Cindy," and done by Teddy Vann (Triple X-101). In March of 1966 a slightly similar song, at least as far as the chorus line and title, was released by Trini Lopez (Reprise 0455), but was, nonetheless, a different composition. This song should not be confused with the earlier hit, "Cindy Oh Cindy."

CITY BY NIGHT (Bill Giant - Bernie Baum - Florence Kaye)
RECORDED: June, 1966
RELEASED: June, 1967
FIRST APPEARANCE: RCA Victor (LP) LPM-3787 (mono) and LSP-3787 (stereo)
HIT PRIOR TO ELVIS: None
HIT AFTER ELVIS: None
OTHER SIGNIFICANT RECORDINGS: None

CLAMBAKE (Ben Weisman - Sid Wayne)
RECORDED: February, 1967
RELEASED: November, 1967
FIRST APPEARANCE: RCA Victor (LP) LPM-3893 (mono) and LSP-3893 (stereo) CLAMBAKE
HIT PRIOR TO ELVIS: None
HIT AFTER ELVIS: None
OTHER SIGNIFICANT RECORDINGS: None

CLEAN UP YOUR OWN BACKYARD (Scott Davis - Strange)

RECORDED: October, 1968
RELEASED: June, 1969
FIRST APPEARANCE: RCA (45rpm single) 47-9747
HIT PRIOR TO ELVIS: None
HIT AFTER ELVIS: None
OTHER SIGNIFICANT RECORDINGS: None

C'MON EVERYBODY (Joy Byers)

RECORDED: July, 1963
RELEASED: June, 1964
FIRST APPEARANCE: RCA Victor (EP) EPA-4382 (mono)
HIT PRIOR TO ELVIS: None
HIT AFTER ELVIS: None
OTHER SIGNIFICANT RECORDINGS: None, however this song should not be confused with "C'mon Everybody" as recorded by Eddie Cochran (Liberty 55166), and released in November, 1958.

COME ALONG (David Hess)

RECORDED: May, 1965
RELEASED: April, 1966
FIRST APPEARANCE: RCA Victor (LP) LPM-3553 (mono) and LSP-3553 (stereo) FRANKIE AND JOHNNY

COME WHAT MAY (Tableporter)

RECORDED: May, 1966
RELEASED: June, 1966
FIRST APPEARANCE: RCA Victor (45rpm single) 47-8870
HIT PRIOR TO ELVIS: April, 1958 by Clyde McPhatter (Atlantic 1185)
HIT AFTER ELVIS: None
OTHER SIGNIFICANT RECORDINGS: None

CONFIDENCE (Sid Tepper - Roy C. Bennett)

RECORDED: February, 1967
RELEASED: November, 1967
FIRST APPEARANCE: RCA Victor (LP) LPM-3893 (mono) and LSP-3893 (stereo) CLAMBAKE
HIT PRIOR TO ELVIS: None
HIT AFTER ELVIS: None
OTHER SIGNIFICANT RECORDINGS: None

COTTON CANDY LAND (Ruth Batchelor - Bob Roberts)

RECORDED: October, 1962
RELEASED: March, 1963
FIRST APPEARANCE: RCA Victor (LP) LPM-2697 (mono) and LSP-2697 (stereo) IT HAPPENED AT THE WORLD'S FAIR
HIT PRIOR TO ELVIS: None
HIT AFTER ELVIS: None
OTHER SIGNIFICANT RECORDINGS: None

COULD I FALL IN LOVE (Randy Starr)

RECORDED: June, 1966. Charlie Hodge joins Elvis in a duet on portions of this song.
RELEASED: June, 1967
FIRST APPEARANCE: RCA Victor (LP) LPM-3787 (mono) and LSP-3787 (stereo) DOUBLE TROUBLE
HIT PRIOR TO ELVIS: None
HIT AFTER ELVIS: None
OTHER SIGNIFICANT RECORDINGS: None

CRAWFISH (Fred Wise - Ben Weisman)

RECORDED: January, 1958
RELEASED: August, 1958
FIRST APPEARANCE: RCA Victor (LP) LPM-1884 (mono)
HIT PRIOR TO ELVIS: None
HIT AFTER ELVIS: None
OTHER SIGNIFICANT RECORDINGS: October, 1958 by The Stone Crushers (RCA Victor 47-7309).

CROSS MY HEART AND HOPE TO DIE (Sid Wayne - Ben Wiseman)

RECORDED: July, 1964
RELEASED: April, 1965
FIRST APPEARANCE: RCA Victor (LP) LPM-3338 (mono) and LSP-3338 (stereo) GIRL HAPPY
HIT PRIOR TO ELVIS: None
HIT AFTER ELVIS: None
OTHER SIGNIFICANT RECORDINGS: None

CRYING IN THE CHAPEL (Darrell Glenn)

RECORDED: October, 1960
RELEASED: April, 1965
FIRST APPEARANCE: RCA Victor (45rpm single) 447-0643
HIT PRIOR TO ELVIS: June, 1953 by Darrell Glenn (Valley 105); July, 1953 by Rex Allen (Decca 28758); July, 1953 by The Orioles, featuring Sonny Til (Jubilee 5122); January, 1965 by Adam Wade (Epic 9753).
HIT AFTER ELVIS: None
OTHER SIGNIFICANT RECORDINGS: Another fine rhythm and blues version, also from 1953, is by the Four Dukes (Duke 116)

D

DANNY (Fred Wise - Ben Weisman)

RECORDED: January, 1958
RELEASED: December, 1978
FIRST APPEARANCE: RCA Victor (LP) CPL1-3078 (mono) ELVIS: A LEGENDARY PERFORMER VOL. 3
HIT PRIOR TO ELVIS: None
HIT AFTER ELVIS: December, 1959 by Conway Twitty with the title "Lonely Blue Boy" used instead of "Danny." (MGM 12857).
OTHER SIGNIFICANT RECORDINGS: None

NOTE: Although Elvis did record the song first (originally intended for inclusion in the "King Creole" soundtrack), Conway was the first to release the song commercially. The reason for the title change was that Twitty's most recent hit, at the time, was "Danny Boy," and another "Danny" song was out of the question. Other than the title change, the lyrics are the same on both the Presley and Twitty versions.

DANNY BOY (Fred E. Weatherly)

RECORDED: February, 1976
RELEASED: May, 1976
FIRST APPEARANCE: RCA (LP) APL1-1506 (stereo)
 FROM ELVIS PRESLEY BOULEVARD, MEMPHIS,
 TENNESSEE
HIT PRIOR TO ELVIS: Believe it or not, from the time this
 song was originally written in 1913, when Fred Weatherly
 added words to the old Irish air, until 1959 when two
 artists released the tune on hit singles, we can find no record
 of any hit recordings. However, as we've pointed out earlier
 in this book, our reference of charted hits doesn't begin un-
 til 1940. The song could very well have been a hit during
 the period 1913 - 1939. In May, 1959 by Sil Austin (instrumental) (Mercury 71442); September, 1959 by Conway
 Twitty (MGM 12826); October, 1961 by Andy Williams
 (Columbia 42199); December, 1964 by Patti LaBelle &
 The Blue Belles (Parkway 935); February, 1965 by Jackie
 Wilson (Brunswick 55277); March, 1967 by Ray Price
 (Columbia 44042).
HIT AFTER ELVIS: None
OTHER SIGNIFICANT RECORDINGS: Although there was
 never a group harmony hit version of this song, it wasn't
 because it wasn't tried. A nice rhythm and blues version
 of the tune was done in 1957 by The Sparks (Hull 723).

DATIN' (Fred Wise - Randy Starr)

RECORDED: August, 1965
RELEASED: June, 1966
FIRST APPEARANCE: RCA Victor (LP) LPM-3643 (mono)
 and LSP-3643 (stereo) PARADISE HAWAIIAN STYLE
HIT PRIOR TO ELVIS: None
HIT AFTER ELVIS: None
OTHER SIGNIFICANT RECORDINGS: None

(YOU'RE THE) DEVIL IN DISGUISE (Bill Giant - Bernie Baum -
 Florence Kaye)
RECORDED: May, 1963
RELEASED: June, 1963
FIRST APPEARANCE: RCA Victor (45rpm single) 47-8188
HIT PRIOR TO ELVIS: None
HIT AFTER ELVIS: None
OTHER SIGNIFICANT RECORDINGS: November, 1963 by
 Rex Gildo (Capitol 5076). Sung in German.

DIDJA' EVER (Sid Wayne - Sherman Edwards)

RECORDED: April, 1960
RELEASED: October, 1960
FIRST APPEARANCE: RCA Victor (LP) LPM-2256 (mono)
 and LSP-2256 (stereo) G.I. BLUES
HIT PRIOR TO ELVIS: None
HIT AFTER ELVIS: None
OTHER SIGNIFICANT RECORDINGS: None

DIRTY, DIRTY FEELING (Jerry Leiber - Mike Stoller)

RECORDED: April, 1960
RELEASED: April, 1960
FIRST APPEARANCE: RCA Victor (LP) LPM-2231 (mono)
 and LSP-2231 (stereo) ELVIS IS BACK!
HIT PRIOR TO ELVIS: None
HIT AFTER ELVIS: None
OTHER SIGNIFICANT RECORDINGS: None

DIXIELAND ROCK (Claude DeMetruis - Fred Wise)*

RECORDED: January, 1958
RELEASED: August, 1958
FIRST APPEARANCE: RCA Victor (LP) LPM-1884 (mono)
HIT PRIOR TO ELVIS: None
HIT AFTER ELVIS: None
OTHER SIGNIFICANT RECORDINGS: None
*The composing team of DeMetruis-Wise is shown on the EP "King
Creole," Vol 2, however, in double checking against the LP, "King
Creole," we note that it credits A. Schroeder - R. Frank. Take your
pick!

DO NOT DISTURB (Bill Giant - Bernie Baum - Florence Kaye)

RECORDED: July, 1964
RELEASED: April, 1965
FIRST APPEARANCE: RCA Victor (LP) LPM-3338 (mono)
 and LSP-3338 (stereo) GIRL HAPPY
HIT PRIOR TO ELVIS: None
HIT AFTER ELVIS: None
OTHER SIGNIFICANT RECORDINGS: None

DO THE CLAM (Sid Wayne - Ben Weisman - Dolores Fuller)

RECORDED: July, 1964
RELEASED: April, 1965
FIRST APPEARANCE: RCA Victor (LP) LPM-3338 (mono)
 and LSP-3338 (stereo) GIRL HAPPY
HIT PRIOR TO ELVIS: None
HIT AFTER ELVIS: None
OTHER SIGNIFICANT RECORDINGS: None

DO THE VEGA (Bill Giant - Bernie Baum - Florence Kaye)

RECORDED: July, 1963
RELEASED: November, 1968
FIRST APPEARANCE: RCA Camden (LP) PRS-279 (stereo)
 SINGER PRESENTS ELVIS SINGING FLAMING STAR
 AND OTHERS
HIT PRIOR TO ELVIS: None
HIT AFTER ELVIS: None
OTHER SIGNIFICANT RECORDINGS: None

DO YOU KNOW WHO I AM (Bobby Russell)

RECORDED: February, 1969
RELEASED: November, 1969
FIRST APPEARANCE: RCA (LP) LSP-6020 (stereo)
 FROM MEMPHIS TO VEGAS/FROM VEGAS TO
 MEMPHIS
HIT PRIOR TO ELVIS: None
HIT AFTER ELVIS: None
OTHER SIGNIFICANT RECORDINGS: None

DOIN' THE BEST I CAN (Doc Pomus - Mort Schuman)

RECORDED: April, 1960
RELEASED: October, 1960
FIRST APPEARANCE: RCA Victor (LP) LPM-2256 (mono)
 and LSP-2256 (stereo) G.I. BLUES
HIT PRIOR TO ELVIS: None
HIT AFTER ELVIS: None
OTHER SIGNIFICANT RECORDINGS: None

DONCHA' THINK IT'S TIME (Clyde Otis - Willie Dixon)

RECORDED: February, 1958
RELEASED: April, 1958
FIRST APPEARANCE: RCA Victor (45rpm single) 47-7240
  and (78rpm single) 20-7240
HIT PRIOR TO ELVIS: None
HIT AFTER ELVIS: None
OTHER SIGNIFICANT RECORDINGS: None

DON'T (Jerry Leiber - Mike Stoller)

RECORDED: September, 1957
RELEASED: January, 1958
FIRST APPEARANCE: RCA Victor (45rpm single) 47-7150
  and (78rpm single) 20-7150
HIT PRIOR TO ELVIS: None
HIT AFTER ELVIS: None
OTHER SIGNIFICANT RECORDINGS: None

DON'T ASK ME WHY (Fred Wise - Ben Weisman)

RECORDED: January, 1958
RELEASED: June, 1958
FIRST APPEARANCE: RCA Victor (45rpm single) 47-7280
  and (78rpm single) 20-7280
HIT PRIOR TO ELVIS: None
HIT AFTER ELVIS: None
OTHER SIGNIFICANT RECORDINGS: None

DON'T BE CRUEL (Otis Blackwell - Elvis Presley)

RECORDED: July, 1956
RELEASED: July, 1956
FIRST APPEARANCE: RCA Victor (45rpm single) 47-6604
  and (78rpm single) 20-6604
HIT PRIOR TO ELVIS: None
HIT AFTER ELVIS: September, 1960 by Bill Black's Combo
  (Hi 2026); February, 1963 by Barbara Lynn (Jamie 1244).
OTHER SIGNIFICANT RECORDINGS: November, 1977 by
  Otis Blackwell on his LP THESE ARE MY SONGS (Inner
  City 1032). January, 1971 by Jerry Foster (Metromedia
  201).

DON'T CRY DADDY (Scott Davis)

RECORDED: January, 1969. Ronnie Milsap joins Elvis
  in a duet on the chorus of this song.
RELEASED: November, 1969
FIRST APPEARANCE: RCA (45rpm single) 47-9768
HIT PRIOR TO ELVIS: None
HIT AFTER ELVIS: None
OTHER SIGNIFICANT RECORDINGS: None

DON'T LEAVE ME NOW (Aaron Schroeder - Ben Weisman)

RECORDED: February, 1957
RELEASED: July, 1957
FIRST APPEARANCE: RCA Victor (LP) LPM-1515 (mono)
  LOVING YOU
HIT PRIOR TO ELVIS: None
HIT AFTER ELVIS: None
OTHER SIGNIFICANT RECORDINGS: None

DON'T THINK TWICE, IT'S ALL RIGHT (Bob Dylan)

RECORDED: May, 1971
RELEASED: July, 1973
FIRST APPEARANCE: RCA (LP) APL1-0283 (stereo)
  ELVIS
HIT PRIOR TO ELVIS: September, 1963 by Peter, Paul &
  Mary (Warner Bros. 5385); October, 1965 by The Wonder
  Who (The Four Seasons) (Phillips 40324).
HIT AFTER ELVIS: None
OTHER SIGNIFICANT RECORDINGS: Like many of the
  songs written by Bob Dylan, his recording of this tune
  was not a single hit for him. He did, however, have his
  original version of it on his first album (August, 1963)
  THE FREEWHEELIN' BOB DYLAN (Columbia CL-1986/
  CS-8786).

DOUBLE TROUBLE (Doc Pomus - Mort Schuman)

RECORDED: June, 1966
RELEASED: June, 1967
FIRST APPEARANCE: RCA Victor (LP) LPM-3787 (mono)
  and LSP-3787 (stereo) DOUBLE TROUBLE
HIT PRIOR TO ELVIS: None
HIT AFTER ELVIS: None
OTHER SIGNIFICANT RECORDINGS: None

DOWN BY THE RIVER SIDE and WHEN THE SAINTS GO
MARCHING IN (Traditional - Arranged by Bill Giant - Bernie
  Baum - Florence Kaye)
RECORDED: May, 1965
RELEASED: April, 1966
FIRST APPEARANCE: RCA Victor (LP) LPM-3553 (mono)
  and LSP-3553 (stereo) FRANKIE AND JOHNNY
HIT PRIOR TO ELVIS: Even though there have been no pre-
  vious hit versions of this two-song medley, the individual
  songs have been hits. DOWN BY THE RIVERSIDE: March,
  1960 by Les Compagnons De La Chanson (Capitol 4342).
  WHEN THE SAINTS GO MARCHING IN: August, 1951 by
  The Weavers (Decca 27670); March, 1956 by Bill Haley &
  His Comets (as "The Saint's Rock & Roll") (Decca 29870);
  February, 1959 by Fats Domino (Imperial 5569).
HIT AFTER ELVIS: None
OTHER SIGNIFICANT RECORDINGS: None

DOWN IN THE ALLEY (Jesse Stone and The Clovers)

RECORDED: May, 1966
RELEASED: October, 1966
FIRST APPEARANCE: RCA Victor (LP) LPM-3702 (mono)
  and LSP-3702 (stereo) SPINOUT
HIT PRIOR TO ELVIS: None
HIT AFTER ELVIS: None
OTHER SIGNIFICANT RECORDINGS: The original
  version, after which Elvis' recording is patterned, was
  issued in August, 1957 (Atlantic 1152).

DRUMS OF THE ISLANDS (Sid Tepper - Roy C. Bennett)

RECORDED: August, 1965
RELEASED: June, 1966
FIRST APPEARANCE: RCA Victor (LP) LPM-3643 (mono)
  and LSP-3643 (stereo) PARADISE HAWAIIAN STYLE
HIT PRIOR TO ELVIS: None
HIT AFTER ELVIS: None
OTHER SIGNIFICANT RECORDINGS: None

EARLY MORNING RAIN (Gordon Lightfoot)

RECORDED: March, 1971
RELEASED: February, 1972
FIRST APPEARANCE: RCA (LP) LSP-4671 (stereo)
ELVIS NOW
HIT PRIOR TO ELVIS: September, 1965 by Peter, Paul
& Mary (Warner Bros. 5659); August, 1966 by George
Hamilton IV (RCA Victor 47-8924).
HIT AFTER ELVIS: None
OTHER SIGNIFICANT RECORDINGS: No doubt, on one
of his albums, Gordon Lightfoot performs this song.

EARTH BOY (Sid Tepper - Roy C. Bennett)

RECORDED: March, 1962
RELEASED: November, 1962
FIRST APPEARANCE: RCA Victor (LP) LPM-2621 (mono)
and LSP-2621 (stereo) GIRLS! GIRLS! GIRLS!
HIT PRIOR TO ELVIS: None
HIT AFTER ELVIS: None
OTHER SIGNIFICANT RECORDINGS: None

EASY COME, EASY GO (Sid Wayne - Ben Weisman)

RECORDED: September, 1966
RELEASED: May, 1967
FIRST APPEARANCE: RCA Victor (EP) EPA-4387) (mono)
EASY COME, EASY GO
HIT PRIOR TO ELVIS: None
HIT AFTER ELVIS: None
OTHER SIGNIFICANT RECORDINGS: None. In February,
1964 Bill Anderson released a completely different song
that was also titled "Easy Come, Easy Go" (Decca 31404).
Another song, different than either of the others, was a
February, 1970, hit for Bobby Sherman. It too was titled
"Easy Come, Easy Go" (Metromedia 177).

(SUCH AN) EASY QUESTION (Otis Blackwell - Winfield Scott)

RECORDED: March, 1962
RELEASED: June, 1962
FIRST APPEARANCE: RCA Victor (LP) LPM-2523 (mono)
and LSP-2523 (stereo) POT LUCK
HIT PRIOR TO ELVIS: None
HIT AFTER ELVIS: None
OTHER SIGNIFICANT RECORDINGS: None

ECHOES OF LOVE (Robert McMains)

RECORDED: May, 1963
RELEASED: March, 1964
FIRST APPEARANCE: RCA Victor (LP) LPM-2894 (mono)
and LSP-2894 (stereo) KISSIN' COUSINS
HIT PRIOR TO ELVIS: None
HIT AFTER ELVIS: None
OTHER SIGNIFICANT RECORDINGS: None. In October,
1977 a completely different song, using the same title, was
a hit for the Doobie Brothers (Warner Bros. 8471).

EDGE OF REALITY (Bill Giant - Bernie Baum - Florence Kaye)

RECORDED: March, 1968
RELEASED: November, 1968
FIRST APPEARANCE: RCA (45rpm single) 47-9670
HIT PRIOR TO ELVIS: None
HIT AFTER ELVIS: None
OTHER SIGNIFICANT RECORDINGS: None

EL TORO (Bill Giant - Bernie Baum - Florence Kaye)

RECORDED: January, 1963
RELEASED: November, 1963
FIRST APPEARANCE: RCA Victor (LP) LPM-2756 (mono)
and LSP-2756 (stereo)
HIT PRIOR TO ELVIS: None
HIT AFTER ELVIS: None
OTHER SIGNIFICANT RECORDINGS: None

EVERYBODY COME ABOARD (Bill Giant - Bernie Baum - Florence Kaye)

RECORDED: May, 1965
RELEASED: April, 1966
FIRST APPEARANCE: RCA Victor (LP) LPM-3553 (mono)
and LSP-3553 (stereo)
HIT PRIOR TO ELVIS: None
HIT AFTER ELVIS: None
OTHER SIGNIFICANT RECORDINGS: None

FADED LOVE (Bob Wills - John Wills)

RECORDED: June, 1970
RELEASED: February, 1971
FIRST APPEARANCE: RCA (LP) LSP-4460 (stereo)
ELVIS COUNTRY
HIT PRIOR TO ELVIS: December, 1962 by Leon McAuliff
(Cimmaron 4057); February, 1963 by Jackie De Shannon
(Liberty 55526); September, 1963 by Patsy Cline (Decca
31522).
HIT AFTER ELVIS: None
OTHER SIGNIFICANT RECORDINGS: The original version,
by Bob Wills & His Texas Playboys, is available on several
of his albums.

FAIRYTALE (Anita Pointer - Bonnie Pointer)

RECORDED: March, 1975
RELEASED: May, 1975
FIRST APPEARANCE: RCA (LP) APL1-1039 (stereo)
ELVIS TODAY
HIT PRIOR TO ELVIS: September, 1974 by The Pointer
Sisters (Blue Thumb 254).
HIT AFTER ELVIS: None
OTHER SIGNIFICANT RECORDINGS: None

FAME AND FORTUNE (Fred Wise - Ben Weisman)

RECORDED: March, 1960
RELEASED: April, 1960
FIRST APPEARANCE: RCA Victor (45rpm single) 47-7740
HIT PRIOR TO ELVIS: None
HIT AFTER ELVIS: None
OTHER SIGNIFICANT RECORDINGS: None

FARTHER ALONG (Traditional Sacred - Arranged and Adapted
by Elvis Presley)
RECORDED: May, 1966
RELEASED: March, 1967
FIRST APPEARANCE: RCA Victor (LP) LPM-3758 (mono)
and LSP-3758 (stereo) HOW GREAT THOU ART
HIT PRIOR TO ELVIS: None
HIT AFTER ELVIS: None
OTHER SIGNIFICANT RECORDINGS: The Stamps
Quartet did this song on a 78rpm release (Okeh 04236)
backed with "A Beautiful Prayer," the label of which reads
"Piano Acc [accompaniment] Presley." A coincidence?

FEVER (John Davenport - Eddie Cooley)

RECORDED: April, 1960
RELEASED: April, 1960
FIRST APPEARANCE: RCA Victor (LP) LPM-2231 (mono)
and LSP-2231 (stereo) ELVIS IS BACK.
HIT PRIOR TO ELVIS: June, 1956 by Little Willie John
(King 4935); June, 1958 by Peggy Lee (Capitol 3998).
HIT AFTER ELVIS: November, 1965 by The McCoys
(Bang 511); December, 1972 by Rita Coolidge (A & M
1398).
OTHER SIGNIFICANT RECORDINGS: None

FIND OUT WHAT'S HAPPENING (Jerry Crutchfield)

RECORDED: July, 1973
RELEASED: November, 1973
FIRST APPEARANCE: RCA (LP) APL1-0388 (stereo)
RAISED ON ROCK
HIT PRIOR TO ELVIS: February, 1968 by Bobby Bare
(RCA Victor 47-9450)
HIT AFTER ELVIS: None
OTHER SIGNIFICANT RECORDINGS: None

FINDERS KEEPERS, LOSERS WEEPERS (Dory Jones - Ollie
Jones)
RECORDED: May, 1963
RELEASED: July, 1965
FIRST APPEARANCE: RCA Victor (LP) LPM-3450 (mono)
and LSP-3450 (stereo) ELVIS FOR EVERYONE
HIT PRIOR TO ELVIS: None
HIT AFTER ELVIS: None
OTHER SIGNIFICANT RECORDINGS: December, 1964 by
Nella Dodds; same title but a different song (Wand 171).
The Elvis song should not be confused with "Finders
Keepers" by The Chairman Of The Board, 1973,
(Invictus 1251).

FIRST IN LINE (Aaron Schroeder - Ben Weisman)

RECORDED: September, 1956
RELEASED: November, 1956
FIRST APPEARANCE: RCA Victor (LP) LPM-1382 (mono)
ELVIS
HIT PRIOR TO ELVIS: None
HIT AFTER ELVIS: None
OTHER SIGNIFICANT RECORDINGS: None

FIVE SLEEPY HEADS (Sid Tepper - Roy C. Bennett)

RECORDED: June, 1967
RELEASED: June, 1968
FIRST APPEARANCE: RCA Victor (LP) LPM-3989 (mono)
and LSP-3989 (stereo) SPEEDWAY
HIT PRIOR TO ELVIS: None
HIT AFTER ELVIS: None
OTHER SIGNIFICANT RECORDINGS: None of this partic-
ular recording, but the melody used for this song is "Brahms
Lullaby" (Johannes Brahms).

FLAMING STAR (Sid Wayne - Sherman Edwards)

RECORDED: August, 1960
RELEASED: April, 1961
FIRST APPEARANCE: RCA Victor (Compact 33 Double)
LPC-128 (mono) ELVIS BY REQUEST
HIT PRIOR TO ELVIS: None
HIT AFTER ELVIS: None
OTHER SIGNIFICANT RECORDINGS: None

FLIP, FLOP AND FLY (Joe Turner - Charles Calhoun)

RECORDED: (For TV) February, 1956 as part of a medley,
"Shake, Rattle and Roll"/"Flip, Flop and Fly."
(For records) March, 1974 as part of a six song medley.
RELEASED: June, 1974
FIRST APPEARANCE: RCA (LP) CPL1-0606 (stereo)
ELVIS RECORDED LIVE ON STAGE IN MEMPHIS
HIT PRIOR TO ELVIS: March, 1955 by Joe Turner
(Atlantic 1053).
HIT AFTER ELVIS: None
OTHER SIGNIFICANT RECORDINGS: None, however it
should be noted that the 1956 recording made of the
"Shake, Rattle and Roll"/"Flip, Flop and Fly" medley
was broadcast on the Jackie Gleason Stage Show, hosted
by Tommy and Jimmy Dorsey (aka "The Dorsey Show").
"Shake, Rattle and Roll" was also done originally by Joe
Turner, thus the medley was two of Joe Turner's hits.

FOLLOW THAT DREAM (Fred Wise - Ben Weisman)

RECORDED: July, 1961
RELEASED: April, 1962
FIRST APPEARANCE: RCA Victor (EP) EPA-4368 (mono)
FOLLOW THAT DREAM
HIT PRIOR TO ELVIS: None
HIT AFTER ELVIS: None
OTHER SIGNIFICANT RECORDINGS: None

FOOL (Carl Sigman - James Last)

RECORDED: March, 1972
RELEASED: April, 1973
FIRST APPEARANCE: RCA (45rpm single) 74-0910
HIT PRIOR TO ELVIS: None
HIT AFTER ELVIS: None
OTHER SIGNIFICANT RECORDINGS: None

FOOLS FALL IN LOVE (Jerry Leiber - Mike Stoller)

RECORDED: May, 1966
RELEASED: January, 1967
FIRST APPEARANCE: RCA Victor (45rpm single) 47-9056
HIT PRIOR TO ELVIS: February, 1957 by The Drifters
 (Atlantic 1123)
HIT AFTER ELVIS: September, 1977 by Jacky Ward
 (Mercury 55003)
OTHER SIGNIFICANT RECORDINGS: June, 1960 by
 Sammy Turner (Big Top 3049). Elvis' version is fast,
 almost identical to The Drifter's recording, whereas the
 Ward and Turner renditions are ballads.

FOOLS RUSH IN (WHERE ANGELS FEAR TO TREAD)
 (Johnny Mercer - Rube Bloom)
RECORDED: May, 1971
RELEASED: February, 1972
FIRST APPEARANCE: RCA (LP) LSP-4671 (stereo)
 ELVIS NOW
HIT PRIOR TO ELVIS: July, 1940 by Glenn Miller
 (Bluebird 10728); November, 1960 by Brook Benton
 (Mercury 71722); September, 1962 by Etta James
 (Argo 5424); September, 1963 by Rick Nelson
 (Decca 31533). The arrangements used by Rick Nelson
 and Elvis are nearly identical. Much of this can be
 attributed to the fact that James Burton was the lead
 guitar player on both recordings. Before joining Elvis'
 band, Burton played lead guitar for Rick Nelson and is
 featured on practically every one of Rick's hits.
HIT AFTER ELVIS: None
OTHER SIGNIFICANT RECORDINGS: None. We should
 point out that Elvis' recording of this song did not carry
 the part of the original title shown in parenthesis, which is
 why it is not shown in bold print. It is included here,
 however, because it was a part of the song title when
 originally written.

(THAT'S WHAT YOU GET) FOR LOVIN' ME (Gordon
 Lightfoot)
RECORDED: March, 1971
RELEASED: July, 1973
FIRST APPEARANCE: RCA (LP) APL1-0283 (stereo)
 ELVIS
HIT PRIOR TO ELVIS: January, 1965 by Peter, Paul & Mary
 (Warner Bros. 5496); August, 1966 by Waylon Jennings
 (RCA Victor 47-8917).
HIT AFTER ELVIS: None
OTHER SIGNIFICANT RECORDINGS: No doubt a version
 by Gordon Lightfoot exists on one of his albums.

FOR OL' TIMES SAKE (Tony Joe White)

RECORDED: July, 1973
RELEASED: September, 1973
FIRST APPEARANCE: RCA (45rpm single) APB0-0088
HIT PRIOR TO ELVIS: None
HIT AFTER ELVIS: None
OTHER SIGNIFICANT RECORDINGS: A version by Tony
 Joe White may have appeared on record.

FOR THE GOOD TIMES (Kris Kristofferson)

RECORDED: March, 1972 (unreleased studio version); June,
 1972 (released live version).
RELEASED: June, 1972
FIRST APPEARANCE: RCA (LP) LSP-4776 (stereo) ELVIS
 AS RECORDED AT MADISON SQUARE GARDEN
HIT PRIOR TO ELVIS: June, 1970 by Ray Price (Columbia
 45178).
HIT AFTER ELVIS: None
OTHER SIGNIFICANT RECORDINGS: It's hard to find a
 singer who hasn't recorded a version of this song, including
 Kristofferson himself.

FOR THE HEART (Dennis Linde)

RECORDED: February, 1976
RELEASED: March, 1976
FIRST APPEARANCE: RCA (45rpm single) PB-10601
HIT PRIOR TO ELVIS: None
HIT AFTER ELVIS: None
OTHER SIGNIFICANT RECORDINGS: None. On this
 recording, the song's composer, Dennis Linde, is featured
 on bass. His bass was overdubbed onto the track after the
 original session, which has Jerry Scheff on bass, was com-
 pleated.

FOR THE MILLIONTH AND THE LAST TIME (Sid Tepper -
 Roy C. Bennett)
RECORDED: October, 1961
RELEASED: July, 1965
FIRST APPEARANCE: RCA Victor (LP) LPM-3450 (mono)
 and LSP-3450 (stereo) ELVIS FOR EVERYONE
HIT PRIOR TO ELVIS: None
HIT AFTER ELVIS: None
OTHER SIGNIFICANT RECORDINGS: None

FORGET ME NEVER (Fred Wise - Ben Weisman)

RECORDED: October, 1960
RELEASED: July, 1965
FIRST APPEARANCE: RCA Victor (LP) LPM-3450 (mono)
 and LSP-3450 (stereo) ELVIS FOR EVERYONE
HIT PRIOR TO ELVIS: None
HIT AFTER ELVIS: None
OTHER SIGNIFICANT RECORDINGS: None

FORT LAUDERDALE CHAMBER OF COMMERCE
 (Sid Tepper - Roy C. Bennett)
RECORDED: July, 1964
RELEASED: April, 1965
FIRST APPEARANCE: RCA Victor (LP) LPM-3338 (mono)
 and LSP-3338 (stereo) GIRL HAPPY
HIT PRIOR TO ELVIS: None
HIT AFTER ELVIS: None
OTHER SIGNIFICANT RECORDINGS: None

FOUNTAIN OF LOVE (Bill Giant - Jeff Lewis)

RECORDED: March, 1962
RELEASED: June, 1962
FIRST APPEARANCE: RCA Victor (LP) LPM-2523 (mono)
 and LSP-2523 (stereo) POT LUCK
HIT PRIOR TO ELVIS: None
HIT AFTER ELVIS: None
OTHER SIGNIFICANT RECORDINGS: None

FRANKFORT SPECIAL (Sid Wayne - Sherman Edwards)

RECORDED: April, 1960
RELEASED: October, 1960
FIRST APPEARANCE: RCA Victor (LP) LPM-2256 (mono) and LSP-2256 (stereo) G.I. BLUES
HIT PRIOR TO ELVIS: None
HIT AFTER ELVIS: None
OTHER SIGNIFICANT RECORDINGS: None

FRANKIE AND JOHNNY (Alex Gottlieb - Fred Karger - Ben Weisman)

RECORDED: May, 1965
RELEASED: March, 1966
FIRST APPEARANCE: RCA Victor (45rpm single) 47-8780
HIT PRIOR TO ELVIS: April, 1959 by Johnny Sea (NRC 019); April, 1959 by Johnny Cash (Columbia 41371); August, 1961 by Brook Benton (Mercury 71859); July, 1963 by Sam Cooke (RCA Victor 47-8215); July, 1964 by The Greenwood County Singers (Kapp 591).
NOTE: Although all versions of this song maintain a similar story line, it seems that each recording is noticably different in both lyrics and arrangement. Both the Johnny Sea and Johnny Cash releases were titled "Frankie's Man Johnny."
HIT AFTER ELVIS: None
OTHER SIGNIFICANT RECORDINGS: None

FROM A JACK TO A KING (Ned Miller)

RECORDED: January, 1969
RELEASED: November, 1969
FIRST APPEARANCE: RCA (LP) LSP-6020 (stereo) FROM MEMPHIS TO VEGAS/FROM VEGAS TO MEMPHIS
HIT PRIOR TO ELVIS: December, 1962 by Ned Miller (Fabor 114).
HIT AFTER ELVIS: None
OTHER SIGNIFICANT RECORDINGS: None

FUN IN ACAPULCO (Ben Weisman - Sid Wayne)

RECORDED: January, 1963
RELEASED: November, 1963
FIRST APPEARANCE: RCA Victor (LP) LPM-2750 (mono) and LSP-2750 (stereo) FUN IN ACAPULCO
HIT PRIOR TO ELVIS: None
HIT AFTER ELVIS: None
OTHER SIGNIFICANT RECORDINGS: None

FUNNY HOW TIME SLIPS AWAY (Willie Nelson)

RECORDED: August, 1969 (live - unreleased); June, 1970 (for record release).
RELEASED: February, 1971
FIRST APPEARANCE: RCA (LP) LSP-4460 (stereo) ELVIS COUNTRY
HIT PRIOR TO ELVIS: October, 1961 by Billy Walker (Columbia 42050); November, 1961 by Jimmy Elledge (RCA Victor 47-7946); October, 1963 by Johnny Tillotson (Cadence 1441); August, 1964 by Joe Hinton (using only "Funny" as its title) (Back Beat 541).
HIT AFTER ELVIS: July, 1976 by Dorothy Moore (Malaco 1033).
OTHER SIGNIFICANT RECORDINGS: Willie Nelson's version can be found on one of his earlier (Liberty) LPs.

G.I. BLUES (Sid Tepper - Roy C. Bennett)

RECORDED: April, 1960
RELEASED: October, 1960
FIRST APPEARANCE: RCA Victor (LP) LPM-2256 (mono) and LSP-2256 (stereo) G.I. BLUES
HIT PRIOR TO ELVIS: None
HIT AFTER ELVIS: None
OTHER SIGNIFICANT RECORDINGS: None

GENTLE ON MY MIND (John Hartford)

RECORDED: January, 1969
RELEASED: May, 1969
FIRST APPEARANCE: RCA (LP) LSP-4155 (stereo)
HIT PRIOR TO ELVIS: June, 1967 by Glen Campbell (Capitol 5539); September, 1968 (reissue) by Glen Campbell (Capitol 5539); February, 1968 by Patti Page (Columbia 44353).
HIT AFTER ELVIS: May, 1969 by Aretha Franklin (Atlantic 2619).
OTHER SIGNIFICANT RECORDINGS: October, 1968 by John Hartford (RCA LSP-4068) on "Gentle On My Mind" LP.

GENTLY (Murray Wizell - Edward Lisbona)

RECORDED: March, 1961
RELEASED: June, 1961
FIRST APPEARANCE: RCA Victor (LP) LPM-2370 (mono) and LSP-2370 (stereo) SOMETHING FOR EVERYBODY
HIT PRIOR TO ELVIS: None
HIT AFTER ELVIS: None
OTHER SIGNIFICANT RECORDINGS: None

GIRL HAPPY (Doc Pomus - Norman Meade)

RECORDED: July, 1964
RELEASED: April, 1965
FIRST APPEARANCE: RCA Victor (LP) LPM-3338 (mono) and LSP-3338 (stereo) GIRL HAPPY
HIT PRIOR TO ELVIS: None
HIT AFTER ELVIS: None
OTHER SIGNIFICANT RECORDINGS: None

GIRL NEXT DOOR WENT A' WALKING: This title appeared only on later pressings of the LP "Elvis Is Back." First pressings —both mono and stereo— give the title as "The Girl Next Door." In each case, titles are identical on both the label and jacket. See THE GIRL NEXT DOOR for this listing.

GIRL OF MINE (Reed - Mason)

RECORDED: July, 1973
RELEASED: November, 1973
FIRST APPEARANCE: RCA (LP) APL1-0388 (stereo) RAISED ON ROCK
HIT PRIOR TO ELVIS: None
HIT AFTER ELVIS: None
OTHER SIGNIFICANT RECORDINGS: None

GIRLS! GIRLS! GIRLS! (Jerry Leiber - Mike Stoller)

RECORDED: March, 1962
RELEASED: November, 1962
FIRST APPEARANCE: RCA Victor (LP) LPM-2621 (mono)
and LSP-2621 (stereo) GIRLS! GIRLS! GIRLS!
HIT PRIOR TO ELVIS: August, 1961 by The Coasters
(Atco 6204).
HIT AFTER ELVIS: None
OTHER SIGNIFICANT RECORDINGS: None

GIVE ME THE RIGHT (Fred Wise - Norman Blagman)

RECORDED: March, 1961
RELEASED: June, 1961
FIRST APPEARANCE: RCA Victor (LP) LPM-2370 (mono)
and LSP-2370 (stereo) SOMETHING FOR EVERYBODY
HIT PRIOR TO ELVIS: None
HIT AFTER ELVIS: None
OTHER SIGNIFICANT RECORDINGS: None

GO EAST, YOUNG MAN (Bill Giant - Bernie Baum - Florence
Kaye)
RECORDED: February, 1965
RELEASED: October, 1965
FIRST APPEARANCE: RCA Victor (LP) LPM-3468 (mono)
and LSP-3468 HARUM SCARUM
HIT PRIOR TO ELVIS: None
HIT AFTER ELVIS: None
OTHER SIGNIFICANT RECORDINGS: None

GOIN' HOME (Joy Byers)

RECORDED: October, 1967
RELEASED: June, 1968
FIRST APPEARANCE: RCA Victor (LP) LPM-3989 (mono)
and LSP-3989 (stereo) SPEEDWAY
HIT PRIOR TO ELVIS: None
HIT AFTER ELVIS: None
OTHER SIGNIFICANT RECORDINGS: None

GOLDEN COINS (Bill Giant - Bernie Baum - Florence Kaye)

RECORDED: February, 1965
RELEASED: October, 1965
FIRST APPEARANCE: RCA Victor (LP) LPM-3468 (mono)
and LSP-3468 (stereo) HARUM SCARUM
HIT PRIOR TO ELVIS: None
HIT AFTER ELVIS: None
OTHER SIGNIFICANT RECORDINGS: None

GONNA GET BACK HOME SOMEHOW (Doc Pomus -
Mort Schuman)
RECORDED: March, 1962
RELEASED: June, 1962
FIRST APPEARANCE: RCA Victor (LP) LPM-2523 (mono)
and LSP-2523 (stereo) POT LUCK
HIT PRIOR TO ELVIS: None
HIT AFTER ELVIS: None
OTHER SIGNIFICANT RECORDINGS: None

GOOD LUCK CHARM (Aaron Schroeder - Wally Gold)

RECORDED: October, 1961
RELEASED: March, 1962
FIRST APPEARANCE: RCA Victor (45rpm single) 47-7992
HIT PRIOR TO ELVIS: None
HIT AFTER ELVIS: None
OTHER SIGNIFICANT RECORDINGS: None

GOOD ROCKIN' TONIGHT (Roy Brown)

RECORDED: September, 1954
RELEASED: September, 1954
FIRST APPEARANCE: Sun (45 and 78rpm single) 210
HIT PRIOR TO ELVIS: February,1948 by Wynonie Harris
(King 4210).
HIT AFTER ELVIS: January, 1959 by Pat Boone (Dot
15888).
OTHER SIGNIFICANT RECORDINGS: January, 1948 by
Roy Brown, the original version (Deluxe 1093). When
the Deluxe label was purchased by King Records, and
the earlier Deluxe releases reissued, the catalog number
was changed to Deluxe 3093 on this issue. It's also
interesting to note that only Brown's original version
gave the title as "Good Rocking Tonight," as compared
to "Good Rockin' Tonight."

GOOD TIME CHARLIE'S GOT THE BLUES (Danny O'Keefe)

RECORDED: December, 1973
RELEASED: March, 1974
FIRST APPEARANCE: RCA (LP) CPL1-0475 (stereo)
GOOD TIMES
HIT PRIOR TO ELVIS: August, 1972 by Danny O'Keefe
(Signpost 70006).
HIT AFTER ELVIS: None
OTHER SIGNIFICANT RECORDINGS: None

GOT A LOT O' LIVIN' TO DO (Aaron Schroeder - Ben Weisman)

RECORDED: January, 1957
RELEASED: July, 1957
FIRST APPEARANCE: RCA Victor (LP) LPM-1515 (mono)
LOVING YOU
HIT PRIOR TO ELVIS: None
HIT AFTER ELVIS: None
OTHER SIGNIFICANT RECORDINGS: None

GOT MY MOJO WORKING (Preston Foster)

RECORDED: June, 1970
RELEASED: May, 1971
FIRST APPEARANCE: RCA (LP) LSP-4530 (stereo)
LOVE LETTERS FROM ELVIS
HIT PRIOR TO ELVIS: March, 1966 by Jimmy Smith
(Verve 10393).
HIT AFTER ELVIS: None
OTHER SIGNIFICANT RECORDINGS: February, 1957 by
Muddy Waters (Chess 1652).

GREEN GREEN GRASS OF HOME (Claude Putman Jr.)

RECORDED: March, 1975
RELEASED: May, 1975
FIRST APPEARANCE: RCA (LP) APL1-1039 (stereo)
TODAY
HIT PRIOR TO ELVIS: July, 1965 by Porter Wagoner
(RCA Victor 47-8622); December, 1966 by Tom Jones
(Parrot 40009).
HIT AFTER ELVIS: None
OTHER SIGNIFICANT RECORDINGS: None

GREENBACK DOLLAR, WATCH AND CHAIN (Ray Harris)

This title is listed here to once and for all dispell the rumor that Elvis plays piano on this recording. The song, recorded by Ray Harris, was recorded during the summer of 1957 (probably June or July) while Elvis was in Hollywood filming and doing studio sessions for RCA. He *was* in Memphis during the Christmas holidays of 1956 at which time the recordings with Jerry Lee Lewis, Carl Perkins and Johnny Cash (aka The Million Dollar Quartet) were made, unofficially of course.

GUADALAJARA (Pepe Guizar)

RECORDED: January, 1963
RELEASED: November, 1963
FIRST APPEARANCE: RCA Victor (LP) LPM-2756 (mono) and LSP-2756 (stereo) FUN IN ACAPULCO
HIT PRIOR TO ELVIS: None
HIT AFTER ELVIS: None
OTHER SIGNIFICANT RECORDINGS: None

GUITAR MAN (Jerry "Reed" Hubbard)

RECORDED: September, 1967
RELEASED: January, 1968
FIRST APPEARANCE: RCA Victor (45rpm single) 47-9425
HIT PRIOR TO ELVIS: May, 1967 by Jerry Reed (RCA Victor 47-9152).
HIT AFTER ELVIS: None
OTHER SIGNIFICANT RECORDINGS: None. Although the label on the Elvis release shows Jerry Reed as the composer, BMI's files give Jerry Hubbard as the writer. Also, this song should not be confused with "The Guitar Man" by Bread (Elektra 45803), a completely different song, or with "(Dance With The) Guitar Man," by Duane Eddy (RCA Victor 47-8087), another totally different song.

HAPPY ENDING (Ben Weisman - Sid Wayne)

RECORDED: October, 1962
RELEASED: March, 1963
FIRST APPEARANCE: RCA Victor (LP) LPM-2697 (mono) and LSP-2697 (stereo)
HIT PRIOR TO ELVIS: None
HIT AFTER ELVIS: None
OTHER SIGNIFICANT RECORDINGS: None

HARBOR LIGHTS (Jimmy Kennedy - Hugh Williams)

RECORDED: July, 1954
RELEASED: January, 1976
FIRST APPEARANCE: RCA Victor (LP) CPL1-1349 (this is a monaural track on what is mostly a stereo album). ELVIS: A LEGENDARY PERFORMER VOL. 2
HIT PRIOR TO ELVIS: August, 1950 by Sammy Kaye (Columbia 38963); September, 1950 by Guy Lombardo (Decca 27208); October, 1950 by Ray Anthony (Capitol 1190); October, 1950 by Ken Griffin (Columbia 38889); October, 1950 by Ralph Flanagan (RCA Victor 20-3911); October, 1950 by Bing Crosby (Decca 27219).
HIT AFTER ELVIS: January, 1960 by The Platters (Mercury 71563). Recorded after Elvis' session, obviously, but issued 16 years before his version became available.
OTHER SIGNIFICANT RECORDINGS: No doubt, between the time the song was written in 1937 and the period our coverage begins (1940) someone had a hit with it. Even though not hits, per se, several fine rhythm and blues groups had versions of this song out in the fifties. Among them was the Federal (12010) release by The Dominoes, featuring Clyde McPhatter on lead vocal (early 1951).

HARD HEADED WOMAN (Claude De Metrius)

RECORDED: January, 1958
RELEASED: June, 1958
FIRST APPEARANCE: RCA Victor (45 rpm single) 47-7280 and (78rpm single) 20-7280
HIT PRIOR TO ELVIS: None
HIT AFTER ELVIS: None
OTHER SIGNIFICANT RECORDINGS: None

HARD KNOCKS (Joy Byers)

RECORDED: February, 1964
RELEASED: October, 1964
FIRST APPEARANCE: RCA Victor (LP) LPM-2999 (mono) and LSP-2999 (stereo) ROUSTABOUT
HIT PRIOR TO ELVIS: None
HIT AFTER ELVIS: None
OTHER SIGNIFICANT RECORDINGS:

HARD LUCK (Ben Weisman - Sid Wayne)

RECORDED: May, 1965
RELEASED: April, 1966
FIRST APPEARANCE: RCA Victor (LP) LPM-3553 (mono) and LSP-3553 (stereo) FRANKIE AND JOHNNY
HIT PRIOR TO ELVIS: None
HIT AFTER ELVIS: None
OTHER SIGNIFICANT RECORDINGS: None

HARUM HOLIDAY (Peter Andreoli - Vince Poncia Jr.)

RECORDED: February, 1965
RELEASED: October, 1965
FIRST APPEARANCE: RCA Victor (LP) LPM-3468 (mono) and LSP-3468 (stereo) HARUM SCARUM
HIT PRIOR TO ELVIS: None
HIT AFTER ELVIS: None
OTHER SIGNIFICANT RECORDINGS: None. In European countries this film, "Harum Scarum," was titled "Harum Holiday," thus tying in more to the title song.

HAVE A HAPPY (Ben Weisman - Florence Kaye - Dolores Fuller)

RECORDED: March, 1969
RELEASED: April, 1970
FIRST APPEARANCE: RCA Camden (LP) CAS-2408 (stereo) LET'S BE FRIENDS
HIT PRIOR TO ELVIS: None
HIT AFTER ELVIS: None
OTHER SIGNIFICANT RECORDINGS: None

HAVE I TOLD YOU LATELY THAT I LOVE YOU (Scott Weisman)
RECORDED: January, 1957
RELEASED: July, 1957
FIRST APPEARANCE: RCA Victor (LP) LPM-1515 (mono) LOVING YOU
HIT PRIOR TO ELVIS: None
HIT AFTER ELVIS: September, 1957 by Ricky Nelson (Imperial 5463); January, 1969 by Kitty Wells & Red Foley (Decca 32427).
OTHER SIGNIFICANT RECORDINGS: Perhaps the most famous recording of this song, from the years prior to our coverage, is by Gene Autry (Columbia 37079).

HAWAIIAN SUNSET (Sid Tepper - Roy C. Bennett)

RECORDED: March, 1961
RELEASED: October, 1961
FIRST APPEARANCE: RCA Victor (LP) LPM-2426 (mono) and LSP-2426 (stereo) BLUE HAWAII
HIT PRIOR TO ELVIS: None
HIT AFTER ELVIS: None
OTHER SIGNIFICANT RECORDINGS: None

HAWAIIAN WEDDING SONG (Al Hoffman - Dick Manning - C. E. King)
RECORDED: March, 1961
RELEASED: October, 1961
FIRST APPEARANCE: RCA Victor (LP) LPM-2426 (mono) and LSP-2426 (stereo) BLUE HAWAII
HIT PRIOR TO ELVIS: December, 1958 by Andy Williams (Cadence 1358).
HIT AFTER ELVIS: None
OTHER SIGNIFICANT RECORDINGS: None. It is interesting to note that while both Elvis' and Andy Williams discs credit C. E. King, as a co-composer, ASCAP's files show only Hoffman and Manning.

HE IS MY EVERYTHING (Dallas Frazier)

RECORDED: June, 1971
RELEASED: April, 1972
FIRST APPEARANCE: RCA (LP) LSP-4690 (stereo) HE TOUCHED ME
HIT PRIOR TO ELVIS: None of this specific composition. See "There Goes My Everything" for more information.
HIT AFTER ELVIS: None
OTHER SIGNIFICANT RECORDINGS: One year earlier (June, 1970), Elvis recorded "There Goes My Everything." This song is simply different lyrics added to the same basic instrumental track used the year before.

HE KNOWS JUST WHAT I NEED: *See JESUS KNOWS WHAT I NEED*

HE TOUCHED ME (William J. Gaither)

RECORDED: May, 1971
RELEASED: March, 1972
FIRST APPEARANCE: RCA (45rpm single) 74-0651
HIT PRIOR TO ELVIS: None
HIT AFTER ELVIS: None
OTHER SIGNIFICANT RECORDINGS: None. This single release was one of only three standard catalog Elvis singles that did not reach one of the major national charts. Excluding Christmas and Gold Standard singles, only "He Touched Me"/"Bosom of Abraham," "How Great Thou Art"/"His Hand in Mine" and "You'll Never Walk Alone"/"We Call on Him," all sacred songs, failed to chart.

HEARTBREAK HOTEL (Mae Axton - Tommy Durden - Elvis Presley)
RECORDED: January, 1956 (Contrary to some opinions, this was the **second** song Elvis recorded for RCA. The first was "I Got A Woman." Note that we're talking only about the order in which they were recorded —not released. Both songs, plus "Money Honey," were recorded on the same day, January 10, 1956.
RELEASED: February, 1956
FIRST APPEARANCE: RCA Victor (45rpm single) 47-6420 and (78rpm single) 20-6420.
HIT PRIOR TO ELVIS: None
HIT AFTER ELVIS: July, 1956 by Stan Freberg, a parody (Capitol 3480); November, 1966 by Roger Miller (Smash 2066); December, 1970 by Frijid Pink (Parrot 352); September, 1979 by Willie Nelson (Columbia - 11023).
OTHER SIGNIFICANT RECORDINGS: None

HEART OF ROME (G. Stephens - A. Blaikley - K. Howard)

RECORDED: June, 1970
RELEASED: July, 1971
FIRST APPEARANCE: RCA (45rpm single) 47-9998
HIT PRIOR TO ELVIS: None
HIT AFTER ELVIS: None
OTHER SIGNIFICANT RECORDINGS: None

HE'LL HAVE TO GO (Joe Allison - Audrey Allison)

RECORDED: October, 1976
RELEASED: July, 1977
FIRST APPEARANCE: RCA Victor (LP) AFL1-2428 (stereo) MOODY BLUE
HIT PRIOR TO ELVIS: December, 1959 by Jim Reeves (RCA Victor 47-7643); January, 1964 by Solomon Burke (Atlantic 2218).
HIT AFTER ELVIS: None
OTHER SIGNIFICANT RECORDINGS: An answer song was issued by Jeanne Black in April, 1960, titled "He'll Have to Stay " (Capitol 4368).

HELP ME (Larry Gatlin)

RECORDED: December, 1973
RELEASED: May, 1974
FIRST APPEARANCE: RCA (45rpm single) APBO-0280
HIT PRIOR TO ELVIS: None
HIT AFTER ELVIS: March, 1977 by Ray Price (Col. 10503)
OTHER SIGNIFICANT RECORDINGS: None. This song should not be confused with completely different recordings, using the same title, by Joni Mitchell (March, 1974 - Asylum 11034) and by The Spellbinders (November, 1966 - Columbia 43830).

HELP ME MAKE IT THROUGH THE NIGHT (Kris Kristofferson)

RECORDED: May, 1971
RELEASED: February, 1972
FIRST APPEARANCE: RCA (LP) LSP-4671 (stereo) ELVIS NOW
HIT PRIOR TO ELVIS: January, 1971 by Sammi Smith (Mega 615 - 0015); May, 1971 by Joe Simon (Spring 113). Joe Simon's version debuted on the charts the same day that Elvis was in the studio doing the session from which his version was taken.
HIT AFTER ELVIS: November, 1971 by O.C. Smith (Columbia 45435); March, 1972 by Gladys Knight & The Pips (Soul 35094).
OTHER SIGNIFICANT RECORDINGS: Kris Kristofferson's version appears on the LP "Country Music in the Modern Era" (New World NW-207 - 1976 issue), which coincidentally enough also contains one Elvis track, "Mystery Train."

HERE COMES SANTA CLAUS (RIGHT DOWN SANTA CLAUS LANE) (Gene Autry - Haldeman - Melka)

RECORDED: September, 1957
RELEASED: November, 1957
FIRST APPEARANCE: RCA Victor (LP) LOC-1035 (mono) ELVIS' CHRISTMAS ALBUM
HIT PRIOR TO ELVIS: December, 1947 by Gene Autry (Columbia 37942).
HIT AFTER ELVIS: None
OTHER SIGNIFICANT RECORDINGS: This Christmas standard has been recorded by dozens of artists.

HE'S YOUR UNCLE, NOT YOUR DAD (Sid Wayne - Ben Weisman)

RECORDED: June, 1967
RELEASED: June, 1968
FIRST APPEARANCE: RCA Victor (LP) LPM-3989 (mono) and LSP-3989 (stereo) SPEEDWAY
HIT PRIOR TO ELVIS: None
HIT AFTER ELVIS: None
OTHER SIGNIFICANT RECORDINGS: None

HEY, HEY, HEY (Joy Byers)

RECORDED: February, 1967
RELEASED: November, 1967
FIRST APPEARANCE: RCA Victor (LP) LPM-3893 (mono) and LSP-3893 (stereo) CLAMBAKE
HIT PRIOR TO ELVIS: None
HIT AFTER ELVIS: None
OTHER SIGNIFICANT RECORDINGS: None

HEY JUDE (John Lennon - Paul McCartney)

RECORDED: January, 1969
RELEASED: February, 1972
FIRST APPEARANCE: RCA (LP) LSP-4671 (stereo) ELVIS NOW
HIT PRIOR TO ELVIS: September, 1968 by The Beatles (Apple 2276); December, 1968 by Wilson Pickett (Atlantic 2591).
HIT AFTER ELVIS: None
OTHER SIGNIFICANT RECORDINGS: None

HEY LITTLE GIRL (Joy Byers)

RECORDED: February, 1965
RELEASED: October, 1965
FIRST APPEARANCE: RCA Victor (LP) LPM-3468 (mono) and LSP-3468 (stereo) HARUM SCARUM
HIT PRIOR TO ELVIS: None
HIT AFTER ELVIS: None
OTHER SIGNIFICANT RECORDINGS: None, however this song should not be confused with any of the other songs with the same title, by such artists as: Dee Clark, Major Lance, Del Shannon, The Techniques and Foster Sylvers.

HIGH HEEL SNEAKERS (Robert Higgenbotham)

RECORDED: September, 1967
RELEASED: January, 1968
FIRST APPEARANCE: RCA Victor (45rpm single) 47-9425
HIT PRIOR TO ELVIS: February, 1964 by Tommy Tucker (Checker 1067); November, 1964 by Jerry Lee Lewis (Smash 1930); August, 1965 by Stevie Wonder (Tamla 54119); March, 1966 by Ramsey Lewis (Cadet 5531).
HIT AFTER ELVIS: October, 1968 by Jose Feliciano (RCA Victor 47-9641).
OTHER SIGNIFICANT RECORDINGS: None

HIS HAND IN MINE (Mosie Lister)

RECORDED: October, 1960
RELEASED: December, 1960
FIRST APPEARANCE: RCA Victor (LP) LPM-2328 (mono) and LSP-2328 (stereo) HIS HAND IN MINE
HIT PRIOR TO ELVIS: None
HIT AFTER ELVIS: None
OTHER SIGNIFICANT RECORDINGS: A favorite of many of the gospel quartets, including The Statesmen, and recorded by several of those groups.

(MARIE'S THE NAME) HIS LATEST FLAME (Doc Pomus - Mort Schuman)

RECORDED: June, 1961
RELEASED: August, 1961
FIRST APPEARANCE: RCA Victor (45rpm single) 47-7908
HIT PRIOR TO ELVIS: None
HIT AFTER ELVIS: None
OTHER SIGNIFICANT RECORDINGS: August, 1961 by Del Shannon on his LP "Runaway" (Big Top 1303).

HOLLY LEAVES AND CHRISTMAS TREES (West - Spreen)

RECORDED: May, 1971
RELEASED: October, 1971
FIRST APPEARANCE: RCA (LP) LSP-4579 (stereo)
HIT PRIOR TO ELVIS: None
HIT AFTER ELVIS: None
OTHER SIGNIFICANT RECORDINGS: None

HOME IS WHERE THE HEART IS (Sherman Edwards - Hal David)

RECORDED: October, 1961
RELEASED: September, 1962
FIRST APPEARANCE: RCA Victor (EP) EPA-4371
KID GALAHAD
HIT PRIOR TO ELVIS: None
HIT AFTER ELVIS: None
OTHER SIGNIFICANT RECORDINGS: None

HOT DOG (Jerry Leiber - Mike Stoller)

RECORDED: February, 1957
RELEASED: July, 1957
FIRST APPEARANCE: RCA Victor (LP) LPM-1515 (mono)
LOVING YOU
HIT PRIOR TO ELVIS: None
HIT AFTER ELVIS: None
OTHER SIGNIFICANT RECORDINGS: None

HOUND DOG (Jerry Leiber - Mike Stoller)

RECORDED: July, 1956
RELEASED: July, 1956
FIRST APPEARANCE: RCA Victor (45rpm single) 47-6604
and (78rpm single) 20-6604.
HIT PRIOR TO ELVIS: March, 1953 by Willie Mae "Big
Mama" Thornton (Peacock 1612).
HIT AFTER ELVIS: None
OTHER SIGNIFICANT RECORDINGS: April, 1953 by
Rufus Thomas, titled "Bear Cat (Hound Dog)."
(Sun 181); July, 1964 by The Candy Johnson Show
(Canjo 102); by Chuck Jackson, a single issued from his Elvis
tribute LP, backed with "Love Me Tender" (Wand 1159).

HOUSE OF SAND (Bill Giant - Bernie Baum - Florence Kaye)

RECORDED: August, 1965
RELEASED: June, 1966
FIRST APPEARANCE: RCA Victor (LP) LPM-3643 (mono)
and LSP-3643 (stereo) PARADISE HAWAIIAN STYLE
HIT PRIOR TO ELVIS: None
HIT AFTER ELVIS: None
OTHER SIGNIFICANT RECORDINGS: None

HOW CAN YOU LOSE WHAT YOU NEVER HAD (Ben Weisman
- Sid Wayne)
RECORDED: February, 1967
RELEASED: November, 1967
FIRST APPEARANCE: RCA Victor (LP) LPM-3893 (mono)
and LSP-3893 (stereo) CLAMBAKE
HIT PRIOR TO ELVIS: None
HIT AFTER ELVIS: None
OTHER SIGNIFICANT RECORDINGS: None

HOW DO YOU THINK I FEEL (Cindy Walker - Webb Pierce)

RECORDED: September, 1956
RELEASED: November, 1956
FIRST APPEARANCE: RCA Victor (LP) LPM-1382 (mono)
ELVIS
HIT PRIOR TO ELVIS: None
HIT AFTER ELVIS: None
OTHER SIGNIFICANT RECORDINGS: November, 1954 by
Jimmie Rodgers Snow (RCA Victor 47-5900).

HOW GREAT THOU ART (Stuart K. Hine)

RECORDED: May, 1966
RELEASED: March, 1967
FIRST APPEARANCE: RCA Victor (LP) LPM-3758 (mono)
and LSP-3758 (stereo) HOW GREAT THOU ART
HIT PRIOR TO ELVIS: None
HIT AFTER ELVIS: None
OTHER SIGNIFICANT RECORDINGS: This gospel standard
has been recorded by nearly everyone who does sacred
recordings.

HOW THE WEB IS WOVEN (Clive Westlake - David Most)

RECORDED: June, 1970
RELEASED: December, 1970
FIRST APPEARANCE: RCA (LP) LSP-4445 (stereo)
THAT'S THE WAY IT IS
HIT PRIOR TO ELVIS: None
HIT AFTER ELVIS: None
OTHER SIGNIFICANT RECORDINGS: None

HOW WOULD YOU LIKE TO BE (Ben Raleigh - Mark Barman)

RECORDED: October, 1962
RELEASED: March, 1963
FIRST APPEARANCE: RCA Victor (LP) LPM-2697 (mono)
and LSP-2697 (stereo) IT HAPPENED AT THE WORLD'S
FAIR
HIT PRIOR TO ELVIS: None
HIT AFTER ELVIS: None
OTHER SIGNIFICANT RECORDINGS: None

HOW'S THE WORLD TREATING YOU (Chet Atkins -
Boudleaux Bryant)
RECORDED: September, 1956
RELEASED: November, 1956
FIRST APPEARANCE: RCA Victor (LP) LPM-1382 (mono)
ELVIS
HIT PRIOR TO ELVIS: None
HIT AFTER ELVIS: October, 1961 by The Louvin Brothers
(Capitol 4628).
OTHER SIGNIFICANT RECORDINGS: None

HURT (Jimmie Craine - Al Jacobs)

RECORDED: February, 1976
RELEASED: March, 1976
FIRST APPEARANCE: RCA (45rpm single) PB-10601
HIT PRIOR TO ELVIS: July, 1961 by Timi Yuro (Liberty
55343); December, 1965 by Little Anthony & The Imperials
(DCP-1154); May, 1975 by The Manhattans (Columbia
10140).
HIT AFTER ELVIS: None
OTHER SIGNIFICANT RECORDINGS: None

I BEG OF YOU (Rose Marie McCoy - Kelly Owens)

RECORDED: February, 1957
RELEASED: January, 1958
FIRST APPEARANCE: RCA Victor (45rpm single) 47-7510 and (78rpm single) 20-7510.
HIT PRIOR TO ELVIS: None
HIT AFTER ELVIS: None
OTHER SIGNIFICANT RECORDINGS: None

I BELIEVE (Ervin Drake - Jimmy Shirl - Al Stillman - Irvin Graham)

RECORDED: January, 1957
RELEASED: March, 1957
FIRST APPEARANCE: RCA Victor (EP) EPA-4054 PEACE IN THE VALLEY
HIT PRIOR TO ELVIS: February, 1953 by Frankie Laine (Columbia 39938); March, 1953 by Jane Froman (Capitol 2332).
HIT AFTER ELVIS: June, 1964 by The Bachelors (London 9672).
OTHER SIGNIFICANT RECORDINGS: None

I BELIEVE IN THE MAN IN THE SKY (Richard Howard)

RECORDED: October, 1960
RELEASED: April, 1965
FIRST APPEARANCE: RCA Victor (45rpm single) 447-0643
HIT PRIOR TO ELVIS: None
HIT AFTER ELVIS: None
OTHER SIGNIFICANT RECORDINGS: None

I CAN HELP (Billy Swan)

RECORDED: March, 1975
RELEASED: May, 1975
FIRST APPEARANCE: RCA (LP) APL1-1039 (stereo) TODAY
HIT PRIOR TO ELVIS: September, 1974 by Billy Swan (Monument 8621).
HIT AFTER ELVIS: None
OTHER SIGNIFICANT RECORDINGS: None

I CAN'T STOP LOVING YOU (Don Gibson)

RECORDED: August, 1969
RELEASED: November, 1969
FIRST APPEARANCE: RCA (LP) LSP-6020 (stereo) FROM MEMPHIS TO VEGAS/FROM VEGAS TO MEMPHIS
HIT PRIOR TO ELVIS: February, 1958 by Don Gibson (RCA Victor 47-7133); March, 1958 by Kitty Wells (Decca 30551); May, 1962 by Ray Charles (ABC/Paramount 10330); May, 1963 by Count Basie (Reprise 20, 170)
HIT AFTER ELVIS: None
OTHER SIGNIFICANT RECORDINGS: None

I DON'T CARE IF THE SUN DON'T SHINE (Mack David)

RECORDED: September, 1954
RELEASED: September, 1954
FIRST APPEARANCE: Sun 210 (45 and 78rpm singles)
HIT PRIOR TO ELVIS: None
HIT AFTER ELVIS: None
OTHER SIGNIFICANT RECORDINGS: Even though this song was written in 1949, we can find no charted hit versions, other than Elvis', ever!

I DON'T WANNA BE TIED (Bill Giant - Bernie Baum - Florence Kaye)

RECORDED: March, 1962
RELEASED: November, 1962
FIRST APPEARANCE: RCA Victor (LP) LPM-2621 (mono) and LSP-2621 (stereo) GIRLS! GIRLS! GIRLS!
HIT PRIOR TO ELVIS: None
HIT AFTER ELVIS: None
OTHER SIGNIFICANT RECORDINGS: None

I DON'T WANT TO (Janice Torre - Fred Spielman)

RECORDED: March, 1962
RELEASED: November, 1962
FIRST APPEARANCE: RCA Victor (LP) LPM-2621 (mono) and LSP-2621 (stereo) GIRLS! GIRLS! GIRLS!
HIT PRIOR TO ELVIS: None
HIT AFTER ELVIS: None
OTHER SIGNIFICANT RECORDINGS: None

I FEEL SO BAD (Chuck Willis)

RECORDED: March, 1961
RELEASED: May, 1961
FIRST APPEARANCE: RCA Victor (45rpm single) 47-7880
HIT PRIOR TO ELVIS: June, 1954 by Chuck Willis (Okeh 7029).
HIT AFTER ELVIS: January, 1967 by Little Milton (Checker 1162); August, 1971 by Ray Charles (ABC 11308).
OTHER SIGNIFICANT RECORDINGS: None

I FEEL THAT I'VE KNOWN YOU FOREVER (Doc Pomus - Alan Jeffries)
RECORDED: March, 1962
RELEASED: June, 1962
FIRST APPEARANCE: RCA Victor (LP) LPM-2523 (mono) and LSP-2523 (stereo) POT LUCK
HIT PRIOR TO ELVIS: None
HIT AFTER ELVIS: None
OTHER SIGNIFICANT RECORDINGS: None

I FORGOT TO REMEMBER TO FORGET (Charlie Feathers - Stanley Kesler)
RECORDED: July, 1955
RELEASED: August, 1955
FIRST APPEARANCE: Sun 223 (45 and 78rpm singles)
HIT PRIOR TO ELVIS: None
HIT AFTER ELVIS: None
OTHER SIGNIFICANT RECORDINGS: April, 1970 by Jerry Foster (Metromedia 184).

I GOT A FEELIN' IN MY BODY (Dennis Linde)

RECORDED: December, 1973
RELEASED: March, 1974
FIRST APPEARANCE: RCA (LP) CPL1-0475 (stereo)
  GOOD TIMES
HIT PRIOR TO ELVIS: None
HIT AFTER ELVIS: None
OTHER SIGNIFICANT RECORDINGS: None

I GOT A WOMAN (Ray Charles)

RECORDED: January, 1956 (This was the first song
  recorded by Elvis for RCA, January 10, 1956).
RELEASED: March, 1956
FIRST APPEARANCE: RCA Victor (EP) EPA-747
  ELVIS PRESLEY (BLUE SUEDE SHOES)
HIT PRIOR TO ELVIS: January, 1955 by Ray Charles
  (Atlantic 1050).
HIT AFTER ELVIS: March, 1963 by Rick Nelson (Decca
  31475); November, 1963 by Freddy Scott (Colpix 709);
  October, 1962 by Jimmy McGriff (Sue 770).
  (On the Ray Charles and Jimmy McGriff issues, the song
  is titled "I've Got A Woman." The McGriff recording is
  an instrumental.)
OTHER SIGNIFICANT RECORDINGS: None

I GOT LUCKY (Fred Wise - Ben Weisman - Dolores Fuller)

RECORDED: November, 1961
RELEASED: September, 1962
FIRST APPEARANCE: RCA Victor (EP) EPA-4371
  KID GALAHAD
HIT PRIOR TO ELVIS: None
HIT AFTER ELVIS: None
OTHER SIGNIFICANT RECORDINGS: None

I GOT STUNG (Aaron Schroeder - David Hill)

RECORDED: June, 1958
RELEASED: November, 1958
FIRST APPEARANCE: RCA Victor (45rpm single) 47-7410
  and (78rpm single) 20-7410
HIT PRIOR TO ELVIS: None
HIT AFTER ELVIS: None
OTHER SIGNIFICANT RECORDINGS: None

I GOTTA KNOW (Paul Evans - Matt Williams)

RECORDED: April, 1960
RELEASED: November, 1960
FIRST APPEARANCE: RCA Victor (45rpm single) 47-7810
HIT PRIOR TO ELVIS: None
HIT AFTER ELVIS: None
OTHER SIGNIFICANT RECORDINGS: None

I, JOHN (Johnson - McFadden - Brooks)

RECORDED: June, 1971
RELEASED: April, 1972
FIRST APPEARANCE: RCA (LP) LSP-4690 (stereo)
  HE TOUCHED ME
HIT PRIOR TO ELVIS: None
HIT AFTER ELVIS: None
OTHER SIGNIFICANT RECORDINGS: None

I JUST CAN'T HELP BELIEVIN' (Barry Mann - Cynthia Weil)

RECORDED: August, 1970
RELEASED: December, 1970
FIRST APPEARANCE: RCA (LP) LSP-4445 (stereo)
  THAT'S THE WAY IT IS
HIT PRIOR TO ELVIS: June, 1970 by B.J. Thomas
  (Scepter 12283).
HIT AFTER ELVIS: October, 1970 by David Frizzell
  (Columbia 45238).
OTHER SIGNIFICANT RECORDINGS: None

I LOVE ONLY ONE GIRL (Sid Tepper - Roy C. Bennett)

RECORDED: June, 1966
RELEASED: June, 1967
FIRST APPEARANCE: RCA Victor (LP) LPM-3787 (mono)
  and LSP-3787 (stereo) DOUBLE TROUBLE
HIT PRIOR TO ELVIS: None
HIT AFTER ELVIS: None
OTHER SIGNIFICANT RECORDINGS: None

I LOVE YOU BECAUSE (Leon Payne) TAKE ONE

RECORDED: July, 1954 (This was the first song recorded
  by Elvis for Sun records, therefore making it the first commercial track in Elvis' career. This version (take one) was
  not released until 1974. The version issued in 1956 (takes
  two and four, spliced) will be listed separately, following
  this.
RELEASED: January, 1974
FIRST APPEARANCE: RCA Victor (LP) CPL1-0341 (this
  track mono) ELVIS: A LEGENDARY PERFORMER
  VOL. 1
HIT PRIOR TO ELVIS: October, 1949 by Leon Payne
  (Capitol 40238); February, 1950 by Ernest Tubb (Decca
  46213).
HIT AFTER ELVIS: February, 1960 by Johnny Cash
  (Sun 334); March, 1963 by Al Martino (Capitol 4930);
  August, 1969 by Carl Smith (Columbia 44939); February,
  1976 by Jim Reeves (RCA PB-10557); September, 1978 by
  Don Gibson (ABC/Hickory 54036).
OTHER SIGNIFICANT RECORDINGS: None

I LOVE YOU BECAUSE (Leon Payne) TAKES TWO/FOUR

RECORDED: July, 1954 (a portion of take two and of take
  four were edited together to form one complete take).
RELEASED: March, 1956
FIRST APPEARANCE: RCA Victor (LP) LPM-1254 (mono)
HIT PRIOR TO ELVIS: See above
HIT AFTER ELVIS: See above
OTHER SIGNIFICANT RECORDINGS: None

I MET HER TODAY (Don Robertson - Hal Blair)

RECORDED: October, 1961
RELEASED: July, 1965
FIRST APPEARANCE: RCA Victor (LP) LPM-3450 (mono)
  and LSP-3450 (stereo) ELVIS FOR EVERYONE
HIT PRIOR TO ELVIS: None
HIT AFTER ELVIS: None
OTHER SIGNIFICANT RECORDINGS: None

MISS YOU (Donnie Sumner)

RECORDED: September, 1973
RELEASED: November, 1973
FIRST APPEARANCE: RCA (LP) APL1-0388 (stereo)
RAISED ON ROCK/FOR OL' TIMES SAKE
HIT PRIOR TO ELVIS: None
HIT AFTER ELVIS: None
OTHER SIGNIFICANT RECORDINGS: None, however this song should not be confused with completely different songs using the same title, by Harold Melvin & The Bluenotes (Philadelphia International 3516) and by The Dells (Cadet 5700).

I NEED SOMEBODY TO LEAN ON (Doc Pomus - Mort Schuman)

RECORDED: July, 1963
RELEASED: June, 1964
FIRST APPEARANCE: RCA Victor (EP) EPA-4382
VIVA LAS VEGAS
HIT PRIOR TO ELVIS: None
HIT AFTER ELVIS: None
OTHER SIGNIFICANT RECORDINGS: None

I NEED YOU SO (Ivory Joe Hunter)

RECORDED: February, 1957
RELEASED: July, 1957
FIRST APPEARANCE: RCA Victor (LP) LPM-1515 (mono)
LOVING YOU
HIT PRIOR TO ELVIS: April, 1950 by Ivory Joe Hunter (MGM 10663).
HIT AFTER ELVIS: None
OTHER SIGNIFICANT RECORDINGS: None

I NEED YOUR LOVE TONIGHT (Sid Wayne - Bix Reichner)

RECORDED: June, 1958
RELEASED: March, 1959
FIRST APPEARANCE: RCA Victor (45rpm single) 47-7506
HIT PRIOR TO ELVIS: None
HIT AFTER ELVIS: None
OTHER SIGNIFICANT RECORDINGS: None

I REALLY DON'T WANT TO KNOW (Don Robertson - Howard Barnes)

RECORDED: June, 1970
RELEASED: December, 1970
FIRST APPEARANCE: RCA (45rpm single) 47-9960
HIT PRIOR TO ELVIS: December, 1953 by Eddy Arnold (RCA Victor 5525); April, 1954 by Les Paul & Mary Ford (Capitol 2735); May, 1960 by Tommy Edwards (MGM 12890); September, 1962 by Solomon Burke (Atlantic 2157); January, 1963 by Esther Phillips (Lenox 5560); August, 1966 by Ronnie Dove (Diamond 208).
HIT AFTER ELVIS: None
OTHER SIGNIFICANT RECORDINGS: None

I SLIPPED, I STUMBLED, I FELL (Fred Wise - Ben Weisman)

RECORDED: October, 1960
RELEASED: June, 1961
FIRST APPEARANCE: RCA Victor (LP) LPM-2370 (mono) and LSP-2370 (stereo) SOMETHING FOR EVERYBODY
HIT PRIOR TO ELVIS: None
HIT AFTER ELVIS: None
OTHER SIGNIFICANT RECORDINGS: None

I THINK I'M GONNA LIKE IT HERE (Don Robertson - Hal Blair)

RECORDED: January, 1963
RELEASED: November, 1963
FIRST APPEARANCE: RCA Victor (LP) LPM-2756 (mono) and LSP-2756 (stereo) FUN IN ACAPULCO
HIT PRIOR TO ELVIS: None
HIT AFTER ELVIS: None
OTHER SIGNIFICANT RECORDINGS: None

I WANT TO BE FREE (Jerry Leiber - Mike Stoller)

RECORDED: June, 1957
RELEASED: October, 1957
FIRST APPEARANCE: RCA Victor (EP) EPA-4114
JAILHOUSE ROCK
HIT PRIOR TO ELVIS: None
HIT AFTER ELVIS: None
OTHER SIGNIFICANT RECORDINGS: None. A completely different song, using the same title, was done by The Ohio Players (April, 1975 - Mercury 73675).

I WANT YOU, I NEED YOU, I LOVE YOU (Maurice Mysels - Ira Kosloff)

RECORDED: April, 1956
RELEASED: May, 1956
FIRST APPEARANCE: RCA Victor (45rpm single) 47-6540 and (78rpm single) 20-6540.
HIT PRIOR TO ELVIS: None
HIT AFTER ELVIS: None
OTHER SIGNIFICANT RECORDINGS: None

NOTE: The 78 singles and first pressings of the 45 incorrectly printed writer Maurice Mysels name as Maurice Myself.

I WANT YOU WITH ME (Woody Harris)

RECORDED: March, 1961
RELEASED: June, 1961
FIRST APPEARANCE: RCA Victor (LP) LPM-2370 (mono) and LSP-2370 SOMETHING FOR EVERYBODY
HIT PRIOR TO ELVIS: None
HIT AFTER ELVIS: None
OTHER SIGNIFICANT RECORDINGS: None

I WAS BORN ABOUT TEN THOUSAND YEARS AGO (Adapted by Elvis Presley)

RECORDED: June, 1970
RELEASED: February, 1971 (excerpts) - February, 1972 (complete song).
FIRST APPEARANCE: RCA (LP) LSP-4460 (excerpts) - RCA (LP) LSP-4671 (complete song) (both stereo).
HIT PRIOR TO ELVIS: None
HIT AFTER ELVIS: None
OTHER SIGNIFICANT RECORDINGS: None

I WAS THE ONE (Aaron Schroeder - Hal Blair - Claude DeMetrius - Peppers)

RECORDED: January, 1956
RELEASED: February, 1956
FIRST APPEARANCE: RCA Victor (45rpm single) 47-6420 and (78rpm single) 20-6420.
HIT PRIOR TO ELVIS: None
HIT AFTER ELVIS: None
OTHER SIGNIFICANT RECORDINGS: None

I WASHED MY HANDS IN MUDDY WATER (Joe Babcock)

RECORDED: June, 1970
RELEASED: February, 1971
FIRST APPEARANCE: RCA (LP) LSP-4460 (stereo) ELVIS COUNTRY
HIT PRIOR TO ELVIS: February, 1965 by Stonewall Jackson (Columbia 43197); June, 1966 by Johnny Rivers (Imperial 66175).
HIT AFTER ELVIS: None
OTHER SIGNIFICANT RECORDINGS: August, 1965 by Charlie Rich (Smash 1993).

I WILL BE HOME AGAIN (Benjamin - Laveen - Singer)

RECORDED: April, 1960 (Charlie Hodge on duet vocals)
RELEASED: April, 1960
FIRST APPEARANCE: RCA Victor (LP) LPM-2231 (mono) and LSP-2231 (stereo) ELVIS IS BACK!
HIT PRIOR TO ELVIS: None
HIT AFTER ELVIS: None
OTHER SIGNIFICANT RECORDINGS: None

I WILL BE TRUE (Ivory Joe Hunter)

RECORDED: May, 1971
RELEASED: July, 1973
FIRST APPEARANCE: RCA (LP) APL1-0283 (stereo) ELVIS
HIT PRIOR TO ELVIS: None
HIT AFTER ELVIS: None
OTHER SIGNIFICANT RECORDINGS: March, 1952 by Ivory Joe Hunter (MGM 11195).

IF EVERYDAY WAS LIKE CHRISTMAS (Red West)

RECORDED: June, 1966
RELEASED: November, 1966
FIRST APPEARANCE: RCA Victor (45rpm single) 47-8950
HIT PRIOR TO ELVIS: None
HIT AFTER ELVIS: None
OTHER SIGNIFICANT RECORDINGS: None

IF I CAN DREAM (W. Earl Brown)

RECORDED: June, 1968
RELEASED: November, 1968
FIRST APPEARANCE: RCA (45rpm single) 47-9670
HIT PRIOR TO ELVIS: None
HIT AFTER ELVIS: None
OTHER SIGNIFICANT RECORDINGS: None

IF I GET HOME ON CHRISTMAS DAY (McCaulay)

RECORDED: May, 1971
RELEASED: October, 1971
FIRST APPEARANCE: RCA (LP) LSP-4579 (stereo) ELVIS SINGS THE WONDERFUL WORLD OF CHRISTMAS
HIT PRIOR TO ELVIS: None
HIT AFTER ELVIS: None
OTHER SIGNIFICANT RECORDINGS: None

IF I WERE YOU (Gerald Nelson)

RECORDED: June, 1970
RELEASED: May, 1971
FIRST APPEARANCE: RCA (LP) LSP-4530 (stereo) LOVE LETTERS FROM ELVIS
HIT PRIOR TO ELVIS: None
HIT AFTER ELVIS: None
OTHER SIGNIFICANT RECORDINGS: None. A completely different song, using the same title, appeared on the first Peter & Gordon LP, "A World Without Love" (June, 1964 - Capitol 2115).

IF I'M A FOOL (FOR LOVING YOU) (Stanley Kesler)

RECORDED: February, 1969
RELEASED: April, 1970
FIRST APPEARANCE: RCA Camden (LP) CAS-2408 (Stereo) LET'S BE FRIENDS
HIT PRIOR TO ELVIS: None
HIT AFTER ELVIS: None
OTHER SIGNIFICANT RECORDINGS: June, 1964 by Jimmy Clanton (Philips 40208). Another 1964 hit by Bobby Wood had the same title (except there were no parenthesis used) but was a completely different song (Joy 285).

IF THAT ISN'T LOVE (Dottie Rambo)

RECORDED: December, 1973
RELEASED: March, 1974
FIRST APPEARANCE: RCA (LP) CPL1-0475 (stereo) GOOD TIMES
HIT PRIOR TO ELVIS: None
HIT AFTER ELVIS: None
OTHER SIGNIFICANT RECORDINGS: None

IF THE LORD WASN'T WALKING BY MY SIDE (Henry Slaughter)

RECORDED: May, 1966
RELEASED: March, 1967
FIRST APPEARANCE: RCA Victor (LP) LPM-3758 (mono) and LSP-3758 HOW GREAT THOU ART
HIT PRIOR TO ELVIS: None
HIT AFTER ELVIS: None
OTHER SIGNIFICANT RECORDINGS: None

IF WE NEVER MEET AGAIN (A.E. Brumley)

RECORDED: October, 1960
RELEASED: December, 1960
FIRST APPEARANCE: RCA Victor (LP) LPM-2328 (mono) and LSP-2328 HIS HAND IN MINE
HIT PRIOR TO ELVIS: None
HIT AFTER ELVIS: None
OTHER SIGNIFICANT RECORDINGS: None

IF YOU DON'T COME BACK (Jerry Leiber - Mike Stoller)

RECORDED: July, 1973
RELEASED: November, 1973
FIRST APPEARANCE: RCA (LP) APL1-0388 (stereo) RAISED ON ROCK/FOR OL' TIMES SAKE
HIT PRIOR TO ELVIS: None
HIT AFTER ELVIS: None
OTHER SIGNIFICANT RECORDINGS: None

F YOU LOVE ME (LET ME KNOW) (John Rostill)
RECORDED: April, 1977
RELEASED: July, 1977
FIRST APPEARANCE: RCA Victor (LP) AFL1-2428 (stereo)
    MOODY BLUE
HIT PRIOR TO ELVIS: April, 1974 by Olivia Newton-John
    (MCA 40209).
HIT AFTER ELVIS: None
OTHER SIGNIFICANT RECORDINGS: None

F YOU TALK IN YOUR SLEEP (Red West - Johnny Christopher)
RECORDED: December, 1973
RELEASED: May, 1974
FIRST APPEARANCE: RCA (45rpm single) APB0-0280
HIT PRIOR TO ELVIS: None
HIT AFTER ELVIS: None
OTHER SIGNIFICANT RECORDINGS: None

IF YOU THINK I DON'T NEED YOU (Bob "Red" West - Joe
    Cooper)
RECORDED: July, 1963
RELEASED: June, 1964
FIRST APPEARANCE: RCA Victor (EP) EPA-4382
    VIVA LAS VEGAS
HIT PRIOR TO ELVIS: None
HIT AFTER ELVIS: None
OTHER SIGNIFICANT RECORDINGS: None

I'LL BE BACK (Sid Wayne - Ben Weisman)
RECORDED: February, 1966
RELEASED: October, 1966
FIRST APPEARANCE: RCA Victor (LP) LPM-3702 (mono)
    and LSP-3702 SPINOUT
HIT PRIOR TO ELVIS: None
HIT AFTER ELVIS: None
OTHER SIGNIFICANT RECORDINGS: None. A completely
    different song, using the same title, appeared on the LP
    "Beatles '65" (Capitol 2228).

I'LL BE HOME FOR CHRISTMAS (Kent - Gannon - Ram)
RECORDED: September, 1957
RELEASED: November, 1957
FIRST APPEARANCE: RCA Victor (LP) LOC-1035 (mono)
    ELVIS' CHRISTMAS ALBUM
HIT PRIOR TO ELVIS: November, 1943 by Bing Crosby
    (Decca 18570).
HIT AFTER ELVIS: None
OTHER SIGNIFICANT RECORDINGS: None

I'LL BE HOME ON CHRISTMAS DAY (Michael Jarrett)
RECORDED: May, 1971
RELEASED: October, 1971
FIRST APPEARANCE: RCA (LP) LSP-4579 (stereo)
    ELVIS SINGS THE WONDERFUL WORLD OF CHRIST-
    MAS
HIT PRIOR TO ELVIS: None
HIT AFTER ELVIS: None
OTHER SIGNIFICANT RECORDINGS: None

I'LL BE THERE (IF YOU EVER WANT ME) (Gabbard -
    Price) (Bobby Darin)
RECORDED: January, 1969
RELEASED: April, 1970
FIRST APPEARANCE: RCA Camden (LP) CAS-2408 (stereo)
    LET'S BE FRIENDS
HIT PRIOR TO ELVIS: December, 1964 by Gerry & The
    Pacemakers (Laurie 3279); July, 1960 by Bobby Darin
    (Atco 6167).
HIT AFTER ELVIS: None
OTHER SIGNIFICANT RECORDINGS: September, 1963
    by Tony Orlando (Epic 9622).

    NOTE: Some confusion exists as to why Elvis' version of this
    song credits the writing team of Gabbard - Price. Both Bobby
    Darin's original version and Gerry & The Pacemakers' hit show
    Bobby Darin as the writer.

**I'LL HOLD YOU IN MY HEART (TILL I CAN HOLD YOU IN
MY ARMS** (Eddy Arnold - Hal Horton - Tommy Dilbeck)
RECORDED: January, 1969
RELEASED: May, 1969
FIRST APPEARANCE: RCA (LP) LSP-4155 (stereo)
    FROM ELVIS IN MEMPHIS
HIT PRIOR TO ELVIS: 1947, by Eddy Arnold (RCA Victor);
    July, 1951 by Eddie Fisher (RCA Victor 4191); June, 1967
    by Freddie Hart (Kapp 820).
HIT AFTER ELVIS: None
OTHER SIGNIFICANT RECORDINGS: None

I'LL NEVER FALL IN LOVE AGAIN (Donegan - Currie)
RECORDED: February, 1976
RELEASED: May, 1976
FIRST APPEARANCE: RCA (LP) APL1-1506 (stereo)
    FROM ELVIS PRESLEY BOULEVARD, MEMPHIS,
    TENNESSEE
HIT PRIOR TO ELVIS: August, 1967 by Tom Jones
    (Parrot 40018); July, 1969 by Tom Jones, re-
    recorded and reissued.
HIT AFTER ELVIS: None
OTHER SIGNIFICANT RECORDINGS: None. This song
    should not be confused with the Dionne Warwick hit,
    from December, 1969, using the same title (Scepter 12273).

I'LL NEVER KNOW (Fred Karger - Sid Wayne - Ben Weisman)
RECORDED: June, 1970
RELEASED: May, 1971
FIRST APPEARANCE: RCA (LP) LSP-4530 (stereo)
    LOVE LETTERS FROM ELVIS
HIT PRIOR TO ELVIS: None
HIT AFTER ELVIS: None
OTHER SIGNIFICANT RECORDINGS: None. A completely
    different song, using the same title, was released by The
    Four Lads in February 1956 (Columbia 40629).

I'LL NEVER LET YOU GO (LITTLE DARLIN') (Jimmy Wakely)
RECORDED: January, 1955
RELEASED: March, 1956
FIRST APPEARANCE: RCA Victor (LP) LPM-1254 (mono)
    ELVIS PRESLEY
HIT PRIOR TO ELVIS: None
HIT AFTER ELVIS: None
OTHER SIGNIFICANT RECORDINGS: By Jimmy Wakely
    (Decca 5973). Probably 1942-43.

I'LL REMEMBER YOU (Kuiokalani Lee)

RECORDED: June, 1966
RELEASED: October, 1966
FIRST APPEARANCE: RCA Victor (LP) LPM-3702 (mono) and LSP-3702 (stereo) SPINOUT
HIT PRIOR TO ELVIS: None
HIT AFTER ELVIS: None
OTHER SIGNIFICANT RECORDINGS: This song has appeared on several albums of Hawaiian favorites.

I'LL TAKE LOVE (Dolores Fuller - Mark Barkan)

RECORDED: September, 1966
RELEASED: May, 1967
FIRST APPEARANCE: RCA Victor (EP) EPA-4387 EASY COME, EASY GO
HIT PRIOR TO ELVIS: None
HIT AFTER ELVIS: None
OTHER SIGNIFICANT RECORDINGS: None

I'LL TAKE YOU HOME AGAIN KATHLEEN (Adapted by Elvis Presley)

RECORDED: May, 1971
RELEASED: July, 1973
FIRST APPEARANCE: RCA (LP) APL1-0283 (stereo) ELVIS
HIT PRIOR TO ELVIS: August, 1957 by Slim Whitman (Imperial 8310). Strangely enough, this was not a country chart hit for Slim. It was, however, on the pop charts.
OTHER SIGNIFICANT RECORDINGS: None

I'M COMIN' HOME (Charlie Rich)

RECORDED: March, 1961
RELEASED: June, 1961
FIRST APPEARANCE: RCA Victor (LP) LPM-2370 (mono) and LSP-2370 (stereo) SOMETHING FOR EVERYBODY
HIT PRIOR TO ELVIS: None
HIT AFTER ELVIS: None
OTHER SIGNIFICANT RECORDINGS: April, 1960 by Carl Mann (Phillips International 3555). This is a completely different song than any of the hits using the same title, by such artists as: Johnny Horton, Tommy James, Dave Edmunds, The Spinners, Johnny Mathis, Stories, Paul Anka, Marv Johnson, Stories, Tom Jones, etc. (Some of these used the similar title "I'm Coming Home," but are listed anyway to eliminate any possible confusion.)

I'M COUNTING ON YOU (Don Robertson)

RECORDED: January, 1956
RELEASED: March, 1956
FIRST APPEARANCE: RCA Victor (LP) LPM-1254 (mono) ELVIS PRESLEY
HIT PRIOR TO ELVIS: None
HIT AFTER ELVIS: November, 1956 by Kitty Wells (Decca 30094).
OTHER SIGNIFICANT RECORDINGS: None

I'M FALLING IN LOVE TONIGHT (Don Robertson)

RECORDED: October, 1962
RELEASED: March, 1963
FIRST APPEARANCE: RCA Victor (LP) LPM-2697 (mono) and LSP-2697 (stereo) IT HAPPENED AT THE WORLD'S FAIR
HIT PRIOR TO ELVIS: None
HIT AFTER ELVIS: None
OTHER SIGNIFICANT RECORDINGS: None

I'M GONNA SIT RIGHT DOWN AND CRY (OVER YOU) (Thomas Biggs)

RECORDED: January, 1956
RELEASED: March, 1956
FIRST APPEARANCE: RCA Victor (LP) LPM-1254 (mono) ELVIS PRESLEY
HIT PRIOR TO ELVIS: None
HIT AFTER ELVIS: None
OTHER SIGNIFICANT RECORDINGS: None

I'M GONNA WALK DEM GOLDEN STAIRS (Adapted by Elvis Presley)

RECORDED: October, 1960
RELEASED: December, 1960
FIRST APPEARANCE: RCA Victor (LP) LPM-2328 (mono) and LSP-2328 (stereo) HIS HAND IN MINE
HIT PRIOR TO ELVIS: None
HIT AFTER ELVIS: None
OTHER SIGNIFICANT RECORDINGS: None

I'M LEAVIN' (Michael Jarrett - Sonny Charles)

RECORDED: May, 1971
RELEASED: July, 1971
FIRST APPEARANCE: RCA (45rpm single) 47-9998
HIT PRIOR TO ELVIS: None
HIT AFTER ELVIS: None
OTHER SIGNIFICANT RECORDINGS: None

I'M LEFT, YOU'RE RIGHT, SHE'S GONE Stanley Kesler - Taylor)

RECORDED: December, 1954
RELEASED: April, 1955
FIRST APPEARANCE: Sun 217 (45 and 78rpm)
HIT PRIOR TO ELVIS: None
HIT AFTER ELVIS: None
OTHER SIGNIFICANT RECORDINGS: January, 1971 by Jerry Foster (Metromedia 201).

I'M MOVIN' ON (Clarence E. "Hank" Snow)

RECORDED: January, 1969
RELEASED: May, 1969
FIRST APPEARANCE: RCA (LP) LSP-4155 FROM ELVIS IN MEMPHIS
HIT PRIOR TO ELVIS: June, 1950 by Hank Snow (RCA Victor 0328); November, 1959 by Ray Charles (Atlantic 2043); December, 1959 by Don Gibson (RCA Victor 47-7629); April, 1963 by Matt Lucas (Smash 1813).
HIT AFTER ELVIS: April, 1972 by John Kay (Dunhill 4309)
OTHER SIGNIFICANT RECORDINGS: It's interesting that Hank Snow's version of this song appears on the same RCA promotional EP (PRO-12) as Elvis' "Old Shep," issued in 1958. Little did anyone know that Elvis would have his own version of this song 11 years later.

'M NOT THE MARRYING KIND (Hal David - Sherman Edwards)

RECORDED: July, 1961
RELEASED: April, 1962
FIRST APPEARANCE: RCA Victor (EP) EPA-4368
    FOLLOW THAT DREAM
HIT PRIOR TO ELVIS: None
HIT AFTER ELVIS: None
OTHER SIGNIFICANT RECORDINGS: None. A completely
    different song, using the same title, was released by Dean
    Martin in late 1966 (Reprise 0538).

I'M SO LONESOME I COULD CRY (Hank Williams)

RECORDED: January, 1973
RELEASED: February, 1973
FIRST APPEARANCE: RCA (LP) VPSX-6089 (quad)
    ALOHA FROM HAWAII VIA SATELLITE
HIT PRIOR TO ELVIS: November, 1949 by Hank
    Williams (MGM 10560); November, 1962 by Johnny
    Tillotson (Cadence 1432); January, 1966 by B.J.
    Thomas (Scepter 12129); January, 1971 by Linda
    Plowman (Janus 146).
HIT AFTER ELVIS: October, 1973 by Hank Wilson
    (aka Leon Russell) (Shelter 7336); February, 1976
    by Terry Bradshaw (Mercury 73760).
OTHER SIGNIFICANT RECORDINGS: None

I'M YOURS (Don Robertson - Hal Blair)

RECORDED: June, 1961
RELEASED: June, 1962
FIRST APPEARANCE: RCA Victor (LP) LPM-2523 (mono)
    and LSP-2523 (stereo) POT LUCK
HIT PRIOR TO ELVIS: None
HIT AFTER ELVIS: None
OTHER SIGNIFICANT RECORDINGS: None. A completely
    different song, using the same title, was recorded by Eddie
    Fisher, by Don Cornell and by The Four Aces. All three
    versions were issued in 1952.

IN MY DREAMS

This song is listed here because it foolishly was included on
an Elvis bootleg album. IT POSITIVELY IS NOT ELVIS!
The origin of the song goes back to a demostration acetate
that was made for Elvis, so that he could listen to the song
and determine whether he wanted to record it. The singer
on the acetate has not yet been identified. It could even
be the composer, as it is not unusual for a songwriter to
record a demo of his/her material when presenting it for
an artists consideration. Regardless, it is not Elvis!

IN MY FATHER'S HOUSE (ARE MANY MANSIONS)
    (Aileene Hanks)
RECORDED: October, 1960
RELEASED: December, 1960
FIRST APPEARANCE: RCA Victor (LP) LPM-2328 (mono)
    and LSP-2328 (stereo) HIS HAND IN MINE
HIT PRIOR TO ELVIS: None
HIT AFTER ELVIS: None
OTHER SIGNIFICANT RECORDINGS: None

IN MY WAY (Fred Wise - Ben Weisman)

RECORDED: October, 1960
RELEASED: July, 1965
FIRST APPEARANCE: RCA Victor (LP) LPM-3450 (mono)
    and LSP-3450 (stereo) ELVIS FOR EVERYONE
HIT PRIOR TO ELVIS: None
HIT AFTER ELVIS: None
OTHER SIGNIFICANT RECORDINGS: None

(See our Elvis novelty/tribute section for information
on the U.K. version of this song by Dave Kaye)

IN THE GARDEN (C. A. Miles)

RECORDED: May, 1966
RELEASED: March, 1967
FIRST APPEARANCE: RCA Victor (LP) LPM-3758 (mono)
    and LSP-3758 (stereo) HOW GREAT THOU ART
HIT PRIOR TO ELVIS: None
HIT AFTER ELVIS: None
OTHER SIGNIFICANT RECORDINGS: None

IN THE GHETTO (Scott Davis)

RECORDED: January, 1969
RELEASED: April, 1969
FIRST APPEARANCE: RCA (45rpm single) 47-9741
HIT PRIOR TO ELVIS: None
HIT AFTER ELVIS: July, 1969 by Dolly Parton (RCA 0192);
    June, 1972 by Candi Staton (Fame 91000).
OTHER SIGNIFICANT RECORDINGS: None

IN YOUR ARMS (Aaron Schroeder - Wally Gold)

RECORDED: March, 1961
RELEASED: June, 1961
FIRST APPEARANCE: RCA Victor (LP) LPM-2370 (mono)
    and LSP-2370 (stereo) SOMETHING FOR EVERYBODY
HIT PRIOR TO ELVIS: None
HIT AFTER ELVIS: None
OTHER SIGNIFICANT RECORDINGS: None

INDESCRIBABLY BLUE (Darrell Glenn)

RECORDED: June, 1966
RELEASED: January, 1967
FIRST APPEARANCE: RCA Victor (45rpm single) 47-9056
HIT PRIOR TO ELVIS: None
OTHER SIGNIFICANT RECORDINGS: None

INHERIT THE WIND (Eddie Rabbitt)

RECORDED: January, 1969
RELEASED: November, 1969
FIRST APPEARANCE: RCA (LP) LSP-6020 (stereo) FROM
    MEMPHIS TO VEGAS/FROM VEGAS TO MEMPHIS
HIT PRIOR TO ELVIS: None
HIT AFTER ELVIS: None
OTHER SIGNIFICANT RECORDINGS: None

IS IT SO STRANGE (Faron Young)

RECORDED: January, 1957
RELEASED: April, 1957
FIRST APPEARANCE: RCA Victor (EP) EPA-4041 JUST
    FOR YOU
HIT PRIOR TO ELVIS: None
HIT AFTER ELVIS: None
OTHER SIGNIFICANT RECORDINGS: None

ISLAND OF LOVE (KAUAI) (Sid Tepper - Roy C. Bennett)

RECORDED: March, 1961
RELEASED: October, 1961
FIRST APPEARANCE: RCA Victor (LP) LPM-2426 (mono) and LSP-2426 (stereo) BLUE HAWAII
HIT PRIOR TO ELVIS: None
HIT AFTER ELVIS: None
OTHER SIGNIFICANT RECORDINGS: None

IT AIN'T NO BIG THING (BUT IT'S GROWING) (Merritt - Joy - Hall)

RECORDED: June, 1970
RELEASED: May, 1971
FIRST APPEARANCE: RCA (LP) LSP-4530 (stereo) LOVE LETTERS FROM ELVIS
HIT PRIOR TO ELVIS: March, 1970 by The Mills Brothers (Dot 17321).
HIT AFTER ELVIS: None
OTHER SIGNIFICANT RECORDINGS: None. A completely different song, using the same title, was done by The Radiants (April, 1965 - Chess 1925)

IT FEELS SO RIGHT (Fred Wise - Ben Weisman)

RECORDED: March, 1960
RELEASED: April, 1960
FIRST APPEARANCE: RCA Victor (LP) LPM-2231 (mono) and LSP-2231 (stereo) ELVIS IS BACK!
HIT PRIOR TO ELVIS: None
HIT AFTER ELVIS: None
OTHER SIGNIFICANT RECORDINGS: None

IT HURTS ME (Joy Byers)

RECORDED: January, 1964
RELEASED: February, 1964
FIRST APPEARANCE: RCA Victor (45rpm single) 47-8307
HIT PRIOR TO ELVIS: None
HIT AFTER ELVIS: None
OTHER SIGNIFICANT RECORDINGS: None. A completely different song, using the same title, was released by Bobby Goldsboro (August, 1966 - United Artists 50056).

IT IS NO SECRET (WHAT GOD CAN DO) (Stuart Hamblen)

RECORDED: January, 1957
RELEASED: March, 1957
FIRST APPEARANCE: RCA Victor (EP) EPA-4054 PEACE IN THE VALLEY
HIT PRIOR TO ELVIS: January, 1951 by Bill Kenny & The Song Spinners (Decca 27326); March, 1951 by Jo Stafford (Columbia 39082).
HIT AFTER ELVIS: None
OTHER SIGNIFICANT RECORDINGS: October, 1950 by Stuart Hamblen (Columbia 20724).

IT KEEPS RIGHT ON A-HURTIN' (Johnny Tillotson)

RECORDED: February, 1969
RELEASED: May, 1969
FIRST APPEARANCE: RCA (LP) LSP-4155 (stereo) FROM ELVIS IN MEMPHIS
HIT PRIOR TO ELVIS: May, 1962 by Johnny Tillotson (Cadence 1418).
HIT AFTER ELVIS: None
OTHER SIGNIFICANT RECORDINGS: None

IT WON'T BE LONG (Sid Wayne - Ben Weisman)

RECORDED: June, 1966
RELEASED: June, 1967
FIRST APPEARANCE: RCA Victor (LP) LPM-3787 (mono) and LSP-3787 (stereo) DOUBLE TROUBLE
HIT PRIOR TO ELVIS: None
HIT AFTER ELVIS: None
OTHER SIGNIFICANT RECORDINGS: None. A completely different song, using the same title, appeared on the first Beatles Capitol LP, "Meet The Beatles" (January, 1964 - Capitol 2047).

IT WON'T SEEM LIKE CHRISTMAS (WITHOUT YOU) (Balthrop)

RECORDED: May, 1971
RELEASED: October, 1971
FIRST APPEARANCE: RCA (LP LSP-4579 (stereo) ELVIS SINGS THE WONDERFUL WORLD OF CHRIST-MAS
HIT PRIOR TO ELVIS: None
HIT AFTER ELVIS: None
OTHER SIGNIFICANT RECORDINGS: None

ITO EATS (Sid Tepper - Roy C. Bennett)

RECORDED: March, 1961
RELEASED: October, 1961
FIRST APPEARANCE: RCA Victor (LP) LPM-2426 (mono) and LSP-2426 (stereo) BLUE HAWAII
HIT PRIOR TO ELVIS: Are you kidding?
HIT AFTER ELVIS: None
OTHER SIGNIFICANT RECORDINGS: None

IT'S A MATTER OF TIME (Clive Westlake)

RECORDED: March, 1972
RELEASED: August, 1972
FIRST APPEARANCE: RCA (45rpm single) 74-0769
HIT PRIOR TO ELVIS: None
HIT AFTER ELVIS: None
OTHER SIGNIFICANT RECORDINGS: None

IT'S A SIN (Fred Rose - Zeb Turner)

RECORDED: March, 1961
RELEASED: June, 1961
FIRST APPEARANCE: RCA Victor (LP) LPM-2370 (mono) and LSP-2370 (stereo) SOMETHING FOR EVERYBODY
HIT PRIOR TO ELVIS: None
HIT AFTER ELVIS: January, 1969 by Marty Robbins (Columbia 44739).
OTHER SIGNIFICANT RECORDINGS: None. This song should not be confused with the huge fifties hit "(It's No) Sin."

IT'S A WONDERFUL WORLD (Sid Tepper - Roy C. Bennett)

RECORDED: February, 1964
RELEASED: October, 1964
FIRST APPEARANCE: RCA Victor (LP) LPM-2999 (mono) and LSP-2999 (stereo) ROUSTABOUT
HIT PRIOR TO ELVIS: None
HIT AFTER ELVIS: None
OTHER SIGNIFICANT RECORDINGS: None

IT'S CARNIVAL TIME (Ben Weisman - Sid Wayne)

RECORDED: February, 1964
RELEASED: October, 1964
FIRST APPEARANCE: RCA Victor (LP) LPM-2999 (mono) and LSP-2999 (stereo) ROUSTABOUT
HIT PRIOR TO ELVIS: None
HIT AFTER ELVIS: None
OTHER SIGNIFICANT RECORDINGS: None

IT'S EASY FOR YOU (Webber - Rice)

RECORDED: October, 1976
RELEASED: July, 1977
FIRST APPEARANCE: RCA Victor (LP) AFL1-2428 (stereo) MOODY BLUE
HIT PRIOR TO ELVIS: None
HIT AFTER ELVIS: None
OTHER SIGNIFICANT RECORDINGS: None

IT'S IMPOSSIBLE (Wayne Manzanero)

RECORDED: February, 1972
RELEASED: July, 1973
FIRST APPEARANCE: RCA (LP) APL1-0283 (stereo) ELVIS
HIT PRIOR TO ELVIS: November, 1970 by Perry Como (RCA 74-0387); September, 1971 by New Birth (RCA 74-0520).
HIT AFTER ELVIS: None
OTHER SIGNIFICANT RECORDINGS: None

IT'S MIDNIGHT (Billy Edd Wheeler - Jerry Chesnut)

RECORDED: December, 1973
RELEASED: October, 1974
FIRST APPEARANCE: RCA (45rpm single) PB-10074
HIT PRIOR TO ELVIS: None
HIT AFTER ELVIS: None
OTHER SIGNIFICANT RECORDINGS: None. A completely different song, using the title "It's Midnight (Do You Know Where Your Baby Is?)" was released by Sandy Posey (December, 1976 - Warner Bros. 8289).

IT'S NOW OR NEVER (Aaron Schroeder - Wally Gold)

RECORDED: April, 1960
RELEASED: July, 1960
FIRST APPEARANCE: RCA Victor (45rpm single) 47-7777
HIT PRIOR TO ELVIS: None
HIT AFTER ELVIS: None
OTHER SIGNIFICANT RECORDINGS: Although ASCAP credits both the words and music to this song to 1960, the tune is based on the Italian "O Sole Mio," a sampling of which can be heard on the LP "Elvis In Concert." The most memorable version of "O Sole Mio" was performed by Enrico Caruso, a 1916 million-seller for him.

IT'S ONLY LOVE (Mark James - Steve Tyrell)

RECORDED: May, 1971
RELEASED: September, 1971
FIRST APPEARANCE: RCA (45rpm single) 48-1017
HIT PRIOR TO ELVIS: March, 1969 by B.J. Thomas (Scepter 12244).
HIT AFTER ELVIS: None
OTHER SIGNIFICANT RECORDINGS: None. Completely different songs, using the same title, have been released by The Beatles, on their "Rubber Soul" LP (Capitol 2442 - December, 1965), and by ZZ Top (September, 1976 - London 241).

IT'S OVER (Jimmie Rodgers)

RECORDED: January, 1973
RELEASED: February, 1973
FIRST APPEARANCE: RCA (LP) VPSX-6089 (quad) ALOHA FROM HAWAII VIA SATELLITE
HIT PRIOR TO ELVIS: May, 1966 by Jimmie Rodgers (Dot 16861).
HIT AFTER ELVIS: None
OTHER SIGNIFICANT RECORDINGS: None. Completely different songs, using the same title, have been released by Roy Orbison (April, 1964 - Monument 837) and by Boz Scaggs (April, 1976 - Columbia 10319). Elvis once sang a portion of the Orbison tune, during a Las Vegas concert, after introducing Orbison, who was in the audience.
NOTE: The earliest known recorded concert wherein Elvis sings "It's Over" was in February, 1972. That version, however, has appeared only on a bootleg release.

IT'S STILL HERE (Ivory Joe Hunter)

RECORDED: May, 1971
RELEASED: July, 1973
FIRST APPEARANCE: RCA (LP) AFL1-0283 (stereo) ELVIS
HIT PRIOR TO ELVIS: None
HIT AFTER ELVIS: None
OTHER SIGNIFICANT RECORDINGS:

IT'S YOUR BABY, YOU ROCK IT (Shirl Milete - Nora Fowler)

RECORDED: June, 1970
RELEASED: February, 1971
FIRST APPEARANCE: RCA (LP) LSP-4460 (stereo) ELVIS COUNTRY
HIT PRIOR TO ELVIS: None
HIT AFTER ELVIS: None
OTHER SIGNIFICANT RECORDINGS: None. This song should not be confused with "It's Your Baby," as recorded by Joe Tex, a completely different song.

I'VE GOT A THING ABOUT YOU BABY (Tony Joe White)

RECORDED: July, 1973
RELEASED: January, 1974
FIRST APPEARANCE: RCA (45rpm single) APBO-0196
HIT PRIOR TO ELVIS: October, 1972 by Billy Lee Riley (Entrance 7508).
HIT AFTER ELVIS: None
OTHER SIGNIFICANT RECORDINGS: None

I'VE GOT CONFIDENCE (Andrae Crouch)

RECORDED: May, 1971
RELEASED: April, 1972
FIRST APPEARANCE: RCA (LP) LSP-4690 (stereo)
HE TOUCHED ME
HIT PRIOR TO ELVIS: None
HIT AFTER ELVIS: None
OTHER SIGNIFICANT RECORDINGS: None

I'VE GOT TO FIND MY BABY (Joy Byers)

RECORDED: July, 1964
RELEASED: April, 1965
FIRST APPEARANCE: RCA Victor (LP) LPM-3338 (mono)
and LSP-3338 (stereo) GIRL HAPPY
HIT PRIOR TO ELVIS: None
HIT AFTER ELVIS: None
OTHER SIGNIFICANT RECORDINGS: None

I'VE LOST YOU (Ken Howard - Alan Blaikley)

RECORDED: June, 1970
RELEASED: July, 1970
FIRST APPEARANCE: RCA (45rpm single) 47-9873
HIT PRIOR TO ELVIS: None
HIT AFTER ELVIS None
OTHER SIGNIFICANT RECORDINGS: None. A completely
different song, using the same title, was released by Jackie
Wilson (April, 1967 - Brunswick 55321).

JAILHOUSE ROCK (Jerry Leiber - Mike Stoller)

RECORDED: June, 1957
RELEASED: October, 1957
FIRST APPEARANCE: RCA Victor (45rpm single) 47-7035
and (78rpm single) 20-7035
HIT PRIOR TO ELVIS: None
HIT AFTER ELVIS: None
OTHER SIGNIFICANT RECORDINGS: None

JUST A LITTLE BIT (Piney Brown - John Thornton - Earl
Washington - Ralph Bass) (D. Gordon)
RECORDED: July, 1973
RELEASED: November, 1973
FIRST APPEARANCE: RCA (LP) APL1-0388 (stereo)
RAISED ON ROCK/FOR OL' TIMES SAKE
HIT PRIOR TO ELVIS: February, 1960 by Roscoe Gordon
(Vee Jay 332); October, 1965 by Roy Head (Scepter 12116).
HIT AFTER ELVIS: None
OTHER SIGNIFICANT RECORDINGS: None. Completely
different songs, using the same title, were released by
Blue Cheer (June, 1968 - Philips 40541) and Little Milton
(May, 1969 - Checker 1217).

NOTE: Elvis' version of this song, and BMI's files, show the
team of Brown, Thornton, Washington and Bass as composers.
Both the Gordon and Head releases credit D. Gordon as the
songs writer.

JESUS KNOWS WHAT I NEED (Mosie Lister)

RECORDED: October, 1960
RELEASED: December, 1960
FIRST APPEARANCE: RCA Victor (LP) LPM-2328 (mono)
and LSP-2328 (stereo) HIS HAND IN MINE
HIT PRIOR TO ELVIS: None
HIT AFTER ELVIS: None
OTHER SIGNIFICANT RECORDINGS: By The Statesmen
Quartet, a version that no doubt inspired Elvis' recording.
NOTE: On the "His Hand In Mine" reissue (ANL1-1319) and on many
foreign pressings, the title of this song is shown as "He Knows Just
What I Need."

JOHNNY B. GOODE (Chuck Berry)

RECORDED: August, 1969
RELEASED: November, 1969
FIRST APPEARANCE: RCA (LP) LSP-6020 (stereo) FROM
MEMPHIS TO VEGAS/FROM VEGAS TO MEMPHIS
HIT PRIOR TO ELVIS: April, 1958 by Chuck Berry (Chess
1691); August, 1964 by Dion (Columbia 43096); May,
1969 by Buck Owens (Capitol 2485).
HIT AFTER ELVIS: January, 1970 by Johnny Winter
(Columbia 45058).
OTHER SIGNIFICANT RECORDINGS: None

JOSHUA FIT THE BATTLE (Arranged and Adapted by
Elvis Presley)
RECORDED: October, 1960
RELEASED: December, 1960
FIRST APPEARANCE: RCA Victor (LP) LPM-2328 (mono)
and LSP-2328 (stereo) HIS HAND IN MINE
HIT PRIOR TO ELVIS: None
HIT AFTER ELVIS: None
OTHER SIGNIFICANT RECORDINGS: None

JUDY (Teddy Redell)

RECORDED: March, 1961
RELEASED: June, 1961
FIRST APPEARANCE: RCA Victor (LP) LPM-2370 (mono)
and LSP-2370 (stereo) SOMETHING FOR EVERYBODY
HIT PRIOR TO ELVIS: None
HIT AFTER ELVIS: None
OTHER SIGNIFICANT RECORDINGS: None. Completely
different songs, using the same title, were released by:
Frankie Vaughn (August, 1958 - Epic 9273); David Seville
(May, 1959 - Liberty 55193); Ray Sanders (December,
1970 - United Artists 50732).

JUST A LITTLE BIT (goes here)

JUST BECAUSE (Bob Shelton - Joe Shelton - Sid Robin)

RECORDED: September, 1954
RELEASED: March, 1956
FIRST APPEARANCE: RCA Victor (LP) LPM-1254 (mono)
ELVIS PRESLEY
HIT PRIOR TO ELVIS: May, 1948 by Frankie Yankovic &
His Yanks (Columbia 12359).
HIT AFTER ELVIS: November, 1961 by The McGuire
Sisters (Coral 62288).
OTHER SIGNIFICANT RECORDINGS: April, 1957 by The
Happy Jesters (Dot 15566), a comedy-parody version.
NOTE: Although Elvis' version shows the writing team of Shelton,
Shelton and Robin, the writing credits on the McGuire Sisters version
list Edna Lewis, Dick Jacobs and Murray Kane as the composing team.

JUST CALL ME LONESOME (Rex Griffin)

RECORDED: September, 1967
RELEASED: November, 1967
FIRST APPEARANCE: RCA Victor (LP) LPM-3893 (mono) and LSP-3893 (stereo) CLAMBAKE
HIT PRIOR TO ELVIS: August, 1955 by Eddy Arnold (RCA Victor 47-6198).
HIT AFTER ELVIS: None
OTHER SIGNIFICANT RECORDINGS: None

JUST FOR OLD TIMES SAKE (Sid Tepper - Roy C. Bennett)

RECORDED: March, 1962
RELEASED: June, 1962
FIRST APPEARANCE: RCA Victor (LP) LPM-2523 (mono) and LSP-2523 (stereo) POT LUCK
HIT PRIOR TO ELVIS: None
HIT AFTER ELVIS: None
OTHER SIGNIFICANT RECORDINGS: None. A completely different song, using the same title, was released by The McGuire Sisters (March, 1961 - Coral 62249).

JUST PRETEND (Doug Flett - Guy Fletcher)

RECORDED: June, 1970
RELEASED: December, 1970
FIRST APPEARANCE: RCA (LP) LSP-4445 (stereo) THAT'S THE WAY IT IS
HIT PRIOR TO ELVIS: None
HIT AFTER ELVIS: None
OTHER SIGNIFICANT RECORDINGS: None

JUST TELL HER JIM SAID HELLO (Jerry Leiber - Mike Stoller)

RECORDED: March, 1962
RELEASED: August, 1962
FIRST APPEARANCE: RCA Victor (45rpm single) 47-8041
HIT PRIOR TO ELVIS: None
HIT AFTER ELVIS: None
OTHER SIGNIFICANT RECORDINGS: None

KENTUCKY RAIN (Eddie Rabbitt - D. Heard)

RECORDED: February, 1969
RELEASED: February, 1970
FIRST APPEARANCE: RCA (45rpm single) 47-9791
HIT PRIOR TO ELVIS: None
HIT AFTER ELVIS: None
OTHER SIGNIFICANT RECORDINGS: None

KING CREOLE (Jerry Leiber - Mike Stoller)

RECORDED: January, 1958
RELEASED: August, 1958
FIRST APPEARANCE: RCA Victor (LP) LPM-1884 (mono) KING CREOLE
HIT PRIOR TO ELVIS: None
HIT AFTER ELVIS: None
OTHER SIGNIFICANT RECORDINGS: None

KING OF THE WHOLE WIDE WORLD (Ruth Batchelor - Bob Roberts)

RECORDED: October, 1961
RELEASED: September, 1962
FIRST APPEARANCE: RCA Victor (EP) EPA-4371 KID GALAHAD
HIT PRIOR TO ELVIS: None
HIT AFTER ELVIS: None
OTHER SIGNIFICANT RECORDINGS: None
NOTE: On both the EP and the special promotional single (SP 45-118), songwriter Ruth Batchelor's name is incorrectly spelled, omitting the "e" in her last name.

KISSIN' COUSINS (Fred Wise - Randy Starr)

RECORDED: October, 1963
RELEASED: March, 1964
FIRST APPEARANCE: RCA Victor (LP) LPM-2894 (mono) and LSP-2894 (stereo) KISSIN' COUSINS
HIT PRIOR TO ELVIS: None
HIT AFTER ELVIS: None
OTHER SIGNIFICANT RECORDINGS: None

KISSIN' COUSINS (NUMBER 2) (Bill Giant - Bernie Baum - Florence Kaye)

RECORDED: October, 1963
RELEASED: March, 1964
FIRST APPEARANCE: RCA Victor (LP) LPM-2894 (mono) and LSP-2894 (stereo) KISSIN' COUSINS
HIT PRIOR TO ELVIS: None
HIT AFTER ELVIS: None
OTHER SIGNIFICANT RECORDINGS: None

KISMET (Sid Tepper - Roy C. Bennett)

RECORDED: February, 1965
RELEASED: October, 1965
FIRST APPEARANCE: RCA Victor (LP) LPM-3468 (mono) and LSP-3468 (stereo) HARUM SCARUM
HIT PRIOR TO ELVIS: None
HIT AFTER ELVIS: None
OTHER SIGNIFICANT RECORDINGS: None. It should be noted that this song was not from, nor was it connected in any way with, the Broadway production "Kismet."

KISS ME QUICK (Doc Pomus - Mort Schuman)

RECORDED: June, 1961
RELEASED: June, 1962
FIRST APPEARANCE: RCA Victor (LP) LPM-2523 (mono) and LSP-2523 (stereo) POT LUCK
HIT PRIOR TO ELVIS: None
HIT AFTER ELVIS: None
OTHER SIGNIFICANT RECORDINGS: None

KNOWN ONLY TO HIM (Stuart Hamblen)

RECORDED: October, 1960
RELEASED: December, 1960
FIRST APPEARANCE: RCA Victor (LP) LPM-2328 (mono) and LSP-2328 (stereo) HIS HAND IN MINE
HIT PRIOR ELVIS: None
HIT AFTER ELVIS: None
OTHER SIGNIFICANT RECORDINGS: None known, however the possibility does exist that Hamblen recorded this song himself. We just have no documentation of such a release.

KU-U-I-PO (HAWAIIAN SWEETHEART) (Hugo Peretti - Luigi Creatore - George Weiss)
RECORDED: March, 1961
RELEASED: October, 1961
FIRST APPEARANCE: RCA Victor (LP) LPM-2426 (mono) and LSP-2426 (stereo) BLUE HAWAII
HIT PRIOR TO ELVIS: None
HIT AFTER ELVIS: None
OTHER SIGNIFICANT RECORDINGS: None
NOTE: The "(Hawaiian Sweetheart)" portion of the title does not appear on the jackets. Nor does it appear on the label of the Pickwick LP "Mahalo From Elvis," which also contains a version of "Ku-u-i-po."

LAWDY, MISS CLAWDY (Lloyd Price)
RECORDED: February, 1956
RELEASED: August, 1956
FIRST APPEARANCE: RCA Victor (45rpm single) 47-6642 and (78rpm single) 20-6642
HIT PRIOR TO ELVIS: May, 1952 by Lloyd Price (Specialty 428).
HIT AFTER ELVIS: February, 1960 by Gary Stites (Carlton 525); March, 1967 by The Buckinghams (U.S.A. 869). The title spelling on the Buckinghams release is "Laudy Miss Claudy."
OTHER SIGNIFICANT RECORDINGS: None

LEAD ME, GUIDE ME (Doris Akers)
RECORDED: May, 1971
RELEASED: April, 1972
FIRST APPEARANCE: RCA (LP) LSP-4690 (stereo) HE TOUCHED ME
HIT PRIOR TO ELVIS: None
HIT AFTER ELVIS: None
OTHER SIGNIFICANT RECORDINGS: None

LET IT BE ME (JE T'APPARTIENS) (Mann Curtis - Gilbert Becaud)
RECORDED: February, 1970
RELEASED: May, 1970
FIRST APPEARANCE: RCA (LP) LSP-4362 (stereo) ON STAGE - FEBRUARY, 1970
HIT PRIOR TO ELVIS: April, 1957 by Jill Corey (Columbia 40878); January, 1960 by The Everly Brothers (Cadence 1376); August, 1964 by Betty Everett & Jerry Burler (Vee Jay 613); July, 1967 by The Sweet Inspirations (Atlantic 2418); January, 1969 by Glen Campbell & Bobbie Gentry (Capitol 2387).
HIT AFTER ELVIS: None
OTHER SIGNIFICANT RECORDINGS: None

NOTE: This song was introduced in the States as the theme song for the mid-fifties television show "Climax." Many readers may have thought that the first hit version was by the Everly Brothers, however, as you can see, it was a nationally charted hit for Jill Corey nearly three years earlier.

LET ME (Elvis Presley - Vera Matson)
RECORDED: August, 1956
RELEASED: November, 1956
FIRST APPEARANCE: RCA Victor (EP) EPA-4006 LOVE ME TENDER
HIT PRIOR TO ELVIS: None
HIT AFTER ELVIS: None
OTHER SIGNIFICANT RECORDINGS: None. A completely different song, using the same title, was released by Paul Revere & The Raiders (May, 1969 - Columbia 44854).

LET ME BE THERE (John Rostill)
RECORDED: March, 1974
RELEASED: June, 1974
FIRST APPEARANCE: RCA (LP) CPL1-0606 (stereo) ELVIS RECORDED LIVE ON STAGE IN MEMPHIS
HIT PRIOR TO ELVIS: November, 1973 by Olivia Newton-John (MCA 40101).
HIT AFTER ELVIS: None
OTHER SIGNIFICANT RECORDINGS: None

LET YOURSELF GO (Joy Byers)
RECORDED: June, 1967
RELEASED: June, 1968
FIRST APPEARANCE: RCA Victor (45rpm single) 47-9547
HIT PRIOR TO ELVIS: None
HIT AFTER ELVIS: None
OTHER SIGNIFICANT RECORDINGS: None. Completely different songs, using the same title, were released by James Brown (April, 1967 - King 6100) and The Friends Of Distinction (July, 1969 - RCA 74-0204).

LET'S BE FRIENDS (Arnold - Morrow - Martin)
RECORDED: March, 1969
RELEASED: April, 1970
FIRST APPEARANCE: RCA Camden (LP) CAS-2408 (stereo) LET'S BE FRIENDS
HIT PRIOR TO ELVIS: None
HIT AFTER ELVIS: None
OTHER SIGNIFICANT RECORDINGS: None

LET'S FORGET ABOUT THE STARS (A. L. Owens)
RECORDED: March, 1969
RELEASED: April, 1970
FIRST APPEARANCE: RCA Camden (LP) CAS-2408 (stereo) LET'S BE FRIENDS
HIT PRIOR TO ELVIS: None
HIT AFTER ELVIS: None
OTHER SIGNIFICANT RECORDINGS: None

LET US PRAY (Ben Weisman - Florence Kaye)
RECORDED: May, 1969
RELEASED: March, 1971
FIRST APPEARANCE: RCA Camden (LP) CALX-2472 YOU'LL NEVER WALK ALONE
HIT PRIOR TO ELVIS: None
HIT AFTER ELVIS: None
OTHER SIGNIFICANT RECORDINGS: None

LIFE (Shirl Milete)

RECORDED: June, 1970
RELEASED: May, 1971
FIRST APPEARANCE: RCA (45rpm single) 47-9985
HIT PRIOR TO ELVIS: None
HIT AFTER ELVIS: None
OTHER SIGNIFICANT RECORDINGS: None. A completely different song, using the same title, was released by Sly & The Family Stone (July, 1968 - Epic 10353)

LIKE A BABY (Jesse Stone)

RECORDED: April, 1960
RELEASED: April, 1960
FIRST APPEARANCE: RCA Victor (LP) LPM-2231 (mono) and LSP-2231 (stereo) ELVIS IS BACK!
HIT PRIOR TO ELVIS: None
HIT AFTER ELVIS: None
OTHER SIGNIFICANT RECORDINGS: January, 1963 by James Brown (King 5710).

LITTLE CABIN ON THE HILL (Bill Monroe - Lester Flatt)

RECORDED: June, 1970
RELEASED: February, 1971
FIRST APPEARANCE: RCA (LP) LSP-4460 (stereo) ELVIS COUNTRY
HIT PRIOR TO ELVIS: None
HIT AFTER ELVIS: None
OTHER SIGNIFICANT RECORDINGS: 1949 by Bill Monroe's Bluegrass Boys (Columbia 20459). This original version carried the title "Little Cabin Home On The Hill."

LITTLE DARLIN' (Maurice Williams)

RECORDED: April, 1977
RELEASED: July, 1977
FIRST APPEARANCE: RCA (LP) AFL1-2428 (stereo) MOODY BLUE
HIT PRIOR TO ELVIS: January, 1957 by The Gladiolas (Excello 2101); February, 1957 by The Diamonds (Mercury 71060).
HIT AFTER ELVIS: None
OTHER SIGNIFICANT RECORDINGS: February, 1961 by Bobby Rydell, "Cherie" uses the same music as "Little Darlin'" but with completely different lyrics (Cameo 186).

LITTLE EGYPT (Jerry Leiber - Mike Stoller)

RECORDED: February, 1964
RELEASED: October, 1964
FIRST APPEARANCE: RCA Victor (LP) LPM-2999 (mono) and LSP-2999 (stereo) ROUSTABOUT
HIT PRIOR TO ELVIS: April, 1961 by The Coasters (Atco 6192).
HIT AFTER ELVIS: None
OTHER SIGNIFICANT RECORDINGS: None

LITTLE SISTER (Doc Pomus - Mort Schuman)

RECORDED: June, 1961
RELEASED: August, 1961
FIRST APPEARANCE: RCA Victor (45rpm single) 47-7908
HIT PRIOR TO ELVIS: None
HIT AFTER ELVIS: None
OTHER SIGNIFICANT RECORDINGS: None

LONESOME COWBOY (Sid Tepper - Roy C. Bennett)

RECORDED: February, 1957
RELEASED: July, 1957
FIRST APPEARANCE: RCA Victor (LP) LPM-1515 (mono) LOVING YOU
HIT PRIOR TO ELVIS: None
HIT AFTER ELVIS: None
OTHER SIGNIFICANT RECORDINGS: None

LONG BLACK LIMOUSINE (Vern Stovall - Bobby George)

RECORDED: January, 1969
RELEASED: May, 1969
FIRST APPEARANCE: RCA (LP) LSP-4155 (stereo)
HIT PRIOR TO ELVIS: October, 1968 by Jody Miller (Capitol 2290).
HIT AFTER ELVIS: None
OTHER SIGNIFICANT RECORDINGS: None

LONG LEGGED GIRL (WITH THE SHORT DRESS ON)
(J. Leslie McFarland - Winfield Scott)
RECORDED: June, 1966
RELEASED: May, 1967
FIRST APPEARANCE: RCA Victor (45rpm single) 47-9115
HIT PRIOR TO ELVIS: None
HIT AFTER ELVIS: None
OTHER SIGNIFICANT RECORDINGS: None

(IT'S A) LONG LONELY HIGHWAY (Doc Pomus - Mort Schuman)
RECORDED: May, 1963
RELEASED: March, 1964
FIRST APPEARANCE: RCA Victor (LP) LPM-2894 (mono) and LSP-2894 (stereo) KISSIN' COUSINS
HIT PRIOR TO ELVIS: None
HIT AFTER ELVIS: None
OTHER SIGNIFICANT RECORDINGS: None

LONG TALL SALLY (Enotris Johnson - Richard Penniman - Robert Blackwell)
RECORDED: September, 1956
RELEASED: November, 1956
FIRST APPEARANCE: RCA Victor (LP) LPM-1382 (mono) ELVIS
HIT PRIOR TO ELVIS: March, 1956 by Little Richard (Richard Penniman) (Specialty 572); April, 1956 by Pat Boone (Dot 15457).
HIT AFTER ELVIS: None
OTHER SIGNIFICANT RECORDINGS: None

LONELY MAN (Benny Benjamin - Sol Marcus)

RECORDED: October, 1960
RELEASED: February, 1961
FIRST APPEARANCE: RCA Victor (45rpm single) 47-7850
HIT PRIOR TO ELVIS: None
HIT AFTER ELVIS: None
OTHER SIGNIFICANT RECORDINGS: None. A completely different song, using the similar title "A Lonely Man" was released by The Chi-Lites (September, 1972 - Brunswick 55483).

LOOK OUT, BROADWAY (Fred Wise - Randy Starr)

RECORDED: May, 1965
RELEASED: April, 1966
FIRST APPEARANCE: RCA Victor (LP) LPM-3553 (mono) and LSP-3553 (stereo) FRANKIE AND JOHNNY
HIT PRIOR TO ELVIS: None
HIT AFTER ELVIS: None
OTHER SIGNIFICANT RECORDINGS: None

LOVE COMING DOWN (Jerry Chesnut)

RECORDED: February, 1976
RELEASED: May, 1976
FIRST APPEARANCE: RCA (LP) APL1-1506 (stereo) FROM ELVIS PRESLEY BOULEVARD, MEMPHIS, TENNESSEE
HIT PRIOR TO ELVIS: None
HIT AFTER ELVIS: None
OTHER SIGNIFICANT RECORDINGS: None

LOVE LETTERS (Edward Heyman - Victor Young)

RECORDED: May, 1966
RELEASED: June, 1966
FIRST APPEARANCE: RCA Victor (45rpm single) 47-8870
HIT PRIOR TO ELVIS: February, 1962 by Ketty Lester (Era 3068).
HIT AFTER ELVIS: None
OTHER SIGNIFICANT RECORDINGS: None, although it is surprising that it took 17 years for this tune to become a pop hit. It was written in 1945.

LOVE ME (Jerry Leiber - Mike Stoller)

RECORDED: September, 1956
RELEASED: November, 1956
FIRST APPEARANCE: RCA Victor (LP) LPM-1382 (mono) ELVIS
HIT PRIOR TO ELVIS: None
HIT AFTER ELVIS: None
OTHER SIGNIFICANT RECORDINGS: 1954 by Willie & Ruth (Spark); December, 1954 by Jimmie Rodgers Snow (RCA Victor 47-5986); April, 1959 by The Jackson Brothers (Atco 6139). Completely different songs, using the same title, were done by: Bobby Hebb (December, 1966 - Philips 40421); The Rascals (June, 1971 - Columbia 45300); The Impressions (July, 1971 - Curtom 1959); Billy Stewart (May, 1966 - Chess 1960); Yvonne Elliman (September, 1976 - RSO 858).

LOVE ME, LOVE THE LIFE I LEAD (Macaulay - Greenaway)

RECORDED: May, 1971
RELEASED: July, 1973
FIRST APPEARANCE: RCA (LP) APL1-0283 (stereo) ELVIS
HIT PRIOR TO ELVIS: None
HIT AFTER ELVIS: None
OTHER SIGNIFICANT RECORDINGS: None

LOVE ME TENDER (Elvis Presley - Vera Matson)

RECORDED: August, 1956
RELEASED: October, 1956
FIRST APPEARANCE: RCA Victor (45rpm single) 47-6643 and 20-6643 (78rpm single).
HIT PRIOR TO ELVIS: None
HIT AFTER ELVIS: November, 1956 by Henri Rene (RCA Victor 47-6728); September, 1962 by Richard Chamberlain (MGM 13097); June, 1967 by Percy Sledge (Atlantic 2414).
OTHER SIGNIFICANT RECORDINGS: March, 1978 by James Brown, as a tribute recording to Elvis (Polydor 14460). A completely different song, using the same title, was released by The Sparrows (1956 - Davis 456).

LOVE ME TONIGHT (Don Robertson)

RECORDED: May, 1963
RELEASED: November, 1963
FIRST APPEARANCE: RCA Victor (LP) LPM-2756 (mono) and LSP-2756 (stereo) FUN IN ACAPULCO
HIT PRIOR TO ELVIS: None
HIT AFTER ELVIS: None
OTHER SIGNIFICANT RECORDINGS: None. Completely different songs, using the same title, were released by Tom Jones (May, 1969 - Parrot 40038) and by Head East (A & M 1784).

LOVER DOLL (Sid Wayne - Abner Silver)

RECORDED: January, 1958
RELEASED: August, 1958
FIRST APPEARANCE: RCA Victor (LP) LPM-1884 (mono) KING CREOLE
HIT PRIOR TO ELVIS: None
HIT AFTER ELVIS: None
OTHER SIGNIFICANT RECORDINGS: None

LOVE SONG OF THE YEAR (Chris Christian)

RECORDED: December, 1973
RELEASED: January, 1975
FIRST APPEARANCE: RCA (LP) APL1-0873 (stereo) PROMISED LAND
HIT PRIOR TO ELVIS: None
HIT AFTER ELVIS: None
OTHER SIGNIFICANT RECORDINGS: None

LOVING ARMS (Tom Jans)

RECORDED: December, 1973
RELEASED: March, 1974
FIRST APPEARANCE: RCA (LP) CPL1-0475 (stereo) GOOD TIMES
HIT PRIOR TO ELVIS: July, 1973 by Dobie Gray (MCA 40100.
HIT AFTER ELVIS: March, 1974 by Kris Kristofferson & Rita Coolidge (A&M 1498).
OTHER SIGNIFICANT RECORDINGS: None

LOVING YOU (Jerry Leiber - Mike Stoller)

RECORDED: February, 1957
RELEASED: June, 1957
FIRST APPEARANCE: RCA Victor (45 rpm single) 47-7000 and (78rpm single) 20-7000
HIT PRIOR TO ELVIS: None
HIT AFTER ELVIS: None
OTHER SIGNIFICANT RECORDINGS: October, 1977 by Donna Fargo, with the Jordanaires, as a tribute to Elvis. (Warner Bros. LP RS-3099 "Shame On Me"). Completely different songs, using the same title, were released by numerous artists (some shown as "Lovin' You").

MAKE ME KNOW IT (Otis Blackwell)

RECORDED: March, 1960
RELEASED: April, 1960
FIRST APPEARANCE: RCA Victor (LP) LPM-2231 (mono) and LSP-2231 (stereo) ELVIS IS BACK!
HIT PRIOR TO ELVIS: None
HIT AFTER ELVIS: None
OTHER SIGNIFICANT RECORDINGS: None

MAKE THE WORLD GO AWAY (Hank Cochran)

RECORDED: June, 1970
RELEASED: February, 1971
FIRST APPEARANCE: RCA (LP) LSP-4460 (stereo) ELVIS COUNTRY
HIT PRIOR TO ELVIS: July, 1963 by Ray Price (Columbia 42827); July, 1963 by Timi Yuro (Liberty 55587); October, 1965 by Eddy Arnold (RCA Victor 47-8679); June, 1975 by Donny & Marie Osmond (MGM 14807).
HIT AFTER ELVIS: None
OTHER SIGNIFICANT RECORDINGS: None

MAMA (Charles O'Curran - Dudley Brooks)

RECORDED: March, 1962
RELEASED: April, 1970
FIRST APPEARANCE: RCA Camden (LP) CAS-2408 (stereo) LET'S BE FRIENDS
HIT PRIOR TO ELVIS: None
HIT AFTER ELVIS: None
OTHER SIGNIFICANT RECORDINGS: None. Completely different songs, using the same title, were released by Connie Francis (February, 1960 - MGM 12878) and B.J. Thomas (May, 1966 - Pacemaker 231 & Scepter 12139)

MAMA DON'T DANCE (Kenny Loggins - Jim Messina)

RECORDED: March, 1974
RELEASED: June, 1974
FIRST APPEARANCE: RCA (LP) CPL1-0606 (stereo) ELVIS RECORDED LIVE ON STAGE IN MEMPHIS (This song is performed as part of a six song medley)
HIT PRIOR TO ELVIS: November, 1972 by Loggins & Messina (Columbia 45719) as "Your Mama Don't Dance."
HIT AFTER ELVIS: None
OTHER SIGNIFICANT RECORDINGS: None

MAMA LIKED THE ROSES (John Christopher)

RECORDED: January, 1969
RELEASED: May, 1970
FIRST APPEARANCE: RCA (45rpm single) 47-9835
HIT PRIOR TO ELVIS: None
HIT AFTER ELVIS: None
OTHER SIGNIFICANT RECORDINGS: None

MANSION OVER THE HILLTOP (Ira Stamphill)

RECORDED: October, 1960
RELEASED: December, 1960
FIRST APPEARANCE: RCA Victor (LP) LPM-2328 (mono) and LSP-2328 (stereo) HIS HAND IN MINE
HIT PRIOR TO ELVIS: None
HIT AFTER ELVIS: None
OTHER SIGNIFICANT RECORDINGS: None

MARGUERITA (Don Robertson)

RECORDED: January, 1963
RELEASED: November, 1963
FIRST APPEARANCE: RCA Victor (LP) LPM-2756 (mono) and LSP-2756 (stereo) FUN IN ACAPULCO
HIT PRIOR TO ELVIS: None
HIT AFTER ELVIS: None
OTHER SIGNIFICANT RECORDINGS: None. A completely different song, using the same title, and done in an Elvis soundalike style was released by Terry Stafford on his LP "Suspicion" (May, 1964 - Crusader 1001).

MARY IN THE MORNING (Johnny Cymbal - Michael Rashkow)

RECORDED: June, 1970
RELEASED: December, 1970
FIRST APPEARANCE: RCA (LP) LSP-4445 (stereo) THAT'S THE WAY IT IS
HIT PRIOR TO ELVIS: May, 1967 by Al Martino (Capitol 5904).
HIT AFTER ELVIS: None
OTHER SIGNIFICANT RECORDINGS: None

MEAN WOMAN BLUES (Claude DeMetrius)

RECORDED: January, 1957
RELEASED: July, 1957
FIRST APPEARANCE: RCA Victor (LP) LPM-1515 (mono) LOVING YOU
HIT PRIOR TO ELVIS: None
HIT AFTER ELVIS: September, 1963 by Roy Orbison (Monument 824).
OTHER SIGNIFICANT RECORDINGS: None

MEMORIES (Scott Davis - Strange)

RECORDED: June, 1968
RELEASED: December, 1968
FIRST APPEARANCE: RCA (LP) LPM-4088 (some mono/ some stereo) ELVIS (NBC-TV SPECIAL)
HIT PRIOR TO ELVIS: None
HIT AFTER ELVIS: December, 1969 by The Lettermen as half of a two song medley, "Traces"/"Memories" (Capitol 2697).
OTHER SIGNIFICANT RECORDINGS: None. A completely different song, using the same title, was written in 1915 by Gus Kahn and Egbert Van Alstyne.

MEMPHIS, TENNESSEE (Chuck Berry)

RECORDED: January, 1964
RELEASED: July, 1965
FIRST APPEARANCE: RCA Victor (LP) LPM-3450 (mono) and LSP-3450 ELVIS FOR EVERYONE
HIT PRIOR TO ELVIS: May, 1963 by Lonnie Mack (instrumental) (Fraternity 906).
HIT AFTER ELVIS: May, 1964 by Johnny Rivers (Imperial 66032).
OTHER SIGNIFICANT RECORDINGS: June, 1959 by Chuck Berry (Chess 1729).
NOTE: Both Elvis' and Chuck Berry's versions used the complete title "Memphis, Tennessee." The Mack and Rivers releases shortened the title to just "Memphis." A sequel tune was released by Chuck Berry, titled "Little Marie," in October of 1964 (Chess 1912).

MERRY CHRISTMAS BABY (Lou Baxter - Johnny Moore)

RECORDED: May, 1971
RELEASED: October, 1971
FIRST APPEARANCE: RCA (LP) LSP-4579 (stereo) ELVIS SINGS THE WONDERFUL WORLD OF CHRISTMAS
HIT PRIOR TO ELVIS: December, 1949 by Johnny Moore's Three Blazers (Exclusive 63); December, 1958 by Chuck Berry (Chess 1714).
HIT AFTER ELVIS: None
OTHER SIGNIFICANT RECORDINGS: December, 1950 by Charles Brown With Johnny Moore's Three Blazers (Swing Time 238); December, 1954 by Charles Brown (Hollywood 1021).
NOTE: The same master recording was used on all of the above issues, except the Chuck Berry version, of course.

MEXICO (Sid Tepper - Roy C. Bennett)

RECORDED: January, 1963
RELEASED: November, 1963
FIRST APPEARANCE: RCA Victor (LP) LPM-2756 (mono) and LSP-2756 (stereo) FUN IN ACAPULCO
HIT PRIOR TO ELVIS: None
HIT AFTER ELVIS: None
OTHER SIGNIFICANT RECORDINGS: None. Completely different songs, using the same title, were recorded by Bob Moore (an instrumental) (August, 1961 - Monument 446) and by James Taylor (September, 1975 - Warner Bros. 8137).
NOTE: Although he is not featured on this particular session, Bob Moore, who had the instrumental hit of "Mexico," was a bass player for Elvis on many of his sixties recording sessions.

MILKCOW BLUES BOOGIE (Kokomo Arnold)

RECORDED: December, 1954
RELEASED: January, 1955
FIRST APPEARANCE: Sun 215 (45 and 78rpm)
HIT PRIOR TO ELVIS: None
HIT AFTER ELVIS: January, 1961 by Rick Nelson (Imperial 5707).
OTHER SIGNIFICANT RECORDINGS: The original recording of this song was done in 1935 by Kokomo Arnold. Both the Arnold and Rick Nelson versions were titled "Milk Cow Blues." Kokomo's release was on Decca (7029) records.

MILKY WHITE WAY (Arranged and Adapted by Elvis Presley)

RECORDED: October, 1960
RELEASED: December, 1960
FIRST APPEARANCE: RCA Victor (LP) LPM-2328 (mono) and LSP-2328 (stereo) HIS HAND IN MINE
HIT PRIOR TO ELVIS: None
HIT AFTER ELVIS: None
OTHER SIGNIFICANT RECORDINGS: None

MINE (Sid Tepper - Roy C. Bennett)

RECORDED: September, 1967
RELEASED: June, 1968
FIRST APPEARANCE: RCA Victor (LP) LPM-3989 (mono) and LSP-3989 (stereo) SPEEDWAY
HIT PRIOR TO ELVIS: None
HIT AFTER ELVIS: None
OTHER SIGNIFICANT RECORDINGS: None

MIRACLE OF THE ROSARY (Lee Denson)

RECORDED: May, 1971
RELEASED: February, 1972
FIRST APPEARANCE: RCA (LP) LSP-4671 (stereo) ELVIS NOW
HIT PRIOR TO ELVIS: None
HIT AFTER ELVIS: None
OTHER SIGNIFICANT RECORDINGS: None

MIRAGE (Bill Giant - Bernie Baum - Florence Kaye)

RECORDED: February, 1965
RELEASED: October, 1965
FIRST APPEARANCE: RCA Victor (LP) LPM-3468 (mono) and LSP-3468 (stereo) HARUM SCARUM
HIT PRIOR TO ELVIS: None
HIT AFTER ELVIS: None
OTHER SIGNIFICANT RECORDINGS: None. A completely different song, using the same title, was released by Tommy James & The Shondells (April, 1967 - Roulette 4736).

MONEY HONEY (Jesse Stone)

RECORDED: January, 1956
RELEASED: February, 1956
FIRST APPEARANCE: RCA Victor (LP) LPM-1254 (mono) ELVIS PRESLEY
HIT PRIOR TO ELVIS: October, 1953 by The Drifters (Atlantic 1006).
HIT AFTER ELVIS: None
OTHER SIGNIFICANT RECORDINGS: None. A completely different song, using the same title, was released by the Bay City Rollers (January, 1976 - Arista 0170).

MOODY BLUE (Mark James)

RECORDED: February, 1976
RELEASED: December, 1976
FIRST APPEARANCE: RCA (45rpm single) PB-10857
HIT PRIOR TO ELVIS: None
HIT AFTER ELVIS: None
OTHER SIGNIFICANT RECORDINGS: None

MOONLIGHT SWIM (Sylvia Dee - Ben Weisman)

RECORDED: March, 1961
RELEASED: October, 1961
FIRST APPEARANCE: RCA Victor (LP) LPM-2426 (mono) and LSP-2426 (stereo) BLUE HAWAII
HIT PRIOR TO ELVIS: August, 1957 by Nick Noble (Mercury 71169); October, 1957 by Tony Perkins (RCA Victor 47-7020), shown as "Moon-Light Swim."
HIT AFTER ELVIS: None
OTHER SIGNIFICANT RECORDINGS: None

MR. SONGMAN (Donnie Sumner)

RECORDED: December, 1973
RELEASED: January, 1975
FIRST APPEARANCE: RCA (LP) APL1-0873 (stereo) PROMISED LAND
HIT PRIOR TO ELVIS: None
HIT AFTER ELVIS: None
OTHER SIGNIFICANT RECORDINGS: None

MY BABE (Willie Dixon)

RECORDED: August, 1969
RELEASED: November, 1969
FIRST APPEARANCE: RCA (LP) LSP-6020 (stereo) FROM MEMPHIS TO VEGAS/FROM VEGAS TO MEMPHIS
HIT PRIOR TO ELVIS: February, 1955 by Little Walter (Checker 811); March, 1966 by Roy Head (Back Beat 560).
OTHER SIGNIFICANT RECORDINGS: April, 1960 by Willie Dixon, titled "My Baby Don't Stand No Cheating" (Folkways LP F-2386). Completely different songs, using the same title, "My Babe," were released by Ronnie Dove (April, 1967 - Diamond 221) and by The Righteous Brothers (August, 1963 - Moonglow 223).

MY BABY LEFT ME (Arthur Crudup)

RECORDED: January, 1956
RELEASED: May, 1956
FIRST APPEARANCE: RCA Victor (45rpm single) 47-6540 and (78rpm single) 20-6540
HIT PRIOR TO ELVIS: None
HIT AFTER ELVIS: None
OTHER SIGNIFICANT RECORDINGS: 1950 by Arthur "Big Boy" Crudup (RCA Victor 130,284.

MY BOY (B. Martin - P. Coulter - C. Francois - Jean-Pierre Boutayre)

RECORDED: December, 1973
RELEASED: March, 1974
FIRST APPEARANCE: RCA (LP) CPL1-0475 (stereo) GOOD TIMES
HIT PRIOR TO ELVIS: November, 1971 by Richard Harris (Dunhill 4293).
HIT AFTER ELVIS: None
OTHER SIGNIFICANT RECORDINGS: None

MY DESERT SERENADE (Stanley J. Gelber)

RECORDED: February, 1965
RELEASED: October, 1965
FIRST APPEARANCE: RCA Victor (LP) LPM-3468 (mono) and LSP-3468 (stereo) HARUM SCARUM
HIT PRIOR TO ELVIS: None
HIT AFTER ELVIS: None
OTHER SIGNIFICANT RECORDINGS: None

MY LITTLE FRIEND (Shirl Milete)

RECORDED: January, 1969
RELEASED: February, 1970
FIRST APPEARANCE: RCA (45rpm single) 47-9791
HIT PRIOR TO ELVIS: None
HIT AFTER ELVIS: None
OTHER SIGNIFICANT RECORDINGS: None

MY WAY (Paul Anka - Revaux - Francois)

RECORDED: January, 1973
RELEASED: April, 1973
FIRST APPEARANCE: RCA (LP) VPSX-6089 (quad) ALOHA FROM HAWAII VIA SATELLITE
HIT PRIOR TO ELVIS: March, 1969 by Frank Sinatra (Reprise 0817); April, 1970 by Brook Benton (Cotillion 44072).
HIT AFTER ELVIS: None
OTHER SIGNIFICANT RECORDINGS: None

MY WISH CAME TRUE (Ivory Joe Hunter)

RECORDED: September, 1957
RELEASED: July, 1959
FIRST APPEARANCE: RCA Victor (45rpm single) 47-7600 and (78rpm single) 20-7600
HIT PRIOR TO ELVIS: None
HIT AFTER ELVIS: None
OTHER SIGNIFICANT RECORDINGS: 1971 on the LP "The Return of Ivory Joe Hunter" (Epic E-30348)

MYSTERY TRAIN (Sam Phillips - Junior Parker)

RECORDED: February, 1955
RELEASED: August, 1955
FIRST APPEARANCE: Sun 223 (45 and 78rpm singles)
HIT PRIOR TO ELVIS: None
HIT AFTER ELVIS: None
OTHER SIGNIFICANT RECORDINGS: 1953 by Little Junior's Blue Flames (Sun 192); December, 1955 by The Turtles (RCA Victor 47-6356).

NOTE: RCA's December (1955) release of BOTH Elvis' version of "Mystery Train" and the Turtles' version is a move that, to this day, we cannot fully understand. "Mystery Train" was, of course, the first Elvis release on RCA Victor, but since the song had already become a hit for Sun, it could be that the Turtles issue was simply an RCA cover of Elvis' Sun hit. This theory might seem logical if it were not for the Turtles (47-6356) and the Presley (47-6357) versions being consecutive release numbers. Obviously, by the time they would have had the cover [Turtles] ready they would have known that they were releasing Presley's version. Perhaps, by the time our second edition of this book is ready, we will know more about this unusual situation.

NEVER AGAIN (Billy Edd Wheeler - Jerry Chesnut)

RECORDED: February, 1976
RELEASED: May, 1976
FIRST APPEARANCE: RCA (LP) APL1-1506 (stereo)
 FROM ELVIS PRESLEY BOULEVARD, MEMPHIS,
 TENNESSEE
HIT PRIOR TO ELVIS: None
HIT AFTER ELVIS: None
OTHER SIGNIFICANT RECORDINGS: None

NEVER BEEN TO SPAIN (Hoyt Axton)

RECORDED: June, 1972
RELEASED: June, 1972
FIRST APPEARANCE: RCA (LP) LSP-4776 (stereo)
 ELVIS AS RECORDED AT MADISON SQUARE GARDEN
HIT PRIOR TO ELVIS: December, 1971 by Three Dog Night
 (Dunhill 4299)
HIT AFTER ELVIS: None
OTHER SIGNIFICANT RECORDINGS: None

NEVER ENDING (Buddy Kaye - Phil Springer)

RECORDED: May, 1963
RELEASED: July, 1964
FIRST APPEARANCE: RCA Victor (45rpm single) 47-8400
HIT PRIOR TO ELVIS: None
HIT AFTER ELVIS: None
OTHER SIGNIFICANT RECORDINGS: None

NEVER SAY YES (Doc Pomus - Mort Schuman)

RECORDED: February, 1966
RELEASED: October, 1966
FIRST APPEARANCE: RCA Victor (LP) LPM-3702 (mono)
 and LSP-3702 (stereo) SPINOUT
HIT PRIOR TO ELVIS: None
HIT AFTER ELVIS: None
OTHER SIGNIFICANT RECORDINGS: None

NEW ORLEANS (Sid Tepper - Roy C. Bennett)

RECORDED: January, 1958
RELEASED: August, 1958
FIRST APPEARANCE: RCA Victor (LP) LPM-1884 (mono)
 KING CREOLE
HIT PRIOR TO ELVIS: None
HIT AFTER ELVIS: None
OTHER SIGNIFICANT RECORDINGS: None. A completely
 different song, using the same title, was recorded by: U. S.
 Bonds (October, 1960 - Legrand 1003); Eddie Hodges
 (June, 1965 - Aurora 153); Neil Diamond (December, 1967
 Bang 554). Another song, still using the same title, was re-
 corded by The Staple Singers (February, 1976 - Curtom
 0113). A country version of the U.S. Bonds record became
 a hit for Anthony Armstrong Jones (October, 1969 - Chart
 5033).

NIGHT LIFE (Bill Giant - Bernie Baum - Florence Kaye)

RECORDED: July, 1963
RELEASED: November, 1968
FIRST APPEARANCE: RCA Camden (LP) PRS-279 SINGER
 PRESENTS ELVIS SINGING FLAMING STAR AND
 OTHERS
HIT PRIOR TO ELVIS: None
HIT AFTER ELVIS: None
OTHER SIGNIFICANT RECORDINGS: None. A completely
 different song, using the same title, was released by Ray
 Price (September, 1963 - Columbia 42827), Rusty Draper
 (September, 1963 - Monument 823) and Claude Gray
 (May, 1968 - Decca 32312).

NIGHT RIDER (Doc Pomus - Mort Schuman)

RECORDED: March, 1962
RELEASED: June, 1962
FIRST APPEARANCE: RCA Victor (LP) LPM-2523 (mono)
 and LSP-2523 (stereo) POT LUCK
HIT PRIOR TO ELVIS: None
HIT AFTER ELVIS: None
OTHER SIGNIFICANT RECORDINGS: None

NO MORE (Don Robertson - Hal Blair)

RECORDED: March, 1961
RELEASED: October, 1961
FIRST APPEARANCE: RCA Victor (LP) LPM-2426 (mono)
 and LSP-2426 BLUE HAWAII
HIT PRIOR TO ELVIS: None
HIT AFTER ELVIS: None
OTHER SIGNIFICANT RECORDINGS: None. A completely
 different song, using the same title, was released by The
 DeJohn Sisters (December, 1954 - Epic 9085) and by The
 McGuire Sisters (January, 1955 - Coral 61323). The full
 title of this particular song was "(My Baby Don't Love Me)
 No More."

(THERE'S) NO ROOM TO RHUMBA IN A SPORTS CAR
 (Fred Wise - Dick Manning)
RECORDED: January, 1963
RELEASED: November, 1963
FIRST APPEARANCE: RCA Victor (LP) LPM-2756 (mono)
 and LSP-2756 (stereo) FUN IN ACAPULCO
HIT PRIOR TO ELVIS: None
HIT AFTER ELVIS: None
OTHER SIGNIFICANT RECORDINGS: None

NOTHINGVILLE (Scott Davis - Strange)

RECORDED: June, 1968
RELEASED: December, 1968
FIRST APPEARANCE: RCA (LP) LPM-4088 (some mono,
 some stereo) ELVIS (NBC-TV SPECIAL)
HIT PRIOR TO ELVIS: None
HIT AFTER ELVIS: None
OTHER SIGNIFICANT RECORDINGS: None

O COME, ALL YE FAITHFUL (Arranged and Adapted by Elvis Presley)
RECORDED: May, 1971
RELEASED: October, 1971
FIRST APPEARANCE: RCA (LP) LSP-4579 (stereo) ELVIS SINGS THE WONDERFUL WORLD OF CHRISTMAS
HIT PRIOR TO ELVIS: None
HIT AFTER ELVIS: None
OTHER SIGNIFICANT RECORDINGS: None

OH LITTLE TOWN OF BETHLEHEM (Arranged by Elvis Presley)
RECORDED: September, 1957
RELEASED: November, 1957
HIT PRIOR TO ELVIS: None
HIT AFTER ELVIS: None
OTHER SIGNIFICANT RECORDINGS: None

OLD MACDONALD (Randy Starr)
RECORDED: June, 1966
RELEASED: June, 1967
FIRST APPEARANCE: RCA Victor (LP) LPM-3787 (mono) and LSP-3787 DOUBLE TROUBLE
HIT PRIOR TO ELVIS: August, 1958 by The Chargers (featuring Jessie Belvin) (RCA Victor 47-7301; November, 1960 by Frank Sinatra (Capitol 4466).
NOTE: As with "Frankie and Johnny," this song is composed using noticeably different lyrics each time it is recorded. Each of these three versions differ greatly from the other two.

OLD SHEP (Red Foley)
RECORDED: September, 1956
RELEASED: November, 1956
FIRST APPEARANCE: RCA Victor (LP) LPM-1382 (mono) ELVIS
HIT PRIOR TO ELVIS: None
HIT AFTER ELVIS: None
OTHER SIGNIFICANT RECORDINGS: 1947 by Red Foley (Decca 46052).

ON A SNOWY CHRISTMAS EVE (Stanley J. Gelber)
RECORDED: May, 1971
RELEASED: October, 1971
FIRST APPEARANCE: RCA (LP) LSP-4579 (stereo) ELVIS SINGS THE WONDERFUL WORLD OF CHRISTMAS
HIT PRIOR TO ELVIS: None
HIT AFTER ELVIS: None
OTHER SIGNIFICANT RECORDINGS: None

ONCE IS ENOUGH (Sid Tepper - Roy C. Bennett)
RECORDED: October, 1963
RELEASED: March, 1964
FIRST APPEARANCE: RCA Victor (LP) LPM-2894 (mono) and LSP-2894 (stereo) KISSIN' COUSINS
HIT PRIOR TO ELVIS: None
HIT AFTER ELVIS: None
OTHER SIGNIFICANT RECORDINGS: None

ONE BOY, TWO LITTLE GIRLS (Bill Giant - Bernie Baum - Florence Kaye)
RECORDED: October, 1963
RELEASED: March, 1964
FIRST APPEARANCE: RCA Victor (LP) LPM-2894 (mono) and LSP-2894 (stereo) KISSIN' COUSINS
HIT PRIOR TO ELVIS: None
HIT AFTER ELVIS: None
OTHER SIGNIFICANT RECORDINGS: None

ONE BROKEN HEART FOR SALE (Otis Blackwell - Winfield Scott)
RECORDED: October, 1962
RELEASED: February, 1963
FIRST APPEARANCE: RCA Victor (45rpm single) 47-8134
HIT PRIOR TO ELVIS: None
HIT AFTER ELVIS: None
OTHER SIGNIFICANT RECORDINGS: None

ONE NIGHT (Dave Bartholomew - Pearl King)
RECORDED: February, 1957
RELEASED: November, 1958
FIRST APPEARANCE: RCA Victor (45rpm single) 47-7410 and (78rpm single) 20-7410
HIT PRIOR TO ELVIS: None
HIT AFTER ELVIS: August, 1976 by Roy Head (ABC/Dot 17650).
OTHER SIGNIFICANT RECORDINGS: March, 1956 by Smiley Lewis (Imperial 5380); September, 1963 by Fats Domino (Imperial 5980).
NOTE: Lyrically, there was quite a difference between the original Smiley Lewis version and Elvis' 1958 release. The original lyrics were considered too risque for an Elvis Presley pop issue, so what was "One night of sin is what I'm now paying for" became the less offensive "One night with you is what I'm now praying for." Elvis did include some of the original lyrics in his version of this song as performed on the 1968 NBC-TV special. The Fats Domino version is patterned after Smiley Lewis' rendition, whereas Roy Head did the song like Elvis did in the fifties.

ONE-SIDED LOVE AFFAIR (Bill Campbell)
RECORDED: January, 1956
RELEASED: March, 1956
FIRST APPEARANCE: RCA Victor (LP) LPM-1254 (mono)
HIT PRIOR TO ELVIS: None
HIT AFTER ELVIS: None
OTHER SIGNIFICANT RECORDINGS: None
NOTE: On some Elvis releases, "One-Sided" is hyphenated, on just as many others it is not.

ONE TRACK HEART (Bill Giant - Bernie Baum - Florence Kaye)
RECORDED: February, 1964
RELEASED: October, 1964
FIRST APPEARANCE: RCA Victor (LP) LPM-2999 (mono) and LSP-2999 (stereo) ROUSTABOUT
HIT PRIOR TO ELVIS: None
HIT AFTER ELVIS: None
OTHER SIGNIFICANT RECORDINGS: None

ONLY BELIEVE (Paul Rader)
RECORDED: June, 1970
RELEASED: May, 1971
FIRST APPEARANCE: RCA (45rpm single) 47-9985
HIT PRIOR TO ELVIS: None
HIT AFTER ELVIS: None
OTHER SIGNIFICANT RECORDINGS: None

ONLY THE STRONG SURVIVE (Jerry Butler - Gamble - Huff)

RECORDED: February, 1969
RELEASED: May, 1969
FIRST APPEARANCE: RCA (LP) LSP-4155 (stereo)
  FROM ELVIS IN MEMPHIS
HIT PRIOR TO ELVIS: February, 1969 by Jerry Butler
  (Mercury 72898).
HIT AFTER ELVIS: None
OTHER SIGNIFICANT RECORDINGS: None

PADRE (Jacques Larue - Paul Francis Webster - Alain Romans)

RECORDED: May, 1971
RELEASED: July, 1973
FIRST APPEARANCE: RCA (LP) APL1-0283 (stereo)
  ELVIS
HIT PRIOR TO ELVIS: May, 1958 by Toni Arden (Decca
  30628); December, 1970 by Marty Robbins (Columbia
  45273).
HIT AFTER ELVIS: None
OTHER SIGNIFICANT RECORDINGS: None

PARADISE HAWAIIAN STYLE (Bill Giant - Bernie Baum -
  Florence Kaye)

RECORDED: August, 1965
RELEASED: June, 1966
FIRST APPEARANCE: RCA Victor (LP) LPM-3643 (mono)
  and LSP-3643 PARADISE HAWAIIAN STYLE
HIT PRIOR TO ELVIS: None
HIT AFTER ELVIS: None
OTHER SIGNIFICANT RECORDINGS: None. Because of
  this songs lyrics, "Aloha Hawaii U.S.A.," it was used as the
  theme song for the worldwide television special "Aloha From
  Hawaii Via Satellite."

PARALYZED (Otis Blackwell - Elvis Presley)

RECORDED: September, 1956
RELEASED: November, 1956
FIRST APPEARANCE: RCA Victor (LP) LPM-1382 (mono)
  ELVIS
HIT PRIOR TO ELVIS: None
HIT AFTER ELVIS: None
OTHER SIGNIFICANT RECORDINGS: None. A completely
  different song, using the same title, was released by The
  Legendary Stardust Cowboy (November, 1968 - Psycho-
  Suave 1033 & Mercury 72862).

PARTY (Don Robertson)

RECORDED: February, 1957
RELEASED: July, 1957
FIRST APPEARANCE: RCA Victor (LP) LPM-1515 (mono)
  LOVING YOU
HIT PRIOR TO ELVIS: None
HIT AFTER ELVIS: August, 1960 by Wanda Jackson
  (Capitol 4397), using the title "Let's Have A Party."
OTHER SIGNIFICANT RECORDINGS: None. Completely
  different songs, using the same title, were released by
  Maceo & The Macks, spelled "Parrty," (August, 1973 -
  People 624) and ["Party"] by Van McCoy (August, 1976
  H&L 4670).

PATCH IT UP (Eddie Rabbitt - Rory Bourke)

RECORDED: June, 1970
RELEASED: October, 1970
FIRST APPEARANCE: RCA (45rpm single) 47-9916
HIT PRIOR TO ELVIS: None
HIT AFTER ELVIS: None
OTHER SIGNIFICANT RECORDINGS: None

(THERE'LL BE) PEACE IN THE VALLEY (FOR ME)
  (Thomas A. Dorsey)
RECORDED: January, 1957
RELEASED: March, 1957
FIRST APPEARANCE: RCA Victor (EP) EPA-4054
  PEACE IN THE VALLEY
HIT PRIOR TO ELVIS: August, 1951 by Red Foley
  (Decca 46319).
HIT AFTER ELVIS: None
OTHER SIGNIFICANT RECORDINGS: None

PETUNIA, THE GARDNER'S DAUGHTER (Sid Tepper -
  Roy C. Bennett)
RECORDED: May, 1965
RELEASED: April, 1966
FIRST APPEARANCE: RCA Victor (LP) LPM-3553 (mono)
  and LSP-3553 (stereo) FRANKIE AND JOHNNY
HIT PRIOR TO ELVIS: None
HIT AFTER ELVIS: None
OTHER SIGNIFICANT RECORDINGS: None

PIECES OF MY LIFE (Troy Seals)

RECORDED: March, 1975
RELEASED: May, 1975
FIRST APPEARANCE: RCA (LP) APL1-1039 (stereo)
  TODAY
HIT PRIOR TO ELVIS: None
HIT AFTER ELVIS: None
OTHER SIGNIFICANT RECORDINGS: November, 1974 by
  Charlie Rich, from the LP "The Silver Fox" (Epic 33250).

PLAYING FOR KEEPS (Stanley Kesler)

RECORDED: September, 1956
RELEASED: January, 1957
FIRST APPEARANCE: RCA Victor (45rpm single) 47-6800
  and (78rpm single) 20-6800
HIT PRIOR TO ELVIS: None
HIT AFTER ELVIS: None
OTHER SIGNIFICANT RECORDINGS: None

PLEASE DON'T DRAG THAT STRING AROUND (Otis
  Blackwell - Winfield Scott)
RECORDED: May, 1963
RELEASED: June, 1963
FIRST APPEARANCE: RCA Victor (45rpm single) 47-8188
HIT PRIOR TO ELVIS: None
HIT AFTER ELVIS: None
OTHER SIGNIFICANT RECORDINGS: None

PLEASE DON'T STOP LOVING ME (Joy Byers)

RECORDED: May, 1965
RELEASED: March, 1966
FIRST APPEARANCE: RCA Victor (45rpm single) 47-8780
HIT PRIOR TO ELVIS: None
HIT AFTER ELVIS: None
OTHER SIGNIFICANT RECORDINGS: None

PLEDGING MY LOVE (Don Robey - Ferdinand Washington)

RECORDED: October, 1976
RELEASED: June, 1977
FIRST APPEARANCE: RCA (45rpm single) PB-10998
HIT PRIOR TO ELVIS: January, 1955 by Johnny Ace
   (Duke 136); February, 1955 by Teresa Brewer (Coral
   61362); November, 1958 by Roy Hamilton (Epic 9294);
   April, 1960 by Johnny Tillotson (Cadence 1377); July,
   1971 by Kitty Wells (Decca 32840).
HIT AFTER ELVIS: None
OTHER SIGNIFICANT RECORDINGS: None

POCKETFUL OF RAINBOWS (Fred Wise - Ben Weisman)

RECORDED: May, 1960
RELEASED: October, 1960
FIRST APPEARANCE: RCA Victor (LP) LPM-2256 (mono)
   and LSP-2256 (stereo) G.I. BLUES
HIT PRIOR TO ELVIS: None
HIT AFTER ELVIS: September, 1961 by Deane Hawley
   (Liberty 55359).
OTHER SIGNIFICANT RECORDINGS: None

POISON IVY LEAGUE (Bill Giant - Bernie Baum - Florence
   Kaye)
RECORDED: February, 1964
RELEASED: October, 1964
FIRST APPEARANCE: RCA Victor (LP) LPM-2999 (mono)
   and LSP-2999 (stereo) ROUSTABOUT
HIT PRIOR TO ELVIS: None
HIT AFTER ELVIS: None
OTHER SIGNIFICANT RECORDINGS: None. A completely
   different song, using the same title, was recorded by Ral
   Donner (1964 - Fontana 1502).

POLK SALAD ANNIE (Tony Joe White)

RECORDED: February, 1970
RELEASED: May, 1970
FIRST APPEARANCE: RCA (LP) LSP-4362 (stereo)
   ON STAGE - FEBRUARY, 1970
HIT PRIOR TO ELVIS: June, 1969 by Tony Joe White
   (Monument 1104).
HIT AFTER ELVIS: None
OTHER SIGNIFICANT RECORDINGS: None

POOR BOY (Elvis Presley - Vera Matson)

RECORDED: August, 1956
RELEASED: November, 1956
FIRST APPEARANCE: RCA Victor (EP) EPA-4006
   LOVE ME TENDER
HIT PRIOR TO ELVIS: None
HIT AFTER ELVIS: None
OTHER SIGNIFICANT RECORDINGS: None. Completely
   different songs, using the same title, were recorded by Casey
   Kelly (September, 1972 - Elektra 45804) and by The Royal-
   tones, an instrumental, (October, 1958 - Jubilee 5338).
   Another version of the instrumental "Poor Boy," that did
   not become a hit, was by The Sugar Canes (November,
   1958 - King 5157).

POWER OF MY LOVE (Bill Giant - Bernie Baum - Florence Kaye)

RECORDED: February, 1969
RELEASED: May, 1969
FIRST APPEARANCE: RCA (LP) LSP-4155 (stereo)
   FROM ELVIS IN MEMPHIS
HIT PRIOR TO ELVIS: None
HIT AFTER ELVIS: None
OTHER SIGNIFICANT RECORDINGS: None

PROMISED LAND (Chuck Berry)

RECORDED: December, 1973
RELEASED: October, 1974
FIRST APPEARANCE: RCA (45rpm single) PB-10074
HIT PRIOR TO ELVIS: December, 1964 by Chuck Berry
   (Chess 1916); December, 1970 by Freddie Weller
   (Columbia 45276).
HIT AFTER ELVIS: None
OTHER SIGNIFICANT RECORDINGS: None

PROUD MARY (John Fogerty)

RECORDED: February, 1970
RELEASED: May, 1970
FIRST APPEARANCE: RCA (LP) LSP-4362 (stereo)
   ON STAGE - FEBRUARY, 1970
HIT PRIOR TO ELVIS: January, 1969 by Creedence Clear-
   water Revival (Fantasy 619); April, 1969 by Solomon
   Burke (Bell 783); June, 1969 by Anthony Armstrong
   Jones (Chart 5017); October, 1969 by Sonny Charles &
   The Checkmates, LTD (A&M 1127).
HIT AFTER ELVIS: January, 1971 by Ike & Tina Turner
   (Liberty 52616).
OTHER SIGNIFICANT RECORDINGS: None

PUPPET ON A STRING (Sid Tepper - Roy C. Bennett)

RECORDED: July, 1964
RELEASED: April, 1965
FIRST APPEARANCE: RCA Victor (LP) LPM-3338 (mono)
   and LSP-3338 (stereo) GIRL HAPPY
HIT PRIOR TO ELVIS: None
HIT AFTER ELVIS: None
OTHER SIGNIFICANT RECORDINGS: None

PUT THE BLAME ON ME (Fred Wise - Norman Blagman -
   Kay Twomey)
RECORDED: March, 1961
RELEASED: June, 1961
FIRST APPEARANCE: RCA Victor (LP) LPM-2370 (mono)
   and LSP-2370 (stereo) SOMETHING FOR EVERYBODY
HIT PRIOR TO ELVIS: None
HIT AFTER ELVIS: None
OTHER SIGNIFICANT RECORDINGS: None

PUT YOUR HAND IN THE HAND (Gene Maclellan)

RECORDED: June, 1971
RELEASED: February, 1972
FIRST APPEARANCE: RCA (LP) LSP-4671 (stereo)
   ELVIS NOW
HIT PRIOR TO ELVIS: January, 1971 by Beth Moore
   (Capitol 3013); March, 1971 by Ocean (Kama Sutra 519);
   May, 1971 by Anne Murray (Capitol 3082).
HIT AFTER ELVIS: None
OTHER SIGNIFICANT RECORDINGS: None

QUEENIE WAHINE'S PAPAYA (Bill Giant - Bernie Baum - Florence Kaye)
RECORDED: August, 1965
RELEASED: June, 1966
FIRST APPEARANCE: RCA Victor (LP) LPM-3643 (mono) and LSP-3643 (stereo) PARADISE HAWAIIAN STYLE
HIT PRIOR TO ELVIS: None
HIT AFTER ELVIS: None
OTHER SIGNIFICANT RECORDINGS: None

RAGS TO RICHES (Richard Adler - Jerry Ross)
RECORDED: September, 1970
RELEASED: March, 1971
FIRST APPEARANCE: RCA (45rpm single) 47-9980
HIT PRIOR TO ELVIS: September, 1953 by Tony Bennett (Columbia 40048); November, 1953 by Billy Ward & The Dominoes (King 1280); November, 1963 by Sunny & The Sunliners (Tear Drop 3022).
HIT AFTER ELVIS: None
OTHER SIGNIFICANT RECORDINGS: None

RAISED ON ROCK (Mark James)
RECORDED: July, 1973
RELEASED: September, 1973
FIRST APPEARANCE: RCA (45rpm single) APBO-0088
HIT PRIOR TO ELVIS: None
HIT AFTER ELVIS: None
OTHER SIGNIFICANT RECORDINGS: None

REACH OUT TO JESUS (Ralph Carmichael)
RECORDED: June, 1971
RELEASED: April, 1972
FIRST APPEARANCE: RCA (LP) LSP-4690 (stereo) HE TOUCHED ME
HIT PRIOR TO ELVIS: None
HIT AFTER ELVIS: None
OTHER SIGNIFICANT RECORDINGS: None

RECONSIDER BABY (Lowell Fulson)
RECORDED: April, 1960
RELEASED: April, 1960
FIRST APPEARANCE: RCA Victor (LP) LPM-2231 (mono) and LSP-2231 (stereo) ELVIS IS BACK!
HIT PRIOR TO ELVIS: November, 1954 by Lowell Fulson (Checker 804).
HIT AFTER ELVIS: None
OTHER SIGNIFICANT RECORDINGS: None

REDDY TEDDY (Robert Blackwell - John Marascalco)
RECORDED: September, 1956
RELEASED: November, 1956
FIRST APPEARANCE: RCA Victor (LP) LPM-1382 (mono) ELVIS
HIT PRIOR TO ELVIS: June, 1956 by Little Richard (Specialty 579).
HIT AFTER ELVIS: None
OTHER SIGNIFICANT RECORDINGS: None

RELAX (Sid Tepper - Roy C. Bennet)
RECORDED: October, 1962
RELEASED: March, 1963
FIRST APPEARANCE: RCA Victor (LP) LPM-2697 (mono) and LSP-2697 (stereo) IT HAPPENED AT THE WORLD'S FAIR
HIT PRIOR TO ELVIS: None
HIT AFTER ELVIS: None
OTHER SIGNIFICANT RECORDINGS: None

RELEASE ME (AND LET ME LOVE AGAIN) (Eddie Miller - W. S. Stevenson)
RECORDED: February, 1970
RELEASED: May, 1970
FIRST APPEARANCE: RCA (LP) LSP-4362 (stereo) ON STAGE - FEBRUARY, 1970
HIT PRIOR TO ELVIS: December, 1953 by Jimmy Heap (Capitol 2518); March, 1954 by Ray Price (Columbia 21214); October, 1962 by Little Esther (Esther Phillips) (Lennox 5555); March, 1967 by Engelbert Humperdinck (Parrot 40011); May, 1967 by Esther Phillips (Atlantic 2411); November, 1968 by Johnny Adams (SSS International 750).
HIT AFTER ELVIS: May, 1974 by Marie Owens (MCA 40241).
OTHER SIGNIFICANT RECORDINGS: None

RETURN TO SENDER (Otis Blackwell - Winfield Scott)
RECORDED: March, 1962
RELEASED: October, 1962
FIRST APPEARANCE: RCA Victor (45rpm single) 47-8100
HIT PRIOR TO ELVIS: None
HIT AFTER ELVIS: None
OTHER SIGNIFICANT RECORDINGS: None

RIDING THE RAINBOW (Fred Wise - Ben Weisman)
RECORDED: October, 1961
RELEASED: September, 1962
FIRST APPEARANCE: RCA Victor (EP) EPA-4371 KID GALAHAD
HIT PRIOR TO ELVIS: None
HIT AFTER ELVIS: None
OTHER SIGNIFICANT RECORDINGS: None

RIP IT UP (Robert Blackwell - John Marascalco)
RECORDED: September, 1956
RELEASED: November, 1956
FIRST APPEARANCE: RCA Victor (LP) LPM-1382 (mono) ELVIS
HIT PRIOR TO ELVIS: June, 1956 by Little Richard (Specialty 579); July, 1956 by Bill Haley & The Comets (Decca 30028).

NOTE: In a highly unusual move, Elvis recorded his own versions of BOTH SIDES of Little Richard's Specialty 579 ("Reddy Teddy"/"Rip It Up").

ROCK-A-HULA BABY (Fred Wise - Ben Weisman - Dolores Fuller)
RECORDED: March, 1961
RELEASED: October, 1961
FIRST APPEARANCE: RCA Victor (LP) LPM-2426 (mono) and LSP-2426 (stereo) BLUE HAWAII
HIT PRIOR TO ELVIS: None
HIT AFTER ELVIS: None
OTHER SIGNIFICANT RECORDINGS: None
NOTE: On its single release, both 45 and 33 Compact, this song was labeled a "Twist Special." The objective was to grasp a piece of the "Twist" dance craze.

ROUSTABOUT (Bill Giant - Bernie Baum - Florence Kaye)
RECORDED: February, 1964
RELEASED: October, 1964
FIRST APPEARANCE: RCA Victor (LP) LPM-2999 (mono) and LSP-2999 (stereo) ROUSTABOUT
HIT PRIOR TO ELVIS: None
HIT AFTER ELVIS: None
OTHER SIGNIFICANT RECORDINGS: None

RUBBERNECKIN' (Dory Jones - Bunny Warren)
RECORDED: January, 1969
RELEASED: November, 1969
FIRST APPEARANCE: RCA (45rpm single) 47-9768
HIT PRIOR TO ELVIS: None
HIT AFTER ELVIS: None
OTHER SIGNIFICANT RECORDINGS: None

RUNAWAY (Del Shannon - Max Crook)
RECORDED: August, 1969
RELEASED: May, 1970
FIRST APPEARANCE: RCA (LP) LSP-4362 (stereo) ON STAGE - FEBRUARY, 1970
HIT PRIOR TO ELVIS: March, 1961 by Del Shannon (Big Top 3067); March, 1961 by Lawrence Welk (Dot 16336).
HIT AFTER ELVIS: January, 1972 by Tony Orlando & Dawn, a part of the "Runaway"/"Happy Together" medley (Bell 45, 175); March, 1975 by Charlie Kulis (Playboy 6023); May, 1977 by Bonnie Raitt (Warner Bros. 8382); March, 1978 by Narvel Felts (ABC 12338).
OTHER SIGNIFICANT RECORDINGS: None
NOTE: This was one of two songs that appeared for the first time on the LP "On Stage - February, 1970" that were actually recorded on stage in August, 1969. The other song recorded in 1969 was "Yesterday."

RUN ON (Arranged and Adapted by Elvis Presley)
RECORDED: May, 1966
RELEASED: March, 1967
FIRST APPEARANCE: RCA Victor (LP) LPM-3758 (mono) and LSP-3758 (stereo) HOW GREAT THOU ART
HIT PRIOR TO ELVIS: None
HIT AFTER ELVIS: None
OTHER SIGNIFICANT RECORDINGS: None

SAND CASTLES (David Hess - Herb Goldberg)
RECORDED: August, 1965
RELEASED: June, 1966
FIRST APPEARANCE: RCA Victor (LP) LPM-3643 (mono) and LSP-3643 (stereo) PARADISE HAWAIIAN STYLE
HIT PRIOR TO ELVIS: None
HIT AFTER ELVIS: None
OTHER SIGNIFICANT RECORDINGS: None

SANTA BRING MY BABY BACK (TO ME) (Aaron Schroeder - Claude DeMetrius)
RECORDED: September, 1957
RELEASED: November, 1957
FIRST APPEARANCE: RCA Victor (LP) LOC-1035 (mono) ELVIS' CHRISTMAS ALBUM
HIT PRIOR TO ELVIS: None
HIT AFTER ELVIS: None
OTHER SIGNIFICANT RECORDINGS: None

SANTA CLAUS IS BACK IN TOWN (Jerry Leiber - Mike Stoller)
RECORDED: September, 1957
RELEASED: November, 1957
FIRST APPEARANCE: RCA Victor (LP) LOC-1035 (mono) ELVIS' CHRISTMAS ALBUM
HIT PRIOR TO ELVIS: None
HIT AFTER ELVIS: None
OTHER SIGNIFICANT RECORDINGS: None

SANTA LUCIA (Arranged by Elvis Presley)
RECORDED: July, 1963
RELEASED: July, 1965
FIRST APPEARANCE: RCA Victor (LP) LPM-3450 (mono) and LSP-3450 (stereo) ELVIS FOR EVERYONE
HIT PRIOR TO ELVIS: None
HIT AFTER ELVIS: None
OTHER SIGNIFICANT RECORDINGS: None

SAVED (Jerry Leiber - Mike Stoller)
RECORDED: June, 1968
RELEASED: December, 1968
FIRST APPEARANCE: RCA (LP) LPM-4088 (some mono- some stereo) ELVIS (NBC-TV SPECIAL)
HIT PRIOR TO ELVIS: April, 1961 by LaVern Baker (Atlantic 2099).
HIT AFTER ELVIS: None
OTHER SIGNIFICANT RECORDINGS: None

SCRATCH MY BACK (THEN I'LL SCRATCH YOURS) (Bill Giant - Bernie Baum - Florence Kaye)
RECORDED: August, 1965
RELEASED: June, 1966
FIRST APPEARANCE: RCA Victor (LP) LPM-3643 (mono) and LSP-3643 (stereo) PARADISE HAWAIIAN STYLE
HIT PRIOR TO ELVIS: None
HIT AFTER ELVIS: None
OTHER SIGNIFICANT RECORDINGS: None

SEE SEE RIDER (Ma Rainey - Chuck Willis)

RECORDED: February, 1970
RELEASED: May, 1970
FIRST APPEARANCE: RCA (LP) LSP-4362 (stereo)
    ON STAGE - FEBRUARY, 1970
HIT PRIOR TO ELVIS: March, 1957 by Chuck Willis, as
    "C. C. Rider" (Atlantic 1130); November, 1962 by LaVern
    Baker, as "See See Rider" (Atlantic 2167); November, 1965
    by Bobby Powell, as "C. C. Rider" (Whit 714); September,
    1966 by The Animals, as "See See Rider" (MGM 13582);

    December, 1965 by Mitch Ryder & The Detroit
    Wheels, as part of the song "Jenny Take A Ride"
    (New Voice 806).
HIT AFTER ELVIS: None
OTHER SIGNIFICANT RECORDINGS: None

NOTE: Although Chuck Willis had the original recording of this song,
it was LaVern Baker's 1962-63 version that Elvis' arrangement was
patterned after. Elvis' arrangement was quite unique, however, as
this song became his opening theme for live appearances.

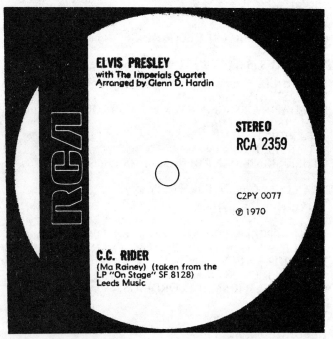

It seems that RCA could never settle on either the title or the
composer of this song.

On most worldwide releases, the title was "See See Rider,"
with no writer shown. What was given where normally the
composer's name goes was "Arranged by Elvis Presley." On
the other hit versions, one would find either Ma Rainey or
Chuck Willis.

Yet, on this British single release, the title is shown as
"C. C. Rider" and the song's writer as Ma Rainey.

SEEING IS BELIEVING (Red West - Glen Spreen)

RECORDED: May, 1971
RELEASED: April, 1972
FIRST APPEARANCE: RCA (LP) LSP-4690 (stereo)
    HE TOUCHED ME
HIT PRIOR TO ELVIS: None
HIT AFTER ELVIS: None
OTHER SIGNIFICANT RECORDINGS: None

SENTIMENTAL ME (Jim Morehead - Jimmy Cassin)

RECORDED: March, 1961
RELEASED: June, 1961
FIRST APPEARANCE: RCA Victor (LP) LPM-2370 (mono)
    and LSP-2370 (stereo) SOMETHING FOR EVERYBODY
HIT PRIOR TO ELVIS: December, 1949 by The Ames Bros.
    (Coral 60140); April, 1950 by Russ Morgan (Decca 24904);
    May, 1950 by Ray Anthony (Capitol 923).
HIT AFTER ELVIS: None
OTHER SIGNIFICANT RECORDINGS: None

SEPARATE WAYS (Red West - Richard Mainegra)

RECORDED: March, 1972
RELEASED: November, 1972
FIRST APPEARANCE: RCA (45rpm single) 74-0815
HIT PRIOR TO ELVIS: None
HIT AFTER ELVIS: None
OTHER SIGNIFICANT RECORDINGS: None

SHAKE A HAND (Joe Morris)

RECORDED: March, 1975
RELEASED: May, 1975
FIRST APPEARANCE: RCA (LP) APL1-1039 (stereo)
    TODAY
HIT PRIOR TO ELVIS: July, 1953 by Faye Adams
    (Herald 416); February, 1960 by LaVern Baker (Atlantic
    2048); June, 1962 by Ruth Brown (Philips 40028);
    May, 1963 by Jackie Wilson & Linda Hopkins (Bruns-
    wick 55243); January, 1958 by Mike Pedicin (Cameo 125).
HIT AFTER ELVIS: None
OTHER SIGNIFICANT RECORDINGS: November, 1959
    by Little Richard (Specialty 670).

NOTE: It's interesting to note that Lavern Baker had three consecutive
nationally charted records, "Shake A Hand," "Saved," and "See See
Rider," and that all three of these were later recorded by Elvis.

SHAKE, RATTLE AND ROLL (Charles Calhoun)

RECORDED: February, 1956
RELEASED: November, 1956
FIRST APPEARANCE: RCA Victor (LP) LPM-1382 (mono)
    ELVIS
HIT PRIOR TO ELVIS: April, 1954 by Joe Turner (Atlantic
    1026); August, 1954 by Bill Haley & His Comets (Decca
    29204).
HIT AFTER ELVIS: June, 1967 by Arthur Conley (Atco
    6494).
OTHER SIGNIFICANT RECORDINGS: None

SHAKE THAT TAMBOURINE (Bill Giant - Bernie Baum - Florence Kaye)
RECORDED: February, 1965
RELEASED: October, 1965
FIRST APPEARANCE: RCA Victor (LP) LPM-3468 (mono) and LSP-3468 (stereo) HARUM SCARUM
HIT PRIOR TO ELVIS: None
HIT AFTER ELVIS: None
OTHER SIGNIFICANT RECORDINGS: None

SHE'S A MACHINE (Joy Byers)
RECORDED: September, 1966
RELEASED: November, 1968
FIRST APPEARANCE: RCA Camden (LP) PRS-279 (stereo) SINGER PRESENTS ELVIS SINGING FLAMING STAR AND OTHERS
HIT PRIOR TO ELVIS: None
HIT AFTER ELVIS: None
OTHER SIGNIFICANT RECORDINGS: None

SHE'S NOT YOU (Doc Pomus - Jerry Leiber - Mike Stoller)
RECORDED: March, 1962
RELEASED: July, 1962
FIRST APPEARANCE: RCA Victor (45rpm single) 47-8041
HIT PRIOR TO ELVIS: None
HIT AFTER ELVIS: None
OTHER SIGNIFICANT RECORDINGS: None

SHE THINKS I STILL CARE (Dickie Lee)
RECORDED: February, 1976
RELEASED: December, 1976
FIRST APPEARANCE: RCA (45rpm single) PB-10857
HIT PRIOR TO ELVIS: April, 1962 by George Jones (United Artists 424).
HIT AFTER ELVIS: None
OTHER SIGNIFICANT RECORDINGS: None

SHE WEARS MY RING (Boudleaux Bryant - Felice Bryant)
RECORDED: December, 1973
RELEASED: March, 1974
FIRST APPEARANCE: RCA (LP) CPL1-0475 (stereo) GOOD TIMES
HIT PRIOR TO ELVIS: September, 1968 by Ray Price (Columbia 44628)
HIT AFTER ELVIS: None
OTHER SIGNIFICANT RECORDINGS: None

SHOPPIN' AROUND (Sid Tepper - Roy C. Bennett - Aaron Schroeder)
RECORDED: May, 1960
RELEASED: October, 1960
FIRST APPEARANCE: RCA Victor (LP) LPM-2256 (mono) and LSP-2256 (stereo) G.I. BLUES
HIT PRIOR TO ELVIS: None
HIT AFTER ELVIS: None
OTHER SIGNIFICANT RECORDINGS: None

SHOUT IT OUT (Bill Giant - Bernie Baum - Florence Kaye)
RECORDED: May, 1965
RELEASED: April, 1966
FIRST APPEARANCE: RCA Victor (LP) LPM-3553 (mono) and LSP-3553 (stereo) FRANKIE AND JOHNNY
HIT PRIOR TO ELVIS: None
HIT AFTER ELVIS: None
OTHER SIGNIFICANT RECORDINGS: None. This song should not be confused with "Shout It Out Loud," by Kiss (March, 1976 - Casablanca 854).

SILENT NIGHT (Joseph Mohr - Franz Gruber)
RECORDED: September, 1957
RELEASED: November, 1957
FIRST APPEARANCE: RCA Victor (LP) LOC-1035 (mono) ELVIS' CHRISTMAS ALBUM
HIT PRIOR TO ELVIS: None
HIT AFTER ELVIS: December, 1957 by Bing Crosby (Decca 23777); December, 1962 by Mahalia Jackson, as "Silent Night, Holy Night" (Apollo 750); December, 1949 by Sister Rosetta Tharpe (Decca 48119).
OTHER SIGNIFICANT RECORDINGS: It's difficult to find an artist who hasn't performed this perennial favorite.

SILVER BELLS (Evans - Livingston)
RECORDED: May, 1971
RELEASED: October, 1971
FIRST APPEARANCE: RCA (LP) LSP-4579 (stereo) ELVIS SINGS THE WONDERFUL WORLD OF CHRISTMAS
HIT PRIOR TO ELVIS: December, 1957 by Bing Crosby with Carol Richards (Decca 27229).
HIT AFTER ELVIS: None
OTHER SIGNIFICANT RECORDINGS: None

SING YOU CHILDREN (Gerald Nelson - Fred Burch)
RECORDED: September, 1966
RELEASED: April, 1967
FIRST APPEARANCE: RCA Victor (EP) EPA-4387 EASY COME, EASY GO
HIT PRIOR TO ELVIS: None
HIT AFTER ELVIS: None
OTHER SIGNIFICANT RECORDINGS: None

SINGING TREE (Owens - Solberg)
RECORDED: September, 1967
RELEASED: November, 1967
FIRST APPEARANCE: RCA Victor (LP) LPM-3893 (mono) and LSP-3893 (stereo) CLAMBAKE
HIT PRIOR TO ELVIS: None
HIT AFTER ELVIS: None
OTHER SIGNIFICANT RECORDINGS: None

SLICIN' SAND (Sid Tepper - Roy C. Bennett)
RECORDED: March, 1961
RELEASED: October, 1961
FIRST APPEARANCE: RCA Victor (LP) LPM-2426 (mono) and LSP-2426 (stereo) BLUE HAWAII
HIT PRIOR TO ELVIS: None
HIT AFTER ELVIS: None
OTHER SIGNIFICANT RECORDINGS: None

SLOWLY BUT SURELY (Sid Wayne - Ben Weisman)

RECORDED: May, 1963
RELEASED: November, 1963
FIRST APPEARANCE: RCA Victor (LP) LPM-2756 (mono) and LSP-2756 (stereo) FUN IN ACAPULCO
HIT PRIOR TO ELVIS: None
HIT AFTER ELVIS: None
OTHER SIGNIFICANT RECORDINGS: None

SMOKEY MOUNTAIN BOY (Lenore Rosenblatt - Victor Millrose)

RECORDED: October, 1963
RELEASED: March, 1964
FIRST APPEARANCE: RCA Victor (LP) LPM-2894 (mono) and LSP-2894 (stereo) KISSIN' COUSINS
HIT PRIOR TO ELVIS: None
HIT AFTER ELVIS: None
OTHER SIGNIFICANT RECORDINGS: None

SMORGASBORD (Sid Tepper - Roy C. Bennett)

RECORDED: February, 1966
RELEASED: October, 1966
FIRST APPEARANCE: RCA Victor (LP) LPM-3702 (mono) and LSP-3702 (stereo) SPINOUT
HIT PRIOR TO ELVIS: None
HIT AFTER ELVIS: None
OTHER SIGNIFICANT RECORDINGS: None

SNOWBIRD (Gene Maclellan)

RECORDED: September, 1970
RELEASED: February, 1971
FIRST APPEARANCE: RCA (LP) LSP-4460 (stereo) ELVIS COUNTRY
HIT PRIOR TO ELVIS: July, 1970 by Anne Murray (Capitol 2738).
HIT AFTER ELVIS: None
OTHER SIGNIFICANT RECORDINGS: None

SO CLOSE, YET SO FAR (FROM PARADISE) (Joy Byers)

RECORDED: February, 1965
RELEASED: October, 1965
FIRST APPEARANCE: RCA Victor (LP) LPM-3468 (mono) and LSP-3468 (stereo) HARUM SCARUM
HIT PRIOR TO ELVIS: None
HIT AFTER ELVIS: None
OTHER SIGNIFICANT RECORDINGS:

SO GLAD YOU'RE MINE (Arthur Crudup)

RECORDED: January, 1956
RELEASED: November, 1956
FIRST APPEARANCE: RCA Victor (LP) LPM-1382 (mono) ELVIS
HIT PRIOR TO ELVIS: None
HIT AFTER ELVIS: None
OTHER SIGNIFICANT RECORDINGS: 1946 by Arthur "Big Boy" Crudup (Victor 20-1949).

SO HIGH (Arranged by Elvis Presley)

RECORDED: May, 1966
RELEASED: March, 1967
FIRST APPEARANCE: RCA Victor (LP) LPM-3758 (mono) and LSP-3758 (stereo) HOW GREAT THOU ART
HIT PRIOR TO ELVIS: None
HIT AFTER ELVIS: None
OTHER SIGNIFICANT RECORDINGS: None containing the exact lyrics and message as Elvis' version, however, in July of 1959, LaVern Baker released "So High, So Low," a hit made up of slightly different lyrics (as a love song rather than a spiritual), but with the same music as heard on Elvis' recording. (Atlantic 2033)

SOFTLY, AS I LEAVE YOU (A. de Vita - Hal Shaper)

RECORDED: Live in Las Vegas (circa 1975-1976)
RELEASED March, 1978
FIRST APPEARANCE: RCA (45rpm single) PB-11212
HIT PRIOR TO ELVIS: August, 1964 by Frank Sinatra (Reprise 0301).
HIT AFTER ELVIS: None
OTHER SIGNIFICANT RECORDINGS: The first American release, a regional hit in the States, was by Matt Monro (April, 1962 - Liberty 55449).

SOLDIER BOY (David Jones - Theodore Williams Jr.)

RECORDED: March, 1960
RELEASED: April, 1960
FIRST APPEARANCE: RCA Victor (LP) LPM-2231 (mono) and LSP-2231 (stereo) ELVIS IS BACK!
HIT PRIOR TO ELVIS: June, 1955 by The Four Fellows (Glory 234).
HIT AFTER ELVIS: None
OTHER SIGNIFICANT RECORDINGS: None. A completely different song, using the same title, was released by The Shirelles (March, 1962 - Scepter 1228).

SOLITAIRE (Neil Sedaka - Cody)

RECORDED: February, 1976
RELEASED: May, 1976
FIRST APPEARANCE: RCA (LP) APL1-1506 (stereo) FROM ELVIS PRESLEY BOULEVARD, MEMPHIS, TENNESSEE
HIT PRIOR TO ELVIS: July, 1975 by The Carpenters (A&M 1721).
HIT AFTER ELVIS: None
OTHER SIGNIFICANT RECORDINGS: November, 1974 by Neil Sedaka, on the LP "Sedaka's Back" (MCA 463).

SOMEBODY BIGGER THAN YOU AND I (Johnny Lane) (Lange - Heath - Burke)

RECORDED: May, 1966
RELEASED: April, 1967
FIRST APPEARANCE: RCA Victor (LP) LPM-3758 (mono) and LSP-3758 (stereo) HOW GREAT THOU ART
HIT PRIOR TO ELVIS: None
HIT AFTER ELVIS: None
OTHER SIGNIFICANT RECORDINGS: April, 1951 by The Ink Spots (Decca 27494).

NOTE: A bit of confusion on RCA's part as to who is the composer(s) of this song, exists here. The monaural copy of "How Great Thou Art" credits Johnny Lane, whereas the stereo issue credits the team of Lange, Heath and Burke. If it means anything, "He Walks Beside Me" also credits Lange, Heath and Burke.

SOMETHING (George Harrison)

RECORDED: January, 1973
RELEASED: February, 1973
FIRST APPEARANCE: RCA (LP) VPSX-6089 (quad) ALOHA FROM HAWAII VIA SATELLITE
HIT PRIOR TO ELVIS: October, 1969 by The Beatles (Apple 2654); July, 1970 by Booker T. & The MG's (Stax 0073); September, 1970 by Shirley Bassey (United Artists 50698).
HIT AFTER ELVIS: March, 1974 by Johnny Rodriguez (Mercury 73471).
OTHER SIGNIFICANT RECORDINGS: None

SOMETHING BLUE (Paul Evans - Al Byron)

RECORDED: March, 1962
RELEASED: June, 1962
FIRST APPEARANCE: RCA Victor (LP) LPM-2523 (mono) and LSP-2523 (stereo) POT LUCK
HIT PRIOR TO ELVIS: None
HIT AFTER ELVIS: None
OTHER SIGNIFICANT RECORDINGS: None

SONG OF THE SHRIMP (Sid Tepper - Roy C. Bennett)

RECORDED: March, 1962
RELEASED: November, 1962
FIRST APPEARANCE: RCA Victor (LP) LPM-2621 (mono) and LSP-2621 (stereo) GIRLS! GIRLS! GIRLS!
HIT PRIOR TO ELVIS: None
HIT AFTER ELVIS: None
OTHER SIGNIFICANT RECORDINGS: None

NOTE: A glance at the month of recording for "Something Blue" and "Song of the Shrimp" might give one the impression that the tracks for the "Pot Luck" album and for "Girls! Girls! Girls!" were recorded during the same session. This was not the case. In fact, the tracks used on the "Pot Luck" LP were recorded in Nashville, whereas the "Girls! Girls! Girls!" tunes were done later that month in Hollywood.

SOUND ADVICE (Bill Giant - Bernie Baum - Florence Kaye)

RECORDED: July, 1961
RELEASED: July, 1965
FIRST APPEARANCE: RCA Victor (LP) LPM-3450 (mono) and LSP-3450 (stereo) ELVIS FOR EVERYONE
HIT PRIOR TO ELVIS: None
HIT AFTER ELVIS: None
OTHER SIGNIFICANT RECORDINGS: None

SPANISH EYES (Bert Kaempfert - Charles Singleton - William Snyder)
RECORDED: December, 1973
RELEASED: March, 1974
FIRST APPEARANCE: RCA (LP) CPL1-0475 (stereo) GOOD TIMES
HIT PRIOR TO ELVIS: June, 1965 by Bert Kaempfert, as "Moon Over Naples," an instrumental (Decca 31812); November, 1965 by Al Martino (Capitol 5542).
HIT AFTER ELVIS: None
OTHER SIGNIFICANT RECORDINGS: None

SPEEDWAY (Tom Glazer - Schlaks)

RECORDED: June, 1967
RELEASED: June, 1968
FIRST APPEARANCE: RCA Victor (LP) LPM-3989 (mono) and LSP-3989 (stereo) SPEEDWAY
HIT PRIOR TO ELVIS: None
HIT AFTER ELVIS: None
OTHER SIGNIFICANT RECORDINGS: None

SPINOUT (Sid Wayne - Ben Weisman - Dolores Fuller)

RECORDED: February, 1966
RELEASED: September, 1966
FIRST APPEARANCE: RCA Victor (45rpm single) 47-8941
HIT PRIOR TO ELVIS: None
HIT AFTER ELVIS: None
OTHER SIGNIFICANT RECORDINGS: None

SPRING FEVER (Bill Giant - Bernie Baum - Florence Kaye)

RECORDED: July, 1964
RELEASED: April, 1965
FIRST APPEARANCE: RCA Victor (LP) LPM-3338 (mono) and LSP-3338 (stereo) GIRL HAPPY
HIT PRIOR TO ELVIS: None
HIT AFTER ELVIS: None
OTHER SIGNIFICANT RECORDINGS: None. A completely different song, using the same title, was released by Little Willie John (May, 1961 - King 5503).

STAND BY ME (Arranged by Elvis Presley)

RECORDED: May, 1966
RELEASED: April, 1967
FIRST APPEARANCE: RCA Victor (LP) LPM-3758 (mono) and LSP-3758 (stereo) HOW GREAT THOU ART
HIT PRIOR TO ELVIS: None
HIT AFTER ELVIS: None
OTHER SIGNIFICANT RECORDINGS: None. A completely different song, using the same title, was released by Ben E. King (May, 1961 - Atco 6194), and many other artists.

STARTIN' TONIGHT (Lenore Rosenblatt Victor Millrose)

RECORDED: July, 1964
RELEASED: April, 1965
FIRST APPEARANCE: RCA Victor (LP) LPM-3338 (mono) and LSP-3338 (stereo) GIRL HAPPY
HIT PRIOR TO ELVIS: None
HIT AFTER ELVIS: None
OTHER SIGNIFICANT RECORDINGS: None

STARTING TODAY (Don Robertson)

RECORDED: March, 1961
RELEASED: June, 1961
FIRST APPEARANCE: RCA Victor (LP) LPM-2370 (mono) and LSP-2370 (stereo) SOMETHING FOR EVERYBODY
HIT PRIOR TO ELVIS: None
HIT AFTER ELVIS: None
OTHER SIGNIFICANT RECORDINGS: None

STAY AWAY (Sid Tepper - Roy C. Bennett)

RECORDED: October, 1967
RELEASED: March, 1968
FIRST APPEARANCE: RCA Victor (45rpm single) 47-9465
HIT PRIOR TO ELVIS: None
HIT AFTER ELVIS: None
OTHER SIGNIFICANT RECORDINGS: The music, or melody, used on this song is the standard "Greensleeves." Using the title "Greensleeves," but completely different lyrics than Elvis, the Beverley Sisters had a hit in December, 1956. In April, 1969, Mason Williams had an instrumental hit, as "Greensleeves." (Warner Bros. 7272).

STAY AWAY, JOE (Sid Wayne - Ben Weisman)

RECORDED: October, 1967
RELEASED: April, 1970
FIRST APPEARANCE: RCA Camden (LP) CAS-2408 (stereo) LET'S BE FRIENDS
HIT PRIOR TO ELVIS: None
HIT AFTER ELVIS: None
OTHER SIGNIFICANT RECORDINGS: None

STEADFAST, LOYAL AND TRUE (Jerry Leiber - Mike Stoller)

RECORDED: January, 1958
RELEASED: August, 1958
FIRST APPEARANCE: RCA Victor (LP) LPM-1884 (mono) KING CREOLE
HIT PRIOR TO ELVIS: None
HIT AFTER ELVIS: None
OTHER SIGNIFICANT RECORDINGS: None

STEAMROLLER BLUES (James Taylor)

RECORDED: January, 1973
RELEASED: February, 1973
FIRST APPEARANCE: RCA (LP) VPSX-6089 (quad) ALOHA FROM HAWAII VIA SATELLITE
HIT PRIOR TO ELVIS: None
HIT AFTER ELVIS: None
OTHER SIGNIFICANT RECORDINGS: March, 1970 by James Taylor on the LP "Sweet Baby James," as "Steamroller" (Warner Bros. 1843).

STEPPIN' OUT OF LINE (Fred Wise - Ben Weisman - Dolores Fuller)

RECORDED: March, 1961
RELEASED: June, 1962
FIRST APPEARANCE: RCA Victor (LP) LPM-2523 (mono) and LSP-2523 (stereo) POT LUCK
HIT PRIOR TO ELVIS: None
HIT AFTER ELVIS: None
OTHER SIGNIFICANT RECORDINGS: None

STOP, LOOK AND LISTEN (Joy Byers)

RECORDED: February, 1966
RELEASED: October, 1966
FIRST APPEARANCE: RCA Victor (LP) LPM-3702 (mono) and LSP-3702 (stereo) SPINOUT
HIT PRIOR TO ELVIS: None
HIT AFTER ELVIS: None
OTHER SIGNIFICANT RECORDINGS: None. A completely different song, using the same title, was released by The Chiffons (September, 1966 - Laurie 3357). A song with the similar title "Stop, Look, Listen," was released by The Stylistics (May, 1971 - Avco Embassy 4572). The complete title of this song was "Stop, Look, Listen (To Your Heart)."

STOP WHERE YOU ARE (Bill Giant - Bernie Baum - Florence Kaye)

RECORDED: August, 1965
RELEASED: June, 1966
FIRST APPEARANCE: RCA Victor (LP) LPM-3643 (mono) and LSP-3643 (stereo) PARADISE HAWAIIAN STYLE
HIT PRIOR TO ELVIS: None
HIT AFTER ELVIS: None
OTHER SIGNIFICANT RECORDINGS: None

STRANGER IN MY OWN HOME TOWN (Percy Mayfield)

RECORDED: February, 1969
RELEASED: November, 1969
FIRST APPEARANCE: RCA (LP LSP-6020 (stereo) FROM MEMPHIS TO VEGAS/FROM VEGAS TO MEMPHIS
HIT PRIOR TO ELVIS: None
HIT AFTER ELVIS: None
OTHER SIGNIFICANT RECORDINGS: October, 1963 by Percy Mayfield (Tangerine 941).

STRANGER IN THE CROWD (Winfield Scott)

RECORDED: June, 1970
RELEASED: December, 1970
FIRST APPEARANCE: RCA (LP) LSP-4445 (stereo) THAT'S THE WAY IT IS
HIT PRIOR TO ELVIS: None
HIT AFTER ELVIS: None
OTHER SIGNIFICANT RECORDINGS: None

STUCK ON YOU (Aaron Schroeder - J. Leslie McFarland)

RECORDED: March, 1960
RELEASED: April, 1960
FIRST APPEARANCE: RCA Victor (45rpm single) 47-7740
HIT PRIOR TO ELVIS: None
HIT AFTER ELVIS: None
OTHER SIGNIFICANT RECORDINGS: None

SUCH A NIGHT (Lincoln Chase)

RECORDED: April, 1960
RELEASED: April, 1960
FIRST APPEARANCE: RCA Victor (LP) LPM-2231 (mono) and LSP-2231 (stereo) ELVIS IS BACK!
HIT PRIOR TO ELVIS: February, 1954 by The Drifters (Atlantic 1019).
HIT AFTER ELVIS: None
OTHER SIGNIFICANT RECORDINGS: March, 1962 by Vince Everett (ABC Paramount 10313). March, 1964 by Conway Twitty (ABC Paramount 10550). A completely different song, using the same title, was released by Dr. John (September, 1973 - Atco 5937).

NOTE: The Vince Everett recording of "Such A Night" is generally thought of as being the single finest duplication of an Elvis recording. His vocal and overall arrangement is nearly identical to Elvis' version. An interesting thing about the Conway Twitty release is that it is backed with "My Baby Left Me," another Elvis song. Of course, the remaining noteworthy point is that both of these versions of "Such A Night" were on ABC Paramount.

176

SUMMER KISSES, WINTER TEARS (Fred Wise - Ben Weisman - Lloyd)
RECORDED: August, 1960
RELEASED: April, 1961
FIRST APPEARANCE: RCA Victor (EP) LPC-128
   ELVIS BY REQUEST
HIT PRIOR TO ELVIS: None
HIT AFTER ELVIS: None
OTHER SIGNIFICANT RECORDINGS: None

SUPPOSE (Dee - Goehring)
RECORDED: June, 1967
RELEASED: June, 1968
FIRST APPEARANCE: RCA Victor (LP) LPM-3989 (mono)
   and LSP-3989 (stereo) SPEEDWAY
HIT PRIOR TO ELVIS: None
HIT AFTER ELVIS: None
OTHER SIGNIFICANT RECORDINGS: None

SURRENDER (Doc Pomus - Mort Schuman)
RECORDED: October, 1960
RELEASED: February, 1961
FIRST APPEARANCE: RCA Victor (45rpm single) 47-7850
HIT PRIOR TO ELVIS: None
HIT AFTER ELVIS: None
OTHER SIGNIFICANT RECORDINGS: This song was based on the melody "Come Back To Sorrento." Different songs, using the same title, were released by Perry Como (June, 1946 - RCA Victor 1877) and by Diana Ross (August, 1971 Motown 1188).

SUSAN WHEN SHE TRIED (Don Reid)
RECORDED: March, 1975
RELEASED: May, 1975
FIRST APPEARANCE: RCA (LP) APL1-1039 (stereo)
   TODAY
HIT PRIOR TO ELVIS: October, 1975 by The Statler Brothers (Mercury 73625).
HIT AFTER ELVIS: None
OTHER SIGNIFICANT RECORDINGS: None

SUSPICION (Doc Pomus - Mort Schuman)
RECORDED: March, 1962
RELEASED: June, 1962
FIRST APPEARANCE: RCA Victor (LP) LPM-2523 (mono)
   and LSP-2523 (stereo) POT LUCK
HIT PRIOR TO ELVIS: None
HIT AFTER ELVIS: February, 1964 by Terry Stafford (Crusader 101).
OTHER SIGNIFICANT RECORDINGS: None
NOTE: After the success of "Suspicion" for Terry Stafford, he released his first album ("Suspicion" Crusader 1001) which has not only the title track and "I'll Touch a Star," the follow-up hit, but "Playing With Fire," a song many fans thought Elvis recorded. There is no evidence to indicate Elvis ever recorded this song, but after hearing Stafford's version, it is easily believable that Elvis may have had a demo of the song done for him [Elvis]. Further, it may have been written especially for Presley, probably for use in one of his movies.

SUSPICIOUS MINDS (Mark James)
RECORDED: January, 1969
RELEASED: September, 1969
FIRST APPEARANCE: RCA (45rpm single) 47-9764
HIT PRIOR TO ELVIS: None
HIT AFTER ELVIS: November, 1970 by Waylon Jennings & Jessie Coulter (RCA 9920); June, 1971 by Dee Dee Warwick (Atco 6810).
OTHER SIGNIFICANT RECORDINGS: None

SWEET ANGELINE (Arnold - Martin - Morrow)
RECORDED: September, 1973
RELEASED: November, 1973
FIRST APPEARANCE: RCA (LP) APL1-0388 (stereo)
   RAISED ON ROCK/FOR OL' TIMES SAKE
HIT PRIOR TO ELVIS: None
HIT AFTER ELVIS: None
OTHER SIGNIFICANT RECORDINGS: None

SWEET CAROLINE (Neil Diamond)
RECORDED: February, 1970
RELEASED: May, 1970
FIRST APPEARANCE: RCA (LP) LSP-4362 (stereo)
   ON STAGE - FEBRUARY, 1970
HIT PRIOR TO ELVIS: June, 1969 by Neil Diamond (Uni 55136).
HIT AFTER ELVIS: November, 1970 by Anthony Armstrong Jones (Chart 5100); August, 1972 by Bobby Womack (United Artists 50946).
OTHER SIGNIFICANT RECORDINGS: None

SWING DOWN, SWEET CHARIOT (Arranged by Elvis Presley)
RECORDED: October, 1960
RELEASED: December, 1960
FIRST APPEARANCE: RCA Victor (LP) LPM-2328 (mono)
   and LSP-2328 (stereo) HIS HAND IN MINE
HIT PRIOR TO ELVIS: None
HIT AFTER ELVIS: None
OTHER SIGNIFICANT RECORDINGS: None

SYLVIA (Geoff Stevens - Les Reed)
RECORDED: June, 1970
RELEASED: February, 1972
FIRST APPEARANCE: RCA (LP) LSP-4671 (stereo)
   ELVIS NOW
HIT PRIOR TO ELVIS: None
HIT AFTER ELVIS: None
OTHER SIGNIFICANT RECORDINGS: None. A completely song, using the same title, was released by Focus (July, 1973 - Sire 708).

TAKE GOOD CARE OF HER (Ed Warren - Arthur Kent)

RECORDED: July, 1973
RELEASED: January, 1974
FIRST APPEARANCE: RCA (45rpm single) APB0-0196
HIT PRIOR TO ELVIS: March, 1961 by Adam Wade
(Coed 546); March, 1966 by Sonny James (Capitol 5612);
September, 1966 by Mel Carter (Imperial 66208).
OTHER SIGNIFICANT RECORDINGS: None

TAKE ME TO THE FAIR (Sid Tepper - Roy C. Bennett)

RECORDED: October, 1962
RELEASED: March, 1963
FIRST APPEARANCE: RCA Victor (LP) LPM-2697 (mono)
and LSP-2697 (stereo) IT HAPPENED AT THE WORLD'S
FAIR
HIT PRIOR TO ELVIS: None
HIT AFTER ELVIS: None
OTHER SIGNIFICANT RECORDINGS: None

TAKE MY HAND, PRECIOUS LORD (Thomas A. Dorsey)

RECORDED: January, 1957
RELEASED: March, 1957
FIRST APPEARANCE: RCA Victor (EP) EPA-4054
PEACE IN THE VALLEY
HIT PRIOR TO ELVIS: None
HIT AFTER ELVIS: None
OTHER SIGNIFICANT RECORDINGS: None

TALK ABOUT THE GOOD TIMES (Jerry Hubbard)

RECORDED: December, 1973
RELEASED: March, 1974
FIRST APPEARANCE: RCA (LP) CPL1-0475 (stereo)
GOOD TIMES
HIT PRIOR TO ELVIS: February, 1970 by Jerry Reed
(RCA 47-9804).
HIT AFTER ELVIS: None
OTHER SIGNIFICANT RECORDINGS: None

(LET ME BE YOUR) TEDDY BEAR (Kal Mann - Bernie Lowe)

RECORDED: February, 1957
RELEASED: June, 1957
FIRST APPEARANCE: RCA Victor (45rpm single) 47-7000
and (78rpm single) 20-7000
HIT PRIOR TO ELVIS: None
HIT AFTER ELVIS: None
OTHER SIGNIFICANT RECORDINGS: None. A completely
different song, using the title "Teddy Bear," was released
by Red Sovine (June, 1976 - Starday 142).

TELL ME PRETTY BABY (Andrew Lee Jackson)

This song is listed only because it was released and wrongfully
publicized as being by Elvis Presley. By now, hopefully, every
fan knows that this was a deliberate attempt to cheat Elvis'
followers. Of course, anyone who was familiar with Elvis'
voice knew immediately that this was a fraud. Those most
susceptible to the scheme were those who ordered by mail,
without having an opportunity to hear the record first. Elvis
had nothing to do with this recording!

TELL ME WHY (Titus Turner)

RECORDED: January, 1957
RELEASED: December, 1965
FIRST APPEARANCE: RCA Victor (45rpm single) 47-8740
HIT PRIOR TO ELVIS: June, 1956 by The Crew Cuts
(Mercury 70890); June, 1956 by Gale Storm (Dot 15470).
HIT AFTER ELVIS: None
OTHER SIGNIFICANT RECORDINGS: March, 1956 by
Marie Knight, the original version (Wing 90069). Complete-
ly different songs, using the same title, were done by:
Bobby Vinton, The Beatles, Eddie Fisher, The Four Aces
and Mathews' Southern Comfort.

TENDER FEELING (Bill Giant - Bernie Baum - Florence Kaye)

RECORDED: October, 1963
RELEASED: March, 1964
FIRST APPEARANCE: RCA Victor (LP) LPM-2894 (mono)
and LSP-2894 (stereo) KISSIN' COUSINS
HIT PRIOR TO ELVIS: None
HIT AFTER ELVIS: None
OTHER SIGNIFICANT RECORDINGS: None

THANKS TO THE ROLLING SEA (Ruth Batchelor - Bob
Roberts)
RECORDED: March, 1962
RELEASED: November, 1962
FIRST APPEARANCE: RCA Victor (LP) LPM-2621 (mono)
and LSP-2621 (stereo) GIRLS! GIRLS! GIRLS!
HIT PRIOR TO ELVIS: None
HIT AFTER ELVIS: None
OTHER SIGNIFICANT RECORDINGS: None

THAT'S ALL RIGHT (Arthur "Big Boy" Crudup)

RECORDED: July, 1954
RELEASED: July, 1954
FIRST APPEARANCE: Sun (45 and 78rpm) 209
HIT PRIOR TO ELVIS: None
HIT AFTER ELVIS: None
OTHER SIGNIFICANT RECORDINGS: 1949 by Arthur
"Big Boy" Crudup (RCA Victor 50-0000); Sun 1129 by
Jimmy Ellis, although not credited on the label (1972).

THAT'S SOMEONE YOU NEVER FORGET (Red West - Elvis
Presley)
RECORDED: June, 1961
RELEASED: June, 1962
FIRST APPEARANCE: RCA Victor (LP) LPM-2523 (mono)
and LSP-2523 (stereo)
HIT PRIOR TO ELVIS: None
HIT AFTER ELVIS: None
OTHER SIGNIFICANT RECORDINGS: None

THAT'S WHEN YOUR HEARTACHES BEGIN (Raskin - Brown - Fisher)

RECORDED: January, 1957
RELEASED: March, 1957
FIRST APPEARANCE: RCA Victor (45rpm single) 47-6870 and (78rpm single) 20-6870
HIT PRIOR TO ELVIS: None
HIT AFTER ELVIS: None
OTHER SIGNIFICANT RECORDINGS: May, 1950 by The Ink Spots (Decca 25505); April, 1952 by Billy Bunn & His Buddies (RCA Victor 20-4657).

NOTE: Of the four songs recorded at the Sun studios in 1953-54, prior to Elvis' first actual session there as an artist, this appears to have been the only tune that he later would record for release. We have never found reason to believe that "My Happiness," "A Casual Love," or "I'll Never Stand In Your Way" were ever recorded again by Elvis.

THE BULLFIGHTER WAS A LADY (Sid Tepper - Roy C. Bennett)

RECORDED: January, 1963
RELEASED: November, 1963
FIRST APPEARANCE: RCA Victor (LP) LPM-2756 (mono) and LSP-2756 (stereo) FUN IN ACAPULCO
HIT PRIOR TO ELVIS: None
HIT AFTER ELVIS: None
OTHER SIGNIFICANT RECORDINGS: None

THE EYES OF TEXAS: *See YELLOW ROSE OF TEXAS/THE EYES OF TEXAS*

THE FAIR IS MOVING ON (Fletcher - Flett)

RECORDED: February, 1969
RELEASED: June, 1969
FIRST APPEARANCE: RCA (45rpm single) 47-9747
HIT PRIOR TO ELVIS: None
HIT AFTER ELVIS: None
OTHER SIGNIFICANT RECORDINGS: None

THE FIRST NOEL (Arranged and Adapted by Elvis Presley)

RECORDED: May, 1971
RELEASED: October, 1971
FIRST APPEARANCE: RCA (LP) LSP-4597 (stereo) ELVIS SINGS THE WONDERFUL WORLD OF CHRISTMAS
HIT PRIOR TO ELVIS: None
HIT AFTER ELVIS: None
OTHER SIGNIFICANT RECORDINGS: None

THE FIRST TIME EVER I SAW YOUR FACE (Ewan MacColl)

RECORDED: March, 1971
RELEASED: April, 1972
FIRST APPEARANCE: RCA (45rpm single) 74-0672
HIT PRIOR TO ELVIS: None
HIT AFTER ELVIS: February, 1972 by Roberta Flack (Atlantic 2864).
OTHER SIGNIFICANT RECORDINGS: An interesting story here! The back cover liner notes on the RCA (DML 1-0348) "The Greatest Show On Earth" album states that Elvis was the first to record this song. This is incorrect. What is true is that Elvis recorded his version of the song before Roberta Flack's version appeared on 45rpm singles. Miss Flack's first LP, "First Take" (Atlantic 8230), contained her version of this song, and this LP was released in July-August, 1969, 19 months before Elvis recorded the tune. It was as a result of Roberta Flack's version being included in the Clint Eastwood film, "Play Misty For Me" that public interest in the song prompted its release as a single.

THE FOOL (Naomi Ford)

RECORDED: June, 1970
RELEASED: February, 1971
FIRST APPEARANCE: RCA (LP) LSP-4460 (stereo) ELVIS COUNTRY
HIT PRIOR TO ELVIS: July, 1956 by Sanford Clark (Dot 15481); August, 1956 by The Gallahads (Jubilee 5252).
HIT AFTER ELVIS: None
OTHER SIGNIFICANT RECORDINGS: 1955 by Sanford Clark (original label) (MCI-1003).

THE GIRL I NEVER LOVED (Randy Starr)

RECORDED: February, 1967
RELEASED: November, 1967
FIRST APPEARANCE: RCA Victor (LP) LPM-3893 (mono) and LSP-3893 (stereo) CLAMBAKE
HIT PRIOR TO ELVIS: None
HIT AFTER ELVIS: None
OTHER SIGNIFICANT RECORDINGS: None

THE GIRL NEXT DOOR (Bill Rice - Thomas Wayne)

RECORDED: April, 1960
RELEASED: April, 1960
FIRST APPEARANCE: RCA Victor (LP) LPM-2231 (mono) and LSP-2231 (stereo) ELVIS IS BACK!
HIT PRIOR TO ELVIS: None
HIT AFTER ELVIS: None
OTHER SIGNIFICANT RECORDINGS: None
NOTE: Later pressings of this LP showed the title of this song as "Girl Next Door Went A' Walking."

THE GIRL OF MY BEST FRIEND (Beverly Ross - Sam Bobrick)

RECORDED: April, 1960
RELEASED: April, 1960
FIRST APPEARANCE: RCA Victor (LP) LPM-2231 (mono) and LSP-2231 (stereo) ELVIS IS BACK!
HIT PRIOR TO ELVIS: None
HIT AFTER ELVIS: April, 1961 by Ral Donner (Gone 5102).
OTHER SIGNIFICANT RECORDINGS: July, 1960 by Eddie Wood (Ember 1064).

THE IMPOSSIBLE DREAM (THE QUEST) (Joe Darion - Mitch Leigh)

RECORDED: June, 1972
RELEASED: June, 1972
FIRST APPEARANCE: RCA (LP) LSP-4776 (stereo) ELVIS AS RECORDED AT MADISON SQUARE GARDEN
HIT PRIOR TO ELVIS: May, 1966 by Jack Jones (Kapp 755); March, 1968 by The Hesitations (Kapp 899); July, 1968 by Roger Williams (Kapp 907).
HIT AFTER ELVIS: None
OTHER SIGNIFICANT RECORDINGS: None.
NOTE: Has it ever occured to you that all three of the hit single versions of this song were on Kapp records?

THE LAST FAREWELL (Roger Whittaker - Webster)

RECORDED: February, 1976
RELEASED: May, 1976
FIRST APPEARANCE: RCA (LP) APL1-1506 (stereo) FROM ELVIS PRESLEY BOULEVARD, MEMPHIS, TENNESSEE
HIT PRIOR TO ELVIS: March, 1975 by Roger Whittaker (RCA PB-50030).
HIT AFTER ELVIS: None
OTHER SIGNIFICANT RECORDINGS: None

THE LOVE MACHINE (Gerald Nelson - Fred Burch - Chuck Taylor)

RECORDED: September, 1976
RELEASED: April, 1967
FIRST APPEARANCE: RCA Victor (EP) EPA-4387 EASY COME, EASY GO
HIT PRIOR TO ELVIS: None
HIT AFTER ELVIS: None
OTHER SIGNIFICANT RECORDINGS: None

THE MEANEST GIRL IN TOWN (Joy Byers)

RECORDED: July, 1964
RELEASED: April, 1965
FIRST APPEARANCE: RCA Victor (LP) LPM-3338 (mono) and LSP-3338 (stereo)
HIT PRIOR TO ELVIS: None
HIT AFTER ELVIS: None
OTHER SIGNIFICANT RECORDINGS: None

THE NEXT STEP IS LOVE (Paul Evans - Paul Parnes)

RECORDED: June, 1970
RELEASED: July, 1970
FIRST APPEARANCE: RCA (45rpm single) 47-9873
HIT PRIOR TO ELVIS: None
HIT AFTER ELVIS: None
OTHER SIGNIFICANT RECORDINGS: None

THE SOUND OF YOUR CRY (Bill Giant - Bernie Baum - Florence Kaye)

RECORDED: June, 1970
RELEASED: September, 1971
FIRST APPEARANCE: RCA (45rpm single) 48-1017
HIT PRIOR TO ELVIS: None
HIT AFTER ELVIS: None
OTHER SIGNIFICANT RECORDINGS: None

THE WALLS HAVE EARS (Sid Tepper - Roy C. Bennett)

RECORDED: March, 1962
RELEASED: November, 1962
FIRST APPEARANCE: RCA Victor (LP) LPM-2621 (mono) and LSP-2621 (stereo) GIRLS! GIRLS! GIRLS!
HIT PRIOR TO ELVIS: None
HIT AFTER ELVIS: None
OTHER SIGNIFICANT RECORDINGS: None. A completely different song, using the same title, was released by Patti Page (April, 1959 - Mercury 71428).

THE WONDER OF YOU (Baker Knight)

RECORDED: February, 1970
RELEASED: May, 1970
FIRST APPEARANCE: RCA (45rpm single) 47-9835
HIT PRIOR TO ELVIS: May, 1959 by Ray Peterson (RCA Victor 47-7513); June, 1964 by Ray Peterson, a reissue of his 1959 release (RCA Victor 47-8333).
OTHER SIGNIFICANT RECORDINGS: None

THE WONDERFUL WORLD OF CHRISTMAS (Fred Tobias - Frisch)

RECORDED: May, 1971
RELEASED: October, 1971
FIRST APPEARANCE: RCA (LP) LSP-4579 (stereo) ELVIS SINGS THE WONDERFUL WORLD OF CHRISTMAS
HIT PRIOR TO ELVIS: None
HIT AFTER ELVIS: None
OTHER SIGNIFICANT RECORDINGS: None

NOTE: Elvis recorded three "Wonderful World" type songs; "The Wonderful World of Christmas," "Wonderful World" and "It's A Wonderful World."

THERE AIN'T NOTHING LIKE A SONG (Joy Byers - Johnston)

RECORDED: June, 1967 (duet with Nancy Sinatra)
RELEASED: June, 1968
FIRST APPEARANCE: RCA Victor (LP) LPM-3989 (mono) and LSP-3989 (stereo) SPEEDWAY
HIT PRIOR TO ELVIS: None
HIT AFTER ELVIS: None
OTHER SIGNIFICANT RECORDINGS: None.

THERE GOES MY EVERYTHING (Dallas Frazier)

RECORDED: June, 1970
RELEASED: December, 1970
FIRST APPEARANCE: RCA (45rpm single) 47-9960
HIT PRIOR TO ELVIS: December, 1966 by Jack Green (Decca 32023); June, 1967 by Engelbert Humperdinck (Parrot 40015).
HIT AFTER ELVIS: None
OTHER SIGNIFICANT RECORDINGS: None

THERE IS NO GOD BUT GOD (Bill Kenny)

RECORDED: June, 1971
RELEASED: April, 1972
FIRST APPEARANCE: RCA (LP) LSP-4690 (stereo) HE TOUCHED ME
HIT PRIOR TO ELVIS: None
HIT AFTER ELVIS: None
OTHER SIGNIFICANT RECORDINGS: None

THERE IS SO MUCH WORLD TO SEE (Sid Tepper - Ben Weisman)

RECORDED: June, 1966
RELEASED: June, 1967
FIRST APPEARANCE: RCA Victor (LP) LPM-3787 (mono) and LSP-3787 (stereo) DOUBLE TROUBLE
HIT PRIOR TO ELVIS: None
HIT AFTER ELVIS: None
OTHER SIGNIFICANT RECORDINGS: None

THERE'S A BRAND NEW DAY ON THE HORIZON (Joy Byers)

RECORDED: February, 1964
RELEASED: October, 1964
FIRST APPEARANCE: RCA Victor (LP) LPM-2999 (mono) and LSP-2999 (stereo) ROUSTABOUT
HIT PRIOR TO ELVIS: None
HIT AFTER ELVIS: None
OTHER SIGNIFICANT RECORDINGS: None

THERE'S A HONKY TONK ANGEL (WHO WILL TAKE MF BACK IN) (Troy Deals - Denny Rice)

RECORDED: December, 1973
RELEASED: January, 1975
FIRST APPEARANCE: RCA (LP) APL1-0873 (stereo) PROMISED LAND
HIT PRIOR TO ELVIS: January, 1974 by Conway Twitty (MCA 40173).
HIT AFTER ELVIS: None
OTHER SIGNIFICANT RECORDINGS: None

NOTE: Elvis recorded his version of this song on December 15, 1973. Because of the release date of Conway Twitty's version, the possibility, although slim, exists that Elvis may have recorded the song before Conway. In all likelyhood, Twitty recorded the song shortly before Presley.

THERE'S ALWAYS ME (Don Robertson)

RECORDED: March, 1961
RELEASED: June, 1961
FIRST APPEARANCE: RCA Victor (LP) LPM-2370 (mono) and LSP-2370 SOMETHING FOR EVERYBODY
HIT PRIOR TO ELVIS: None
HIT AFTER ELVIS: February, 1979 by Ray Price (Monument 45-277).
OTHER SIGNIFICANT RECORDINGS: None

THERE'S GOLD IN THE MOUNTAINS (Bill Giant - Bernie Baum - Florence Kaye)

RECORDED: October, 1963
RELEASED: March, 1964
FIRST APPEARANCE: RCA Victor (LP) LPM-2894 (mono) and LSP-2894 (stereo) KISSIN' COUSINS
HIT PRIOR TO ELVIS: None
HIT AFTER ELVIS: None
OTHER SIGNIFICANT RECORDINGS: None

THEY REMIND ME TOO MUCH OF YOU (Don Robertson)

RECORDED: October, 1962
RELEASED: March, 1963
FIRST APPEARANCE: RCA Victor (LP) LPM-2697 (mono) and LSP-2697 (stereo) IT HAPPENED AT THE WORLD'S FAIR
HIT PRIOR TO ELVIS: None
HIT AFTER ELVIS: None
OTHER SIGNIFICANT RECORDINGS: None

THINKING ABOUT YOU (Tim Baty)

RECORDED: December, 1973
RELEASED: January, 1975
FIRST APPEARANCE: RCA (45rpm single) PB-10191
HIT PRIOR TO ELVIS: None
HIT AFTER ELVIS: None
OTHER SIGNIFICANT RECORDINGS: None

THIS IS LIVING (Fred Wise - Ben Weisman)

RECORDED: October, 1961
RELEASED: September, 1962
FIRST APPEARANCE: RCA Victor (EP) EPA-4371 KID GALAHAD
HIT PRIOR TO ELVIS: None
HIT AFTER ELVIS: None
OTHER SIGNIFICANT RECORDINGS: None

THIS IS MY HEAVEN (Bill Giant - Bernie Baum - Florence Kaye)

RECORDED: August, 1965
RELEASED: June, 1966
FIRST APPEARANCE: RCA Victor (LP) LPM-3643 (mono) and LSP-3643 (stereo) PARADISE HAWAIIAN STYLE
HIT PRIOR TO ELVIS: None
HIT AFTER ELVIS: None
OTHER SIGNIFICANT RECORDINGS: None

THIS IS OUR DANCE (Les Reed - Geoff Stephens)

RECORDED: June, 1970
RELEASED: May, 1971
FIRST APPEARANCE: RCA (LP) LSP-4530 (mono) LOVE LETTERS FROM ELVIS
HIT PRIOR TO ELVIS: None
HIT AFTER ELVIS: None
OTHER SIGNIFICANT RECORDINGS: None

THIS IS THE STORY (Arnold - Morrow - Martin)

RECORDED: July, 1969
RELEASED: November, 1969
FIRST APPEARANCE: RCA (LP) LSP-6020 (stereo) FROM MEMPHIS TO VEGAS/FROM VEGAS TO MEMPHIS
HIT PRIOR TO ELVIS: None
HIT AFTER ELVIS: None
OTHER SIGNIFICANT RECORDINGS: None

THREE CORN PATCHES (Jerry Leiber - Mike Stoller)

RECORDED: July, 1973
RELEASED: November, 1973
FIRST APPEARANCE: RCA (LP) APL1-0388 (stereo) RAISED ON ROCK/FOR OL' TIMES SAKE
HIT PRIOR TO ELVIS: None
HIT AFTER ELVIS: None
OTHER SIGNIFICANT RECORDINGS: None

THRILL OF YOUR LOVE (Stanley Kesler)

RECORDED: April, 1960
RELEASED: April, 1960
FIRST APPEARANCE: RCA Victor (LP) LPM-2231 (mono) and LSP-2231 (stereo) ELVIS IS BACK!
HIT PRIOR TO ELVIS: None
HIT AFTER ELVIS: None
OTHER SIGNIFICANT RECORDINGS: None

TIGER MAN (Lewis - Burns)

RECORDED: June, 1968
RELEASED: November, 1968
FIRST APPEARANCE: RCA Camden (LP) PRS-279 (stereo)
SINGER PRESENTS ELVIS SINGING FLAMING STAR
AND OTHERS
HIT PRIOR TO ELVIS: None
HIT AFTER ELVIS: None
OTHER SIGNIFICANT RECORDINGS: August, 1953 by
Rufus Thomas (Sun 188).

TODAY, TOMORROW AND FOREVER (Bill Giant - Bernie
Baum - Florence Kaye)
RECORDED: July, 1963
RELEASED: June, 1964
FIRST APPEARANCE: RCA Victor (EP) EPA-4382
VIVA LAS VEGAS
HIT PRIOR TO ELVIS: None
HIT AFTER ELVIS: None
OTHER SIGNIFICANT RECORDINGS: None

TOMORROW IS A LONG TIME (Bob Dylan)

RECORDED: May, 1966
RELEASED: October, 1966
FIRST APPEARANCE: RCA Victor (LP) LPM-3702 (mono)
and LSP-3702 (stereo) SPINOUT
HIT PRIOR TO ELVIS: None
HIT AFTER ELVIS: None
OTHER SIGNIFICANT RECORDINGS: November, 1971 by
Bob Dylan, on the LP "Bob Dylan's Greatest Hits Vol. 2"
(Columbia KG-31120).

TOMORROW NEVER COMES (Ernest Tubb - Johnny Bond)

RECORDED: June, 1970
RELEASED: February, 1971
FIRST APPEARANCE: RCA (LP) LSP-4460 (stereo)
ELVIS COUNTRY
HIT PRIOR TO ELVIS: May, 1949 by Ernest Tubb (Decca
46106); April, 1970 by Slim Whitman (Imperial 66441);
September, 1966 by B.J. Thomas (Scepter 12165).
HIT AFTER ELVIS: None
OTHER SIGNIFICANT RECORDINGS: None

TOMORROW NIGHT (Sam Coslow - Will Grosz)

RECORDED: July, 1955*
RELEASED: July, 1965
FIRST APPEARANCE: RCA Victor (LP) LPM-3450 (mono)
and LSP-3450 (stereo) ELVIS FOR EVERYONE
HIT PRIOR TO ELVIS: None
HIT AFTER ELVIS: None
OTHER SIGNIFICANT RECORDINGS: 1948 by Lonnie
Johnson (The Lonnie Johnson theme song) (King 4201);
December, 1954 by LaVern Baker (Atlantic 1047).

* We are giving the 1955 recording date because most observers and
Elvis discographers agree that this song was recorded at Sun, probably
during his July session. We have no solid reason to disagree with this
theory, but we are faced with some nagging doubts. Everyone agrees
that the sound, less the overdubbed guitars, bass, harmonica, drums,
and background vocals by the Anita Kerr Singers, is the "Sun sound."
However, in listening to the tape of Elvis visiting and jamming at the
home of Eddie Fadal (circa May, 1958) "Tomorrow Night" by Lavern
Baker is played in its entirety. During the song Elvis does not sing
along —at all— as he did on many of the other songs that were played.
Prior to its playing, Elvis is asked if he likes the song. His reply is
simply "oh yeah." Never does he even hint to the fact that he had
ever recorded the song himself! Can you imagine him resisting the
opportunity to mention that he had recorded the song while he was
at Sun. It's just very difficult to conceive his silence, and seeming
total uninterest in this song at that time. Again, we're not disputing
the Sun recording date. Just questioning what seems to be an interesting inconsistency. Perhaps, before our second edition of this
book goes to press, the actual recording date on this song will be
conclusively revealed.

TONIGHT IS SO RIGHT FOR LOVE (Sid Wayne - Abner Silver)

RECORDED: April, 1960
RELEASED: October, 1960
FIRST APPEARANCE: RCA Victor (LP) LPM-2256 (mono)
and LSP-2256 (stereo) G. I. BLUES
HIT PRIOR TO ELVIS: None
HIT AFTER ELVIS: None
OTHER SIGNIFICANT RECORDINGS: None

TONIGHT'S ALL RIGHT FOR LOVE (Sid Wayne - Abner Silver -
Lilly)
RECORDED: May, 1960
RELEASED: January, 1974
FIRST APPEARANCE: RCA (LP) CPL1-0341 (stereo)
ELVIS: A LEGENDARY PERFORMER VOL. 1
HIT PRIOR TO ELVIS: None
HIT AFTER ELVIS: None
OTHER SIGNIFICANT RECORDINGS: None

NOTE: As the story goes, RCA was unable, for copyright reasons,
to release this song in the European countries, as originally recorded
"Tonight Is So Right For Love." On that recording the melody used
is "The Barcarolle," or "A Venetian Boat Song." For the version to
then be issued in Europe, the melody "Tales From Vienna Woods"
replaced The Barcarolle. The lyrics were pretty much the same.
Although not released in the U.S. until 1974 —and then only an
edited version— this version appeared in 1960 in Europe, and on a
45rpm single, backed with "Wooden Heart," in Germany.

TOO MUCH (Bernard Weinman - Lee Rosenberg)

RECORDED: September, 1956
RELEASED: January, 1957
FIRST APPEARANCE: RCA Victor (45rpm single) 47-6800
and (78rpm single) 20-6800
HIT PRIOR TO ELVIS: None
HIT AFTER ELVIS: None
OTHER SIGNIFICANT RECORDINGS: 1954 by Bernard
Hardison (Republic 7111).

NOTE: BMI's files credit only Bernard Weinman for this composition,
leaving us to assume that Lee Rosenberg may have only contributed
to Elvis' version of this song. We also recognize the possibility that
Bernard Hardison was none other than Bernard Weinman.

TOO MUCH MONKEY BUSINESS (Chuck Berry)

RECORDED: January, 1968
RELEASED: November, 1968
FIRST APPEARANCE: RCA Camden (LP) PRS-279 (stereo)
SINGER PRESENTS ELVIS SINGING FLAMING STAR
AND OTHERS
HIT PRIOR TO ELVIS: October, 1956 by Chuck Berry
(Chess 1635).
HIT AFTER ELVIS: None
OTHER SIGNIFICANT RECORDINGS: None

TREAT ME NICE (Jerry Leiber - Mike Stoller)

RECORDED: September, 1957
RELEASED: September, 1957
FIRST APPEARANCE: RCA Victor (45rpm single) 47-7035
and (78rpm single) 20-7035.
HIT PRIOR TO ELVIS: None
HIT AFTER ELVIS: None
OTHER SIGNIFICANT RECORDINGS: None

T-R-O-U-B-L-E (Jerry Chesnut)

RECORDED: March, 1975
RELEASED: May, 1975
FIRST APPEARANCE: RCA (45rpm single) PB-10278
HIT PRIOR TO ELVIS: None
HIT AFTER ELVIS: None
OTHER SIGNIFICANT RECORDINGS: None

TROUBLE (Jerry Leiber - Mike Stoller)

RECORDED: January, 1958
RELEASED: August, 1958
FIRST APPEARANCE: RCA Victor (LP) LPM-1884 (mono)
KING CREOLE
HIT PRIOR TO ELVIS: None
HIT AFTER ELVIS: None
OTHER SIGNIFICANT RECORDINGS: None

TRUE LOVE (Cole Porter)

RECORDED: February, 1957
RELEASED: July, 1957
FIRST APPEARANCE: RCA Victor (LP) LPM-1515 (mono)
LOVING YOU
HIT PRIOR TO ELVIS: August, 1956 by Jane Powell
(Verve 2018); August, 1956 by Bing Crosby & Grace Kelly
(Capitol 3507). Surprising to many, the Jane Powell version
was both released and charted before Bing & Grace, who
sang the song in the movie "High Society."
OTHER SIGNIFICANT RECORDINGS: July, 1963 by
Richard Chamberalin (MGM-13148).

TRUE LOVE TRAVELS ON A GRAVEL ROAD (Dallas Frazier -
Al Owens)
RECORDED: February, 1969
RELEASED: May, 1969
FIRST APPEARANCE: RCA (LP) LSP-4155 (stereo)
FROM ELVIS IN MEMPHIS
HIT PRIOR TO ELVIS: December, 1968 by Duane Dee
(Capitol 2332).
HIT AFTER ELVIS: None
OTHER SIGNIFICANT RECORDINGS: None

TRYIN' TO GET TO YOU (Margie Singleton - Rose Marie
McCoy)
RECORDED: July, 1955
RELEASED: March, 1956
FIRST APPEARANCE: RCA Victor (LP) LPM-1254 (mono)
ELVIS PRESLEY
HIT PRIOR TO ELVIS: None
HIT AFTER ELVIS: None
OTHER SIGNIFICANT RECORDINGS: June, 1954 by The
Eagles (Mercury 70391). A completely different song,
with the similar title "Trying To Get To You," was released
by The Teen Kings (featuring Roy Orbison) on Jewel 101
(1956).

TUTTI FRUTTI (Richard Penniman - Dorothy LaBostrie)

RECORDED: January, 1956
RELEASED: March, 1956
FIRST APPEARANCE: RCA Victor (LP) LPM-1254 (mono)
ELVIS PRESLEY
HIT PRIOR TO ELVIS: December, 1955 by Little Richard
(Specialty 561); January, 1956 by Pat Boone (Dot 15443).
HIT AFTER ELVIS: None
OTHER SIGNIFICANT RECORDINGS: None

TWENTY DAYS AND TWENTY NIGHTS (Ben Weisman - Clive
Westlake)
RECORDED: June, 1970
RELEASED: December, 1970
FIRST APPEARANCE: RCA (LP) LSP-4445 (stereo)
THAT'S THE WAY IT IS
HIT PRIOR TO ELVIS: None
HIT AFTER ELVIS: None
OTHER SIGNIFICANT RECORDINGS: None

UNCHAINED MELODY (Hy Zaret - Alex North)

RECORDED: April, 1977
RELEASED: July, 1977
FIRST APPEARANCE: RCA (LP) AFL1-2428 (stereo)
MOODY BLUE
HIT PRIOR TO ELVIS: March, 1955 by Les Baxter, an
instrumental (Capitol 3055); March, 1955 by Al Hibbler
(Decca 29441); April, 1955 by Roy Hamilton (Epic 9102);
April, 1955 by June Valli (RCA Victor 47-6078); October,
1963 by Vito & The Salutations (Herald 583); July, 1965
by The Righteous Brothers (Philles 129); August, 1968 by
The Sweet Inspirations (Atlantic 2551).
HIT AFTER ELVIS: None
OTHER SIGNIFICANT RECORDINGS: None

NOTE: This is one of those songs wherein the actual title is never
mentioned in its lyrics. The reason for such an unusual title, for a
vocal, is that the music was the title theme for the film "Unchained."

UNTIL IT'S TIME FOR YOU TO GO (Buffy Sainte-Marie)

RECORDED: May, 1971
RELEASED: January, 1972
FIRST APPEARANCE: RCA (45rpm single) 74-0619
HIT PRIOR TO ELVIS: February, 1970 by Neil Diamond (Uni 55204).
HIT AFTER ELVIS: August, 1973 by New Birth (RCA APB0-0003).
OTHER SIGNIFICANT RECORDINGS: November, 1970 by Buffy Sainte-Marie (Vanguard 35116).

UP ABOVE MY HEAD (Brown)

RECORDED: June, 1968
RELEASED: December, 1968
FIRST APPEARANCE: RCA (LP) LPM-4088 (some mono/ some stereo) ELVIS (NBC-TV SPECIAL)
HIT PRIOR TO ELVIS: October, 1964 by Al Hirt, a vocal (RCA Victor 47-8439).
HIT AFTER ELVIS: None
OTHER SIGNIFICANT RECORDINGS: None

U.S. MALE (Jerry Hubbard)

RECORDED: January, 1968
RELEASED: March, 1968
FIRST APPEARANCE: RCA Victor (45rpm single) 47-9465
HIT PRIOR TO ELVIS: None
HIT AFTER ELVIS: None
OTHER SIGNIFICANT RECORDINGS: February, 1967 by Jerry Reed, on the LP "The Unbelievable Guitar and Voice of Jerry Reed," which also contains his version of "Guitar Man." (RCA LPM/LSP-3756)

VINO, DINERO Y AMOR (Wine, Money & Love) (Sid Tepper - Roy C. Bennett)
RECORDED: January, 1963
RELEASED: November, 1963
FIRST APPEARANCE: RCA Victor (LP) LPM-2756 (mono) and LSP-2756 (stereo) FUN IN ACAPULCO
HIT PRIOR TO ELVIS: None
HIT AFTER ELVIS: None
OTHER SIGNIFICANT RECORDINGS: None

VIVA LAS VEGAS (Doc Pomus - Mort Schuman)

RECORDED: July, 1963
RELEASED: April, 1964
FIRST APPEARANCE: RCA Victor (45rpm single) 47-8360
HIT PRIOR TO ELVIS: None
HIT AFTER ELVIS: None
OTHER SIGNIFICANT RECORDINGS: None

NOTE: Since this song appeared on 45rpm single, and not on the "Viva Las Vegas" EP, it creates a situation whereby the "Viva Las Vegas" EP becomes the only Elvis EP or LP to NOT contain the song that is the title of the EP or LP, if, indeed, such a title was ever a song. Obviously, such releases as "Loving You VOL. 2" and "King Creole VOL. 2" do not even break this rule, since there was never a song bearing those complete titles.

WALK A MILE IN MY SHOES (Joe South)

RECORDED: February, 1970
RELEASED: May, 1970
FIRST APPEARANCE: RCA (LP) LSP-4362 (stereo) ON STAGE - FEBRUARY, 1970
HIT PRIOR TO ELVIS: December, 1969 by Joe South (Capitol 2704).
HIT AFTER ELVIS: None
OTHER SIGNIFICANT RECORDINGS: None

WAY DOWN (Layng Martine Jr.)

RECORDED: October, 1976
RELEASED: June, 1977
FIRST APPEARANCE: RCA (45rpm single) PB-10998
HIT PRIOR TO ELVIS: None
HIT AFTER ELVIS: None
OTHER SIGNIFICANT RECORDINGS: None

WEAR MY RING AROUND YOUR NECK (Bert Carroll - Russell Moody)
RECORDED: February, 1958
RELEASED: April, 1958
FIRST APPEARANCE: RCA Victor (45rpm single) 47-7240 and (78rpm single) 20-7240
HIT PRIOR TO ELVIS: None
HIT AFTER ELVIS: None
OTHER SIGNIFICANT RECORDINGS: None

WEARIN' THAT LOVED ON LOOK (Dallas Frazier - Al Owens)

RECORDED: January, 1969
RELEASED: May, 1969
FIRST APPEARANCE: RCA (LP) LSP-4155 (stereo) FROM ELVIS IN MEMPHIS
HIT PRIOR TO ELVIS: None
HIT AFTER ELVIS: None
OTHER SIGNIFICANT RECORDINGS: None

WE CALL ON HIM (Fred Karger - Ben Weisman - Sid Wayne)

RECORDED: September, 1967
RELEASED: April, 1968
FIRST APPEARANCE: RCA Victor (45rpm single) 47-9600
HIT PRIOR TO ELVIS: None
HIT AFTER ELVIS: None
OTHER SIGNIFICANT RECORDINGS: None

WE CAN MAKE THE MORNING (Jay Ramsey)

RECORDED: May, 1971
RELEASED: January, 1972
FIRST APPEARANCE: RCA (45rpm single) 74-0619
HIT PRIOR TO ELVIS: None
HIT AFTER ELVIS: None
OTHER SIGNIFICANT RECORDINGS: None

WELCOME TO MY WORLD (Ray Winkler - John Hathcock)

RECORDED: January, 1973
RELEASED: February, 1973
FIRST APPEARANCE: RCA (LP) VPSX-6089 (quad)
   ALOHA FROM HAWAII VIA SATELLITE
HIT PRIOR TO ELVIS: January, 1964 by Jim Reeves
   (RCA Victor 47-8289); June, 1971 by Eddy Arnold
   (RCA Victor 47-9993).
HIT AFTER ELVIS: None
OTHER SIGNIFICANT RECORDINGS: None

WE'LL BE TOGETHER (Charles O'Curran - Dudley Brooks)

RECORDED: March, 1962
RELEASED: November, 1962
FIRST APPEARANCE: RCA Victor (LP) LPM-2621 (mono)
   and LSP-2621 (stereo) GIRLS! GIRLS! GIRLS!
HIT PRIOR TO ELVIS: None
HIT AFTER ELVIS: None
OTHER SIGNIFICANT RECORDINGS: None, however we
   do know that the melody of this song was around many
   years before Elvis. We also believe that it begins with
   the letter "C," and would be delighted if someone would
   give us its title.

   PS: I believe it was a girl's name, something like
   CARMELITA.
   —Editor

WE'RE COMING IN LOADED (Otis Blackwell - Winfield Scott)

RECORDED: March, 1962
RELEASED: November, 1962
FIRST APPEARANCE: RCA Victor (LP) LPM-2621 (mono)
   and LSP-2621 (stereo) GIRLS! GIRLS! GIRLS!
HIT PRIOR TO ELVIS: None
HIT AFTER ELVIS: None
OTHER SIGNIFICANT RECORDINGS: None

WE'RE GONNA MOVE (Vera Matson - Elvis Presley)

RECORDED: August, 1956
RELEASED: November, 1956
FIRST APPEARANCE: RCA Victor (EP) EPA-4006
   LOVE ME TENDER
HIT PRIOR TO ELVIS: None
HIT AFTER ELVIS: None
OTHER SIGNIFICANT RECORDINGS: None

WESTERN UNION (Sid Tepper - Roy C. Bennett)

RECORDED: May, 1963
RELEASED: June, 1968
FIRST APPEARANCE: RCA Victor (LP) LPM-3989 (mono)
   and LSP-3989 (stereo) SPEEDWAY
HIT PRIOR TO ELVIS: None
HIT AFTER ELVIS: None
OTHER SIGNIFICANT RECORDINGS: None. A completely
   different song, using the same title, was released by The
   Five Americans (February, 1967 - Abnak 118).

WHAT A WONDERFUL LIFE (Sid Wayne - Jerry Livingston)

RECORDED: July, 1961
RELEASED: April, 1962
FIRST APPEARANCE: RCA Victor (EP) EPA-4368
   FOLLOW THAT DREAM
HIT PRIOR TO ELVIS: None
HIT AFTER ELVIS: None
OTHER SIGNIFICANT RECORDINGS: None

WHAT'D I SAY (Ray Charles)

RECORDED: July, 1963
RELEASED: May, 1964
FIRST APPEARANCE: RCA Victor (45rpm single) 47-8360
HIT PRIOR TO ELVIS: July, 1959 by Ray Charles (Atlantic
   2031); March, 1961 by Jerry Lee Lewis (Sun 356); March,
   1962 by Bobby Darin (Atco 6221).
HIT AFTER ELVIS: March, 1972 by Rare Earth (Rare
   Earth 5043).
OTHER SIGNIFICANT RECORDINGS: January, 1962 by
   Calvin Carter, a fine instrumental version (Vee Jay 419).

WHAT EVERY WOMAN LIVES FOR (Doc Pomus - Mort
   Schuman)
RECORDED: May, 1965
RELEASED: April, 1966
FIRST APPEARANCE: RCA Victor (LP) LPM-3553 (mono)
   and LSP-3553 (stereo) FRANKIE AND JOHNNY
HIT PRIOR TO ELVIS: None
HIT AFTER ELVIS: None
OTHER SIGNIFICANT RECORDINGS: None

WHAT NOW MY LOVE (Carl Sigman - Gilbert Becaud -
   P. Delanoe)
RECORDED: January, 1973
RELEASED: February, 1973
FIRST APPEARANCE: RCA (LP) VPSX-6089 (quad)
   ALOHA FROM HAWAII VIA SATELLITE
HIT PRIOR TO ELVIS: January, 1966 by Sonny & Cher
   (Atco 6395); March, 1966 by Herb Alpert & The Tijuana
   Brass (A&M 792); September, 1966 by Richard "Groove"
   Holmes (Prestige 427).
HIT AFTER ELVIS: None
OTHER SIGNIFICANT RECORDINGS: January, 1966 by
   Gilbert Becaud, the LP "What Now My Love" (Kapp 1353).
   Actually, none of the first recordings of this song became
   hits. Prior to Sonny & Cher's (1/66) release, in October,
   November and December of '65, came these versions:
   Al Martino (Capitol 5506), Vic Dana (Dolton 313),
   Peter Duchin (Decca 31863) and Richard Anthony
   (V.I.P. 25022).

WHAT NOW, WHAT NEXT, WHERE TO (Don Robertson - Hal
   Blair)
RECORDED: May, 1963
RELEASED: June, 1967
FIRST APPEARANCE: RCA Victor (LP) LPM-3787 (mono)
   and LSP-3787 (stereo) DOUBLE TROUBLE
HIT PRIOR TO ELVIS: None
HIT AFTER ELVIS: None
OTHER SIGNIFICANT RECORDINGS: None

WHAT'S SHE REALLY LIKE (Sid Wayne - Abner Silver)

RECORDED: April, 1960
RELEASED: October, 1960
FIRST APPEARANCE: RCA Victor (LP) LPM-2256 (mono)
   and LSP-2256 (stereo) G.I. BLUES
HIT PRIOR TO ELVIS: None
HIT AFTER ELVIS: None
OTHER SIGNIFICANT RECORDINGS: None

WHEELS ON MY HEELS (Sid Tepper - Roy C. Bennett)

RECORDED: February, 1964
RELEASED: October, 1964
FIRST APPEARANCE: RCA Victor (LP) LPM-2999 (mono) and LSP-2999 (stereo) ROUSTABOUT
HIT PRIOR TO ELVIS: None
HIT AFTER ELVIS: None
OTHER SIGNIFICANT RECORDINGS: None

WHEN I'M OVER YOU (Shirl Milete)

RECORDED: June, 1970
RELEASED: May, 1971
FIRST APPEARANCE: RCA (LP) LSP-4530 (stereo) LOVE LETTERS FROM ELVIS
HIT PRIOR TO ELVIS: None
HIT AFTER ELVIS: None
OTHER SIGNIFICANT RECORDINGS: None

WHEN IT RAINS IT REALLY POURS (William Emerson)

RECORDED: February, 1957
RELEASED: July, 1965
FIRST APPEARANCE: RCA Victor (LP) LPM-3450 (mono) and LSP-3450 (stereo) ELVIS FOR EVERYONE
HIT PRIOR TO ELVIS: None
HIT AFTER ELVIS: None
OTHER SIGNIFICANT RECORDINGS: January, 1955 by Billy "The Kid" Emerson (Sun 214), as "When It Rains, It Pours."

WHEN MY BLUE MOON TURNS TO GOLD AGAIN (Wiley Walker - Gene Sullivan)

RECORDED: September, 1956
RELEASED: November, 1956
FIRST APPEARANCE: RCA Victor (LP) LPM-1382 (mono) ELVIS
HIT PRIOR TO ELVIS: None
HIT AFTER ELVIS: None
OTHER SIGNIFICANT RECORDINGS: April, 1970 by Jerry Foster (Metromedia 184).

WHEN THE SAINTS GO MARCHING IN: *See DOWN BY THE RIVERSIDE and WHEN THE SAINTS GO MARCHING IN*

WHERE COULD I GO BUT TO THE LORD (J.B. Coats)

RECORDED: May, 1966
RELEASED: April, 1967
FIRST APPEARANCE: RCA Victor (LP) LPM-3758 (mono) and LSP-3758 (stereo) HOW GREAT THOU ART
HIT PRIOR TO ELVIS: None
HIT AFTER ELVIS: None
OTHER SIGNIFICANT RECORDINGS: None

WHERE DID THEY GO LORD (Dallas Frazier - A. L. "Doodle" Owens)

RECORDED: September, 1970
RELEASED: March, 1971
FIRST APPEARANCE: RCA (45rpm single) 47-9980
HIT PRIOR TO ELVIS: None
HIT AFTER ELVIS: None
OTHER SIGNIFICANT RECORDINGS: None

WHERE DO I GO FROM HERE (Williams)

RECORDED: March, 1972
RELEASED: July, 1973
FIRST APPEARANCE: RCA (LP) APL1-0283 (stereo) ELVIS
HIT PRIOR TO ELVIS: None
HIT AFTER ELVIS: None
OTHER SIGNIFICANT RECORDINGS: None

WHERE DO YOU COME FROM (Ruth Batchelor - Bob Roberts)

RECORDED: March, 1962
RELEASED: October, 1962
FIRST APPEARANCE: RCA Victor (45rpm single) 47-8100
HIT PRIOR TO ELVIS: None
HIT AFTER ELVIS: None
OTHER SIGNIFICANT RECORDINGS: None

WHERE NO ONE STANDS ALONE (Mosie Lister)

RECORDED: May, 1966
RELEASED: April, 1967
FIRST APPEARANCE: RCA Victor (LP) LPM-3758 (mono) and LSP-3758 (stereo) HOW GREAT THOU ART
HIT PRIOR TO ELVIS: None
HIT AFTER ELVIS: None
OTHER SIGNIFICANT RECORDINGS: None

WHITE CHRISTMAS (Irving Berlin)

RECORDED: September, 1957
RELEASED: November, 1957
FIRST APPEARANCE: RCA Victor (LP) LOC-1035 (mono) ELVIS' CHRISTMAS ALBUM
HIT PRIOR TO ELVIS: September, 1942 by Bing Crosby (Decca 18429); December, 1946 by Bing Crosby (Decca 23778); December, 1946 by Frank Sinatra (Columbia 37132); December, 1949 by Ernest Tubb (Decca 46186); November, 1954 by The Drifters (Atlantic 1048).
HIT AFTER ELVIS: None
OTHER SIGNIFICANT RECORDINGS: November, 1948 by The Ravens (National 9062); November, 1954 by The Ravens (Mercury 70505).

WHO AM I (Charles "Rusty" Goodman)

RECORDED: February, 1969
RELEASED: March, 1971
FIRST APPEARANCE: RCA Camden CALX-2472 (stereo) YOU'LL NEVER WALK ALONE
HIT PRIOR TO ELVIS: None
HIT AFTER ELVIS: None
OTHER SIGNIFICANT RECORDINGS: None. A completely different song, using the same title, was released by Petula Clark (October, 1966 - Warner Bros. 5863).

WHO ARE YOU (WHO AM I?) (Sid Wayne - Ben Weisman)

RECORDED: June, 1967
RELEASED: June, 1968
FIRST APPEARANCE: RCA Victor (LP) LPM-3989 (mono) and LSP-3989 (stereo) SPEEDWAY
HIT PRIOR TO ELVIS: None
HIT AFTER ELVIS: None
OTHER SIGNIFICANT RECORDINGS: None

WHO NEEDS MONEY (Randy Starr)
RECORDED: February, 1967 (a duet*)
RELEASED: November, 1967
FIRST APPEARANCE: RCA Victor (LP) LPM-3893 (mono) and LSP-3893 (stereo) CLAMBAKE
HIT PRIOR TO ELVIS: None
HIT AFTER ELVIS: None
OTHER SIGNIFICANT RECORDINGS: None
NOTE: In the film, Elvis sings this duet with Will Hutchins, the actor. But, as would be expected in filming, Hutchins only lip syncs to the song. Therefore, the question remains, whose voice is really on the record with Elvis? Is it Will Hutchins, or another —so far unidentified— singer? The LP offers no help. Rarely did RCA credit those who dueted with Presley unless they were also well known, such as Nancy Sinatra. Even Charlie Hodge was uncredited for his duets with Elvis.

WHOLE LOT-TA SHAKIN' GOIN' ON (Dave Williams - Sonny David)
RECORDED: September, 1970
RELEASED: February, 1971
FIRST APPEARANCE: RCA (LP) LSP-4460 (stereo) ELVIS COUNTRY
HIT PRIOR TO ELVIS: June, 1957 by Jerry Lee Lewis (Sun 267); October, 1960 by Chubby Checker (Parkway 813); November, 1960 by Conway Twitty (MGM 12962).
HIT AFTER ELVIS: None
OTHER SIGNIFICANT RECORDINGS: November, 1955 by The Commodores (Dot 15439).

WHY ME, LORD (Kris Kristofferson)
RECORDED: March, 1974
RELEASED: June, 1974
FIRST APPEARANCE: RCA (LP) CPL1-0606 (stereo) ELVIS RECORDED LIVE ON STAGE IN MEMPHIS
HIT PRIOR TO ELVIS: March, 1973 by Kris Kristofferson (Monument 8571), as "Why Me."
HIT AFTER ELVIS: None
OTHER SIGNIFICANT RECORDINGS: None

WILD IN THE COUNTRY (Hugo Peretti - Luigi Creatore - George Weiss)
RECORDED: October, 1960
RELEASED: May, 1961
FIRST APPEARANCE: RCA Victor (45rpm single) 47-7880
HIT PRIOR TO ELVIS: None
HIT AFTER ELVIS: None
OTHER SIGNIFICANT RECORDINGS: None

WINTER WONDERLAND (Dick Smith - Felix Bernard)
RECORDED: May, 1971
RELEASED: October, 1971
FIRST APPEARANCE: RCA (LP) LSP-4579 (stereo) ELVIS SINGS THE WONDERFUL WORLD OF CHRISTMAS
HIT PRIOR TO ELVIS: December, 1946 by Perry Como (RCA Victor 1968).
HIT AFTER ELVIS: None
OTHER SIGNIFICANT RECORDINGS: None
NOTE: This song was written in 1934.

WISDOM OF THE AGES (Bill Giant - Bernie Baum - Florence Kaye)
RECORDED: February, 1965
RELEASED: October, 1965
FIRST APPEARANCE: RCA Victor (LP) LPM-3468 (mono) and LSP-3468 (stereo) HARUM SCARUM
HIT PRIOR TO ELVIS: None
HIT AFTER ELVIS: None
OTHER SIGNIFICANT RECORDINGS: None

WITCHCRAFT (Dave Bartholomew - Pearl King)
RECORDED: May, 1963
RELEASED: October, 1963
FIRST APPEARANCE: RCA Victor (45rpm single) 47-8243
HIT PRIOR TO ELVIS: November, 1955 by The Spiders (Imperial 5366).
HIT AFTER ELVIS: None
OTHER SIGNIFICANT RECORDINGS: None. A completely different song, using the same title, was a hit for Frank Sinatra (January, 1958 - Capitol 3859), and, coincidentally enough, was also performed by Elvis, in a duet with Sinatra, on ABC-TV's Sinatra special (March, 1960). Elvis never made a studio recording of this "Witchcraft."

WITHOUT HIM (Mylon R. LeFevre)
RECORDED: May, 1966
RELEASED: April, 1967
FIRST APPEARANCE: RCA Victor (LP) LPM-3758 (mono) and LSP-3758 (stereo) HOW GREAT THOU ART
HIT PRIOR TO ELVIS: None
HIT AFTER ELVIS: None
OTHER SIGNIFICANT RECORDINGS: None

WITHOUT LOVE (THERE IS NOTHING) (Danny Small)
RECORDED: January, 1969
RELEASED: November, 1969
FIRST APPEARANCE: RCA (LP) LSP-6020 (stereo) FROM MEMPHIS TO VEGAS/FROM VEGAS TO MEMPHIS
HIT PRIOR TO ELVIS: January, 1957 by Clyde McPhatter (Atlantic 1117); June, 1963 by Ray Charles (ABC Paramount 10453); December, 1967 by Oscar Toney Jr. (Bell 699).
HIT AFTER ELVIS: December, 1969 by Tom Jones (Parrot 40045).
OTHER SIGNIFICANT RECORDINGS: None

WOLF CALL (Bill Giant - Bernie Baum - Florence Kaye)
RECORDED: July, 1964
RELEASED: April, 1965
FIRST APPEARANCE: RCA Victor (LP) LPM-3338 (mono) and LSP-3338 (stereo) GIRL HAPPY
HIT PRIOR TO ELVIS: None
HIT AFTER ELVIS: None
OTHER SIGNIFICANT RECORDINGS: None

WOMAN WITHOUT LOVE (Jerry Chesnut)

RECORDED: March, 1975
RELEASED: May, 1975
FIRST APPEARANCE: RCA (LP) APL1-1039 (stereo)
 TODAY
HIT PRIOR TO ELVIS: November, 1968 by Johnny Darrell
 (United Artists 50481).
HIT AFTER ELVIS: None
OTHER SIGNIFICANT RECORDINGS: None

WONDERFUL WORLD (Fletcher - Flett)

RECORDED: March, 1968
RELEASED: November, 1968
FIRST APPEARANCE: RCA Camden (LP) PRS-279 (stereo)
 SINGER PRESENTS ELVIS SINGING FLAMING STAR
 AND OTHERS
HIT PRIOR TO ELVIS: None
HIT AFTER ELVIS: None
OTHER SIGNIFICANT RECORDINGS: None. A completely
 different song, using the same title, was released by Sam
 Cooke (May, 1960 - Keen 8-2112), Herman's Hermits
 (MGM 13354 - May, 1965) and by Art Garfunkle with
 James Taylor and Paul Simon (January, 1978 - Columbia
 10676), as "(What A) Wonderful World."

WOODEN HEART (Fred Wise - Ben Weisman - Bert Kaempfert -
 Kay Twomey)
RECORDED: April, 1960
RELEASED: October, 1960
FIRST APPEARANCE: RCA Victor (LP) LPM-2256 (mono)
 and LSP-2256 (stereo) G. I. BLUES
HIT PRIOR TO ELVIS: None
HIT AFTER ELVIS: June, 1961 by Joe Dowell (Smash 1708);
 June, 1975 by Bobby Vinton (ABC 12100).
OTHER SIGNIFICANT RECORDINGS: None

WORDS (Barry Gibb - Robin Gibb - Maurice Gibb)

RECORDED: August, 1969
RELEASED: November, 1969
FIRST APPEARANCE: RCA (LP) LSP-6020 (stereo)
 FROM MEMPHIS TO VEGAS/FROM VEGAS TO
 MEMPHIS
HIT PRIOR TO ELVIS: January, 1968 by The Bee Gees
 (Atco 6548).
HIT AFTER ELVIS: None
OTHER SIGNIFICANT RECORDINGS: None. Completely
 different songs, using the same title, were released by The
 Monkees (July, 1967 - Colgems 1007); Pat Boone (March,
 1960 - Dot 16048); Margie Joseph (December, 1974 -
 Atlantic 3220) and by Donny Gerrard (March, 1976 -
 Greedy 101). The latter two were titled "Words
 (Are Impossible)."

WORKING ON THE BUILDING (Hoyle - Bowles)

RECORDED: October, 1960
RELEASED: December, 1960
FIRST APPEARANCE: RCA Victor (LP) LPM-2328 (mono)
 and LSP-2328 (stereo) HIS HAND IN MINE
HIT PRIOR TO ELVIS: None
HIT AFTER ELVIS: None
OTHER SIGNIFICANT RECORDINGS: None

YELLOW ROSE OF TEXAS/THE EYES OF TEXAS
 (Fred Wise - Randy Starr) (Sinclair)
RECORDED: July, 1963
RELEASED: November, 1968
FIRST APPEARANCE: RCA Camden (LP) PRS-279 (stereo)
 SINGER PRESENTS ELVIS SINGING FLAMING STAR
 AND OTHERS
HIT PRIOR TO ELVIS: ("Yellow Rose of Texas" only) July,
 1955 by Mitch Miller (Columbia 40540); July, 1955 by
 Johnny Desmond (Coral 61476); October, 1955 by Stan
 Freberg, a parody (Capitol 3249); September, 1955
 by Ernest Tubb (Decca 29633).
HIT AFTER ELVIS: None
OTHER SIGNIFICANT RECORDINGS: None
NOTE: The composers shown on Elvis' version of "Yellow Rose of
Texas" are responsible for the Presley adaptation. Writer/adapter of
the Mitch Miller/Johnny Desmond version was Don George. Of course,
Stan Freberg created his zany version.

YESTERDAY (John Lennon - Paul McCartney)

RECORDED: August, 1969
RELEASED: May, 1970
FIRST APPEARANCE: RCA (LP) LSP-4362 (stereo)
 ON STAGE - FEBRUARY, 1970
HIT PRIOR TO ELVIS: September, 1965 by The Beatles
 (Capitol 5498); October, 1967 by Ray Charles (ABC
 11009).
HIT AFTER ELVIS: None
OTHER SIGNIFICANT RECORDINGS: This was, perhaps,
 the most recorded song of the sixties.
NOTE: This song, and "Runaway," were recorded during the August,
1969 Las Vegas engagement, and NOT February, 1970, as the LP would
lead one to believe.

YOGA IS AS YOGA DOES (Gerald Nelson - Fred Burch)

RECORDED: September, 1966
RELEASED: May, 1967
FIRST APPEARANCE: RCA Victor (EP) EPA-4387
 EASY COME, EASY GO
HIT PRIOR TO ELVIS: None
HIT AFTER ELVIS: None
OTHER SIGNIFICANT RECORDINGS: None

YOU ASKED ME TO (Waylon Jennings - Billy Joe Shaver)

RECORDED: December, 1973
RELEASED: January, 1975
FIRST APPEARANCE: RCA (LP) APL1-0873 (stereo)
 PROMISED LAND
HIT PRIOR TO ELVIS: September, 1973 by Waylon
 Jennings (RCA APB0-0086).
HIT AFTER ELVIS: None
OTHER SIGNIFICANT RECORDINGS: None

YOU CAN'T SAY NO IN ACAPULCO (Dolores Fuller -
 Morris - Feller)
RECORDED: January, 1963
RELEASED: November, 1963
FIRST APPEARANCE: RCA Victor (LP) LPM-2756 (mono)
 and LSP-2756 (stereo) FUN IN ACAPULCO
HIT PRIOR TO ELVIS: None
HIT AFTER ELVIS: None
OTHER SIGNIFICANT RECORDINGS: None

YOU DON'T HAVE TO SAY YOU LOVE ME (Vicki Wickham - Simon Napier-Bell - P. Donaggio - V. Pallavicni)
RECORDED: June, 1970
RELEASED: October, 1970
FIRST APPEARANCE: RCA (45rpm single) 47-9916
HIT PRIOR TO ELVIS: May, 1966 by Dusty Springfield (Philips 40371); January, 1968 by The Four Sonics (Sport 110).
HIT AFTER ELVIS: None
OTHER SIGNIFICANT RECORDINGS: None

YOU DON'T KNOW ME (Eddy Arnold - Cindy Walker)
RECORDED: February, 1967
RELEASED: October, 1967
FIRST APPEARANCE: RCA Victor (45rpm single) 47-9341
HIT PRIOR TO ELVIS: June, 1956 by Jerry Vale (Columbia 40710); August, 1956 by Eddy Arnold (RCA Victor 47-6502)); February, 1960 by Lenny Welch (Cadence 1373); July, 1962 by Ray Charles (ABC Paramount 10345).
HIT AFTER ELVIS: March, 1970 by Ray Pennington (Monument 1194).
OTHER SIGNIFICANT RECORDINGS: None

YOU GAVE ME A MOUNTAIN (Marty Robbins)
RECORDED: January, 1973
RELEASED: February, 1973
FIRST APPEARANCE: RCA (LP) VPSX-6089 (quad) ALOHA FROM HAWAII VIA SATELLITE
HIT PRIOR TO ELVIS: January, 1969 by Frankie Laine (ABC 11174); March, 1969 by Johnny Bush (Stop 257).
HIT AFTER ELVIS: None
OTHER SIGNIFICANT RECORDINGS: June, 1969 by Marty Robbins, on the LP "It's A Sin" (Columbia 9811).
NOTE: Contrary to popular opinion, Marty Robbins did not release this song first. As you can see, his version didn't appear on the market until May (at the earliest) or June, 1969. Frankie Laine's version was released in January.

YOU GOTTA STOP (Bill Giant - Bernie Baum - Florence Kaye)
RECORDED: September, 1966
RELEASED: April, 1967
FIRST APPEARANCE: RCA Victor (EP) EPA-4387 EASY COME, EASY GO
HIT PRIOR TO ELVIS: None
HIT AFTER ELVIS: None
OTHER SIGNIFICANT RECORDINGS: None

YOU'LL BE GONE (Elvis Presley - Charlie Hodge - Red West)
RECORDED: March, 1962
RELEASED: February, 1965
FIRST APPEARANCE: RCA Victor (45rpm single) 47-8500
HIT PRIOR TO ELVIS: None
HIT AFTER ELVIS: None
OTHER SIGNIFICANT RECORDINGS: None

YOU'LL NEVER WALK ALONE (Richard Rodgers - Oscar Hammerstein)
RECORDED: September, 1967
RELEASED: April, 1968
FIRST APPEARANCE: RCA Victor (45rpm single) 47-9600
HIT PRIOR TO ELVIS: December, 1963 by Patti LaBelle & The Blue Belles (Nicetown 5020 & Parkway 896); May, 1965 by Gerry & The Pacemakers (Laurie 3302).
HIT AFTER ELVIS: September, 1969 by The Brooklyn Bridge (Buddah 139).
OTHER SIGNIFICANT RECORDINGS: 1954 by Roy Hamilton (Epic 9015).
NOTE: This song was written in 1945.

YOU'LL THINK OF ME (Mort Schuman)
RECORDED: January, 1969
RELEASED: September, 1969
FIRST APPEARANCE: RCA (45rpm single) 47-9764
HIT PRIOR TO ELVIS: None
HIT AFTER ELVIS: None
OTHER SIGNIFICANT RECORDINGS: None

YOUNG AND BEAUTIFUL (Aaron Schroeder - Abner Silver)
RECORDED: June, 1957
RELEASED: October, 1957
FIRST APPEARANCE: RCA Victor (EP) EPA-4114 JAILHOUSE ROCK
HIT PRIOR TO ELVIS: None
HIT AFTER ELVIS: None
OTHER SIGNIFICANT RECORDINGS: None

YOUNG DREAMS (Aaron Schroeder - Martin Kalmanoff)
RECORDED: January, 1958
RELEASED: August, 1958
FIRST APPEARANCE: RCA Victor (LP) LPM-1884 (mono) KING CREOLE
HIT PRIOR TO ELVIS: None
HIT AFTER ELVIS: None
OTHER SIGNIFICANT RECORDINGS: None

YOUR CHEATIN' HEART (Hank Williams)
RECORDED: February, 1958
RELEASED: July, 1965
FIRST APPEARANCE: RCA Victor (LP) LPM-3450 (mono) and LSP-3450 (stereo) ELVIS FOR EVERYONE
HIT PRIOR TO ELVIS: February, 1953 by Hank Williams (MGM 11416); February, 1953 by Joni James (MGM 11426).
HIT AFTER ELVIS: September, 1958 by George Hamilton IV (ABC Paramount 9946); March, 1959 by Billy Vaughn, an instrumental (Dot 15936); November, 1962 by Ray Charles (ABC Paramount 10375).

YOUR LOVE'S BEEN A LONG TIME COMING (Rory Bourke)

    RECORDED: December, 1973
    RELEASED: January, 1975
    FIRST APPEARANCE: RCA (LP) APL1-0873 (stereo)
      PROMISED LAND
    HIT PRIOR TO ELVIS: None
    HIT AFTER ELVIS: None
    OTHER SIGNIFICANT RECORDINGS: None

YOUR TIME HASN'T COME YET BABY (Hirschhorn - Kasha)

    RECORDED: June, 1967
    RELEASED: June, 1968
    FIRST APPEARANCE: RCA Victor (45rpm single) 47-9547
    HIT PRIOR TO ELVIS: None
    HIT AFTER ELVIS: None
    OTHER SIGNIFICANT RECORDINGS: None

YOU'RE A HEARTBREAKER (Jack Sallee)

    RECORDED: December, 1954
    RELEASED: January, 1955
    FIRST APPEARANCE: Sun (45 and 78rpm) 215
    HIT PRIOR TO ELVIS: None
    HIT AFTER ELVIS: None
    OTHER SIGNIFICANT RECORDINGS: None

YOU'VE LOST THAT LOVIN' FEELIN' (Phil Spector - Barry Mann - Cynthia Weil)

    RECORDED: August, 1970
    RELEASED: December, 1970
    FIRST APPEARANCE: RCA (LP) LSP-4445 (stereo)
    THAT'S THE WAY IT IS
    HIT PRIOR TO ELVIS: December, 1964 by The Righteous Brothers (Philles 124); September, 1969 by Dionne Warwick (Scepter 12262).
    HIT AFTER ELVIS: October, 1971 by Roberta Flack & Donny Hathaway (Atlantic 2837).
    OTHER SIGNIFICANT RECORDINGS: None

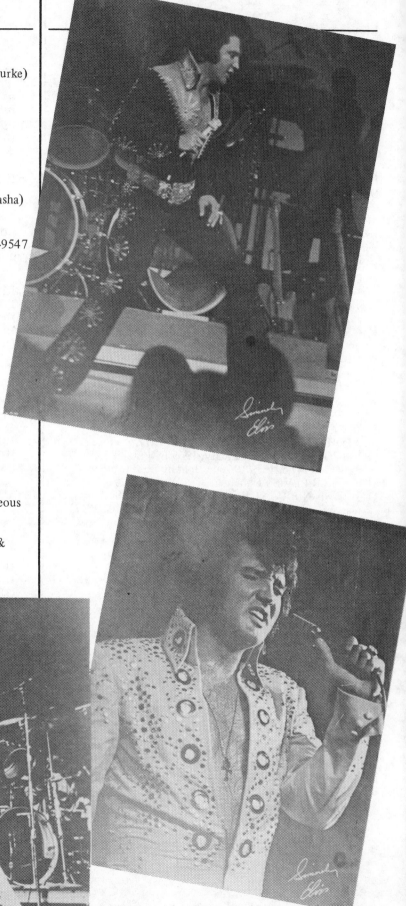

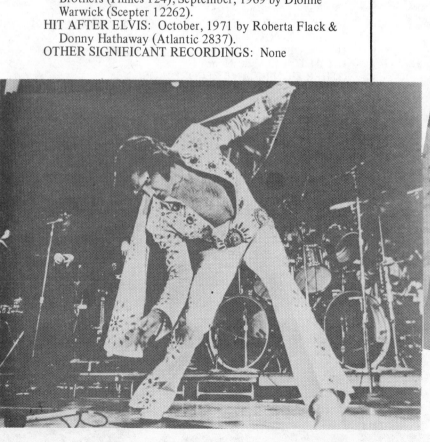

10216-015-B/1

ALTERNATES & VARIATIONS

SONGS THAT HAVE BEEN RELEASED IN MORE THAN ONE FORM.

Each of the following Elvis songs has been made available in more than form. The alternate version(s) may be legitimate, such as those released or authorized by RCA, or unauthorized, as are privately issued bootleg recordings.

As you no doubt know, the degree of quality on bootleg discs can range from absolutely dreadful to perfect "studio" quality. Only those releases meeting a mininum standard of quality will be listed in this section. To put this into perspective, the audio fidelity should be at least as good as that of the 1961 "Hawaii Benefit Concert." Anything less cannot truly be enjoyed.

We have limited the listings to albums as much as possible. Nearly every worthwhile track has been included on one LP or another.

Since only a small percentage of the bootleg releases, and none of the counterfeits, are truly worthwhile to the Elvis fan, we have chosen not to do a separate discography on them.

Instead, within the pages of this chapter, you'll find those unauthorized releases that are, from a content standpoint, a usefull addition to one's collection.

By exercising a little care and through an analysis of this data, one can also avoid the costly duplication of buying more than one album of the same material. For example, the recordings made by Elvis on the Ed Sullivan show are available on at least three or four different albums. You only need one. Likewise with the songs from the Louisiana Hayride and the Eagle's Hall shows. Hopefully, the time spent in preparing this section will assist you in planning for valuable additions to your collection, while avoiding unwanted duplications.

We would like to make it clear that the listing of unauthorized recordings in this publication is neither a recommendation to buy them or a solicitation of any type. The information is provided for no reason other than a desire to offer a more comprehensive publication.

Become familiar with the following terms, as they are used in this chapter, extensively, and, more and more, in fandom.

ALTERNATE TAKE: Generally speaking, the alternate take is the most desirable of the variant forms. To be included in this catagory requires a separate and different vocal rendering of the song by Elvis! Songs tagged as alternate takes cannot be from any of Elvis' live concert appearances. These many songs will be dealt with as "Concert Versions." In many cases, the difference between the original version and the alternate take is very obvious. At other times, the difference may be quite subtle and, perhaps, un-noticed by most fans. For this reason, a description of the variation will be included when needed.

In compiling this section, many hours were spent pouring over Elvis' many recordings. The emphisis is placed on Elvis' standard U.S. catalog, however, as often as deemed necessary, we will include special releases and foreign pressings. One important source of alternate takes, and alternate mixes too, for that matter, is the many acetates that have found their way into the hands of collectors. But, for consistency's sake, we will not attempt to list song variations that are only known to exist on acetate. For every acetate we know about, there are probably a hundred that we know nothing about; an impossible area to document comprehensively at this time. This section will stick to those discs that were actually pressed and released.

ALTERNATE MIX: If one version of an Elvis song sounds different to you than another recording of the same song, yet you'd swear that Elvis' vocal is the same, you're probably listening to an alternate *mix*. Sometimes an alternate mix can sound varied enough to give the impression of an alternate take. We will distinguish between these two forms in every case.

Even though all of RCA's electronically reprocessed albums, from monaural originals, are truly alternate mixes, they are not included in this section. It's simple enough to just remember that they *all* are. On the other hand, many of RCA's monaural albums contained beefed-up versions (alternate mixes) of mono originals. Usually, the difference is the addition of reverberation, or echo. These changes will be noted individually.

In recent times, a new type of mix has become popular with both RCA and the fans; the "pure Elvis" sound. These are the songs exactly as recorded by Elvis and his combo, prior to any overdubbing of background vocals, horns, strings and other forms of orchestration. All of these will fall into the "alternate mix" catagory.

FALSE START: When an unsuccessful attempt to record a particular song is released, it will be termed a false start. Even if the false start only falls short of being a complete take by a few seconds, it is still only a "start." If the number is completed, to the planned ending, it is a "take."

CONCERT VERSION: These are recordings that feature a version of a song performed by Elvis during a live concert. If the same song was made available from several different concerts, each one will be listed as a separate "concert version." When more than one version appears on the same album, each track will be given a number, in parenthesis, so that the reader knows exactly which track is being described.

In those cases where a rehersal version of a song appears on disc, it will be classified as a concert version if the rehersal is for a live concert. If a rehersal is for a studio session, or results in a studio recording, it would be found under the heading of "alternate take."

(Continued on the following page)

TV AUDIO TRACK: During the period beginning January 28, 1956 and ending March 26, 1960, Elvis made 13 guest appearances on television. All but one of these appearances can be heard on an assortment of bootleg albums. The one that has never turned up is Elvis' first appearance on the Milton Berle show, April 3, 1956. This is the catagory where what material is available will be listed. Any Elvis performance after 1960 on television would be a concert and not a guest appearance. And any recordings made from those concerts will appear as "concert versions."

FILM VERSION: These are songs that were made by recording from the audio during one of Elvis' movies. Usually, off of a television showing or, in more recent years, a pre-recorded video cassette. Mostly done with songs that appeared in a film but were never made available on records and with songs that, in the film, differed significantly from previously available versions.

A BIG HUNK O' LOVE

- *ORIGINAL VERSION:* Any RCA release that is not taken from a live concert.
- *CONCERT VERSION:* "Aloha From Hawaii Via Satellite" RCA (VPSX-6089).
- *FILM VERSION:* "From The Dark To The Light" and "Rock My Soul," bootleg albums. Taken from the film "Elvis On Tour."
- *CONCERT VERSION:* "The Legend Lives On" and "Superstar Out-takes Vol. 2," bootleg albums. Taken from a February, 1972 Las Vegas concert.

A DOG'S LIFE

- *ORIGINAL VERSION:* All RCA releases.
- *ALTERNATE TAKE:* "A Dog's Life," a bootleg album.

A FOOL SUCH AS I

- *ORIGINAL VERSION:* All RCA releases.
- *CONCERT VERSION:* "Hawaii Benefit Concert" a bootleg album. From a 1961 live appearance.

A WHISTLING TUNE

- *ORIGINAL VERSION:* All RCA releases.
- *FALSE STARTS:* "Behind Closed Doors," a bootleg album, contains two false starts that feature Elvis and a couple more that end before he begins to sing.

ALL SHOOK UP

- *ORIGINAL VERSION:* Any RCA release that is not taken from a live concert.
- *CONCERT VERSION:* "Elvis (NBC-TV Special)" RCA (LPM-4088).
- *CONCERT VERSION:* "From Memphis To Vegas/From Vegas To Memphis" RCA (LSP-6020) and "Elvis In Person At The International Hotel, Las Vegas, Vevada" RCA (LSP-4428)
- *CONCERT VERSION:* "Elvis As Recorded At Madison Square Garden" RCA (LSP-4776).
- *CONCERT VERSION:* "Hawaii Benefit Concert," a bootleg album.
- *CONCERT VERSION (1):* "The Burbank Sessions Vol. 2," a bootleg album. This is the version (side one) that appears on the RCA LP "Elvis (NBC-TV Special)." In this case, the song is part of a medley.
- *CONCERT VERSION (2):* "The Burbank Sessions Vol. 2," a bootleg album. Again, the song is part of a medley.

ALMOST

- *ORIGINAL VERSION:* All RCA releases.
- *ALTERNATE TAKE:* "Behind Closed Doors," a bootleg album.

ALMOST ALWAYS TRUE

- *ORIGINAL VERSION:* All RCA releases.
- *ALTERNATE TAKE:* "Behind Closed Doors," a bootleg album.
- *FALSE START:* "Behind Closed Doors," a bootleg album.

ALOHA OE

- *ORIGINAL VERSION:* All RCA releases.
- *ALTERNATE TAKE:* "Leavin' It Up To You," a bootleg album.

AMERICAN TRILOGY

- *ORIGINAL VERSION:* RCA 45rpm single 74-0672, a concert version.
- *CONCERT VERSION:* "Elvis As Recorded At Madison Square Garden" RCA (LSP-4776).
- *CONCERT VERSION:* "Aloha From Hawaii Via Satellite" RCA (VPSX-6089).
- *CONCERT VERSION:* "Elvis Recorded Live On Stage In Memphis" RCA (CPL1-0606).
- *CONCERT VERSION:* "A Dog's Life," a bootleg album. This version is from the "Aloha From Hawaii" TV rehersal show, performed in concert prior to the concert that was actually aired.

AND I LOVE YOU SO

- *ORIGINAL VERSION:* "Today" RCA (APL1-1039).
- *CONCERT VERSION:* "Elvis In Concert" RCA (APL2-2587).

ARE YOU LONESOME TO-NIGHT

- *ORIGINAL VERSION:* Any RCA release that is not taken from a live concert.
- *CONCERT VERSION:* "From Memphis To Vegas/From Vegas To Memphis" RCA (LSP-6020) and "Elvis In Person At The International Hotel, Las Vegas, Nevada" RCA (LSP-4428).
- *CONCERT VERSION:* "A Legendary Performer Vol. 1" RCA (CPL1-0341). Recorded for possible use in the '68 TV special.
- *CONCERT VERSION:* "Hawaii Benefit Concert," a bootleg album.
- *CONCERT VERSION (1):* "The Burbank Sessions Vol. 1," a bootleg album.
- *CONCERT VERSION (2):* "The Burbank Sessions Vol. 1," a bootleg album. This is the same version that appears on the RCA LP "A Legendary Performer, Vol. 1," and it is the one on side three of this album.

ARE YOU SINCERE

- *ORIGINAL VERSION:* "Raised On Rock/For Ol' Times Sake" RCA (APL1-0388).
- *ALTERNATE TAKE:* "Our Memories Of Elvis Vol. 1" RCA (AQL1-3279) and the 45rpm single RCA PB-11533.

AS LONG AS I HAVE YOU

- *ORIGINAL VERSION:* All RCA releases.
- *ALTERNATE TAKE (1):* "From The Beach To The Bayou," a bootleg album.
- *ALTERNATE TAKE (2):* "From The Beach To The Bayou," a bootleg album.
- *ALTERNATE TAKE (3):* "From The Beach To The Bayou," a bootleg album.
- *ALTERNATE TAKE:* "The Rockin' Rebel Vol. 1," a bootleg album.

ASK ME

- *ORIGINAL VERSION:* All RCA releases in the
- *ALTERNATE MIX:* On the RCA 45rpm version issued in France (45-567). One of the two stereo channels is missing, and so, as a result, are the Jordanaires (vocal backing) and the orchestration. What's left, on this release, is Elvis' vocal and Floyd Cramer's (keyboard) accompaniment.

(YOU'RE SO SQUARE) BABY, I DON'T CARE

- *ORIGINAL VERSION:* "Jailhouse Rock" EP RCA (EPA-4114) and "Worldwide Gold Award Hits, Vol. 2" RCA (LPM-6402).
- *ALTERNATE MIX:* "A Date With Elvis" RCA (LPM-2011).
- *FILM VERSION:* "Got A Lot O' Livin' To Do," a bootleg album.

BABY, LET'S PLAY HOUSE

- *ORIGINAL VERSION:* Sun single (217) and RCA single (20/47-6383).
- *ALTERNATE MIX:* All RCA albums.
- *TV AUDIO TRACK:* "The Dorsey Shows" and "Superstar Out-takes Vol. 2," bootleg albums.
- *CONCERT VERSION:* "The First Years," an unauthorized album. "The Entertainer" and "Rockin' Rebel Vol. 2," bootleg albums. These three albums contain a version recorded at a 1955 Houston, Texas performance.

BABY, WHAT YOU WANT ME TO DO

- *ORIGINAL VERSION:* "Elvis (NBC-TV Special" RCA (LPM-4088), a concert version.
- *CONCERT VERSION:* "A Legendary Performer Vol. 2" RCA (CPL1-1349).
- *CONCERT VERSION (1):* "The Burbank Sessions Vol. 1," a bootleg album.
- *CONCERT VERSION (2):* "The Burbank Sessions Vol. 1," a bootleg album. It is this version (side one - track eight) that is heard on the RCA LP "Elvis (NBC-TV Special)."
- *CONCERT VERSION (3):* "The Burbank Sessions Vol. 1," a bootleg album. It is this version (side two) that a portion of was used on the RCA LP "A Legendary Performer Vol. 2." This bootleg album contains the complete song.
- *CONCERT VERSION (4):* "The Burbank Sessions Vol. 1," a bootleg album.
- *CONCERT VERSION:* "The Burbank Sessions Vol. 2," a bootleg album.

BEACH BOY BLUES

- *ORIGINAL VERSION:* All RCA releases.
- *ALTERNATE TAKE:* "Behind Closed Doors," a bootleg album.
- *ALTERNATE TAKE:* "From The Beach To The Bayou," a bootleg album.
- *FALSE START:* "Behind Closed Doors" and "From The Beach To The Bayou," bootleg albums.

BIG BOOTS

- *ORIGINAL VERSION:* "G.I. Blues" RCA (LPM/LSP-2256).
- *ALTERNATE TAKE:* "Elvis Sings For Children And Grown-ups Too" RCA (CPL1-2901).

BIG BOSS MAN

- *ORIGINAL VERSION:* All RCA releases prior to December, 1968.
- *ALTERNATE TAKE:* "Elvis (NBC-TV Special)" RCA (LPM-4088).

BLUE CHRISTMAS

- *ORIGINAL VERSION:* Any RCA release that is not taken from a live concert.
- *CONCERT VERSION:* "Elvis (NBC-TV Special)" RCA (LPM-4088).
- *CONCERT VERSION (1):* "The Burbank Sessions Vol. 1," a bootleg album.
- *CONCERT VERSION (2):* "The Burbank Sessions Vol. 1," a bootleg album. It is this version (side four) that appears on RCA's "Elvis (NBC-TV Special)."

BLUE HAWAII

- *ORIGINAL VERSION:* "Blue Hawaii" RCA (LPM/LSP-2426).
- *ALTERNATE TAKE:* "A Legendary Performer, Vol. 2" RCA (CPL1-1349) and "Mahalo From Elvis" Pickwick (ACL-7064).

BLUE MOON OF KENTUCKY

- *ORIGINAL VERSION:* Sun single (209) and RCA single (20/47-6380).
- *ALTERNATE MIX:* All RCA albums and on the extended play "A Touch Of Gold Vol. 3" RCA (EPA-5141).
- *CONCERT VERSION:* "The Entertainer" and "Rockin' Rebel Vol. 2," both bootleg albums, and "Elvis Presley Live On The Louisiana Hayride," a bootleg EP. These releases contain Elvis' version of the song that he performed in December, 1954 on the Louisiana Hayride.
- *CONCERT VERSION:* "The First Years," an unauthorized album and "Rockin' Rebel Vol. 2," a bootleg album. These releases contain a version recorded in a 1955 Houston, Texas appearance.

BLUE RIVER

- *ORIGINAL VERSION:* All RCA releases in the United States.
- *ALTERNATE MIX:* Actually, it isn't really a different mix but we have no term for a speed variation, so it goes here. It's the French EP "Elvis Presley" (86508), and the version of this song it contains runs about four seconds longer, giving the appearance of sounding slightly different than on other RCA releases.

BLUE SUEDE SHOES

- *ORIGINAL VERSION:* Except for "G.I. Blues" LP, any RCA release that is not taken from a live concert.
- *ALTERNATE TAKE:* "G.I. Blues" RCA (LPM/LSP-2256).
- *CONCERT VERSION:* "From Memphis To Vegas/From Vegas To Memphis" RCA (LSP-6020) and "Elvis In Person At The International Hotel, Las Vegas, Nevada" RCA (LSP-4428).
- *CONCERT VERSION:* "Aloha From Hawaii Via Satellite" RCA (VPSX-6089).
- *CONCERT VERSION:* "A Legendary Performer Vol. 2" RCA (CPL1-1349).
- *CONCERT VERSION (1):* "The Burbank Sessions Vol. 1," a bootleg album.
- *CONCERT VERSION (2):* "The Burbank Sessions Vol. 1," a bootleg album. It is this version (side three) that appears on "A Legendary Performer Vol. 2."
- *CONCERT VERSION (1):* "The Burbank Sessions Vol. 2," a bootleg album.
- *CONCERT VERSION (2):* "The Burbank Sessions Vol. 2," a bootleg album.
- *TV AUDIO TRACK (1):* "The Dorsey Shows" and "Superstar Out-takes Vol. 2," bootleg albums. From Elvis' January 28, 1956 appearance on the Dorsey Bros. show.
- *TV AUDIO TRACK (2):* "The Dorsey Shows" and "Superstar Out-takes Vol. 2," bootleg albums. From Elvis' March 17, 1956 appearance on the Dorsey show.

BLUEBERRY HILL

- *ORIGINAL VERSION:* All RCA releases prior to June, 1974.
- *CONCERT VERSION:* "Elvis Recorded Live On Stage In Memphis" RCA (CPL1-0606).

BOSOM OF ABRAHAM

- *ORIGINAL VERSION:* All RCA releases.
- *FILM VERSION:* "From The Dark To The Light" and "Rock My Soul," bootleg albums. Recorded from the film "Elvis On Tour."

BRIDGE OVER TROUBLED WATER

- *ORIGINAL VERSION:* "That's The Way It Is" RCA (LSP-4445).
- *CONCERT VERSION:* "The Legend Lives On," a bootleg album. Recorded during a

BRIDGE OVER TROUBLED WATER

- *ORIGINAL VERSION:* "That's The Way It Is" RCA (LSP-4445).
- *ALTERNATE TAKE:* "The Legend Lives On" and "Superstar Out-takes Vol. 1," bootleg albums.
- *FILM VERSION:* "From The Dark To The Light," a bootleg album. Contains segments of the song, as appeared in the film "That's The Way It Is."

BURNING LOVE

- *ORIGINAL VERSION:* On any RCA release that is not a live concert recording.
- *CONCERT VERSION:* "Aloha From Hawaii Via Satellite" RCA (VPSX-6089).
- *CONCERT VERSION:* "Leavin' It Up To You," a bootleg album. From the "Aloha" rehersal show.
- *FILM VERSION:* "From The Dark To The Light," a bootleg album. Recorded from the film "Elvis On Tour."

CANE AND A HIGH STARCHED COLLAR

- *ORIGINAL VERSION:* "A Legendary Performer Vol. 2" RCA (CPL1-1349).
- *FALSE START:* "A Legendary Performer Vol. 2" RCA (CPL1-1349).
- *FILM VERSION:* "Cane And A High Starched Collar" and "I Wanna Be A Rock 'N' Roll Star," bootleg albums.

CAN'T HELP FALLING IN LOVE

- *ORIGINAL VERSION:* On any RCA release that is not a live concert recording.
- *CONCERT VERSION:* "Elvis (NBC-TV Special)" RCA (LPM-4088).
- *CONCERT VERSION:* "From Memphis To Vegas/From Vegas To Memphis" RCA (LSP-6020) and "Elvis In Person At The International Hotel, Las Vegas, Nevada" RCA (LSP-4428).
- *CONCERT VERSION:* "Elvis As Recorded At Madison Square Garden" RCA (LSP-4776).
- *CONCERT VERSION:* "Aloha From Hawaii Via Satellite" RCA (VPSX-6089).
- *CONCERT VERSION:* "Elvis Recorded Live On Stage In Memphis" RCA (CPL1-0606).
- *CONCERT VERSION:* "Elvis In Concert" RCA (APL2-2587).
- *CONCERT VERSION:* "The Legend Lives On" and "Superstar Out-takes Vol. 1," bootleg albums. Recorded live in Las Vegas, 1969.
- *CONCERT VERSION:* "A Dog's Life," a bootleg album. From the "Aloha" rehersal show.
- *ALTERNATE TAKE (1):* "From The Beach To The Bayou," a bootleg album.
- *ALTERNATE TAKE (2):* "From The Beach To The Bayou," a bootleg album.
- *ALTERNATE TAKE (3):* "Behind Closed Doors" and "From The Beach To The Bayou," bootleg albums.
- *ALTERNATE TAKE (4):* "From The Beach To The Bayou," a bootleg album.
- *ALTERNATE TAKE (5):* "From The Beach To The Bayou," a bootleg album. This is the track that RCA released as a single and included on the "Blue Hawaii" LP; it is the "original version" listed above.
- *FALSE STARTS:* "From The Beach To The Bayou" contains 12 false starts of this song. "Behind Closed Doors" has three of the 12 on it, and "Plantation Rock" has two false starts that do not appear on either of the other albums. These are all bootlegs.
- *ALTERNATE TAKE:* "Plantation Rock," a bootleg album.

C'MON EVERYBODY

- *ORIGINAL VERSION:* All RCA releases.
- *FILM VERSION:* "Eternal Elvis" and "Viva Las Vegas," bootleg albums.

CRAWFISH

- *ORIGINAL VERSION:* All RCA releases.
- *ALTERNATE MIX:* "From The Beach To The Bayou," a bootleg album. This version contains the complete beginning and ending vocal by Kitty White.
- *FILM VERSION:* "Loving You," a bootleg album.

DIXIELAND ROCK

- *ORIGINAL VERSION:* "King Creole" RCA (LPM-1884).
- *ALTERNATE MIX:* "King Creole Vol. 2" RCA EP (EPA-4321) and "Worldwide Gold Award Hits, Vol. 2" RCA (LPM-6402). This version was made by eliminating a few opening beats from the original version. It is a few seconds shorter in length.

DONCHA' THINK IT'S TIME

- *ORIGINAL VERSION:* RCA single release (20/47-7240) and "Worldwide Gold Award Hits, Vol. 2" RCA (LPM-6402).
- *ALTERNATE TAKE:* "Elvis Gold Records, Vol. 2" RCA LPM-2075).

DON'T BE CRUEL

- *ORIGINAL VERSION:* On any RCA release that is not a live concert recording.
- *CONCERT VERSION:* "Elvis As Recorded At Madison Square Garden" RCA (LSP-4776).
- *CONCERT VERSION:* "Elvis In Concert" RCA (APL2-2587). In both of the RCA LP issues, containing the concert version, this song is coupled with "Teddy Bear" in a medley.
- *CONCERT VERSION (1):* "The Burbank Sessions Vol. 2," a bootleg album.
- *CONCERT VERSION (2):* "The Burbank Sessions Vol. 2," a bootleg album.
- *CONCERT VERSION:* "Hawaii Benefit Concert," a bootleg album.
- *TV AUDIO TRACK (1):* "The King Goes Wild," "From The Waist Up," "The Hillbilly Cat 1954-1974, " "Rock My Soul " and "The Rockin' Rebel Vol 3." From the September 9, 1956 appearance on the Ed Sullivan show.
- *TV AUDIO TRACK (2):* "The King Goes Wild," "From The Waist Up " and "The Hillbilly Cat 1954-1974," all bootleg albums. From the October 28, 1956 appearance on the Ed Sullivan show.
- *TV AUDIO TRACK (3):* "The King Goes Wild" and "From The Waist Up," bootleg albums. From the January, 6, 1957 appearance on the Ed Sullivan show.

DON'T CRY DADDY

- *ORIGINAL VERSION:* Any RCA release.
- *ALTERNATE MIX:* "King of Rock And Roll, Elvis Presley's Golden Album, Vol. 1," an unauthorized album from China.
- *CONCERT VERSION:* "Behind Closed Doors" and "The Entertainer," bootleg albums. From a Las Vegas rehersal session.

DON'T LEAVE ME NOW

- *ORIGINAL VERSION:* "Loving You" RCA (LPM-1515).
- *ALTERNATE TAKE:* "Jailhouse Rock" RCA EP (EPA-4114).
- *FILM VERSION:* "Got A Lot O' Livin' To Do," a bootleg album.

DON'T THINK TWICE, IT'S ALL RIGHT

- *ORIGINAL VERSION:* "Elvis" RCA (APL1-0283).
- *ALTERNATE MIX:* "Our Memories Of Elvis Vol. 2" RCA (AQL1-3448). This version runs almost six minutes longer than the first release on the LP "Elvis."
- *ALTERNATE MIX:* "Behind Closed Doors," a bootleg album. This recording runs about two minutes longer than the version on "Our Memories Of Elvis." Actually the length of the song, as originally recorded by Elvis, was close to 15 minutes, and the entire track has yet to be issued by anyone.

DRUMS OF THE ISLANDS

- *ORIGINAL VERSION:* All RCA releases.
- *ALTERNATE TAKE:* "Behind Closed Doors," a bootleg album. This is a complete "take" despite it's lack of length.
- *FALSE STARTS:* "Behind Closed Doors," a bootleg album, contains two false starts of this song.

EARLY MORNING RAIN

- *ORIGINAL VERSION:* "Elvis Now" RCA (LSP-4761).
- *ALTERNATE TAKE:* "Mahalo From Elvis" Pickwick (ACL-7064).
- *CONCERT VERSION:* "Elvis In Concert" RCA (APL2-2587).

EYES OF TEXAS, THE: *See YELLOW ROSE OF TEXAS/THE EYES OF TEXAS*

FADED LOVE

- *ORIGINAL VERSION:* "Elvis Country" RCA (LSP-4460).
- *ALTERNATE MIX:* "From Elvis With Love" RCA Record Club (R234340). The second instrumental bridge is faded out earlier on this version, making the overall length shorter. Also, there is no overlapping of "I Was Born About Ten Thousand Years Ago," as there is on "Elvis Country."
- *ALTERNATE TAKE:* "Behind Closed Doors," a bootleg album, has an alternate take that runs over four minutes in length.

FAIRYTALE

- *ORIGINAL VERSION:* "Today" RCA (APL1-1039).
- *CONCERT VERSION:* "Elvis In Concert" RCA (APL2-2587).

FAME AND FORTUNE

- *ORIGINAL VERSION:* Any RCA release prior to December, 1978.
- *ALTERNATE TAKE:* "A Legendary Performer Vol. 3" RCA (CPL1-3078/3082).
- *TV AUDIO TRACK:* "TV Guide Presents Elvis" and "Eternal Elvis," bootleg albums. From the 1960 Sinatra show.

FEVER

- *ORIGINAL VERSION:* On any RCA release that is not a live concert recording.
- *CONCERT VERSION:* "Aloha From Hawaii Via Satellite" RCA (VPSX-6089).
- *CONCERT VERSION:* "Leavin' It Up To You," a bootleg album. From the "Aloha" rehersal show.

ELVIS PRESLEY

FIND OUT WHAT'S HAPPENING

- *ORIGINAL VERSION:* "Raised On Rock/For Ol' Times Sake" RCA (APL1-0388).
- *ALTERNATE MIX:* "Our Memories Of Elvis Vol. 2" RCA (AQL1-3448). The so-called "pure Elvis" sound; lacks overdubbing.

FIRST TIME EVER I SAW YOUR FACE, THE

- *ORIGINAL VERSION:* All RCA releases.
- *ALTERNATE TAKE:* "Behind Closed Doors," a bootleg album. This take has a female voice, who could be Kathy Westmoreland, overdubbed with Elvis to form a duet.

FLAMING STAR

- *ORIGINAL VERSION:* All RCA releases in the United States.
- *ALTERNATE MIX:* "Flaming Star And Summer Kisses," an album released in England (RCA RD-7723), has a shorter version of this tune. Some of the beginning notes are missing, and the song is simply "faded in" just prior to the vocal.

FLIP, FLOP AND FLY: *See SHAKE, RATTLE AND ROLL/ FLIP, FLOP AND FLY*

FOR THE HEART

- *ORIGINAL VERSION:* All RCA releases prior to 1979.
- *ALTERNATE MIX:* "Our Memories Of Elvis Vol. 2" RCA (AQL1-3448). No overdubbing is heard on this release; the "pure Elvis" sound.

FORGET ME NEVER

- *ORIGINAL VERSION:* All RCA releases.
- *ALTERNATE TAKE:* "Behind Closed Doors," a bootleg album.
- *FALSE START:* "Behind Closed Doors," a bootleg album.

FRANKFORT SPECIAL

- *ORIGINAL VERSION:* "G.I. Blues" RCA (LPM/LSP-2256).
- *ALTERNATE TAKE:* "A Legendary Performer Vol. 3" RCA (CPL1-3078/3082).

FUNNY HOW TIME SLIPS AWAY

- *ORIGINAL VERSION:* "Elvis Country" RCA (LSP-4460).
- *CONCERT VERSION:* "Elvis As Recorded At Madison Square Garden" RCA (LSP-4776).
- *ALTERNATE TAKE:* "Behind Closed Doors," a bootleg album.
- *ALTERNATE MIX:* "Country Memories" RCA Record Club (R244069). There is no overlapping of "I Was Born About Ten Thousand Years Ago" on this version. It is sloppily faded in at the beginning and faded out before the true ending.

GENTLE ON MY MIND

- *ORIGINAL VERSION:* All RCA releases.
- *ALTERNATE TAKE:* Appears on a various artists LP, whose title we cannot set in type, from the U.S.S.R., an unauthorized album. This same version is also on "Behind Closed Doors," a bootleg album.

GIRL OF MINE

- *ORIGINAL VERSION:* "Raised On Rock/For Ol' Times Sake" RCA (APL1-0388).
- *ALTERNATE MIX:* "Our Memories Of Elvis Vol. 1" RCA (AQL1-3279). No overdubbing is heard on this release; the "pure Elvis" sound.

GOOD ROCKIN' TONIGHT

- *ORIGINAL VERSION:* Sun single (210), RCA single (20/47-6381) and the extended play "A Touch Of Gold, Vol. 1" RCA EPA-5088).
- *ALTERNATE MIX:* All RCA album releases.
- *CONCERT VERSION:* "The First Years," an unauthorized album, "The Entertainer" and "Rockin Rebel Vol. 2," both bootleg albums. This version is from the 1955 Houston, Texas appearance.

GOT A LOT O' LIVIN' TO DO

- *ORIGINAL VERSION:* All RCA releases.
- *FILM VERSION (1):* "Got A Lot O' Livin' To Do" and "Loving You," bootleg albums.
- *FILM VERSION (2):* "Got A Lot O' Livin' To Do" and "Loving You," bootleg albums.

GREEN GREEN GRASS OF HOME

- *ORIGINAL VERSION:* "Today" RCA (APL1-1039).
- *ALTERNATE MIX:* "Our Memories Of Elvis Vol. 2" RCA (AQL1-3448). No overdubbing is heard on this release; the "pure Elvis" sound.

GUITAR MAN

- *ORIGINAL VERSION:* Any RCA release other than on the LP "Elvis (NBC-TV Special)."
- *ALTERNATE TAKE:* "Elvis (NBC-TV Special)" RCA (LPM-4088). Three segments of this song are heard on this LP.
- *ALTERNATE TAKE (1):* "The Burbank Sessions Vol. 2," a bootleg album.
- *ALTERNATE TAKE (2):* "The Burbank Sessions Vol. 2," a bootleg album.

NOTE: The two takes of this song on the bootleg album are only of the reprise version, similar to, but not the same take as is heard prior to "If I Can Dream" on the RCA TV Special LP. The complete song, heard on side one of the TV Special LP, is not included on any bootleg releases.

GUADALAJARA

- *ORIGINAL VERSION:* All RCA releases prior to December, 1978.
- *ALTERNATE TAKE:* "A Legendary Performer Vol. 3" RCA (CPL1-3078/3082).

HAWAIIAN SUNSET

- *ORIGINAL VERSION:* All RCA releases.
- *ALTERNATE TAKE:* "Plantation Rock," a bootleg album.

HAWAIIAN WEDDING SONG

- *ORIGINAL VERSION:* "Blue Hawaii" RCA (LPM/LSP-2426).
- *CONCERT VERSION:* "Elvis In Concert" RCA (APL2-2587).
- *ALTERNATE TAKE:* "Behind Closed Doors," a bootleg album.

HEART OF ROME

- *ORIGINAL VERSION:* "Love Letters From Elvis" RCA (LSP-4530).
- *ALTERNATE MIX:* RCA 45rpm single 47-9998. The single has added overdubbing not heard on the LP.

HEARTBREAK HOTEL

- *ORIGINAL VERSION:* Any RCA release that is not taken from a live concert.
- *CONCERT VERSION:* "Elvis (NBC-TV Special)" RCA (LPM-4088). Performed as part of a medley.
- *CONCERT VERSION:* "Elvis As Recorded At Madison Square Garden" RCA (LSP-4776).
- *CONCERT VERSION:* "Hawaii Benefit Show," a bootleg album. From a 1961 live appearance.
- *CONCERT VERSION:* "The Burbank Sessions Vol. 1," a bootleg album.
- *CONCERT VERSION (1):* "The Burbank Sessions Vol. 2," a bootleg album.
- *CONCERT VERSION (2):* "The Burbank Sessions Vol. 2," a bootleg album. Performed as part of a medley. It is this track that appears on the RCA LP "Elvis (NBC-TV Special)."
- *CONCERT VERSION (3):* "The Burbank Sessions Vol. 2," a bootleg album. Performed as part of a medley.
- *TV AUDIO TRACK (1):* "The Dorsey Shows" and "Superstar Out-takes Vol. 2," bootleg albums. From Elvis' January 28, 1956 appearance.
- *TV AUDIO TRACK (2):* "The Dorsey Shows" and "Superstar Out-takes Vol. 2," bootleg albums. From Elvis' March 17, 1956 appearance.
- *TV AUDIO TRACK (3):* "The Dorsey Shows" and "Superstar Out-takes Vol. 2," bootleg albums. From Elvis' March 24, 1956 appearance.
- *TV AUDIO TRACK:* "The King Goes Wild" and "From The Waist Up," bootleg albums.

HEY JUDE

- *ORIGINAL VERSION:* All RCA releases.
- *CONCERT VERSION:* "The Legend Lives On" and "Superstar Out-takes Vol. 1," bootleg albums. Coupled with "Yesterday" as a two song medley.

HOME IS WHERE THE HEART IS

- *ORIGINAL VERSION:* All RCA releases.
- *ALTERNATE TAKE:* "Behind Closed Doors," a bootleg album.
- *ALTERNATE TAKE:* "A Dog's Life," a bootleg album.

HOT DOG

- *ORIGINAL VERSION:* All RCA releases.
- *FILM VERSION:* "Loving You," a bootleg album.

HOUND DOG

- *ORIGINAL VERSION:* Any RCA release that is not taken from a live concert.
- *CONCERT VERSION:* "Elvis (NBC-TV Special)" RCA (LPM-4088).
- *CONCERT VERSION:* "From Memphis To Vegas/From Vegas To Memphis" RCA (LSP-6020) and "Elvis In Person At The International Hotel, Las Vegas, Nevada" RCA (LSP-4428).
- *CONCERT VERSION:* "Elvis As Recorded At Madison Square Garden" RCA (LSP-4776).
- *CONCERT VERSION:* "Aloha From Hawaii Via Satellite" RCA (VPSX-6089).
- *CONCERT VERSION:* "Elvis Recorded Live On Stage In Memphis" RCA (CPL1-0606).
- *CONCERT VERSION:* "Elvis In Concert" RCA (APL2-2587).
- *CONCERT VERSION (1):* "The Burbank Sessions, Vol. 2," a bootleg album. It is this version (side one) that is heard on the RCA LP "Elvis (NBC-TV Special)." On this album, the TV Special album and the Memphis album, this song is part of a medley.
- *CONCERT VERSION (2):* "The Burbank Sessions Vol. 2," a bootleg album.
- *CONCERT VERSION:* "Hawaii Benefit Show," a bootleg album. From a 1961 appearance.
- *TV AUDIO TRACK (1):* "The King Goes Wild," "From The Waist Up," "Rockin' Rebel Vol. 3" and "The Hillbilly Cat 1954-1974," all bootleg albums. From Elvis' September 9, 1956 appearance on the Ed Sullivan show.
- *TV AUDIO TRACK (2):* "The King Goes Wild," "From The Waist Up" and "The Hillbilly Cat 1954-1974," bootleg albums. From Elvis' October 28, 1956 appearance on the Ed Sullivan show.
- *TV AUDIO TRACK (3):* "The King Goes Wild" and "From The Waist Up," bootleg albums. From Elvis' January 6, 1957 appearance on the Ed Sullivan show.
- *TV AUDIO TRACK:* "TV Guide Presents Elvis," Rockin' Rebel Vol. 3" and "Superstar Out-takes Vol. 1," bootleg albums. From Elvis' July 1, 1956 appearance on the Steve Allen show.
- *TV AUDIO TRACK:* "Rockin' Rebel Vol. 2," a bootleg album. From Elvis' June 5, 1956 appearance on the Milton Berle show.

HOW GREAT THOU ART

- *ORIGINAL VERSION:* Any RCA release that is not taken from a live concert.
- *CONCERT VERSION:* "Elvis Recorded Live On Stage In Memphis" RCA (CPL1-0606).
- *CONCERT VERSION:* "Elvis In Concert" RCA (APL2-2587).

HOW THE WEB WAS WOVEN

- *ORIGINAL VERSION:* All RCA releases.
- *FILM VERSION:* "From The Dark To The Light," a bootleg album. Only a portion of this song was used in the film, "That's The Way It Is," and it is included here.

HURT

- *ORIGINAL VERSION:* Any RCA release that is not taken from a live concert.
- *CONCERT VERSION:* "Elvis In Concert" RCA (APL2-2587).

I CAN HELP

- *ORIGINAL VERSION:* "Today" RCA (APL1-1039).
- *ALTERNATE MIX:* "Our Memories Of Elvis Vol. 2" RCA (AQL1-3448). No overdubbing used; the "pure Elvis" sound.

I CAN'T STOP LOVING YOU

- *ORIGINAL VERSION:* "From Memphis To Vegas/From Vegas To Memphis" RCA (LSP-6020) and "Elvis In Person At The International Hotel, Las Vegas, Nevada." RCA (LSP-4428).
- *CONCERT VERSION:* "Elvis As Recorded At Madison Square Garden" RCA (LSP-4776).
- *CONCERT VERSION:* "Aloha From Hawaii Via Satellite" RCA (VPSX-6089).
- *CONCERT VERSION:* "Elvis Recorded Live On Stage In Memphis" RCA (CPL1-0606).
- *CONCERT VERSION:* "Welcome To My World" RCA (APL1-2274).

I DON'T CARE IF THE SUN DON'T SHINE

- *ORIGINAL VERSION:* Sun single (210), RCA single (20/47-6381) and RCA extended play "Anyway You Want Me" (EPA-965).
- *ALTERNATE MIX:* "The Sun Sessions" RCA (AMP1-1675).
- *ALTERNATE TAKE:* "Good Rockin' Tonight" and "Rockin' Rebel Vol. 1," bootleg albums. Both contain the last half of an alternate take.
- *FALSE START:* "Good Rockin' Tonight" and "Rockin' Rebel Vol. 1," bootleg albums.

I FORGOT TO REMEMBER TO FORGET

- *ORIGINAL VERSION:* Sun (223) and RCA (20/47-6357) singles and "Heartbreak Hotel" EP (EPA-821).
- *ALTERNATE MIX:* Any RCA long play (LP) release. The reverberation is greater on the LP versions.

I GOT A FEELIN' IN MY BODY

- *ORIGINAL VERSION:* "Good Times" RCA (CPL1-0475).
- *ALTERNATE MIX:* "Our Memories Of Elvis, Vol. 2" RCA (AQL1-3448) and RCA 45rpm single (PB-11679). No overdubbing; the "pure Elvis" sound.

I GOT A WOMAN

- *ORIGINAL VERSION:* Any RCA release that is not taken from a live concert.
- *CONCERT VERSION:* "Elvis Recorded Live On Stage In Memphis" RCA (CPL1-0606). Contains the "Amen" tag.
- *CONCERT VERSION:* "Elvis In Concert" RCA (APL2-2587). Contains the "Amen" tag.
- *CONCERT VERSION:* "Hawaii Benefit Show," a bootleg album. From a 1961 appearance.
- *CONCERT VERSION:* "The Entertainer" and "Behind Closed Doors," bootleg albums. From an August, 1969 Las Vegas show.
- *FILM VERSION:* "From The Dark To The Light" and "Rock My Soul," bootleg albums. With the "Amen" tag. From "Elvis On Tour."
- *TV AUDIO TRACK:* "The Dorsey Shows" and "Superstar Out-takes Vol. 2," bootleg albums. From Elvis' February 11, 1956 appearance on the Dorsey Brothers show.
- *CONCERT VERSION:* "The First Years," an unauthorized album, "The Entertainer," "Rockin' Rebel Vol. 2" and "Elvis Presley On The Louisiana Hayride (EP), all bootlegs. From Elvis' 1955 Houston appearance.

I GOT LUCKY

- *ORIGINAL VERSION:* All RCA releases.
- *ALTERNATE TAKE:* "Behind Closed Doors," a bootleg album.

I, JOHN

- *ORIGINAL VERSION:* Any RCA release.
- *FILM VERSION:* "From The Dark To The Light," a bootleg album.

I JUST CAN'T HELP BELIEVIN'

- *ORIGINAL VERSION:* Any RCA release.
- *FILM VERSION:* "From The Dark To The Light," a bootleg album. From the film "That's The Way It Is."

I LOVE YOU BECAUSE

- *ORIGINAL VERSION:* All RCA releases prior to January, 1974. "The Sun Sessions" RCA (AMP1-1675) contains both this version and the alternate take.
- *ALTERNATE TAKE:* "A Legendary Performer Vol. 1" RCA (CPL1-0341) and "The Sun Sessions" RCA (AMP1-1675).

I NEED SOMEBODY TO LEAN ON

- *ORIGINAL VERSION:* All RCA releases.
- *FILM VERSION:* "Viva Las Vegas," a bootleg album.

I NEED YOUR LOVE TONIGHT

- *ORIGINAL VERSION:* All RCA releases.
- *CONCERT VERSION:* "Hawaii Benefit Show," a bootleg album. From a 1961 concert.

I REALLY DON'T WANT TO KNOW

- *ORIGINAL VERSION:* RCA 45rpm single 47-9960.
- *ALTERNATE MIX:* "Elvis Country" RCA (LSP-4460). Although it's less offensive on this track than some of the others on this LP, there is still some slight overlapping of "I Was Born About Ten Thousand Years Ago."

I SLIPPED, I STUMBLED, I FELL

- *ORIGINAL VERSION:* All RCA releases.
- *ALTERNATE TAKE:* "Behind Closed Doors," a bootleg album.
- *ALTERNATE TAKE:* "Leavin' It Up To You," a bootleg album.
- *FALSE STARTS:* "Behind Closed Doors," a bootleg album, contains two false starts of this song.

I WANT TO BE FREE

- *ORIGINAL VERSION:* "Jailhouse Rock" RCA EP (EPA-4114) and "Worldwide Gold Award Hits, Vol. 2" RCA (LPM-6402).
- *ALTERNATE MIX:* "A Date With Elvis" RCA (LPM-2011).
- *FILM VERSION:* "Got A Lot O' Livin' To Do" and "Loving You," bootleg albums.

I WANT YOU, I NEED YOU, I LOVE YOU

- *ORIGINAL VERSION:* Any RCA release prior to January, 1976.
- *ALTERNATE TAKE:* "A Legendary Performer Vol. 2" RCA (CPL1-1349).
- *TV AUDIO TRACK:* "TV Guide Presents Elvis Presley" and "Rockin' Rebel Vol. 3," bootleg albums. From Elvis' July 1, 1956 appearance on the Steve Allen show.
- *TV AUDIO TRACK:* "Rockin' Rebel Vol. 2" and "Superstar Out-takes Vol. 1," bootleg albums. From Elvis' June 5, 1956 appearance on the Milton Berle show.

I WAS BORN ABOUT TEN THOUSAND YEARS AGO

- *ORIGINAL VERSION:* "Elvis Country" RCA (LSP-4460). Even in its disected state, this was still the first release of this song.
- *ALTERNATE TAKE:* "Elvis Now" RCA (LSP-4671).

I WAS THE ONE

- *ORIGINAL VERSION:* All RCA releases.
- *TV AUDIO TRACK:* "The Dorsey Shows" and "Superstar Out-takes Vol. 2," bootleg albums. From Elvis' February 4, 1956 appearance on the Dorsey show.
- *CONCERT VERSION:* "Rockin' Rebel Vol. 3," a bootleg album. From a 1956 concert appearance.

I WASHED MY HANDS IN MUDDY WATER

- *ORIGINAL VERSION:* "Elvis Country" RCA (LSP-4460).
- *ALTERNATE MIX:* "Country Memories" RCA (R244069), RCA record club issue. This version does not have the overlapping "I Was Born About Ten Thousand Years Ago."
- *ALTERNATE TAKE:* "Behind Closed Doors," a bootleg album.

IF I CAN DREAM

- *ORIGINAL VERSION:* Any RCA release prior to April, 1978.
- *ALTERNATE TAKE:* "He Walks Beside Me" RCA (AFL1-2772).
- *TV AUDIO TRACK:* "Eternal Elvis," a bootleg album.
- *CONCERT VERSION (1):* "The Burbank Sessions Vol. 2," a bootleg album.
- *CONCERT VERSION (2):* "The Burbank Sessions Vol. 2," a bootleg album. It is this version (side four) that is heard on the "Elvis (NBC-TV Special)" LP.

IF I WERE YOU

- *ORIGINAL VERSION:* All RCA releases.
- *ALTERNATE TAKE:* "A Dog's Life," a bootleg album.

IF YOU LOVE ME (LET ME KNOW)

- *ORIGINAL VERSION:* "Moody Blue" RCA (AFL1-2428).
- *CONCERT VERSION:* "Elvis In Person" RCA (APL2-2587).

IF YOU THINK I DON'T NEED YOU

- *ORIGINAL VERSION:* All RCA releases.
- *FILM VERSION:* "Viva Las Vegas," a bootleg album.
- *FALSE STARTS:* "Viva Las Vegas," a bootleg album. Contains three lengthy false starts.

I'LL NEVER FALL IN LOVE AGAIN

- *ORIGINAL VERSION:* "From Elvis Presley Boulevard, Memphis, Tennessee" RCA (APL1-1506).
- *ALTERNATE MIX:* "Our Memories Of Elvis" RCA (AQL1-3279). No overdubbing; the "pure Elvis" sound.

I'LL NEVER LET YOU GO (LITTLE DARLIN')

- *ORIGINAL VERSION:* All RCA releases.
- *ALTERNATE TAKE:* "Good Rockin' Tonight" and "Rockin' Rebel Vol. 1," bootleg albums. The first half of the song is missing on these releases.

I'LL REMEMBER YOU

- *ORIGINAL VERSION:* Any RCA release that is not taken from a live concert.
- *CONCERT VERSION:* "Aloha From Hawaii Via Satellite" RCA (VPSX-6089).
- *CONCERT VERSION:* "Plantation Rock," a bootleg album. From the "Aloha" rehersal show.

I'M LEFT, YOU'RE RIGHT, SHE'S GONE

- *ORIGINAL VERSION:* Sun (217) and RCA (20/47-6383) singles and the RCA extended play "Anyway You Want Me" (EPA-965).
- *ALTERNATE MIX:* Any RCA long play (LP) version of this song. Stronger reverberation is used on the LP versions.
- *ALTERNATE TAKE:* The bootleg albums "Good Rockin' Tonight," "I Wanna Be A Rock 'n' Roll Star" and "Rockin' Rebel Vol. 1" contain a song that is such an alternate take of "I'm Left, You're Right, She's Gone" that it even has a different title. While the backing and instrumentation is much different, the lyrics are pretty close to the familiar version. Its title is "My Baby's Gone," and it has never been released in an authorized form.

I'M SO LONESOME I COULD CRY

- *ORIGINAL VERSION:* All RCA releases.
- *CONCERT VERSION:* "Plantation Rock," a bootleg album. From the "Aloha" rehersal show.

I'M YOURS

- *ORIGINAL VERSION:* "Pot Luck" RCA (LPM/LSP-2523).
- *ALTERNATE MIX:* RCA 45rpm single 47-8657. Elvis' narration over the instrumental bridge is missing from the single.

IMPOSSIBLE DREAM, THE   (The Quest)

- *ORIGINAL VERSION:* "Elvis As Recorded At Madison Square Garden" RCA (LSP-4776).
- *CONCERT VERSION:* "He Walks Beside Me" RCA (AFL1-2772).
- *CONCERT VERSION:* "The Legend Lives On" and "Superstar Out-takes Vol. 2," bootleg albums. From Elvis' February, 1972 Las Vegas appearance.

IN MY WAY

- *ORIGINAL VERSION:* All RCA releases.
- *ALTERNATE TAKE:* "Behind Closed Doors," a bootleg album.

IN THE GHETTO

- *ORIGINAL VERSION:* Any RCA release that is not taken from a live concert.
- *CONCERT VERSION:* "From Memphis To Vegas/From Vegas To Memphis" RCA (LSP-6020) and "Elvis In Person At The International Hotel, Las Vegas, Nevada" RCA (LSP-4428).
- *CONCERT VERSION:* "The Legend Lives On" and "Superstar Out-takes Vol. 1," bootleg albums. From Elvis' August, 1969 Las Vegas appearance.

IS IT SO STRANGE

- *ORIGINAL VERSION:* "Just For You" RCA EP (EPA-4041).
- *ALTERNATE MIX:* Any RCA long play (LP) version. Stronger reverberation is used on the LP versions.

ISLAND OF LOVE (KAUAI)

- *ORIGINAL VERSION:* All RCA releases.
- *ALTERNATE TAKE:* "Behind Closed Doors," a bootleg album.
- *FALSE START:* "Behind Closed Doors," a bootleg album.

IT HURTS ME

- *ORIGINAL VERSION:* All RCA releases in the United States, prior to December, 1978.
- *ALTERNATE MIX:* One of the two stereo channels is missing, and so, as a result, are the Jordanaires (vocal backing) and the orchestration. What's left, on this release, is Elvis' vocal and Floyd Cramer's (piano) accompaniment. This version appeared on an RCA 45rpm single released in Italy (N-1410) and on the bootleg album "Eternal Elvis."
- *ALTERNATE TAKE:* "A Legendary Performer Vol. 3" RCA (CPL1-3078/3082). A portion (omitting the unusual instrumental bridge) of the song, as recorded for possible use in the '68 TV special. Ultimately not included in the special.
- *ALTERNATE TAKE:* "The '68 Comeback" and "Superstar Out-takes Vol. 1," bootleg albums. The complete song, including the instrumental bridge.

IT'S IMPOSSIBLE

- *ORIGINAL VERSION:* All RCA releases.
- *CONCERT VERSION:* "The Legend Lives On" and "Superstar Out-takes Vol. 2," bootleg albums. From Elvis' February, 1972 Las Vegas appearance.

IT'S MIDNIGHT

- *ORIGINAL VERSION:* RCA 45rpm single (PB-10074) and "Promised Land" LP (APL1-0873).
- *ALTERNATE MIX:* "Our Memories Of Elvis Vol. 1" RCA (AQL1-3279). No overdubbing; the "pure Elvis" sound.

IT'S NOW OR NEVER

- *ORIGINAL VERSION:* Any RCA release that is not from a live concert.
- *CONCERT VERSION:* "Elvis In Concert" RCA (APL2-2587).
- *CONCERT VERSION:* "Hawaii Benefit Show," a bootleg album. From Elvis' 1961 concert.

IT'S OVER

- *ORIGINAL VERSION:* All RCA releases.
- *CONCERT VERSION:* "A Dog's Life," a bootleg album. From the "Aloha" rehersal show.
- *CONCERT VERSION:* "The Legend Lives On" and "Superstar Out-takes Vol. 2," bootleg albums. From Elvis' February, 1972, Las Vegas appearance.

IT'S YOUR BABY, YOU ROCK IT

- *ORIGINAL VERSION:* "Elvis Country" RCA (LSP-4460).
- *ALTERNATE TAKE:* "The Entertainer" and "Behind Closed Doors," bootleg albums. Both have edited versions of this take. The complete version exists on an acetate from RCA in Nashville.

I'VE LOST YOU

- *ORIGINAL VERSION:* Any RCA release that is not from a live concert.
- *CONCERT VERSION:* "That's The Way It Is" RCA (LSP-4445).

JAILHOUSE ROCK

- *ORIGINAL VERSION:* Any RCA release that is not taken from a live concert.
- *CONCERT VERSION:* "Elvis (NBC-TV Special)" RCA (LPM-4088).
- *CONCERT VERSION:* "Elvis Recorded Live On Stage In Memphis" RCA (CPL1-0606). Part of a medley.
- *CONCERT VERSION:* "Elvis In Concert" RCA (APL2-2587).
- *CONCERT VERSION (1):* "The Burbank Sessions Vol. 2," a bootleg album.
- *CONCERT VERSION (2):* "The Burbank Sessions Vol. 2," a bootleg album. It is this version (side three) that appears on RCA's "Elvis (NBC-TV Special)" LP.
- *FILM VERSION:* "Got A Lot O' Livin' To Do," a bootleg album.

JOHNNY B. GOODE

- *ORIGINAL VERSION:* "From Memphis To Vegas/From Vegas To Memphis" RCA (LSP-6020) and "Elvis In Person At The International Hotel, LasVegas, Nevada" RCA (LSP-4428).
- *CONCERT VERSION:* "Aloha From Hawaii Via Satellite" RCA (VPSX-6089).
- *CONCERT VERSION:* "Elvis In Concert" RCA (APL2-2587).

KENTUCKY RAIN

- *ORIGINAL VERSION:* All RCA releases.
- *CONCERT VERSION:* "Behind Closed Doors" and "The Entertainer," bootleg albums. From a February, 1970 Las Vegas rehersal session.

KING CREOLE

- *ORIGINAL VERSION:* All RCA releases.
- *ALTERNATE TAKE (1):* "From The Beach To The Bayou," a bootleg album.
- *ALTERNATE TAKE (2):* "From The Beach To The Bayou" and "Rockin' Rebel Vol. 1," bootleg albums.

KING OF THE WHOLE WIDE WORLD

- *ORIGINAL VERSION:* All RCA releases.
- *ALTERNATE TAKE:* "Behind Closed Doors," a bootleg album.
- *ALTERNATE TAKE:* "Leavin' It Up To You," a bootleg album.

KISS ME QUICK

- *ORIGINAL VERSION:* All RCA releases in the United States.
- *ALTERNATE MIX:* "Elvis Presley Canta" RCA EP (3-20820). This Spanish EP has one of the two stereo channels missing, and, as a result, the vocal backing and part of the orchestration.

KU-U-I-PO

- *ORIGINAL VERSION:* All RCA releases.
- *ALTERNATE TAKE:* "Mahalo From Elvis" Pickwick (ACL-7064).
- *ALTERNATE TAKE:* "Plantation Rock, " a bootleg album.

LAWDY, MISS CLAWDY

- *ORIGINAL VERSION:* Any RCA release that is not taken from a live concert.
- *CONCERT VERSION:* "Elvis (NBC-TV Special)" RCA (LPM-4088).
- *CONCERT VERSION:* "Elvis Recorded Live On Stage In Memphis" RCA (CPL1-0606).
- *CONCERT VERSION (1):* "The Burbank Sessions Vol. 1," a bootleg album.
- *CONCERT VERSION (2):* "The Burbank Sessions Vol. 1," a bootleg album. This version is used on RCA's TV special LP.

LEAD ME, GUIDE ME

- *ORIGINAL VERSION:* All RCA releases.
- *FILM VERSION:* "From The Dark To The Light" and "Rock My Soul," bootleg albums. From the film "Elvis On Tour."

LET IT BE ME (JE T'APPARTIENS)

- *ORIGINAL VERSION:* "On Stage - February, 1970" RCA (LSP-4362).
- *CONCERT VERSION:* "A Legendary Performer,Vol. 3" RCA (CPL1-3078/3082).

LET YOURSELF GO

- *ORIGINAL VERSION:* Any RCA release prior to December, 1978.
- *ALTERNATE TAKE:* "A Legendary Performer Vol. 3" RCA (CPL1-3078/3082).
- *ALTERNATE TAKE:* "The '68 Comeback" and "Superstar Out-takes Vol. 1," bootleg albums. Contains the song as used in actual filming of the bordello scene, including the female voice intro.

LIFE

- *ORIGINAL VERSION:* RCA 45rpm single (47-9985).
- *ALTERNATE MIX:* "Love Letters From Elvis" RCA (LSP-4530). This version allows a bit of Elvis' singing at the end that does not appear on the single.

LITTLE EGYPT

- *ORIGINAL VERSION:* "Roustabout" RCA (LPM/LSP-2999).
- *ALTERNATE TAKE:* "Elvis (NBC-TV Special)" RCA (LPM-4088). A portion of the song is used in a medley on this LP.

LITTLE SISTER

- *ORIGINAL VERSION:* Any RCA release that is not taken from a live concert.
- *CONCERT VERSION:* "Elvis In Concert" RCA (APL2-2587).
- *FILM VERSION:* "From The Dark To The Light," a bootleg album. Contains a brief version of the song, as performed in "That's The Way It Is."

LONELY MAN

- *ORIGINAL VERSION:* All RCA releases.
- *ALTERNATE TAKE:* "Behind Closed Doors," a bootleg album.

LONESOME COWBOY

- *ORIGINAL VERSION:* All RCA releases.
- *FILM VERSION:* "Loving You," a bootleg album.

LONG LEGGED GIRL

- *ORIGINAL VERSION:* RCA 45rpm single 47-9115. This mix was later issued on the LP "Almost In Love" RCA/Camden (CAS-2440).
- *ALTERNATE MIX:* "Double Trouble" RCA (LPM/LSP-3787). This version later issued on the RCA/Camden LP "Elvis sings hits from his movies, Vol. 1." Listen to the slight difference in instrumentation and the sharpness of the electric guitar, and you'll hear the difference in the two versions.

(IT'S A) LONG LONELY HIGHWAY

- *ORIGINAL VERSION:* "Kissin' Cousins" RCA (LPM/LSP-2894).
- *ALTERNATE TAKE:* " RCA 45rpm single release (47-8657).

LONG TALL SALLY

- *ORIGINAL VERSION:* Any RCA release that is not taken from a live concert.
- *CONCERT VERSION:* "Aloha From Hawaii Via Satellite" RCA (VPSX-6089).
- *CONCERT VERSION:* "Elvis Recorded Live On Stage In Memphis" RCA (CPL1-0606). Included as part of a rock & roll song medley.

LOVE ME

- *ORIGINAL VERSION:* Any RCA release that is not taken from a live concert.
- *CONCERT VERSION:* "Elvis As Recorded At Madison Square Garden" RCA (LSP-4776).
- *CONCERT VERSION:* "Aloha From Hawaii Via Satellite" RCA (VPSX-6089).
- *CONCERT VERSION:* "Elvis Recorded Live On Stage In Memphis" RCA (CPL1-0606).
- *CONCERT VERSION:* "Elvis In Concert" RCA (APL2-2587).
- *CONCERT VERSION:* "Hawaii Benefit Show," a bootleg album. From a 1961 appearance.
- *CONCERT VERSION (1):* "The Burbank Sessions Vol. 1," a bootleg album.
- *CONCERT VERSION (2):* "The Burbank Sessions Vol. 1," a bootleg album.
- *TV AUDIO TRACK:* "The King Goes Wild," "From The Waist Up" and "The Hillbilly Cat 1954-1974," bootleg albums. From Elvis' October 28, 1956 appearance on the Ed Sullivan show.

LOVE ME TENDER

- *ORIGINAL VERSION:* Any RCA release that is not taken from a live concert.
- *CONCERT VERSION:* "Elvis (NBC-TV Special)" RCA (LPM-4088).
- *CONCERT VERSION:* "Elvis As Recorded At Madison Square Garden" RCA (LSP-4776).
- *CONCERT VERSION (1):* "The Burbank Sessions Vol. 2," a bootleg album.
- *CONCERT VERSION (2):* "The Burbank Sessions Vol. 2," a bootleg album. This is the version (side four) that appears on the RCA album "Elvis (NBC-TV Special)."
- *CONCERT VERSION:* "Rockin' Rebel Vol. 2," a bootleg album. From a 1956 concert.
- *TV AUDIO TRACK (1):* "The King Goes Wild," "From The Waist Up" and "The Hillbilly Cat 1954-1974," bootleg albums. From Elvis' September 9, 1956 appearance on the Ed Sullivan show.
- *TV AUDIO TRACK (2):* "The King Goes Wild," "From The Waist Up" and "The Hillbilly Cat 1954-1974," bootleg albums. From Elvis' October 28, 1956 appearance on the Ed Sullivan show.
- *TV AUDIO TRACK (3):* "The King Goes Wild" and "From The Waist Up," bootleg albums. From Elvis' January 6, 1957 appearance on the Ed Sullivan show.

NOTE: Since we have no category for "Concocted Versions," we'll simply make note that several bootleg releases contained the version of this song that featured the voices of Elvis and Linda Ronstadt. This recording, and other manufactured phony duets, are not real releases, and therefore will not be listed in this book.

LOVER DOLL

- *ORIGINAL VERSION:* "King Creole" RCA (LPM-1884).
- *ALTERNATE TAKE:* "King Creole" extended play, RCA (EPA-4319) and "Worldwide Gold Award Hits, Vol. 2" RCA (LPM-6402).
- *ALTERNATE TAKE:* "From The Beach To The Bayou," a bootleg album.

LOVING YOU

- *ORIGINAL VERSION:* All RCA releases.
- *ALTERNATE TAKE (1):* "Rockin' Rebel Vol. 3," a bootleg album. Uptempo version.
- *ALTERNATE TAKE (2):* "Rockin' Rebel Vol. 3," a bootleg album. Ballad version.
- *ALTERNATE TAKE (3):* "Rockin' Rebel Vol. 3," a bootleg album. Uptempo version.
- *FALSE STARTS:* "Rockin' Rebel Vol. 3," a bootleg album. Contains three false starts of the ballad version.
- *FILM VERSION:* "Loving You," a bootleg album. Also on this album is the verse, sung by Elvis in the uptempo style, that is heard over the film's opening credits.

MAKE THE WORLD GO AWAY

- *ORIGINAL VERSION:* "Elvis Country" RCA (LSP-4460).
- *ALTERNATE MIX:* "Country Memories" RCA Record Club issue (R244069). Faded in late and faded out early to avoid any overlapping from "I Was Born About Ten Thousand Years Ago."
- *ALTERNATE MIX:* "Welcome To My World" RCA (APL1-2274). Even though the jacket states that this is a "live" track, it is not! This is a studio track, and, we might add, the only one of these three versions that lets you hear the complete song; no overlapping or annoying fades.

MARY IN THE MORNING

- *ORIGINAL VERSION:* All RCA releases.
- *ALTERNATE MIX:* "Leavin' It Up To You," a bootleg album. No overdubbing; the "pure Elvis" sound.

MEMORIES

- *ORIGINAL VERSION:* All RCA releases.
- *CONCERT VERSION (1):* "The Burbank Sessions Vol. 1," a bootleg album.
- *CONCERT VERSION (2):* "The Burbank Sessions Vol. 1," a bootleg album.

NOTE: Neither of the concert versions of this song, as heard on this album, were used by RCA for their release. Each of these two versions has a change in lyrics when compared to RCA's version.

MERRY CHRISTMAS BABY

- *ORIGINAL VERSION:* "Elvis Sings The Wonderful World Of Christmas" RCA (LSP-4579).
- *ALTERNATE MIX:* RCA 45rpm single 74-0572. The song runs for a minute and a half longer on the LP.

MILKCOW BLUES BOOGIE

- *ORIGINAL VERSION:* All Sun and RCA singles.
- *ALTERNATE MIX:* On any RCA album.

MONEY HONEY

- *ORIGINAL VERSION:* All RCA releases.
- *TV AUDIO TRACK:* "The Dorsey Shows" and "Superstar Out-takes Vol. 2," bootleg albums. From Elvis' March 24, 1956 appearance.

MOONLIGHT SWIM

- *ORIGINAL VERSION:* Any RCA release.
- *ALTERNATE TAKE:* "Behind Closed Doors," a bootleg album.
- *FALSE START:* "Behind Closed Doors," a bootleg album.

MY BABY'S GONE: *See I'M LEFT, YOU'RE RIGHT, SHE'S GONE*

MY BOY

- *ORIGINAL VERSION:* "Good Times" RCA (CPL1-0475) and 45rpm single, RCA (PB-10191).
- *ALTERNATE MIX:* "Our Memories Of Elvis, Vol. 1" RCA (AQL1-3279).

MY WAY

- *ORIGINAL VERSION:* "Aloha From Hawaii Via Satellite" RCA (VPSX-6089).
- *CONCERT VERSION:* "Elvis In Concert" RCA (APL2-2587) and 45rpm single, RCA (PB-11165).
- *CONCERT VERSION:* "A Dog's Life," a bootleg album. From the "Aloha" rehersal show.

MYSTERY TRAIN

- *ORIGINAL VERSION:* Sun (223) and RCA (20/47-6357) singles and the EP "Anyway You Want Me" RCA (EPA-965);
- *CONCERT VERSION:* "From Memphis To Vegas/From Vegas To Memphis" RCA (LSP-6020) and "Elvis In Person At The International Hotel, Las Vegas, Nevada" RCA (LSP-4428). Performed as part of a "Mystery Train"/"Tiger Man" medley.
- *ALTERNATE MIX:* Any RCA release on LP that is not taken from a live concert.

NEVER AGAIN

- *ORIGINAL VERSION:* "From Elvis Presley Boulevard, Memphis, Tennessee" RCA (APL1-1506).
- *ALTERNATE MIX:* "Our Memories Of Elvis, Vol. 1" RCA (AQL1-3279). No overdubbing; the "pure Elvis" sound.

NEVER BEEN TO SPAIN

- *ORIGINAL VERSION:* All RCA releases.
- *CONCERT VERSION:* "Superstar Out-takes Vol. 2," a bootleg album. From a 1972 Las Vegas appearance.

NEXT STEP IS LOVE, THE

- *ORIGINAL VERSION:* All RCA releases.
- *FILM VERSION:* "From The Dark To The Light," "Eternal Elvis," and "Special Delivery," bootleg albums. From the film "That's The Way It Is."

NO MORE

- *ORIGINAL VERSION:* All RCA releases.
- *ALTERNATE TAKE:* "Mahalo From Elvis" Pickwick (ACL-7064).
- *ALTERNATE TAKE:* "Plantation Rock," a bootleg album.

OLD SHEP

- *ORIGINAL VERSION:* All RCA releases.
- *ALTERNATE TAKE:* "Eternal Elvis" and "Rockin' Rebel Vol. 3," bootleg albums. The original source from which this version was taken, we believe, was the HMV album "Elvis Presley No. 2," from England. Reportedly, only a limited number of pressings contained this version of the song, as the original version qucikly replaced it on the LP.

ONE NIGHT

- *ORIGINAL VERSION:* Any RCA release that is not taken from a live concert.
- *CONCERT VERSION:* "Elvis (NBC-TV Special)" RCA (LPM-4088).
- *CONCERT VERSION (1):* "The Burbank Sessions Vol. 1," a bootleg album.
- *CONCERT VERSION (2):* "The Burbank Sessions Vol. 1," a bootleg album. This is the version (second time done on side two) that is heard on the RCA LP "Elvis (NBC-TV Special)."
- *CONCERT VERSION (3):* "The Burbank Sessions Vol. 1," a bootleg album.
- *CONCERT VERSION:* "The Burbank Sessions Vol. 2," a bootleg album.
- *CONCERT VERSION:* "Hawaii Benefit Show," a bootleg album.
- *FILM VERSION:* "From The Dark To The Light," a bootleg album. From the film "That's The Way It Is."

ONLY BELIEVE

- *ORIGINAL VERSION:* All RCA releases.
- *ALTERNATE TAKE:* "Plantation Rock," a bootleg album.

PARADISE HAWAIIAN STYLE

- *ORIGINAL VERSION:* All RCA releases.
- *ALTERNATE TAKE:* "A Dog's Life," a bootleg album. On this release the title is mistakenly given as "Hawaii U.S.A."

PARTY

- *ORIGINAL VERSION:* All RCA releases.
- *FILM VERSIONS:* "Loving You" and "Got A Lot O' Livin' To Do," bootleg albums. Elvis sang the song twice in the film and both are included on these albums.

PATCH IT UP

- *ORIGINAL VERSION:* RCA 45rpm single (47-9916) and "Worldwide Gold Award Hits, Vol. 2" RCA (LPM-6402).
- *CONCERT VERSION:* "That's The Way It Is" RCA (LSP-4445).
- *ALTERNATE TAKE:* "Leavin' It Up To You," a bootleg album.

(THERE'LL BE) PEACE IN THE VALLEY (FOR ME)

- *ORIGINAL VERSION:* All RCA releases.
- *TV AUDIO TRACK:* "The King Goes Wild" and "From The Waist Up," bootleg albums. From Elvis' January 6, 1957 appearance on the Ed Sullivan show.

POLK SALAD ANNIE

- *ORIGINAL VERSION:* "On Stage" RCA (LSP-4362).
- *CONCERT VERSION:* "Elvis As Recorded At Madison Square Garden" RCA (LSP-4776).
- *CONCERT VERSION:* "The Entertainer" and "Behind Closed Doors," bootleg albums. From a February, 1970 Las Vegas session.
- *FILM VERSIONS:* "From The Dark To The Light," a bootleg album. Elvis sang the song one and a half times in "That's The Way It Is," and it's all on this LP.

POOR BOY

- *ORIGINAL VERSION:* "Love Me Tender" RCA extended play (EPA-4006) and "Worldwide Gold Award Hits, Vol. 2" RCA (LPM-6402).
- *ALTERNATE MIX:* "For LP Fans Only" RCA (LPM-1990). Stronger reverberation is used on the LP version.

PROUD MARY

- *ORIGINAL VERSION:* "On Stage - February, 1970" RCA (LSP-4362).
- *CONCERT VERSION:* "Elvis As Recorded At Madison Square Garden" RCA (LSP-4776).

QUEENIE WAHINE'S PAPAYA

- *ORIGINAL VERSION:* Any RCA release.
- *FALSE START:* "Leavin' It Up To You," a bootleg album. This track still falls into the catagory of false starts, even though Elvis nearly completes the tune. It's almost an alternate take.

RAGS TO RICHES

- *ORIGINAL VERSION:* Any RCA release.
- *ALTERNATE TAKE:* "Superstar Out-takes Vol 2" and "Special Delivery," bootleg albums.

RECONSIDER BABY

- *ORIGINAL VERSION:* Any RCA release.
- *CONCERT VERSION:* "Hawaii Benefit Show," a bootleg album.

REDDY TEDDY

- *ORIGINAL VERSION:* Any RCA release.
- *TV AUDIO TRACK:* "The King Goes Wild," "From The Waist Up," "The Hillbilly Cat 1954-1974," and "Rock My Soul," bootleg albums. From Elvis' September 9, 1956 appearance on the Ed Sullivan show.

RIDING THE RAINBOW

- *ORIGINAL VERSION:* Any RCA release.
- *FALSE STARTS:* "A Dog's Life," a bootleg album. Two false starts are included on this LP, the second of which lacks only a few seconds, at the very end, of being an alternate take.

ROCK-A-HULA BABY

- *ORIGINAL VERSION:* All RCA releases.
- *ALTERNATE TAKE:* "A Dog's Life," a bootleg album.
- *FALSE STARTS:* "A Dog's Life," a bootleg album. Two false starts are included.

ROUSTABOUT

- *ORIGINAL VERSION:* Any RCA release.
- *ALTERNATE TAKE:* "Paramount Pictures Presents 'Roustabout' - Theatre Lobby Spot." (45rpm single)

SAND CASTLES

- *ORIGINAL VERSION:* Any RCA version.
- *ALTERNATE TAKE:* "Leavin' It Up To You," a bootleg album.

SANTA CLAUS IS BACK IN TOWN

- *ORIGINAL VERSION:* All RCA releases.
- *CONCERT VERSION:* "The Burbank Sessions Vol. 1," a bootleg album. Only a portion of the song is done by Elvis in an impromptu version.

SCRATCH MY BACK (THEN I'LL SCRATCH YOURS)

- *ORIGINAL VERSION:* Any RCA release.
- *ALTERNATE TAKE:* "A Dog's Life," a bootleg album.

SEE SEE RIDER

- *ORIGINAL VERSION:* "On Stage - February, 1970" RCA (LSP-4362).
- *CONCERT VERSION:* "Aloha From Hawaii Via Satellite" RCA (VPSX-6089).
- *CONCERT VERSION:* "Elvis Recorded Live On Stage In Memphis" RCA (CPL1-0606).
- *CONCERT VERSION:* "Elvis In Concert" RCA (APL2-2587).

SEPARATE WAYS

- *ORIGINAL VERSION:* All RCA releases.
- *FILM VERSION:* "Special Delivery," a bootleg album. From the film "Elvis On Tour."

SHAKE, RATTLE AND ROLL/FLIP, FLOP AND FLY

- *ORIGINAL VERSION:* No RCA original exists for the pairing of these two songs, but, individually, "Shake, Rattle and Roll" is an original version on any RCA release. "Flip, Flop and Fly" appears originally on "Elvis Recorded Live On Stage In Memphis," in medley form (RCA CPL1-0606).
- *TV AUDIO TRACK:* "The Dorsey Shows" and "Superstar Out-takes Vol. 2," bootleg albums. From Elvis' February 11, 1956 appearance.

SHE THINKS I STILL CARE

- *ORIGINAL VERSION:* RCA 45rpm single (PB-10857) release and the "Moody Blue" LP (AFL1-2428).
- *ALTERNATE MIX:* "Our Memories Of Elvis Vol. 1" RCA (AQL1-3279). No overdubbing; the "pure Elvis" sound.

SHE WEARS MY RING

- *ORIGINAL VERSION:* "Good Times" RCA (CPL1-0475).
- *ALTERNATE MIX:* "Our Memories Of Elvis Vol. 2," RCA (AQL1-3448). No overdubbing; the "pure Elvis" sound.

SIGNS OF THE ZODIAC

- *ORIGINAL VERSION:* Since there was never an authorized version of this song released, we'll call the actual studio version the original release. That track appears on the bootleg album "Behind Closed Doors."
- *FILM VERSION:* "Eternal Elvis," a bootleg album, which was actually issued prior to "Behind Closed Doors," has the overdubbed version that was used in the film "The Trouble With Girls."

SLICIN' SAND

- *ORIGINAL VERSION:* Any RCA release.
- *ALTERNATE TAKE:* "Plantation Rock," a bootleg album.

SOLITAIRE

- *ORIGINAL VERSION:* "From Elvis Presley Boulevard, Memphis, Tennessee" RCA (APL1-1506).
- *ALTERNATE MIX:* "Our Memories Of Elvis Vol. 1" RCA (AQL1-3279). No overdubbing; the "pure Elvis" sound.

SOMETHING

- *ORIGINAL VERSION:* All RCA releases.
- *CONCERT VERSION:* "Plantation Rock," a bootleg album. From the "Aloha" rehersal show.

SOUND OF YOUR CRY, THE

- *ORIGINAL VERSION:* Any RCA release.
- *ALTERNATE TAKE:* "Superstar Out-takes Vol. 2" and "Special Delivery," bootleg albums.

SPANISH EYES

- *ORIGINAL VERSION:* "Good Times" RCA (CPL1-0475).
- *ALTERNATE MIX:* "Our Memories Of Elvis, Vol. 1" RCA (AQL1-3279). No overdubbing; the "pure Elvis" sound.

STAY AWAY JOE

- *ORIGINAL VERSION:* "Let's Be Friends" RCA/Camden (CAS-2408)
- *ALTERNATE TAKE:* "Almost In Love" RCA/Camden (CAS-2440). There need not be any confusion about the fact that only first [1970] pressings of this LP contain this track. Quite simply, if the title is "Stay Away Joe," you've got the alternate. If the title reads "Stay Away," you've got a completely song.

STEADFAST, LOYAL AND TRUE

- *ORIGINAL VERSION:* Any RCA release.
- *ALTERNATE TAKE:* "From The Beach To The Bayou," a bootleg album.

STEPPIN' OUT OF LINE

- *ORIGINAL VERSION:* Any RCA release.
- *ALTERNATE TAKE:* "Behind Closed Doors," a bootleg album.
- *FALSE START:* "Behind Closed Doors," a bootleg album.
- *ALTERNATE TAKE:* "Plantation Rock," a bootleg album.
- *FALSE STARTS:* "Plantation Rock," a bootleg album. Two false starts are included.

STOP WHERE YOU ARE

- *ORIGINAL VERSION:* Any RCA release.
- *ALTERNATE TAKE:* "Leavin' It Up To You," a bootleg album.

STRANGER IN THE CROWD

- *ORIGINAL VERSION:* Any RCA release.
- *FILM VERSION:* "From The Dark To The Light," a bootleg album. Elvis sang only a portion of the song, in the film "That's The Way It Is," and it's on this LP.

STUCK ON YOU

- *ORIGINAL VERSION:* All RCA releases.
- *TV AUDIO TRACK:* "Eternal Elvis" and "TV Guide Presents Elvis Presley," bootleg albums. From Elvis' March 26, 1960 appearance on the Frank Sinatra special.

SUCH A NIGHT

- *ORIGINAL VERSION:* Any RCA release that is a complete take of the song.
- *FALSE STARTS:* "A Legendary Performer, Vol. 2" RCA (CPL1-1349). Two false starts are included on this LP.
- *CONCERT VERSION:* "Hawaii Benefit Show," a bootleg album. From a 1961 appearance.

SUSPICION

- *ORIGINAL VERSION:* All RCA releases in the United States.
- *ALTERNATE MIX:* "Elvis Presley Canta" RCA EP (3-20820). This Spanish EP has one of the two stereo channels missing, and, as a result, the vocal backing and part of the orchestration.

SUSPICIOUS MINDS

- *ORIGINAL VERSION:* Any RCA release that is not taken from a live concert.
- *CONCERT VERSION:* "From Memphis To Vegas/From Vegas To Memphis" RCA (LSP-6020) and "Elvis In Person At The International Hotel, Las Vegas, Nevada" RCA (LSP-4428).
- *CONCERT VERSION:* "Elvis As Recorded At Madison Square Garden" RCA (LSP-4776).
- *CONCERT VERSION:* "Aloha From Hawaii Via Satellite" RCA (VPSX-6089).
- *CONCERT VERSION:* "Behind Closed Doors," a bootleg album. From a February, 1970 Las Vegas appearance.
- *CONCERT VERSION:* "The Legend Lives On" and "Superstar Out-takes Vol. 1," bootleg albums. From an August, 1969 Las Vegas appearance.

SWING DOWN, SWEET CHARIOT

- *ORIGINAL VERSION:* All RCA releases.
- *CONCERT VERSION:* "Hawaii Benefit Show," a bootleg album. From a 1961 appearance.
- *FILM VERSION:* "Eternal Elvis," a bootleg album. From the film "The Trouble With Girls."
- *ALTERNATE TAKE:* "Behind Closed Doors," a bootleg album. Respective to the original version, this is an alternate take. This is the studio recording from which the film version, shown above, was made.

SYLVIA

- *ORIGINAL VERSION:* Any RCA release.
- *ALTERNATE TAKE:* "Plantation Rock," a bootleg album.

SPRING FEVER

- *ORIGINAL VERSION:* Any RCA release.
- *ALTERNATE TAKE:* "Special Delivery," a bootleg album.

TAKE GOOD CARE OF HER

- *ORIGINAL VERSION:* RCA 45rpm single (APBO-0196) and "Good Times" RCA LP (CPL1-0475).
- *ALTERNATE MIX:* "Our Memories Of Elvis, Vol. 1" RCA (AQL1-3279). No overdubbing; the "pure Elvis" sound.

(LET ME BE YOUR) TEDDY BEAR

- *ORIGINAL VERSION:* Any RCA release that is not taken from a live concert.
- *CONCERT VERSION:* "Elvis As Recorded At Madison Square Garden" RCA (LSP-4776). As part of a "Teddy Bear"/"Don't Be Cruel" medley.
- *CONCERT VERSION:* "Elvis In Concert" RCA (APL2-2587). As part of a "Teddy Bear"/"Don't Be Cruel" medley.
- *FILM VERSIONS:* "Loving You" and "Got A Lot O' Livin' To Do," bootleg albums.

THAT'S ALL RIGHT

- *ORIGINAL VERSION:* Sun (209) and RCA (20/47-6380) singles and, surprisingly enough, "A Legendary Performer, Vol. 1" RCA (CPL1-0341).
- *ALTERNATE MIX:* Any other RCA release, on EP or LP, that is not from a live concert.
- *CONCERT VERSION:* "Elvis As Recorded At Madison Square Garden" RCA (LSP-4776).
- *CONCERT VERSION:* "Elvis In Concert" RCA (APL2-2587).
- *CONCERT VERSION:* "Rockin' Rebel Vol. 2" and "Elvis Presley On The Louisiana Hayride" EP, bootleg releases. From Elvis' December, 1954 appearance on the Louisiana Hayride.
- *CONCERT VERSION:* "The First Years," "Rockin' Rebel Vol. 2" and "The Entertainer," bootleg albums. From Elvis' 1955 Houston, Texas appearance.
- *CONCERT VERSION:* "The Burbank Sessions Vol. 1," a bootleg album. This version was not used in the '68 Special, nor ever released by RCA. It was, however, included in the "Memories Of Elvis" TV special, hosted by Ann-Margret.
- *CONCERT VERSION:* "Hawaii Benefit Show," a bootleg album. From a 1961 appearance.
- *FILM VERSION:* "From The Dark To The Light," a bootleg album. Includes the portion of the song, as performed in the film "That's The Way It Is."

THERE GOES MY EVERYTHING

- *ORIGINAL VERSION:* RCA 45rpm single (47-9960) and "Worldwide Gold Award Hits, Vol. 2" RCA (LPM-6402).
- *ALTERNATE MIX:* "Elvis Country" RCA (LSP-4460). The ending of the song is overlapped with "I Was Born About Ten Thousand Years Ago."
- *ALTERNATE TAKE:* "A Dog's Life," a bootleg album.

THERE'S A HONKY TONK ANGEL (WHO WILL TAKE ME BACK IN)

- *ORIGINAL VERSION:* "Promised Land" RCA (APL1-0873).
- *ALTERNATE MIX:* "Our Memories Of Elvis, Vol. 2" RCA (AQL1-3448) and RCA 45rpm single PB-11679.

THINKING ABOUT YOU

- *ORIGINAL VERSION:* RCA 45rpm single (PB-10191) and "Promised Land" LP (APL1-0873).
- *ALTERNATE MIX:* "Our Memories Of Elvis, Vol. 2" (AQL1-3448). No overdubbing; the "pure Elvis" sound.

THIS IS LIVING

- *ORIGINAL VERSION:* All RCA releases.
- *ALTERNATE TAKE:* "Behind Closed Doors," a bootleg album.

THIS IS MY HEAVEN

- *ORIGINAL VERSION:* Any RCA release.
- *ALTERNATE TAKE:* "Behind Closed Doors," a bootleg album.

TIGER MAN

- *ORIGINAL VERSION:* "Singer Presents Elvis Singing Flaming Star And Others" RCA/Camden (CAS-2304).
- *CONCERT VERSION:* "From Memphis To Vegas/From Vegas To Memphis" RCA (LSP-6020) and "Elvis In Person At The International Hotel, Las Vegas, Nevada" RCA (LSP-4428). Performed as part of a "Mystery Train"/"Tiger Man" medley.

TODAY, TOMORROW AND FOREVER

- *ORIGINAL VERSION:* All RCA releases.
- *FILM VERSION:* "Viva Las Vegas," a bootleg album.

TOMORROW NEVER COMES

- *ORIGINAL VERSION:* "Elvis Country" RCA (LSP-4460).
- *ALTERNATE MIX:* "Behind Closed Doors," a bootleg album. No overdubbing or overlapping; the "pure Elvis" sound.

TONIGHT IS SO RIGHT FOR LOVE

- *ORIGINAL VERSION:* All RCA releases bearing *this* title.
- *ALTERNATE TAKE:* Pretty much the same lyrics were put to a completely different melody and titled "Tonight's All Right For Love." The newer arrangement was, from 1960 through 1973, available only on foreign (mostly European) RCA releases. See "Tonight's All Right For Love" for more information.

TONIGHT'S ALL RIGHT FOR LOVE

- *ORIGINAL VERSION:* Any RCA release, from any country, that is timed at 2:10 (or thereabouts). Some examples that come immediately to mind are the "G.I. Blues" LP from Italy and Germany and the RCA 45rpm single release, in Germany (with picture sleeve) of "Tonight's All Right For Love"/"Wooden Heart."
- *ALTERNATE MIX:* A shortened version appears on the U.S. LP "A Legendary Performer, Vol. 1," as well as on a few foreign releases containing this song. This version will show a time of approximately 1:20.

TOO MUCH

- *ORIGINAL VERSION:* All RCA releases.
- *TV AUDIO TRACK:* "The King Goes Wild" and "From The Waist Up," bootleg albums. From Elvis' January 6, 1957 appearance on the Ed Sullivan show.

TREAT ME NICE

- *ORIGINAL VERSION:* All RCA releases.
- *FILM VERSION:* "Got A Lot O' Livin' To Do," a bootleg album. From "Jailhouse Rock." This is not the only time in the film when Elvis did this song, but it's the only one on this album, and it is the complete version.

ElVIS PRESLEY M-G-M 1241

TROUBLE

- *ORIGINAL VERSION:* Any RCA release that is not taken from a live concert.
- *CONCERT VERSION:* "Elvis (NBC-TV Special)" RCA (LPM-4088).
- *CONCERT VERSION (1):* "The Burbank Sessions Vol. 2," a bootleg album.
- *CONCERT VERSION (2):* "The Burbank Sessions Vol. 2," a bootleg album.
- *CONCERT VERSION (3):* "The Burbank Sessions Vol. 2," a bootleg album.
- *CONCERT VERSION (4):* "The Burbank Sessions Vol. 2," a bootleg album.

NOTE: None of these four tracks match, perfectly, the versions used by RCA on their TV special album. As with "Memories," they probably did additional recording until they were satisfied with the results.

TRYIN' TO GET TO YOU

- *ORIGINAL VERSION:* Any RCA release that is not taken from a live concert.
- *CONCERT VERSION:* "A Legendary Performer, Vol. 1" RCA (CPL1-0341).
- *CONCERT VERSION:* "Elvis Recorded Live On Stage In Memphis" RCA (CPL1-0606).
- *CONCERT VERSION (1):* "The Burbank Sessions Vol. 1," a bootleg album.
- *CONCERT VERSION (2):* "The Burbank Sessions Vol. 1," a bootleg album. It is this version (side four) that appears on "A Legendary Performer, Vol. 1."

TUTTI FRUTTI

- *ORIGINAL VERSION:* All RCA releases.
- *TV AUDIO TRACK (1):* "The Dorsey Shows" and "Superstar Out-takes Vol. 2," bootleg albums. From Elvis' February 4, 1956 appearance.
- *TV AUDIO TRACK (2):* "The Dorsey Shows" and "Superstar Out-takes Vol. 2," bootleg albums. From Elvis' February 18, 1956 appearance.

UNCHAINED MELODY

- *ORIGINAL VERSION:* "Moody Blue" RCA (AFL1-2428).
- *CONCERT VERSION:* RCA 45rpm single PB-11212.

VIVA LAS VEGAS

- *ORIGINAL VERSION:* All RCA releases in the United States.
- *ALTERNATE MIX:* This song is available in true stereo, but not on any U.S. releases. For some strange reason, albums from Japan and New Zealand have the stereo recording of this song, but we never have. Why not?
- *FILM VERSIONS:* "Viva Las Vegas," a bootleg album. The song appeared three times in the film, and they are all included on this LP.

WAY DOWN

- *ORIGINAL VERSION:* RCA 45rpm single (PB-10998) and "Moody Blue" LP (AFL1-2428).
- *ALTERNATE MIX:* "Our Memories Of Elvis, Vol. 1," RCA (AQL1-3448). No overdubbing; the "pure Elvis" sound.

WE'RE GONNA MOVE

- *ORIGINAL VERSION:* "Love Me Tender" RCA extended play (EPA-4006) and "Worldwide Gold Award Hits, Vol. 2" RCA (LPM-6402).
- *ALTERNATE MIX:* "A Date With Elvis" RCA (LPM-2011). Stronger reverberation is used on the LP version.

WHAT'D I SAY

- *ORIGINAL VERSION:* Any RCA release that is not taken from a live concert.
- *CONCERT VERSION:* "Elvis In Concert" RCA (APL2-2587). A rather brief rendering, but it's the only live version released by RCA.
- *FILM VERSION:* "Viva Las Vegas," a bootleg album.
- *CONCERT VERSION:* "The Legend Lives On" and "Superstar Out-takes Vol. 1," bootleg albums. From Elvis' August, 1969 Las Vegas appearance.
- *FILM VERSION:* "From The Dark To The Light," a bootleg album. A portion of the song was done in "That's The Way It Is," and it is included on this LP.

WHEN MY BLUE MOON TURNS TO GOLD AGAIN

- *ORIGINAL VERSION:* All RCA releases.
- *CONCERT VERSION (1):* "The Burbank Sessions Vol. 1," a bootleg album.
- *CONCERT VERSION (2):* "The Burbank Sessions Vol. 1," a bootleg album.
- *TV AUDIO TRACK:* "From The Waist Up" and "The King Goes Wild," bootleg albums.

WHOLE LOT-TA SHAKIN' GOIN' ON

- *ORIGINAL VERSION:* "Elvis Country" RCA (LSP-4460).
- *ALTERNATE MIX:* "Country Memories" RCA Record Club issue (R244069), has late fade-in and early fade-out to avoid overlapping "I Was Born About Ten Thousand Years Ago."

WILD IN THE COUNTRY

- *ORIGINAL VERSION:* All RCA releases in the United States.
- *ALTERNATE MIX:* "Elvis For Everyone," as released in England (7752) and "From The Beach To The Bayou," a bootleg album contain a version that highlights the use of the maracas.
- *ALTERNATE TAKE:* "Behind Closed Doors," a bootleg album.
- *FALSE START:* "Behind Closed Doors," a bootleg album.

WORDS

- *ORIGINAL VERSION:* All RCA releases.
- *FILM VERSION:* "From The Dark To The Light," a bootleg album. A portion of the song was done in the film "That's The Way It Is," and is included in this LP.

YELLOW ROSE OF TEXAS/THE EYES OF TEXAS

- *ORIGINAL VERSION:* All RCA releases.
- *FILM VERSION:* "Viva Las Vegas," a bootleg album.

YESTERDAY

- *ORIGINAL VERSION:* All RCA releases.
- *CONCERT VERSION:* "The Legend Lives On" and "Superstar Out-takes," bootleg albums. From Elvis' August, 1969 Las Vegas appearance.

YOU DON'T HAVE TO SAY YOU LOVE ME
- *ORIGINAL VERSION:* Any RCA release that is not taken from a live concert.
- *CONCERT VERSION:* "Elvis As Recorded At Madison Square Garden" RCA (LSP-4776).
- *FILM VERSION:* "From The Dark To The Light," a bootleg album. From the film "That's The Way It Is."
  NOTE: RCA's original acetate for this song had a brief piano opening that is not heard on any of the released versions.

YOU DON'T KNOW ME
- *ORIGINAL VERSION:* All RCA releases.
- *FILM VERSION:* "Eternal Elvis," a bootleg album.

YOU GAVE ME A MOUNTAIN
- *ORIGINAL VERSION:* "Aloha From Hawaii Via Satellite" RCA (VPSX-6089).
- *CONCERT VERSION:* "Elvis In Concert" RCA (APL2-2587)
- *CONCERT VERSION:* "Leavin' It Up To You," a bootleg album. From the "Aloha" rehersal show.
- *CONCERT VERSION:* "Superstar Out-takes Vol. 2," a bootleg album. From a 1972 Las Vegas appearance.
- *FILM VERSION:* "Rock My Soul," a bootleg album. From the movie "Elvis On Tour."

YOU'LL THINK OF ME
- *ORIGINAL VERSION:* RCA 45rpm single 47-9764
- *ALTERNATE MIX:* "From Memphis To Vegas/From Vegas To Memphis" RCA (LSP-6020) and "Back In Memphis" RCA (LSP-4429). Here's one you'll miss if you don't listen carefully. The album version eliminates the "da-da, da-da" that Elvis sings over the instrumental bridge, prior to the last verse "then in your warm, etc. etc."

YOUNG AND BEAUTIFUL
- *ORIGINAL VERSION:* "Jailhouse Rock" EP (EPA-4114) and on "Worldwide Gold Award Hits, Vol. 2" RCA (LPM-6402).
- *ALTERNATE MIX:* "A Date With Elvis" RCA (LPM-2011). This version has a noticable increase in reverberation (echo) and the result is that he sounds about 10 years older than he does on the EP version.
- *FILM VERSION:* "Got A Lot O' Livin' To Do," a bootleg album. Contains the three versions sang in the film "Jailhouse Rock."

YOUR LOVE'S BEEN A LONG TIME COMING
- *ORIGINAL VERSION:* "Promised Land" RCA (APL1-0873).
- *ALTERNATE MIX:* "Our Memories Of Elvis, Vol. 1" RCA (AQL1-3279). No overdubbing; the "pure Elvis" sound.

YOU'RE A HEARTBREAKER
- *ORIGINAL VERSION:* Sun (215) and RCA (20/47-6382) singles.
- *ALTERNATE MIX:* All RCA versions on long play (LP) releases. Additional overdubbing is used.

YOU'VE LOST THAT LOVIN' FEELIN'
- *ORIGINAL VERSION:* "That's The Way It Is" RCA (LSP-4445).
- *CONCERT VERSION:* "Elvis As Recorded At Madison Square Garden" RCA (LSP-4776).

ADDITIONAL SONG INFORMATION

Thus far, RCA has released 36 songs by Elvis, taken from his live appearances, that are available in no other form other than as concert recordings.

Here is a handy listing of those three dozen tunes. . . none of which have ever been available from studio recordings. Of course, many of them were never recorded in the studio by Elvis, but a few were.

AMEN
AMERICA (THE BEAUTIFUL)
AN AMERICAN TRILOGY
BABY, WHAT YOU WANT ME TO DO
FLIP, FLOP AND FLY
FOR THE GOOD TIMES (March, 1972)
I CAN'T STOP LOVING YOU
IF YOU LOVE ME (LET ME KNOW)
I JUST CAN'T HELP BELEVIN' (August, 1970)*
I'M SO LONESOME I COULD CRY
IT'S IMPOSSIBLE
IT'S OVER
JOHNNY B. GOODE
LET IT BE ME
LET ME BE THERE
LITTLE DARLIN'
(YOUR) MAMA DON'T DANCE
MY BABE
MY WAY
NEVER BEEN TO SPAIN
POLK SALAD ANNIE
PROUD MARY
RUNAWAY
SEE SEE RIDER
SOFTLY, AS I LEAVE YOU
STEAMROLLER BLUES
THE IMPOSSIBLE DREAM
THE WONDER OF YOU
TIGER MAN
UNCHAINED MELODY
WHAT NOW MY LOVE
WHY ME (LORD)
WORDS (August, 1970)*
YESTERDAY
YOU GAVE ME A MOUNTAIN
YOU'VE LOST THAT LOVIN' FEELIN'

*These songs were, in a technical sense, recorded in a studio session. It's just that the studio versions were only rehersals for an upcoming live appearance. Dates given are for those studio rehersal sessions.

Titles in lighter type face were recorded in the studio, but those recordings have never been made available on records.

The following songs have appeared on unauthorized record releases only. Some are complete songs, some only pieces. A few are studio quality, others so bad it's hard to justify listing them. But, again for the sake of being comprehensive, they are all here.

DAINTY LITTLE MOONBEAMS: A piece of a song from the film "Girls! Girls! Girls! Included on the bootleg album "Eternal Elvis." Quality: good.

DOMINIC: Lifted from the film "Stay Away Joe." Appears on the bootleg album "I Wanna Be A Rock 'N' Roll Star." Quality: good

FOLSOM PRISON BLUES: *See I WALK THE LINE/FOLSOM PRISON BLUES*

GET BACK: Performed as part of a "Little Sister"/"Get Back" medley. Included on the bootleg album "Command Performance." Quality: fair.

HAPPY BIRTHDAY: Elvis sang this familiar tune on a couple of occasions when someone was having a birthday. Can be heard on "Elvis Presley Is Alive And Well And Singing In Las Vegas," "Cadillac Elvis," "The Legend Lives On" and "Superstar Out-takes Vol. 1." Quality: excellent on "Superstar Out-takes.

HAPPY, HAPPY BIRTHDAY BABY: Recorded at the home of a friend, in 1958. Heard on "Forever Young, Forever Beautiful," a bootleg album. Quality: fair.

HUSKY DUSTY DAY: Elvis sang this duet with Hope Lange, in "Wild In The Country," and it's on the bootleg album "Eternal Elvis." Quality: good.

I UNDERSTAND (JUST HOW YOU FEEL): Recorded at the home of a friend, in 1958. Heard on "Forever Young, Forever Beautiful," a bootleg album. Quality: fair.

I WALK THE LINE/FOLSOM PRISON BLUES: An unrehersed pairing of two Johnny Cash tunes. Included on "The Entertainer" and "To Know Him Is To Love Him," bootleg albums. Quality: fair.

I'M LEAVIN' IT UP TO YOU: Probably from a Las Vegas show rehersal session. Only a couple of verses were available, but on "Leavin It Up To You" (bootleg album) you get to hear them twice, edited one time after another. Quality: fair.

JAMBALAYA: Recorded during a 1975 live appearance in (wouldn't ya' know it) Louisiana. Included on the bootleg album "Eternal Elvis." Quality: poor.

JUST A CLOSER WALK WITH THEE: Recorded at the home of a friend, in 1958. Heard on "Forever Young, Forever Beautiful," a bootleg album. Quality: fair.

MacARTHUR PARK: During a moment of clowning around, Elvis sings a few lines from this song. Available on the bootleg album "The Burbank Sessions Vol. 2." Quality: excellent.

M-I-C-K-E-Y M-O-U-S-E: Elvis had fun with this well-known melody. It can be heard on "Cadillac Elvis," a bootleg album. Quality: fair.

MORE: A few seconds of this song, from a live concert, appear on the bootleg album "To Know Him Is To Love Him." Quality: poor.

MY BABY'S GONE: The alternate approach to "I'm Left, You're Right, She's Gone." Included on "Rockin' Rebel Vol. 1" and "Good Rockin' Tonight," just to name a couple. Quality: excellent.

OH HAPPY DAY: Recorded during one of Elvis' live concert appearances. Heard on the bootleg album "Command Performance." Quality: fair

PLANTATION ROCK: Recorded for the film "Girls! Girls! Girls!," but never used in the movie, or in any way by RCA. Heard on the bootleg LP of the same name. Quality: excellent.

PORTRAIT OF MY LOVE: From a backstage (informal) rehersal session, probably in Las Vegas. Included on the bootleg album "Special Delivery." Quality: poor.

SIGNS OF THE ZODIAC: Used in the film "The Trouble With Girls," but a studio version (prior to overdubbing for the film) is found on the bootleg album "Behind Closed Doors." Quality: excellent.

SWEET INSPIRATION: The giant hit by The Sweet Inspirations received Elvis' treatment during one of his concerts. It can be heard on "To Know Him Is To Love Him." Quality: poor.

THE LADY LOVES ME: This duet (Elvis and Ann-Margret) was taken from the flim "Viva Las Vegas," and appears on the bootleg LP "Viva Las Vegas." Quality: good.

TIP-TOE THRU THE TULIPS: One humorously delivered line of this Tiny Tim hit is heard on "The Burbank Sessions Vol. 2," a bootleg album. Quality: excellent.

TWEEDLE DEE: From a 1955 Louisiana Hayride appearance, and heard on "Rockin' Rebel Vol. 2," "Elvis On The Louisiana Hayride" and "The Entertainer" just to name a few. All issues of this song, thus far, are unauthorized.. Quality: excellent.

VIOLET, VIOLET (FLOWER OF N.Y.U.): A studio version of this brief tune, later to appear in "The Trouble With Girls," is heard on "Behind Closed Doors," a bootleg album. Quality: excellent.

WHEN THE SNOW IS ON THE ROSES: This Ed Ames hit was sung by Elvis during one of his live shows. It's on the bootleg albums "The Hillbilly Cat Live," "Special Delivery" and "Sold Out." Quality: fair.

WIFFENPOOF SONG, THE: A few lines from this standard are on the bootleg album "Behind Closed Doors." Quality: excellent.

WITCHCRAFT: The Frank Sinatra song, performed by Elvis in a duet with Sinatra; from the 1960 "Welcome Home Elvis" TV show. On the bootleg album "TV Guide." Quality: good.

YIPPIE YI YO: Elvis sang a few lines in a comedy skit on the Steve Allen TV show, in 1956. It's on "Rockin' Rebel Vol. 3" and "Superstar Out-takes," bootleg albums. Quality: good.

Most of the songs released on single records have also appeared on an LP, either before or after the single issue. The following songs, however, have never appeared on any RCA album released as part of Elvis' standard U.S. catalog.

The last time we discussed the possibility of putting all of the songs on one LP, with RCA, we were told that it was being given serious thought. The possibility does therefore exist that, before long, there will be no Elvis songs from single releases that are not also available on long play.

AMERICA
COME WHAT MAY
FIRST TIME EVER I SAW YOUR FACE
HIGH HEEL SNEAKERS
I'M LEAVIN'
IT'S ONLY LOVE
RAGS TO RICHES
SOFTLY, AS I LEAVE YOU
SOUND OF YOUR CRY, THE

True stereo recordings of most of Elvis' post-army tracks are easily found among RCA's U.S. catalog. The two dozen exceptions, tunes that have not been issued in true stereo here, are listed below.

The odds are that true stereo masters are in RCA's file on most of these, but a couple are probably mastered only in mono. They are noted with as asterisk.

A WHISTLING TUNE
AMERICA*
ANGEL
C'MON EVERYBODY
COME WHAT MAY
EASY COME, EASY GO ▪
FIRST TIME EVER I SAW YOUR FACE
FOLLOW THAT DREAM
FOOLS FALL IN LOVE
HIGH HEEL SNEAKERS
HOME IS WHERE THE HEART IS
I GOT LUCKY
I NEED SOMEBODY TO LEAN ON
IF YOU THINK I DON'T NEED YOU
I'LL TAKE LOVE ▪
I'M LEAVIN'
I'M NOT THE MARRYING KIND
IT'S ONLY LOVE
KING OF THE WHOLE WIDE WORLD
LOVE MACHINE, THE ▪
RAGS TO RICHES
RIDING THE RAINBOW
SING YOU CHILDREN ▪
SOFTLY, AS I LEAVE YOU*
SOUND OF YOUR CRY, THE
SUSPICIOUS MINDS (The 45rpm version of this song)
THIS IS LIVING
TODAY, TOMORROW AND FOREVER
VIVA LAS VEGAS ▪
WHAT A WONDERFUL LIFE
YOGA IS AS YOGA DOES ▪
YOU GOTTA STOP ▪

▪ These songs have appeared
in true stereo on foreign releases.

RCA'S CATALOG...TODAY

The current numbering system for RCA's available Elvis catalog is one that was recently revised, and in most cases will differ somewhat from the letters and numbers used on the originals.

The following chart will provide a handy checklist, not only to know what is now available and what is not, but to be able to convert the earlier catalog numbers to the ones now in use.

REVISION OF CATALOG NUMBERS FOR AVAILABLE ELVIS PRESLEY RECORDINGS FROM RCA*

*Effective: Spring, 1980.

TITLE:	PREVIOUS NUMBER:	CURRENT NUMBER: RECORDS:	8-TRACK TAPE:	QUAD 8-TRACK:	CASSETTE TAPE:
Elvis Presley	LPM-1254	Deleted	—	—	—
Elvis Presley	LSP(e)-1254	AFL1-1254(e)	APS1-0382	—	—
Elvis	LPM-1382	Deleted	—	—	—
Elvis	LSP-1382(e)	AFL1-1382(e)	APS1-0383	—	—
Loving You	LPM-1515	Deleted	—	—	—
Loving You	LSP-1515(e)	AFL1-1515(e)	APS1-0384	—	—
Elvis' Christmas Album	LOC-1035	Deleted	—	—	—
Elvis' Christmas Album	LPM-1951	Deleted	—	—	—
Elvis' Christmas Album	LSP-1951(e)	Deleted	—	—	—
Elvis' Christmas Album (RCA/ Camden)	CAL-2428	CAS-2428†	—	—	—
Elvis' Golden Records	LPM-1707	Deleted	—	—	—
Elvis' Golden Records	LSP-1707(e)	AFL1-1707(e)	1244	—	1244
King Creole	LPM-1884	Deleted	—	—	—
King Creole	LSP-1884(e)	AFL1-1884(e)	APS1-0385	—	
For LP Fans Only	LPM-1990	Deleted	—	—	—
For LP Fans Only	LSP-1990(e)	AFL1-1990(e)	APS1-0386	—	—
A Date With Elvis	LPM-2011	Deleted	—	—	—
A Date With Elvis	LSP-2011(e)	AFL1-2011(e)	APS1-0387	—	—
50,000,000 Elvis Fans Can't Be Wrong - Elvis' Gold Records, Vol. 2	LPM-2075	Deleted	—	—	—
50,000,000 Elvis Fans Can't Be Wrong - Elvis' Gold Records, Vol. 2	LSP-2075(e)	AFL1-2075(e)	2093	—	AFK1-2075
Elvis Is Back	LPM-2231	Deleted	—	—	—
Elvis Is Back	LSP-2231	AFL1-2231	1135	—	—
G. I. Blues	LPM-2256	Deleted	—	—	—
G. I. Blues	LSP-2256	AFL1-2256	1169	—	1169
His Hand In Mine	LPM-2328	Deleted	—	—	—
His Hand In Mine	LSP-2328	ANL1-1319	ANS1-1319	—	ANK1-1319
Something For Everybody	LPM-2370	Deleted	—	—	—
Something For Everybody	LSP-2370	AFL1-2370	1137	—	1137
Blue Hawaii	LPM-2426	Deleted	—	—	—
Blue Hawaii	LSP-2426	AFL1-2426	1019	—	1019

TITLE:	PREVIOUS NUMBER:	CURRENT NUMBER: RECORDS:	8-TRACK TAPE:	QUAD 8-TRACK:	CASSETTE TAPE:
Pot Luck	LPM-2523	Deleted	—	—	—
Pot Luck	LSP-2523	AFL1-2523	1138	—	—
Girls! Girls! Girls!	LPM-2621	Deleted	—	—	—
Girls! Girls! Girls!	LSP-2621	AFL1-2621	1139	—	—
It Happened At The World's Fair	LPM-2697	Deleted			
It Happened At The World's Fair	LSP-2697	AFL1-2568	APS1-2568	—	APK1-2568
Elvis' Golden Records, Vol. 3	LPM-2765	Deleted	—	—	—
Elvis' Golden Records, Vol. 3	LSP-2765	AFL1-2765	1057	—	1057
Fun In Acapulco	LPM-2756	Deleted	—	—	—
Fun In Acapulco	LSP-2756	AFL1-2756	1141	—	—
Kissin' Cousins	LPM-2894	Deleted	—	—	—
Kissin' Cousins	LSP-2894	AFL1-2894	1142	—	—
Roustabout	LPM-2999	Deleted	—	—	—
Roustabout	LSP-2999	AFL1-2999	1143	—	—
Girl Happy	LPM-3338	Deleted	—	—	—
Girl Happy	LSP-3338	AFL1-3338	1018	—	1018
Elvis For Everyone	LPM-3450	Deleted	—	—	—
Elvis For Everyone	LSP-3450	AFL1-3450	1078	—	1078
Harum Scarum	LPM-3468	Deleted	—	—	—
Harum Scarum	LSP-3468	AFL1-2558	APS1-2558	—	APK1-2558
Frankie And Johnny	LPM-3553	Deleted	—	—	—
Frankie And Johnny	LSP-3553	Deleted†	—	—	—
Paradise Hawaiian Style	LPM-3643	Deleted	—	—	—
Paradise Hawaiian Style	LSP-3643	AFL1-3643	1165	—	1165
Spinout	LPM-3702	Deleted	—	—	—
Spinout	LSP-3702	AFL1-2560	APS1-2560	—	APK1-2560
How Great Thou Art	LPM-3758	Deleted	—	—	—
How Great Thou Art	LSP-3758	AFL1-3758	1218	—	1218
Double Trouble	LPM-3787	Deleted	—	—	—
Double Trouble	LSP-3787	AFL1-2564	AFS1-2564	—	APK1-2564
Clambake	LPM-3893	Deleted	—	—	—
Clambake	LSP-3893	AFL1-2565	AFS1-2565	—	APK1-2565
Elvis' Gold Records, Vol. 4	LPM-3921	Deleted	—	—	—
Elvis' Gold Records, Vol. 4	LSP-3921	AFL1-3921	1297	—	1297
Speedway	LPM-3989	Deleted	—	—	—
Speedway	LSP-3989	AFL1-3989	1335	—	1335
Singer Presents Elvis Singing Flaming Star And Others	PRS-279	Deleted°	—	—	—
Elvis (NBC-TV Special)	LPM-4088	AFM1-4088	1391	—	1391
Elvis Sings Flaming Star (RCA/ Camden)	CAS-2304	CAS-2304†	—	—	—

TITLE:	PREVIOUS NUMBER:	CURRENT NUMBER: RECORDS:	8-TRACK TAPE:	QUAD 8-TRACK:	CASSETTE TAPE:
From Elvis In Memphis	LSP-4155	AFL1-4155	1456	1456 ■	1456
From Memphis To Vegas/ From Vegas To Memphis	LSP-6020	LSP-6020	5076	–	APK2-2656
Let's Be Friends (RCA/ Camden)	CAS-2408	CAS-2408 †	–	–	–
On Stage - February, 1970	LSP-4362	AFL1-4362	1594	1594 ■	1594
Worldwide 50 Gold Award Hits, Vol. 1	LPM-6401	LPM-6401	–	–	–
Worldwide 50 Gold Award Hits, Vol. 1	–	Deleted ●	P8S-6401	–	PK-6401
Worldwide 50 Gold Award Hits, Vol. 1 - No. 1	–	–	1773	–	1773
Worldwide 50 Gold Award Hits, Vol. 1 - No. 2	–	–	1774	–	1774
Worldwide 50 Gold Award Hits, Vol. 1 - No. 3	–	–	1775	–	1775
Worldwide 50 Gold Award Hits, Vol. 1 - No. 4	–	–	1776	–	1776
Almost In Love	CAS-2440	CAS-2440 †	–	–	–
Elvis In Person At The International Hotel, Las Vegas, Nevada	LSP-4428	AFL1-4428	1634	–	1634
Elvis Back In Memphis	LSP-4429	AFL1-4429	1632	–	1632
Elvis: That's The Way It Is	LSP-4445	AFL1-4445	1652	1652 ■	1652
Elvis Country	LSP-4460	AFL1-4460	1655	–	1655
You'll Never Walk Alone	CALX-2472	CAS-2472 †	–	–	–
Love Letters From Elvis	LSP-4530	AFL1-4530	1748	–	1748
Worldwide Gold Award Hits, Vol. 2	LPM-6402	LPM-6402	–	–	–
Worldwide Gold Award Hits, Vol. 2 - No. 1	–	–	1793	–	1793
Worldwide Gold Award Hits, Vol. 2 - No. 2	–	–	1794	–	1794
Worldwide Gold Award Hits, Vol. 2 - No. 3	–	–	1795	–	1795
Worldwide Gold Award Hits, Vol. 2 - No. 4	–	–	1796	–	1796
C'mon Everybody	CAL-2518	CAS-2518 †	–	–	–
I Got Lucky	CAL-2533	CAS-2533 †	–	–	–
Elvis Sings The Wonderful World Of Christmas	LSP-4579	ANL1-1936	ANS1-1936	–	ANK1-1936
Elvis Now	LSP-4671	AFL1-4671	1898	–	1898
He Touched Me	LSP-4690	AFL1-4690	1923	–	1923

TITLE:	PREVIOUS NUMBER:	CURRENT NUMBER: RECORDS:	8-TRACK TAPE:	QUAD 8-TRACK:	CASSETTE TAPE:
Elvis Sings Hits From His Movies, Vol. 1	CAS-2567	CAS-2567†	–	–	–
Elvis As Recorded At Madison Square Garden	LSP-4776	AFL1-4776	2054	2054 ■	2054
Burning Love (And Hits From His Movies, Vol. 2)	CAS-2595	CAS-2595†	–	–	–
Separate Ways	CAS-2611	CAS-2611†	–	–	–
Aloha From Hawaii Via Satellite (Quad)	VPSX-6089	CPD2-2642	CPS2-2642	Vol. 1: 2140 Vol. 2: 2141	CPK2-2642
Almost In Love	CAS-2440	CAS-2440†	–	–	–
Elvis (Including "Fool")	APL1-0283	Deleted	–	–	–
Raised On Rock/For Ol' Times Sake	APL1-0388	AFL1-0388	APS1-0388	–	APK1-0388
Elvis: A Legendary Performer, Vol. 1	CPL1-0341	CPL1-0341	CPS1-0341	–	CPK1-0341
Good Times	CPL1-0475	AFL1-0475	CPS1-0475	–	CPK1-0475
Elvis Recorded Live On Stage In Memphis	CPL1-0606	AFL1-0606	CPS1-0606	–	CPK1-0606
Elvis Recorded Live On Stage In Memphis (Quad)	APD1-0606	Deleted □	–	–	–
Having Fun With Elvis On Stage	CPM1-0818	AFM1-0818	CPS1-0818	–	CPK1-0818
Promised Land	APL1-0873	AFL1-0873	APS1-0873	–	APK1-0873
Promised Land (Quad)	APD1-0873	APD1-0873	–	APT1-0873	–
Today	APL1-1039	AFL1-1039	APS1-1039	–	APK1-1039
Today (Quad)	APD1-1039	APD1-1039	–	APT1-1039	–
Pure Gold	ANL1-0971(e)	ANL1-0971(e)	ANS1-0971	–	ANK1-0971
Elvis: A Legendary Performer, Vol. 2	CPL1-1349	CPL1-1349	CPS1-1349	–	CPK1-1349
The Sun Sessions	APM1-1675	AFM1-1675	APS1-1675	–	APK1-1675
From Elvis Presley Boulevard, Memphis, Tennessee	APL1-1506	AFL1-1506	APS1-1506	–	APK1-1506
Welcome To My World	APL1-2274	AFL1-2274	APS1-2274	–	APK1-2274
Moody Blue	AFL1-2428	AFL1-2428	AFS1-2428	–	AFK1-2428
Elvis In Concert	APL2-2587	APL2-2587	APS2-2587	–	APK2-2587
He Walks Beside Me	AFL1-2772	AFL1-2772	AFS1-2772	–	AFK1-2772
Elvis Sings For Children And Grownups Too	CPL1-2901	CPL1-2901	CPS1-2901	–	CPK1-2901

TITLE:	PREVIOUS NUMBER:	CURRENT NUMBER: RECORDS:	8-TRACK TAPE:	QUAD 8-TRACK:	CASSETTE TAPE:
Elvis: A Legendary Performer, Vol. 3 (Picture Disc Edition)	CPL1-3078	CPL1-3078	–	–	–
Elvis: A Legendary Performer, Vol. 3	CPL1-3082	CPL1-3082	CPS1-3082	–	CPK1-3082
Our Memories Of Elvis	AQL1-3279	AQL1-3279	AQS1-3279	–	AQK1-3279
Our Memories Of Elvis, Vol. 2	AQL1-3448	AQL1-3448	AQS1-3448	–	AQK1-3448
Elvis: A Canadian Tribute	KKL1-7065	KKL1-7065	KKS1-7065	–	KKK1-7065

Symbols Key:

† These are recordings sold to Pickwick. Any records or tapes currently available would be on Pickwick's label.

° Originally appeared as a special product on RCA, and was sold only at Singer Sewing Centers in conjunction with the televised 1968 Elvis special. Shortly thereafter, this album was retitled "Elvis Sings Flaming Star" and issued on RCA's Camden series.

■ Indicates an 8-track tape cartridge available in quad of a title that was never available in quad on disc.

▯ Of the four albums made available in quad, this is the only one that was never repressed. It is a good possibility that when existing quad LP inventory is exhausted, quad will be dropped from the catalog.

● A special LP-size box set was marketed for both 8-track and cassette tapes, containing all 50 of the "Gold Award" hits. Available for a limited time only, in 1970.

ADDITIONAL NOTE: When identical numbers are shown for any or all of the available tape formats, the actual difference is in the prefix. A P8S prefix identifies an 8-track cartridge, a Q8 or PQ8 is a quad 8-track and PK designates a cassette release.

ELVIS NOVELTY/TRIBUTE SONGS

BY: HOWARD F. BANNEY

August 16, 1977 is the date used to determine whether a song about Elvis is a "novelty" or a "tribute" recording. Regardless of content, any record released prior to that date will be classified as a novelty.

The broad scope of the term novelty requires, for our purposes, a further breakdown, placing each recording into one of the following sub-catagories:

ELVIS NOVELTY: The complete recording, be it serious or comedy, is about Elvis.

MENTIONS ELVIS: Elvis is mentioned or unquestionably refered to in the song.

MENTIONS ELVIS SONG(S): One or more of songs made famous by Elvis Presley are mentioned.

ELVIS PARODY: A parody of Elvis' style and/or one of his songs.

ELVIS ANSWERED: Those songs that answer or respond to one of Elvis' songs.

BREAK-IN: Usually a comedy recording, contains one or more break-ins taken from Elvis' songs. May also contain his speaking voice used as a break-in.

ELVIS BREAK-IN: **All** of the break-in tracks are taken from Elvis' songs.

Many of the songs listed in this section could easily fit into more than one of the above groups, but only the catagory that best describes the recording will be used. For example, an "Elvis Break-in" would also be an "Elvis Novelty," using the key above. But using the term "Elvis Break-in" tells you much more than just lumping the record in with the Elvis novelties would.

When known, we will give the flip side (on 45rpm singles) and the year of release. Naturally, any information you may have to help us fill in the holes in this section, or any part of this book, would be both appreciated and acknowledged.

Not included in these listings are "cover versions" of Elvis' songs that are neither novelties nor tributes.

ELVIS NOVELTY SINGLES

Alaimo, Steve
☐ AMERIKAN MUSIC/Nobody's Fool. . . Entrance 7505   *1972*
Mentions Elvis

Arbogast & Ross
☐ CHAOS/CHAOS (Part 2). . . Liberty 55197   *1959*
Break-in

Adams, Billy
☐ RETURN OF THE ALL AMERICAN BOY/That's My Baby. . . NauVoo 45-805
Elvis Novelty

Angel, Johnny
☐ TEENAGE WEDDING/Baby, It's Love. . . Vin 1004
Mentions Elvis

Annonymous
☐ WHERE'S ELVIS/Flip not known. . . Planet 1001   *1958*
Elvis Novelty

Audrey, (With Love From)
☐ DEAR ELVIS/DEAR ELVIS (Part 2). . . Plus 104   *1956*
Break-in (although entire record is about Elvis)

Baker, LaVern
☐ HEY MEMPHIS!/Voodoo Voodoo. . . Atlantic 2119   *1961*
Elvis Answered ("Little Sister")

Bare, Bobby
☐ I'M HANGIN' UP MY RIFLE/That's Where I Want To Be. . . Fraternity 861   *1959*
Elvis Novelty
☐ BROOKLYN BRIDGE/Zig-Zag Twist. . . Fraternity 890   *1961*
Mentions Elvis
☐ PUT A LITTLE LOVIN' ON ME/Flip not known. . . RCA 10718   *1976*
Mentions Elvis

Barlby, Steve
☐ ELVIS/I'VE LOST YOU. . . RCA 2131 (England)
Elvis Novelty

Bash, Otto
☐ THE ELVIS BLUES/Later. . . RCA Victor 47-6585   *1956*
Elvis Novelty

Beaumont, Jimmy
☐ EV'RYBODY'S CRYIN'/Camera. . . May 112   *1961*
Mentions Elvis

Beavers
☐ ROCKIN' AT THE DRIVE-IN/Sack Dress. . . Capitol 3956   *1958*
Mentions Elvis

Berries
☐ THE KING (DON'T BE CRUEL)/If I Had The Wings Of A Dove. . . Epic 7645 (Foreign)   *1971*
Elvis Novelty

Billy & Eddie
☐ THE KING IS COMING BACK/Come Back, Baby. . . Top Rank 2017   *1959*
Elvis Novelty

Blenders
☐ WAKE UP TO MUSIC/New Sensations In
Sound. . . RCA Victor 47-6712   *1956*
Break-in

Blockbusters
☐ HI HON!/Boogie Bop. . . Crystalette 725   *1959*
Mentions Elvis

Blur, Ben
☐ THE CHARIOT RACE/The Flight (by Aaron
Plane). . . Mark X 8007   *1960*
Break-in

Bobolinks
☐ (I WANNA BE) ELVIS PRESLEY'S SERGEANT/Your
Cotton Pickin' Heart. . . Key 573   *1958*
Elvis Novelty

Boyle, Billy
☐ MY BABY'S CRAZY 'BOUT ELVIS/Held
For Questioning. . . Decca 11503 (England)   *1962*
Elvis Novelty

Buchanan & Ancell
☐ BUCHANAN & ANCELL MEET THE CREATURE/The
Creature. . . Flying Saucer 1232   *1957*
Break-in

Buchanan & Goodman
☐ THE FLYING SAUCER/The Flying Saucer
(Part 2). . . Luniverse 101   *1956*
Break-in
☐ BUCHANAN & GOODMAN ON TRIAL/
Crazy. . . Luniverse 102   *1956*
Break-in
☐ FLYING SAUCER THE 2ND/Martian
Melody. . . Luniverse 105   *1957*
Break-in
☐ SANTA AND THE SATELLITE/SANTA AND THE
SATELLITE (Part 2). . . Luniverse 107   *1957*
Break-in
☐ THE FLYING SAUCER GOES WEST/Saucer
Serenade. . . Luniverse 108   *1958*
Break-in
☐ FRANKENSTEIN OF '59/FRANKENSTEIN
RETURNS. . . Novelty 301   *1959*
Break-in

Bush, Dick
☐ HOLLYWOOD PARTY/Ezactly. . . Era 1067   *1958*
Mentions Elvis

Byrnes, Edward
☐ YOU'RE THE TOP/Kookie, Kookie (Lend Me
Your Comb). . . Warner Bros. 5047   *1959*
Mentions Elvis

Cannon, Freddy
☐ ROCK 'N ROLL ABC'S/Superman. . . MCA 40269   *1974*
Mentions Elvis

Carpenter, Thelma
☐ YES, I'M LONESOME TONIGHT/Gimmie A
Little Kiss. . . Coral 62241   *1961*
Elvis Answered

Checker, Chubby
☐ THE CLASS/Schooldays, Oh Schooldays. . . Parkway
804   *1959*
Mentions Elvis

Checker, Chubby & Bobby Rydell
☐ JINGLE BELL IMITATIONS/Jingle Bell
Rock. . . Cameo 205   *1961*
Mentions Elvis

Chestnuts, The (And Band)
☐ ROCK 'N ROLL TRAGEDY/I'm So
Blue. . . Night Train 906
Break-in

Clark, Alan
☐ ROCK AND ROLL/What A Heck Of A Mess. . . Clark
003   *1975*
Mentions Elvis

Cole, Sonny
☐ I DREAMED I WAS ELVIS/Curfew Cops. . . Rollin'
Rock
Elvis Novelty

Crum, Simon (Ferlin Husky)
☐ DON'T BE MAD/LITTLE RED WEBB. . . Capitol 4966   *1963*
Elvis Parody ("Don't Be Cruel")/Mentions Elvis

Cymbal, Johnny
☐ TEENAGE HEAVEN/Cinderella
Baby. . . Kapp 524   *1963*
Mentions Elvis

Dallon, Lee
☐ STAR OF A ROCK AND ROLL BAND/Too
Young To Jive. . . Tara 104   *1974*
Mentions Elvis

Davids, Janie & The 4 Lettermen
☐ GONNA GET EVEN (WITH ELVIS PRESLEY'S
SERGEANT/Big Deal. . . Key 576   *1958*
Elvis Novelty

DeBree, Peter & The Wanderers
☐ HEY! MR. PRESLEY/Honey, Won't You
Love Me. . . Fortune 200   *1958*
Elvis Novelty

Dees, Rick & His Cast Of Idiots
☐ HE ATE TOO MANY JELLY DONUTS/Barely
White (That'll Get It Baby). . . RSO 870   *1977*
Elvis Novelty

DeHoney, Jimmy With Carson Smith's Roadrangers
☐ MAIN ATTRACTION/I Was A Truck
Driver. . . Nabir 134
Mentions Elvis

Dinning, Mark
☐ TOP FORTY, NEWS, WEATHER AND SPORTS/
Suddenly. . .MGM 12980   1961
Mentions Elvis Song ("Are You Lonesome Tonight")

Dion
☐ MIDTOWN AMERICAN MAIN STREET GANG/
MIDTOWN AMERICAN MAIN STREET GANG
(Long version/short version). . .Lifesong 1770
Mentions Elvis

Dufresne, Diame
☐ CHANSON POUR ELVIS/J' Ai Vendu Mon Ame
Au Rock 'N Roll. . .Kebec Disc 10104 (Canadian release,
sung in French)   1975
Elvis Novelty

Emperor's Friends, The
☐ THE CROSSING GAME/I'm Normal. . . Current 111   1966
Mentions Elvis

Fabares, Shelly & Paul Peterson
☐ WHAT DID THEY DO BEFORE ROCK AND ROLL/
Very Unlikely. . . Colpix 631   1962
Mentions Elvis

Fabulous McClevertys
☐ DON'T BLAME IT ON ELVIS/Tickle, Tickle. . . Verve
10029   1956
Elvis Novelty

Fairchild, Barbara
☐ LITTLE GIRL FEELING/His Green Eyes. . . Columbia
10047   1974
Mentions Elvis

Flares
☐ ROCK AND ROLL HEAVEN/Rock And Roll
Heaven (Part 2). . . Press 2800   1962
Mentions Elvis

Forman, David
☐ DREAM OF A CHILD/DREAM OF A CHILD. . .Arista
0214   1976
Mentions Elvis

Fontaine, Louie
☐ ELVIS IS THE KING/Don't Look, Virginia. . .Emerald
1001   1977
Elvis Novelty

Ford, Jim
☐ THE STORY OF ELVIS PRESLEY/Desert
Walk. . .Drumfire 2   1960
Break-in

Freberg, Stan
☐ HEARTBREAK HOTEL/Rock Island Line. . . Capitol
3480   1956
Elvis Parody
☐ TELE-VEE-SHUN/Banana Boat (Day-O). . . Capitol
3687   1957
Mentions Elvis

Goodman, Dickie
☐ ON CAMPUS/Mambo Suzie. . . Cotique 158   1969
Break-in
☐ THE TOUCHABLES/Martian Melody. . . Mark X
8009   1961
Break-in
☐ THE TOUCHABLES IN BROOKLYN/
Mystery. . . Mark X 8010   1961
Break-in

Granger, Gerri
☐ JUST TELL HIM JANE SAID HELLO/What's Wrong
With Me. . . Big Top 3150   1963
Elvis Answered ("Just Tell Her Jim Said Hello")

Grayzell, Rudy
☐ JUDY/I Think Of You. . . Sun 290   1958
Mentions Elvis

Greats
☐ MARCHING ELVIS/Fiddler's Rock. . . Ebb 145   1958
Elvis Novelty

Gregory, Ivan & The Blue Notes
☐ ELVIS PRESLEY BLUES/Kathy. . . G&G 110   1956
Elvis Novelty

Guerrero, Lalo
☐ POUND DOG/Pancho Claus. . . L&M 1000   1956
Elvis Parody ("Hound Dog")
☐ ELVIS PEREZ/Lola. . . L&M 1001   1956
Elvis Novelty

Harris, Dave
☐ ELVIS AND THE UNMENTIONABLES/The Mad 40
Show By The Mad Dee Jay. . . Town 2004   1962
Break-in

☐ ELVIS AND THE UNMENTIONABLES/Bicentenential
Blitz Election '76. . . Fun-E-Bone 816   1976
Break-in

Hamilton, George IV
☐ IF YOU DON'T KNOW/A Rose And A Baby
Ruth. . . ABC-Paramount 9765   1956
Mentions Elvis

Harper, Reed & The Three Notes
☐ OH ELVIS!/O Sole Mia — Rock & Roll. . . Pyramid
4012
Elvis Novelty

Harris, Genee
☐ BYE, BYE ELVIS/You're Like A Jumpin'
Jack. . . ABC-Paramount 9900   1958
Elvis Novelty

Hart, Don
☐ PRESLEY ON HER MIND/Pledge Of Love. . . Reserve
118   1957
Elvis Novelty

Hawley, Deane
☐ NEW FAD/Pretty Little Mary. . .Dore 524   *1959*
Mentions Elvis

Holly Twins
☐ I WANT ELVIS FOR CHRISTMAS/The Tender
Age. . . Liberty 55048   *1957*
Elvis Novelty

Homer & Jethro
☐ HART BRAKE MOTEL/TWO-TONE SHOES. . . RCA
Victor 47-6542   *1956*
Elvis Parodies ("Heartbreak Hotel" and "Blue Suede Shoes")
☐ HOUN DAWG/Screen Door. . . RCA Victor 47-6706   *1956*
Elvis Parody ("Hound Dog")
☐ ARE YOU LONESOME TONIGHT/I Love Your
Pizza. . . RCA 47-7852   *1961*
Elvis Parody

Hook, Dr.
☐ THE MILLIONAIRE/Flip not known. . . Capitol 4101   *1975*
Mentions Elvis

Hugo & Luigi
☐ ROCKABILLY PARTY/Shenandoah Rose. . . Roulette
4012   *1957*
Mentions Elvis

Hunt Sisters & Mark, with Roy Hall & His Boys
☐ ELVIS IS ROCKING AGAIN/Teardrops. . . Fortune
210   *1960*
Elvis Novelty

Jackson, Sammy
☐ ARE YOU MY BABY/Live Fast. . . Orbit 536   *1959*
Mentions Elvis

Jarvis, Felton
☐ DON'T KNOCK ELVIS/Honest John. . . Viva 1001   *1959*
Elvis Novelty

Jay, Jerry (Osborne)
☐ THE KING'S COUNTRY/Merry Christmas To You
(instrumental). . . Quality 201   *1966*
Elvis Break-in

Jo
☐ I DON'T WANT TO BE ANOTHER GOOD LUCK
CHARM/She Can Have You. . . Capitol 4745   *1962*
Elvis Answered ("Good Luck Charm")

Johnny & Donna
☐ OH JOHNNY/THE DECISION. . . Titanic 5006
Mentions Elvis

Jones, Tom
☐ TUPELO, MISSISSIPPI FLASH/Daughter Of
Darkness. . . Parrot 40048   *1970*
*Elvis Novelty (Exactly how much, if any, of this song
relates to Elvis is questionable)*

Katz, Mickey
☐ YOU'RE A DOITY DOG/Litvak Square Dance. . . Capitol
3607   *1956*
Elvis Answered ("Hound Dog")

Kaye, Dave
☐ IN MY WAY/Flip not known. . . Decca 12073
(England)   *1965*
Mentions Elvis (and dedicates this song to him)

Kayli, Bob
☐ EVERYONE WAS THERE/I Took A
Dare. . . Carlton 482   *1958*
Mentions Elvis

Keegan, Sky
☐ MEMPHIS MIRACLE/Rock & Roll Heaven
U.S.A. . . Claridge 406   *1975*
Elvis Novelty

Kids
☐ ELVIS AND ME/So Shy/Juke Box Is Broken/Please
Don't Nag. . . RCA Victor (EP) EPA-4188   *1957*
Elvis Novelty

Klein, Mo & The Sergeants
☐ ALRIGHT PRIVATE/Flying Loxbox. . . Crystalette
722   *1958*
Elvis Novelty

Lang, Julie
☐ ELVIS/Woman Need De Man. . . Deluxe 6111   *1957*
Elvis Novelty

Lawrence, Syd
☐ THE ANSWER TO THE FLYING SAUCER/Haunted
Guitar. . . Cosmic 1001   *1956*
Break-in

Le Blanc, Lenny
☐ HOUND DOG MAN (Play It Again)/Sharing The Night
Together. . . Big Tree 1606   *1976*
Elvis Novelty (although he is not mentioned by name)

Lee, Linda
☐ ARE YOU LONESOME TONIGHT/There He
Goes. . . Shasta 146   *1960*
Elvis Answered

Lewis, Gary & The Playboys
☐ I SAW ELVIS PRESLEY LAST NIGHT/Something
Is Wrong. . . Liberty 56144   *1969*
Elvis Novelty

Lewis, Jerry Lee
☐ LEWIS BOOGIE/The Return Of Jerry Lee. . . Sun 301   *1958*
Mentions Elvis
☐ IT WON'T HAPPEN WITH ME/Cold, Cold Heart. . . Sun
364   *1961*
Mentions Elvis

Lowe, Virginia
☐ I'M IN LOVE WITH ELVIS PRESLEY/Empty
Feeling. . . Melba 107   *1956*
Elvis Novelty

Maddox Brothers And Rose
☐ THE DEATH OF ROCK AND ROLL/Flip not
known. . . Columbia 21559   *1956*
Elvis Parody ("I Got A Woman")

Mad Martians
☐ OUTER SPACE LOOTERS/OUTER SPACE LOOTERS (No. 2). . . Satellite 33617   *1957*
Break-in

Mad Milo
☐ ELVIS ON TRIAL/A DATE WITH ELVIS. . . Combo 131   *1957*
Break-in
☐ ELVIS FOR CHRISTMAS/Happy New Year (By Roy Tan & The Combo). . . Million 20018   *1957*
Break-in

Martin, Janis
☐ MY BOY ELVIS/Little Bit. . . RCA Victor 47-6652   *1956*
Elvis Novelty

Marty
☐ MARTY ON PLANET MARS/Marty On Planet Mars (Part 2). . . Novelty 101   *1956*
Break-in

Memphis Mill
☐ ELVIS IS THE KING/ELVIS IS THE KING (instrumental). . . W.B. Sound 1621
Elvis Novelties

Monte, Lou
☐ ELVIS PRESLEY FOR PRESIDENT/If I Was A Millionaire. . . RCA Victor 47-6704   *1956*
Elvis Novelty

Nazy, Ron Cameron
☐ THE GREAT DEBATE/THE GREAT DEBATE. . .Trey 3013   *1960*
Break-in

Newton, Wayne
☐ LITTLE JUKEBOX/Wild. . . George 7778   *1961*
Mentions Elvis

Nino & The Ebb Tides
☐ JUKE BOX SATURDAY NIGHT/(Someday) I'll Fall In Love. . . Madison 166   *1961*
Mentions Elvis

Noel, Sid
☐ FLYING SAUCER/FLYING SAUCER (Part 2). . . Aladdin 3331
Break-in (using Elvis' songs as sung by other artists)

Osborne, Jerry & Bruce Hamilton
☐ THE COUNTRY SIDE OF '76/THE COUNTRY SIDE OF '76. . . Jellyroll 10676   *1976*
Break-in

Oshins, Milt
☐ ALL ABOUT ELVIS/ALL ABOUT ELVIS (Part 2). . . Pelvis 169   *1956*
Elvis Novelty

Page, Ricky
☐ YES, I'M LONESOME TONIGHT/Standing On A Mountain Top. . . Rendezvous 139   *1961*
Elvis Answered ("Are You Lonesome Tonight")

Parsons, Bill (Bobby Bare)
☐ THE ALL AMERICAN BOY/Rubber Dolly. . . Fraternity 835   *1958*
Elvis Novelty (although doesn't mention him by name)

Paula, Marlena
☐ I WANNA SPEND CHRISTMAS WITH ELVIS/Once More It's Christmas. . . Regent 7506   *1956*
Elvis Novelty

Penn, Little Lambsie
☐ I WANNA SPEND CHRISTMAS WITH ELVIS/Painted Lips And Pigtails. . . Atco 6082   *1956*
Elvis Novelty

Perkins, Carl
☐ THE E.P. EXPRESS/Big Bad Blues. . . Mercury 73609   *1974*
Mentions Elvis Songs (Entire song made up of Elvis' song titles)

Perry, Jo-Ann
☐ YES, I'M LONESOME TONIGHT/Flip not known. . .Glad 1006   *1961*
Elvis Answered ("Are You Lonesome Tonight")

Phantom Of Rock (Wayne Stierle)
☐ THE ROCK ERA/THE ROCK ERA (Part 2). . .Patti 10000   *1973*
Elvis Novelty

Plane, Aaron
☐ THE FLIGHT/THE CHARIOT RACE (By Ben Blur). . . Mark X 8007   *1960*
Break-in

Quaker City Boys
☐ WON'T YA COME OUT, MARYANN/Teasin'. . . Swan 4023   *1958*
Mentions Elvis

Randal, Paul
☐ I'M LONESOME FOR YOU/What Is A Grandmother?. . . Roulette 4352   *1961*
Mentions Elvis (done to the tune of "Are You Lonesome Tonight")

Ray, Anita & The Nature Boys
☐ ELVIS PRESLEY BLUES/Frankie's Song. . . Dream 1300   *1958*
Elvis Novelty

Real Pros
☐ IN LOVE WITH ELVIS/My Love For You. . . Conema 7516   *1975*
Elvis Novelty

Red River Dave
☐ A TRIBUTE TO ELVIS' MOTHER/Flip not known. . . Marathon 101   *1958*
Elvis Novelty

Reed, Jerry
☐ TUPELO, MISSISSIPPI FLASH/Wabash Cannonball. . . RCA Victor 47-9334   *1967*
Elvis Novelty (Exactly how much, if any, this song relates to Elvis Presley is questionable)

Rivers, Johnny
☐ IT WON'T HAPPEN WITH ME/Memphis,
Tennessee. . . Imperial 66032   1964
Mentions Elvis

Rosella, Carmela
☐ OH! IT WAS ELVIS/Where. . . Nancy 1004   1961
Elvis Novelty

Ruff & Reddy
☐ HENRY GOES TO THE MOON/Henry Goes To
The Moon (Part 2). . . Cavalier 876   1958
Break-in

Sawyer, Steve
☐ HEY FONZIE/Flip not known. . . Casablanca 855 1976
Mentions Elvis

Schickel, Steve
☐ LEAVE MY SIDEBURNS BE/Cry Baby Boogie. . . Mercury
70999   1956
Elvis Parody ("Blue Suede Shoes")

Scott Brothers
☐ CELEBRITY PARTY/Do You Want My
Love. . . N.Y. Skyline 501
Mentions Elvis

Senn, Tony
☐ THE KING IS COMING HOME/Flip not
known. . . McDowell   1960
Elvis Novelty

Shields, Bobby
☐ THE LAND OF ROCK AND ROLL/I Wouldn't
Change You For The World. . . Melba 105   1956
Mentions Elvis

Shorr, Mickey & The Cut-ups
☐ DR. BEN CASEY/Roaring 20's Rag. . . Tuba 11636 1962
Break-in

Sicknics
☐ PRESIDENTIAL PRESS CONFERENCE/PRESIDENTIAL
PRESS CONFERENCE (Part 2). . . Amy 824   1961
Break-in

Slinky, Ratmore (Jerry Osborne)
☐ PLANE CRAZY/POLITICAL CIRCUS '72. . . Jellyroll
69   1975
Break-ins (recorded in 1972; released in 1975)

Smith, Mack Allen
☐ KING OF ROCK AND ROLL/Lonely Street. . . Ace
3011
Elvis Novelty

Sophisticates
☐ WHEN ELVIS MARCHES HOME AGAIN/Woody's
Place. . . Viva 61   1960
Elvis Novelty

Starr, Freddie
☐ WHITE CHRISTMAS/White Christmas (Part 2). . . Thunder-
bird 102   1975
Mentions Elvis

Stevens, Dodie
☐ YES, I'M LONESOME TONIGHT/Too Young. . . Dot
16167   1961
Elvis Answered

Tennant, Jimmie
☐ SALUTE/The Big Retreat. . . Warwick 533   1960
*Elvis Novelty (all break-ins are Elvis songs, but are sung on
this record by Jimmie Tennant)*

Threeteens
☐ DEAR 53310761/Doowaddie. . . Rev 4516   1958
Elvis Novelty

Tubes
☐ PROUD TO BE AN AMERICAN/Don't Touch Me
There. . . A&M 1826   1976
Mentions Elvis

Tully, Lee With Milt Moss
☐ AROUND THE WORLD WITH ELWOOD PRETZEL/
AROUND THE WORLD WITH ELWOOD PRETZEL (Part
2. . . Flair X 3007   1956
Elvis Novelty

Turner, Titus
☐ WHEN THE SERGEANT COMES MARCHING HOME/
Flip not known. . . Glover 302   1960
Elvis Novelty

Twisters
☐ ELVIS LEAVES SORRENTO/Street Dance. . . Campus
125   1961
Elvis Novelty (both sides are instrumentals)

Unknown, The (Jimmy Fields)
☐ I HAVE RETURNED/Keep Talking Baby. . . Autograph
206   1960
Elvis Novelty

Valentines
☐ THE SOCK/Sixteen Senoritas. . .Iona 1003
Mentions Elvis

Vincent, Gene
☐ STORY OF THE ROCKERS/Pickin' Popies. . . Playground
100 (reissued on Forever 6001)   1968
Mentions Elvis

Wakelin, Johnny
☐ TENNESSEE HERO (ELVIS)/Say Hello To Mister
Blues. . . Pye 45460   1975
Elvis Novelty

Walker, L. A.
☐ THEY GAVE US ROCK AND ROLL/Ooh, Shucks
Baby. . . Original Sound 108   1973
Mentions Elvis

Wallace, Bobby
☐ TRIBUTE TO A KING/Don't Hurry, Don't
Worry. . . Okie 5597
Elvis Novelty

Wasden, Jaybee
☐ ELVIS IN THE ARMY/De Castrow. . . Trepur 1011   *1959*
Elvis Novelty

Wheelie & The Hubcaps
☐ ELVIS PRESLEY MEDLEY/Chuck Berry Medley. . . Scepter
12375   *1973*

Winkley & Nutley (Jim Stag & Bob Mitchell)
☐ REPORT TO THE NATION/Report To The Nation
(Part 2). . . MK 101   *1960*
Break-in

Wood, Anita (Elvis' girlfriend, circa '57-'58)
☐ MEMORIES OF YOU/Two Young Fools In
Love. . . Santo 9008   *1961*
Elvis Novelty
☐ I'LL WAIT FOREVER/I Can't Show How I Feel. . . Sun
361   *1961*
Elvis Novelty

NOTE: When both sides of a record relate to Elvis, all capital
letters will be used on both titles. If only the first title is in
capitals, the flip is not related to Elvis in any way. If the flip
side is an instrumental, that word will appear after the flip side's
title. If both sides are instrumentals, then that information will
appear in italics below the listing.

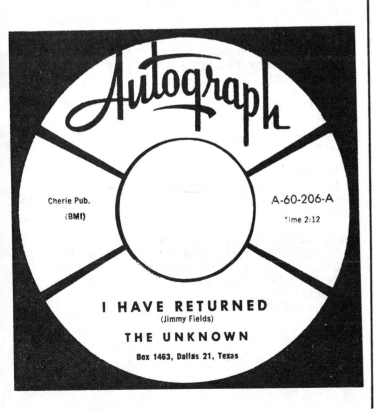

ALBUMS CONTAINING ELVIS NOVELTIES

Beach Boys
☐ LP: ALL SUMMER LONG (Capitol 2110). Contains the
song DO YOU REMEMBER? *1964*
Mentions Elvis

Big Ross & The Memphis Sound
☐ LP: ELVIS PRESLEY'S GOLDEN HITS (Pickwick 3292).
Contains songs made famous by Elvis. *1970*
Elvis Novelty

Boone, Pat
☐ LP: PAT BOONE SINGS. . .GUESS WHO? (Dot 25501).
Contains songs made famous by Elvis. *1964*
Elvis Novelty

Buchanan & Goodman
☐ LP: THE ORIGINAL FLYING SAUCERS (IX Chains
9000). Contains novelty break-in recordings. *1972*
Break-in (Elvis used on several tracks)
☐ LP: THE FLYING SAUCER STORY (Buchanan & Good-
man 716). Contains novelty break-in recordings.
Break-in (Elvis used on several tracks)
☐ LP: THE MANY HEADS OF DICKIE GOODMAN (Rori
3301). Contains novelty break-in recordings.
Break-in (Elvis used on several tracks)
NOTE: The first and third albums above are shown on the cover
as by Dickie Goodman, but since Bill Buchanan is featured on
many of the tracks they are all listed under Buchanan & Goodman.
In addition, the novelty "Flying Saucers" has appeared on several
"oldies" LP compilations, such as "Original Hits Vol. 6" (Liberty
3260).

Caddy, Alan
☐ EP: A TRIBUTE TO ELVIS PRESLEY'S GREATEST
HITS (Avenue 162). Contains six songs made famous
by Elvis (England). *1971*

Castaway Strings
☐ LP: THE CASTAWAY STRINGS PLAY THE ELVIS
PRESLEY SONG BOOK (Vee Jay 1113). Instrumental
versions of songs made famous by Elvis. *1964*
Elvis Novelty

Chartbusters
☐ LP: THE CHARTBUSTERS SALUTE THE HITS OF
ELVIS PRESLEY (Pye 8004). Contains songs made
famous by Elvis. *1973*
Elvis Novelty

Donner, Ral
☐ LP: THE PRESLEY STYLE OF RAL DONNER (Gypsy
1000). Contains songs not recorded by Elvis, but done in
a Presley style. *1979*
Elvis Novelty

Dragon, Paul
☐ LP: GOLDEN MEMORIES (Belle Meade 1002).
Contains songs made famous by Elvis. *1977*
Elvis Novelty

Dylan, Bob
☐ LP: NEW MORNING (Columbia 30290). Contains the
song WENT TO SEE THE GYPSY. *1970*
Mentions Elvis

Eager, Vince
☐ LP: VINCE EAGER PAYS TRIBUTE TO ELVIS PRESLEY
(Avenue 093). Contains songs made famous by Elvis.
Elvis Novelty

Emi & Hamlyn Group
☐ LP: SMASH HITS, PRESLEY STYLE (MFP-5114).
Contains songs made famous by Elvis.
Elvis Novelty
☐ LP: SMASH HITS, PRESLEY STYLE (MFP-50095).
Contains more songs made famous by Elvis.
Elvis Novelty

Farago, Johnny
☐ LP: POUR LES FANS D' ELVIS SEU EMENT (For Elvis
Fans Only) (Nobel 508/9). Contains songs made famous
by Elvis, sung in French.
Elvis Novelty

Golden Ring
☐ LP: THE GOLDEN RING TRIBUTE TO ELVIS (Arc
832). Contains songs made famous by Elvis.
Elvis Novelty
☐ LP: A TRIBUTE TO ELVIS (Arc 832). Contains more
songs made famous by Elvis.
Elvis Novelty

Hachey, Bobby
☐ LP: BOBBY HACHEY SINGS ELVIS (London 5113).
Contains songs made famous by Elvis.
Elvis Novelty

Hollyridge Strings
☐ LP: THE HOLLYRIDGE STRINGS PLAY INSTRUMENTAL
VERSIONS OF HITS MADE FAMOUS BY ELVIS PRESLEY
(Capitol 2221). The title says it all. *1964*
Elvis Novelty
☐ EP: THE HOLLYRIDGE STRINGS PLAY ELVIS (Capitol
SXA-2221). An EP with six selections from the
above LP. *1964*
Elvis Novelty

Jackson, Chuck
☐ LP: DEDICATED TO THE KING (Wand 680). Contains
songs made·famous by Elvis. *1968*
Elvis Novelty

Joseph And The Amazing Technicolor Dreamcoat
☐ LP: JOSEPH AND THE AMAZING TECHNICOLOR
DREAMCOAT (MCA 399). Contains the song, SONG
OF THE KING, which mentions four Elvis songs and is
done in an Elvis style. *1974*
Mentions Elvis Songs

Kennedy, Jerry
☐ LP: JERRY KENNEDY'S DANCING GUITARS ROCK THE HITS OF THE KING (Smash 27004). Contains songs made famous by Elvis. *1961*
Elvis Novelty

King, Albert
☐ LP: KING DOES THE KING'S THINGS (Stax 2015). Contains songs made famous by Elvis. *1969*
Elvis Novelty

Lewis, Gary & The Playboys
☐ LP: I'M ON THE RIGHT ROAD NOW (Liberty 7633). Contains the song I SAW ELVIS PRESLEY LAST NIGHT. *1970*
Elvis Novelty

Lincolns
☐ LP: A TRIBUTE TO ELVIS PRESLEY (Canadian). Contains songs made famous by Elvis.
Elvis Novelty

Little Richard
☐ LP: THE KING OF ROCK AND ROLL (Reprise 6462). Contains the song THE KING OF ROCK AND ROLL. *1971*
Mentions Elvis (the "King" refered to in this song is Little Richard, himself)

Mann, Johnny (Singers)
☐ LP: BALLADS OF THE KING (Liberty 3198). Contains ballads made famous by Elvis. *1961*
Elvis Novelty

Meyer, Alan
☐ LP: ALAN PRESENTS THE ELVIS PRESLEY STORY (Worldwide Presentation). Contains songs made famous by Elvis. *1974*
Elvis Novelty

Moore, Scotty
☐ LP: THE GUITAR THAT CHANGED THE WORLD (Epic 24103). Contains songs made famous by Elvis. *1964*
Elvis Novelty

Muller, Werner
☐ LP: WERNER MULLER PLAYS ELVIS PRESLEY (London 44217). Contains songs made famous by Elvis Presley. *1974* (A German release in 1974, reissued and exported in 1977)
Elvis Novelty

Nashville Country Singers
☐ LP: THE HITS OF ELVIS PRESLEY & JIM REEVES (Mountain Dew 7029). Contains songs made famous by Elvis on one side of the LP.
Elvis Novelty

Nelson, Dave
☐ LP: DAVE NELSON SINGS THE BEST OF ELVIS (Stereo Gold Award 388). Contains songs made famous by Elvis.
Elvis Novelty

Ochs, Phil
☐ LP: GUNFIGHT AT CARNEGIE HALL (A&M 9010). Contains seven songs made famous by Elvis.
Elvis Novelty

O'Doherty, Cahir
☐ LP: SALUTE TO ELVIS (CBS 9221). Contains songs made famous by Elvis (Ireland). *1976*
Elvis Novelty

Original Artists
☐ LP: ALL ABOUT ELVIS (no label or number). Contains songs about Elvis from previously issued singles. A bootleg album.
Elvis Novelty
☐ LP: ELVIS PRESLEY FOR PRESIDENT (Vantage 2). Contains songs about Elvis from previously issued singles. A bootleg album.
Elvis Novelty
☐ LP: FOR THE LOVE OF ELVIS (Superstar 110). Contains songs about Elvis from previously issued singles. A bootleg album.
Elvis Novelty
☐ LP: SONGS ABOUT ELVIS (8135-1/2). Contains songs about Elvis from previously issued singles. A bootleg album.
Elvis Novelty
☐ LP: ALL AMERICAN BOY (Vantage 6695). Contains songs about Elvis from previously issued singles. A bootleg album.
Elvis Novelty

Perry, Eden & The Nashville Pops Orchestra
☐ LP: THE HITS OF ELVIS PRESLEY (Windmill 125). Contains songs made famous by Elvis.
Elvis Novelty

Presley, Rick
☐ LP: RICK PRESLEY LIVE (Elvis II 1002). Contains songs made famous by Elvis. *1976*
Elvis Novelty

Reilly, Betty
☐ LP: CAUGHT IN THE ACT (RKO 118). Contains the song SAGA OF ELVIS PRESLEY.
Elvis Novelty

☐ LP: THE EXPLOSIVE BETTY REILLY (Golden Tone 4067). Contains the song THE SAGA OF ELVIS PRESLEY.
Elvis Novelty

Rusk, Johnny
☐ LP: A TRIBUTE TO ELVIS (Comstock Prod.). Contains song made famous by Elvis.
Elvis Novelty

Saucedo, Rick
☐ LP: RICK SAUCEDO LIVE (Reality 555). Contains songs made famous by Elvis.
Elvis Novelty

Seth, Larry
☐ LP: BIG EL SHOW "IN CONCERT" (Castle 1007). Contains songs made famous by Elvis.
Elvis Novelty

Stafford, Terry
☐ LP: SUSPICION (Crusader 1001). Contains four songs made
famous by Elvis, and other songs in an Elvis style.   *1964*
Elvis Novelty

Stierle, Wayne
☐ LP: THE REAL HISTORY OF ROCK 'N' ROLL (Candlelite
1002). Contains a review of Elvis' career, 1954-1969, in
words and music.   *1970*
Elvis Novelty

Scotty Moore was there when it happened. He heard the screams. There was Elvis in the spotlight. And at his right hand from the beginning—from ragged rehearsals in a boardinghouse room and first record sessions to barnstorming the flatbed truck circuit, from flat-broke to that historic first appearance with Tommy Dorsey, from roadhouse to the glittering spotlight in Las Vegas, from hillbilly honky-tonk to Hollywood—Scotty was there.

ELVIS TRIBUTE SINGLES

A Tint Of Darkness
☐ GOODBYE ELVIS/I'm Leaving. . . XClusive 104.   *1978*

Adkins, Paul
☐ THERE'S A BRAND NEW STAR/Hey There Lonely Girl. . . Owl 197712.   *1977*

Alexander, Arthur
☐ HOUND DOG MAN'S GONE HOME/So Long Baby. . . Music Mill 1012.   *1977*

Allen, Frankie
☐ JUST A COUNTRY BOY/I Need You Every Hour (England). . . Rockfield 6337.   *1977*

Angelo, Bonnie
☐ ELVIS MAGIC/The Ballad Of Sam Diamond. . . Bonny T.S.S. 3253.   *1978*

Archer, Con
☐ ELVIS IS GONE (BUT NOT FORGOTTEN)/Let's Start A New Tomorrow (Canada). . . QCA 463.   *1977*
NOTE: This song was privately recorded at QCA's studios, in Cincinnati, for Canadian release. Never issued by QCA, and only available in the U.S. as an import.

Ardesana, Rick
☐ ANGEL FROM HEAVEN/Flip not known. . . Magic Touch 9009.   *1978*

Arthurs, Neil
☐ KING UPON THE THRONE/Nashville's Got My Heart (Canada). . . Neil Arthur's Quest 1.   *1977*

Bellamy Brothers
☐ MEMORABILIA/Flip not known. . . Warner Bros. 8462.   *1977*
Mentions Elvis

Birds Of A Feather
☐ ELVIS, HOW COULD I RESIST/ELVIS, HOW COULD I RESIST (Instrumental) (Canada). . . Amour 8425.   *1977*
☐ NOTE: A longer version of this song was issued on a special 12-inch disco single.

Black Paul
☐ THE KING IN BLACK DISCO/Cosmic Waves. (Belgium). . . Dolphine 64501. A 12-inch single.   *1977*

Boyer, Brendon
☐ THANK YOU ELVIS/Stagger Lee (Ireland). . . Hawk 411.   *1977*

Brand, Jack
☐ ELVIS, WE'RE SORRY WE FENCED YOU IN/ELVIS, WE'RE SORRY WE FENCED YOU IN (Instrumental) Shane 7101.   *1977*

Brown, James
☐ LOVE ME TENDER/Have A Happy Day. . . Polydor 14460.   *1978*

Burnette, Billy Joe
☐ WELCOME HOME ELVIS/I Haven't Seen Mama In Years. . . Gusto-Starday 167   *1977*
☐ THE COLONEL AND THE KING/THE COLONEL AND THE KING. . . Gusto-Starday 4-9009. Promotional copy; same song on both sides. This song may have only appeared on promo copies, as we know of no commercial singles being released.   *1978*

Busby, Jimmy
☐ AUGUST 16TH (ELVIS PRESLEY DAY)/KING ELVIS, THE GREATEST. . . GUR 3378.   *1978*

Bush Band
☐ TOO MANY KINGS/Sun, Sail Away. . . Encore 178.   *1977*

California Gold
☐ THE BALLAD OF ELVIS PRESLEY/Wine In The Pines. . . Larupin 100.   *1977*

Camilli, Jim
☐ A TRIBUTE TO THE KING OF ROCK & ROLL (From The King Of The Golden Oldies)/A TRIBUTE TO THE KING OF ROCK & ROLL. . . No label name or number.   *1977*

Campbell, Glen
☐ HOUND DOG MAN

Canterbury, Chip
☐ A TRIBUTE TO ELVIS/A Proud Man Cries. . . Riverside 047.   *1977*

Cash, Johnny
☐ I WILL ROCK AND ROLL WITH YOU/A Song For The Life. . . Columbia 3-10888.   *1978*
Mentions Elvis

Cassidy, Pam
☐ THE LIFE OF ELVIS/God Can't Lie. . . Moon 1003   *1977*

Channel, Bruce
☐ THE KING IS FREE (LOVE ME)/Funky Dude (by Andy & The Dude). . . LeCam 7277.   *1977*
☐ A PRESLEY MEDLEY/A Man Without A Woman. . . LeCam 1117.   *1978*

Clark, Pet
☐ I'L NE CHANTERA PLUS SAMAIS/55 MILLIONS DeGARULOIS (France). . . CBS (number not known)

Clay, Clifford
☐ ROCK ELVIS, ROCK/Flip not known. . . MCM 7527

Cody, Michele
☐ MERRY CHRISTMAS ELVIS/All I Want For Christmas Is My Daddy. . . Safari 601.   *1978*

Copeland, Tony
☐ THE PASSING OF A KING/Rambler. . . Arco 104   *1977*

Craig, Greer
☐ LOVE ME/LITTLE SISTER. . . Trail 1862.   *1977*

Crain, Billy
☐ A TRIBUTE TO ELVIS/Calling You. . . Demo 8695   *1977*

Crouch, Dub
☐ THE LEGEND OF ELVIS PRESLEY/Dallas
Blues. . . Professional Artists 774588.   *1977*

Daddy Bob
☐ WELCOME HOME ELVIS/Pappa's Gone. . . Bertram
International 1835.   *1977*

Demarche, Doug
☐ LISA/I WAS THE ONE. . . Mimi 2-26.   *1978*

Donner, Ral
☐ THE DAY THE BEAT STOPPED/Rock On
Me. . . Thunder 7801.   *1978*

Drafti
☐ THE KING OF ROCK 'N' ROLL (WHY MUST A
YOUNG MAN DIE)/Hard Rain. . . CBS 5713.   *1977*

Durden, Tom
☐ ELVIS/ELVIS. . . Westbound 55405.   *1977*

Edwards, Gary
☐ KING OF ROCK & ROLL/Flip not known. . . Dover 1001

Eldorado
☐ JUST FOR YOU DAD/JUST FOR YOU DAD. . . Thor
1120.   *1979*

Ellis, Jimmy
☐ I'M NOT TRYING TO BE LIKE ELVIS/Games You've
Been Playing. . . Boblo 536.   *1978*

Everette, Leon
☐ GOODBYE KING OF ROCK & ROLL/When The
Daisies Grow Wild. . . True 107.   *1977*

Fagen, Jim
☐ THE LAST ENCORE/The Night My Lady Learned To
Love. . . Webcore 101   *1977*

Farago, Johnny
☐ THE KING IS GONE/SURRENDER (Canada). . . Concorde
18.   *1977*
☐ LE KING N'EST PLUS/DONNE NOI UN PEU DE
TENDRESSE (Canada). . . Concorde 17.   *1977*
☐ BLUE CHRISTMAS/Blue Christmas (instrumental). . . Con-
corde 23.   *1977*

Fillingane, H.
☐ A TRIBUTE TO THE KING/A TRIBUTE TO THE
KING. . . Tribute 001.   *1977*

Fishburn, Mack
☐ THE GRACELAND KING OF ROCK/Roads. . . Sweet-
land 001.   *1978*

Fisher, Danny
☐ A TRIBUTE TO ELVIS (BLUE SUEDE SHOES)/
REDDY TEDDY (Belgium). . . Marc 003.   *1977*

Fowler, Wally
☐ A NEW STAR IN HEAVEN/A Wonderful Time Up
There. . . Dove 100.   *1977*
☐ PRISCILLA/HE'LL NEVER BE LONELY AGAIN. . . Dove
2177.   *1977*

Freeman, Bobby
☐ ELVIS GOODBYE/IMPRESSIONS (including Elvis). . . Kim-
ray 81677.   *1977*

Gibson, Billy
☐ LITTLE LISA/Yellow Hound. . . Columbia 2324.   *1979*

Gillespie, Wesley
☐ THE WORLD LOVES YOU ELVIS/Early Sunday
Morning. . . Rome 1017.   *1977*

Grady, Leigh
☐ BLUE CHRISTMAS (WITHOUT ELVIS)/How Great
Thou Art. . . Appaloosa 112.   *1977*

Grimmett, Tink
☐ A TRIBUTE TO ELVIS/Don't Leave Me Now. . . Tink
736.   *1977*

Guardino, L.
☐ ROCKIN' ROLLIN' MAN/Red Planet Mars, Sign Of
Aires. . . LVG 336.   *1978*

Haggard, Merle
☐ FROM GRACELAND TO THE PROMISED LAND/
Are You Lonesome Tonight. . . MCA 40804.   *1977*

Hansen Brothers
☐ YOUR MEMORY IN MY MIND/MY FRIEND ELVIS/
IF IT WASN'T FOR ELVIS. . . Starfire 102.   *1978*
NOTE: Three songs are included on the above single.
☐ MY FRIEND ELVIS/Tonight's The Time. . . AAA-
Aron 001.   *1977*
☐ IF IT WASN'T FOR ELVIS/Dancin' At The Disco. . . Paul,
Dale, Tom & Ray 001. With Deke Rivers.   *1977*

Harris, Joe
☐ AL WEET JE NIET WIE PRESLEY IS/Onbekend Is
Onbemind. . . RKM 4B006-99551.

Harrison, Bob "Lil Elvis"
☐ ELVIS IS GONE/Yellow Moon. . . Lil' Elvis
World 114-62.   *1977*

Haywood, Ann
☐ TO THE MEMORY OF ELVIS/LISA MY LOVE (by
Dorris Haywood). . . Brougham 0009.   *1978*

Hebel, Ray
☐ (ELVIS) HIS LEGEND'S STILL ALIVE (IT'S GREAT TO
HAVE AN IDOL/(ELVIS) HIS LEGEND'S STILL ALIVE
(IT'S GREAT TO HAVE AN IDOL). . . Encore 1775.   *1977*

Hess, Bennie
☐ ELVIS PRESLEY BOOGIE/Make My Dreams Come True Tonight. . . Showland 2202.   *1978*

Hickcox, Jack
☐ WE'RE SURE GONNA MISS YOU, OLD FRIEND/ Your Memory Sure Does Get Around. . . Constellation 001.   *1977*

Himes, Vernon
☐ WE LOVED HIM TENDER/Believe In My Jesus. . . Artist 780529.   *1978*

Hutchison, Terry
☐ REFLECTIONS OF A MAN (ELVIS)/Lord, Give Me A New Song. . . Tap 5378.

Holbrook, Tom
☐ OH YES, HE'S GONE/A NEW BEGINNING. . . Hillside 7708.   *1977*

Hughes, Linda
☐ ELVIS WON'T BE HERE FOR CHRISTMAS/Here Comes That Hurt Again (Canada). . . Great Northwest Music.   *1979*

Jacks, Warren
☐ THE LEGEND OF A KING/Dream, only dream. . . Paper Dragon 438.   *1977*

Jackson, Skip
☐ THE GREATEST STAR OF ALL/Kent In Kentucky (United Kingdom). . . Alaska 2010.   *1977*

Jefferson, Buzz
☐ A LONELY CHRISTMAS (WITHOUT ELVIS PRESLEY)/ A LONELY CHRISTMAS (WITHOUT ELVIS PRESLEY) (instrumental) (Canada). . . Monpole 618.   *1977*

Jenkins, Jimmy
☐ FAREWELL TO THE KING/Only Myself. . . Seatbelts Fastened EP 60.   *1977*
Elvis Break-in

Jewell, Nancy
☐ A TRIBUTE TO ELVIS (A Memory - We Didn't Get Enough Of You)/Marriage: A 50-50 Deal. . . Pickin' Post 8830.   *1977*

Jones, Carl
☐ ROCK AND ROLL KING/ROCK AND ROLL KING (instrumental). . . CJ 675.   *1977*

Jones, Gene
☐ NEVER AGAIN (WILL THERE BE ANOTHER KING OF ROCK & ROLL)/Fools Hall Of Fame. . . Little Gem 1042.   *1977*

Joyce, Brenda
☐ TO ELVIS/TRIBUTE. . . Treehouse 12510.   *1979*

Kaye, Ronnie
☐ THE KING IS DEAD/THE KING IS DEAD. . . The Scene 1487.   *1977*

Knight, Vicki
☐ TO ELVIS IN HEAVEN/Learning To Love Again. . . American Sound 3096.   *1977*

Kahane, Jackie
☐ REQUIEM FOR ELVIS/REQUIEM FOR ELVIS (instrumental). . . Raintree 2206.   *1977*

Karr, Eddie
☐ ELVIS/ELVIS. . . Memory 38655.   *1977*

Klaus, Oliver
☐ ROCK & ROLL HEAVEN/Flip not known (Canada). . . Aquarius.   *1978*
Mentions Elvis

Koempel, Doug
☐ ROCK ON, AND ON, AND ON/Cold, Cold Ground. . . Chart Action 114.   *1977*

King, Sherry
☐ OUR ELVIS/Pretend. . . MCM 007531.   *1977*

Larry & Vicky
☐ SOUL SALUTE TO ELVIS/How I Wish You Were Here. . . Fraternity 3406.

Lee & Lowe
☐ HOUND DOG MAN'S GONE HOME/Living Without You. . . Music Mill 1011.   *1977*

Lee, Terry
☐ I SING THIS SONG FOR ELVIS/Love Me Tonight (Holland). . . Mercury 6198,171.   *1977*

Leroux, Kelly
☐ MY LITTLE GIRL'S PRAYER (FOR ELVIS)/Wallisville County Jail. . . King's International 5099.   *1977*

Linda Sue
☐ YOU'RE STILL THE KING/OUR MAN ELVIS. . . Clark Country 38818.   *1977*

Lloyd, Melody
☐ ELVIS, A LEGENDARY ANGEL/FORGET ME NEVER. . . Starr 9277.   *1977*

Long, Huey
☐ ELVIS STOLE MY BABY/The Ballad Of John Glenn. . . Rock-it 17077.   *1978*
NOTE: A song recorded before Aug. 16, 1977, but issued on this label after Elvis' death.

Loyd, Harold
☐ A PRAYER FOR ELVIS/A MESSAGE FROM HAROLD. . . Modern Age Enterprises.   *1979*

Luke, Jimmy & Bruce Channel
☐ MY DARLING GINGER [Alden] /Soul Of A Man. . . Le-Cam 512.   *1978*

☐ MY DARLING GINGER [Alden] /THE PASSING OF THE KING. . . LeCam 512/615.   *1978*

Luman, Bob
☐ A CHRISTMAS TRIBUTE/Give Someone You
Love. . . Polydor 14444. This song pays tribute to
both Elvis and Bing Crosby. *1977*
NOTE: It's ironic that, after recording this tribute to the
fallen superstars, death claimed Bob Luman as one of its
next victims.

Lynne, Connie
☐ A TRIBUTE TO ELVIS: MEMORIES OF YOU/A
TRIBUTE TO ELVIS: MEMORIES OF YOU. . . American
Sound 102. *1977*

Magical Music Circus
☐ AMICO ELVIS/TO ELVIS (Italy). . . CGD 10040.
(Side one: Italian - Side two: English) *1977*

Mann, Elgin
☐ IT'S BEEN A YEAR ELVIS/Why Me, Lord (by
Jane Benger) (Canada). . . "E" 77203. *1978*

Marshon, Chris
☐ GOD CALLED ELVIS HOME/ELVIS FOR JUST AN
HOUR OR TWO. . . Nif 1000. *1977*

☐ GOD CALLED ELVIS HOME/ELVIS FOR JUST AN
HOUR OR TWO. . . Phono 2657. *1977*

☐ ELVIS, GOD'S READY FOR A SONG/BLUEST
CHRISTMAS EVER (Without Elvis). . . Phono 2658. *1977*

Matthews (M.D.), Jim
☐ ELVIS THE KING/I Just Can't Leave Your Love
Alone. . . Music Emporium 1176. *1977*

☐ WE'LL HAVE A BLUE CHRISTMAS, ELVIS/Gone
The Old, Come The New. . . Music Emporium 7029. *1977*

McDowell, Roger
☐ STATUE OF A KING/Teach Me Not To
Cry. . . Compass 009. *1977*

McDowell, Ronnie
☐ THE KING IS GONE/Walking Through Georgia
In The Rain. . . Scorpion 135 *1977*

☐ I JUST WANTED YOU TO KNOW/Animal. . . Scorpion
0553, *1978*

McKee, Ron
☐ ELVIS, WE MISS YOU TONIGHT/Be-Bop A Lula. . . American Sound 3090. *1977*

McQueen, Gerri
☐ HIS MISSION/HE MUST BE SINGIN'. . . Geri-Mac
36865. *1979*

Michaels, Andy
☐ WE'LL REMEMBER YOU/Take These Memories
Away. . . El Vee 1355. *1978*

Minter, Pat
☐ LET'S LET ELVIS GET SOME SLEEP/Dog Man. . . Show-
case 1023. *1979*

Mirror, Danny
☐ I REMEMBER ELVIS PRESLEY/I REMEMBER ELVIS
PRESLEY (instrumental) (Holland). . . Poker 15023. *1977*

☐ I REMEMBER ELVIS PRESLEY/I REMEMBER ELVIS
PRESLEY, INCLUDING "ARE YOU LONESOME
TONIGHT" & "CAN'T HELP FALLING IN LOVE"
(United Kingdom). . . Stone 2121. *1977*

☐ I REMEMBER ELVIS PRESLEY/Don't Cry
(Hungary). . . SPKS 70321. *1978*

☐ I REMEMBER ELVIS PRESLEY/Don't Cry
(Czechoslovakia). . . Tonpress 0797. *1978*

☐ I REMEMBER ELVIS PRESLEY/I'm Gonna Love
You (U.S. & Canada). . . Redwood 1001. *1978*

Misty
☐ D.O.A./That's All Right & Blue Moon Of
Kentucky (by Jimmy Ellis). . . Sun 1136. *1977*

Mitchell, Eddy
☐ ET LA VOIX D' ELVIS/La Derniere Seance
(France). . . Barclay 620,373. *1977*

Morgan, Josh
☐ HERE'S TO THE KING/Feelings. . . Fable 310. *1977*

Moseley, John
☐ TUPELO, MISSISSIPPI SON/TUPELO, MISSISSIPPI
SON. . . Moon Pie 1980. *1977*

Munley, Terry
☐ ELVIS, GONE BUT NOT FORGOTTEN/The Dress In
The Window At The Store. . . Fleetwood 7711. *1978*

Murrell, Johnny
☐ ELVIS IN HEAVEN/ELVIS IN HEAVEN. . . B.I. 5043.

Nicholas, Jenny
☐ ELVIS/DADDY GONE BYE-BYE. . . Blue Candle
1525. *1977*

☐ ELVIS/DADDY GONE BYE-BYE (Japan). . . Canyon
Spark 600. *1978*

Nichols, Pamala
☐ DON'T CRY LISA/Don't Think It's Wrong. . . Heart-
song 458. *1977*

North, Angelmaye
☐ PRESLEY, THE KING CADILLAC MAN/PRESLEY,
THE KING CADILLAC MAN. . . High Country 108. *1977*

Norton, Shelia/Evang. Al Ragsdale
☐ ELVIS HAD TWO ANGELS/ELVIS DREAMED AND IT
CAME TRUE (by Evang. Al Ragsdale)/SHE PLACED A
ROSE ON ELVIS PRESLEY'S GRAVE/HE LEFT BEHIND
SO MANY MEMORIES (by Evang. Al Ragsdale). . . Dale
9950. Songs 1 and 3 are by Shelia Norton, 2 and 4 by
Evang. Al Ragsdale. *1978*

Offerman, Gustoav
☐ I REMEMBER ELVIS PRESLEY/Dodzi Nocas
(Czechoslovakia). . . Opus 91330483. *1978*

Olson
☐ KING OF ROCK AND ROLL/I Want Your Loving
Too (Germany). . . Polydor 2054-201. *1978*

Orsi, Phil
☐ A FRIEND I NEVER KNEW/Love Is Slipping
Away. . . Sonic 3030. *1977*

Osborne, Jerry
☐ THE GRACELAND TOUR/No flip side; a one-sided
soundsheet. . . Record Digest 25794. Limited edition,
600 copies made; given as a preimum with the feature
book "Our Best To You." *1979*
Elvis Break-in

Owens, Nell
☐ TO ELVIS, LOVE/I Lost In The Game Of
Love. . . Music City 102878. *1978*

Palmer, Odie
☐ A LETTER TO ELVIS/All I Can See Is You. . . Little
Gem 1020. *1977*

Pascale, Valery & The Soul Affair Orch.
☐ ELVIS SERENADE/ELVIS SERENADE (instrumental)
(Belgium). . . Best Seller 60122.

Peterson, Beth
☐ FOR ELVIS, THE WORLD CRIES/You Say It's All
Over. . . Sound Studios 665. *1977*

Pickard, George
☐ ELVIS, THE MAN FROM TUPELO/ELVIS, THE MAN
FROM TUPELO. . . Bar-Tone 77169. *1977*

Polidori
☐ DO YOU REMEMBER THE KING?/DO YOU REMEMBER
THE KING? (instrumental). . . Vandor 13. *1977*

Prehle, Michelle
☐ A LETTER TO ELVIS/A Little Bit Of Heaven. . . Magic
Carpet 506. *1979*
NOTE: This song was recorded prior to Aug. 16, 1977, but issued
on this label after Elvis' death.

Presley, Grandpa Jesse
☐ THE ROOTS OF ELVIS: "Who's That Kickin' My Dog
Around"/"The Billy Goat Song" / "Swingin' In The
Orchard". . . Legacy Park 2000. From a recording
made in 1958. *1978*

Presley, Vester (Uncle)
☐ A MESSAGE TO ELVIS FANS AND MY FRIENDS/A
MESSAGE TO ELVIS FANS AND MY FRIENDS. . . Ves-
Pres 1. *1979*

Price, David
☐ LOVE HIM TENDER, SWEET JESUS/I Need A
Friend. . . Rice 5075. *1977*

Radcliffe, P. Sterling (With His Sterling Sounds)
☐ THE LONELY KING OF ROCK 'N' ROLL/Roamin'
(Till I Find The One I Love). . . Via 81677. *1977*

Ramos, Juan
☐ (ELVIS PRESLEY) EL REY DEL ROCK 'N' ROLL/Te
Vas Angel Mio (sung in Spanish). . . Teardrop 3397. *1977*

Ray, Leda
☐ CRY, CRY A FEW TEARS FOR ELVIS/Think I'm
Gonna Love You. . . Allied Artists 008. *1977*

Raynor, Wilguis J.C.
☐ MY HEART'S CONTENT (GOODBYE FROM THE KING)/
Just Before Dawn. . . RTF 100. *1977*
☐ A CHRISTMAS LETTER TO DADDY/My Christmas
Came Early. . . RTF 101 (with Donna Jo). *1977*

Real Pros
☐ THE MEMORY OF ELVIS PRESLEY/We Got The
Blues. . . Cinema 7836. *1978*

Reed, Denny
☐ THE KING OF ROCK (HAS MET THE KING)/Ridin'
On Empty. . . Aspire 334. *1977*

Regina
☐ REQUIEM FOR ELVIS/REQUIEM FOR ELVIS (instrumental). . . Phillips 6202,006. (Germany) *1978*

Rich, Frankie
☐ FOR ELVIS/Lori. . . Texas 1004. *1977*

Ringo (not to be confused with Ringo Starr)
☐ GOODBYE ELVIS/GOODBYE ELVIS (instrumental). . . Formule 49-307. (France) *1977*

Rivers, Deke: *See HANSEN BROTHERS*

Roberts, Danny
☐ THE MEMPHIS COWBOY/THE MEMPHIS COW-
BOY. . . Honey Bee 2007. *1977*

Rock Odyssey
☐ A TRIBUTE TO ELVIS/A TRIBUTE TO ELVIS
(Part 2) (France). . . Barclay 620,386.

Romain
☐ ELVIS/Canzonnetta (France). . . Motors 2097226.

Roy, Douglas
☐ DISCO TO THE KING/DISCO TO THE KING
(Canada). . . Smash Disco 8888. A 12-inch single. *1977*

Russell, Leon
☐ ELVIS AND MARILYN/Anita Bryant. . . Paradise
8667. *1978*

Sampson, Jana
☐ (MERRY CHRISTMAS) FROM LISA MARIE/(We've
Got) Christmas On Our Mind (with Randall Parr). . . Rock-
It 501. *1979*

Sampson, Jean
☐ THE TROUBADOUR FROM MEMPHIS/Do You
Believe... Lighthouse 3000. *1977*

Saucedo, Rick
☐ THE KING OF BLUE SUEDE SOUL/JAILHOUSE
ROCK... Eclipse 1732. *1977*

☐ THE LEGEND LIVES ON/HOW GREAT THOU
ART... Fraternity 3416. *1978*

Schilt, Norman
☐ ELVIS IN HEAVEN/It's Not In The Book... Texas
Tornado 4845. *1978*

Scott, Ken
☐ ELVIS' GREATEST SHOW/I Had To Call You
Darlin'... K.E.Y. 8666. *1978*

Scott, Ron
☐ GOODBYE ELVIS/Mrs. Turner (Belgium)... Arti
Bano 1062.

Sexton, Patsy
☐ CHRISTMAS WITHOUT ELVIS/CHRISTMAS CARD
FOR ELVIS... Delta 1151. *1978*

Shilo
☐ GOD BROUGHT THE CURTIN DOWN/Midnight
Music... Shane 001. *1977*

Smith, Chris
☐ KING OF THE ROCK & ROLL SONG/Hank... CMA
001. *1978*

Smith, David
☐ HEROES AND IDOLS (Don't Come Easy)/Loraine
Phillips... MDJ 1004. *1979*

Snow, B.F.
☐ ELVIS IS A LEGEND/LISA IS HER NAME... Dee-
Bee 20. *1977*

Songwriters
☐ CRYING 'BOUT ELVIS/No Night In Heaven... Indian-
head 1112. *1977*

Sovine, Red
☐ THE KING'S LAST CONCERT/Lay Down Sally... Gusto-
Starday 180. *1978*

Staggs, Jimmy
☐ DEAR ELVIS/I DON'T KNOW WHERE I'M GOING
(GOODBYE TO THE KING)... Sagitario 500. *1977*

Summers, Gene
☐ GOODBYE PRISCILLA (BYE BYE BLUE BABY)/
World Of Illusion... Teardrop 3405. *1977*
NOTE: Label was mis-printed; should have read "Bye Bye
Baby Blue."

Sumner, J.D.
☐ ELVIS HAS LEFT THE BUILDING/Sweet, Sweet
Spirit... QCA 461. *1977*

Teardrops
☐ GOODNIGHT ELVIS/Hey Gingerbread... Laurie
3660. *1977*

Tiffin, Barry
☐ CANDY BARS FOR ELVIS/CANDY BARS FOR
ELVIS... Tiffin International 300. *1977*

Tigre, Terry
☐ ELVIS, WE LOVE YOU/ELVIS, WE LOVE
YOU... Gusto-Starday 166. *1977*
NOTE: This single was issued to promote Tigre's album,
bearing the same title. It was never commercially released
to the general public.

Todd, Don
☐ ELVIS DREAMED AND IT CAME TRUE/I DREAMED
ELVIS SANG MY SONG... Dale 437. *1977*

Tollison, Johnny
☐ DARK CLOUD OVER MEMPHIS/DARK CLOUD OVER
MEMPHIS... Klub 5515. *1977*

Tolson, Bill & The Jordanaires
☐ THE LETTER FROM ELVIS/Ain't Love Grand... East-
ern 01. *1978*

Tucker, Tanya
☐ A BIG HUNK O' LOVE/BREAK-UP (by Charlie
Rich) (bootleg release)... Rooster 5002. *1978*

Tune Timers
☐ DEAR ELVIS PRESLEY, GOODBYE/A Mother... Command Performance 390. *1979*

☐ ELVIS, OUR KING/Fantastic Voyage... Command
Performance 404. *1979*

Tunstall, Arkey
☐ IS THE KING DEAD?/As I See It... Brand X 00 *1978*

Turner, Terry
☐ DEDICATION TO A KING/You're Gone... S.D.B.
1198. *1977*

☐ DEDICATION TO A KING/You're Gone... MCM
007533. *1977*

Tura, Will
☐ GOODBYE ELVIS/Hoboken U.S.A... Topkapi
2103 127. (Sung in Flemish) *1977*

☐ GOODBYE ELVIS/Addio... Topkapi 2103 128.
(Sung in English) *1978*

☐ GOODBYE ELVIS/One-sided phonocard, similar
to a soundsheet (Czechoslovakia)... Tonpress 0838. *1978*

Wade, Elvis
☐ MEMORIES OF THE KING/MEMORIES OF THE
KING... Memory 244. *1977*

Wages, Ben
☐ ELVIS IN MEMORIAM/ELVIS IN MEMORIAM... International 2536. *1978*

Westley, Tarry
☐ HE LIVES/You Don't Know Me... Chapman 1118. *1977*

Westmoreland, Kathy
☐ YOU WERE THE MUSIC/What Would I Do Without
My Music. . . Age Of Woman 5789.   *1978*
☐ MY FATHER WATCHES OVER ME/What Am I
Living For. . . Age Of Woman 7144.   *1978*
NOTE: Even though "My Father Watches Over Me" has no
lyrics pertaining directly to Elvis, Kathy sang the song at his
funeral and released it as a tribute to Elvis.

White, Paul
☐ MERRY CHRISTMAS ELVIS/I'm So Lonesome I
Could Cry. . . Spin Chek 16021.
☐ ELVIS, CHRISTMAS WON'T BE CHRISTMAS
WITHOUT YOU/Midnight Girl. . . Country Jubilee
0101.   *1977*

White, Perry
☐ HAPPY BIRTHDAY ELVIS (We Wish You Were
Here)/HAPPY BIRTHDAY ELVIS (We Wish You
Were Here) (instrumental). . . Jet Sounds 16004/5.   *1978*

Whitehouse, Bill
☐ ELVIS: FROM US TO YOU/Two More Days Till
Christmas. . . Independent Sound 101.   *1978*

Whittington, Jim
☐ GOODBYE ELVIS/Will The Circle Be Unbroken. . . Lew
Breyer Productions 178.   *1977*

Williams, Diane
☐ GOODBYE BING, ELVIS, AND GUY/One More
Christmas. . . Little Gem 1022. Pays tribute to Bing
Crosby and Guy Lombardo also.   *1978*

Williams, Roy
☐ I REMEMBER ELVIS/The Fire Of Love Has Gone
Out. . . WB Country Sound 7700.   *1977*

Wright, Lee
☐ CAPRICORN KINGS/Wait Til' Morning. . . Praire
Dust 7628.

Yates, Bill
☐ ELVIS, WE MISS YOU/Golden Guitar. . . Emery
8809.   *1978*

Since nearly all of the songs listed in this section are Elvis
tributes, there is no need to list that beneath every entry. We
will, however, point out those that are not Elvis tributes but
do mention him. An occasional break-in or Elvis break-in
will also be noted in these after-August 16, 1977 releases.
Year of release is given when known.

ELVIS TRIBUTE ALBUMS AND ALBUMS CONTAINING ELVIS TRIBUTES

Most of the albums contained in this section are albums wherin the entire contents is dedicated, in one way or another, to Elvis. In those cases where only a portion of the album pertains to Elvis, we will identify those particular tracks by listing them in capital letters.

Blance, Burt & The King Creoles
☐ LP: TRIBUTE TO ELVIS PRESLEY (National 16 200) (France). Contains songs made famous by Elvis. *1978*

Burnette, Billy Joe
☐ LP: WELCOME HOME ELVIS (Gusto 994). Contains the songs WELCOME HOME ELVIS and THE COLONEL AND THE KING. *1977*

Chavis, Danny
☐ LP: THE KING AND I (Roc-co 77-673). Contains 10 songs made famous by Elvis. *1978*

Donner, Ral
☐ LP: RAL DONNER'S ELVIS SCRAPBOOK (Gone 5033). Contains songs performed in a style similar to Elvis'.

Duty Free
☐ LP: DUTY FREE (EMI 064-18315) (Italy). Contains 24 songs made famous by Elvis.

Ellis, Jimmy
☐ LP: BY REQUEST, ELLIS SINGS ELVIS (Boblo 78-829). Contains songs made famous by Elvis. *1978*
   NOTE: Jimmy Ellis was also featured on the Sun record albums "Duets" (Jerry Lee Lewis & Friends) and "Trio Plus Friends" (Jerry Lee Lewis, Charlie Rich & Carl Perkins). His is the Elvis sound-alike voice. Elvis does not appear on these albums.

Everett, Leon
☐ LP: GOODBYE KING OF ROCK N' ROLL (True 1002). Contains the title song plus THE WORLD'S GREATEST STAR HAS GONE HOME. *1977*

Everett, Vince
☐ LP: ELVIS ON MY MIND - THE LEGEND LIVES ON (States Of America 231). Contains previously issued songs by Everette, some of which are among the best Elvis sound-alikes ever recorded. *1978*

Farago, Johnny
☐ LP: POUR LES AMATEUR D' ELVIS (K-tel 131) (Canada). Contains songs made famous by Elvis, one side sung in French the other in English. *1977*

☐ LP: POUR LES AMATEUR D' ELVIS VOL. 2 (K-tel 136) (Canada). Contains songs made famous by Elvis, some in French. *1978*

Fargo, Donna
☐ LP: SHAME ON ME (Warner Bros. 3099). Contains her Elvis tribute song LOVING YOU, with special narration. *1978*

Fisher, Bobby
☐ LP: CANADA'S OWN ELVIS (GC 2001) (Canada). Contains 15 songs made famous by Elvis. *1977*

Fowler, Wally
☐ LP: A TRIBUTE TO ELVIS (Dove 1000). Contains the song A NEW STAR IN HEAVEN. *1977*

Granberg, Per "Elvis"
☐ LP: ROCKABYE, ROLLABYE (Phillips 6478013) (Norway). Contains songs made famous by Elvis.

☐ LP: I CAN'T STOP LOVING YOU (Phillips 9114017) (Norway). Contains more songs made famous by Elvis.

☐ LP: THE BEST OF PER "ELVIS" GRANBERG (Phillips 6478031) (Norway). Contains eight songs made famous by Elvis, plus other rock standards.

Haggard, Merle
☐ LP: FROM GRACELAND TO THE PROMISED LAND (MCA 2314). Contains Elvis tributes and songs made famous by Elvis. *1977*

Harrison, Bob "Lil' Elvis"
☐ LP: LIL' ELVIS (Lil' Elvis World). Contains five songs made famous by Elvis. *1977*

James, Bucky Dee & The Nashville Explosion
☐ LP: ELVIS: A TRIBUTE TO THE KING (Springboard 6015). Contains songs made famous by Elvis. *1978*

Jordanaires
☐ LP: CHRISTMAS TO ELVIS (Classic 1935). Contains songs made famous by Elvis. *1978*

Little Tony
☐ LP: TRIBUTE TO ELVIS (International Kris 2004) (Italy). Contains songs made famous by Elvis. *1978*

☐ LP: TONY CANTA ELVIS (RCA 1190) (Italy). Contains songs made famous by Elvis, sung in Italian. *1978*

McDowell, Ronnie
☐ LP: THE KING IS GONE (Scorpion 8021). Contains the title hit plus his version of "Heartbreak Hotel." *1977*

☐ LP: A TRIBUTE TO THE KING, IN MEMORY (Scorpion 0015). Contains THE KING IS GONE plus songs made famous by Elvis. *1979*

☐ LP: SOUNDTRACK FROM "ELVIS THE MOVIE" (DCP 79). Contains the songs from the film, all of which relate to Elvis' life story. *1979*

Offerman, Gustav
☐ LP: A JEHO SOLISTI (Opus 91130677) (Czechoslovakia). Contains the song I REMEMBER ELVIS PRESLEY. *1978*

101 Strings
☐ LP: 101 STRINGS PLAY A TRIBUTE TO ELVIS PRESLEY (Alshire 5348). Contains eight instrumental versions of Elvis' songs.

Perry, Eden & The Nashville Pops
☐ LP: THE HITS OF ELVIS PRESLEY (Windmill 255) (England). Contains songs made famous by Elvis.

Peterson, Beth
☐ LP: FOR ELVIS THE WORLD CRIES (Sound Studios 5230). Contains tribute songs and songs made famous by Elvis.

Schaeffer, Randy
☐ LP: JUST LIKE ELVIS (Olympus 1004). Contains songs made famous by Elvis.   *1978*

Sexton, Patsy
☐ LP: ELVIS ON MY MIND (Delta 1002). Contains 12 tracks about Elvis' life.   *1978*

Smith, S. Presley
☐ LP: REMEMBA ME (Celestial Sound 8074). Contents too strange to describe!

Sumner, J.D. & The Stamps
☐ LP: ELVIS' FAVORITE GOSPEL SONGS (QCA 362). Contains gospel songs. First pressing.   *1977*

☐ LP: ELVIS' FAVORITE GOSPEL SONGS (QCA 362). Later pressings had a disclaimer on the cover stating that Elvis' voice was not heard on the LP.   *1977*

☐ LP: MEMORIES OF OUR FRIEND ELVIS (Blue Mark 373). Double album containing a live appearance by J.D. Sumner and the Stamps, doing their Elvis tribute show.   *1978*

Tigre, Terry
☐ LP: ELVIS, WE LOVE YOU (Gusto-Starday 993). Contains title track plus songs made famous by Elvis.   *1977*

Thunderbird Singers
☐ LP: THE KING'S MUSIC (Thunderbird Prod. Inc. 34234). Contains 28 songs made famous by Elvis.

Various Artists
☐ LP: TO ELVIS: LOVE STILL BURNING (Fotoplay 1001). An Elvis picture disc that does not feature his voice. Contains 11 songs of tribute by 11 different artists. First pressings; white cover.   *1978*

☐ LP: TO ELVIS: LOVE STILL BURNING (Fotoplay 1001). Later pressings; black cover.   *1978*

Wild Honey Singers
LP: A CHILD'S INTRODUCTION TO ELVIS PRESLEY (Kid Stuff 1002). Contains songs made famous by Elvis.

ELVIS ACETATES

For those who may not be familiar with the world of Elvis acetates, a brief explanation is in order.

An acetate is basically a phonograph record that is individually "cut," as compared to the "stamping" process used on mass-produced records. Each disc receives a coating of cellulose acetate, thus the origin of the term acetate. Once in awhile, an old-timer in the industry will refer to acetates as a "lacquer." Again, this is in reference to the lacquer or cellulose derivative finish on the disc.

Film studios used acetates in the fifties to be able to program a certain song into a script at a given moment. Since Elvis did so many films that included his singing (lip sync) of songs, there were many acetates containing his voice, although by the time he got out of the army tapes had pretty much replaced the discs.

Recording studios had many uses for the acetate. One of the most common was that they were given to the artists and musicians involved in a particular session, in order to either become more familiar with the material or just to hear the final results.

Elvis acetates can be found in several sizes, but the 7-inch, 8-inch and 12-inch discs seem to be the most common. Some are recorded on both sides, others just on one side. Each one will bear the label (if a label is used) of its manufacturer.

When it comes to value, there could be a world of difference between two seemingly identical acetates. The most important consideration, among collectors, is the specific material. If the song(s) are exactly the same as the commonly available version, then the acetate will only be of novelty interest.

On the other hand, if the acetate contains a song that has not yet been overdubbed (the "pure Elvis" sound), it will be in great demand. Most acetates fall into this catagory.

If you've uncovered an acetate that has an alternate take of a known Elvis song, or better yet, a song that has never been heard by Elvis fans, then you've struck gold. The most astonishing discovery of this type is probably the Louisiana Hayride demonstration acetate that featured Elvis singing "Maybellene" the Chuck Berry classic.

Based on the divergent prices paid, and asked, for the few Elvis acetates that have surfaced, we have arrived at the following price guidelines.

All prices are given for discs in near-mint condition. Use and abuse will cause the values to drop proportionately.

SMALL ACETATES: (Up to 8-inches)

Same material as commonly released: *$25 - $100 range*
Without overdubbing ("pure Elvis"): *$100 - $300 range*
Alternate take(s): *$200 - $500 range*
Unreleased material: *$500 and up range*

LARGE ACETATES: (10-inch and 12-inch)

Simply double the appropiate price range given for samll the small acetates.

Remember, these are only a range of prices, given as a guideline to assist you in buying, selling and trading.

And don't be surprised if the value drops on certain acetates that contain material that has appeared on unauthorized releases.

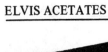

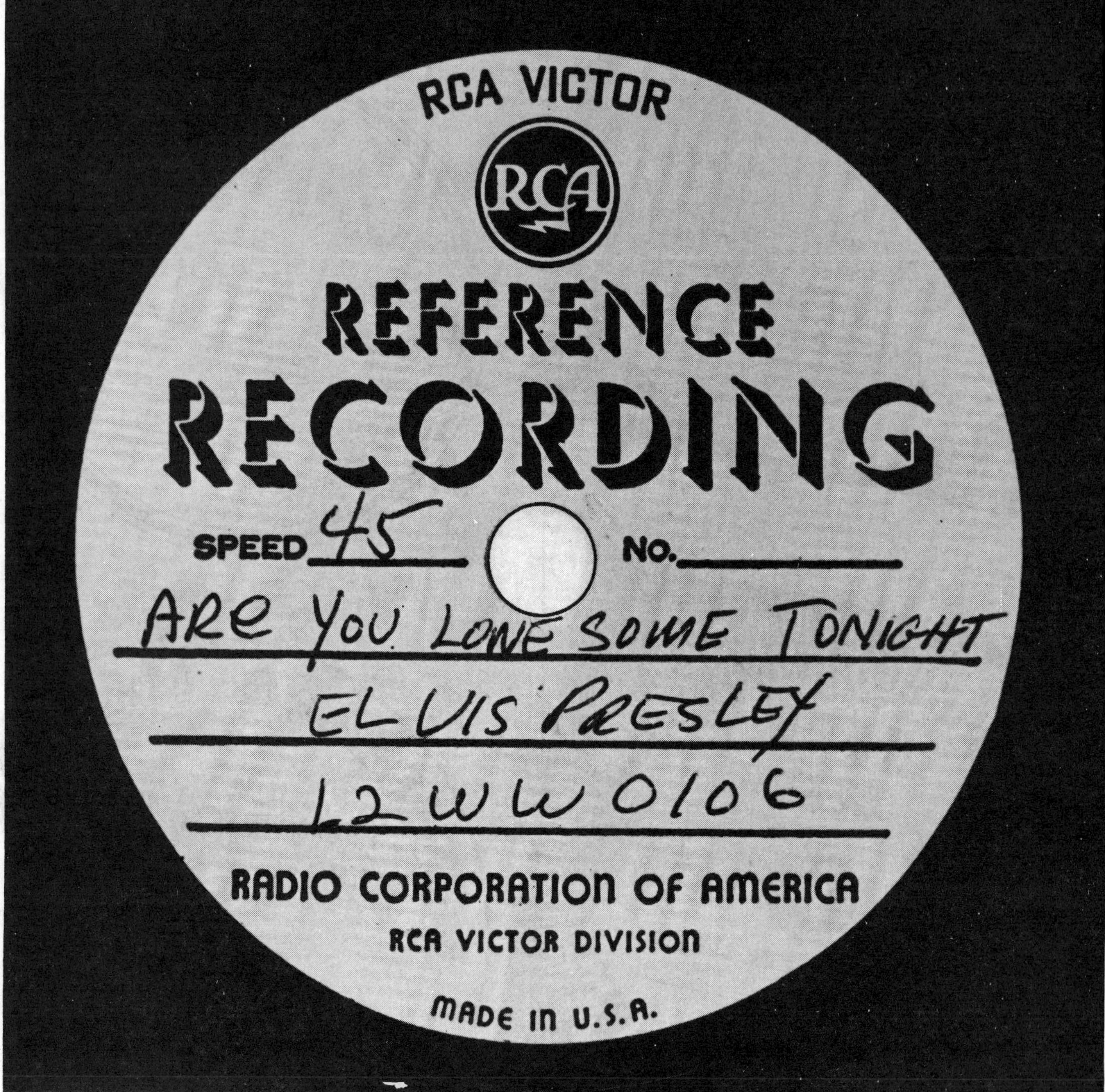

RCA VICTOR

REFERENCE RECORDING

SPEED 45 NO.

ARE YOU LONESOME TONIGHT

ELVIS PRESLEY

L2 WW 0106

RADIO CORPORATION OF AMERICA

RCA VICTOR DIVISION

MADE IN U.S.A.

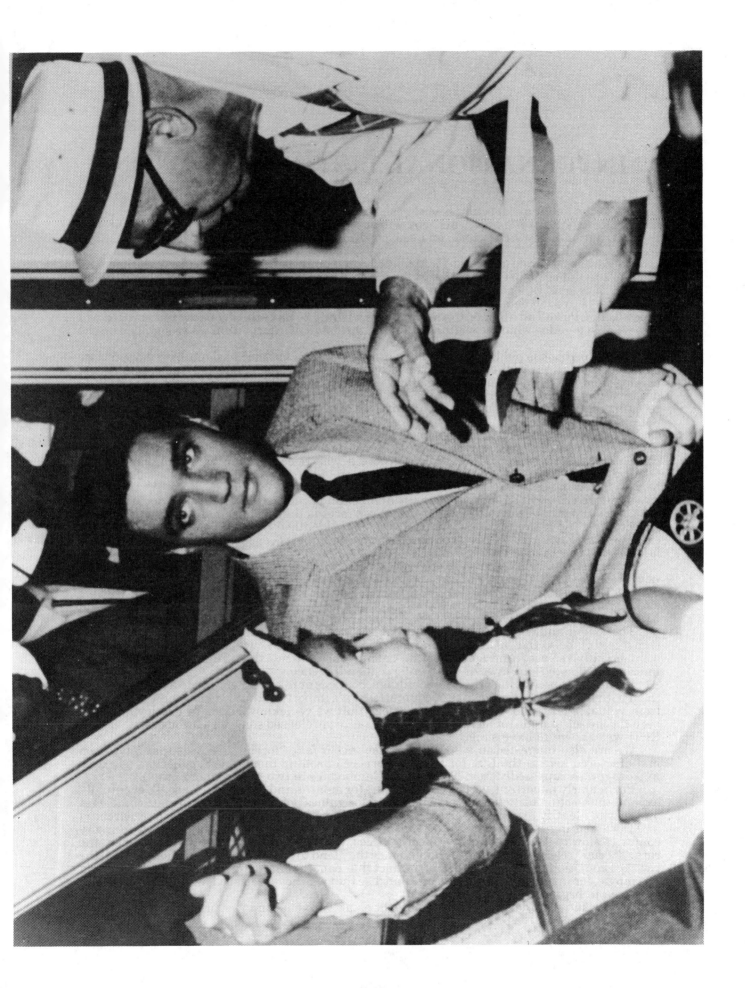

INTERNATIONAL LISTINGS SECTION

Growth in the hobby of collecting Elvis Presley records has great serious potential from putting his friends together worldwide. This book will accomplish much towards that end, first through the International Elvis Directory, and second through expanding the International Listings section that follows.

These listings from randomly-contributed key countries have begun the task they said "couldn't be done," to list every record ever released by Elvis anywhere in the world! All credit sources, of course, who contribute towards this goal will be acknowledged in print!

No facts are too detailed or of no interest. We want all information on all singles (at all speeds), all EPs and all albums. Correspondents wishing to have their country represented will be best able to judge what we want by studying the detail of information we've supplied on the U.S. listings.

Since this book is published in English (and its authors not multi-lingual), we'd appreciate English translations of the songs and/or album titles submitted, as well as label names and catalog numbers (if not in arabic numerals, as used in this guide). It is also very important to describe physical characteristics of the labels, sleeves or jackets, information that would be recognizable to someone from another part of the world—not just English speaking—who might obtain copies.

In other words, we want this guide to be useful to anybody, anywhere, who understands English. We want any reader, worldwide, to be able to identify, authenticate and determine the contents of any Elvis record, regardless where it was released or in what language it was labelled! Photographs, in addition to descriptions, would be helpful and in some few cases we'll be able to reproduce them in future editions.

What we print will be dependent on the number and accuracy of our sources. So far, some of our contributors have submitted to us only those records they feel would be of interest to U.S. collectors and have omitted their country's versions of identical U.S. releases. Actually, we want to know of *all* Elvis product in all countries (except for imports), even if the only difference is the labelled country of manufacture!

Any information is better than none, even if it is only to settle once and for all that a country never released an Elvis record of its own. Then we can stop looking and wondering! We received a nice letter, for instance, from Harri Salo, who resides in Espoo, Finland, informing us that his country produced no Elvis records, only importing them mostly from West Germany and Great Britain, and occasionally from the U.S., Canada, Italy and possibly a few other countries.

The extent and depth of our interest extends to the unauthorized as well as to legitimate, franchised labels and RCA subsidiaries. By "unauthorized" we mean labels that were commercially released and sold over the counter in countries that either don't subscribe to international copyright laws or don't enforce its adherence.

We have no interest in "private" recordings, bootlegs or fakes, other than to avoid confusing them with real product. In the case of counterfeits, it's important that we know how to tell them from valuable originals. The few U.S. bootlegs that we've acknowledged in Presleyana have been for the sole purpose of identifying commercially unreleased songs or various versions that Elvis was known to have sung.

We are also interested in stopping the issuance if fake "foreign" records that have been manufactured here in the U.S. for the sole purpose of selling them to U.S. collectors as exotic imports (fakes supposedly from Turkey and Cambodia are two that come to mind).

Particularly important, we feel, are the years (or months and years) of release. To eventually expand this section to include established collector values on these records, the dates of release and how to identify first pressings will have to be known. Since the difficulties in researching and documenting later pressings and reissues may make the commercial releases in many countries slow to develop accurate collector prices, we feel that it is important to document the rare "special" releases as soon as possible, since they tend to set the precedents and establish the trends. Promotional releases or special product that came out in commemoration of the opening of a movie, for instance, or any short-lifespan disc that was never reissued, will be the surest and best area to begin.

As we cautiously delve into and explore the establishment of market prices on international releases, we face the instant question: what are they worth *here* versus what are they worth *there*? The money a collector will pay must always be more in the U.S. Obviously, if a Japanese release, for instance, is worth a certain amount on the open market in Tokyo, an American collector will expect to have to pay that amount, plus what it costs to get it here, plus what will be lost in the money exchange, plus compensation for the extra effort in making the sale.

We are interested, too, in international tributes to Elvis (many are already documented in Presleyana) and songs from other countries *about* Elvis. In some cases, if the lyrics are particularly noteworthy, a translation would be appreciated, though not expected.

Among the countries we hope to include in the expanded second edition of Presleyana, but not limited to these, are: Argentina, Australia, Belgium, Brazil, Canada, China, Denmark, Egypt, France, Greece, India, Italy, Japan, Malaysia, Mexico, The Netherlands, New Zealand, Peru, The Philippines, Portugal, South Africa, Spain, Taiwan, Uruguay, Venezuela, and Yugoslavia.

To correspondents in the countries already published: remember, additional listings are equally important!

We wish again to thank our first correspondents and to solicit lists from individuals and fan clubs worldwide. We are especially interested in obtaining the names and addresses of all fan clubs, since through their memberships we may be able to trace and get answers to the inevitable puzzles that will arise as we near our goals. Address all correspondence to:

Jellyroll Productions
Box 3017
Scottsdale, Arizona 85257
U.S.A.

ENGLAND

By Tony Neale

ELVIS' SINGLE RELEASES IN GREAT BRITAIN

The first 13 British Elvis singles appeared on the HMV label. HMV was essentially His Masters Voice, and the HMV label had the familiar RCA dog, Nipper, on it.

HMV POP 182: HEARTBREAK HOTEL/I WAS THE ONE (March 1956)
HMV POP 213: BLUE SUEDE SHOES/TUTTI FRUTTI (June 1956)
HMV POP 235: I WANT YOU, I NEED YOU, I LOVE YOU/MY BABY LEFT ME (July 1956)
HMV POP 249: DON'T BE CRUEL/HOUND DOG (October 1956)
HMV POP 272: BLUE MOON/I DON'T CARE IF THE SUN DON'T SHINE (November 1956)
HMV POP 253: LOVE ME TENDER/ANYWAY YOU WANT ME (THAT'S HOW I'LL BE) (December 1956)
HMV POP 295: MYSTERY TRAIN/LOVE ME (February 1957)
HMV POP 305: BABY, LET'S PLAY HOUSE/RIP IT UP (March 1957)
HMV POP 330: TOO MUCH/PLAYING FOR KEEPS (April 1957)
HMV POP 359: ALL SHOOK UP/THAT'S WHEN YOUR HEARTACHES BEGIN (June 1957)
HMV POP 378: PARALYSED/WHEN MY BLUE MOON TURNS TO GOLD AGAIN (August 1957)
HMV POP 408: LAWDY MISS CLAWDY/TRYING TO GET TO YOU (October 1957)
HMV POP 428: I'M LEFT, YOU'RE RIGHT, SHE'S GONE/HOW DO YOU THINK I FEEL (January 1958)

There was an additional HMV single —a European issue, not officially issued in Great Britain— that appeared only on 45rpm single. It should also be noted that this is the rarest of all the HMV single releases.

HMV 7MC42: MYSTERY TRAIN/I FORGOT TO REMEMBER TO FORGET

RCA Victor 1013: TEDDY BEAR/LOVING YOU (July 1957)
RCA Victor 1020: PARTY/GOT A LOT O' LIVIN' TO DO (October 1957)
RCA Victor 1025: SANTA BRING MY BABY BACK TO ME/SANTA CLAUS IS BACK IN TOWN (November 1957)
RCA Victor 1028: JAILHOUSE ROCK/TREAT ME NICE (January 1958)
RCA Victor 1043: DON'T/I BEG OF YOU (February 1958)
RCA Victor 1058: WEAR MY RING AROUND YOUR NECK/DONCHA' THINK IT'S TIME (May 1958)
RCA Victor 1070: HARD HEADED WOMAN/DON'T ASK ME WHY (July 1958)
RCA Victor 1081: KING CREOLE/DIXIELAND ROCK (September 1958)
RCA Victor 1088: ALL SHOOK UP/THAT'S WHEN YOUR HEART-ACHES BEGIN (October 1958)
RCA Victor 1095: HOUND DOG/BLUE SUEDE SHOES (October 1958)
RCA Victor 1100: I GOT STUNG/ONE NIGHT (January 1959)
RCA Victor 1113: I NEED YOUR LOVE TONIGHT/(NOW AND THEN THERE'S) A FOOL SUCH AS I (April 1959)
RCA Victor 1136: A BIG HUNK O' LOVE/MY WISH CAME TRUE (July 1959)
RCA Victor 1187: STUCK ON YOU/FAME AND FORTUNE (1960)
RCA Victor 1194: A MESS OF BLUES/GIRL OF MY BEST FRIEND (1960)
RCA Victor 1207: IT'S NOW OR NEVER/MAKE ME KNOW IT (1960)
RCA Victor 1216: ARE YOU LONESOME TO-NIGHT/I GOTTA KNOW (1961)
RCA Victor 1226: WOODEN HEART/TONIGHT IS SO RIGHT FOR LOVE (1961)
RCA Victor 1227: SURRENDER/LONELY MAN (1961)
RCA Victor 1244: WILD IN THE COUNTRY/I FEEL SO BAD (1961)
RCA Victor 1258: LITTLE SISTER/(MARIE'S THE NAME) HIS LATEST FLAME (1961)
RCA Victor 1270: CAN'T HELP FALLING IN LOVE/ROCK-A-HULA BABY (1961)
RCA Victor 1280: GOOD LUCK CHARM/ANYTHING THAT'S PART OF YOU (1962)
RCA Victor 1303: SHE'S NOT YOU/JUST TELL HER JIM SAID HELLO (1962)
RCA Victor 1320: RETURN TO SENDER/WHERE DO YOU COME FROM (1962)

RCA Victor 1337: ONE BROKEN HEART FOR SALE/THEY REMIND ME TOO MUCH OF YOU (1963)
RCA Victor 1355: DEVIL IN DISGUISE/PLEASE DON'T DRAG THAT STRING AROUND (1963)
RCA Victor 1374: BOSSA NOVA BABY/WITCHCRAFT (1963)
RCA Victor 1375: KISS ME QUICK/SOMETHING BLUE (1963)
RCA Victor 1390: VIVA LAS VEGAS/WHAT'D I SAY (1964)
RCA Victor 1404: KISSIN' COUSINS/IT HURTS ME (1964)
RCA Victor 1411: SUCH A NIGHT/NEVER ENDING (1964)
RCA Victor 1422: AIN'T THAT LOVING YOU BABY/ASK ME (1964)
RCA Victor 1430: BLUE CHRISTMAS/WHITE CHRISTMAS (1964)
RCA Victor 1443: DO THE CLAM/YOU'LL BE GONE (1965)
RCA Victor 1455: CRYING IN THE CHAPEL/I BELIEVE IN THE MAN IN THE SKY (1965)
RCA Victor 1489: TELL ME WHY/PUPPET ON A STRING (1965)
RCA Victor 1504: BLUE RIVER/DO NOT DISTURB (1965)
RCA Victor 1509: FRANKIE AND JOHNNY/PLEASE DON'T STOP LOVING ME (1966)
RCA Victor 1526: LOVE LETTERS/COME WHAT MAY (1966)
RCA Victor 1545: ALL THAT I AM/SPINOUT (1966)
RCA Victor 1557: IF EVERY DAY WAS LIKE CHRISTMAS/HOW WOULD YOU LIKE TO BE (1966)
RCA Victor 1565: INDESCRIBABLY BLUE/FOOLS FALL IN LOVE (1967)
RCA Victor 1593: THE LOVE MACHINE/YOU GOTTA STOP (1967)
RCA Victor 1616: LONG LEGGED GIRL (WITH A SHORT DRESS ON)/ THAT'S SOMEONE YOU NEVER FORGET (1967)
RCA Victor 1628: THERE'S ALWAYS ME/JUDY (1967)
RCA Victor 1642: BIG BOSS MAN/YOU DON'T KNOW ME (1968)
RCA Victor 1663: GUITAR MAN/HIGH HEEL SNEAKERS (1968)
RCA Victor 1688: U.S. MALE/STAY AWAY (1968)
RCA Victor 1714: YOUR TIME HASN'T COME YET BABY/LET YOURSELF GO (1968)
RCA Victor 1747: YOU'LL NEVER WALK ALONE/WE CALL ON HIM (1968)
RCA Victor 1768: A LITTLE LESS CONVERSATION/ALMOST IN LOVE (1968)
RCA 1795: IF I CAN DREAM/MEMORIES (1969)
RCA 1831: IN THE GHETTO/ANY DAY NOW (1969)
RCA 1869: CLEAN UP YOUR OWN BACKYARD/THE FAIR IS MOVING ON (1969)
RCA 1900: SUSPICIOUS MINDS/YOU'LL THINK OF ME (1969)
RCA 1916: DON'T CRY DADDY/RUBBERNECKIN' (1970)
RCA 1949: KENTUCKY RAIN/MY LITTLE FRIEND (1970)
RCA 1974: THE WONDER OF YOU/MAMA LIKED THE ROSES (1970)
RCA 1999: I'VE LOST YOU/THE NEXT STEP IS LOVE (1970)
RCA 2046: YOU DON'T HAVE TO SAY YOU LOVE ME/PATCH IT UP (1970)
RCA 2060: THERE GOES MY EVERYTHING/I REALLY DON'T WANT TO KNOW (1971)
RCA 2084: RAGS TO RICHES/WHERE DID THEY GO LORD (1971)
RCA (Maximillion) 2104: HEARTBREAK HOTEL/HOUND DOG-DON'T BE CRUEL (1971) (a multi-track single)
RCA 2125: I'M LEAVIN'/HEART OF ROME (1971)
RCA (Maximillion) 2153: JAILHOUSE ROCK-ARE YOU LONESOME TO-NIGHT/TEDDY BEAR-STEADFAST, LOYAL AND TRUE (1971)
RCA 2158: I JUST CAN'T HELP BELIEVIN'/HOW THE WEB IS WOVEN (1971)
RCA 2188: UNTIL IT'S TIME FOR YOU TO GO/WE CAN MAKE THE MORNING (1972)
RCA 2229: AN AMERICAN TRILOGY/THE FIRST TIME EVER I SAW YOUR FACE (1972)
RCA 2267: BURNING LOVE/IT'S A MATTER OF TIME (1972)
RCA 2304: SEPARATE WAYS/ALWAYS ON MY MIND (1972)
RCA 2359: POLK SALAD ANNIE/C.C. RIDER (1973)
RCA 2393: FOOL/STEAMROLLER BLUES (1973)
RCA 2435: RAISED ON ROCK/FOR OLD TIMES SAKE (1973)
RCA APBO-0196: I'VE GOT A THING ABOUT YOU BABY/TAKE GOOD CARE OF HER (1974)
RCA APBO-0280: IF YOU TALK IN YOUR SLEEP/HELP ME (1974)
RCA 2458: MY BOY/LOVING ARMS (1974)
RCA PB-10074: PROMISED LAND/IT'S MIDNIGHT (1975)

RCA 2562: T-R-O-U-B-L-E/MR. SONGMAN (1975)
RCA (Maximillion) 2601: BLUE MOON/YOU'RE A HEARTBREAKER/
    I'M LEFT, YOU'RE RIGHT, SHE'S GONE (a multi-track
    single)
RCA 2635: GREEN GREEN GRASS OF HOME/THINKING ABOUT
    YOU (1975)
RCA 2674: HURT/FOR THE HEART (1976)
RCA 2694: ALL SHOOK UP/HEARTBREAK HOTEL (1977)
RCA 2695: JAILHOUSE ROCK/TREAT ME NICE (1977)
RCA 2696: I GOT STUNG/ONE NIGHT (1977)
RCA 2697: I NEED YOUR LOVE TONIGHT/(NOW AND THEN
    THERE'S) A FOOL SUCH AS I (1977)
RCA 2698: IT'S NOW OR NEVER/MAKE ME KNOW IT (1977)
RCA 2699: ARE YOU LONESOME TO-NIGHT/I GOTTA KNOW (1977)
RCA 2700: WOODEN HEART/TONIGHT IS SO RIGHT FOR LOVE
    (1977)
RCA 2701: SURRENDER/LONELY MAN (1977)
RCA 2702: (MARIE'S THE NAME) HIS LATEST FLAME/LITTLE
    SISTER (1977)
RCA 2703: CAN'T HELP FALLING IN LOVE/ROCK-A-HULA BABY
    (1977)
RCA 2704: GOOD LUCK CHARM/ANYTHING THAT'S PART OF
    YOU (1977)
RCA 2705: SHE'S NOT YOU/JUST TELL HER JIM SAID HELLO (1977)
RCA 2706: RETURN TO SENDER/WHERE DO YOU COME FROM
    (1977)
RCA 2707: DEVIL IN DISGUISE/PLEASE DON'T DRAG THAT
    STRING AROUND (1977)
RCA 2708: CRYING IN THE CHAPEL/I BELIEVE IN THE MAN IN
    THE SKY (1977)
RCA 2709: THE WONDER OF YOU/MAMA LIKED THE ROSES (1977)
RCA 2729: GIRL OF MY BEST FRIEND/A MESS OF BLUES (1977)
RCA 2768: SUSPICION/(IT'S A) LONG LONELY HIGHWAY (1977)
RCA PB-0857: MOODY BLUE/SHE THINKS I STILL CARE (1977)
RCA PB-0998: WAY DOWN/PLEDGING MY LOVE (1977)
RCA PB-9265: DON'T BE CRUEL/HOUND DOG (1978)
RCA PB-9334: OLD SHEP/PARALYSED (1978)
RCA PB-1165: MY WAY/AMERICA (1977)
RCA PB-9464: IT WON'T SEEM LIKE CHRISTMAS/MERRY
    CHRISTMAS BABY (1979)
RCA PC-9464: IT WON'T SEEM LIKE CHRISTMAS/MERRY
    CHRISTMAS BABY (1979) (special 12-inch edition)

MORE ON BRITISH SINGLES:

The HMV 78s came in a plain brown cover, while the 45s had a cream
and scarlet sleeve. The 78 labels were light blue with black and white lettering. The 45rpm labels were pink; first pressed with gold lettering, then
issued with white letters.

The RCA singles, up until the late sixties, were issued in a red and white
paper sleeve. In case you're wondering, the picture sleeves that you had in
the States were not issued here. The pre-army singles had the triangular
centres (small hole, but could be punched out to make larger hole), on the
originals, although were repressed using the standard 45rpm size hole.

The popular
Elvis talking
disc, "The
Truth About
Me," as issued
in England.

ELVIS' EXTENDED PLAYS IN GREAT BRITAIN

HMV 7EG-8199: LOVE ME TENDER (February 1957)
HMV 7EG-8256: GOOD ROCKIN' TONIGHT (September 1957)
RCA Victor RCX-101: PEACE IN THE VALLEY (1957)
RCA Victor RCX-104: ELVIS PRESLEY (I NEED YOU SO) (1957)
RCA Victor RCX-106: JAILHOUSE ROCK (1958)
RCA Victor RCX-117: KING CREOLE VOL. 1 (1958)
RCA Victor RCX-118: KING CREOLE VOL. 2 (1958)
RCA Victor RCX-121: ELVIS SINGS CHRISTMAS SONGS (1958)*
RCA Victor RCX-131: ELVIS SAILS (1958)
RCA Victor RCX-135: ELVIS IN A TENDER MOOD (1959)
RCA Victor RCX-175: STRICTLY ELVIS (OLD SHEP) (1959)
RCA Victor RCX-1045: A TOUCH OF GOLD, VOL. 1 (1959)
RCA Victor RCX-1048: A TOUCH OF GOLD, VOL. 2 (1960)
RCA Victor RCX-190: SUCH A NIGHT (1960)
RCA Victor RCX-211: FOLLOW THAT DREAM (1962)
RCA Victor RCX-7106: KID GALAHAD (1963)
RCA Victor RCX-7141: LOVE IN LAS VEGAS (1964)
RCA Victor RCX-7142: ELVIS FOR YOU, VOL. 1 (1964)
RCA Victor RCX-7143: ELVIS FOR YOU, VOL. 2 (1964)
RCA Victor RCX-7173: TICKLE ME, VOL. 1 (1965)
RCA Victor RCX-7174: TICKLE ME, VOL. 2 (1965)
RCA Victor RCX-7187: EASY COME, EASY GO (1967) †

* First pressings of the "Elvis Sings Christmas Songs" EP had a fold-away
back cover, showing the same photo of Elvis as seen on the back cover of
the (U.K.) "Elvis' Golden Records" LP.

† The British version of "Easy Come, Easy Go" EP had only four tracks,
as the 45rpm single of "The Love Machine"/"You Gotta Stop" offered
the other two songs.

ELVIS' LONG PLAYS IN GREAT BRITAIN

HMV CLP-1093: ELVIS PRESLEY-ROCK & ROLL (1956)
HMV CLP-1105: ELVIS-ROCK & ROLL No. 2 (1957)
HMV DLP-1159: THE BEST OF ELVIS (10-inch LP) (1957)
RCA Victor RC-24001: LOVING YOU (10-inch LP) (1957)
RCA Victor RD-27052: ELVIS' CHRISTMAS ALBUM (1957)
RCA Victor RD-27088: KING CREOLE (1958)
RCA Victor (Red Seal) RB-16069: ELVIS' GOLDEN RECORDS (1958)
RCA Victor RD-27120: ELVIS (1959)
RCA Victor RD-27128: A DATE WITH ELVIS (1959)
RCA Victor RD-27159: ELVIS' GOLDEN RECORDS, VOL. 2 (1960)
RCA Victor RD-27171/SF-6060: ELVIS IS BACK (1960)
RCA Victor RD-27192/SF-5078: G.I. BLUES (1960)
RCA Victor RD-27211/SF-5094: HIS HAND IN MINE (1960)
RCA Victor RD-27244/SF-5106: SOMETHING FOR EVERYBODY (1961)
RCA Victor RD-27238/SF-5115: BLUE HAWAII (1961)
RCA Victor RD-27265/SF-5135: POT LUCK WITH ELVIS (1962)
RCA Victor RD-7528/SF-7528: ROCK & ROLL No. 2 (reissue) (1963)
RCA Victor RD-7534/SF-7534: GIRLS! GIRLS! GIRLS! (1963)
RCA Victor RD-7565/SF-7565: IT HAPPENED AT THE WORLD'S FAIR
    (1963)
RCA Victor RD-7609/SF-7609: FUN IN ACAPULCO (1963)
RCA Victor RD-7630/SF-7630: ELVIS' GOLDEN RECORDS, VOL. 3
    (1964)
RCA Victor RD-7645/SF-7645: KISSIN' COUSINS (1964)
RCA Victor RD-7678/SF-7678: ROUSTABOUT (1964)
RCA Victor RD-7714/SF-7714: GIRL HAPPY (1965)
RCA Victor RD-7723: FLAMING STAR & SUMMER KISSES (1965)
    (reissue of 10-inch "Loving You" LP, plus newer songs)
RCA Victor RD-7752/SF-7752: ELVIS FOR EVERYONE (1965)
RCA Victor RD-7767/SF-7767: HAREM HOLIDAY (1966)
RCA Victor RD-7793/SF-7793: FRANKIE AND JOHNNY (1966)
RCA Victor RD-7810/SF-7810: PARADISE HAWAIIAN STYLE (1966)
RCA Victor RD-7820/SF-7820: CALIFORNIA HOLIDAY (1966)
    (issued in the States as "Spinout")
RCA Victor RD-7867/SF-7867: HOW GREAT THOU ART (1967)
RCA Victor RD-7892/SF-7892: DOUBLE TROUBLE (1967)
RCA Victor RD-7917/SF-7917: CLAMBAKE (1967)
RCA Victor RD-7924/SF-7924: ELVIS' GOLD RECORDS, VOL. 4 (1968)
RCA International INTS-1012: ELVIS SINGS FLAMING STAR (1969)
RCA RD-8011/PL-42370: ELVIS (NBC-TV SPECIAL) (1969)
RCA RD-8029/SF-8029: FROM ELVIS IN MEMPHIS (1969)
RCA International INTS-1103: LET'S BE FRIENDS (1970)
RCA SF-8080/I: FROM MEMPHIS TO VEGAS/FROM VEGAS TO
    MEMPHIS (1970)

RCA SF-8128: ON STAGE - FEBRUARY, 1970 (1970)
RCA International INT-1126: ELVIS' CHRISTMAS ALBUM (1970)
RCA LPM-6401: WORLDWIDE 50 GOLD AWARD HITS, VOL. 1 (1970)
RCA International INTS-1206: ALMOST IN LOVE (1970)
RCA SF-8162: THAT'S THE WAY IT IS (1971)
RCA Camden CDM-1088: YOU'LL NEVER WALK ALONE (1971)
RCA SF-8172: ELVIS COUNTRY (I'M 10,000 YEARS OLD) (1971)
RCA International INTS-1286: C'MON EVERYBODY (1971)
RCA SF-8202: LOVE LETTERS FROM ELVIS (1971)
RCA LPM-6402: WORLDWIDE GOLD AWARD HITS, VOL. 2 - THE
        OTHER SIDES (1971)
RCA SF-8221: ELVIS SINGS THE WONDERFUL WORLD OF
        CHRISTMAS (1971)
RCA International INT-1322: I GOT LUCKY (1971)
RCA SF-8233: ROCK & ROLL (reissue of HMV CLP-1093) (1972)
RCA SF-8266: ELVIS NOW (1972)
RCA SF-8275: HE TOUCHED ME (1972)
RCA SF-8296: ELVIS AS RECORDED AT MADISON SQUARE
        GARDEN (1972)
RCA Camden CDS-1110: BURNING LOVE AND HITS FROM HIS
        MOVIES, VOL. 2 (1972)
RCA DPS-2040: ALOHA FROM HAWAII VIA SATELLITE (1973)
RCA Camden CDS-1118: SEPARATE WAYS (1973)
RCA SF-8378: ELVIS (INCLUDING "FOOL") (1973)
RCA APM1-0818: HAVING FUN WITH ELVIS ON STAGE (1974)
RCA LPL1-7527: HITS OF THE 70'S (1974)
RCA APL1-0388: RAISED ON ROCK (1974)
RCA CPL1-0341: A LEGENDARY PERFORMER, VOL. 1 (1974)
RCA SPL1-0475: GOOD TIMES
RCA APL1-0606: ELVIS LIVE ON STAGE IN MEMPHIS (1974)
RCA APL1-0873: PROMISED LAND (1975)
ARCADE ADE-P-12: ELVIS' 40 GREATEST (1975)
RCA RS-1011: ELVIS TODAY (1975)
RCA Camden CDS-1146: EASY COME, EASY GO (1975)
RCA Camden CDS-1150: ELVIS - U.S. MALE (1975)
RCA Starcall HY-1001: THE SUN COLLECTION (1975)
RCA GELV-6A: ELVIS PRESLEY'S GREATEST HITS (1975)
        (Reader's Digest 6-LP box set, plus a bonus LP)
RCA Starcall HY-1023: PICTURES OF ELVIS (1976)
RCA CPL1-1349: A LEGENDARY PERFORMER, VOL. 2 (1976)
RCA RS-1060: FROM ELVIS PRESLEY BOULEVARD, MEMPHIS,
        TENNESSEE (1976)
RCA Camden PDA-009: THE ELVIS COLLECTION (1976)
        (Combined Camden LPs 1088 and 1110)
RCA Camden PDA-042: THE ELVIS COLLECTION, VOL. 2
        (Combined Camden LPs 1118 and 1146) (1976)
RCA PL-42003: ELVIS IN DEMAND (1977)
REDWOOD/CHISWICK R1: THE ELVIS TAPES (1977)
RCA PL-12274: WELCOME TO MY WORLD (1977)
RCA PL-12428: MOODY BLUE (1977)
CHARLEY/SUN 1001: THE SUN YEARS (1977)
RCA PL-42356: ROUSTABOUT (reissue) (1977)
RCA PL-42354: GIRLS! GIRLS! GIRLS! (reissue) (1977)
RCA PL-42357: FUN IN ACAPULCO (reissue) (1977)
RCA PL-42355: KISSIN' COUSINS (reissue) (1977)
RCA PL-42358: LOVING YOU (reissue) (1977)
RCA PL-02587: ELVIS IN CONCERT (1977)
RCA PL-12772: HE WALKS BESIDE ME (1978)
RCA PL-42101: THE '56 SESSIONS, VOL. 1 (1978)
RCA PL-42370: ELVIS (NBC-TV SPECIAL) (reissue) (1978)
RCA PL-42102: THE '56 SESSIONS, VOL. 2 (1979)
RCA PL-42691: ELVIS' 40 GREATEST (1979)
        (special pink vinly pressing)
RCA PL-13279: OUR MEMORIES OF ELVIS, VOL. 1 (1979)
RCA PL-13082: A LEGENDARY PERFORMER, VOL. 3 (1979)
RCA PL-13448: OUR MEMORIES OF ELVIS, VOL. 2 (1979)
RCA PL-42371: ELVIS SINGS THE WONDERFUL WORLD OF
        CHRISTMAS (reissue) (1979)
VIRGIN-KING 1: THE FIRST YEAR (1979)
RCA PDA-054: THE ELVIS COLLECTION, VOL. 3 (1979)
RCA Camden CDS-1182: DOUBLE DYNAMITE (1980)
RCA Camden CDS-1185: FLAMING STAR (1980)
RCA Camden CDS-1188: DOUBLE DYNAMITE (1980)
HAMMER HMR-9005: ELVIS-THE KING SPEAKS (1980)
RCA NL-43054: ELVIS PRESLEY TWIN-PACK (1980)

CHILE

By Carlos Arancibia & Eugenio Torres

ELVIS' 78rpm SINGLES IN CHILE

RCA Victor 92-5252: JUGUEMOS A LOS NOVIOS (Baby Let's Play House)/FIESTA DE ROCK N' ROLL ESTA NOCHE (Good Rockin' Tonight)

RCA Victor 92-5261: NO SEAS CRUEL (Don't Be Cruel)/PERRO SABUESO (Hound Dog)

RCA Victor 95-5262: AMAME TIERNAMENTE (Love Me Tender)/TRISTEZAS DE LA VACA LECHERA (Milkcow Blues Boogie)

RCA Victor 9252: HOTEL NOSTALIGICO (Heartbreak Hotel)/TREN DE MISTERIO (Mystery Train)

ELVIS' 45rpm SINGLES IN CHILE

All of the 78rpm singles and nearly all of the 45s were issued without picture covers. Any exceptions will be noted.

In the early stages of Elvis' career, RCA executives here were very reluctant to issue his records. For that reason you'll see an occasional flip side by another artist, usually a non-rock, well-established singer.

Considering the small Chilean market and the small quantity of each record pressed, it is easy to understand why Chilean Elvis records are so rare. And if they're rare here, they must be next to impossible to find in other corners of the world. In addition, very few Elvis records were ever reissued or went into second pressings.

RCA Victor 94-0080: HOUND DOG (Elvis)/YOUR HEART'S DANGER (by The Laurie Sisters)

RCA Victor 94-0082: DON'T BE CRUEL (Elvis)/SOMEBODY UP THERE LIKES ME (by Perry Como)

RCA Victor 47-7150: DON'T/I BEG OF YOU

RCA Victor 47-7240: WEAR MY RING AROUND YOUR NECK/DONCHA' THINK IT'S TIME

RCA Victor 47-7280: HARD HEADED WOMAN/DON'T ASK ME WHY

RCA Victor 47-7410: ONE NIGHT/I GOT STUNG

RCA Victor 47-7600: A BIG HUNK O' LOVE/MY WISH CAME TRUE

RCA Victor 94-0222: MAKE ME KNOW IT/LIKE A BABY

RCA Victor 94-0249: THE GIRL OF MY BEST FRIEND/DIRTY, DIRTY FEELING

RCA Victor 47-7740: STUCK ON YOU/FAME AND FORTUNE

RCA Victor 47-7777: IT'S NOW OR NEVER/A MESS OF BLUES

RCA Victor 47-7810: ARE YOU LONESOME TO-NIGHT/I GOTTA KNOW

RCA Victor 94-0275: SURRENDER/LONELY MAN

RCA Victor 47-7880: I FEEL SO BAD/WILD IN THE COUNTRY

RCA Victor 94-0308: NO MORE/SENTIMENTAL ME

RCA Victor 47-7908: LITTLE SISTER/(MARIE'S THE NAME) HIS LATEST FLAME

RCA Victor 47-7968: CAN'T HELP FALLING IN LOVE/ROCK-A-HULA BABY

RCA Victor 47-7992: GOOD LUCK CHARM/ANYTHING THAT'S PART OF YOU

RCA Victor 47-8100: RETURN TO SENDER/WHERE DO YOU COME FROM

RCA Victor 47-8188: (YOU'RE THE) DEVIL IN DISGUISE/PLEASE DON'T DRAG THAT STRING AROUND

RCA Victor 94-0344: WE'LL BE TOGETHER/THE WALLS HAVE EARS

RCA Victor 94-0415: ASK ME/ECHOES OF LOVE

RCA Victor 47-8243: BOSSA NOVA BABY/WITCHCRAFT

RCA Victor 94-0395: WHAT'D I SAY/VIVA LAS VEGAS

RCA Victor 47-8400: SUCH A NIGHT/NEVER ENDING

RCA Victor 47-8941: ALL THAT I AM/SPINOUT

RCA Victor 47-0639: SUSPICIUOS (Suspicion)/KISS ME QUICK

RCA Victor 14-0006: CRYING IN THE CHAPEL/I BELIEVE IN THE MAN IN THE SKY

RCA Victor 47-8500: DO THE CLAM/YOU'LL BE GONE

RCA Victor 47-8585: (IT'S SUCH AN) EASY QUESTION/IT FEELS SO RIGHT

RCA Victor 47-8698: PUPPET ON A STRING/TELL ME WHY

RCA Victor 47-8870: LOVE LETTERS/COME WHAT MAY

RCA 47-9670: IF I CAN DREAM/EDGE OF REALITY

RCA 47-9731: MEMORIES/CHARRO

RCA 47-9741: IN THE GETHO (In The Ghetto)/ANY DAY NOW

RCA 47-9764: SUSPICIOUS MINDS/YOU'LL THINK OF ME

RCA 47-9835: THE WONDER OF YOU/MAMA LIKED THE ROSES

RCA 47-9873: I'VE LOST YOU/THE NEXT STEP IS LOVE

RCA 47-9916: PATCH IT UP/YOU DON'T HAVE TO SAY YOU LOVE ME

RCA 47-9998: I'M LEAVIN'/HEART OF ROME

RCA APBO-0280: IF YOU TALK IN YOUR SLEEP/HELP ME (This was the first Chilean 45 issued in stereo)

RCA JB-10857: MOODY BLUE/SHE THINKS I STILL CARE

RCA PB-10998: WAY DOWN/PLEDGING MY LOVE

RCA PB-11165: AMERICA/MY WAY (with picture sleeve)

ELVIS' 33-COMPACT SINGLES IN CHILE

RCA Victor 7-33-001: ELVIS IN COMPACT (with cover)

RCA Victor C-27: ELVIS PRESLEY HITS (with cover)

ELVIS' 45rpm EXTENDED PLAYS IN CHILE

RCA Victor CME-65: HEARTBREAK HOTEL/I WAS THE ONE I FORGOT TO REMEMBER TO FORGET/MYSTERY TRAIN

RCA Victor CME-91: I WANT YOU, I NEED YOU, I LOVE YOU/MY BABY LEFT ME
FLIP: Two songs by Julius LaRosa

RCA Victor CME-92: LOVE ME TENDER/ANY WAY YOU WANT ME I DON'T CARE IF THE SUN DON'T SHINE/THAT'S ALL RIGHT

RCA Victor CME-93: TUTTI FRUTTI/ONE SIDED LOVE AFFAIR I'LL NEVER LET YOU GO/THAT'S WHEN YOUR HEARTACHES BEGIN

RCA Victor CME-99: TOO MUCH/PLAYING FOR KEEPS YOU'RE A HEARTBREAKER/I GOT A WOMAN

RCA Victor CME-101: LOVE ME/HOW DO YOU THINK I FEEL PARALYZED/ANYPLACE IS PARADISE

RCA Victor CME-123: TEDDY BEAR/GOT A LOT O' LIVING TO DO LOVING YOU/HOT DOG

RCA Victor CME-130: MEAN WOMAN BLUES/LONESOME COWBOY PARTY/TRUE LOVE

RCA Victor CME-131: JAILHOUSE ROCK/TREAT ME NICE DON'T LEAVE ME NOW/I NEED YOU SO

RCA Victor CME-134: I'M GONNA SIT RIGHT DOWN AND WRITE MYSELF A LETTER (by Bing Crosby/BLUEBERRY HILL (Elvis)
FIRST ROMANCE (by Tony Perkins)/ANGELIQUE-O (by Harry Belefonte)

NOTE: On this EP, Elvis actually sings "Hard Headed Woman." This is a real collector's item here.

RCA Victor CME-145: DIXIELAND ROCK/YOUNG DREAMS CRAWFISH/TROUBLE

RCA Victor EPA-4319: KING CREOLE/NEW ORLEANS AS LONG AS I HAVE YOU/LOVER DOLL

RCA Victor EPA-4368: FOLLOW THAT DREAM/ANGEL WHAT A WONDERFUL LIFE/I'M NOT THE MARRYING KIND

All of the Chilean EP releases have regular picture covers, except for EPA-4368, "Follow That Dream."

ELVIS' 10-INCH LONG PLAYS IN CHILE

RCA Victor CML-3006: HITS AND NORTH AMERICAN STARS (contains one Elvis track, "Good Rockin' Tonight")

RCA Victor CML-3009: ELVIS PRESLEY - Y SU CONJUNTO (there are two covers for this LP, one with Elvis' photo on the front, and one without photo)

RCA Victor CML-3012: ELVIS PRESLEY

ELVIS' STANDARD LONG PLAYS IN CHILE

RCA Victor LOC-1035: ELVIS SINGS CHRISTMAS SONGS (two versions; one with Elvis' photo on cover and one without. Not issued with the photo booklet, as was U.S. version)
RCA Victor LPM-1707: ELVIS' GOLDEN RECORDS
RCA Victor LPM-2011: A DATE WITH ELVIS
RCA Victor LPM-2075: ELVIS' GOLD RECORDS, VOL. 2
RCA Victor LPM-2231: ELVIS IS BACK
RCA Victor LPM-2256: G.I. BLUES
RCA Victor LPM-2370: SOMETHING FOR EVERYBODY
RCA Victor LPM-2426: BLUE HAWAII
RCA Victor LPM-2523: POT LUCK
RCA Victor LPM-2621: GIRLS! GIRLS! GIRLS!
RCA Victor LPM-2756: FUN IN ACAPULCO
RCA Victor LPM-2765: ELVIS' GOLDEN RECORDS, VOL. 3
RCA Victor LPM-2999: ROUSTABOUT
RCA Victor LPM-3338: GIRL HAPPY
RCA Victor LPM-3468: HARUM SCARUM
RCA Victor LPM-3553: FRANKIE AND JOHNNY
RCA Victor LPM-3643: PARADISE HAWAIIAN STYLE
RCA LPM-4088: ELVIS (NBC-TV SPECIAL)
RCA LPM-4155: FROM ELVIS IN MEMPHIS
RCA LPM-4362: ON STAGE (mono/stereo)
RCA LPM-4445: THAT'S THE WAY IT IS (stereo)
RCA LPM-4776: ELVIS AS RECORDED AT MADISON SQUARE GARDEN (stereo)
RCA APL2-0008: ALOHA FROM HAWAII VIA SATELLITE (stereo)
RCA LSP-3921: ELVIS' GOLDEN RECORDS, VOL. 4 (stereo)
RCA APL1-2274: WELCOME TO MY WORLD (stereo)
RCA APL1-2428: MOODY BLUE (stereo)
RCA CPL1-2901: ELVIS SINGS FOR CHILDREN AND GROWNUPS TOO
RCA ACL1-3279: OUR MEMORIES OF ELVIS (stereo)

GERMANY

By Peter Baumann

ELVIS' SINGLES IN GERMANY

A good many of the German Elvis releases were notably different than those issued in the U.S. It is those that were different that would be of greatest interest to fans outside Germany, and, for that reason, we will not list releases that are the same as what you've seen in the States.

First pressings were on the black RCA label, using silver lettering. Many were reissued on the black RCA VICTOR label, followed by the more recent orange label. The RCA dog, "Nipper," has not been used in Germany. We also have never had a Gold Standard Series.

All original issues of 47-6383 through 47-7600 (U.S. catalog numbers) came in a white paper sleeve with a red RCA logo.

When we began to get Elvis picture sleeves, they were often different than their U.S. counterparts. The same is true with the reissues of the earlier songs.

The reissue, on the orange label, of 47-6420 uses the same picture as on the U.S. release of 47-9998. Our 47-6604 has the same photo as the U.S. LPM-1382 and the German 47-7035 sleeve uses the photo that was on the U.S. LPM-1515. These are just some examples of how, sometimes, foreign issues will vary from U.S. product.

Here is a listing of interesting and unusual singles released in Germany, all different in some way than the U.S. releases.

RCA 47-9109: LOVE ME/RIP IT UP
RCA 47-9129: TOO MUCH/TEDDY BEAR
RCA 47-9143: SANTA CLAUS IS BACK IN TOWN/SANTA BRING MY BABY BACK TO ME
RCA 47-9144: PARTY/GOT A LOT O' LIVIN' TO DO
RCA 47-9154: BABY, I DON'T CARE/I WANT TO BE FREE
RCA 47-9200: LOVER DOLL/DIXIELAND ROCK
RCA 47-9201: DIXIELAND ROCK/KING CREOLE (reissued with picture sleeve)
RCA 47-9224: YOUNG AND BEAUTIFUL/LOVER DOLL
RCA 47-9227: THAT'S ALL RIGHT/YOU'RE A HEARTBREAKER
RCA 47-9279: WHITE CHRISTMAS/SILENT NIGHT
RCA 47-9314: IT'S NOW OR NEVER/MAKE ME KNOW IT
RCA 47-9333: A MESS OF BLUES/THE GIRL OF MY BEST FRIEND
RCA 47-9340: WOODEN HEART (MUSS I DENN)/TONIGHT'S ALL RIGHT FOR LOVE
RCA 47-9399: NO MORE/SENTIMENTAL ME
RCA 47-9417: KING OF THE WHOLE WIDE WORLD/HOME IS WHERE THE HEART IS (sleeve similar to EPA-4371)
RCA 47-9429: KISS ME QUICK/NO MORE
RCA 47-9443: I BELIEVE/IT IS NO SECRET
RCA 47-9452: KISS ME QUICK/NIGHT RIDER (sleeve similar to U.S. 47-7850)
RCA 47-9459: I GOT LUCKY/GIRLS! GIRLS! GIRLS! (sleeve similar to U.S. 47-7908)
RCA 47-9466: THE WALLS HAVE EARS/SONG OF THE SHRIMP
RCA 47-9508: MEXICO/YOU CAN'T SAY NO IN ACAPULCO (sleeve is similar to picture on back of "Acapulco" LP)
RCA 47-9533: IT HURTS ME/SUSPICION (sleeve similar to U.S. 47-8188)
RCA 47-9546: KISSIN' COUSINS/ONE BOY, TWO LITTLE GIRLS (sleeve similar to U.S. 47-8307)
RCA 47-9686: BLUE RIVER/YOU'LL BE GONE (sleeve similar to U.S. 47-8740)
RCA 74-16126: I JUST CAN'T HELP BELIEVIN'/HOW THE WEB WAS WOVEN (with sleeve)
RCA 74-16177: POLK SALAD ANNIE/C. C. RIDER
RCA 74-16194: IT'S NOW OR NEVER/ARE YOU LONESOME TONIGHT
RCA 74-16384: TEDDY BEAR/LOVING YOU
RCA 74-16386: ALL SHOOK UP/THAT'S WHEN YOUR HEARTACHES BEGIN
RCA PPBO-4111: HEARTBREAK HOTEL/I GOT STUNG
RCA PPBO-4112: CAN'T HELP FALLING IN LOVE/LOVE ME TENDER
RCA PPBO-4113: CRYING IN THE CHAPEL/ONE NIGHT
RCA PPBO-7006: SUSPICIOUS MINDS/THAT'S ALL RIGHT
RCA PPBO-7224: GREEN GREEN GRASS OF HOME/MAKE THE WORLD GO AWAY (with sleeve)

RCA PPBO-7047: ROCK-A-HULA BABY/SHAKE, RATTLE & ROLL
RCA PPBO-7048: GOOD LUCK CHARM/SURRENDER
RCA PPBO-7074: A MESS OF BLUES/THE GIRL OF MY BEST FRIEND (with sleeve)
RCA PB-09001: WOODEN HEART/KISS ME QUICK
RCA PB-09002: DEVIL IN DISGUISE/SUSPICION
RCA PB-09022: BOSSA NOVA BABY/MY BABY LEFT ME

"WOODEN HEART" – THE ENGLISH TRANSLATION
By Dieter Boek

As most fans know, Elvis did sing a portion of one of his songs in the German language. The song was "Wooden Heart" and it was one of the tunes used in the Germany-oriented film "G.I. Blues."

One might assume that the German lyrics were none other than the simple translation of the English lyrics heard in the song. This is not the case. In fact, with the exception of the last few lines, the German lyrics seem to have nothing to do with the remainder of the song.

For your convenience, we offer the following line-for-line translation:

Muss i denn	*Must I then,*
muss i denn	*must I then*
zum Stadtele hinaus	*go out to town,*
Stadtele hinaus	*out to town*
und Du mein Schatz bleibst hier	*and you my darling (love) stay here.*
Muss i denn	*Must I then,*
muss i denn	*must I then*
zum Stadtele hinaus	*go out to town,*
Stadtele hinaus	*out to town*
und Du mein Schatz bleibst hier	*and you my darling (love) stay here.*
Sei mir gut	*Treat me nice,*
sei mir gut	*treat me good.*
sei mir wie Du wirklich sollst	*Treat me like you really should.*

. . . cause I don't have a wooden heart.

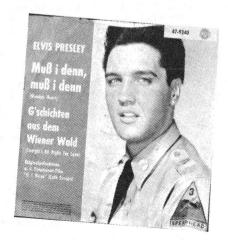

263

ELVIS' EXTENDED PLAYS IN GERMANY

All of the German Elvis extended plays were issued on the black RCA (or RCA Victor) label. The lettering is silver in color. There have been no orange label EP issues and no Gold Standard reissues.

Most of the RCA special products were issued only in the U.S., however SPA 7-37, "Perfect For Parties," was released in Germany. On it, the song "Anchors Aweigh," by Tony Cabot, is replaced by "Ring Out Then Your Hoiahs," also by Tony Cabot.

The following are standard German catalog releases that are different than those issued in the U.S.

RCA EPB-1035: SANTA CLAUS IS BACK IN TOWN/HERE COMES
          SANTA CLAUS
          WHITE CHRISTMAS/I'LL BE HOME FOR CHRISTMAS
RCA EPB-1035-2: BLUE CHRISTMAS/SANTA BRING MY BABY BACK
          TO ME
          SILENT NIGHT/OH LITTLE TOWN OF BETHLEHEM
RCA EPC-1515-3: BLUEBERRY HILL/DON'T LEAVE ME NOW
          HAVE I TOLD YOU LATELY THAT I LOVE YOU/I
          NEED YOU NOW
RCA EPA-2426: NO MORE/BLUE HAWAII
          MOONLIGHT SWIM/ALMOST ALWAYS TRUE
RCA EPA-4361: SUCH A NIGHT/IT FEELS SO RIGHT
          LIKE A BABY/MAKE ME KNOW IT
RCA EPA-9009: FLAMING STAR/WILD IN THE COUNTRY
          FRANKFORT SPECIAL/G.I. BLUES
RCA EPA-9011: FLAMING STAR/SUMMER KISSES, WINTER TEARS
          FRANKFORT SPECIAL/G.I. BLUES
RCA EPA 9068: THIS IS LIVING/RIDING THE RAINBOW
          I GOT LUCKY/A WHISTLING TUNE
RCA EPA-9073: KISS ME QUICK/NIGHT RIDER
          JOSHUA FIT THE BATTLE/JUDY
RCA EPA-9105: BOSSA NOVA BABY/RELAX
          WITCHCRAFT/FEVER
RCA EPA-9106: FUN IN ACAPULCO/NO ROOM TO RHUMBA
          I THINK I'M GONNA LIKE IT HERE/MEXICO
RCA EPA-9500: HOUND DOG/DON'T BE CRUEL
          I WANT YOU, I NEED YOU, I LOVE YOU/HEART-
          BREAK HOTEL
RCA EPA-9541: TREAT ME NICE/I BEG OF YOU
          ALL SHOOK UP/DON'T
RCA EPA-9561: PLAYING FOR KEEPS/TOO MUCH
          WEAR MY RING AROUND YOUR NECK/DONCHA'
          THINK IT'S TIME
RCA EPA-9562: GOOD ROCKIN' TONIGHT/BLUE MOON OF
          KENTUCKY
          MILKCOW BLUES BOOGIE/THAT'S ALL RIGHT
RCA EPA-9617: HARD HEADED WOMAN/STEADFAST, LOYAL AND
          TRUE
          THAT'S WHEN YOUR HEARTACHES BEGIN/DON'T
          ASK ME WHY
RCA EPA-9644: ONE NIGHT/YOU'RE A HEARTBREAKER
          I GOT STUNG/BABY LET'S PLAY HOUSE
          (Original has photo similar to that which is on the
          cover of U.S. LPM-1990, whereas reissues have a
          completely different photo)
RCA EPA-9656: JUST BECAUSE/IS IT SO STRANGE
          A FOOL SUCH AS I/I NEED YOUR LOVE TONIGHT
RCA EPA-9673: A BIG HUNK O' LOVE/MONEY HONEY
          MY WISH CAME TRUE/REDDY TEDDY
          (cover shows a picture of Elvis taken when he was in
          Germany)
RCA EPA-9775: IT'S NOW OR NEVER/A MESS OF BLUES
          FAME AND FORTUNE/STUCK ON YOU

Collectors may be interested to know that we did manage to get one Elvis EP issued on the popular maroon label, in Germany. It was EPA-5088 ("A Touch Of Gold").

There also exists a series called "Klingende Post," made for record dealers, that contains some Elvis. I have no specific information on this series but would welcome any input from readers on the subject.

ELVIS' LONG PLAYS IN GERMANY

As we have done with the other German Elvis releases, we will list only those albums that are different than the Elvis LPs issued in the U.S.

RCA LOC-1035: ELVIS' CHRISTMAS ALBUM (not issued with a double-pocket jacket or with photo booklet insert)
RCA LSP-2256: G.I. BLUES (German LP has the long version of "Tonight's All Right For Love" instead of either "Tonight Is So Right For Love" or the short version of "Tonight's All Right For Love," as was issued in the U.S. on the "Legendary Performer" series.
HOR ZU SHZT-521: GOLDEN BOY ELVIS
HOR ZU SHZE-128: SCHLAGER SCHLAGEN EIN (a various artists LP that contains one song, "Mexico," by Elvis)
ARCADE ADEG-6: ELVIS' 40 GREATEST (double album)
RCA MU-120: RCA SAMPLER (contains one Elvis track, "Guitar Man")
RCA MU-121: RCA SAMPLER (contains one Elvis track, "U.S. Male")
RCA 16,30007/1-7: ELVIS PRESLEY'S GREATEST HITS (Reader's Digest 7-LP box set)
RCA SRS-558: A PORTRAIT IN MUSIC
RCA LSP-10204: THE ROCKIN' DAYS
RCA LSP-10220: TODAY, TOMORROW AND FOREVER
RCA LPL1-7527: ELVIS' HITS OF THE 70'S
RCA POL1-8078: PURE GOLD (has two additional songs, "Frankie And Johnny" and "Clean Up Your Own Backyard," that did not appear on U.S. version)
RCA POL1-8079: PICTURES OF ELVIS
RCA PPL1-8081: ELVIS IN HOLLYWOOD
RCA POL2-8024: ELVIS FOREVER (this double LP was awarded two gold records for sales in Germany, on March 16, 1978)
RCA PL-42101: THE '56 SESSIONS, VOL. 1
RCA PL-42102: THE '56 SESSIONS, VOL. 2
RCA PL-42232: 100 SUPER ROCKS (a 7-LP set with 100 songs)
RCA PL-42935: THE RARE ELVIS
RCA 4711,000: ELVIS' RECORD COVERS (a lavish 180-page book that reproduces, actual size, every LP cover, front and back, released in Germany on Elvis, plus the disc "A Portrait In Music," all bound together)
RCA LSP-10380: ROCK 'N' ROLL

The following albums were made available in Germany through various record and book clubs.

RCA 27-261-7: 20 FANTASTIC GOLDEN HITS
RCA 27-480-3: 20 FANTASTIC HITS
RCA 27-511-5: BLUE HAWAII
RCA 27-558-6: ELVIS IN HOLLYWOOD
RCA 27-626-1: ELVIS SINGS THE WONDERFUL WORLD OF
          CHRISTMAS
RCA 27-637-8: FROM MEMPHIS TO VEGAS/FROM VEGAS TO
          MEMPHIS
RCA 27-092-6: ROCK HISTORY (a 5-LP set with one LP, "A Portrait In Music," by Elvis)
RCA 63-070-20: 20 FANTASTIC HITS
RCA 65-896-3: BURNING LOVE
RCA 66-479-7: MEIN STAR ELVIS PRESLEY (a triple LP)

EASTERN-BLOC COUNTRIES
CZECHOSLOVAKIA·U.S.S.R.·EAST GERMANY·POLAND

By Ing. Miloslav Soch

Right away, you'll notice that the quantity of Elvis releases from the Eastern-bloc countries falls way short of what you'll find his output to be in the rest of the world. But, at the same time, there's a good chance that the Presley product from our side of the globe will provide fascinating viewing, as most have never appeared in print before.

Perhaps, more than anything, however, the reader will gain even greater insight and confidence into the oft-repeated claim that. . . collecting Elvis is universal.

CZECHOSLOVAKIA

We have only one Elvis release to report from Czechoslovakia, an LP:
Opus (S) 91 13 0625: PURE GOLD (Three known variations)
1) Green label with pressing code 78 1 on label
2) Blue label with pressing code 78 2 on label
3) Green label with pressing code 79 2 and "RCA Italiana" on label

U.S.S.R.

All Russian releases appear on Melodija, the State's recording company. There have been three albums (one on 10-inch disc) and one EP. Until his death, there had never been an Elvis recording issued in the U.S.S.R.
Melodija (M) 33D-18305-06: MUZYKALNYJ KALEJDOSKOP NO. 7
A 10-inch LP with various artists; contains "I Believe In The Man In The Sky" by Elvis (an interesting choice. . . when you think about it).
Melodija (S) 33C-04739-40: MELODII I RITMY
A various artists LP, contains "I'm Movin' On" by Elvis.
Melodija (S) C60-05007-08: ESTRADNAJA ORBITA
A various artists LP, containing "True Love Travels On A Gravel Road" and an alternate take of "Gentle On My Mind" that has never been released in any other country (but has appeared on an American bootleg album).
Melodija (S) C62-04951-52 (33 1/3rpm): ESTRADNJA ORBITA
Four tracks from the LP of the same name, including both of the above mentioned Elvis songs.

EAST GERMANY (G.D.R.)

Amiga (S) 8 55 630: ELVIS
This is a selection of 16 of Elvis' golden hits.
RCA International (S) INTS-1126: ELVIS' CHRISTMAS ALBUM
For inter-shop (free currency) sale only. Same songs (12) as the U.S. LOC-1035/LPM-1951 but with a cover similar to "Elvis Sings the Wonderful World of Christmas."

POLAND

There are no standard Elvis records from Poland to document, but this country has issued quite a few 'Phono-cards' that contain Elvis' singing voice.

The phono-card recording is similar to the flexi-discs, or soundsheets, that you have seen in the U.S., with a photographic scene covering the entire card (playing surface) a la the picture disc concept. Each phono-disc is packaged in a (very) plain white sleeve with the artist and song titles printed on the front.

Regarding the photos used on the phono-discs, they are most likely to remind one of picture postcards, depicting various Polish scenes or scenery. They do not pertain to the artist or songs at all.

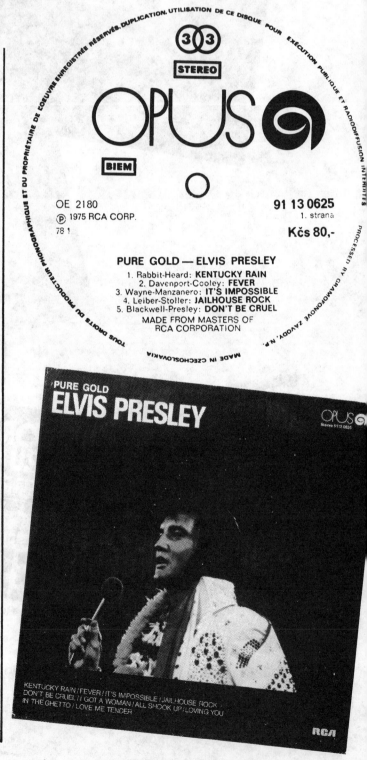

МИНИСТЕРСТВО КУЛЬТУРЫ СССР

МЕЛОДИЯ

СТЕРЕО ВСЕСОЮЗНАЯ ФИРМА ГРАМПЛАСТИНОК ○ 33

АПРЕЛЕВСКИЙ ОРДЕНА ЛЕНИНА ЗАВОД

ГОСТ 5289-73   1 сторона
33С—04739   Гр. 3. 1-90

МЕЛОДИИ И РИТМЫ
ЗДРАВСТВУЙ И ДО СВИДАНИЯ (Мирреа)
ТЫ ТАКОЙ ЧЕЛОВЕК (Герот)
РОЗОВЫЙ САД (И. Саут). В ЛЕТНИЙ ДЕНЬ (Дорси)
Я ИДУ (К. Сноу). ВОКРУГ ОРКЕСТРА (Фэгерти)
ЖЕЛТАЯ РЕКА (Христи). СУЛЕЙМАН (Диманд)
ЗЕЛЕНЫЕ РУКАВА (муз. нар.)
ПОЗДНО НОЧЬЮ (Блэкмор)
ЗАГЛЯНИ КО МНЕ (Фогерти)
ЭНДИ ВИЛЬЯМС (3), ЭЛВИС ПРЕСЛИ (5)
«ХЭППИ БИТ БОЙЗ» (9)
Орк. и хор ДЖЕЙМСА ЛАСТА

R-0610-II

IT'S NOW OR NEVER
GUITAR MAN

śpiewa E. PRESLEY

NIE ZGINAĆ
CENA ZŁ 14.—

tonpress

267

ISRAEL

By P. Zilbergeld

ELVIS' SINGLES IN ISRAEL

Nearly every Israeli single was exactly the same as the U.S. release. The only noteworthy exceptions are noted below.

RCA APBO-0196: TAKE GOOD CARE OF HER/I'VE GOT A THING ABOUT YOU BABY (issued with different picture sleeve than in U.S.)

RCA 47-9873: I'VE LOST YOU/THE NEXT STEP IS LOVE (issued with different picture sleeve than in U.S.)

ELVIS' EXTENDED PLAYS IN ISRAEL

All singles and extended plays were issued on RCA's black label. Most were pressed without the RCA dog.

Most extended plays were issued here. Some had Israeli covers and numbers, others had French covers with Israeli numbers. Those that differ from standard U.S. issues are listed below.

RCA Victor EPA-8107: ONE NIGHT/I GOT STUNG
I NEED YOUR LOVE TONIGHT/A FOOL SUCH AS I

RCA Victor EPA-8101: LITTLE SISTER/ARE YOU LONESOME TO-NIGHT
HIS LATEST FLAME/I GOTTA KNOW

RCA Victor EPA-8102: IT'S NOW OR NEVER/A MESS OF BLUES
FAME AND FORTUNE/STUCK ON YOU

RCA Victor EPA-8103: SURRENDER/LONELY MAN
FLAMING STAR/SUMMER KISSES, WINTER TEARS

RCA Victor EPA-8104: DEVIL IN DISGUISE/ONE BROKEN HEART FOR SALE
RELAX/PLEASE DON'T DRAG THAT STRING AROUND

RCA Victor EPA-8105: BOSSA NOVA BABY/VINO, DINERO Y AMOR
FUN IN ACAPULCO/NO ROOM TO RHUMBA IN A SPORTS CAR

RCA Victor EPA-8106: RETURN TO SENDER/I DON'T WANNA BE TIED
GIRLS! GIRLS! GIRLS!/I DON'T WANT TO

RCA Victor EPA-8107: ONE NIGHT/I GOT STUNG
I NEED YOUR LOVE TONIGHT/A FOOL SUCH AS I

RCA Victor EPA-86285: G.I. BLUES/DID'JA EVER
TONIGHT'S ALL RIGHT FOR LOVE/WOOD-EN HEART

RCA Victor EPA-86393: KISSIN' COUSINS/SMOKY MOUNTAIN BOY
THERE'S GOLD IN THE MOUNTAINS/CATCHIN' ON FAST

RCA Victor EPA-86411: AIN'T THAT LOVING YOU BABY/IT HURTS ME
WHAT'D I SAY/SLOWLY BUT SURELY

RCA Victor EPA-86434: DO THE CLAM/CROSS MY HEART AND HOPE TO DIE
GIRL HAPPY/THE MEANEST GIRL IN TOWN

RCA Victor EPA-7174: IT FEELS SO RIGHT/EASY QUESTION
LONG LONELY HIGHWAY/I'M YOURS (titled "Tickle Me, Vol. 2")

ROYAL 611104: SUSPICIOUS MINDS/YOU'LL THINK OF ME
CLEAN UP YOUR OWN BACKYARD/THE FAIR IS MOVING ON (This EP is a Persian import. The word "Suspicious" is incorrectly spelled "Suspiclous," on the sleeve. Another error is in the number, which is given as 612104 on the sleeve)

ELVIS' LONG PLAYS IN ISRAEL

We've found that most U.S. standard commercial albums were issued here, using the same number and cover as appeared in the States. A few exceptions, however, should be listed. They are below.

RCA CS-2595: BURNING LOVE AND HITS FROM HIS MOVIES (issued here on RCA's regular orange label; not on the Camden label. Also has different back cover than U.S. version)

RCA LPL1-7527: ELVIS' HITS OF THE 70'S

RCA PPL1-8087: ELVIS IN HOLLYWOOD

INTERNATIONAL ELVIS DIRECTORY

YOUR NAME SHOULD BE IN NEXT YEAR'S INTERNATIONAL ELVIS DIRECTORY

The second edition of *Presleyana* will list names in two categories, collector and dealer, with a section for each. You can be listed as a dealer by your store name (a limit of four lines for the name and address), or your personal name and mailing address, even if you deal part time and only through mail order. The choice is yours.

All names in each section will be listed alphabetically by name under country, state and city headings. Not only will this become a mailing list for the collectors to receive offers from other collectors, dealers and interested parties worldwide, but it will serve as a handy and easy-to-find reference of location for those travelling through an area who might want to contact Elvis fans in a certain area.

It will be up to each person submitting their name to decide:

(1) Do you want your home address or a post office mailing address? Name and address must not take over four lines.

(2) Do you want to list your phone number?

TERMS: a $5.00 registration fee is required to cover the enormous costs of cataloging and printing. You must also *sign* your letter giving us authorization to print your name as submitted. If you want to think of this as a "classified ad," which it really isn't (it's much more than that), you'll never in any other way reach so many interested people in such an *in*expensive way. Collectors should reflect that most catalogs cost from 50¢ to $3.00, and many of these will doubtless be sent to the names in this Directory free.

Jellyroll Productions
Box 3017
Scottsdale, Arizona 85257
U.S.A.

Each of the following record collectors and dealers is either partially or exclusively interested in Elvis' recordings. Those who have indicated that they sell, or deal, Elvis records are so noted with an asterisk following the name.

A

AJ'S Record-Go-Round*
2240 16th St., N.E., Canton, OHIO 44705 - (216) 453-5500

ALDEN, Leach
32430 Diamond Ave., Mission, B.C., CANADA V2V 1M2
(604) 826-9805

ALLAN, Edward
118 Hedgewood Rd., Lutherville, MARYLAND 21093

AMES, Elizabeth E.
9 Overlook Dr., Belford, MASSACHUSETTS 01730

ARBOGAST, Robert Mike
P.O. Box 483, Covington, VIRGINIA 24426

ASHWOOD, Paul
P.O. Box 376, Bloomsburg, PENNSYLVANIA 17815

B

B & B Sales*
1014 Joseph St., P.O. Box 7038, Shreveport, LOUISIANA 71107

BAKER, Dave
1102 E. 4th St., West Fargo, NORTH DAKOTA 58078

BANNEY, Howard F.
RD 7, Hopewell Jct., NEW YORK 12533 - (914) 226-5233

BAY, Robert W.
1426 Jaywood Dr., St. Louis, MISSOURI 63141

BECK, Larry E.
P.O. Box 611, High Point, NORTH CAROLINA 27261

BELKNAP, Burt
183 Palmdale Dr. Apt. 4, Williamsville, NEW YORK 14221

BENNETT, Randall
P.O. Box 52, Amboy, MINNESOTA 56010 - (507)674-3745

BLACK, Frank
108 Webster Apts., Clinton, ILLINOIS 61727 - (217) 935-8603

BOST, Jim
313 Shumate Dr., Cleveland, MISSISSIPPI 38732 - (601) 846-6716

BOUCHER, Philip
128 Treeview Dr., Toronto 510, Ontario, CANADA M8W 4C3

BRAM, Bill
2 Spruce St., Great Neck, NEW YORK 11021

BROWN, Jean
3114 Redfield, Pasadena, TEXAS 77503 - (713) 472-0952

BROZ, Robert L.
6820 46th Ave. N., Crystal, MINNESOTA 55428 - (612) 537-4467

BWANA DISC Records*
1921 N. Keystone, Chicago, ILLINOIS 60639 - (312) 384-2350

C

CABRERA, Rene A.
240 N.E. Sanchez, Apt. 7, Ocala, FLORIDA 32670

CAB'S Collections
RD 5, Box 240, Duncansville, PENNSYLVANIA 16635

CAMPA, Frank F.
15824 East Arrow Hwy., Irwindale, CALIFORNIA 91706

CARTER, Ann
10718 Louise Ave., Granada Hills, CALIFORNIA 91344

CATTANEO, Bob*
P.O. Box 240, Daly City, CALIFORNIA 91406

CELON, Jim
26 Patmar Dr., Monroe, CONNECTICUT 06468

CHATMAN, Christopher
1400½ J St., Sacramento, CALIFORNIA 95814 - (916) 446-6026

COLLECTIBLES*
4547 Gravois, St. Louis, MISSOURI 63116

COLLECTOR'S Exchange
300 W. Peachtree 3E, Atlanta, GEORGIA 30308 - (404) 524-4669

COSBY, Jean
1020 N. Mariposa St., Apt. H, Burbank, CALIFORNIA 91506

COTTON, Lee
806 K St., Sacramento, CALIFORNIA 95814 - (916) 446-3973

CURTIN, Jim
1018 Lawrence Rd., Darby, PENNSYLVANIA 19023 - (215) 534-5232

CUTSHAW, Wayne
326 Bellevue, Round Lake, ILLINOIS 60073

CZAPKAY, Mike
640 Calero Ave., San Jose, CALIFORNIA 95123 - (408) 224-D381

DANS, Dennis
3026 Lone Oak Dr., Shreveport, LOUISIANA 71118

DEAN, Richard
714 Forest Dr., Gages Lake, ILLINOIS 60030 - (312) 223-6076

DEE, Tony
P.O. Box 432, East Elmhurst, NEW YORK 11369 - (212) 699-7116

DE POALO, F.
30 S. Cole Ave., Spring Valley, NEW YORK 10977

DODSON, Jerry & Susan
Columbia Garden Apts. H-68, Columbia, TENNESSEE 38401 - (615) 388-3683

DOWLING, Paul
6 Malvern Court, Ruxton, MARYLAND 21204 - (301) 825-6057

DROUIN, Bruce
332 Terrace Ave., Hasbrouck Heights, NEW JERSEY 07604

DUNN, Donald D.*
170 Beech St., Patterson, NEW JERSEY 07501

EDWARDS, Ray
1650 N. Hermitage, Ft. Myers, FLORIDA 33907

EICHEL, Andreas
Fredericlastrabe 13, 1000 Berlin 19, WEST GERMANY - 030/302-6408

EISENSTEIN, Len
7610 N. 34th Ave., Phoenix, ARIZONA 85021 - (602) 242-0243

ELVIS Store, The*
P.O. Box 7143, Shreveport, LOUISIANA 71107 - (318) 226-0105

ELVIS, Warehouse, The*
323 Franklin Blvd. So. Suite 804, Chicago, ILLINOIS 60606

ELVIS Unlimited*
2323 San Jacinto, Houston, TEXAS 77002

EMPORIUM, The*
629 S. Poplar, Centralia, ILLINOIS 62801 - (618) 5321312

FENSKE, Jerry
919 N. 8th Ave., Wausau, WISCONSIN 54401

FEUSER, Karla
Spangenberger Str. 21, D-3500 Kassel-B., WEST GERMANY

FISCHER, Joe
RT. 2 Box 337, Mukwongo, WISCONSIN

FOLEY, Joan
P.O. Box 513, Scarbrough, MAINE 04074

FROM, Helen R.
910 Stuart Ave., Mamaroneck, NEW YORK 10543

FULL MOON Records*
1400½ J St., Sacramento, CALIFORNIA 95814 - (916) 446-6026

GARDNER, Nelson
P.O. Box 1082, Portland, MAINE 04104

GEISER, Jerry
5883 Sterwerf Dr., Cleveland, OHIO 45002

GELORMINE, Phil
P.O. Box 388, Bound Brook, NEW JERSEY 08805

Goff, Sharron
2523 NE 134th, Seattle, WASHINGTON 98125 - (206) 362-7968

GOIN' BACK Enterprises*
P.O. Box 7161, Honolulu, HAWAII 96821

GOLDEN GROOVES Records*
P.O. Box 432, East Elmhurst, NEW YORK 11369 - (212) 699-7116

GOLDEN OLDIES Records*
4538 Roosevelt Wy. NE, Seattle, WASHINGTON 98105

GRAY, Robert
74 Country Club Blvd., Worcester, MASSACHUSETTS 01605

GREGORY, Chuck
17 Chavenson St., Fall River, MASSACHUSETTS 02723

GREIG, Barry J.
55 Chester Ave., Toronto, Ontario, CANADA M4K 2Z8

GROSH, Thomas R.*
P.O. Box 241, Ephrata, PENNSYLVANIA 17522

HABEL, Vince
RD 3 Box 72, Columbia, PENNSYLVANIA 17512 - (717) 684-5816

HAFEMAN, Buck
1603 W. College Ave., Appleton, WISCONSIN 54911

HANNAFORD, Jim
RR 2 Box 3, Alva, OKLAHOMA 73717

HANSEN, Paul
59 Mission Lane, Walnut Creek, CALIFORNIA 94596

HARROWBY, Marlowe
Warren, Manitoba, CANADA R0C 3E0

HEINZMAN, Ed
14204 Terminal Ave., Cleveland, OHIO 44135

HENDLEY, Dennis R.
4260 N. 49th St., Milwaukee, WISCONSIN 53216

HILBURN, Larry*
P.O. Box 308, West Plains, MISSOURI 65776

HODGE, Joe
3701 Anderson Ave., Chattanooga, TENNESSEE 37412

HOMISKI, Raymond B.
151 Shelley Ave., Elizabeth, NEW JERSEY 07208

HOUSE Of Oldies*
33 Bonair Ave., Hampton, NEW HAMPSHIRE 03842 - (603) 926-4129

HOWARD, Louis
3821 Ingleside St., Olney, MARYLAND 20832 - (301) 774-7912

ICARD, Sheila
P.O. Box 187, Rutherford College, NORTH CAROLINA 28671

J

JOHNSON, William B.
1838 W. Claremont St., Phoenix, ARIZONA 85015

JONES, Debbie
823 S. Seneca, Bartlesville, OKLAHOMA 74003

JONES, Larry
48 Mustang Village, Greenville, SOUTH CAROLINA 29611

JONES, Randy
9358 Frankfort Ave., Fontana, CALIFORNIA 92335

JONES, Wayne
7 Ellington Rd., E. Hartford, CONNECTICUT 06108

K

KAYSINGER, Jim
P.O. Box 211, Whitesville, KENTUCKY 42378

KEIFER, Kathy
2745 Barbour Dr., Fairfield, CALIFORNIA 94533

KELLEY, Wayne*
P.O. Box 1337, Clanton, ALABAMA 35045

KERN, Andy
2323 San Jacinto, Houston, TEXAS 77002

KLINE, June
44 North St. Box 56, North Lewisburg, OHIO 43060

KOWACHEK, Mrs. Victor
35420 Hatherly Pl., Sterling Heights, MICHIGAN 48077

KUBIK, Carl
5855 Bonnie Brea St., Indianapolis, INDIANA - (317) 257-3691

L

LABBATE, Anna
P.O. Box 1233, Church St. Station, New York, NEW YORK 10008

LACEY, B.
14349 Lawndale, Midlothian, ILLINOIS 60445

LADD, Jerry
7255 Jethve Lane, Cincinnati, OHIO 45243

LARSEN, Gregory
901 East Lake St., Aurora, ILLINOIS 60506

LA VERGNE, Bob
Rt. 1, South Whitley, INDIANA 46787 - (219) 723-5521

LEONARDO, Edward
P.O. Box 86, Tiverton, RHODE ISLAND 02878

LITTLE NELL'S Records*
N-711 Monroe St., Spokane, WASHINGTON 99201

LODATO, Frank
P.O. Box 272, Arlington, MASSACHUSETTS 02174

LUTHER, Rick
29047 220th Pl. S.E., Kent, WASHINGTON - (206)

M

MACDONALD, Doug
Box 84, Gordon, WISCONSIN 54838 - (715) 376-2218

MAIONE, Mike
47-23 164th St., Flushing, NEW YORK 11358

MARSOLAIS, Patricia
6 No. Pine Ave., Albany, NEW YORK 12203

MC AULIFFE, Jon
24 Bowen St., Newton, MASSACHUSETTS 02159

MC MANUS, Tim
2308 Galley Ct., Woodbridge, VIRGINIA 22192

MC QUISTIN, Alan
1267 Ramsey View Ct., Sudbury, Ontario, CANADA P3E 2E5

MENTCH, Tom
3325 20th St., Racine, WISCONSIN 53405 - (414) 634-1461

MILLS, Johnnie Louise
9420 Sabre Lane, Westminster, CALIFORNIA 92683

MISCIONE, Vincent
5840 NE 22nd Way, Fort Lauderdale, FLORIDA 33308

MOHR, Ken
1635 Dover St., Broomfield, COLORADO 80020

MORRISON, Richard D.
706 E. Lake Shore Dr., Ocoee, FLORIDA 32761

N

NOSKO, Martin
418 E. Iowa St., Evansville, INDIANA 47711

NEUMANN, George
84 Payson St., Portland, MAINE 04102

NICHOLSON, William R.
P.O. Box 398, Kirkland, ILLINOIS 60146 - (815) 965-9926

NORMAN, Steven
1846 Chamberlain SE, Grand Rapids, MICHIGAN 49506

O

OGUCHI, Norihisa
1-2-14 Kyonancho, Musashino City, Tokyo 180, JAPAN

OCHOA, Richard
1206 N. 15th St., Coeur d'Alene, IDAHO 83814 - (208) 664-4549

OSBORNE, Jerry
P.O. Box 28312, Tempe, ARIZONA 85282

P

PARROTT, Steve
525 Terrace Rd., Iowa City, IOWA 52240

PATTERSON, Thomas
2028 W. 41st Ave., Gary, INDIANA 46408

PAULSON, Philip
2715 Station St., Indianapolis, INDIANA 46218

PCOLINSKY, Joseph G.
126 Mark Rd., Birch Hill Est., Hazleton, PENNSYLVANIA 18201
(717) 459-0877

PETROVICH, Pete
5748 Heming Ave., Springfield, VIRGINIA 22151

PIERCE, Alex R.
335 Wayland Rd., Cherryhill, NEW JERSEY 08034

POLWORT, Steve
787 Portland, Collinsville, ILLINOIS 62234

PORTER, Richard
8004 Brooklyn, Kansas City, MISSOURI 64132

PRIOSTE, Larry J.
3025 Balmoral Dr., San Jose, CALIFORNIA 95132 - (408) 923-8344

RAYNER, Anthony
100 Rectory Grove, Hampton, Middx. TW12 1EF, United Kingdom

RECORDS*
806 K St., Sacramento, CALIFORNIA - (916) 446-3973

REESE, Richard L.
11403 SE Stanley, Milwaukee, OREGON 97222

ROSE, Nancy
7590 46th St., R1 - Box 144E, Augusta, MICHIGAN 49012

ROY, Leo
244 Des Lilas O. App. 6, Quebec, CANADA O1L 1B3

RUPERT, Sheldon R.
24 Slate Ridge Dr., York, PENNSYLVANIA 17404

RUSSO, Joe
161 Haase Ave., Paramus, NEW JERSEY 07652

RUSSO, Richard P.
22 Columbia Ave., Kenilworth, NEW JERSEY 07033

SALEM, Thomas*
P.O. Box 921, Framingham, MASSACHUSETTS 01701

SALINETRO, Lillian
25 Riverview Ave., Pittsburgh, PENNSYLVANIA 15214

SACHES, Lynn
5090 Yucca, Edwards, CALIFORNIA 93523

SCHALK, Fritz
Triesterstrabe 82/1023, 2620 Neunkirchen, AUSTRIA - (02635) 38194

SINCLAIR, Ron & Barb
1339 S. Clarence, Berwyn, ILLINOIS 60402 - (312) 795-8551

SMITH, Spencer
Box 139 - RD 4, Mountain Top, PENNSYLVANIA 18707

SONGER, Gary
1702 Westminister, Mexico, MISSOURI 65265

STUESSE, Herb
145 N. 91st Pl., Milwaukee, WISCONSIN - (414) 774-3170

STURM, Adriaan J.
7750 St. Anthony Church Rd., Louisville, KENTUCKY 40214 - (502) 366-0055

SWANSON, Matt
2149 Hartley Ave., Evanston, ILLINOIS 60201

TAILOR, Danny
1633 E. Kelly, Indianapolis, INDIANA 46203 - (317) 783-4431

TAUSCHER, Pete
212 Wheeler Ave., Redwood City, CALIFORNIA 94061

TETREAULT, Brian
101 S.E. 3rd St., Washington, INDIANA 47501 - (812) 254-4721

TOKASH, Stephen J.*
G.P.O. Box 2302, New York, NEW YORK 10001

TREMBLAY, Omer
185 Moody St. Apt. B, Lowell, MASSACHUSETTS 01854

TURNER, Rick
359 Averett Pl., Danville, VIRGINIA 24541

TURPEN, Mrs. T. E.
327 La Vega Dr. S.W., Albuquerque, NEW MEXICO 87105

URGOLA, Philip G.
327 Davis Ave. Apt. 1, Kearny, NEW JERSEY 07032 - (201) 997-1409

VACANTI, Michael
522 Wisconsin St., San Francisco, CALIFORNIA 94107 - (415) 826-4177

VANHOLLEBEKE, Jim
19367 Poinciana, Redford Township, MICHIGAN 48240

VAN ZANT, Bobbi
P.O. Box 387, Phelan, CALIFORNIA 92371

WARNER, Robb
256B Central Ave., San Francisco, CALIFORNIA 94117 or Gilead Street, Gilead, CONNECTICUT 06248

WEAVER, Lynn
P.O. Box 803, Grand Island, NEBRASKA 68801 - (308) 382-1621

WHEELER, James V.
P.O. Box 1552, Summerville, SOUTH CAROLINA 29483

WHITMER, Clinton C.
P.O. Box 86, Wolf Point, MONTANA 59201

WOUNLUND, Jorn
Brsewitzg 6, Gothenburg 411 40, SWEDEN

WRAY, Evelyn
925 Beachum St., Arlington, TEXAS 76011

Z

ZIADIE, Abe
3180 65th Way North, St. Petersburg, FLORIDA 33710

ZOELLER, Sandra
10837 Damond Ave., Bloomington, CALIFORNIA 92316

A FREE LISTING IN OUR COLLECTOR'S DIRECTORY

For the present we are still able to offer free listings in the annual Collector's Directory that appears in our Popular & Rock price guides (both our book for single 45s and our album guide). If you want listed in next year's edition, indicate in 20 words or less what you sell or collect. To be listed in the Collector's Directory, you must submit this information *each year* and *separately* from your listing in the International Elvis Directory. Please submit in separate envelopes or cards to insure that your name goes where you want it. Thank you.

WHOLESALE PRICE LIST

FOR
RECORD SLEEVES

SIZES	NUMBERS OF SLEEVES PER CARTON	WEIGHT PER CTN	YOUR COST PER CARTON
7" White Sleeves	2,500/ctn	20 lbs	$28.75/ctn
7" Green Sleeves	1,000/ctn	15 lbs	$25.00/ctn
10" Green Sleeves	750/ctn	27 lbs	$41.25/ctn
12" Green Sleeves	500/ctn	28 lbs	$32.00/ctn
12" White Sleeves	1,000/ctn	27 lbs	$28.25/ctn
12" White Polylined Sleeves	600/ctn	30 lbs	$45.00/ctn

MINIMUM ORDER 2 CARTONS ANY SIZE

TERMS AND CONDITIONS

FULL PAYMENT WITH ORDER. Checks must clear before sleeves are shipped. Please allow sufficient time for delivery.

FREIGHT — NOTE CAREFULLY

ALL SHIPMENTS WILL BE SENT VIA UPS COLLECT (Cash Only).
Over 100 lbs. will be sent via truck, freight collect.
Please include Street Address and Telephone Number.

BILL COLE

P.O. BOX 60, DEPT. LP-10
WOLLASTON, MA 02170   TEL. (617) 963-5510

Prices subject to change
without notice.

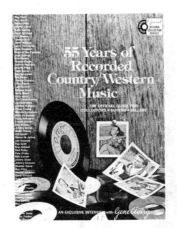

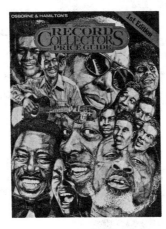

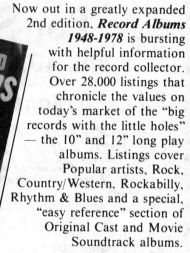

DO YOU KNOW IF YOUR RECORD COLLECTION IS ADEQUATELY PROTECTED AGAINST LOSS?

LIST YOUR RECORD COLLECTION UNDER A GENERAL HOMEOWNERS POLICY

If you do not have your record collection listed separately in your general homeowners policy, in the event of a loss, you would be paid only a fraction of your collection's actual value.

For example, if your Elvis Presley, Milkcow Blues Boogie, (Sun 215) worth $300.00 in mint condition, is destroyed in a fire, the insurance company would only be able to give you 10% of the ORIGINAL COST of the record. Since this record was released in 1955 and sold for 89¢, you would receive 9¢ for your record!

OBTAIN COMPLETE COVERAGE FOR YOUR COLLECTION

Getting FULL coverage for your record valuables is SIMPLE. It can be accomplished in two easy steps:

1. Make a list of your records. Using the Osborne/Hamilton Price Guide for Collectible Records, write down:

*
1. **Name of artist**
2. **Title of record**
3. **Label and number**
4. **Price value**

2. Call your insurance agent and tell him you have an itemized list of records that you want protected with your household goods on your homeowners or renters policy or highlight your record collection in the Osborne/Hamilton Guide and turn the guide in to your agent.

* If you do not have all the information listed above, simply inform your insurance agent that you have records which need to be listed with your general household goods. Many insurance companies are currently using the Record Collector's Price Guides to appraise collections.

The brightest star on earth has now become the brightest star in Heaven, and left us with a love…still burning.

Jerry Osborne
Author-Publisher

"To Elvis: Love Still Burning"

THIS IS THE PICTURE DISC THAT PAVED THE WAY FOR THE DOZENS THAT FOLLOWED!

"TO ELVIS: LOVE STILL BURNING" WAS THE FIRST COMMERCIALLY RELEASED PICTURE DISC ALBUM, BUT ITS PRESS RUN WAS MICROSCOPIC COMPARED TO MANY OTHER PICTURE DISC RELEASES. IT WAS A "LIMITED EDITION" THAT TRULY WAS LIMITED!

WE ARE NOW OFFERING, WHILE THEY LAST, THE REMAINING MANUFACTURER'S INVENTORY OF THIS HISTORIC RELEASE. THESE ARE ALL MINT COPIES AND ARE STILL SEALED. WHEN THEY'RE GONE. . . THEY'RE GONE FOREVER! THEN YOU'LL SEE THIS LP SELLING FOR BIG BUCKS ON THE COLLECTOR'S MARKET.

"TO ELVIS: LOVE STILL BURNING" OFFERS THE COLLECTOR-INVESTOR AN UNBEATABLE COMBINATION:

- THIS LP IS CONSIDERED A "MUST" FOR ELVIS COLLECTORS, AND COLLECTING ELVIS IS THE FASTEST GROWING AREA OF RECORD COLLECTING!

- "LOVE STILL BURNING" WAS THE WORLD'S FIRST ELVIS PRESLEY PICTURE DISC. . . OF ANY TYPE. THERE ARE NO EXCEPTIONS!

- ITS SOUND QUALITY IS SUPERB. NOT LIKE MANY OF THE PICTURE DISCS THAT HAD POOR AUDIO QUALITY.

THE RECENT (1978-1979) PICTURE DISC CRAZE WAS SHORT-LIVED AND NOW ALMOST ANY PICTURE DISC FROM THAT PERIOD IS VALUABLE. ESPECIALLY THE FIRST ONE! ORDER YOUR COPY NOW!

TO ORDER: SEND JUST $12 FOR ONE COPY, PLUS POSTAGE, TO: LARRY HILBURN, P.O. BOX 308, WEST PLAINS, MO 65775 U.S.A.

SPECIAL OFFER! TAKE TWO COPIES FOR ONLY $20. SAVE $4
(Please remember to add sufficient postage)

POSTAGE RATES (For 1 or 2 copies)

U.S. by surface - add $1 to purchase price
U.S. by air - add $3 to purchase price
Foreign by surface - add $2 to purchase price
Foreign by air - add $4 to purchase price

FLEUR DE LIES
Larry Hilburn
P.O. Box 308
West Plains, MO 65775

QUANTITY DISCOUNTS BEGIN AT 10 PIECES - WRITE FOR DETAILS

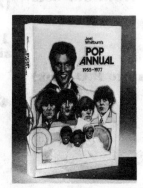

THE ELVIS SUN

6 Malvern Court, Ruxton, Maryland 21204

$ WORLD RENOWNED COLLECTOR OFFERS BIG REWARD $

DOWLING NEEDS PRESLEY RECORDS

The man responsible for Dowling's obsession.

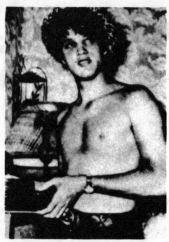

Presley holding discs Dowling seeks.

Dowling on phone with one of his contacts.

Paul Dowling, 6 Malvern Court, Ruxton, Maryland 21204, noted worldwide Elvis Presley record collector and authority, is desperately seeking more Elvis Presley records for his collection. Anyone who might possess items like United States promotional discs or any foreign records is advised to contact him. Considered the top man in his field, Mr. Dowling has informed us that he will pay top dollar for the following Presley material:

U.S.

—MARCH OF DIMES PRESENTS ELVIS—promotional 45 r.p.m.
—TV GUIDE PRESENTS ELVIS—promotional 45.
—EPB 1035—double Xmas EP (Extended Play with picture cover).
—SPD 23—triple EP (with cover).
—SPD 15—10EP BOXED SET (entire set of 10 records plus box).
—SPD 19—8EP BOXED SET (all records plus box).
—33 R.P.M. singles numbered with a "37" prefix.
—33 R.P.M. singles in STEREO with "68" prefix.
—45 R.P.M. singles in STEREO with "61" prefix.
—SP 76—Don't/Wear My Ring (with picture cover).
—SP 139—Roustabout/One Track Heart (with picture cover).
—HO 0808—Blue Christmas promotional single.
—SUN record label 45's and 78's.
—Any 10-inch LP's (Long Plays, promotional or otherwise).
—LPM 1254—the 10-inch version (with the picture cover).
—Any triple EP's with one or more Elvis songs and picture cover.
—Any one-sided promotional singles.
—Any SP-type promotionals; any "NOT FOR SALE" record labels; dust jackets only; singles, EP's, LP's, etc., with one or more cuts by Elvis (with picture covers).
—Basically, anything unusual or of a promotional nature on Elvis.
—Unreleased songs on SUN or RCA.
—Also, tapes and films of live shows in the 50's; Louisiana Hayride; Grand Ole Opry: Dorsey Shows; Milton Berle Shows; Sinatra Show; Hawaii Benefit Show; etc.

FOREIGN

LONG PLAY'S (LP's) ESPECIALLY WANTED ARE:
—T31-077 JANIS & ELVIS 10" (South Africa).
—31-212 ELVIS PRESLEY ROCKS (South Africa).
—31.673 KING OF THE WHOLE WIDE WORLD (South Africa).
—31.118 CHRISTMAS LP (LPM 1382 picture) (South Africa).
—HEW 7605 GOLDEN HITS OF ELVIS PRESLEY (South Africa).
—LS 5048 LOVING YOU (Japan).
—LS 5086 KING CREOLE (Japan).
—LS 5038 CHRISTMAS LP (Japan).
—SHP 5494 CHRISTMAS LP (Japan).
—Any 10" Long Play's from Japan!!
—WESTERN VOL. 6 (Japan).
—SAP 3001 BEST OF ELVIS (Boxed set) (Japan).
—10" and 12" COCKTAIL LP's (Italy).
—BKL 60 ELVIS PRESLEY (Brazil).
—130.252 GOOD ROCKIN' 10" (Cartoon) (France).
—Any 10" LP's from any country except England!!

PLUS: Singles, EP's, LP's with different covers from Spain, Chile, Peru, India, Egypt, Turkey, Japan, Mexico, Brazil, New Zealand, South Africa, Italy, Germany, Bolivia, Columbia, Greece, Uruguay, etc. Would also appreciate listings of current and deleted Elvis records from these countries. Send details of whatever you have for sale/trade!!

Let me hear from you! Make a friend!

Paul Dowling

RARE ELVIS RECORDS

SPECIAL ELVIS COLLECTIBLES FROM JELLYROLL

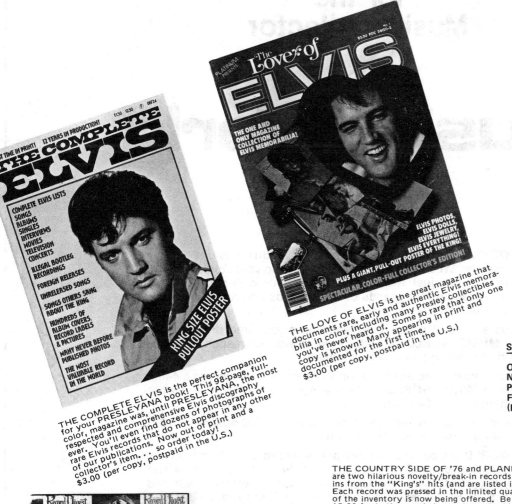

ELVIS IN UNIFORM is still available while supplies last. This giant 18 X 30-inch, full color, Elvis poster is a must for every fan. $3.00 (per poster, postpaid in the U.S.)

THE COMPLETE ELVIS is the perfect companion for your PRESLEYANA book! This 98-page, full-color, magazine was, until PRESLEYANA, the most respected and comprehensive Elvis discography ever. You'll even find dozens of photographs of rare Elvis records that do not appear in any other of our publications. Now out of print and a collector's item. . . so order today! $3.00 (per copy, postpaid in the U.S.)

THE LOVE OF ELVIS is the great magazine that documents rare, early and authentic Elvis memorabilia in color, including many Presley collectibles you've never heard of. Some so rare that only one copy is known! Many appearing in print and documented for the first time. $3.00 (per copy, postpaid in the U.S.)

SPECIAL PACKAGE OFFER:

ORDER BOTH ELVIS MAGAZINES, BOTH NOVELTY RECORDS AND THE ELVIS POSTER — A $14.00 TOTAL VALUE— FOR ONLY $11.00. SAVE $3.00! (PRICE INCLUDES POSTAGE IN THE U.S.)

THE COUNTRY SIDE OF '76 and PLANE CRAZY/POLITICAL CIRCUS '72 are two hilarious novelty/break-in records that Elvis fans love. All feature cut-ins from the "King's" hits (and are listed in the Elvis Novelty section of this book). Each record was pressed in the limited quantity of 500 copies, and the remainder of the inventory is now being offered. Be sure to add these to your collection! $5.00 for both records (per pair, postpaid in the U.S.)

OUR BEST TO YOU is the outstanding feature book published by Jerry Osborne's legendary Record Digest service. A giant 272 page volume crammed with fascinating stories about Elvis, record collecting and much more! Only 500 signed, numbered, copies were printed and we have less than 100 left. Order soon, before they're all gone! Each copy is shipped with the limited edition Elvis novelty/break-in soundsheet, "The Graceland Tour," pressed on red vinyl, included as a bonus. Satisfaction guaranteed! $14.95 (per copy, postpaid in the U.S.)

jp

jellyroll productions
box 3017
scottsdale, arizona 85257

ON ALL FOREIGN ORDERS. . . PLEASE REMEMBER TO ADD SUFFICIENT POSTAGE!